THE SCIENCE OF EDUCATIONAL RESEARCH

second edition

THE SCIENCE OF EDUCATIONAL RESEARCH

second edition

George J. Mouly
University of Miami

VAN NOSTRAND REINHOLD COMPANY
NEW YORK   CINCINNATI   TORONTO   LONDON   MELBOURNE

Van Nostrand Reinhold Company Regional Offices:
Cincinnati, New York, Chicago, Millbrae, Dallas

Van Nostrand Reinhold Company Foreign Offices:
London, Toronto, Melbourne

Published by Van Nostrand Reinhold Company
450 West 33rd Street, New York, N.Y. 10001

Published simultaneously in Canada by
D. Van Nostrand Company (Canada), Ltd.

10 9 8 7 6 5 4 3 2 1

PREFACE

A number of significant developments on the educational scene have occurred since the publication of the first edition of *The Science of Educational Research,* with the result that education today is nothing less than a top priority for American society. Dissatisfaction with the schools, triggered by *Sputnik,* has culminated in loud demands for quality education, which, in turn, have precipitated an expanding series of innovations affecting every aspect of the schools' operation. Equally significant is the new view of education as a vehicle for bold sociological and cultural measures, a departure from its function as a vehicle for the furtherance of scientific and technological progress in the past few years. We have truly entered a new and exciting phase of our national history, wherein education, from Head Start to graduate school, is the focus of a social revolution. Society now places urgent demands on educators for meaningful answers to sociological problems engendered by a complex technological system operating within a rapidly shrinking world. These answers education must provide, if our way of life is to prosper or even, perhaps, to endure.

Fortunately, the research thrust which has characterized America's industrial and technological spheres is now being applied to the improvement of education, ushering in a new educational climate and a new commitment to educational progress. Recent conceptions of the relatively unlimited nature of human potential, together with an awareness of the role of environmental forces in determining such potential, have supplied the schools with a mandate to conduct "engineering-level" studies that will convert results of psychological research into operational programs to promote maximum development of pupil potential. Modern research techniques and tools, ranging from improved experimental designs to computerized data-retrieval and data-processing, now allow us to conduct studies that would have been inconceivable even twenty years ago. Education has been further altered as a result of the federal government's large-scale entry into the research area, through its financial support for the beginnings of long-range systematic programs of educational research.

Our problems are by no means resolved, but we have begun to lay a foundation for later progress: we have a better appreciation of what we know, what we don't know, and how we might proceed to find out. We also have a new awareness that the development of education as an art must rest on the concurrent—perhaps prerequisite—development of education as a science. This realization should facilitate meaningful future dialogue between researchers and practitioners, each of whom will be more aware of the other's viewpoint and more sensitive to their mutual interdependence. We know enough to guard against unrealistic expectations, but we can nevertheless look ahead in educational research today with some degree of optimism.

A textbook in educational research ought to reflect all these current aspects of the profession. This second edition attempts to promote appreciation of the opportunities presented by the new educational climate and to encourage the sense of personal commitment to research which is such a vital factor in the improvement of educational practice. It therefore treats both the producer and the consumer of research in our present phase of education; for we need not only more adequate research but more discriminative interpretation and better use of research results. We need not only a greater appreciation of the value of research but a firmer understanding by everyone in education of the nature of research strategies and of their underlying rationale. We delude ourselves if we imagine that first-rate research—in education or in any other field—can be an amateur undertaking or that the significance of research can be evaluated with no more than "common sense."

The author has been guided throughout this revision by continued adherence to the fundamental objectives of the first edition: namely, to develop in the student an understanding of the essential nature of the scientific approach to the solution of man's problems, to imbue him with respect and appreciation for the spirit of scientific inquiry within the context of the immense complexities of social phenomena, and to help him develop some degree of competence in the techniques and strategies of educational research. This edition, in short, retains as its aim something the author has long regarded as vital to an introductory text: the supplying of a foundation and a tone which can permeate all graduate study and further activity in education.

Probably best used in the one-semester course required at the beginning of graduate work in education, the book may also offer important concepts for some of the undergraduate teacher-education programs of this new era.

The organization is essentially that of the first edition, covering, in turn: the nature of science, the principles of sampling, the rationale of statistical inference, and the elements of the various research methods. These are fundamental to educational research and are relatively unchanging. On the other hand, recent developments have added new dimensions to the introductory course and have pushed others into more advanced study, necessitating new material on the status of educational research as a whole and on experimentation, whereas the treatment of statistics, tests and measurements, data-processing, and the more advanced experimental designs has undergone some entrenchment in this edition. There is obviously need for further study, and for supervised first-hand experience, in these areas, all of which are readily available in other sources concerned more specifically with them rather than with an introduction to the field as a whole.

A *Student's Workbook*, comprising over 2100 five-alternative multiple choice questions, one pretest, and two posttests exploring the content of educational research, has been prepared to accompany this edition. Organized along the general lines of the text, it is intended primarily as a resource for the student rather than the instructor, in that it provides the research student with material for promoting his understanding of the basic concepts of educational research and for evaluating his mastery thereof.

Although, strictly speaking, the work of a single author, this edition has been a joint enterprise with many collaborators. References in the text acknowledge the author's indebtedness to the many scholars whose studies contribute to the book's content. The author also wishes to express his sincere appreciation to numerous colleagues and friends whose suggestions and comments concerning the first edition have been most helpful. Special thanks go to the author's students who, in more ways than one, have taught him educational research.

Coral Gables, Florida   G.J.M.

CONTENTS

The scientific method is the strategy of scientific research: it bears on any whole research cycle and is independent of subject matter. The actual execution of every one of the strategic moves will, on the other hand, depend on the subject matter and on the state of our knowledge regarding that subject matter.——Mario Bunge (1967)

PART ONE

THE SCIENTIFIC METHOD

In his interaction with his environment over the centuries, man has been perpetually beset with problems—which he has proceeded to resolve through various means at his disposal and, of course, with varying degrees of success. Having left behind the gods and demons of his forebears and even their overreliance on tradition and authority, modern man is finally settling more and more on science as the most dependable approach to the solution of the problems characteristic of an advanced level of civilization. And with good reason. The accomplishments of science pervade every aspect of our existence, to the continued amazement of even the most sophisticated. Science has been a most significant factor in the betterment of man's lot; it has raised our standards of living and enabled us to live a longer, healthier, more productive and enjoyable life. By relieving us of the struggle for survival, it has freed us to strive for human dignity and personal fulfillment.

Unfortunately, despite its importance, there is still more confusion than clarity as to the specific nature of science. The man on the street typically has but a vague and often erroneous conception of what science is all about. He is likely to equate science with its products, and particularly with the more spectacular medical successes, space flights, and technological breakthroughs. Science as a process is often cast into the stereotype of a rigid, formalized ritual which, if followed step by step, is guaranteed to provide the required solutions. Rarely do people realize that research is typically a rather inefficient endeavor. An exploration into the unknown cannot be scheduled with the precision of assembly-line production. Rarely do they realize the flounderings and the groping for ideas, the long hours of groundwork, the dead ends, and the tiny gains that lie behind the rare successes that get the headlines. Nor do people appreciate the crucial role played by intuition, whether in selecting a worthwhile problem, in identifying fruitful hypotheses, in deriving effective modes of attack, or in generating meaningful interpretation of the data as the basis for further exploration. There is especially a lack of appreciation of the tentative nature of the results of science and the consequent need for the verification and extension of research findings in the ever-continuing process of obtaining deeper insights and more dependable answers.

The fact that science is traditionally associated in the public mind with the physical and biological sciences is reflected in the tendency for research in the social sciences to subscribe to the basic univariate design, despite the inappropriateness of such a model for the study of behavioral phenomena. The unfortunate consequent has been the concentration of our research efforts on problems selected not in terms of their significance but rather because of their amenability to investigation by the traditional "scientific method." While this is certainly not the time to minimize the importance of competence in library, sampling, statistical, and other research skills, we must especially recognize that science is defined more by its essence than by its mechanics, that science is more than the routine application of mechanical procedures to "standard" problems. This point is of particular importance as it relates to education which, at its present stage of development, calls for a broad multidimensional approach rather than a rigid adherence to a narrow, mechanical conception of science. If we are to make the most of current opportunities, we need to address ourselves by whatever means are appropriate to the study of the more significant problems that constitute the true substance of education as a science. Meanwhile, as we turn to science as an ongoing process through which the understanding, prediction, and control of educational phenomena are to be achieved, we need to keep clearly in mind that the successful application of the scientific method to the investigation of the complex problems we face in education demands a high level of proficiency in its use.

1
THE WORLD
OF SCIENCE
AND TECHNOLOGY

We Americans are a self-improving people. This is the source of our strength and our genius.——Francis Keppel (1964)

MODERN SCIENTIFIC ADVANCES

Material Progress

The scientific productivity that has characterized the past few decades is continuing at an accelerating pace. It is also taking interesting and significant directions. Just as the twentieth century can be considered the atomic century and is now becoming the age of electronics and cybernation, so undoubtedly the twenty-first century will be the genetic century—the DNA age—with the generation of life in a test tube a distinct probability. Equally important, the twenty-first century may also be the century in which man—assuming a satisfactory resolution of the present social unrest—will achieve a full measure of human dignity, in which concern for social welfare will match the emphasis on material progress of the past few decades. We already have many indications of things to come: some are actually in limited production, some are still experimental, others are currently just out of reach. Our progress, whether in the area of transportation, space, medicine, or industrial output, has been truly fantastic. Many of the "spectaculars" of the 1950's are now taken for granted. Half of the scientific knowledge of today was unknown a quarter-century ago; by the year 2000, current contributions will be largely of historical interest as a foundation for the really interesting things that are to come.

Our current space program will undoubtedly lead to relatively routine space travel by the end of the century. Von Braun (1967) predicts a sizable lunar colony by the year 2000. General Electric is devising a nuclear-fueled power plant to generate electricity for the disintegration of water into oxygen and hydrogen to support life on the moon. At the other end of the continuum, as our next target of development, we are exploring the ocean, whose resources in relation to man's needs are relatively inexhaustible. On earth, transportation will take such unusual forms as vacuum-tube propulsion—pipelines that will carry people and freight at tremendous speeds. Air-cushion (flying-carpet) cars will skim over land and water (Floyd, 1966). The computer will become standard in all operations from banking and credit-card buying to booking a flight on a supersonic jet or buying a ticket to the theater. Even more exciting gains will be made in medicine. The transplant of human organs will become even more prevalent when the rejection problem is resolved. Bloodless surgery through laser light beams is already a reality. In time, we will conquer cancer and other diseases, just as we have conquered smallpox and polio. Extending human life to 100, perhaps 120 and even beyond, is a definite possibility. We are indeed at the threshold of an age in which the possibilities of human progress through scientific research simply stagger the imagination.

In a fascinating and scholarly speculation, Kahn and Wiener (1967) list 100 significant technological innovations likely to occur by the year 2000. Some of these, e.g., the drastic reduction in the incidence of congenital defects, human "hibernation" for medical purposes, and a flexible penal system using modern methods of surveillance and control, will be of immense social benefit. The authors also consider the possibility of automated highways, chemical or biological control of human temperament and intelligence, direct input into human memory banks, and effective biochemical treatment of most mental illnesses. They further mention as possible achievements by the year 2000, lifelong immunization against practically all diseases, major genetic modification of the human species, and routine use of extrasensory phenomena.

Progress in Education

More pertinent in the present context are the implications of modern scientific advances for education—and even more crucial, the implications of the advances in education itself, for education cannot be simply the recipient, the object of scientific progress. Rather, it must be the instigator, the primary determinant of scientific progress in all aspects of human endeavor—including education. To the extent that the scientifically productive nation is the educated nation, education cannot afford to drag. This is especially true at the more advanced levels of development for, as our current emphasis on social welfare suggests, an affluent society's welfare is, in the final analysis, a function of social rather than simply material well-being. As Gores (1967) points out, "It is apparent that education will be the new dynamics of our nation's growth industry—that learning is the new growth industry." And ' indeed, education must be the science of tomorrow if scientific progress is to continue at its present accelerating pace.

Educational practice will most likely undergo a drastic change from its present formal arrangement to a much more flexible, individualized arrangement. At the operational level, it is not difficult to conceive of self-contained electronically equipped booths dispensing both instruction and reinforcement, while the teacher of tomorrow is engaged in an entirely different concept of "teaching" than that prevailing today. The possibilities of "learning pills" to accelerate the educational process are entirely believable in light of the chemistry of learning (Jacobson, 1966; Krech, 1968) or even the possible relation between uric acid and intelligence (Nyhan, 1968). As Weir (1967) suggests, imagine the tremendous advantage a nation would have if it could double the intellectual capacity of its citizens by chemical, surgical, or electronic means. At the psychological level, Skinner's success with pigeons, rats, and other animals suggests new horizons in learning (1958):

> It is dangerous to assert that an organism of a given species or age cannot solve a given problem. As a result of careful scheduling, pigeons, rats, and monkeys have done things during the past five years which members of their species have never done before. It is not that their forebears were incapable of such behavior; nature simply never arranged effective sequences of schedules.

The content of education will have to be different—and this, in turn, will necessitate that the approach to education be different. With the current knowledge explosion and the correspondingly rapid technological changes, formal schooling will become a lifelong process of continual updating of tools and skills in order to keep abreast of our rapidly changing world (Martin, 1967).

Bonner (1967) suggests that, even now, a biomedical scientist who does not spend one-third of his time in continuing education is simply becoming obsolete. There may indeed come a time when he will have to devote most of his time to keeping abreast. It is obvious, as Estes (1967) points out, that "We simply can't continue to provide the facts needed to make decisions in a world where most of the facts we'll need are still unknown." With the obvious prospect that classroom learnings will be essentially outdated before the youngster sets out into the world to use them, the school needs to concern itself primarily with teaching students how to learn. This is the only justifiable approach to a functional education.*

The whole concept of formal education will also undergo drastic reconsideration. While formal education might well extend from the age of four or five to include junior college or its equivalent in vocational training, the school will probably cease to be the exclusive—or even the primary—locale of the educational process. With the increased availability of telecast lessons, programed instructional materials, and various other teaching devices and learning aids, the true classroom of the future might typically be the home, the dorm, or even the business or industrial plant. The library of the future will become more and more a remote-access storage-and-retrieval center (see ALA, 1963). The educational system of the future will include adults as well as children utilizing a wide network of facilities both on-site and in nonschool centers operating on an extended school day 52 weeks a year. In these facilities, people will study as their needs suggest, in much the same way as people use a library today. Under this system of continuous education, admission to and graduation from school will probably become essentially irrelevant—as even college graduates engage in continuous maintenance and upgrading of their "education."

Research and the Future

These many scientific advances, covering the whole gamut of human life, will unquestionably bring man immense benefits. But they will also carry a price tag: some will introduce serious side effects ranging from accelerating nuclear proliferation

---

* This in no way implies that all current data are to be scrapped. Certainly, a good part of the basic knowledge of any field can be expected to hold as the foundation for the continued upgrading of the more advanced phases.

to critical invasion of privacy and increased control of the individual by governmental and private agencies. With computer capacity currently increasing exponentially by a factor of 10 every two or three years, computer efficiency by the year 2000 will have increased a billionfold over that of present computers. Under those circumstances, the achievement of what can justifiably be called "artificial intelligence" (Minsky, 1966) becomes much more plausible than any current concept of "computer limitation." All this is potentially good. But, increased computer capacity will also permit, for example, a single national information file containing all educational, medical, employment, legal, credit, security, etc., data on each and every citizen and will, *ipso facto* introduce the very real danger of abuse. It will certainly necessitate the development of strict guidelines for its use.

In fact, it seems that discoveries which are inherently good often introduce serious unforeseen consequences that make their discovery a mixed blessing. Medical advances—acting in conjunction with other forces—have created a critical problem of over-population that already threatens us with imminent disaster: poverty, slums, riots, pollution, loss of privacy, not to mention possible distortion of the species (Van Vleck, 1966) and possibly irreversible alienation among socio-economic classes leading to a major confrontation, with annihilation of one or the other as a likely consequence (Weir, 1967). At any rate, having to live in a society of "wall-to-wall" people calls for considerable readjustment from our present way of life. In a carefully considered treatise, scientists assembled at California Institute of Technology (Bonner et al., 1957; Schuster, 1967) voiced real concern over water pollution, air pollution, thermal pollution, soil erosion, etc., all of which threaten the very existence of man on this earth. Many of our rivers and lakes are already polluted, perhaps beyond recovery; many can only be described as too thick to swim in, too thin to plow. The air in many of our cities is no longer fit for "human consumption."

Yet, it seems logical to assume that scientific ingenuity will be equal to the challenge of solving the problems it has created.* Our space program is an indication of what can be accomplished when massive efforts are exerted in the pursuit of a

---

* Underlying our present difficulties is that we can only look upon present (and anticipated) problems from the perspective of 1970 premises. Approached from the improved insights which the future will inevitably provide, currently *insurmountable* problems will undoubtedly take on a different complexion.

goal. It has been costly, but probably worthwhile in the long run. As Draper (1967) suggests: "I personally think that we will find out that the environment of space is the easiest environment man has ever encountered, once you pay the price of admission." In the short period of eight years from 1960 to 1967, the Polaris missile system was initiated and successfully completed; during the same period, lasers were developed to their present level of relatively universal use in military weapons, computers, data storage, spectroscopy, and chemical research. Our problems of stream and air pollution will eventually be resolved; so will the problem of depletion of our natural resources. Not only will our energy supply of the future be sufficient to convert night into day, heat our homes, and power machinery that will all but eliminate physical labor, but it will do so from power derived from solar energy or extracted from sea water—which, according to Bishop (1966), is sufficient to supply the earth with energy at a thousand times the current rate of consumption for 20 million years. The generating plant of the year 2000 envisaged by Westinghouse Electric (Hartley, 1966) will convert daily as "an almost incidental by-product" over a billion gallons of salt water into fresh water.

The question is one of balance: the resolution of one problem introduces other problems, so that it can be said that the "cause" of *problems* is *solutions*. Spilhaus (1967), in his description of the model city of the future, cautions that the wholesale use of electrical power along present lines will inevitably lead to thermal pollution—and disaster in the form of flood as the earth's temperature increases and ice floes melt. Disposition of millions of gallons of hot water used to cool giant generators on the shore of every river, lake, sea, and ocean can hardly be a matter of insignificance to life as we know it. He points out that with increased urbanization, the use of home air-conditioners throwing out heat as refuse will be no more acceptable in the city of the future than was throwing out slop into the street of the small town of a century ago. In fact, we might have to turn out that light when we are not using it!

Such physical problems will undoubtedly be resolved scientifically—perhaps only to introduce others which, in turn, will also be resolved. Their socio-ethical and sociological implications may be more far-reaching and critical. The fact that the car population of the United States in the year 2000 is estimated at 250 million may mean that private ownership of two or three cars per family may have to give way to social ownership, with everyone simply using the nearest car to take him from place to place. We certainly cannot afford 250 million cars parked 90 percent of the time. At the human level, the fact that an increasing proportion of the population will be "old people" will undoubtedly create problems in the effective operation of the social order. On a more complicated plane, what moral-philosophical stance might society take with regard to the major biochemical, electrical, or surgical alteration of the individual? Will man's rejuvenation through one organ transplant after another carry him to a point where, like an old bicycle, the frame is the only part of the original structure that remains? With the increased ability to delay death, might life be prolonged beyond the point of human dignity, involving a denial of man's right to die and also of society's rights in the matter? Already the Social Security Agency is concerned (UPI, 1968) with the problem of having to pay benefits to the "immortal beneficiary," e.g., the individual with a fatal disease who elects to be placed in deep freeze while waiting for medical science to find a cure. Yet, we cannot deny society access to scientific advances, even though the final outcome, as we see it now, may have catastrophic possibilities. Presumably, the focus must be on present progress—combined with the hope that solutions will be found for possible dangers. Meanwhile, we need to be prepared to face ever more complicated problems, perhaps of a nature and scope beyond our present imagination.

Of particular interest from the standpoint of education—and indeed from the standpoint of the welfare, if not the survival, of man—is the control over his fellowmen which modern science is inevitably going to confer on the social scientist. Medical discoveries will enable us to drastically reduce diseases, both physical and mental. Already biochemical and other forms of treatment have created new possibilities of cure as well as insight into the nature of psychosis. Electrodes imbedded into the septal region of the brain of psychotic patients can alleviate their symptoms by the simple pressing of a button; the same procedure will stop an enraged bull in its tracks. Biochemical treatment, or even a systematic schedule of reinforcement, can likewise effect drastic changes in behavior. New understanding of the electrochemistry of the brain has given the scientist fantastic powers; it has made man's previous attempts at social control "seem like a child's toys in a game that could be as disastrous as it could be rewarding" (Barbour, 1966). Such control could "prove as awesomely good or bad as atomic energy." As discussed in Chapter 3, the increased power of science has brought the danger of abuse and misuse into sharp focus; as long as man pursued his goals—whether noble or sinister—inefficiently, there was apparently no cause for alarm. But now that the atomic bomb has replaced the musket-loader, the wire-trap eavesdropping, and brainwashing soap-box oratory, public concern over possible abuse has become very real. The danger of possible abuse of social control will be of particular concern with regard to education, which typically deals with impressionable and defenseless children. As Powell (1964) points out:

> Most teachers fail because they do not know how to change pupils in distinct ways—and they might be uncomfortable if they did. Consider the extraordinary consequences if teachers were ever made really effective. Education would then have a degree of control over the human mind that the physicians possess, to some extent, over the human body. . . . Perhaps the very substantial academic freedom of most American teachers today rests in their ineffectiveness.

THE ROLE OF RESEARCH

The Nature of Research

Although the fact that the tremendous progress that has characterized our society over the past half-century has been largely the result of research, science, and technology is fully recognized and accepted, the exact meaning of these terms defies precise definition. Research to most people, for example, is far too narrowly and exclusively associated with experimentation as conducted in the physical or biological sciences. Too frequently, science is perceived exclusively in the context of the discovery of a new drug or the invention of a new product.

Actually, research is best conceived as the process of arriving at dependable solutions to problems through the planned and systematic collection, analysis, and interpretation of data. Research is a most important tool for advancing knowledge, for promoting progress, and for enabling man to relate more effectively to his environment, to accomplish his purposes, and to resolve his conflicts. Although it is not the only way, it is certainly one of the more effective ways of solving scientific problems. For our purposes, we can define educational research as the systematic and scholarly application of the scientific method *interpreted in its broadest sense* to the solution of educational problems; conversely, any systematic study designed to promote the development of education as a science can be considered educational research.

Our culture puts such a premium on scientific progress that the terms *science, technology,* and *research* are frequently misused. *Research* is often used in contexts where little research, in the true sense of the word, is actually done. Many agencies claiming to do research, for example, are engaged in nothing more than fact-finding. If it is to be meaningful, the term *research* used within the context of the social sciences should be restricted to activities designed to promote the development of a science of behavior. Accordingly, the term *educational research,* as used in the present text, will likewise be restricted to systematic studies designed to provide educators with more effective means of attaining worthwhile educational goals. It will not include the routine application of what is already known (as in *teaching*); rather, it will be reserved to refer to activities designed to discover facts and relationships that will enable educators to make the educational process more effective.

Rationale Underlying Research

Research is oriented toward the discovery of functional relationships existing among the phenomena of the world in which we live. The fundamental assumption is that invariant relationships exist between certain *antecedents* and certain *consequents* so that, under a specific set of conditions, a certain consequent can be expected to follow the introduction of a given antecedent. Thus, under normal conditions, throwing an object out of the window of a tall building will result in its falling with accelerating speed—and this will be as true tomorrow as it is today or as it was yesterday; as true in Brooklyn as it is in Hong Kong or Timbuktu. That this invariance in time and space prevails is logical: to deny its existence would mean subscribing to a view that phenomena are haphazard, capricious, chaotic, and, consequently, unpredictable—that research and science are impossible.

From the beginning of time, man has noted certain regularities among the phenomena and events of his experience and has attempted to devise laws and principles that express these regularities. These laws and principles are not without exception, of course; any law is valid only under the conditions under which it was derived. Even though objects tend to fall, they have been known to rise when acted upon by other forces—but this does not deny the basic principle of gravity. Research is devoted to the discovery of the conditions under which a given phenomenon occurs, and the conditions under which it does not occur in what might appear to be similar circumstances. Science is based on the premise that, if a given situation could be duplicated in the entirety of its relevant aspects, the phenomenon would also be duplicated without fail. To the extent that the situation is duplicated only in part, on the other hand, the phenomenon may or may not be duplicated. This complication can be frustrating to the beginner who expects to have pat answers to complicated problems—who is interested in *the* solution without all the *if*'s, *when*'s, or *but*'s.

Research and the Social Sciences

Man has come to place more and more reliance on scientific research for the answers to his problems and, judging from his success in the physical and biological sciences, it appears that this trust has been well placed. To be questioned, however, is the extent to which a similar reliance can be placed on scientific research for the answers to problems in the social sciences where, because of the complexity of the variables under consideration, exceptions are more frequent and often more drastic and damaging. In fact, the many exceptions to the generalizations of the social sciences have led some people to question whether a science of human behavior is possible. The point is frequently made that human behavior is not subject to scientific determination and control, that, because man is possessed of a free will and is capable of choice, he is master of his own destiny—i.e., that he operates independently of the forces that surround him.

This view is difficult to accept for the very reason that it denies the concept of orderliness that must characterize all phenomena, including human behavior. It postulates that human behavior is inexplicable, unpredictable, and uncontrollable, a proposition that even the layman would reject, for one is constantly making interpretations and predictions of the behavior of his fellowmen. In fact, above all else, man must be predictable. It is true that human behavior is complex and that, from our present limited level of understanding, it frequently appears disorganized and self-contradictory—but that is simply because we do not understand it. It does not mean that human behavior is incapable of scientific determination any more than prehistoric man's inability to understand his physical world constituted proof that physical phenomena could never be brought under law.

We might go further and suggest that it is not so much that human behavior is complex as it is that our understanding of human phenomena is so extremely limited. Our position today with respect to the science of human behavior is not unlike that of the chemist or the geologist at the turn of the century. Rocks and fossils, when viewed individually, are as different as human beings; yet they have been brought under law. It is just as likely that the differences among human beings and their behavior patterns lie largely at the peripheral level and that, when viewed in perspective, significant regularities, uniformities, and generalities in underlying dynamics will begin to appear. In fact, a good deal of relatively definite knowledge of human behavior has already been accumulated in the science of psychology, and progress has been made both in integrating these uniformities into a systematic framework and in predicting and controlling outcomes.

Much of our present knowledge regarding human behavior exists at the level of empirical description, and we are just now beginning to orient our knowledge to the task of prediction and control. This does not deny—or minimize—the fact that, because of the complex nature of human beings and the way their differences are revealed in behavior, the prediction of this behavior will be subject to numerous exceptions, and that the laws that will eventually be derived from the study of human behavior will probably never be as simple as those that govern the physical elements. Nevertheless and notwithstanding, human behavior is undeniably as legitimate a subject for scientific investigation and determination as are the phenomena of the physical world. In fact, in view of the focus which man must occupy in our world, knowing about himself becomes man's primary task. One might even suggest that research in human behavior must subscribe to the same basic principles of science, though it may not necessarily be amenable to the same specific modes of attack as the other areas of scientific investigation.

Also to be questioned is the extent to which educational research represents a unified field of endeavor of sufficient homogeneity to warrant a common term and common training on the part of those who engage in it. Or, is education so broad and complex that it requires a variety of research techniques which are most appropriately taught in separate courses? The complementary question is whether a single course in research in the behavioral sciences might make better sense.

While there are many answers to these questions, it could be argued that, though the techniques involved in the various social sciences are based on the same principles, the differences in application of these principles often warrant somewhat different emphases and, hence, separate courses of training.* The differences among the various areas of education, on the other hand, appear relatively less crucial and, if education is to make a concerted attack on its problems, a common course is to be recommended. This course would have to be supplemented by special emphasis on the research into specific problems of various areas of specialization within education.

Implied in the preceding paragraph is the fact that, in view of the infinitely more complex phenomena with which social research, in general, and educational research, in particular, have to deal, we must be prepared to adapt our research techniques to the problems with which we are faced. Indeed, it seems likely that much of the difficulty encountered in the social sciences has stemmed from our attempts to mimic the research procedures of the physical sciences. To the extent that the techniques we have borrowed are relatively inappropriate to the problems for which they have been used, our answers have been correspondingly inadequate, and our progress toward the development of education as a science has been correspondingly delayed.

Although it may be more difficult to relate the principles of science to social phenomena, these principles apply to both physical and social phenomena with equal force and effectiveness. Furthermore, in contrast to such sciences as geology, seismology, and astronomy where, even after a problem has been solved, there is not very much that can be done about controlling the phenomena involved, the social sciences generally provide an opportunity for control of any situation whose nature is sufficiently understood.

* A strong case is being presented for an interdisciplinary approach to the training of educational researchers to parallel the interdisciplinary approach used so successfully in industry. There is also a strong argument for recruiting students and scholars from the other social disciplines on the premise that there is no research methodology to which the term *educational* can be applied exclusively (see Chapter 13).

Our task, then, is to discover the uniformities under-lying social phenomena so that they can be integrated into a mean-ingful structure which will eventually permit the prediction and control of consequences. Although this may be a long, complicated process, it seems logical that, in time, we will be able to predict human behavior with an acceptable level of accuracy. In fact, with the newer tools available to us from other disciplines, we should be able to make more rapid progress than did many of the other sciences. This is precisely the task to which we must address our-selves as we join our colleagues who only recently were graduated from alchemy, astrology, and bloodletting.

Highlights of the Chapter

1.   The scientific advances which characterize our modern world in the physical and material domain have been achieved through thorough and painstaking research, the key to scientific progress. Unfortunately, by contrast, the social sciences have lagged far behind.

2.   Since ancient times, man has noted certain regularities in the phenomena and events of his experience and has attempted to de-vise laws and generalizations expressing these regularities and uniformities.

3.   Research is oriented toward the discovery of functional rela-tionships that exist among phenomena. It is predicated on the premise that certain invariant relationships exist between certain antecedents and certain consequents, an assumption which must be accepted; its alternative would be to deny the concept of order-liness and lawfulness in the world about us.

4.   Scientific laws are valid only under the conditions under which they have been derived. If two situations could be dupli-cated in their entirety, their consequents would also be duplicated —invariably and in full. However, to the extent that the conditions postulated in the statement of the law are duplicated only in part in a real situation, the phenomena may or may not be duplicated.

5.   Social phenomena are as subject to scientific investigation and determination as are the phenomena of the physical world. That

human behavior should appear complex and relatively unpredictable and uncontrollable is simply a reflection of the inadequacy of our present knowledge.

6.   There is need to adapt research methods to the complexity and the nature of the research problems that exist in education.

7.   Our progress to date has been slow. If education is to prosper, we need to bring to educational problems the zeal and the competence that has characterized research in the physical and biological sciences.

Questions and Projects

1.   The major project to be associated with a course in educational research is obviously the thesis or dissertation; undoubtedly, nothing can make a course in research more meaningful than the experience of applying its principles in the solution of an actual research problem. Unfortunately, many students will not be writing a thesis. Three alternatives suggest themselves:

(a) A class project which would involve the close cooperation of the members of the class in every phase of its selection and execution, and, if conducted in a nearby school, close coordination, through a steering committee, with the school personnel.

(b) Individual projects may be selected and planned but not carried out to completion. Each student might be expected to select a topic capable of development into a master's thesis and to write up what might normally be the chapters on the problem, the review of the literature, and the design of the study (including the construction of the instruments and their pretesting on a small pilot group, where special instruments are required).

(c) Assistance to a professor conducting research, or affiliation with the R & D unit of the local school system on an internship or field experience basis.

2.   It is essential that the student enrolled in a course in educational research become oriented toward the nature of research through a thorough survey of research studies actually conducted. This is best done by perusing *Dissertation Abstracts* for studies that appear both interesting and worthwhile. The student might

be expected to read the microfilm of at least two or three dissertations in order to understand what constitutes acceptable research.

3.   Make a survey of the basic research materials in education and related fields. Be sure to include new publications as they become available, the earlier books in the field, and the more pertinent general sources and periodicals of interest to educational researchers.

4.   Specifically, what changes have taken place in educational practice since the turn of the century? How many of these changes actually rest on a firm foundation of research? How many of these changes are relatively impossible to validate empirically?

5.   Visualize the classroom of 2000 A.D. What changes do you anticipate in the physical plant, the school furniture, teaching aids, and especially, teaching procedures. Specifically, how might research expedite and ensure the validity of the changes that take place in educational practice? What role might education play in this progress and how can it best orient itself to promote and to guide progress in desirable directions?

Selected References

American Library Association. *The Library and Information Networks of the Future.* Chicago: The Assn., 1963.

Bonner, James et al. *The Next Hundred Years.* Pasadena: Calif. Inst. Technology, 1957.

Brickell, Henry M. "The dynamics of educational change," *Theory into Practice,* 1: 81–88, 1962.

Brownell, William A. "Educational research in the decade ahead," *Calif. J. educ. Res.,* 14: 51–66; 1963.

"Education, population, the pill," *Phi Delta Kappan,* 49: 473–516; 1968.

Elam, Stanley M. (ed.) *Education and the Structure of Knowledge.* Chicago: Rand McNally, 1964.

——— and William P. McClure (eds.) *Education in the 1970's.* Bloomington: Phi Delta Kappa, 1967.

Fund for the Advancement of Education. *Decade of Experiment.* New York: The Fund, 1961.

Gage, N.L. "Can science contribute to the art of teaching?" *Phi Delta Kappan,* 49: 399–403; 1968.

Hook, Sidney (ed.) *Determinism and Freedom in the Age of Modern Science.* New York: New York Univ. Press, 1958.

Hunt, Earl. "Computer simulation: Artificial intelligence studies and their relevance to psychology," *Ann. Rev. Psychol.*, 19: 135–68; 1968.

Kahn, Herman and Anthony J. Wiener. *The Year 2000: A Framework for Speculation on the Next Thirty-Three Years.* New York: Macmillan, 1967.

Krech, David. "Psychoneurobiochemeducation," *Phi Delta Kappan,* 50: 370–75, 1969.

Lundberg, George A. *Can Science Save Us?* New York: Longmans, Green, 1961.

Morison, E.E. *Men, Machines, and Modern Times.* Cambridge: M.I.T. Press, 1966.

Popper, K.R. *The Logic of Scientific Discovery.* New York: Basic Books, 1959.

Rogers, Carl R. and B.F. Skinner. "Some issues concerning the control of human behavior," *Sci.*, 124: 1057–66; 1956.

Russell, Bertrand. *The Impact of Science on Society.* New York: Simon & Schuster, 1953.

Schuster, Richard P. (ed.) *The Next Ninety Years.* Pasadena: Calif. Inst. Technology, 1967.

Silberman, Harry F. et al., "The effect of educational research on classroom instruction," *Harv. educ. Rev.*, 36: 295–317; 1966.

Van Tassel, David D. and Michael G. Hall (eds.) *Science and Society in the United States.* Homewood: Dorsey, 1966.

General Sources in Educational Research

That no introductory text can hope to provide a complete coverage of an area as broad and complex as educational research is self-evident. It is, therefore, imperative for the student to consult other sources in order to gain a more adequate insight into the concepts presented and to obtain greater background in areas of special interest. The following is a representative list of the more relevant general references in the research methodology of education and related fields. Additional sources can be found in references at the end of each chapter. The conscientious student will undoubtedly want to make liberal use of these in broadening his perspective of research. He will also want to attain a reasonable grasp of the content of educational research by becoming familiar with such standard sources as the *Encyclo-*

pedia of Educational Research, the *Review of Educational Research,* and the various professional journals.

Ackoff, Russell L. *The Design of Social Research.* Chicago: Univ. of Chicago Press, 1953.

American Council on Education. *Educational Research: Its Nature, Essential Conditions, and Controlling Concepts.* Series 1, Vol. 3, No. 10. Washington: The Council, 1939.

American Educational Research Association. *Growing Points in Educational Research.* 1949 Official Report. Washington: The Assn., 1949.

————. *Encyclopedia of Educational Research.* 1st ed.: Walter S. Monroe (ed.) 1941; 2nd ed.: Walter S. Monroe (ed.) 1950; 3rd ed.: Chester W. Harris (ed.) 1960; 4th ed.: Robert L. Ebel (ed.) 1969. New York: Macmillan.

———— and Department of Classroom Teachers. *The Implications of Research for the Classroom Teacher.* Joint Yrbk. Washington: Nat. Educ. Assn., 1939.

————. *What Research Says to the Teacher.* Washington: Nat. Educ. Assn., 1953-(Continuing Series).

Anderson, Barry F. *The Psychology Experiment: An Introduction to the Scientific Method.* Belmont: Wadsworth, 1966.

Association for Supervision and Curriculum Development. *Research for Curriculum Improvement.* 1957 Yrbk. Washington: The Assn., 1957.

Bachrach, A.J. *Psychological Research: An Introduction.* New York: Random House, 1962.

Barnes, Fred P. *Research for the Practitioner in Education.* Washington: Dept. Elem. Sch. Princ., NEA, 1964.

Barnes, John B. *Educational Research for Classroom Teachers.* New York: Putnam, 1960.

Barr, Arvil S. et al. *Educational Research and Appraisal.* Philadelphia: Lippincott, 1953.

Best, John W. *Research in Education.* Englewood Cliffs: Prentice-Hall, 1959.

Beveridge, William I.B. *The Art of Scientific Investigation.* New York: Norton, 1951.

Brown, Clarence W. and Edwin E. Ghiselli. *Scientific Method in Psychology.* New York: McGraw-Hill, 1955.

Canadian Education Association. *Invitational Conference on Educational Research.* Toronto: The Assn., 1959–date.

Chapanis, Alphonse. *Research Techniques in Human Engineering.* New York: Harper & Row, 1959.

Doby, John T. (ed.) *An Introduction to Social Research.* Harrisburg: Stackpole, 1954.

Festinger, Leon and Daniel Katz. *Research Methods in the Behavioral Sciences.* New York: Holt, Rinehart & Winston, 1965.

Fox, David J. *The Research Process in Education.* New York: Holt, Rinehart & Winston, 1969.

Freedman, Paul. *The Principles of Scientific Research.* New York: Pergamon, 1960.

Gage, N.L. (ed.) *Handbook of Research on Teaching.* Chicago: Rand McNally, 1963.

Gee, Wilson. *Social Science Research Methods.* New York: Appleton-Century-Crofts, 1950.

Good, Carter V. *Introduction to Educational Research.* New York: Appleton-Century-Crofts, 1963.

———— and Douglas E. Scates. *Methods of Research.* New York: Macmillan, 1954.

Griffiths, Daniel E. *Research in Educational Administration.* New York: Bur. Publ., T.C., Columbia Univ., 1959.

Hillway, Tyrus. *Introduction to Research.* Boston: Houghton-Mifflin, 1964.

Hullfish, H.G. and P.G. Smith. *Reflective Thinking: The Method of Education.* New York: Dodd, Mead, 1961.

Hyman, Herbert H. *The Nature of Psychological Inquiry.* Englewood Cliffs: Prentice-Hall, 1964.

Jackson, Robert W.B. *Educational Research in Canada Today and Tomorrow.* Toronto: Gage, 1961.

Kerlinger, Fred N. *Foundations of Behavioral Research.* New York: Holt, Rinehart & Winston, 1964.

Kurtz, Kenneth H. *Foundations of Psychological Research.* Boston: Allyn & Bacon, 1965.

Larrabee, Harold A. *Reliable Knowledge.* Boston: Houghton Mifflin, 1945.

McConnell, Thomas R. et al. *The Conceptual Structure of Educational Research.* Chicago: Univ. of Chicago Press, 1942.

McCormick, Thomas C. and Roy G. Francis. *Methods of Research in the Behavioral Sciences.* New York: Harper & Row, 1958.

McGrath, G.D. et al. *Educational Research Methods.* New York: Ronald Press, 1963.

Madge, John. *The Tools of Social Science.* New York: Longmans, Green, 1953.

Morrison, J.E. et al. "Twenty-five years of educational research," *Rev. educ. Res.,* 26: 199–344; 1956.

Mussen, Paul H. (ed.) *Handbook of Research Methods in Child Development.* New York: Wiley, 1960.

National Society for the Study of Education. *The Scientific Movement in Education.* 37th Yrbk., Pt. 2. Bloomington: Public School Pub. Co., 1938.

Phi Delta Kappa. Annual Symposia on Educational Research. 1. Frank W. Banghart (ed.) *Educational Research,* 1960; 2. Raymond O.

Collier and Stanley M. Elam (eds.) *Research Designs and Analysis*, 1961; 3. Keith Goldhammer and Stanley M. Elam (eds.) *Research Dissemination and Implementation*, 1962; 4. Nicholas A. Fattu and Stanley M. Elam (eds.) *Simulation Models for Education*, 1963; 5. Stanley M. Elam (ed.) *Education and the Structure of Knowledge*, 1964; 6. G. Guba and Stanley M. Elam (eds.) *The Training and Nurture of Educational Researchers*, 1965; 7. Julian C. Stanley (ed.) *Improving Experimental Design and Statistical Analysis*, 1967; 8. Robert M. Gagné and William J. Gephart (eds.) *Learning Research and School Subjects*, 1968; 9. Donald L. Meyer and Raymond O. Collier (eds.) *Bayesian Statistics*, 1969. Bloomington: Phi Delta Kappa.

Plutchik, Robert. *Foundations of Experimental Research*. New York: Harper & Row, 1968.

Rummel, J. Francis. *Introduction to Research Procedures in Education*. New York: Harper & Row, 1958.

Sax, Gilbert. *Empirical Foundations of Educational Research*. Englewood Cliffs: Prentice-Hall, 1968.

Scott, M. Gladys (ed.) *Research Methods in Health, Physical Education, and Recreation*. Washington: Amer. Assn. Health, Phys. Educ. & Rec., 1959.

Scott, William A. and Michael Wertheimer. *Introduction to Psychological Research*. New York: Wiley, 1962.

Selltiz, Claire et al. *Research Methods in Social Relations*. New York: Holt, Rinehart & Winston, 1959.

Shontz, F.C. *Research Methods in Personality*. New York: Appleton-Century-Crofts, 1965.

Smith, Henry L. and Johnnie R. Smith. *An Introduction to Research in Education*. Bloomington: Educational Publications, 1959.

Travers, Robert M.W. *An Introduction to Educational Research*. New York: Macmillan, 1969.

Underwood, Benton J. *Psychological Research*. New York: Appleton-Century-Crofts, 1957.

Van Dalen, Deobold B. *Understanding Educational Research*. New York: McGraw-Hill, 1966.

Wilson, E. Bright. *Introduction to Scientific Research*. New York: McGraw-Hill, 1952.

Young, Pauline V. *Scientific Social Survey and Research*. Englewood Cliffs: Prentice-Hall, 1966.

2
THE EVOLUTION
OF SCIENCE

All but the most thoughtless and impulsive will . . . use their minds before giving credence to others' reports and try to collect evidence before trusting their own surmises. The world is too full of error and falsehood to make any other course mentally or physically safe.——Jacques Barzun and Henry F. Graff (1957)

From earliest times, man has been curious about his environment. Life is full of intriguing phenomena: from the rain, thunder, and lightning which aroused the curiosity—to say nothing of the terror—of primitive man to the nuclear and cosmic phenomena of today which have a direct bearing on man's welfare and, even, on his survival. Therein lies the raw material from which science is born.

MAN'S SEARCH FOR TRUTH

The means by which man seeks answers to his problems can be classified under three broad categories: *experience, reasoning,* and *experimentation.* These three categories are, of course, complementary and overlapping. Experimentation, for instance, is perhaps best conceived as a combination of experience and reasoning. In fact most problems—and certainly most research problems—call for the operation of all three in varying degrees.

Experience

Perhaps the most primitive, and yet the most fundamental source of the solution to man's many problems is personal experience. Confronted with a sudden flow of water down a ravine, prehistoric man could have saved his life had he remembered one of the first lessons in basic science: water does not generally stay on hills—an elementary version of the law of gravity.

When one has not had personal experience with a phenomenon, the obvious recourse is to consult someone who has. Thus, children consult their parents, teachers, or even older siblings for answers to problems with which they are not familiar. Throughout the history of science, certain persons were recognized as authorities—i.e., there emerged a class of people who were credited with having many of the answers to the problems that perplexed their less enlightened contemporaries. Frequently, these authorities were merely persons of status or power whose word was accepted as law, not because of any great wisdom or communion with truth, but because of prestige derived through strength, birth, wealth, association with magic, or some other form of public acceptance. A few of these authorities attained historical renown. Plato and Aristotle are still considered authorities in many areas of knowledge. Until recently, the name of John Dewey was often invoked as the last word on what should be done in education. Closely related to personal experience are custom and tradition, which provide a large percentage of the answers to everyday, as well as professional, problems. Much of what goes on in the class-room, for example, is justified by "This is the way we have always done it."

Obviously, experience is a basic part of the founda-tion on which science must rest. Experience can be considered one of the two arms of science: it is a prerequisite—a necessary, if not a sufficient—condition to intelligent behavior. On the other hand, as a tool in the discovery of truth, experience has very definite limitations that must be appreciated by those who rely on it. Primary among these limitations is the fact that one frequently has an inadequate, if not inaccurate, conception of his experiences. Too often, our understanding of our experiences are at the level of the blind men looking at the elephant.

Likewise, to accept unconditionally the pronounce-ments of authorities is a dangerous practice. Experts are essential, particularly in a complex culture such as ours, and obviously certain individuals have such wide experience and deep insight that their advice can be of benefit to many people. Yet, it must be remembered that no one is infallible, and even the best and most competent are not exclusive possessors of "the truth, the whole truth, and nothing but the truth." The matter is complicated further by the tendency for authorities to go beyond their area of competence. Actresses, for example, endorse soap and sundry other products, while the athlete becomes an authority on razor blades and supersedes the medical doctor as a judge of the nutritional value of breakfast cereal.

It is also likely that a man who is an authority in one era will be surpassed by very ordinary persons at the next stage of cultural development, and that he will become a liability if cited as an authority past the life of his contribution. As long as people felt that Aristotle had answered all questions, there was no need for seeking more adequate solutions. Since he had discovered the final truth, all scholarship, education, and wisdom up to the Renaissance consisted largely of mastering his answers and techniques of reasoning. In fact, history suggests that it was not prudent to question Aristotle's conclusions: note, for example, the suppression of such theories as heliocentricity and evolution and of the discoveries of Galileo, Copernicus, and other early scientists. In fact, probably the only scholars who were secure in the Middle Ages were the mathematicians, inasmuch as their "discoveries" were unlikely to conflict with any of the established beliefs of the period. Even today, in the U.S.S.R., the writings of Marx and Lenin are considered to be *truth,* and again it is not prudent to disagree. Even in democratic countries, courts of law subscribe to the concept of experts and authority; and in our schools, policy and practice are frequently based on the opinions of the veteran teacher or administrator.

Custom and tradition also must be evaluated carefully. A person cannot investigate everything for himself and must, therefore, rely somewhat on the discoveries of others. Furthermore, anything which has stood the test of time can be expected to possess some element of truth, so that tradition and custom can often be considered reasonably dependable. But that custom and tradition are not infallible guides to truth can be seen from the number of classical errors in history, e.g., the belief that the world was flat. The phonetic approach to the teaching of reading was a parallel error, which attained general acceptance in education. Nothing could be more logical, nothing could be more simple: all a child had to do was to "sound" his letters and to "blend" them and he could read. But then, educators soon realized that this is not the way people *begin* to read. Other educational "truths" that have had widespread acceptance at one time or another include the theory of mental discipline, emphasis on drill in learning, and the schedule approach to baby care.

We must not understate the role of experience and authority in the discovery of truth. Both have a crucial role in promoting man's understanding of his world. They must not be considered as sources of ultimate truth, however, but rather sources of suggestions and hypotheses to be questioned and subjected to more rigorous test. It might be pointed out that, in general, our culture does not encourage this questioning of authority, particularly on the part of children. Even adults who are "from Missouri" are not generally too popular. Teachers, for example, expect their students to accept what they are told, and verbatim parroting of what the teacher or the book has said is generally the royal road to good grades, teacher acceptance, and other rewards. In fact, even at the college level, disagreement with the instructor is rarely encouraged.

Reasoning

A more sophisticated approach to truth is reasoning, which is considered the second of the two arms of science. One of the first major contributions to the systematic discovery of knowledge was made by Aristotle, who perfected the syllogistic method of *deductive reasoning*. In its simplest form, the syllogism consists of a major premise based on a self-evident truth or previously established fact or relationship; a minor premise concerning a particular case to which the fact or relationship inescapably applies; and a conclusion. Thus,

> All men are mortal;
> John is a man;
> therefore, John is mortal.

The procedure is based on the concept of internal consistency; it operates on the assumption that, through a series of formal steps of logic, valid conclusions can be deduced from valid premises.

The next milestone in the progress of science was the inductive process of reasoning introduced by Francis Bacon. In contrast to deductive reasoning, induction proceeds from the analysis of a number of individual cases to a hypothesis, and eventually to a conclusion concerning the general case. The modern method of reasoning, generally attributed to Charles Darwin, combines Aristotelian deduction with Baconian induction. In essence, it consists of a back-and-forth movement in which experience is analyzed inductively to provide hypotheses whose implications are then studied deductively in order to test their validity.

The role of reasoning as an aspect of science must not be minimized: it is an indispensable tool in its operation and development. On the other hand, the limitations of reason must also be clearly recognized. A conclusion is no more adequate than the premises (major or minor) on which it is based; false premises can lead only to false conclusions. Errors can also stem from violations of the rules of logic. Barring such errors, reasoning can point to new relationships in what is already known, but it cannot derive new truths. It can indicate that two propositions are in conflict, but it cannot tell which, if either, is correct, and reasoning from analogy is generally unacceptable as a method of deriving truth. Thus, the empirical fact that compounds of elements which are individually combustible in an atmosphere containing oxygen are themselves combustible, and that compounds of elements which individually are incombustible in oxygen are themselves incombustible would not enable us to reason whether these rules are exception-free—which, indeed, they are not. In general, the contributions of reasoning to the development of science fall into three categories: 1. the suggestion of hypotheses; 2. the logical development of these hypotheses; and 3. the clarification and interpretation of scientific findings and their synthesis into a conceptual framework.

Experimentation

The third and most scientifically sophisticated means by which man seeks to discover truth is experimentation, which is generally considered—perhaps erroneously—to be the scientific method *par excellence*. Chapter 11 will be devoted to a presentation of the various aspects of experimentation, but it might be pointed out here that, in its simplest form, experimentation consists of isolating the effects of the operation of a given factor by assigning that factor to one of two groups which are otherwise equal in all respects. This is, of course, an oversimplified design which is rarely approached even in the physical sciences and probably never in the social sciences.

HISTORICAL DEVELOPMENT

Early Contributions

The beginning of science dates back to the beginning of man. Undoubtedly early man discovered a large number of empirical relationships which enabled him to understand his world with varied degrees of success. The first recorded attempts at science were those of the Egyptians who, partially in response to the annual flooding of the Nile, developed the calendar, geometry, and surveying. These achievements were followed by the less concentrated, but nonetheless valuable, contributions of the Babylonian and Hindu civilizations. Then came the Greeks who, with their emphasis on organization, gave us not only astronomy, medicine, and the Aristotelian system of classification, but also the syllogism as the basis for further deductive systematization of experience. Despite their overemphasis on the theoretical at the expense of the empirical, and their neglect of experimentation as the prime source of scientific evidence, the Greeks can be credited with the first systematic approach to the development of science.

The syllogism was the basic tool of systematic and scholarly reasoning throughout the Hellenistic, Roman, and early Christian period to the time of Galileo and the Renaissance. It reached a peak of misuse in the Middle Ages, when, in disregard of the admonitions of Aristotle, it lost contact with basic observation and experience and degenerated into an exercise in mental gymnastics. For example, if the problem concerned the number of teeth in a horse's mouth, the solution was sought through logic rather than through simple observation, an error of which even Aristotle apparently was guilty. To quote Bertrand Russell (1953):

> To modern educated people, it seems matters of fact have to be ascertained by observation, not by consulting ancient authorities. But this is an entirely modern conception, which hardly existed before the 17th century. Aristotle maintained that women have fewer teeth than men; although he was twice married, it never occurred to him to verify the statement by examining his wives' mouths. He also said that children would be healthier if conceived when the wind is in

the north . . ., that the bite of a shrewmouse is dangerous to
horses, especially if the mouse is pregnant . . . and so on and
so on.

Up to the Renaissance, Aristotle's teachings were considered to be
true, relevant, satisfactory, and at once adequate for all purposes,
and "science" fell to a new low in sterility and futility.

Bacon and the Inductive Method

In the early 1600's, Francis Bacon led a rebellion
against the tendency of philosophers first to agree on a conclusion
and then to marshall the facts in its support—in the manner of a
debate where presenting a convincing argument in support of a
point of view, rather than discovering the truth, is the main concern. He felt strongly that logic could never suffice for the discovery of truth, since "the subtlety of nature is greater many times
over than the subtlety of argument," and that logic began with a
preconceived notion and therefore biased the results obtained. He
posited that if one collected enough data without any preconceived
notion about their significance and orientation—thus maintaining
complete objectivity—inherent relationships pertaining to the general case would emerge to be seen by the alert observer.

Bacon's contribution to the advancement of science
is significant in that he broke the stranglehold of the deductive
method, whose abuse had brought scientific progress to a standstill. His ideas ushered in a period in which scientists such as
Galileo, Lavoisier, Harvey, and Darwin turned from logic and
authority as a source of truth to nature for the solution to man's
problems. These men did not reject logic, experience, and authority; they simply used them as sources of hypotheses rather than of
proof and insisted on empirical proof for verification.

Bacon was essentially incorrect in his basic premise
that a hypothesis was prejudicial to complete objectivity. This
need not be so—if one sets out to test a tentative position and not
to prove a point. Bacon's method at best was obviously wasteful;
at worst it was essentially ineffective. An investigation not guided
by a hypothesis is more likely to result in confusion than enlightenment. In general, data should be collected for research purposes
only after the problem has been clarified sufficiently to suggest a

hypothesis worth exploring. The point is clearly made by Larrabee (1945):

> Unless he is a mere collector of odds and ends, the seeker of knowledge cannot go through life looking *at* things; he must look *for* some things; that means active inquiry with some directing factor in control.

The limitations of induction in the more advanced stages of science are noted by Einstein (1936), who points out that:

> There is no inductive method that could lead to the fundamental concepts of physics. Failure to understand this fact constitutes the basic philosophical error of so many investigators of the 19th century. . . . We now realize with special clarity how much in error are those theorists who believe that theory comes inductively from experience.

The Modern Inductive-Deductive Approach

Bacon's inductive method was superseded by the *inductive-deductive* method—generally attributed to Charles Darwin—which combines Aristotelian deduction with Baconian induction. It consists of a back-and-forth movement in which the investigator first operates inductively from observations to hypotheses, and then deductively from these hypotheses to their implications in order to check their validity from the standpoint of the compatibility of the implications with accepted knowledge. After revision, where necessary, these hypotheses are submitted to further test through the collection of data specifically designed to test their validity at the empirical level.

This approach is the essence of the modern scientific method and marks the last stage of man's progress toward empirical science—a path that took him through folklore and mysticism, dogma and tradition, unsystematic observation, and finally to systematic observation. Although, in practice, the process involves a back-and-forth motion from induction to deduction, in its simplest form, it consists of working inductively from experience to hypotheses, which are elaborated deductively from implications on the basis of which they can be tested. Thus, the modern scientist uses facts and theories as interdependent tools to gain greater scientific insight into his problems. This dual approach is necessary because, though the scientist is interested in a class rather than in the individuals who comprise it, he can never observe the class in its entirety and must, therefore, generalize from a few instances concerning the properties of the whole class.

THE DEVELOPMENT OF SCIENCE

Animism

Man continually strives to understand the phenomena he encounters in order to find means for dealing more effectively with the problems they pose. Primitive man, hearing thunder and seeing flashes of lightning accompanied by violent rain and, perhaps, floods, must have spent many anxious moments wondering when it would all cease and what it was all about.

Anthropology and history indicate that man first explained such phenomena as the work of gods, spirits, demons, and other supernatural agents. Ancient mythology is full of gods and goddesses, who obviously played a significant role in the lives of these primitive people. The Indians, for example, attributed sickness, famine, and other misfortunes to the displeasure of the spirits. The ceremonials of the various "savage" tribes were typically designed to appease angry spirits or to secure their help. This supernatural or animistic stage also survives in current belief in ghosts, gremlins, Lady Luck, and various other beings invented to explain phenomena of unknown origin. Irish folklore is particularly filled with such mythology.

Empirical Science

In time, man came to realize that natural phenomena could be explained by natural *causes*—a most important step marking the beginning of science as a systematic approach to the solution of problems. This development has been a slow process. Crude, unsystematic conjectures gradually gave way to more systematic and critical observations; then to systematic and precise testing of isolated hypotheses under controlled conditions; and finally, in some sciences at least, to the development of theories incorporating the findings of isolated "experiments" into an integrated structure and to the formulation of systematic and precise tests of integrated hypotheses derived through such theories. This process can be divided into two overlapping stages of development: 1. the *empirical* level, in which science consists of discovering empirical relations among phenomena of the variety of "X leads to Y," without understanding *why* this is so; and 2. the *explained* (theoretical) level, which involves the development of a theoretical structure that not only explains isolated empirical relationships, but also integrates them into a meaningful pattern. This theoretical level represents the most advanced stage of science, one which is not completely attained in any of the academic disciplines and which is, of course, barely approached in the social sciences.

1. Experience   Obviously, the starting point of science at its most elementary level is experience, whether the phenomena be a thunderstorm or snowstorm, a vessel broken as a result of the expansion of water as it freezes, an eclipse, or the more commonplace regularity of day and night. Science starts with an observation, to which are added other observations both of a similar and dissimilar nature. Eventually, a system of basic principles is derived that explains both the occurrence and the nonoccurrence of a given set of experiences. The goal of science is the acquisition and the systemization of knowledge concerning the phenomena experienced.

In its early stages, science must concern itself with augmenting and criticizing experience. The accumulation of individual experiences, no matter how clarified, is not sufficient, however, for as long as these experiences remain isolated, they tend to have no meaning from the standpoint of science. The number and diversity of these isolated experiences must be reduced to their underlying unitary basis of organization through the process of classifying and systematizing them into a small number of basic principles of ever-greater generalizability and application.

2. Classification   The most basic procedure for reducing isolated data to a functional basis is classification, a procedure which is fundamental to all research—and indeed, to all mental life—for it constitutes a simple and parsimonious way of comprehending large masses of data. Knowing the class to which a given phenomenon belongs provides us with a basis for understanding it. The classification of a forthcoming storm as a hurricane, for example, gives us the basis for anticipating much of its probable behavior. The identification of an object or phenomenon as a member of a class immediately implies certain attributes already associated with the class. Thus, the words *fish, bird,* and *diamond* carry certain meanings with them. And, the more precise the classification, the clearer the meaning and the more specific the properties associated with the classification. The properties associated with the class *acids* are more precise than those associated with the general class *chemicals,* for example.

To be meaningful, classification must be based on one's purpose. Thus, whether an orange should be classified with a banana or with a baseball depends on whether one is interested in eating it or in rolling it along the floor. Complications arise from the fact that most objects and phenomena have a large number of properties and characteristics which makes it possible to categorize them in any number of classification systems; rarely is the classification system used the only one possible. For example, although telephone directories are organized by surname and by business affiliation, they could also be organized by street address. The problem is to distinguish between a crucial and a superficial basis of classification. In fact, it is characteristic of the early phases of classification to be based on superficial properties; more crucial bases emerge only gradually as greater insight into the phenomena in question is achieved. Thus, from the standpoint of the effect a teacher has on his students, classification of teachers as task-oriented and ego-oriented is probably more meaningful than their classification according to the more tangible factors of age, sex, and degree status.

Classification systems can range from the most simple to the most complex and elaborate—perhaps involving multiple bases of classification and even classification within classification.* Probably the most advanced classification in existence is the periodic table in chemistry, which evolved from the early Greek classification of elements into earth, air, water, and fire. Another major classification system divides living things into plants and animals, a system which, despite its high level of refinement, becomes somewhat difficult to apply in the case of marine animals. More closely related to the present text is the Library of Congress (or the Dewey-Decimal) system of classifying library materials.

---

* The modern emphasis on the concept of sets in mathematics, which is essentially a system of mathematical logic based on classification, e.g., the set of odd numbers or of prime numbers, is of interest in this connection.

The actual allocation of phenomena to different classes—whatever the merit of the classification system may be—is relatively easy if their properties can be appraised and if the basis of classification is known in advance, or if agreement can be reached about the classes where such classification is arbitrary. Since a frog is a frog and a lizard is a lizard because they have the properties of a frog and a lizard respectively, correct classification poses no problem. Classifying a whale as a mammal, rather than as a fish, is likewise a matter of agreeing on which characteristics are fundamental, just as classifying people as tall, average, and short is simply a matter of agreeing on the limits of these classes.

3.   Quantification   While the first step in the development of science is the accumulation and clarification of experiences, it soon becomes necessary to quantify these observations, for only quantification can provide the precision necessary for classification in a more mature science. In fact, the more advanced the science, the greater is the need for it to go beyond enumeration toward evergreater precision in measurement in order to permit the more adequate analysis of phenomena through mathematical manipulation. On the other hand, one must not lose sight of the fact that, though quantification permits an infinite set of fine distinctions, mathematical refinement does not endow data with a precision and significance they did not possess in the first place.

4.   Discovery of Relationships   Through the classification of phenomena along different continua, it is frequently possible to note certain functional relationships among their component aspects. Classifying children simultaneously by sex and physical strength, for instance, is likely to emphasize the fact that boys tend to be stronger than girls. Functional relationships among phenomena can also be observed through temporal sequences. For example, hot days tend to be followed by electrical storms and showers. At a more advanced level, empirical science attempts to express natural laws in the form of a numerical equation relating the quantitative aspects of certain variables to those of other variables—for example, $d = \frac{1}{2}gt^2$ or $V = IR$.

Many of the relationships so discovered represent nothing more than functional co-appearances among phenomena. Such relationships are often crude and indirect. Thus, the relationship between the physical size of an unselected group of children and their reading ability is an indirect relationship: the more correct version is that physical size is related to chronological age which is, in turn, related to mental age and to reading competence. Many similar examples can be given, as, for instance, that of the drunk who, having become intoxicated on water and gin, water and bourbon, and water and rye concluded that water, being the common element, was the cause of his difficulty. The fact that the mortality rate among inmates of jails and penitentiaries is lower than that of the nation as a whole can be explained on the basis of the age bracket of the people incarcerated. By the same token, an increase in delinquency may simply reflect more adequate law enforcement.

5.   Approximations to the Truth   Scientists are generally interested in more fundamental relationships than those representing mere concomitance. However, events are frequently so complex that any fundamental relationship that may exist among them is blurred. It is, therefore, necessary to analyze events into their basic constituents with the idea of discovering a more precise relationship. Accordingly, a major task of science consists of the analysis of phenomena to determine more clearly the relevance of their many aspects.

Involved here are two very fundamental steps in the development of science: the process of successive approximations to the truth and the parallel process of redefinition of the problem in the light of the success or failure of such approximations. This has been particularly evident in connection with the polio vaccine, where we have had, in succession, the Salk, the Coxe, and the Sabin vaccines, each looking like *the* solution and each later found to be wanting. Numerous examples of this kind can be found in any scientific field—in agriculture, for example, better varieties of wheat are discovered every year. Whether in the end, as far as it pertains to natural phenomena, the ultimate truth can be attained is a matter of debate; the issue is relatively academic and probably serves no useful purpose. In many cases, we have come to an approximation to the truth which is sufficient for our purpose—e.g., the immunization against smallpox.

The concept of science as a series of approximations to the truth, which is rarely, if ever, attained, is not particularly satisfying to those who conceive of science as something absolute and who fail to appreciate that all that science can do is provide us with greater understandings. Of interest in this connection is the relatively prevalent tendency, in the field of medicine, for example, to use a "shotgun" approach. The patient is given a general drug, such as penicillin, which may bring about a recovery but which, since it does not help identify the curative agent, does not provide the basis for the future treatment of similar cases, except for the repetition of the general approach. To be of maximum scientific value, the approach should be to try one drug at a time or, if it were possible to obtain a sufficient number of cases, to try a variety of drugs in combinations of one, two, three, etc., in a more elaborate experimental design.

Theoretical Science

The ultimate level of science is *theoretical* science, in which the relationships and phenomena discovered in empirical science are explained on the basis of underlying causation. This is a step toward predicting and determining the methods of controlling their operation so that desirable outcomes can be promoted. For a long time, for instance, chemists realized that certain substances burned, giving up heat and smoke and leaving ashes. This was worth knowing in itself, but it did not explain what was occurring. They proposed various theories to explain the phenomenon, among which was the postulation of a substance called *phlogiston* present in the atmosphere and apparently responsible for the burning. This theory was later rejected in favor of the modern oxidation theory which relates the burning of wood to the rotting of wood, the rusting of iron, and other chemical reactions.

The superiority of the theoretical over the empirical level of science is best understood through an appreciation of the limitations of the latter. Empirical science is awkward and unwieldy since it deals with phenomena in relative isolation, and thus entails the relatively impossible task of grasping each phenomenon individually. Empirical science is particularly limited from the standpoint of predictability and control, which are the ultimate purposes and goals of science. Consider the story related by Charles Lamb of little Bobo, who, having accidentally set fire to his hut, was apparently the first human being to taste roast pork. He had an empirical fact; whatever had happened had provided him with roast pork. However, should he want to taste roast pork again, must he burn the hut again? Must he duplicate all the

circumstances that anteceded the roast pork? His empirical findings might lead him to believe that he could also improve the taste
of rice by setting fire to the hut. Bobo's empirical knowledge was
of restricted usefulness, though, to be sure, he now had a goal that
he might pursue. He might have correctly identified the reason for
the roast pork through intuition, or he might have attempted by
trial and error to eliminate one factor after another and, eventually
have been able to simplify the procurement of roast pork.

Theoretical science can shortcut the process of arriving at solutions. When the individual understands the causes of an
occurrence, he can transfer his knowledge to the solution of similar
problems. Explained science has obvious advantages from the
standpoint of stimulating research and providing worthwhile hypotheses. In fact, the ultimate in scientific excellence is found in
such sciences as physics, in which theory has advanced sufficiently
(on the basis of previous empirical discoveries) so that it can now
anticipate and lead in the discovery of empirical facts. The atomic
bomb, for example, was not devised empirically and then explained; on the contrary, Einstein and his co-workers developed it
theoretically and turned to empirical verification largely for the
purpose of eliminating flaws in its execution. Our space program
also operates largely at the theoretical level.

The transition from empirical to theoretical science
is, of course, a difficult step. It is often relatively easier to find out
what occurs than to explain why. This is particularly true in the
social sciences where, for example, we still do not have a scientific
explanation for the bulk of even the most elementary aspects of
what occurs when a child learns. In some of the more advanced
physical sciences, considerable theoretical progress has been made,
though in none of the sciences is there complete agreement on all
aspects. Physics explains the phenomenon of light by two conflicting theories of wave motion and particle movement, for instance.
In the social sciences, psychology has postulated a number of
theories to explain psychological phenomena, but none has won
universal acceptance. Nor is any one complete; most theories of
learning to date have avoided the question of its neuro-physiologi-
cal basis, for example (see Hebb, 1949; Krech, 1969).

As a science, education is almost exclusively at the
empirical level. In fact, we have yet to discover many of the empirical relationships that apparently exist among the variables op-

erating in the classroom. Probably our greatest lack, however, is our failure to devise a theoretical framework within which we can synthesize educational findings obtained thus far. It might be said that to date the social sciences have suffered from an overemphasis on empiricism and a corresponding neglect of theory. Recently, however, there has been a strong and encouraging trend toward theory development and a more adequate realization that empiricism represents an incomplete stage of science.

CAUSATION

Goals of Science

The purpose of science is to establish functional relationships among phenomena with a view to predicting and, if possible, to controlling their occurrence. Of course, even in some of the more developed sciences—astronomy or geology, for example—the difficulty of manipulating the variables restricts us to the prediction of phenomena and, at best, to an adaptation to their occurrence. Nevertheless, it might be highly desirable and useful to predict in advance the likely occurrence of a hurricane so that we can prepare for it, even if we cannot forestall it. It is likewise profitable to anticipate that the dull child will encounter academic difficulties.

Unfortunately, many of the functional relationships that have been established among phenomena to date are relatively crude and imprecise, incorporating many irrelevant aspects, while some of the more crucial aspects go unrecognized, or are only partially understood. Consequently, the resulting predictions frequently have been unnecessarily clumsy and unwieldy, on the one hand, and frequently in error, on the other. This is evident, for instance, in the relationship which has been established between ability and achievement. Furthermore, even if it were possible to recognize all of the factors involved in a phenomena, they could not all be controlled, and prediction still would be inaccurate to some degree. For this reason, the laws of science are always approximate, especially in the social sciences where the prediction of whether a child will get a certain answer or react in a given way, for example, frequently is determined by some small and unrecognized aspect of the overall situation.

Causation as Probability of Occurrence

Until recently, research was oriented toward the establishment of cause-and-effect relationships among phenomena. Unfortunately, the concept of causation has been troublesome to the scientist and the philosopher as well as to the layman. The latter is likely to consider any antecedent or concomitant of a situation as its causative agent. As Bertrand Russell (1938) pointed out, the people of every country attributed the depression of the 1930's to the sins of their own governments, and, as a result, there was a movement toward the right where the government in power had been leftist and toward the left where the government had leaned to the right. The modern scientist, on the other hand, is more aware of the difficulties the concept presents. The term *causation*, in its strict sense, is gradually disappearing from the vocabulary of science.* This view was anticipated by Russell, who in 1929 wrote:

> All philosophers of every school imagine that causation is one of the fundamental axioms of science, yet, oddly enough, in advanced sciences, such as gravitational astronomy, the word "cause" never occurs . . . . The reason why physics has ceased to look for causes is that, in fact, there is no such thing. The Law of Causality, I believe, like much that passes among philosophers, is a relic of a bygone age, surviving . . . only because it is erroneously supposed to do no harm.

The refinement of functional relationships into their minimal essentials and, of course, their theoretical explanation is much more difficult than the mere establishment of these relationships. The difficulty stems from the fact that phenomena generally occur as a result of multiple causation, each cause contributing to the occurrence as a vector force both singly and in interaction with others—e.g., intelligence contributes only indirectly to teacher effectiveness. Conversely, the occurrence of a given phenomenon as anticipated is a function of the simultaneous operation of all the contributing forces exactly as postulated. However, inasmuch as

---

* Social scientists are somewhat less reluctant to use the term *cause* and *causation* today than they were some ten years ago—with the understanding, of course, that what is involved is a complex system of interaction rather than a simple one-to-one "causal relationship." No confusion needs to result from the use of the terms as long as they incorporate the concept of multiplicity of contributing conditions which together make the occurrence of a given phenomenon probable.

the fulfillment of the latter condition in a given situation is relatively a matter of chance, the emphasis in research, particularly in the social sciences, has shifted toward the discovery of functional relationships which can be expressed as probability of occurrence. This is particularly true in those sciences in which it is not possible to manipulate variables so that relevant factors can be isolated from irrelevant factors.

Even in sciences where variables can be manipulated, it is almost impossible to control all the factors of a situation to the point of identifying the causal agent or agents, and to preclude with certainty the operation of extraneous factors and thus to guarantee the occurrence of the cause-effect sequence exactly as postulated. Science is now reconciled to the idea that all that can be expected in the situational realities under which science must operate is prediction—and eventual control—at a high level of probability. It must, of course, be realized that the establishment of causation is not essential. Thus we can predict that learning will take place even though we cannot identify its "causes," and we can predict the movement of the planets though we cannot control such movements. This is not to minimize the desirability of establishing rigorous cause-and-effect relationships, if this were possible: such relationships would be much more conducive to the development of control and complete explanation than is simple concomitance. It is simply a recognition of the fact that science rarely has complete insight into the nature of such relationships and that it is invariably incapable of precluding all influences that can vitiate the prediction. It is a recognition that, at best, science can only approximate what might be the ideal statement of the relationship between an effect and its cause or causes.

Mill's Canons

Probably the most systematic of the early analyses of causation was presented about a hundred years ago by John Stuart Mill (1873), who postulated five basic canons governing the identification of causes and effects. Although their now obvious limitations have led to their relative rejection by modern scientists, Mill's canons constitute one of the major advances in scientific inference. In fact, their contribution to the clarification of the all-important concept of causation probably puts them on a par with Aristotle's syllogism in the logic of science.

The best known and, in a sense, the most basic are Mill's first two canons.

> *1. The Method of Agreement*   If two or more instances of the phenomenon under investigation have only one circumstance in common, the circumstance in which alone all the instances agree is the cause (or effect) of the given phenomenon.

Thus, if the people who fell sick after having attended a certain banquet have in common the fact that they ate the same food, it may be suspected that the food is the cause of their illness.

> *2.   The Method of Difference*   If an instance in which the phenomenon under investigation occurs, and an instance in which it does not occur, have every circumstance save one in common, that one occurring only in the former; the circumstance in which alone the two instances differ, is the effect, or cause, or a necessary part of the cause, of the phenomenon.

These canons have been subjected to numerous and thorough critical reviews. Cohen and Nagel (1934) point out that they cannot be used either as instruments of discovery or proof. For example, using the method of agreement in the case of baldness, it would be impossible to find two men different in every respect except that both are bald. If we modify the statement to include only relevant respects, we would have to decide what is relevant, and thus would have to start with a hypothesis as to the likely causes of baldness. Using the method of agreement as a method of proof, we would not know whether to expect single or multiple causes and, even if we were to locate one single point of difference between two instances, we could not be sure that it would be present in all cases. Then, too, there is the possibility that the crucial factor has been overlooked and is not included in the consideration—e.g., in this instance, the existence of an unknown fungus as the cause of baldness.

From the standpoint of scientific rigor, the method of difference suffers from much the same limitations as the method of agreement. As a method of discovery, it is limited by the fact that two circumstances can never be alike in all respects save one. Restricting the statement to relevant circumstances necessitates a hypothesis, which may overlook the agent causing the phenomenon directly or acting as a catalytic agent in the operation of other variables. Nor can the method of difference be used as a means of proof, inasmuch as other factors which are not included may be the crucial agents. The problem is further complicated by the fact that, in practice, causal factors are generally complex rather than single. The factors that make for good teaching, for example, probably operate only in interaction with one another.

In summary, the method of agreement is of relatively little value in research since it is almost impossible to fulfill the required conditions. The method of difference, on the other hand, is somewhat more realistic and is essentially the model of the simple experimental design involving the operation of a single experimental factor. Mill's first two canons display their greatest validity and usefulness when considered in terms of their converse, viz., a circumstance which is not common to all instances of a given phenomenon cannot be its cause, and a circumstance cannot be the cause of a phenomenon if, when it is present, the phenomenon fails to occur. An example of the use of this converse would be the identifying of the cause of an allergy by eliminating, one by one, potential causes so that the true cause is finally identified through the process of elimination of non-causes. This converse can be utilized, for example, in a trial-and-error approach to the diagnosis of academic difficulties. It should also be noted that it is easier to disprove than it is to prove. A confirming event by itself adds rather little to the validity of a given proposition. A single contradictory instance, if it can be substantiated, is, on the other hand, enough to disprove it.

3.   The Joint Method of Agreement and Disagreement

If two or more instances in which the phenomenon occurs have only one circumstance in common, while two or more instances in which it does not occur have nothing in common save the absence of that circumstance; the circumstance in which alone the two sets of instances differ is the effect, or cause, or a necessary part of the cause, of the phenomenon.

The third canon simply represents the double application of the Method of Agreement. It might be illustrated by pointing out that one event preceding another does not prove that the first is the cause of the second, unless it can also be shown that the suppression of the first also suppresses the occurrence of the second. In a sense, the third canon comes closer to the concept of cause and effect than either of the other two, if chance fluctuations are eliminated through replication and randomness. On the other hand, the joint method is not much of an improvement over the preceding canons, for it has essentially the same weaknesses as a source of both discovery and proof.

> *4.   The Method of Residue*   Subduct from any phenomenon such part as is known by previous inductions to be the effect of certain antecedents, and the residue of the phenomenon is the effect of the remaining antecedent.

If ABC is the cause of XYZ, and further, if AB is the cause of XY, then C must be the cause of Z. This canon arrives at the specific cause by the process of elimination and is interesting as a source of hypotheses in the more advanced sciences. For example, chemists measuring a mole of chlorine consistently found its weight to be approximately 35.5 grams, which did not make sense since its atomic weight had been calculated on the periodic table to be 35. The problem was solved by the discovery that common chlorine is really a mixture of Chlorine 35 and its isotope Chlorine 37 in the approximate ratio of 3:1. A parallel situation in education would be the case of the gifted child who, because of the interference of emotional factors, is not living up to academic expectations. Useful as this canon is in a highly developed science, it is somewhat less valuable in the social sciences where the expected values are relatively unknown, and the existence, magnitude, and direction of any deviation from the expected cannot always be appraised. It is useful only to the extent that one can detect interference with an established relationship.

> *5.   The Method of Concomitant Variation*   Whatever phenomenon varies in any manner whenever another phenomenon varies in some particular manner is either the cause or an effect of that phenomenon, or is connected with it through some fact of causation.

This canon also has serious weaknesses. Besides requiring valid and reliable measurements, it cannot provide proof since it does not eliminate the possibility of the two factors being caused by a third factor (which is allowed for in the latter part of the statement). It is possible to obtain a correlation of some degree between almost any two variables—e.g., teachers' salaries and the annual consumption of intoxicating liquors, or the number of teachers in a given community and the number of traffic violations, marriages, and other factors that accompany an increase in population. The value of the concept of concomitant variation probably lies in its negative statement—i.e., phenomena that do not vary concomitantly cannot be related causally. This canon, like the others, can suggest hypotheses for investigation. The failure of the canon of concomitance to isolate the operation of a third factor as the mutual cause of the covariation of the two variables is evident in the Hawthorne studies (Roethlesberger and Dickson, 1939) in which industrial production was shown to go up with both an increase and later a decrease in the relative intensity of illumination in the plant. On the other hand, concomitant variation is frequently the only way we can deal with certain problems in which, because of the impossibility of the physical manipulation of the variables, we must rely on statistical analysis.

Evaluation of Mill's Canons

Despite their limitations, Mill's canons represent important landmarks in the history of science. They mark an important gain in the successive definition and redefinition through which science must pass on its way to greater accuracy and truth. As instruments of present-day science, the use of Mill's canons is restricted largely to the derivation of hypotheses and their elimination through logic and, thus, to the reduction of the number of hypotheses to be tested empirically.

Mill's canons were oriented toward the establishment of causation in the sense of attributing the occurrence or non-occurrence of a phenomenon to the operation of a given factor. Their basic weakness stemmed from overlooking the fact that phenomena generally occur in response to a multiplicity of causes, and that what in practice appears to be the same cause frequently leads to varying outcome, with the result that the occurrence of a given phenomenon is a matter of probability rather than certainty. Science is now oriented toward the concept of concomitance and probability, and modern developments in multivariate analysis have made the use of Mill's canons relatively restricted, inadequate, and generally naïve.

PROOF

Nature of Proof

Closely related to cause and effect is the concept of *proof*. The determination of precisely what constitutes proof is sometimes difficult, since proof implies the possibility of establishing truth, a concept which conflicts with the modern view of science as a series of steps toward or approximations to the truth, i.e., a parallel series of partial proofs rather than proof itself. In fact, even if truth were attainable, it would be difficult to establish with any degree of confidence that it had been attained in any one instance; it could never be done with certainty. From an empirical point of view, proof parallels the concept of causation and poses the same problems in its establishment, and again, we find a great deal of looseness in the use of the term. As pointed out by Burton et al. (1958), the layman makes comments without proof and does not expect proof of the comments which he hears; he neither realizes the necessity for proof nor understands the nature of conclusive proof.

It is first necessary to realize that there are different kinds of proof. For example, in the legal sense, the accused may be considered "proved" guilty when his guilt is shown beyond reasonable doubt. Corroboration of adverse testimony, preponderance of evidence and failure to establish an adequate alibi are generally adequate grounds for conviction. An important consideration is the general reputation of the key witness. However, legal "proof" generally requires the establishment of a motive as the center of a conceptual scheme within which the offense can be viewed in perspective. This tends to be necessary even when the accused postulates his guilt.

Deductive Proof

Of greater interest is mathematical proof; for instance, in geometry, each theorem ends with the usual Q.E.D. Analysis of such proofs shows them to be based on internal consistency. Each theorem follows logically from the premise established in its statement and from the proof of the preceding theorems, all the way back to Theorem One, which derives its proof from self-evident postulates and axioms. Barring errors of deductive reasoning, each theorem is as sound as the theorems on which it is based. Proof in mathematics, since it is based on specific assumptions, is much more rigorous than proof in the empirical sense, but its applicability is restricted to the situation specified in its premises. This type of deductive proof is also found in logic; in both cases, proof is absolute: if we accept the premises, barring errors in the process, the conclusions that follow are indisputable.

Empirical Proof

The proof with which research is most directly concerned is empirical proof. What constitutes proof that teaching by Method A leads to greater pupil gain than does teaching by Method B? Or that treating wood with Chemical X increases its tensile strength. Here proof is based on the systematic observation of empirical events. In the latter case, for example, we might take two identical boards, impregnate one of the boards with Chemical X and leave the other untreated, and then test both pieces for strength. The essence of proof in empirical science consists of empirical observations confirming a given hypothesis. Thus, if the investigator hypothesizes that Chemical X increases the strength of wood, and if, when he subjects his hypothesis to a test, his observations are in line with that hypothesis, proof seems to have been established. Such proof is supplied by nature; the investigator simply notes the answer that is provided.

In practice, establishing empirical proof is invariably complicated, since it requires the establishment of control in an attempt to preclude the operation of extraneous factors. Obviously all biasing factors must be controlled since these would vitiate any proof derived. However, even after reasonable control of biasing factors has been effected, the investigator must still consider the operation of chance factors. These are generally controlled through replication and randomization so that whatever effects such uncontrolled factors have on the operation of the factor under study will tend to neutralize themselves—at least at a level that can be allowed for. This means, of course, that empirical proof, even at best, is always a matter of probability, never certainty.

Proof in Modern Science

Actually, no scientific investigation ever proves anything. Proof is a deductive matter, not an experimental operation. All that empiricism can do is to bring evidence to bear on the probable truth of a given proposition at a given level of probability.

There is no way of proving that factor X is the cause of juvenile delinquency. Other variables which are apparently involved are bound to bring about exceptions which will then need to be brought under trend. Research can only demonstrate that, within the context of a given set of basic assumptions, a stated proposition is tenable in the light of the interpretation given the facts known at that time.

This orientation of science toward probability of occurrence is undoubtedly the most crucial distinction between modern science and that of previous times. Until recently, the search for knowledge was an attempt to discover irrevocable truth and scientific effort was directed toward the derivation of immutable laws of a cause-and-effect nature. Modern scientific thought, in contrast, subscribes to the concept of general regularities on an overall basis. In other words, as pointed out by Burt and Gregory (1958), instead of thinking of Newton's Law as an exact or universal law of nature, we might better conceive of it as simply a postulate describing a particular model which, for purposes of certain *approximate* predictions, we find it convenient to accept. Implied here is the very real possibility—in fact, the general expectancy—that values will comply with a given law only in the general sense, that science is a matter of general regularity rather than exception-free relationships expressed in precise mathematical formulas.* Mathematics, on the other hand, is a logical tool and not a substance of science at all. It is rigorous and precise, but this makes it all the less applicable. In fact, its certainty and complete exactitude depend precisely on its detachment from empirical facts.

Acknowledging the concept of probability as the basis of scientific proof is an admission that the last word of science has yet to be said. It attests to the incompleteness of our knowledge and the inadequacy of our control of extraneous factors. The fact that we cannot predict certain phenomena with precision implies that we are not controlling all of the factors involved in their occurrence, just as the occurrence of an event from several alternative causes indicates that we have not defined the exact nature of the cause or of the effect. It must not be inferred that the concep-

---

* To be noted in this connection is the vital contribution of statisticians such as Gauss and LaPlace in placing the concept of error under law (the law of error) and thus permitting the interpretation of data on the basis of their relative agreement with the general law as postulated. It is interesting that we have here a case of converting ignorance into knowledge.

tion of scientific knowledge as merely probable is a denigration of science. Rather it is a recognition that this is the only kind of knowledge possible. Even in the most advanced sciences, experience shows that the actual occurrence of a phenomenon is not in precise agreement with the laws describing its operation. Boyle's Law, for example, expresses an ideal situation which is only approximated in practice. Two missiles fired from the same gun under "identical" conditions rarely, if ever, follow the same trajectory; landing on a target is strictly a matter of probability. For the same reason, actuarial laws, despite their overall accuracy, are almost completely inapplicable in the individual case, just as prediction of academic success is, and must remain, a group concept. On the other hand, there is no cause for discouragement: barring gross errors, workable parts are manufactured, bridges are built, and satellites orbited. We merely acknowledge that they do so not according to exact specifications, but within the tolerance limits postulated by the law of chance.

It is interesting to note that mathematics, as a pure discipline, is independent of empirical proof or disproof. That two and two make four is not proved or disproved by showing that two oranges plus two oranges make four oranges or that two gallons of sand plus two gallons of water do not make four gallons of anything. Nor do mathematicians care: when practice confirms theory, it is to be expected; when it does not agree, it simply reflects failure in the fulfillment of the assumptions on which the mathematical expressions rest. Nevertheless, it is worth noting that the principles of mathematics are generally supported by empirical evidence. For example, the weight that can be supported on a clothesline is a function of the angle of declination and the tensile strength of the line as represented by the equation $w = t \sin \theta$. This, of course, does not "prove" the validity of trigonometry as a discipline, since mathematical proof is not empirical; it simply "proves" that the assumptions upon which trigonometry is based are apparently sound and that the results are, therefore, useful.

Highlights of the Chapter

1.   Man's attempts to arrive at truth concerning his environment have been based on three complementary approaches—*experience*, *reasoning*, and *experimentation*.

2.   Experience—our own or that of others—is obviously a prerequisite to the development of science. However, the number of false beliefs attests to its limitations as a source of scientific truth. Experience makes its greatest contribution in the derivation and the verification of hypotheses.

3.   Reasoning is an indispensable tool in the derivation of scientific truth but it cannot generate, or even identify, truth. Its contribution to the development of science lies in suggesting hypotheses, in evaluating the compatibility of hypotheses with accepted knowledge, in devising a research design capable of testing these hypotheses, and in interpreting the results of such a test.

4.   Historically, syllogistic reasoning, as perfected by Aristotle, represents the first systematic attempt at the discovery of truth. The syllogism degenerated during the Middle Ages into an exercise in mental gymnastics divorced from basic experience. It was superseded in the early 1600's by the inductive approach advocated by Francis Bacon, who objected to what he considered to be the prejudicial influence of hypotheses in orienting the scientist to a prejudged conclusion. Bacon's approach—which was undoubtedly wasteful, if not unproductive—was, in turn, superseded by the modern inductive-deductive method, generally credited to Charles Darwin.

5.   Experimentation is undoubtedly the most rigorous approach to scientific truth. It is designed to test the validity of hypotheses under strict conditions of control.

6.   In its development, science went through three relatively identifiable, although overlapping, stages. Primitive man explained phenomena on the basis of gods, spirits, and other supernatural agents. Later, man came to realize that natural phenomena had natural causes and eventually undertook the task of deriving empirical generalizations relating the occurrence of phenomena to their causes. The third stage consists of developing a logical framework to explain the empirical relationships noted and to permit the deduction of hypotheses concerning the other aspects of the phenomenon in question. This represents the highest level—and the goal—of scientific endeavor.

7. Empirical science operates through such steps as: (a) the accumulation and clarification of experience; (b) classification; (c) quantification; (d) discovery of relationships; and (e) successive approximations to (and successive redefinitions of) the truth.

8. Early science—as exemplified by Mill's canons—was oriented toward the discovery of cause-and-effect relationships of the one-to-one variety between a certain antecedent and a certain consequent. Modern science, in contrast, recognizes that a multiplicity of interacting "causes" are involved in the occurrence of a phenomenon and that its actual occurrence as anticipated is a function of the simultaneous operation of all contributing factors exactly as postulated, and, therefore, always a matter of probability, never certainty.

9. What constitutes proof needs clarification. Deductive proof—like that in mathematics and logic—is simply a matter of internal consistency. Legal proof is generally a matter of plausibility and general credibility. Empirical proof, on the other hand, is invariably a troublesome concept, since it implies the establishment of cause-and-effect relationships (or truth)—which, as we have seen, is relatively impossible. Modern science is oriented toward successive approximations to the truth and partial (tentative) proofs. In contrast to the earlier view, modern science views empirical proof —like causation—as a matter of general expectancy or probability of occurrence at a given level of confidence.

Questions and Projects

1. Investigate and report the contributions of the Greeks—especially Plato and Aristotle—to the development of modern science. Pay particular attention to their system of classification and to the syllogism.

2. List ten false beliefs that were widely accepted, even by the intelligentia, at one time or another in our cultural development. Trace the developments that led to their eventual rejection.

3. How much of our behavior rests on a substantial scientific basis? Log your behavior for a day; classify your experiences as to

their basis in (a) authority; (b) custom and tradition; (c) logical reasoning; and (d) experimentation.

4.   List the ten men in history you feel have made the greatest contribution to man's progress and welfare. To what extent did "science" feature in their contributions?

Selected References

Brown, Clarence W. and Edwin E. Ghiselli. *Scientific Method in Psychology.* New York: McGraw-Hill, 1955.

Cohen, I.B. *Science, Servant of Man.* Boston: Little, Brown, 1950.

Cohen, Morris R. and Ernest Nagel. *An Introduction to Logic and Scientific Method.* New York: Harcourt, Brace, 1934.

Dingle, Herbert (ed.) *A Century of Science,* 1851–1951. New York: Roy, 1951.

Fawcett, Harold P. *The Nature of Proof.* 13th Yrbk., National Council, Teachers of Mathematics. New York: T.C., Columbia Univ., 1938.

Grunbaum, Adolf. "Causality and the science of human behavior," *Amer. Sci.,* 40: 665–76; 1952.

Kantor, J.R. *The Logic of Modern Science.* Bloomington: Principia Press, 1953.

Kaufman, Felix. "The nature of scientific method," *Soc. Res.,* 12: 464–80; 1954.

Kuhn, Thomas S. "Historical structure of scientific discovery," *Sci.,* 136: 760–64; 1962.

Lewin, Kurt. "The conflict between Aristotelian and Galilean modes of thought in contemporary psychology," *J. gen. Psychol.,* 5: 141–77; 1931.

Nagel, Ernest. *The Structure of Science: Problems in the Logic of Scientific Explanation.* New York: Harcourt, Brace & World, 1961.

Merton, Robert K. "Priorities in scientific discovery: A chapter in the sociology of science," *Amer, sociol. Rev.,* 22: 635–59; 1957.

Northrop, F. Stuart C. *The Logic of the Sciences and the Humanities.* New York: Macmillan, 1947.

Russell, Bertrand. "On the notion of cause with applications to the free-will problem," in Herbert Feigl (ed.) *Readings in the Philosophies of Science.* New York: Appleton-Century Crofts, 1953, pp. 387–407.

Sarton, George. *A Guide to the History of Science.* Waltham: Chronica Botanica, 1952.

Scates, Douglas E. "The parallel roles of physical and social science," *Sci. Monthly*, 14: 14–20; Jan. 1947.

Storer, Norman W. *The Social System of Science*. New York: Holt, Rinehart & Winston, 1966.

Thomson, George. "The two aspects of science," *Sci.*, 132: 996–1000; 1960.

Walker, Marshall. *The Nature of Scientific Thought*. Englewood Cliffs: Prentice-Hall, 1966.

Wightman, William P.D. *The Growth of Scientific Ideas*. New Haven: Yale Univ. Press, 1953.

3
THE NATURE
OF SCIENCE

Nothing is more curious than the self-satisfied dogmatism with which mankind at each period of its history cherishes the delusion of the finality of existing modes of knowledge.——Alfred North Whitehead (1954)

Purpose of Science

The basic purpose of science is the accumulation and clarification of experience, and the systematization of such experience into a relatively small number of broad systems of knowledge into which the various categories of phenomena can be structured. It is not merely a matter of cataloging one's experiences or of describing their nature and characteristics in detail, but rather one of discovering or establishing a structural system into which phenomena can be ordered and on the basis of which they can be predicted and, eventually, controlled. In the early stages of science, the task is to gather, define, and catalog experiences in order to obtain an understanding of their interrelationships. In the later stages of science, the task is to reduce to a minimum the number of laws necessary to express these relationships.

Interpreted broadly, the scientific method constitutes the most adequate approach to the discovery of truth, and certainly it has demonstrated its worth, particularly in the physical sciences. On the other hand, the limitations of the scientific method must be clearly understood. For instance, science cannot deal directly with values. It can define some of the issues involved in making value-judgments, but the judgments themselves are outside the scope of science. Even the interpretation of the results of research is outside the realm of science. And, while science attempts to minimize errors and guarantee valid results, errors have been made by persons using the scientific method. Usually, however, the errors were in the use of the method rather than in the method itself. It must also be noted that the scientific method does not lead to truth directly, but proceeds through a series of successive approximations to the isolation of more and more precise relationships and to more adequate formulation of these relationships.

Science as a Method of Discovery

Science can be defined both as an organized body of knowledge and a method and system of deriving truth, with the latter the more crucial and significant. As Dewey (1933) suggests: "The heart of science lies not in the conclusions reached, but in the method of observation, experimentation, and mathematical reasoning by which conclusions are established." While the layman focuses on the facts, laws, and relationships discovered by science, these are really the outcomes of science, i.e., the consequences of "*behaving* scientifically" (Gorlow and Katkovsky, 1959).

The scientific method can be delineated into a number of steps, the exact formulation of which varies somewhat from writer to writer. The general pattern is: certain phenomena are observed; a problem situation develops, is noted, and clarified; crude relationships are tentatively identified and elaborated; a more or less formal hypothesis is derived; a design is developed to test the hypothesis; the hypothesis is verified or refuted; the results are subjected to further tests and refinements; and finally the conclusions are integrated with the previous concepts of science. The process involves such subsidiary steps as the review of relevant experience, the manipulation of factors, the measurement of quantities, the scaling of variables, and the analysis and interpretation of data.

On the other hand, the scientific method must not be conceived as a set of procedures by which all problems of life can be solved. It is not a formula that can be applied mechanically or even computerized in the pursuit of scientific knowledge. Its formal steps, while listed in numerical order, rarely occur in that sequence, since the effective use of the scientific method does not allow for this sort of rigidity. As Skinner (1956) points out:

But it is a mistake to identify scientific practice with the

> formalized constructions of statistics and scientific method.
> These disciplines have their place, but it does not coincide
> with the place of scientific research . . . .

Skinner points out that these disciplines arose very late in the history of science and most of the facts of science were discovered
without their aid.

> It is no wonder that the laboratory scientist is puzzled and
> often dismayed when he discovers how his behavior has been
> reconstructed in formal analyses of the scientific method.
> He is likely to protest that this is not at all a fair represen-
> tation of what he does.

In a similar vein, Kruglak (1949) notes that the very
method of science is not subject to scientific proof. "If it were a
method, all a person would have to do is to memorize its steps
and then everyone would arrive at the same proof or conclusions."
He points out that there is no satisfactory definition of the scientific
method and that the momentous scientific achievements of the past
were realized by procedures in violation of, rather than conformity
with, the formal steps of the scientific method as taught in our
schools, where the spirit of scientific inquiry too frequently de-
generates into collecting the same data that millions of other bored
students have collected for years.

Certainly, not all attempts at discovering truth comply with the specific formulation presented above. Some scientists
suggest that we ought to think of scientific *methods* rather than of
the scientific method. They feel that using the term in the singular
implies that there is only one right way to attack a problem, and
that it leads people to confuse the scientific method with experimentation, which is only one of its forms. Other scientists do not
agree. They realize that, though there are different ways of treating
different problems, the need is for many different scientific *techniques* subsumed under the scientific method.

The difficulty is one of definition. If we hold rigidly
to the scientific method described above as the criterion for inclusion or exclusion in the select club of science, we would have to
exclude Einstein's contributions since they were almost exclusively
organizational and deductive rather than experimental. And, unless we extend the concept of verification to include proof by ob-

servation, we also exclude such sciences as astronomy and geology in which manipulation of variables is basically impossible. We also eliminate historical and other studies in which control is relatively limited. The scientific method must not be interpreted so narrowly that it excludes all approaches except those in which the investigator actually manipulates—either physically or statistically—the conditions of his "experiment," and "causes" the occurrence of the events he wishes to observe as would, for example, the chemist testing a chemical reaction. In fact, this behavior frequently characterizes more adequately the laboratory assistant than it does the scientist. In the later stages of a science, scientific progress and excellence are obtained not through experimentation as such but through the organization and systematization of scientific thought, with experimentation simply confirming what logical deduction has led the scientist to expect.

The Products of Science

The final products of empirical science are the laws and generalizations which place into a unitary conceptual framework a number of relatively isolated relationships discovered through the various techniques of science. Science is generally oriented toward the derivation of laws which are of a nomothetic nature, i.e., general laws which apply to all individuals of a given class or a given set. For example, bright children learn faster than dull children. Such laws are derived statistically and apply statistically—i.e., the relationship is one of probability, and though they are stated as absolutes, it is more correct to state that bright children *tend* to learn . . . , or that, *in general*, bright children . . . .

Such generalizations are not exception-free. They express a useful relationship, but they are generally of limited value in the individual case, since they are derived on the basis of an average set of conditions which no one can duplicate. To the extent that the individual complies with the conditions postulated in the law only in the general sense, the law applies to him only in a general way and, therefore, can be interpreted only on the basis of probability. This is perhaps more obvious in the social sciences where, for example, predicting which student applicant will be successful and which will be unsuccessful is always a precarious undertaking. The predicament, however, is not restricted to the social sciences; it pertains equally well to the bombardment of alpha particles where it is impossible to tell which particle will fly free and which direction it will take.

The degree to which a generalization can be applied to the individual case depends to a great degree on the extent of the clear-cut, nonoverlapping distinctions stated in the conclusions. Thus, the generalization that adults are taller than children can be applied in the individual case with a high degree of probability, while the generalization that executive positions are occupied by persons who are taller than average has only a slightly greater than 50–50 probability of successful prediction in the individual case. The number of conditions included in the statement of the law also affects its applicability: the more of the relevant conditions in the antecedent of the law which are specified, the greater the probability of its validity in cases meeting those specifications. In fact, a law would be exception-free if its statement covered all antecedent conditions involved. However, then there would be no "new" cases and the law would be useless. Thus the more conditions we specify in the statement of a law, the more precise it becomes (under the conditions of its statement), but also the more restricted it is in its application—and the more useless it is as a tool of prediction.

Of particular interest to social scientists are the laws known as *idiographic*—i.e., laws pertaining to the individual case. The clinical psychologist, for example, would rely on idiographic laws in predicting the behavior of his client on the basis of the specific characteristics that make this client like, and yet different from, other counselees. Each child in the classroom also is a unique individual whose behavior is governed by idiographic as well as nomothetic laws.

Hypothetical Constructs

The task confronting the scientist is to formulate laws and principles which express functional relationships among phenomena. The ultimate goal is the relatively complete understanding of such phenomena and their antecedents so as to permit the prediction and eventually the control of their occurrence. In an experiment, for example, the investigator is interested in the effect which a certain *independent* variable has upon some aspect of the *dependent* variable.

However, the operation of the independent variable

with respect to the dependent variable is not a matter of a one-to-one direct-line connection. Rather, scientists generally find it necessary to postulate *hypothetical constructs* to account for the relationships noted among the variables in the situation under observation. Chemists, for example, postulated the existence of molecules long before their actual existence was verified under microscope. They simply found that chemical relationships could be explained more logically and meaningfully when matter was assumed to be made of molecules. Chemists also postulated the concept of valence to account for the attraction of atoms in a chemical reaction.

Hypothetical constructs are used in all sciences: force, mass, or density in physics; genes in genetics; attitudes, motivation, and aptitude in psychology. We postulate mechanical aptitude to account for individual differences in performance on certain tests. Learning, itself, is a hypothetical construct. We speak loosely when we say that practice causes learning; practice is related in a functional way to performance, from which we simply infer that learning has taken place. The scientist's task is to discover laws that govern the operation of these hypothetical constructs. The psychologist, for example, has to specify the factors that determine behavioral changes that occur and to formulate laws pertaining to the relationships involved.

Hypothetical constructs are really products of the scientist's imagination. They are imaginary concepts which provide a structure around which he can order his thinking. In the early stages of the development of a science, these constructs are generally taken from personal experience; in the later stages, they are postulated in terms of events that are inferred rather than directly observed. They may be borrowed from any number of sources, e.g., neurology (S–R bonds), physics (forces, moments), physics and mathematics (vectors, topology), astronomy (life space, phenomenal field), etc. Some are quite elaborate: Hebb (1949) speaks of a conceptual nervous system, complete with synaptic knobs, cell assemblies, and phase sequences. Smith and Carrigan (1959) present a synaptic transmission model in which chemical action activates nerve impulse transmission across synapses.

Hypothetical constructs facilitate our understanding of phenomena, but we must be careful not to use them as if they had a physical counterpart. It is easy to speak of gravity as if it really existed. That is what we did with the construct *instinct* years ago. We spoke of maternal instinct as if it explained maternal behavior when, in reality, we had simply exchanged one level of verbal ignorance for another—we had described what we were alleging to explain. We must also be careful not to get involved in circular arguments: we cannot define problem-solving ability as a function of the hypothetical construct *intelligence* and, at the same time, define intelligence in terms of problem-solving ability.

Hypothetical constructs can also be conceived as *intervening* variables, i.e., variables assumed to intervene between stimulus and response variables. Motives, for example, are said to be intervening variables whose existence is inferred from observable behavior in response to a given situation. Intervening variables, in turn, can be categorized as experiential variables, transfer variables, and various process (mediating) variables, e.g., the ability to discriminate.

Also used to promote a greater understanding of phenomena are what scientists call *models*. Although relatively synonymous in meaning with hypothetical constructs, *models* tend to be used to refer to concrete representations of an object—for example, the tinkertoy model of a complex molecule or the normal curve as the representation of the distribution of IQ's in the general population. *Hypothetical constructs* are generally used to refer to the more abstract representation of the unobservable aspects of phenomena. A parallel distinction might be made between *concept* and *hypothetical construct* which, again, are relatively equivalent. A point of difference might be that a concept expresses an abstraction formed by generalizations from particulars, e.g., weight. A construct is also a concept but one which is postulated for a specific scientific purpose: intelligence (normally a concept) becomes a construct when it enters the theoretical scheme as an intervening variable in explaining school achievement.

Models, just as hypothetical constructs, can be valuable assets in the pursuit of scientific clarity, although certainly an inaccurate model, (e.g., a flat-earth model) can be as much a hindrance as bad theories (e.g., phlogiston) were to early chemists. An interesting new development is experimentation with the model itself and the use of the knowledge so obtained to deal with the real phenomenon—for example, simulation of the learning process through the use of the computer in solving the problems of Euclidean geometry.

Operationalism

To be of scientific value, a concept must be verifiable. This means that it must be defined in terms of an empirical referent or operation. Conversely, any concept that cannot be demonstrated in measurable operations is scientifically meaningless. Freud's concepts of the *id* and the *death instinct,* while not necessarily wrong, are unverifiable and, therefore, outside the realm and scope of science. Repression, on the other hand, can be defined in terms of a measurable decrease in ability to recall. Such an "operational" definition reduces phenomena to the level of some empirical event that actually occurs or exists. In keeping with a basic principle of tests and measurements that learning be defined in terms of measurable changes in pupil behavior, an operational definition of academic growth would refer to what the child can actually do with respect to educational objectives considered valid from the standpoint of the purposes of the investigation.

According to Bridgman (1927, 1961), who first introduced operationalism, the starting point of any science is a set of phenomena that have been operationally defined. In their simplest form, operational definitions are specified in terms of the measuring operations used to identify the phenomenon. Musical pitch, for example, can be defined in units of the scale through which differences in pitch are recognized. Similarly, a stimulus can be defined operationally in terms of what it causes people to do.

Operational definitions identify a given phenomenon by specifying the basic dimensions or operations through which its existence can be ascertained. It follows that, if two concepts can be defined only in terms of the same set of operations, they do not have a separate existence and must be one. It must also be recognized that operational definitions rarely touch upon all the significant dimensions of a given phenomenon. Many concepts (e.g., progressive education, team teaching, etc.) are typically used in educational research in a very sloppy way. On the other hand, insistence on operational terms frequently causes the investigator to settle for superficial or peripheral aspects of the situation. Teacher effectiveness, for example, is often evaluated in terms of pupil progress as measured on a standardized achievement test. The danger of circularity must also be recognized: defining intelligence as whatever a given test of 'intelligence' (of unproven validity) measures is, according to Cattell (1966), the limit of scientific and conceptual bankruptcy.

THEORY AND SCIENTIFIC PROGRESS

The Need for Organization

In its early stages of development, the major concern of science is the accumulation and refinement of experience and the discovery of functional relationships among phenomena. As long as the relationships so derived remain isolated, however, they are of limited value except in the solution of a problem identical to those which led to their discovery. To be useful, knowledge must be organized, and the primary responsibility of a science is to develop a system of organization which will make the facts, as they are accumulated, meaningful from the standpoint of their ultimate purpose.

Science must remain close to facts; yet it is only when isolated facts are placed into perspective by being integrated into some conceptual scheme which promotes a greater understanding of their nature and significance that we approach a science. Thus, Conant (1948) suggests that unless progress is made in reducing the degree of empiricism in an area, the rate of advance in that area will be relatively slow and highly capricious. Similarly, McConnell (1942) points out that the development of a science depends as much on the continuous formulation and revision of theory as it does on investigation and experimentation.

Science is committed to a continuous process of ever-expanding clarification and systematization of its findings. Through continuous observation and experimentation, it attempts to evaluate the adequacy of previous generalizations and to isolate the conditions under which these previous generalizations can be expected to hold. Thus, in sequence, from simple experiences come simple hypotheses, which lead to further experience, further clarification, and more sophisticated hypotheses. As these hypotheses are substantiated, they become laws and principles which, as a result of being mirrored against further facts, hypotheses, and laws, become integrated theories. The ultimate goal is a systematization not only of facts into laws but of laws into ever-expanding conceptual schemes of science. Thus, the method of science is essentially one of a back-and-forth movement—from facts, to hypotheses, to laws, and back to facts as the basis for the testing and refinement of more adequate hypotheses; thus leading to the derivation of more general and comprehensive principles and theories. It must also be noted that generally the steps are rather small; progress in science is made by the slow accumulation of small steps and, frequently, the correction of missteps (Underwood, 1957).

Purpose of Theory

The purposes to be served by theory in the development of science have been implied repeatedly in the previous sections. They can be summarized as follows:

1. Theory synthesizes isolated bits of empirical data into a broader conceptual scheme of wider applicability and predictability. It permits deeper understanding of data and translates empirical findings into more readily understood, more readily retained, and more readily adaptable form. The theory of oxidation, for instance, places into focus many of the chemical reactions common to everyday life. Theory provides facts with meaning and significance by clarifying them and placing them in perspective with one another and with pre-existing theories. It actually determines the kinds of facts that are relevant to a given study, for facts do not identify themselves as relevant. Only theory can help the investigator decide what to observe and what to ignore.

2. Theory permits the prediction of the occurrence of phenomena and enables the investigator to postulate and, eventually, to discover hitherto unknown phenomena. At the time the periodic table was being completed, for instance, certain gaps were noted in the sequence of the elements. Since, according to theory, there should have been no gaps, scientists were spurred to look for the missing elements. In time these were found, probably much earlier than they would have been had their presence not been anticipated by theory.

3. Theory acts as a guide to discovering facts; it pinpoints crucial aspects to be investigated and crucial questions to be answered. By identifying areas in need of exploration, it stimulates research in fields that are lagging.

4. Theory is based on the assumption that detailed empirical findings are special cases of more general laws, and that progress cannot be made as long as observations are

simply accumulated. Theories cannot develop without experimental facts any more than the discovery of experimental facts can proceed far on the basis of grossly inadequate or incorrect theories. For example, the progress of psychiatry as a science was bound to be limited as long as the insane were viewed as possessed by devils. Just as facts underlie theories, theories underlie facts—each raising the other on a spiral to increasingly precise scientific formulations. Research and theory go hand in hand; theory guides and stimulates research while research tests and stimulates theory development, resulting in more adequate theories and more accurate and precise empirical data. This is again a statement of the successive approximations and redefinitions on the basis of which scientific progress is made. Facts derive their significance from the theoretical framework into which they fit, just as theories derive their acceptability from the extent to which they bring facts into clearer focus. This is well stated by Van Dalen (1959):

> . . . there is a constant and intricate relationship between facts and theory. Facts without theory or theory without facts lack significance. Facts take their significance from the theories which define, classify and predict them. Theories possess significance when they are built upon, classified, and tested by facts. Thus, the growth of science is dependent upon the accumulation of facts and the formulation of new or broader theories. To conduct research without theoretical interpretations or to theorize without research is to ignore the essential functions of theory as a tool for achieving economy of thought.

This is particularly true, since in its early stages research must confine its efforts to seeking answers to highly specific and particularized problems. In its later stages, it tends to strive toward unity by breaking down the very barriers that have made its earlier progress possible. Scientific theories attempt to organize the tiny, rigorously defined bits of knowledge into a more realistically meaningful structure. This is precisely the function of theory.

The Modern Acceptance of Theory

The potential value of theory is readily acknowledged by such notable scientists as Einstein and Conant and attested to by the fact that many of the world's leading scientists, e.g., Newton, Poincaré, Whitehead, and Einstein, were philosophers of science rather than experimenters. In fact, it is the feeling of many scientists that we are limited not so much by the inadequacies of our techniques of research as by the inadequacy of our theoretical framework. There are, however, others who are more reserved in their support of theory. A relatively strong stand against theory is taken by Skinner (1950) who questions the need for theories of learning on the grounds that they are not essential to the designing of significant experiments, and further that they actually retard the growth of science by diverting time and effort from research proper and by limiting research to predetermined areas, while discouraging the investigation of those aspects which are not in line with current theory.

The layman, and even the professional educator, frequently displays a lack of appreciation of the complementary nature of theory and practice. Burton et al. (1960) gives a number of reasons for this distrust of theory, ranging from a glorification of factualism, i.e., an undeserved respect for the so-called scientific *fact* and a corresponding disrespect for the impractical "thinker," to a tendency to get involved with one's own experience as the answer to all problems. Many also lack understanding of what theory really is. It is true, of course, that many theories have not been well formulated and that many are based on speculation rather than on scientific fact. This is understandable: in the early stages of his work, the theorist must be blind to exceptions and discordant aspects; otherwise he would never be able to get his theory off the ground. He must bypass certain problems until he has gathered enough facts to resolve them. A theory at first must, of necessity, be oversimplified, self-contradictory, incomplete, with overlapping categories and equivocal definitions. Its first loyalty is to include all the facts within its scope, and this can make for sloppiness. Any of the current theories, particularly in the social sciences, are relatively lacking in validity and scope as well as in practicality, simply because they are not sufficiently advanced. As we look back with our current perspective, the various theories of science in the past —whether in physics, chemistry, medicine, or psychology—appear particularly unenlightened and unhelpful. Early investigators were seriously hampered by the inadequacies of their theories, e.g., the geocentric concept of the universe which Copernicus discredited by showing that planetary movements could be described much more simply by assuming that the stationary center of the universe was the sun and not the earth. Lavoisier, likewise, set an important foundation for chemistry when he abandoned the phlogiston theory of combustion and replaced it with the more adequate concept of oxidation. Boyle made a similar contribution to physics by substituting for the inadequate "Nature abhors a vacuum," the more correct conceptual scheme that air has weight.

No theory is ever complete; no theory incorporates all that is involved in a given phenomenon. Invariably, scientific theories are replaced by more sophisticated theories embodying more of the advanced state of the question so that science widens its horizons to include more and more of the facts as they accumulate. No doubt, many of the things about which there is unanimous agreement today will be found especially inadequate by future standards. But, in terms of theoretical development, we must begin where we are. In the meantime, it must not be assumed that theory consists of blind speculation. On the contrary, a theory is an attempt at synthesizing empirical data for maximal clarification and unification, and some degree of theoretical orientation is generally justified, even if theory is not sufficiently developed for precise implications for practice. Certainly, nothing can be more practical than a sound theory.

Actually, everyone has a number of personal theories based on postulates and assumptions of varying degrees of adequacy and truth from which he makes deductions of various degrees of cruciality and, of course, of accuracy. The school principal, for instance, has many theories about education. These are based partially on personal experience, partially on his reading of relevant literature, and partially on his personal philosophy. But he looks upon these theories as practical facts, and he bases decisions on them as if they were truth. Rarely, if ever, does he subject his theories to a test through a valid experiment of their logical deductions.

Probably the most fundamental determinant of the potential contribution of theory to a given science is the state of development of that science. It seems logical that, in the early stages of any science, the empirical approach—i.e., the accumulation of data—must be paramount. In the later stages, on the other hand, theory is likely to become progressively more vital to its further growth. The question, then, is not one of whether one believes in the crucial role of theory in the advancement of science, but whether a given science is ready for emphasis on theory. This is the position taken by Traxler (1954) and also by MacKinnon (1953), who questions the practice of requiring a doctoral candidate to take a definite theoretical stand in his doctoral dissertation, when the various members of his committee would probably not agree on a single theoretical position themselves.

It is fully recognized that a premature subscription to a theory may blind the scientist to the correct solution in much the same way as the *flat-world* concept or the veneration of Aristotle probably retarded the development of science for centuries. Furthermore, the fact that a discovery which is compatible with an existing theory is easier to accept than one which is not may lead to the perpetuation of false theories supported by prejudged evidence. This was evident in the Dark Ages when even scientists resisted scientific advances. However, truth will eventually prevail, recantations notwithstanding. Premature attempts to reach a formalized theoretical position are likely not only to delimit the areas explored but also to lead to the investigation of the more trivial aspects of science, e.g., conditioning, habit formation, rote memory, simply because they are easier to conceptualize and to test, or perhaps because they lend themselves more readily to mathematical formalization. The result is a neglect of the more theoretically complex but also more scientifically significant aspects of a problem. Another difficulty which arises in the social sciences is that the formulation of a theory immediately leads to its contamination, in the sense that people are affected by knowledge of the theory and, reacting to this knowledge, interfere with its realization. It must also be realized that a theory does not provide answers; it may stimulate and direct research, but it is through significant research and not through theory that significant answers are obtained.

The emphasis to be placed on theory in the development of a given science at a particular stage of development is difficult to establish, since it revolves around the question of when enough is enough. Undoubtedly, science is always ready for theory —at its own level, of course, but ready, nevertheless. The alternative, to gather all the facts and then to theorize, is clearly illogical. It is not fruitful to concentrate on the accumulation of data without some (perhaps vague) idea of what is sought. The accumulation of data and the organization of these data into theoretical structure must go hand in hand, and any lag in one is bound to cause a corresponding lag in the other.

Theory as a Point of Reference

All sciences make use of deduction to some degree. Though in the beginning a given science must concentrate on the accumulation of evidence and the inductive development of tentative hypotheses, in its later stages the relative ratio of induction to deduction leans more toward deduction. Much of the efforts of the physicist, for example, are devoted to the mathematical manipulation of previously derived formulas concerning the relationship among phenomena. In fact, in the more advanced sciences, scientists place their maximum concern on the development of theory, on the basis of which empirical observations are to be guided and explained. A physicist would look with some degree of suspicion on any result that he could not integrate with previously established theory. His first reaction would be to look upon a discordant result, not as a revolutionary concept likely to overthrow all pre-existing knowledge but rather as simply an error, a chance result, or a special case. This is not to imply that physics is fully explored and complete, but rather that it is sufficiently stable and integrated that the next improvements are likely to be small changes, and, furthermore, changes that are compatible with present views. Thus, Einstein's theory of relativity gained early acceptance because it was a better explanation, rather than a refutation, of what was already known about gravity and electrical theories and because it reconciled some of the contradictions of earlier theories.

When exceptions to theories arise, they must be integrated into more adequate theories. A classic example of the resolution of such exceptions can be found in the case of the Dulong-Petit Law, which stated that the specific heat of a solid element multiplied by its atomic weight is a constant (approximately 2 calories per degree). At first, this was simply an empirical observation, with no scientific explanation. Two notable exceptions were carbon and silicon. Later, with the development of the Quantum Theory, not only was the relationship explained, but the exceptions themselves were also explained as special cases.

Data in agreement with theory do not prove a theory, but merely support it; the existence of a single item of negative evidence, on the other hand, is logically sufficient for its rejection or its modification. However, scientists have operated on the premise that a theory is not so much true or false as it is useful or useless, and that an inadequate theory is probably better than no theory at all. Generally, an exception calls for some adjustment in a theory rather than its complete scrapping. As Conant (1951) points out, "A conceptual scheme is never discarded merely because of a few stubborn facts with which it cannot be reconciled; a conceptual scheme is either modified or replaced by a better one, never abandoned with nothing left to take its place."

Exceptions to a theory actually serve a very useful purpose in promoting crucial research and, eventually, in improving the theory. This is not to imply that a theory, once established, except for minor refinements, will stand forever. Certainly the phlogiston theory had to be abandoned completely in favor of the oxidation theory, but in the usual case a refinement or perhaps an extension of the theory can incorporate new evidence. Actually, a theory is rarely, if ever, complete: as new facts appear—and in most theories new facts appear endlessly—theories have to undergo some modification. Rarely, however, is there need for a completely new conceptual scheme.

A particularly important change that probably needs to be made in the future is the unification of the theories used in the different disciplines to explain their own particular data. Each field has developed a considerable amount of specialized knowledge, and a major task of science seems to be that of building bridges from one discipline to another in order to integrate this specialized knowledge into a single conceptual structure. This assumes the unity of science—i.e., it assumes not only that the universe is subject to law and order, but also that various components are subject to the same set of principles of law and order. This seems reasonable—at least more reasonable than to assume that the principles that govern the aspects of one discipline are independent of or in conflict with those of another. Some basis for such unification already exists in the common allegiance of the various disciplines to the scientific method. There is also considerable communality among the basic concepts fundamental to the various fields. The clinical psychologists facing his client, for example, may well be reminded of Newton's third law of motion—i.e., that an object will continue at rest if at rest, or in motion if in motion, until it is affected by a force. Nor are such concepts as *field forces* and *valence* used by Gestalt psychologists too remote from their counterparts in the physical sciences. In recent years, there has been a major rapprochement in the principles and laws of the sciences of the physical and social order, and theoretical unity has become a feature of the more advanced sciences.

Psychologists have developed a number of "schools of psychology" which are not only in disagreement with each other, but which have yet to develop a wholly consistent and satisfactory explanation of all psychological phenomena. There is, of course, a major need for the unification of the various theories and a start has been made in this direction. McConnell (1942), for example, attempted to identify the crucial points of difference among the various theories of learning and the issues which need to be resolved in their reconciliation. Education is almost completely lacking in a consistent theory. Whereas, in the days of Thorndike, much of the work of education was coordinated on the basis of connectionism, present-day educators tend to subscribe to an eclectic and, at times, self-contradictory approach. A teacher may, for example, talk of the "whole child" while drilling arithmetic combinations!

It is not inconceivable that some day a single theoretical system—obviously, unknown at this time—will be used to explain the behavior of molecules, of animals, and of people. Even today, some of the features of the field theory, for example, with its concept of field forces, apply to people in their environment as well as to electrons in their various shells and to heavenly bodies in orbit. Hartmann (1942) points out that field theories claim such scientists as Whitehead, Planck, and Einstein in the physical sciences; Cannon, Lashley, Woodger in physiology; Wertheimer, Köhler, and Koffka in Gestalt psychology; and Lewin in topological psychology. Thus, in a sense, field theory is more a theory of science than it is simply a school of psychology, and it might conceivably contain the seed for a more complete unification of scientific phenomena.

Characteristics of a Good Theory

Whether a given theory can be expected to fulfill its purposes depends on the extent to which it meets certain basic criteria. Among these are:

   1. A theoretical system must permit deductions which can be tested empirically—i.e., it must provide the means for its

own interpretation and verification. Much of the work of Freud, for instance, does not provide testable deductions and is, therefore, a matter of speculation rather than of scientific theory.

2. Theory must be compatible both with observation and with previously validated theories. It must be grounded in empirical data which have been verified and must rest on sound postulates and hypotheses. The better the theory, the more adequately it can explain the phenomena under consideration, and the more facts it can incorporate into a meaningful structure of ever-greater generalizability. A good theory is one that has as wide applicability as the present state of knowledge will permit.

3. Theories must be stated in simple terms; that theory is best which explains the most in the simplest form. This is the *law of parsimony*. A theory must explain the data adequately and yet must not be so comprehensive as to be unwieldy. On the other hand, it must not overlook variables simply because they are difficult to appraise. A theory must be stated precisely and clearly, if it is to serve as an adequate guide to research.

4. Scientific theories must be based on empirical facts and relationships. The mere accumulation of empirical data, however, constitutes neither theory nor science until the data have been organized into general principles that permit the interpretation of particular phenomena on the basis of the operation of more fundamental underlying factors. In complexity and sophistication, theories range from highly formalized examples involving fully developed mathematical relationships to others, such as those in education, which are as yet informal and incomplete.

The Role of the Theorist

In view of the complementary nature of research and theory, both need to be pursued with equal zeal if science, as a unitary discipline, is to progress. Researching and theorizing go hand in hand, and it is generally desirable to begin the report of an investigation by fitting the study into the framework of existing theory, and to end it by pointing out the implications of the findings and conclusions with respect to their theoretical as well as their practical significance. Thus, the scientist is both an investigator and a theorist.

It does not follow, however, that a scientist is equally skilled in these two essential but somewhat independent aspects of science. Without subscribing to the stereotype of the scientist as a man of solitude, few words, and a very specialized and restricted background who is not too well suited for theory development, we need to recognize that it may be difficult for a scientist to perform both as investigator and as theorist. On the other hand, there are scientists with good general background and insight into a particular field and special ability at organization and expression, who could make a significant contribution to science by developing its theoretical framework. This would leave to others the task of delving more deeply and intensively into some of its more precise and restricted aspects.

RESEARCH AS AN ASPECT OF SCIENCE

Nature of Research

The confusion which surrounds the meaning of *research* is even greater than that which surrounds the term *science*. First, it must be repeated that at no time in history did man *begin* to do research; even primitive man attempted to seek truth from his environment and, in a sense, was doing research. The term, as it is used today, is restricted to the more systematic and formal search for orderliness among phenomena. Research may be defined as the systematic, objective, and accurate search for the solution to a well-defined problem; in its broad sense, educational research refers to any activity which is oriented toward the development of education as a science. It is characterized primarily by the scholarliness with which the investigator attacks his problem.

A somewhat narrower definition restricts research to the fifth step of the scientific method—i.e., to the testing of the hypothesis—and places the remaining steps of the scientific method more or less outside the realm of true research. Most people would reject this narrow definition, for it takes research out of the overall context of science and makes it meaningless and unprofitable. Such a definition raises the question: Was the derivation of the atomic bomb research or Dewey's formulation of the steps of critical thinking? A question could also be raised as to whether the testing of the hypothesis is the crucial aspect of research. What if Einstein knew beforehand that the atomic bomb could be devised, so that the testing of the bomb was simply a formality for the purpose of working out a few technical details?

The worth of a scholarly enterprise is not gauged exclusively by its compliance with the criteria of the scientific method in its narrowest sense. With the increasing urgency for the synthesis of research findings, for instance, scholarly writing (though not research in the usual sense) may constitute a greater contribution to science than does research on a trivial problem no matter how adequately it meets the criteria of science. Might it not be more profitable to define research on the basis of its contribution to the attainment of truth—either through discovering heretofore unknown relationships among phenomena or through establishing a greater degree of orderliness among what is already known? It is all a matter of semantics; there is, however, no point in defining research so narrowly as to rob it of its significance.

Pure and Applied Research

Progress in science is best promoted by proper emphasis on the dual processes of deriving knowledge and of organizing such knowledge into theoretical structure. The scientist must devote himself with equal vigor to the pursuit of both, and both must be held in equal honor. In practice, however, it is frequently difficult to maintain such a balance.

Man is always faced with problems, some immediate and some remote. He hopes that eventually most of his problems will be solved. In the meantime, he has to cope with the present as well as the future, with the present frequently having priority. It seems logical that he will accomplish more in solving his problems—both remote and immediate—by developing the required theory and deducing the solution to immediate problems from theoretical premises. However, the problems he faces are here and now, pressing him for an immediate answer—action must be taken, whether in planting crops, curing the sick, or teaching the young. And this action must be taken on the basis of the best evidence available *now*. There is a very definite possibility that the solution can be obtained more quickly by going after it directly rather than indirectly through the development of the required theoretical framework. The present-day emphasis on operations research in industry and on action research in education is an outgrowth of this need for the empirical solution to problems in the immediate situation. In a sense, the practitioner leads; it is he who contributes to early scientific advance. The theorist follows. It is only when science is further advanced that pure science can take the lead in developing practice, as it is doing in the space program, for example. It is consequently natural that, in the early development of science, the technologist will tend to be eclectic, picking up a plausible idea here and there and using it somewhat inventively in the practical situation.

Both pure and applied research are oriented toward the discovery of truth, and both are practical in the sense that they lead to the solution of man's problems. Research is research even though it has no immediate, or even forseeable, field application. Furthermore, all research will probably be useful and practical eventually, no matter how pure and removed from practicality it is at the moment. The contributions of the archeologist or the astronomer are of equal scientific significance as those of the physicist. In fact, many experiments in physics, e.g., the nature of light, were at the time oriented toward the discovery of truth; that they should have come to have a practical value was not unanticipated but they were not undertaken with that immediate purpose in mind.

Nevertheless, from the standpoint of the directness with which the solution to an immediate problem is sought, a distinction needs to be made between pure research, which is interested in the fundamental aspects of science and only indirectly in the practical application which the findings may have, and applied research, which has exactly the opposite orientation. The major question seems to be whether a greater contribution to the development of science and the welfare of mankind can be made by concentrating on pure research than by devoting the same amount of time and energy to the solution of immediate and practical problems. Most scientists would reply that pure research contributes more to the long-range advancement of science. They would point out, for example, that the great advances in the physical sciences have come from pure research rather than from an attempt to resolve an immediate problem. In fact, it might be suggested that the inability to postpone immediate problems may be involved in our failure to advance educational science. Kerlinger (1959), for example, cautions against overemphasis on the desire to solve practical problems.

The practitioner, faced with problems here and now,

cannot wait. Furthermore, he has discovered that theory is not always right, or, more specifically, that while a solution may be right for the conditions under which it was derived, it may not apply to his particular case so that he will still have to solve his own problem—perhaps with improved insight, but nevertheless on his own. He is frequently impatient with the artificial nature of the theoretician's problems and his neglect of real problems. Periodical reactions set in against theory. For example, the depression of the 1930's saw a movement toward the M.Ed. and the Ed.D. as "practical" degrees for educators in contrast to the M.A. and Ph.D. with their greater emphasis on theoretical considerations. To the extent to which any real difference exists between these degrees, there is an implication that the cause of education is best served by emphasis on the solution of practical problems rather than on the derivation of theoretical structure. Action research is another indication of the educator's impatience with theory.

It must be recognized that, though systematic theory has contributed directly to the solution of practical problems, the contribution has not been entirely one-sided. Applied research in the solution of immediate problems has also contributed not only tools and equipment, e.g., the transistor, but has also helped to clarify theory through suggesting valuable hypotheses and general insights that can be incorporated into a more sophisticated attempt at pure research. In fact, a successful attack on theoretical concepts often must await the development of a certain degree of lower-level applied research. Unfortunately, pure and applied research have often operated in relative isolation from each other, much to the detriment of both. The scientific benefits that might accrue from practical research, for example, are frequently lost through failure to relate empirical findings to their theoretical implications. Too often, all that is derived from such studies is the solution to an immediate problem—plus a vague set of rules of thumb that are of doubtful, limited, and restricted validity.

THE RELATION OF SCIENCE TO PHILOSOPHY

The conflict between empiricism and theory finds a parallel in the conflict between the roles of science and philosophy. The former distinction is between the accumulation of data relative to natural phenomena and the integration and unification of the relationships obtained into an underlying conceptual structure. The present distinction is between the proper understanding of the empirical and theoretical nature of phenomena and the interpretation of such phenomena with respect to human goals and purposes.*

Although science and philosophy exist in an interdependent and complementary role, this has not always been reflected in the behavior of either the philosopher or the scientist. The philosopher seems to feel that human goals and values are not subject to scientific determination. He tends to look down on the scientist whose concern is often materialistic and who frequently attempts to discover truth through consensus, statistical manipulation, and the concept of probability. The scientist, on the other hand, seems to feel that science has led to our material progress and welfare, and that philosophers are dreamers whose concern with values frequently takes the form of speculative and intuitive deductions boosted to the level of dogma through emphatic pronouncement. This opinion is frequently shared by the layman, who thinks that "what research says" is accurate and dependable, while "what philosophy says" is speculative and generally undependable.

From the standpoint of their respective functions, science answers the question "what?" while philosophy answers the question "to what end?" Science is concerned with the discovery of knowledge; it can tell what is and why. But this is only a means to an end; philosophy begins where science leaves off, and is concerned with the use of this knowledge. The task of science is to determine the most efficient way of attaining a certain goal; whether that goal is worthy of attainment is a philosophical consideration. Thus, philosophy is concerned with the ultimate ends toward which research needs to be oriented. Science can improve the efficiency of the process, but it cannot adjudicate the desirability of the end.

Science is efficient but amoral and can work as effectively toward the attainment of evil goals as it can toward the promotion of desirable ones. It can provide the most efficient means for promoting competitive behavior or cooperative behavior, just as it can be used in concentration-camp experiments on human

* The term *philosophy* is frequently confused with the concept of *theory development,* which is often referred to as the *philosophical method* of research. Philosophy is also concerned with basic issues such as whether or not invariant relationships between antecedents and their consequents actually exist or whether man's behavior is subject to scientific determination.

beings or in the cure of cancer. On the other hand, to the extent that science operates in a social context and relates to this context, all scientific problems have both a socio-philosophical as well as a scientific component. This is especially true in the behavioral sciences where science, as the servant of man, is primarily devoted to the promotion of a better life.

While it is true that social decisions—whether to go to college, whether to marry or to remain single—are, in the final analysis, value-judgments resting on philosophical rather than strictly scientific considerations, such decisions cannot be made in ignorance of the relative benefits, obstacles, hazards, and consequences of the alternatives. Science can provide the knowledge on which value-judgments can be based. It can provide information about the effects of various courses of action and thus provide a perspective from which the desirability of each can be seen in clearer focus. It cannot deal directly with the values themselves; but neither can philosophy make value-judgments without considering their scientific foundation. Any attempt to do so is bound to result in poor judgment. In the words of Freeman (1929), "Bad science is not cured by good philosophy, nor can good philosophy arise from bad facts." Thus, the philosophical decision to orient our schools toward progressivism or traditionalism cannot be made without considering the scientific evidence regarding the likely outcomes of the two approaches. In the same way, the decision to use the atomic bomb is outside the particular province of science, but science provides the facts that need to be considered in deciding whether or not to use it.

Science also has the responsibility for generating alternatives, e.g., eliminating the cancer-producing effects of tobacco, or developing immunization or cure for possible cancer. Conversely, it can, in a sense, be blamed for failure to provide the necessary data so that crucial decisions have to be made on inadequate or even inaccurate data. Scientific findings can also be misused, of course, but there the fault lies with socio-philosophical misorientation rather than with any evil inherent in science itself. It can be faulted only to the extent that it has allowed itself to be misread—as, for example, allowing society to give tentative research findings a status to which they are not entitled.

Science and philosophy play a complementary role and every problem has both a scientific and a philosophical component. The purpose of science is to derive knowledge; it defines that, under stated conditions, certain events will occur or can be made to occur. Philosophy, on the other hand, is concerned with the ends this knowledge will serve and its relation to the major goals of the social order. Philosophy helps to define and clarify the problems to be solved, the priorities to be assigned, and the assumptions under which the conclusions derived from science are true, and, of course, it interprets what has been found with respect to the goals of society.

Another aspect of the situation is the extent to which values are themselves suitable subjects for scientific investigation. More specifically, the issue is the current stand that values do not meet the standards of scientific objectivity which American psychologists have imposed upon themselves as a criterion of science. The consequence has been a strong denial of this area as a legitimate topic of research, much to the chagrin of such clinicians as Shoben (1957) and Smith (1961), who lament the rejection of values from the concept of personality adjustment, and Bowman (1945), and, more recently, Maslow (1966), in the area of ethics and values themselves. As Maslow points out:

> If there is any primary rule of science, it is, in my opinion, acceptance of the obligation to acknowledge and describe all of reality, all that exists, everything that is the case. Before all else, science must be comprehensive and all-inclusive. It must accept within its jurisdiction even that which it cannot understand or explain, that for which no theory exists, that which cannot be measured, predicted, controlled, or ordered.

Yet, as Bowman points out, ethical issues and morals are falsely cast aside because they do not fit the frame of reference of science as defined by over-zealous devotees to the scientific method, who pride themselves on a high degree of moral detachment from human affairs. All of this, Bowman considers false intellectualism and sterile scientism.

Certainly, there is need for some bench mark as to what constitutes acceptable scientific investigation. But then we make the mistake of assuming that what does not fit our narrow definition of science is automatically nonscience. Because certain methods work well with the physical elements, or with animals, or even with certain aspects of human behavior, we have come to insist that these methods constitute the sole, the exclusive avenue to scientific knowledge. Maslow decries

> . . . the ultimate absurdity of bureaucratic science, in which some portions of the truth may have to be defined as 'unscientific,' in which truth is really true only when gathered by properly certified and uniformed 'truth collectors' and according to traditionally sanctioned methods or ceremonials.

The unfortunate aspect of the situation is that ruling out human values in science can amount to a denial of man himself. Man in his very essence just does not fit this narrow mold. Yet, on what grounds can we say that the experiential world of the phenomenologist is any less real than the abstract world of the physicist? Psychologists, according to Maslow, have displayed a tendency to set up a false reality in terms of trivial externals and to deny the rest because it is not amenable to the methods and tools at hand. He argues that the consequent amoral technologizing of all science is as dangerous as the outright rejection of orthodox science on the grounds that it is too cool, skeptical, and therefore dangerous to human values. Scientific progress requires the collaboration of scientists of different points of view and different interests. Maslow suggests that psychologists concentrate their research efforts on man as the point of reference rather than centering on the impersonal components of reality simply because the scientific study of man is ". . . a more difficult, more exasperating application of the methodology of physics, astronomy, biology, etc. to an irritatingly unsuitable object."

THE SCIENTIST

Status of the Modern Scientist

Since Hiroshima, and especially since *Sputnik I*, American society (if not the world) has become progressively more conscious of the crucial role of the scientist in the progress and survival of mankind. Scientists have found themselves in such high esteem that their opinions, even on nonscientific issues, are sought and frequently accepted unquestioningly. In fact, as pointed out by Michels (1948), scientists now have a voice far out of proportion to their numbers in shaping national and international thought and policy. Furthermore, their opinions, which make the headlines and have such powerful political and sociological influence, frequently fall directly outside the area of competence of its author.

If he is to wield such influence, it is necessary for the scientist to appreciate the nature of his role. First, it must be recognized that science itself is amoral, and that the scientist per se has neither obligation nor responsibility. The scientist is, however, also a person—or, more specifically, a citizen—which, at once, puts him under both obligation and responsibility. In fact, since prestige is invariably bought at the expense of greater responsibility, the scientist is faced with moral problems beyond those of the average citizen. Society has the right to expect him to contribute to its welfare and advancement in keeping with his talents—as it does all of its citizens—both by producing the means for such advancement and by providing whatever leadership his potentialities and status permit him to provide. He is expected to contribute toward its goals, regardless of what his personal views may be. For example, he has a right to object to the use of the atomic bomb, but he must do so as a citizen. He has no right to jeopardize its development through his lack of cooperation any more than a soldier has the right to sabotage plans for the attainment of a military objective. This position, of course, is not one of unanimous agreement; there are those who argue that the scientist is also a person who must live with his conscience, and, just as the conscientious objector can refuse to bear arms in the defense of his country, so the scientist should be free to withhold his services and discoveries if he fears their misuse.

The social scientist is not engaged in anything quite so spectacular as the development of the atomic bomb, but he too has definite responsibilities of perhaps even greater impact than does the physical scientist. With the growing emphasis on social welfare and human dignity, the social scientist will, undoubtedly, have a major role to play in the destiny of our nation and the world. But it will also bring grave responsibilities. As Oppenheimer suggested in 1956, the powerful control that will be made available to psychologists will pose far graver problems than any with which the physicists have had to cope. The social scientist has the obligation of conducting whatever research into social phenomena his status, position, and competence permit and to make known his findings for the enlightenment and betterment of the social order. However, he has a special problem in that not only do his findings affect people directly but, unfortunately, since he usually cannot exert adequate control over his research subjects, rarely are his "discoveries" and his interpretations ironclad. This puts on his shoulders a special responsibility to have at his command a sufficient understanding of the philosophical and sociological issues underlying his problem, on the one hand, and a special grasp of the problem itself and the limitations underlying his findings, on the other hand, so that he can see his conclusions in proper perspective. He must be particularly careful in presenting his findings to avoid the possibility of misinterpretation.

Having convinced himself of the action dictated by his findings, the scientist has the further responsibility of striving for the adoption of his viewpoint. Two cases present themselves here: 1. If his findings and interpretations are matters of agreement among scientists, he can proceed as a scientist to present the scientific position and to urge action. 2. If, on the other hand, there is not complete scientific agreement, he can operate only as a private citizen expressing a personal opinion. He must, then, be careful not to abuse his status and prestige as a scientist in order to promote personal views. In all cases, he must remember that science must be the servant and not the master of man; it must never replace judgment but simply define the issues involved.

The scientist must be careful not to use his position in his own field to promote personal views in a field in which he has no right to speak as an expert. A nuclear physicist violates ethics when he advertises his status as a scientist to support his opinions on educational practices or psychological testing, for example. The scientist will determine by the way he discharges his responsibilities and the way his behavior complies with high ethical standards whether he deserves the prestige accorded to him by our present society.

There is also the opposite problem of the scientist becoming so "scientifically objective" in his views that he develops a moral detachment and skepticism to the point of losing moral perspective. This sometimes occurs, for example, among undergraduate students in psychology, who overextend the need to see behavior as a natural phenomenon to the point of conceiving of behavior as devoid of moral implications. Although the scientist must repress subjectivity and personal feelings when acting in his professional capacity, for him to carry a similar attitude into his social world represents an abuse of science, a false intellectualism.

Likewise, the scientist must not allow feelings of inadequacy in fields outside of his specialty to cause him to withdraw from the affairs of society. He needs to realize that he has a responsibility as a citizen to participate in the resolution of social issues and that his views are probably as adequate as those of many of the people who do take part. He can not avoid his civic responsibilities, for in a democracy the abdication of good men from active citizenship is an open invitation for the forces of evil and incompetence to take over. Bowman (1945) advocates an emphasis on courses in sociology and philosophy as the means of counteracting the development of such skepticism. It would seem that if one ceases to be a human being, there is hardly any point in being a scientist.

Professional Ethics

The necessity for professional ethics has been recognized by society, in general, and by professional groups, in particular. The American Psychological Association, for instance, has a code of ethics defining the responsibility of a psychologist to the profession, to the client, and to the sponsoring agency. Most everything the scientist does has definite and often far-reaching implications. The ethical implications are particularly crucial in the social sciences, where all aspects of research—from the use of people as research subjects to the social and moral implications of the research findings themselves—tend to have more direct ethical significance than they do in the physical sciences. Ethics is even more clearly involved in such problems as the coding of questionnaires in order to identify respondents when they have been "allowed to remain anonymous."

A point of major concern in doing research with human beings, particularly in the personal area of values, is that of the individual's right to privacy, a matter which has achieved such importance as to receive close governmental and professional scrutiny.* The problem presents a basic conflict between two sets of values, both of which are held in high esteem in American society—and particularly in the academic community: 1. the individual's inalienable right to dignity and freedom within the broad limits set by consideration for others; and 2. society's right to discovery, its right to know as the basis for social progress and increased social welfare. Research lies at the very root of the conflict. Respect for the individual will undoubtedly restrict certain types

* See the special issue of the *American Psychologist,* Vol. 22, May 1967.

of research, but, then, democratic society cannot purchase scientific progress at the expense of the individual; nor, as Conrad (1967) suggests, can the social sciences afford to become identified in the public mind with snooping, prying, and the unwarranted invasion of privacy. The resolution of the conflict seems to revolve around what is known as "informed consent," i.e., consent based on the subject's understanding of the nature of the commitment or, where this is not consistent with the objectives of the study, on trust in the qualifications and integrity of the investigator.

Matters of ethics are also involved in the use of school children as experimental guinea pigs, particularly when such experiments interfere with the teacher's effectiveness in fulfilling his primary responsibility of teaching children. It would have to be assumed that any harm done is more than compensated for by the greater good that comes from the discovery of more effective methods. The difficulty is increased in the social sciences by the possibility of error arising from limited control in a research situation that involves human beings. It must be recognized that the social scientist cannot be held accountable for his Frankensteins any more than the physical scientist. Nor is the scientist the keeper of the public conscience. He cannot deprive society of the benefit of knowledge on the grounds that it could possibly be in error or could possibly be misused. Certainly at no time is ignorance to be preferred to knowledge.

On the other hand, the scientist as a special citizen has responsibilities beyond that of the average man in the street. The ethical problems facing the psychologist, for example, will be multiplied a hundredfold as a result of psychology's new power to control behavior, just as they were for the physicist when the power of the atom was first unleashed. As long as the psychologist was relatively inept at accomplishing his avowed purposes of controlling behavior, he received not only freedom but even social blessings and encouragement. Now that he has perfected his skills to the point of truly being able to "influence people," the threat of possible misuse of this power becomes a cause for alarm. To the extent that science simply permits the achievement of whatever goal society has set up, there is need to identify more clearly the issues involved in the use of this power. It might be argued, for example, that psychologists need to be subjected to considerable training in ethics, philosophy, and sociology so as to prevent the possible misuse of this power.

It must be recognized that, although science per se is amoral and has been accused of being cold, materialistic, and inhuman, and even blamed for atrocities, deterioration of morals, etc., these accusations overlook the fact that science is simply the servant and not the master of man. As such, it can be used for good or for evil with equal efficiency. Whereas we can point to many instances of the misuse of science, we must not overlook the fact that science has been largely responsible for the progress from primitive man with his chronic disease, starvation, and other hardships associated with environmental inclemencies to that of civilized man and the intellectual and cultural freedom which befit human dignity.

Characteristics of the Scientist

Although many of the characteristics of scientists can be inferred from the previous discussion, there is no standard "scientific personality" that characterizes all scientists, least of all the stereotype of the scientist as a nonsocial "intellectual" who seldom goes out of his laboratory. There is, of course, a basic core of such fundamental traits as intellectual integrity, professional responsibility, and scientific skepticism which motivate all scientists. The list of such traits is so long and the degree to which they are involved so flexible, however, that there is an unlimited range of individual differences even among the top scientists in a given field.

Many writers have presented lists of the characteristics they considered typical of scientists, but these lists are so comprehensive that they merely include most of the desirable scholarly traits. A more meaningful approach is that of Shannon (1947) who investigated the personality characteristics of 250 world-renowned research workers. Among the traits he found common to this illustrious group, were: 1. enthusiasm and research zeal; 2. intelligence, adaptability, resourcefulness, and versatility; 3. creativity, initiative, originality, ingenuity, and intuitiveness; 4. expertise and competence in their area of investigation; and 5. determination and drive. Other specific traits frequently encountered in the literature describing scientists—many of which overlap those mentioned above—include intellectual curiosity, open-mindedness, freedom from bias, persistence, and thoroughness.

Generally the university atmosphere is considered

most conducive to the maximum development and productivity of the scientist. While industry frequently ties the scientist to the task of providing desired products, the university generally imposes fewer restrictions on his freedom. The ready availability of stimulation and of consultation with colleagues, as well as the continuous challenge provided by students, especially at the graduate level, are significantly favorable factors which tend to be denied the man in the field. This is probably especially true of education. The superintendent of schools, for example, is generally too busy for his own good, and he often lacks the challenge of other experts who can help sharpen his thinking.

On the other hand, if the university is to capitalize on the creative talents of its faculty, it needs to provide for the exercise of these talents by keeping teaching and other responsibilities to a level where creative activities are possible. Education seems to suffer from excessive teaching loads, and many professors grow old without having engaged in any professional activities other than those connected with meeting their classes and attending committee meetings and conventions. The problem deserves serious consideration if education is to derive the full benefits of the talents of its members.

Highlights of the Chapter

1.   The basic purpose of science is the systematization of experience into a structural framework on the basis of which the significance of phenomena can be understood.

2.   The scientific method, interpreted broadly, constitutes the most systematic and generally the most adequate approach to the discovery of empirical truth. It generally encompasses a series of steps consisting of the selection and clarification of a problem, the derivation and elaboration of a hypothesis, the collection of data and the testing of the hypothesis, and finally the generalization of the results. However, the scientific method cannot be equated with the application of a series of steps in rigid sequence; to be effective, it must allow for considerable flexibility in its use.

3.   The problem of empirical science is the acquisition and systematization of knowledge concerning the phenomena experienced in nature. Empirical science augments, systematizes, and criticizes

everyday experience. The initial objects of science are the things experienced in perception. The basic procedure is observation. Scientific description starts with observation; it ends when phenomena postulated by hypotheses are actually observed and eventually explained.

4.   Empirical laws are the expression of certain regularities existing among phenomena. They are best conceived as simply working hypotheses which enable us to grasp phenomena more adequately but whose validity is only tentative. Empirical laws can be idiographic or nomothetic.

5.   The scientist often finds it helpful to postulate hypothetical constructs to account for the relationships he notes among variables. These are simply products of his imagination which—along with models—provide a structure around which he can organize his thinking. Care must be taken not to give such constructs physical existence or to use them in a circular argument.

6.   To be of scientific value, concepts must be defined in terms of specific operations that can actually be demonstrated. Operational definitions also must avoid the danger of circularity and especially of misorientation of research toward the trivial and superficial components of the phenomena under study.

7.   Even though in its early stages, science concentrates on the discovery of empirical relationships among phenomena, empirical science has definite limitations; to be of maximum value, its isolated findings must be structured into a meaningful conceptual framework. The ultimate goal of science is not only the systematization of facts into broad empirical laws and principles, but also the systematization of empirical laws into an ever-smaller number of theories explaining the basis for the relationships noted. The ultimate need is for the unification of the laws and theories of the various disciplines into a single, overall, scientific—empirical and theoretical—framework.

8.   Theory permits a deeper understanding of the significance of phenomena, anticipates hitherto unknown relationships, and acts as a guide to meaningful research in productive areas. In practice,

there must be a back-and-forth movement from the discovery of empirical facts to the structuring of these facts into a conceptual scheme and the orientation of research toward the discovery of further facts that will permit the derivation of more adequate theories. Although premature theoretical rigidity can lead research astray, there is a need in education for a greater appreciation of the complementary role of the empirical and theoretical phases of science.

9.   A theory can never be proved; it can only be accepted if it provides an adequate explanation of empirical facts, or it can be rejected. In practice, however, a theory is not so much true or false as it is useful or useless, and theories, even though apparently false, at least in part, tend to last until modified or replaced by more adequate theories. Meanwhile, the very process of verifying a theory frequently serves a definite purpose in clarifying underlying concepts and in orienting research efforts in meaningful directions.

10.   A good theory—just as a good hypothesis—must provide a more parsimonious explanation of the empirical facts discovered than any competing theory. It must especially be amenable to empirical validation.

11.   Research has been defined as the systematic, objective, and accurate search for the solution of a well-defined problem. Any systematic and scholarly activity designed to promote the development of education as a science can be considered educational research. Research may be classified as pure research and applied research. The latter is the more immediately practical, but the former generally makes the greater contribution to scientific progress.

12.   Science and philosophy exist in interdependent and complementary roles. Science provides knowledge concerning the most efficient means of attaining certain goals; philosophy is concerned with the value of these goals.

13.   The scientist plays a crucial role in the welfare and progress of mankind. He needs to appreciate the special responsibilities that accompany the prestige which modern society has accorded him.

Questions and Projects

1.   What are some of the scientific premises on which the educational enterprise rests? Some of the philosophical and sociological premises? What are some of the more significant laws, principles, and theories of interest to educators?

2.   How valid are the various theories presented in the educational literature, e.g., curriculum theories, theories of communication, theories of supervision, etc.? Of what benefit might they be to educational practice?

3.   Science, we are told, is probably best defined as a process. Explain what this means.

Selected References

Battig, William F. "Parsimony in psychology," *Psychol. Rep.,* 11 (Monogr. Suppl., 3): 555–72; 1962.

Becker, Gordon M. and Charles G. McClintock. "Value: Behavioral decision theory," *Ann. Rev. Psychol.,* 18: 239–56; 1967.

Bellack, Arno A. (ed.) *Theory and Research in Teaching.* New York: Bur. Publ., T.C., Columbia Univ., 1963.

Brodbeck, May. "Toward a fabric of knowledge—Common elements among fields of learning," *Educ. Rec.,* 43: 217–22; 1962.

————. "Logic and the scientific method," in N.L. Gage (ed.) *Handbook of Research on Teaching.* Chicago: Rand McNally, 1963. pp. 44–93.

Bronowski, Jacob. "Scientific and human values," *Univ. Quart.,* 10: 247–59, 1956; 11: 26–42, 1956.

Bruner, Jerome S. "Needed: A theory of instruction," *Educ. Lead.,* 20: 523–32; 1963.

Chapanis, Alphonse. "Men, machines, and models," *Amer. Psychol.,* 16: 113–31; 1961.

Commoner, Barry et al. "Science and human welfare," *Sci.,* 132: 68–73; 1960.

Conant, James B. *Science and Common Sense.* New York: Yale Univ. Press, 1951.

Dorfman, Robert. "Operations research," *Amer. econ. Rev.,* 50: 575–623; 1960.

Dubarle, Daniel. "The scientist and his responsibilities," *Bull. atomic Sci.,* 12: 253–57; 1956.

Edel, Abraham. *Science and the Structure of Ethics.* International Encyclopedia of Unified Science. Vol. 2, No. 3. Chicago: Univ. of Chicago Press, 1961.

Ennis, Robert H. "The 'impossibility' of neutrality," *Harv. educ. Rev.,* 29: 128–36; 1959.

———. "Operational definitions," *Amer. educ. Res. J.,* 1: 183–201; 1964.

Feigl, Herbert. "Aims of education for our age of science: Reflections of a logical empiricist," in John S. Brubacher (ed.) *Modern Philosophies and Education.* 54th Yrbk. N.S.S.E., Pt. I. Chicago: Univ. of Chicago Press, 1955. pp. 304–41.

Frank, Phillip G. (ed.) *The Validation of Scientific Theories.* New York: Collier, 1961.

Griffiths, Daniel E. "Some assumptions underlying the use of models in research," in Jack A. Culbertson and Stephen P. Hencley (eds.) *Educational Research: New Perspectives.* Danville: Interstate, 1963. pp. 121–39.

———. "The nature and meaning of theory," in Daniel E. Griffiths (ed.) *Behavioral Science and Educational Administration.* 63rd Yrbk., N.S.S.E., Pt. II. Chicago: Univ. of Chicago Press, 1964. pp. 95–118.

Guilford, J.P. "The structure of intellect," *Psychol. Bull.,* 53: 267-93, 1956.

Haddow, Alexander. "The scientist as a citizen," *Bull. atomic Sci.,* 12: 247–52; 1956.

Hardie, Charles D. *Truth and Fallacy in Educational Theory.* New York: Bur. Publ., T.C., Columbia Univ., 1962.

Harrison, F.R. "Constructing theories in education," *Sch. Rev.,* 74: 123–38; 1966.

Hempel, Carl G. *Fundamentals of Concept Formation in Empirical Science.* International Encyclopedia of Unified Science. Vol. 2, No. 7. Chicago: Univ. of Chicago Press, 1952.

———. "A logical appraisal of operationalism," in Philip G. Frank (ed.) *The Validation of Scientific Theories.* Chicago: Univ. of Chicago Press, 1961. pp. 56–69.

Horowitz, Irving L. *Philosophy, Science, and the Sociology of Knowledge.* Springfield: Thomas, 1961.

Horsfall, Frank L. "On the unity of the sciences," *Sci.,* 133: 1059–60; 1961.

Hotelling, Harold. "The statistical method and the philosophy of science," *Amer. Stat.,* 12: 9–14; 1958.

Jones, W.T. *The Sciences and the Humanities: Conflict and Reconciliation.* Berkeley: Univ. of Calif. Press, 1965.

Kelman, Herbert C. "Human use of human subjects: The problem of deception in social psychological experiments," *Psychol. Bull.,* 67: 1–11; 1967.

Kemeny, J.G. *A Philosopher Looks at Science.* Princeton: Van Nostrand, 1959.

Lachman, Roy. "The model in theory construction," *Psychol Rev.*, 87: 113–29; 1960.

Lazarsfeld, Paul F. and Wagner Thielens. *The Academic Mind: Social Scientists in a Time of Crisis*. New York: Free Press, 1958.

Longstreth, B. "Behavioral research using students: A primary issue for schools," *Sch. Rev.*, 76: 1–22; 1968.

Maslow, Abraham H. *The Psychology of Science*. New York: Harper & Row, 1966.

Merritt, James W. "The province of philosophy of education," *Educ. Theory*, 11: 45–51; 1961.

Merton, Robert K. "Priorities in scientific discovery: A chapter in the sociology of science," *Amer. sociol. Rev.*, 22: 635–59; 1957.

Miller, James G. "Toward a general theory for the behavioral sciences," *Amer. Psychol.*, 10: 513–31; 1955.

Nagel, Ernest. *The Structure of Science: Problems in the Logic of Scientific Explanations*. New York: Harcourt, Brace & World, 1961.

Newsome, George L. "In what sense is theory a guide to practice in education?" *Educ. Theory*, 14: 31–39; 1964. (See also 14: 93–94; 1964)

Perkinson, H.J. "The methodological determination of the aims of education," *Educ. Theory*, 11: 61–64; 1961.

Restle, Frank. "A theory of discrimination learning," *Psychol. Rev.*, 62: 11–19; 1955.

———. "Relevance of mathematical models for education," in E.R. Hilgard (ed.) *Theories of Learning and Instruction*. 63rd Yrbk., N.S.S.E., Pt. I. Chicago: Univ. of Chicago Press, 1964. pp. 111–32.

Roe, Anne. "The psychology of a scientist," *Sci.*, 134: 456–59; 1961.

Ruebhausen, Oscar M. and Orville G. Brim. "Privacy and behavioral research," *Amer. Psychol.*, 21: 423–37; 1966.

Skinner, B.F. "Are theories of learning necessary?" *Psychol. Rev.*, 57: 193–216; 1950.

———. "The science of learning and the art of teaching," *Harv. educ. Rev.*, 24: 86–97; 1954.

Snow, Charles P. "The moral un-neutrality of science," *Sci.*, 133: 256–59; 1961.

Spence, Kenneth W. "Relation of learning theory to the technology of education," *Harv. educ. Rev.*, 29: 84–95; 1959.

Taylor, Albert J. "What is philosophy of education?", *Educ. Theory*, 13: 95–104, 118; 1963.

Taylor, J.G. "Experimental design: A cloak for intellectual sterility," *Brit. J. Psychol.*, 49: 105–16; 1958.

Thomas, Lawrence G. et al. "Prospects of scientific research into values," *Educ. Theory*, 6: 193–214; 1956.

Turner, Merle B. *Philosophy and the Science of Behavior.* New York: Appleton-Century-Crofts, 1967.

Valois, A.J. *Study of Operationalism and Its Implications for Educational Psychology.* Washington: Catholic Univ. Press, 1960.

Van den Haag, Ernest. "Man as an object of science," *Sci.,* 129: 243–47; 1959.

Winthrop, Henry. "Some neglected considerations concerning the problem of value in psychology," *J. gen. Psychol.,* 64: 37–59; 1961.

4
STEPS OF THE SCIENTIFIC METHOD

Human energy is never more extravagantly wasted than in the persistent effort to answer conclusively questions that are vague and meaningless.——Wendell Johnson (1946)

As Americans we are justifiably proud of our many scientific advances. Not only has science helped us attain a position of international prestige, but it has also provided us with the highest standard of living in the world. Unfortunately, our claim to science as a personal attribute and a way of life are not so clear. The average American still harbors misconceptions, superstitions, prejudices, and numerous other unscientific notions. Too frequently, he reveals that his scientific attitude is really quite superficial. Not only is he governed more directly by hunches, feelings, and opinions than by facts, but he is not sure of what science is— either as a product or as a procedure.

Even our high school and undergraduate students, despite two or more years of "science," generally have only a superficial (if not erroneous) conception of its nature. They frequently equate science with dissecting frogs or with "discovering" the chemical composition of compounds. Rarely are they sufficiently aware of the unity of science or of the philosophical and sociological setting in which it operates.

Although the objectives of science education have been formulated by a number of writers, they are, unfortunately, inadequately incorporated into science courses. Too often, students are introduced to the glamor of science by a lab manual with step-by-step directions for reaching the predetermined answer to their "problem." The textbook is too frequently the same unquestioned authority it is in other classes—with the content equally, if not more, indisputable. Too often, it not only represents a source of anything and everything from phylae and chemical formulae to numberless "laws" to be memorized, but it is also apparently supposed to provide a basis for making students scientists by the page and by the chapter—while instructors lecture on science as a method of "discovery." Fortunately, there has been a definite trend toward science teaching that insures a greater understanding of the tentative and relative nature of scientific laws and of the need for flexibility in the application of the scientific method. There is need for a greater understanding of the nature of science as something to be lived rather than something simply to be learned.

It is sometimes disconcerting to see students who use opinion and fact with the same tone of dogmatic finality and cannot tell one from the other, who cannot substantiate an opinion except by locating another individual who holds the same views, and who equate consensus with truth. Few graduate students in education, for example, appreciate the scientific basis on which education must rest. Research is often considered a competitor of, or a substitute for, constituted authority rather than a means of discovering knowledge. Too frequently students view research as a formalized process of applying a rigid sequence of steps to the solution of a problem. If we are to gain maximum benefit from the present orientation of education toward research, we need, first of all, to develop in our students a more adequate understanding of its nature and its procedures.

THE RESEARCH PROBLEM

Selecting a Topic

Probably no aspect of graduate study is more unnerving to the student than the selection of a research topic; indeed, finding a suitable problem is often a problem in itself. Unfortunately, the student is frequently expected to select a topic early in his graduate work, at a time when he is not ready to make such a selection. To make matters worse, he finds his range of selection restricted by his lack of competence in the more advanced statistical techniques necessary to deal with the more significant educational problems. Too frequently, after anxious conferences with his advisor, the student "chooses" a topic suggested by the latter, often because any topic is better than no topic at all. Some students, after many hours of exploration, abandon their study and start afresh, while others continue despite the unsuitability of the problem and end up with nothing but the satisfaction of having met another requirement. Many students who show exceptional competence in classwork somehow lack whatever is involved in identifying a major project on their own. Unfortunately, graduate education is so organized that the student's first attempt at an individual research project comes at the very end of his program, when it seems a little late to be recognizing weaknesses. It may also be that present selection policies based on previous academic work favor the compulsive grade-getter rather than his more creative counterpart. It must also be recognized that formal instruction in educational research has consistently emphasized the hypothesis-testing rather than the idea-getting phase of research.

Although, as faculty advisors would like to have their students believe, the field of education is "just bristling with problems to be solved," this alleged abundance is not particularly obvious to the poor student who often finds that all of his ideas on the subject fall in the category of "too big," "too small," "already done," "incapable of solution," "beyond his resources and talents," etc. The little anecdote by Buckingham (1927), reproduced in part below, describing the student who comes to discuss a thesis problem and who finally retires "a discouraged seeker after truth in a world where all the problems have been solved" is unfortunately far too familiar to graduate advisors.

> "I've got to write a Master's thesis," says he, "and I'd like to talk to you about a topic." The statement ends with a slight upward inflection as if, in spite of its grammatical form, a sort of question were implied. After an awkward pause Mr. Blank (the student) repeats that he would like to talk about a thesis topic. Whereupon the editor (and professor) suggests that he go ahead and do so.
>
> It transpires, however, that the editor-professor has misconceived Mr. Blank's meaning. He has no topic to talk about. In fact, instead of coming with a topic, he has come to get one. He looks so expectant, too; purely, as one might say, in a receptive mood.
>
> No, he has no problems to suggest. He gives one the impression of having just learned about this thesis business, and of being entirely open-minded on the subject. At least,

one gathers that he has no bias toward any particular topic and certainly no preconceived notions . . . .

Actually, the plight of the student described above is very real. Though the anecdote may be both humorous and depressing, it can perhaps be appreciated when the overall situation is taken into consideration. On the other hand, topic selection is an area of primary importance, for the secret of success in research is frequently as much a matter of selecting an appropriate problem as it is of being able to solve the problem that has been selected. Furthermore, this is an area in which the student is really on his own, and this is precisely the purpose of the thesis or dissertation requirement, for it is here that the aspirant of high professional status demonstrates that he has the necessary initiative, originality, and good judgment. It should be his prerogative, rather than simply his responsibility, to select his problem, to plan its investigation, and to derive its solution, drawing on outside help only in emergencies and for confirmation of the decisions he has made. He can, of course, draw on the experience of his advisor and his major professors, but he must not cast himself in the role of a clerical assistant.

Duplication

Unfortunate indeed is the graduate student who finds that the problem in which he has invested time and effort has already been solved or is the object of a prior claim, for a basic consideration in the choice of a research problem is the avoidance of duplication. It, therefore, behooves the prospective investigator to survey the literature carefully before he begins his study to insure that his problem is not currently under investigation or already solved so that his contribution to existing knowledge would be relatively trivial.

The interpretation of what constitutes duplication is, however, a matter of some debate. It is recognized that some studies can be repeated profitably, either to check their validity or to extend the applicability of their conclusions. Duplication is acceptable, for instance, if the student can bring new evidence to bear on the subject by using an improved design, or if changed circumstances make verification under the new conditions desirable. For example, the four-quarter school year, the subject of numerous studies in the 1920's and 1930's, would bear re-investigation now that air-conditioning has minimized the debilitating effect of summer heat and increased emphasis on family travel has complicated the coordination of summer vacations. In fact, many of the problems solved years ago are in need of verification, extension or re-evaluation now that newer and better psychometric tools, research designs, and statistical procedures are available.

The question of duplication must be considered in the light of the principle that, to be acceptable, a thesis or dissertation must make a contribution to the advancement of education as a science. There are educators who feel that a master's candidate will not make any great contribution at this point in his career and that he might as well be allowed to repeat a good study merely as an exercise in scholarship. They point out that the taboo on duplication deters students from investigating any problem which has been studied before, thus depriving them of many opportunities for significant investigations and resulting in a lack of continuity in the research on a given problem. It is their feeling that master's candidates probably are best employed in respading the grounds from a number of angles. These contentions have some merit in suggesting a somewhat liberal interpretation of what constitutes duplication, but they probably do not justify mere repetition. Although thousands of studies are conducted every year, problems are not getting any scarcer. On the contrary, every study that provides a tentative answer to a problem simply uncovers a multitude of other problems that need investigation. There is, therefore, no point in going over what is already known when there is so much new territory to be explored.

Of course, this does not deny the fact that rarely are problems in education solved with such finality that further verification is unwarranted. Furthermore, rarely are all the aspects of a given problem solved, and it is sometimes possible to carry the investigation of a problem area beyond the first study to the next step. Problems under investigation are frequently fruitful sources of suggestions for parallel studies that could be conducted in related areas without involving objectionable duplication.

Criteria for Selection of a Research Problem

Although there are no standard rules that, either singly or collectively, will guarantee the suitability of a research problem, a number of criteria in the sense of necessary—albeit not

sufficient—conditions might be listed for guidance in the selection
of such a problem.

1. Is the topic of interest? While interest sometimes develops with familiarity, it does not seem likely that the
student can do his best work on a problem that has no personal meaning for him.

2. Is the problem sufficiently original that it does not involve objectionable duplication?

3. Is the problem amenable to research? Many problems
are of a philosophical nature; they can be discussed but not to
the point where objective evidence can provide a solution.
Thus, the problem, "Should high school boys work?" having
no referent is, as stated, a philosophical issue not subject to
scientific determination. Before it could be investigated, it
would have to be oriented toward a criterion—for example,
"Do high school boys who work suffer academically?"

4. Is the problem significant? Specifically, what will it add
to the present state of knowledge or the development of
education as a science? Overemphasis on rigorous statistical
research methodology sometimes encourages the elaborate
investigation of the trivial at the expense of the more significant. Wolfle (1957), for instance, ridicules some of the trivial
problems that have been subjected to research. Referring to
Longfellow's poem, "I shot an arrow into the air; it fell to
earth I knew not where. I breathed a song into the air; it fell
to earth I knew not where," he points out that some people
would not go about the task so lightheartedly; they would
want to have a control group of poets who do not breathe
songs into the air—or would want to conduct a survey to
determine the differential effects of song-breathing and non-
song-breathing poets, for example.

5. Is research into the problem feasible? Many significant
educational problems must be bypassed, perhaps because
they would not get the necessary clearance or perhaps because they are not appropriate from the standpoint of the
competence of the investigator. The investigation of many
worthwhile problems is likewise handicapped by the lack of
adequate tools.

Sometimes, despite all precautions, the problem
selected turns out to be unsuitable. No matter how annoying this
may be, it is generally better for the investigator to abandon his
project and to move on to a different problem. Although an un-

suitable problem sometimes can be converted into a suitable one of a similar or parallel nature, and part of the effort salvaged, it is usually foolish to continue to invest time and effort in a project discovered to be marginal.

Sources of Problems

Although there are a number of sources from which leads to the selection of a problem can be obtained, there is no standard prescription that can be given that will provide each and every student with a suitable research problem. Nor is there a standard source from which a student can simply choose even a tentative topic. While students sometimes just seem to stumble on a problem, it is far more logical to suspect that a good research problem is more directly the outcome of hard work and persistence than of good luck or perhaps even genius; the former is unquestionably the surer way. To the extent that ideas are more likely to thrive on a foundation of experience and knowledge than to emerge from an intellectual and academic vacuum, any student seeking a research problem simply has no alternative but to become thoroughly familiar with the accumulated knowledge of his field.

A complete and critical review of the professional literature is bound to point to a number of contradictions that need to be resolved or perhaps findings that "just don't seem right," both of which suggest the operation of extraneous factors and the need for a replication of the study under conditions of more rigorous control. A study of the literature will undoubtedly point to a number of gaps and inconsistencies: some studies need to be verified; studies dealing with a significant problem are sometimes lacking in scope or perhaps statistical sophistication and should be repeated. There is always the need to extend research findings by determining the limits of their applicability: Is a certain method found effective with middle-class children equally effective with the culturally disadvantaged? It is often desirable for a study conducted under one set of conditions to be repeated under other equally legitimate conditions. Authors of research articles and theses often present ideas concerning factors worth considering in the further exploration of their topic. Granted, some of the ideas they present are not easily pursued, yet progress in science is made by the accumulation of small gains and it may be possible to find some aspect worthy of investigation.

Critical reviews of the literature, as might be found in *Annual Review of Psychology* or the yearbooks of the various professional societies often provide a good perspective from which to grasp the dimensions of a problem, its basic issues, and the methods found productive in its investigation. Often they list problems in need of study. It may be helpful for the student to peruse the titles listed in *Education Index* on topics of interest for ideas to be adapted into a parallel study involving a somewhat different population, or perhaps a different subject area. Not to be overlooked in the search for a problem is the student's personal experience and the educational situation in which he finds himself. Also helpful are the suggestions of administrators, supervisors, and other persons of wide background. Administrators, for example, often lack the means and the personnel necessary for research into some of their problems and might welcome the research efforts of the graduate student. Authors of textbooks and instructors of graduate classes typically point to areas in which answers are lacking or in need of verification. Seminars and informal discussions with fellow-students are also bound to bring out conflicting points of view that can sometimes lead to good research ideas.

It has been suggested that educational research must not be restricted to the solution of immediate problems at the empirical level, but rather must also be oriented toward the integration of research findings into a conceptual framework that gives them meaning and broad usefulness. There is nothing unscientific, however, about solving a practical problem if it can be given conceptual perspective, and it is sometimes better for the graduate student to work on such a problem than to attempt to deal with the more complex organizational or theoretical aspects of science which frequently require a greater insight into the overall field than he is likely to possess.

While it is undoubtedly true that some people are more sensitive than others to the existence of problems, it seems logical to suspect that their sensitivity stems in large part from a clear understanding of the theoretical, empirical, and practical aspects of the field, derived from personal experience and a critical study of the literature. In the same way, creativity and other personality attributes that make for originality, flexibility, ingenuity, foresight, and initiative—and thus contribute to the wise choice of a research problem—must also operate within the framework of what is already known. In short, familiarity with the field is crucial to the selection of an appropriate research problem. Whereas history records a number of instances where the ideas for inventions have come spontaneously to certain people, these were invariably people with a good background in the subject. It would seem logical that anyone untrained in a given field would not be able to see its problems nor the means by which they could be solved. The student must also recognize that, although faculty members are invariably delighted when a student takes the initiative and locates a suitable problem on his own, the acceptability of a topic is a decision for the advisor and his committee. Thus, there are bound to be occasional differences of opinion as to what constitutes an adequate research problem. While this arrangement exerts an influence towards conformity which is perhaps stifling in rare instances, it usually works to the student's benefit.

It may be of advantage to the student seeking a problem for investigation to attempt to structure the field on the basis of such questions as those presented by Holmes et al. (1939):

1. In your field of interest, what practical problems have to be met by those individuals who do the actual work?

2. In current and recent research, what problems are under active attack?

3. What facts, principles, generalizations, and other findings have resulted from research in your field?

4. What practical implications for schoolwork may be drawn from the results?

5. To what extent have the findings of research actually been applied in your field?

6. What problems remain to be subjected to research and what problems are now emerging?

7. What are the chief difficulties to be met in prosecuting the researches yet to be conducted in your field?

8. What are the interrelations between research in your field and research in adjacent fields?

9. What research techniques or procedures have been developed in your field?

10. What concepts have been operative, either explicitly or implicitly, in the research in your field?

11. What assumptions have been implicit or openly avowed in the research in your field?

Clarifying and Stating the Problem

Before the student can proceed with his study, it is essential that he convert his tentative topic into a precise researchable problem, for a vague idea as to what the study is all about is more likely to lead to untold difficulties than to significant outcomes. It is only natural to the student to want to get started, but nothing can be more dangerous and detrimental to the quality of the output than to jump right in without having first made a thorough critical analysis of every aspect of the overall venture. Contrary to what many beginners in research seem to believe, effective research is not a matter of aiming in the general direction of the target with a double-barreled shotgun in the hope that the resulting debris can somehow be fashioned into a significant contribution to the cause of education. Certainly, there is more to good research than collecting copious notes from the library, giving tests to anyone available, and subjecting the tons of data to statistical procedures of sufficient complexity to guarantee an impressive computer output.

To the extent that success in research is better defined by the clarity with which the problem is seen in all its complexity than by the commotion it engenders, the student would be well-advised to concentrate on seeing his problem in perspective, anticipating difficulties, and blueprinting the whole operation so as to make sure that everything will proceed according to plans. This is not an easy task; good planning never is. But this willingness to plan down to the last detail, rather than leave things to chance and hope, is often what distinguishes the scholar from the amateur. While the neophyte is likely to identify research with the collection and analysis of data, the professional researcher is more likely to look on planning and pilot-testing of these plans as the crucial components of research. The actual conduct of the study he is more likely to see as mechanical and routine, often requiring more patience, perseverance, and legwork than genius.

The variety of errors that can be made in the formulation of a research project is relatively unlimited. A common fault, for example, is to list a field or topic rather than to state a specific problem. A study of "Juvenile Delinquency" or of "Teacher Effectiveness" would become more researchable if it were restricted to the comparison of certain aspects of the personality of delinquent and nondelinquent boys, or of the professional attitudes of "good" and "poor" teachers. Another common fault is to state a problem in such a way that its investigation is essentially impossible, e.g., "The desirability of introducing typing in the elementary school," or "The effects of working mothers on the academic achievement of their offspring." Beginning students often choose a problem that is too broad, e.g., "How to teach reading," or "How to promote self-actualization," both of which are obviously impossible to investigate precisely. Conversely, the problem must not be so narrow as to become artificial. In practice, it is better to begin with a semi-broad problem which can be gradually restricted as one proceeds to review the literature. The major delimitation should, of course, take place before the data are collected and preferably before the literature is surveyed in detail.

Following are a few examples of problems that have been reformulated into somewhat more feasible studies. They probably could be altered further and are presented simply as illustrations.

Problem: The role of the principal in American public education.
Restatement: The supervisory practices of principals in the high schools of . . . City.

Problem: A survey of factors affecting pupil progress.
Restatement: A survey of the level of aspiration of overachievers among the culturally disadvantaged in junior high school.

Problem: The relation of socio-economic status to intelligence.
Restatement: A comparative study of the performance of children of different socio-economic status on the items of the Stanford-Binet.

Problem: The value of a remedial reading problem at the college level.
Restatement: A study of the effects of a remedial reading program on the academic achievement of college freshmen.

Problem: A study of the factors that relate to college achievement.

Restatement: A study of the effect of part-time employment on the scholastic achievement of freshmen women at College X.

A good grasp of the problem should provide the student with insight into what can be done in the study he is contemplating, not only in defining his problem but also in deriving hypotheses and likely methods of attack. Such a background can generally be obtained from a thorough review of the literature. If the operation of the variables involved is not known, however, it is highly desirable to conduct a pilot study in order to clarify both their nature and the means of their investigation before the final statement of the problem is made. This takes time, but it is invariably a wise investment because it provides greater insight into the nature of the problem and permits its more precise and adequate formulation.

If the problem is to serve as a guide in planning the study and interpreting its results, it is essential that it be stated in precise terms. Only then can it give direction to the collection of the data and the manner in which they must be processed in order to provide the required answer. To the extent that a study is only as good as the clarity with which it is seen in all its ramifications, the student would be well-advised not only to place his problem in theoretical perspective, whenever possible, but also to identify its basic components as postulates from which specific hypotheses can be deduced. Particularly to be avoided are meaningless clichés and verbalisms which have no relationship to measurable operations, e.g., "The effects of emotional security on the child's all-round growth." In the same way, such terms as "self-actualization," "democracy," or "socialization" are relatively meaningless. To be of scientific value, as we have seen, a concept must be defined in terms of an empirical referent or operation. Learning, for example, must be defined in precise terms of measurable changes in pupil behavior: specifically, what can the student do with respect to the educational objectives considered valid from the standpoint of the investigation? The study must specify the basic operations through which the existence of relevant phenomena can be ascertained. Is teacher effectiveness, for example, to be evaluated in terms of supervisor ratings or on the basis of pupil progress as measured on standardized achievement tests?

Not only must a problem be defined clearly but the

procedure to be used in its solution and the nature and source of the evidence considered satisfactory and pertinent to its solution must also be specified. Such a definition must be made when the problem is selected, inasmuch as it may be found that there is no way of solving the problem as stated, and that it will have to be restated according to what is feasible from the standpoint of method. Thus, sometimes it is the nature of the data that can be collected that determines the problem to be selected for research. It is almost impossible, for example, to compare the relative effectiveness of the newer School Mathematics Study Group program with the traditional approach to the teaching of mathematics, simply because they do not cover the same content and are not oriented toward the same immediate objectives.

In the final analysis, it is the problem as defined that determines the data that are needed, and only data that fit the framework of the problem as stated should be collected. It follows that the whole problem must be explicitly defined—from the standpoint of both the specific question to be answered and the techniques to be followed in providing the required answer—before any attempt is made to gather the data.

THE HYPOTHESIS

The Nature and Purpose of Hypotheses

Going hand in hand with the selection of a research problem is the formulation of a suitable hypothesis as to its likely solution. Operationally, a hypothesis can be considered a tentative generalization about the problem under investigation; it is an assumption or proposition whose tenability is to be tested on the basis of the compatability of its implications with previous knowledge and with specially gathered empirical evidence.

Whenever possible, research should proceed from a hypothesis, for without a hypothesis an investigation is a relatively aimless search for data of vague relevance and significance. Hypotheses are particularly necessary in the search for cause-and-effect relationships. They are perhaps less crucial in studies in which the task is that of determining the status of a given phenomenon, although even in such studies the investigator is likely to need some tentative hypothesis to guide him to the areas worth exploring. Actually, hypotheses are not essential to research, particularly in the early stages of the exploration of a problem. Scientific discoveries can emerge from investigations not directed by hypotheses, and, though hypotheses are generally useful guides to effective research, it must not be assumed that failure to have a hypothesis is necessarily a sign of a lack of scientific sophistication.

The major objection to beginning research with a hypothesis is that postulated over 300 years ago by Bacon, who felt that a hypothesis biased the investigator toward a given position and caused him to lose his objectivity. This need not be so: a hypothesis must be conceived as an assumption which merits consideration, not as a position to be defended. Furthermore, the scientific method puts such restrictions on the investigator that the extent to which he can distort the evidence to fit his personal views is minimal. While it may be true that hypotheses can blind the investigator to other more fruitful hypotheses and cause him to ignore data which are not compatible with his hypothesis, this is the exception rather than the rule in good research.

Actually, it is almost impossible for a person who has a clear picture of his problem not to have one or more hypotheses in mind. The only question, therefore, is the degree to which those hypotheses are recognized at the conscious level and elaborated, screened, refined, and, finally, used as a pivot around which the investigation is to center. Conversely, if the investigator is not capable of formulating a hypothesis about his problem, he may not be ready to undertake its investigation. As Burton et al. (1960) point out, the derivation of the hypothesis should precede the collection of the data. This is indisputable in the usual case, but only to the extent that the investigator of a given topic would generally have enough background to derive intelligent, albeit tentative, hypotheses.

The arguments in favor of well-developed hypotheses as a framework for research center around the fact that the aimless collection of data is not likely to lead anywhere. Since a multitude of possible relationships exist among phenomena, generalizations and relationships significant from the standpoint of a given problem do not just emerge from data. More specifically:

1. Hypotheses provide direction to research and prevent the review of irrelevant literature and the collection of useless or excess data. They enable the investigator to classify the information he has collected from the standpoint of both relevance and organization, for a given fact may be relevant

with respect to one hypothesis and irrelevant with respect to another. Hypotheses not only prevent waste in the collection of data, but they also ensure the collection of data necessary to answer the question posed in the statement of the problem.

2. Hypotheses sensitize the investigator to certain aspects of the situation which are relevant from the standpoint of the problem at hand. In general, hypotheses spell the difference between precision and haphazardness, between fruitful and fruitless research.

3. Hypotheses permit the investigator to understand with greater clarity the problem and its ramifications as well as the data which bear on it. They enable him to identify the procedures and methods to be used in solving his problem and to rule out methods which are incapable of providing the data necessary to test the hypothesis posited.

4. Hypotheses act as a framework for the conclusions. They guide the collection of relevant data and make possible the interpretation of these data in the light of the potential solution. Hypotheses provide the framework for stating conclusions in a meaningful way—i.e., as a direct answer to the hypothesis being tested.

Sources of Hypotheses

The task of deriving adequate hypotheses is essentially parallel to that of selecting suitable problems, since the selection of a problem can hardly be considered apart from the hypothesis that might be tested in its solution. And just as there is no royal road to the location of a suitable problem, there is no royal road to the discovery of fruitful hypotheses. There is also a parallel in the characteristics of experience and creativity that make certain persons capable of deriving adequate hypotheses. Though hypotheses should precede the gathering of data, a good hypothesis can come only from experience. Some degree of data-gathering, such as the recall of past experience, the review of the literature, or a pilot study, must, therefore, precede the development and gradual refinement of the hypothesis. It would be difficult, for example, to derive meaningful hypotheses regarding the various aspects of teacher effectiveness without some background in the psychology of learning.

The factor of persistence must not be overlooked. Success at discovery is invariably predicated on the expenditure of considerable time and effort in tracing various leads and refining tentative hypotheses. Unfortunately, the general pattern is for the investigator to report his final hypothesis and the success to which it led; he never mentions the dozens of hypotheses which he discarded. As a result, other investigators may waste time on the same fruitless leads, although, to be sure, hypotheses which have been discarded too quickly may prove useful when approached from a different point of view.

Actually, a good investigator must have not only an alert mind capable of deriving relevant hypotheses, but also a critical mind capable of rejecting faulty hypotheses. Interestingly enough, the person who is "full of ideas" may also be the person who is lacking in critical analysis—i.e., originality may be somewhat incompatible with a critical attitude.

Although reasoning by analogy is generally considered unacceptable as a source of proof, it is a very fertile source of hypotheses. The premise is that if the two situations are alike in certain aspects relevant from the standpoint of the problem under consideration, they are probably similar in other relevant aspects. It is assumed that the existence of similarities between two situations is not a matter of accident, but rather that it is the result of the operation of some law common to the two situations so that the other similarities governed by the same law also obtain in both instances. Analogy is never based on complete likeness, but the differences are assumed to be in those aspects which are independent of the common law and therefore to be ignored. This cannot be shown through logic, of course, and reasoning by analogy is suspect until its outcomes have been verified through empirical proof. Meanwhile, the insights that analogy provides are useful inasmuch as they lead to their own refinement and verification through the acquisition of relevant data and the formulation of more adequate hypotheses.

Criteria for Judging Hypotheses

The merits of a given hypothesis can be judged only by its effectiveness in the particular problem under investigation, and its final validity cannot be appraised except through an empirical test. Nevertheless, one can set up certain general criteria on the basis of which to judge the relative worth of a hypothesis.

(These criteria, it will be noted, parallel rather closely the criteria of a good theory presented in Chapter 3.)

1. A good hypothesis must be based directly on existing data. It might even be expected to predict or anticipate previously unknown data.

2. A good hypothesis must explain existing data in simpler terms than any competing hypothesis. The law of parsimony favors the hypothesis that explains the most in the simplest terms.

3. A good hypothesis must be stated as simply and concisely as the complexity of the concepts involved will allow. Note, for example, how simply some of the major laws of science—gravity, motion, survival of the fittest, and others—are stated.

4. A good hypothesis must, above all, be testable. It must be stated so that its implications can be deduced in the form of empirical operations with respect to which the relationship can either be validated or refuted. For instance, if the world is round, one can reach the East by sailing west. The statement of the hypothesis must permit the development of a research design capable of providing the data necessary for testing its validity. For example, one of the basic premises of the Montessori system of education—that freedom of movement within the classroom is an essential condition for effective learning—lent itself readily to an empirical test. On the contrary, the proposition that kindergarten promotes social maturity is difficult to validate because of the relative unavailability of adequate means for the valid appraisal of such maturity and for the isolation of other factors which also contribute to social and emotional growth.

Testing the Hypothesis

The proof of the worth of a hypothesis lies in its ability to meet the test of its validity. Validity is established in two stages: 1. The statement of the hypothesis allows the investigator to develop deductively certain implications which, when stated in operational terms, can lead to the rejection of hypotheses that are in conflict with accepted knowledge at the logical level. For example, the notion of a perpetual-motion machine capable of continued work without external power input would have to be rejected since it conflicts with the well-established principle of the conservation of energy. 2. If a hypothesis passes the test of logic, it then must be subjected to an empirical test, perhaps through an experiment or a series of measurements. The hypothesis that boys are stronger or taller in general than girls, for example, can be verified through measurements. In a complex study, such as the comparisons of the relative effectiveness of different combinations of instructional procedures and class size, a research worker may consider three or four hypotheses simultaneously.

The scientist relies on two types of hypotheses. He generally first postulates a *research* hypothesis, which relates to expected outcomes or relations among variables, e.g., children with Head Start experience will outperform comparable children without such experience. However, in order to test the validity of the research hypothesis, he must convert it into operational terms. This is usually done through translating the research hypothesis into the *null* hypothesis which, in effect, says, "No, there is no relation here; the difference between the two groups is simply a matter of chance." This is frequently the opposite of what the investigator believes, and it is usually postulated with the expectation that it will be rejected. He then proceeds to test the null hypothesis on the basis of probability, thereby leading to its acceptance or rejection. If the data in question cannot be accounted for on the basis of chance, they apparently reflect a relationship as postulated in the research hypothesis (see Chapter 6).

A hypothesis that fails to meet the test of its validity must be modified or rejected. However, just like a theory, a hypothesis can be useful even though it is partly incorrect and, in practice, hypotheses are not so much rejected as they are replaced by more adequate hypotheses. Negative instances suggest the presence of other considerations that need to be isolated or incorporated in the statement of the hypothesis so that the exceptions can become part of the relationship at a more sophisticated level. The confirmation of a hypothesis, on the other hand, is always tentative and relative, subject to later revision—and even rejection—as further evidence appears or as more adequate hypotheses are introduced. Evidence can prove neither the research hypothesis nor its counterpart, the null hypothesis; it can only confirm or refute the tenability of one position or the other. Proof would imply certainty, and the investigator cannot be sure that an exception to his hypothesis will never occur, nor can he be sure that his hypothesis is the only hypothesis capable of covering the phenomenon in question. The research design is developed to generate crucial evidence on the alternatives, but confirmation or refutation must always be a matter of probability. This is essentially the pattern we noted in connection with theories, although hypotheses, since they are more tentative and less fully developed than theories, are more subject to modification and to rejection.

Hypotheses, Laws, and Principles

A hypothesis which is sustained by logical and empirical tests provides the basis for generalizations or conclusions. As further research provides greater confirmation and clarification of the conditions under which the hypothesis holds, a generalization (whose importance warrants it) may become a law or a principle. The distinction between a hypothesis, a generalization, a law, and a principle is generally a matter of *dependability*, based on such factors as logical and theoretical plausibility, repeated verification, and adequate definition and delineation of the conditions under which it holds true; and *complexity, scope* and *relative importance*. Thus, Galileo probably began with a simple hunch (*hypothesis*) that the rate of free fall of a body is independent of its size and weight. A few confirming instances may have led him to a generalization (*conclusion*). Later as its importance and scope became recognized, the discovery was given the status of a *principle* or *law*. The point at which the transition from one to the other takes place is, of course, imprecise. The terms *law* and *principle* are generally used interchangeably to refer to the statement of an invariant—as far as it is known at the present—relationship among phenomena. The concept of parsimony, for example, is variously referred to as a law or a principle. Technically, however, a principle is more comprehensive than a law and may serve as a basis from which laws are derived.

A scientific law may be defined as a hypothesis whose scientific validity is relatively unquestioned. It represents as close an approximation to empirical truth as has been derived to date, although, to be sure, occasionally a "law" has to be recalled for revision and extension, and perhaps, rejection. In fact, it may be suspected that most laws, at least in their original statement, incorporate some degree of error and/or incompleteness. As more and more data are accumulated, laws become progressively broader in application, covering more of the known aspects of phenomena more adequately. In their later stages, laws are best explained as the logical outgrowths of theories. Thus, science involves an increasingly adequate explanation of events and phenomena through a complex of more and more useful hypotheses, laws, principles, and theories, logically interrelated into a meaningful whole.

Although the distinction between theories and hypotheses is not always clear or free of overlapping, a theory is broader in scope and rests on a somewhat more sophisticated basis than does a hypothesis. Thus, while a hypothesis may be postulated on the basis of relatively haphazard observations, a theory generally attempts to unify a number of previously established generalizations. This is, of course, most evident in such advanced theories as the theory of evolution or the theory of relativity.

THE COLLECTION AND ANALYSIS OF DATA

Scientific problems can be resolved only on the basis of data, and a major responsibility of the scientist is to set up a research design capable of providing the data necessary to the solution of his problem. While the unity of research makes it impossible to say that one aspect is more crucial than another, the collection of data is of paramount importance in the conduct of research, since, obviously, no solution can be more adequate than the data on which it is based.

The more clearly and thoroughly a problem and its many ramifications are identified, the more adequately the study can be planned and carried to successful completion. Thus, the task is to synchronize the statement of the problem with the design to be used in its solution, and every aspect of the study down to the last detail of execution must be planned before the study is undertaken. It is senseless to select a problem, no matter how adequate, if circumstances preclude the collection of the data required for its solution. The student who just leaves the statistical treatment of his data for "When I get there" may find that the data, as collected, are impossible to analyze.

The problems involved in the accumulation of adequate data are far too technical to be reviewed here; the discussion, therefore, will be restricted to a brief overview of the fundamental aspects of measurements as they relate to research. The student is referred to more adequate treatment to be found in texts in educational and psychological tests and measurements, with the reminder that the field is of primary importance. No one interested in research can afford to be without thorough training in this area.

The Nature of Data

Data can be classified into two broad categories: *qualitative data* or *attributes,* e.g., color, motivation, maladjustment, and honesty, and *quantitative data* or *variables,* e.g., IQ score, grade-point average, and height. The distinction frequently is based on processes rather than on the properties inherent in the phenomena, for generally properties considered qualitative can be made quantitative by measuring them with an instrument designed to assign numerical values to the various degrees to which they exist. Thus, intelligence, height and personality adjustments can exist both as attributes and as variables. As a result, the decision to research a given phenomenon on the basis of its attributes or on the basis of its quantitative aspects is frequently a matter of choice, depending on such considerations as the need for precision and the ease of manipulation of the data. In general, the latter alternative is the more functional and the more adequate, since quantification provides a greater refinement in classification and possesses definite advantages by virtue of its amenability to treatment by modern statistical processes. In fact, the quantification of phenomena is generally considered essential to the progress of a science, particularly at the more advanced levels.

Unfortunately, at present we do not have the instruments necessary for the precise quantification of many of the characteristics with which educational research is concerned, e.g., honesty, health, adjustment, or motivation. Although we are devising progressively more adequate techniques and instruments with which to "measure" what years ago could only be studied as attributes, we still have a long way to go, particularly in the more intangible aspects of human behavior. It appears that by their very nature certain properties and characteristics, e.g., such concepts as married, widowed, and dead, must remain attributes for which the only quantification possible is that of counting the frequency of occurrence. On the other hand, it may be possible to convert even such attributes as sex into what is probably the more meaningful psychological dimension of "masculinity–femininity," and thus convert what is essentially a dichotomous attribute into a measurable quantity.

Variables

Variables can be classified as *continuous* or *discrete*. Continuous variables are those for which fractional values exist and have meaning, *e.g.*, distance, age, and weight, where 4.87 miles, 68.167 years, or any other fraction of a whole unit is logical and measurable within the precision of the instrument used. Discrete variables, on the other hand, exist only in units (usually units of one). For example, there are 29, 30, 31, . . . students in a class, 800, 801, 802, . . . volumes in a library, and so on. Here, fractional values cannot exist; one cannot have 11.25 eggs in a basket; nor can a couple have 2.5 children, in the usual sense of the words *eggs* or *children*. This distinction is somewhat more complicated in practice: What should a college, reporting its enrollment, do with students carrying a half-load? How does a library enumerate three booklets bound into one volume, since it could have as easily had three volumes by binding each separately? The problem is generally resolved—though not entirely satisfactorily—by defining the unit of operation. Thus, the library would have to indicate whether it is referring to the number of volumes separately indexed in the card catalog or to the number of separate titles as listed in the *Cumulative Book Index*, or it might possibly present the data both ways.

The typical problem in educational research deals with test scores. These are generally reported as discrete variables, though they are often fundamentally continuous. Thus, a child having 19 out of 20 words correct on a spelling test gets a score of 19, but inasmuch as he may have missed the twentieth word by a "country mile" or by a mere slip, it is possible to conceive of his true score as ranging anywhere from 19.00 to 19.99. IQ's also are recorded as discrete, though, by their very computation, they are technically continuous. It should be noted in this connection that a major reason for avoiding fractional values in many instances is that the accuracy of measurement does not warrant consideration of fractional values, not that the variables are constitutionally discrete.

In research, where the concern is with group measures which almost invariably are fractional, continuous variables appear somewhat more acceptable than discrete variables. Thus, it seems easier to conceptualize the average distance traveled by commuters to City X as 9.28 miles, or of the average age of freshmen at College Y as 18.34 years, than to think of the average family as having 2.6 children.

Perhaps more pertinent to research is the classification of variables as *independent* and *dependent*. When the investigator is concerned with the school achievement of students in relation to their IQ, the IQ is considered the independent variable; the grades or achievement test scores are the dependent variables in the sense that they depend on the IQ. In an experiment investigating the effect of practice time on performance, time would be the independent variable and performance the dependent variable. In an experiment, we also need to be concerned with independent variables that can be manipulated as against those that can only be assigned. Practice time, teaching methods, or the intensity of an electric shock, for example, can be manipulated; sex, intellectual level, neurotic tendencies, or visual deficiencies, on the other hand, already exist in certain individuals and cannot be randomized. These concepts will be considered in greater detail in connection with experimentation in Chapter 11.

Measurement

Man's first attempt to appraise the properties and characteristics of phenomena probably was made on the basis of a dichotomy. For instance, early attempts at studying the weather were probably restricted to noting whether or not it rained in a given day. Later this was probably extended to counting the number of times it rained in a given period, thereby providing a discrete series. The next step in the development of science was measurement, which provides a relatively unlimited number of categories into which phenomena can be ordered and which permits a more adequate and facile manipulation of the categories by virtue of their susceptibility to mathematical treatment.

Success in research, and in science, depends on the availability of instruments and techniques of sufficient precision to measure the phenomenon under study. Much greater progress in this connection has been made in the physical than in the social sciences. Most of the measurements with which educational research is concerned are derived through pencil-and-paper tests which are, as yet, relatively imprecise. This is particularly true in such areas as motivation, attitudes, values, creativity, etc., all of which are generally considered more psychologically and educationally significant than many of the variables which can be measured with greater accuracy. In fact, many educators would agree with Brown (1942) that the ease and accuracy with which educational outcomes are measured is frequently in direct proportion to their unimportance. What we measure most precisely is precisely what it matters least whether we measure or not! The problems connected with the devising of adequate instruments for measuring the more meaningful psychological dimensions are so complex, however, that their consideration here is inadvisable.

Characteristics of a Good Measuring Instrument

Measurement is effected by means of some instrument, e.g., a gauge, a rule, a scale, or a test. If they are to provide dependable measurements, such instruments, regardless of their specific nature and purpose, must all possess certain qualities, of which *validity* is by far the most important—especially as the results apply to research. There is an important distinction to be made between measurement on an individual basis, as in guidance, and measurement on a group basis. In the first situation, scores must be individually dependable; in the second, we are interested in group averages and do not particularly object to individual errors—provided they cancel out.

A measuring instrument must be *reliable,* i.e., it must be consistent in the measurement of whatever it measures. A test of intelligence, for example, would be lacking in reliability if, in a test-retest situation,* legitimately handled, a child's IQ shifted haphazardly from say, 70 to 140. Reliability is, of course, most important in guidance where the focus is on an individual child. In research, errors of unreliability, representing random errors, tend to cancel out so that in a fairly large sample, group values are not too greatly affected. Of course, a test relatively devoid of reliability, *e.g.,* an elastic yardstick to measure distance, can hardly

---

* Different methods of calculating reliability measure essentially different things. For example, test-retest reliability actually estimates the extent to which John's score at a given time can be used as the basis for inferring his score at a later date. The Kuder-Richardson reliability, on the other hand, is essentially a measure of the internal consistency (homogeneity) of the test, i.e., the extent to which all of the items contribute to the measurement of a common factor. The various measures yield indexes which are not computationally or logically equivalent. Some people advocate abandoning reliability as a concept and substituting indexes of *stability, homogeneity,* or *equivalence* depending on the method used. The point is beyond the scope of the present discussion.

be used as the basis for scientific conclusions.

A good measuring instrument should also be *usable*. From an administrative point of view, usability is a consideration of practical importance. Research is especially concerned with usability because inadequacies in this area are readily transferred into errors of invalidity. Thus, if two groups are compared on the basis of their performances on a test of excessive length, the comparison will incorporate an element of motivation and persistence which will confound the difference in the relative competence of the two groups. Similarly, excessive length in a questionnaire, for instance, is likely to result in a loss of validity by encouraging nonresponse.

Validity refers to the extent to which an instrument measures what it purports to measure.* Operationally, an instrument is valid to the extent to which differences in test performance represent corresponding true differences among individuals in the characteristic the instrument is designed to measure. A test of history would be invalid, for instance, if it incorporated such a high level of reading proficiency that difficulties in understanding the vocabulary interfered with a student's performance on the test.

Failure to appreciate the importance of validity is one of the most common errors vitiating research, particularly in the social sciences where validity is sometimes subtle and difficult to establish. It is frequently reported, for example, that a school is low in arithmetic competence, simply because its students did not perform at expected levels on a test bearing a title suggestive of arithmetic competence. It is essential to note that validity is a specific concept—a test is valid not in general, but is valid for a particular group under particular circumstances. The arithmetic test

---

* Psychologists define four types of validity (APA, 1967): 1. predictive validity. The College Boards have predictive validity to the extent that the scores which they provide are indicative of later success in college; 2. concurrent validity. This is very much like predictive validity but relates to some concurrent rather than future performance; the College Boards would have concurrent validity to the extent that the scores they provide agree in general with high school rank; 3. content validity. This refers to the extent to which the situations incorporated in the test are a representative sample of the trait or characteristic the test is designed to appraise. A test of history would have content validity to the extent that it samples the various contents of the course; 4. construct validity. Except for special situations, construct validity is the most basic in that it ties psychometric concepts to their theoretical (scientific) counterparts. A person scoring high in anxiety would be expected to display behavioral rigidity, close-mindedness, and other characteristics research has associated with anxiety. Again, the discussion is beyond the scope of the present text.

mentioned may not have been valid for the students of the particular school; their curriculum may not have been oriented toward the development of the competencies expected in the test. The norms of a standardized test are accumulated by administering the test to a large sample representative of the grade level or group for whom the test is intended. Since norms are simply standards of comparison, it is inevitable that a given class will not coincide with the norm group in every respect. The lack of compatibility between the two groups may be sufficient to account for the discrepancy in the performance of the class from that of the norm group.

Since validity is specific to a given situation, the legitimacy of the use that is made of a test cannot be considered apart from the purpose for which it is being used. In an experiment where the purpose is to compare the relative performance of two groups, for instance, there may be no invalidity introduced by giving the two groups a short break, even though this is in violation of standardization procedures. Such a step, however, would invalidate any comparison of the performance of the two groups with the norms of the test.

"Test-wiseness" on the part of children who have been tested repeatedly may invalidate a test score in relation to the norms. Whenever the purpose is to compare the performance of a group against the test norms, it must be remembered that a test score is valid only to the extent that the background of the testee is similar to the background of the group on which the test was standardized. For example, a high school, eager to have its graduates accepted into college, may encourage its students to take the College Boards two or three times during the course of their junior and senior years in order to get acquainted with the general nature of the tests and to orient their studies accordingly. To the extent that practice with the tests improved their performance, the scores made by these students on the third and fourth testing would automatically be higher by an indeterminate amount than they should legitimately be. At the other end of the continuum are the culturally disadvantaged children for whom many of our current instruments are relatively invalid.

A difficult problem involving the concept of validity is that of the *fairness* (i.e., the validity) of the instruments used to measure status in an experiment. For example, the relative effectiveness of drill and the project approach in promoting academic growth may well hinge on the emphasis of the test on the basis of which this growth is measured. A comparison of the relative superiority of large *versus* small classes may also depend in no small measure on whether the criterion of the study is the memorization of facts or the development of critical thinking and favorable attitudes toward the subject. In such cases, the investigator must determine what constitutes a valid criterion for the particular purpose of the investigation being conducted. Generally, this requires a clarification of the objectives of the study and a translation of these objectives into a test or a series of tests representing a legitimate criterion of the comparison in question. Such an approach was particularly evident in the Eight Year Study (Aikin, 1942). In any event, there is a need for a clear statement of the nature of the criterion with reference to which one method was found superior to another, since, if a different criterion were used, the relative superiority of the two methods might be reversed.

The concept of validity is not restricted to test scores; it applies to all data-gathering instruments and techniques. Thus, invalidity in research data might result from incompleteness of the returns or ambiguity in the items in a questionnaire study, the very presence of the interviewer or observer in an interview or observation study, the personal biases of the investigator, etc. The admissions requirements listed in university bulletins likewise are not necessarily valid indexes of a given university's actual admissions policies. Sampling is another important consideration affecting the validity of the data gathered for research purposes (see Chapter 7).

THE INTERPRETATION OF THE DATA

The interpretation of research data cannot be considered in the abstract. In view of the diversity of the research methods used in education and the corresponding diversity of the data they seek, the interpretation of data is best considered within the context of each of the methods. The analysis and interpretation of historical data, for example, is best viewed in the light of the historical method, its objectives, and its limitations. For the present it is important to note that, regardless of the adequacy of the data and of the procedures by which they are processed, data do not interpret themselves. It is the investigator who must pass judgment on their meaning from the standpoint of the problem under investigation. Since he cannot examine all members of the class under investigation, in the final analysis, he must make some judgment on the basis of a sample. This always involves a risk. Statistics can restrict the range in which judgment can be made, but there is no substitute for imagination and good sense.

It is essential to recognize that errors can be made in interpretation—just as they can in any of the other steps of the scientific method—and the specific errors to be guarded against vary with the different research methods. The following are among the more common errors of interpretation:

> 1. Failure to see the problem in the perspective of its theoretical and empirical setting, perhaps as a result of an inadequate grasp of the problem in its broad sense and too close a focus on its immediate aspects. Thus, the Hartshorne and May (1928) studies are not to be interpreted as supporting the view that human behavior is inconsistent and haphazard, but rather that the consistency is internal rather than external.

> 2. Failure to appreciate the relevance of the various elements of the situation, resulting from such factors as an inadequate grasp of the problem, too rigid a mind-set, or even a lack of imagination. This may cause the investigator to overlook the operation of significant factors, *e.g.,* motivation and teacher competence in studies of the effectiveness of teaching methods, or selective migration and test fairness in studies of class differences in intellectual ability. Consequently, the outcomes of the study are attributed to the wrong antecedent. A parallel error is the failure to see crucial relationships to be pursued, and the resulting failure to obtain data vital to the investigation.

> 3. Failure to recognize limitations in the research evidence such as: nonrepresentativeness in sampling; biases almost inevitable in the data concerning certain phenomena; inadequacies in the research design, the data-gathering instruments, and/or the statistical analysis; or the inappropriateness of the criterion. Particularly incapacitating from the standpoint of the study is the common failure on the part of the investigator to see that the research design could not possibly lead to any other results than those that were obtained. Thus, the interviewing of students or parents regarding their attitude toward the school is almost sure to lead to endorsement. Similarly, it is said that personality is a more important consideration in teacher effectiveness than is knowledge of subject. Inasmuch as teachers cannot be

certified to teach unless they know their subject well enough to pass the required college courses, the operation of the factor of knowledge of subject-matter is restricted sufficiently to give precedence to other, more unlimited factors in the situation.*

Of a parallel nature is failure on the part of the investigator to make the relative limitations of his study sufficiently explicit so that, while the study is correct, it promotes misinterpretations and/or overextension of its findings and conclusions. A similar error can arise from failure to report the study in sufficient detail to permit the reader to gain an adequate grasp of its nature.

SYNTHESIS AND ORIENTATION

The discussion of the steps of the scientific method presented in this chapter has been restricted to an overview designed to provide continuity and to bring out the unity of educational research. Inasmuch as the implementation of the scientific method is specific to the particular type of research in which it functions, it seems more appropriate to integrate the treatment of these more detailed aspects in the context of the presentation of the various types of research that follows.

On the other hand, what is significant is not the peculiarities of the application of the scientific method to a specific situation, but rather its universality. What needs to be stressed is that science cuts across the arbitrary lines that separate the various disciplines, and that scientists, regardless of disciplinary allegiance, subscribe to a common core of procedures and attitudes in their search for truth. That the general level of sophistication at which the various disciplines operate should vary is inescapable in view of the degree of relative development of each and the complexity of the material with which they deal, but the coordination of their efforts toward a common objective to be attained by subscription to a common method makes the difference one of degree rather than of kind.

In this connection, Hillway (1956) presents the role of the investigator as that of detective. Developing this parallel,

---

* A similar error, noted by Russell (1927) in connection with the classic studies in learning, is reported in Chapter 11. There is also the story of the man who, having removed a grasshopper's legs and finding that it no longer jumped in response to a loud noise, concluded that the removal of its legs had apparently rendered the poor insect deaf.

he points out that the scientist must be alert and trained to seek clues that will develop into fruitful hypotheses, that he must be familiar with sources of information, and that he must be able to use these sources quickly and effectively. Like his detective counterpart, the scientist must not solve his problem on the basis of opinions, no matter how logical they may appear. While he will have to start with hunches and opinions, these are only hypotheses which he must check for validity. He must evaluate all the information he gathers before attempting to synthesize it with respect to his hypotheses. Finally, both the scientist and the detective must test their hypotheses against objective evidence, not mere plausibility. Hillway points out further that, just as detectives differ in their ability to sense important clues and to develop them through logical and empirical considerations, so do researchers differ in their ability to derive fruitful hypotheses and to develop them through the accumulation of the data collected in line with those hypotheses.

Highlights of the Chapter

1.   Even though we depend so critically on science for our material and social welfare and progress, most people have only an inadequate conception of its nature and purpose. We are especially lacking in appreciation of the role of systematic research in the development of the social sciences.

2.   The wise selection of a research problem is among the most crucial aspects of success in research. Unfortunately, the student selecting a problem for thesis or dissertation purposes is generally restricted by personal inadequacies in the areas of problem-awareness, knowledge and perspective of the field, research and statistical competence, and access to data.

3.   The question of its possible contribution and feasibility are among the more important criteria for the selection of a research problem. There is, however, no standard set of rules that will provide the student with a suitable problem. Familiarity with the field and imagination are among the more important attributes facilitating the wise selection of a research topic.

4.   If a problem is to serve its function as a guide in the planning

and conduct of a research study, it must be clearly delineated. It must strike a balance between excessive scope—and resulting unmanageability—and overrestriction—and consequent artificiality.

5.   Whenever possible, the problem should be converted into a hypothesis to be tested, for hypotheses highlight the direction in which the study is to go, the data that need to be collected in its investigation, and the way these data are to be processed to provide an adequate answer. Not only does a hypothesis alert the investigator to relevant aspects of the situation and permit him to refine his research design, but it also provides him with the framework for the interpretation of the findings and the derivation of conclusions. Imagination and familiarity with the field—as well as persistence and a critical attitude—are important factors in the formulation of a good hypothesis.

6.   The most important criterion of a good hypothesis is its testability. Are its implications, when stated in operational terms, compatible with known facts, and, further, are they compatible at the empirical level with the results of research specifically designed to test their validity? A hypothesis is never proven; it is simply sustained or rejected, and, like a theory, a hypothesis may be useful even though it is partially in error. On the other hand, if its significance and scope warrant it, a hypothesis that is sustained may eventually attain the status of a law or principle.

7.   The research design must be capable of providing data on the basis of which the problem can be resolved. Inasmuch as no study can be more adequate than the data on which it is based, competence in research requires familiarity with the principles of tests and measurements—particularly with the concept of validity. The researcher must also be familiar with statistical procedures capable of the adequate analysis of the data that have been collected.

8.   Among the more common errors in the interpretation of the results of research are failing to see the significance of the data, failing to see the limitations of the research design, overlooking contrary evidence, mistaking coincidence for cause-and-effect, and reversing the cause and the effect. The best safeguards against such errors are common sense and insight into the field.

9.   Each of the different methods of educational research presents special problems. However, what is significant is not the unique nature of the different methods but rather the universality of the scientific principles that underlie the various approaches necessary to deal with the varied problems encountered in a field as broad and scientifically undeveloped as education.

Questions and Projects

1.   (a) List five broad areas in the field of education. With respect to each, identify one question in need of an answer.

(b) Develop a research proposal with regard to one of the problems listed above. Follow the format required by the graduate school for master's theses (e.g., problem, justification, etc.).

2.   (a) Make a survey of the theses, projects, and dissertations presented at your school over the years in partial fulfillment of the requirements for the master's and doctoral degrees in education. What is your estimate of the value of these contributions individually and collectively?

(b) Estimate the research orientation of a select group of universities from the caliber of their dissertations as synthesized in *Dissertation Abstracts*.

3.   "Unfortunately, some writers make their facts conform to their hypotheses rather than vice versa." (Brickman, *A Guide to Research in Educational History*, p. 116.) Evaluate the above statement. What safeguard might be taken to prevent this from occurring? Would refraining from starting with a hypothesis be the answer?

Selected References

Bechtoldt, H.P. "Construct validity: A critique," *Amer. Psychol.*, 14: 619–29; 1959. (See reply: Donald T. Campbell. "Recommendations for APA test standards regarding construct, trait, or discriminant validity," *Amer. Psychol.*, 15: 546–53; 1960.)

Bloom, Benjamin S. "Testing cognitive ability and achievement," in N.L. Gage (ed.) *Handbook of Research on Teaching*. Chicago: Rand McNally, 1963. pp. 379–97.

Cattell, Raymond B. and Andrew R. Baggaley. "The objective measurement of attitude motivation: Development and evaluation of principles and devices," *J. Pers.*, 24: 401–23; 1956.

Chamberlin, Thomas C. "The method of multiple working hypotheses," *Sci. Monthly,* 59: 357–62; 1944.

Coombs, Clyde H. "Theory and methods of social measurement," in Leon Festinger and Daniel Katz (eds.) *Research Methods in the Behavioral Sciences.* New York: Holt, Rinehart & Winston, 1965. pp. 471–535.

Cronbach, Lee J. and Paul E. Meehl. "Construct validity and psychological tests," *Psychol. Bull.,* 52: 281–302; 1955.

Davis, Gary A. "Current status of research and theory in human problem solving," *Psychol. Bull.,* 66: 36–54; 1966.

Dewey, John. *How We Think.* Boston: Heath, 1933.

Good, Carter V. "Criteria for selection of the research problem," *Peabody J. Educ.,* 19: 242–56; 1942.

Hall, Roy M. "Research priorities in school administration," in Jack A. Culbertson and Stephen P. Hencley (eds.) *Educational Research: New Perspectives.* Danville: Interstate, 1963. pp. 19–30.

Harris, Chester W. (ed.) *Problems in Measuring Change.* Madison: Univ. of Wisconsin Press, 1963.

Klopsteg, Paul. "The indispensable tools of science," *Sci.,* 132: 1913–22; 1960.

Lindvall, C.M. (ed.) *Defining Educational Objectives.* Pittsburgh: Univ. of Pittsburgh Press, 1964.

Mayo, George D. and Winton H. Manning. "Motivation measurement," *Educ. psychol. Measmt.,* 21: 73–83; 1961.

Rose, Arnold M. "The selection of problems for research," *Amer. J. Sociol.,* 54: 219–27; 1948.

Ryans, David G. "Research designs for the empirical validation of tests and inventories," *Educ. psychol. Measmt.,* 17: 175–84; 1957.

Skinner, B.F. "Pigeons in a pelican," *Amer. Psychol.,* 15: 28–37; 1960.

Stern, George G. "Measuring noncognitive variables in research on teaching," in N.L. Gage (ed.) *Handbook of Research on Teaching.* Chicago: Rand McNally, 1963. pp. 398–447.

Taton, R. *Reason and Chance in Scientific Discovery.* New York: Science Editions, 1962.

Van Dalen, Deobold B. "Role of hypotheses in educational research," *Educ. Admin. Superv.,* 42: 457–60; 1955.

Webb, Eugene J. et al. *Unobtrusive Measures: Nonreactive Research in the Social Sciences.* Chicago: Rand McNally, 1966.

Webb, Wilse B. "The choice of the problem," *Amer. Psychol.,* 16: 223–27; 1961.

———. "A 'couple' of experiments," *Amer. Psychol.,* 23: 428–33; 1968.

5
THE LIBRARY

If we are stupid, we are stupid by choice—for well within walking distance of any of us stands a library with its unlimited knowledge and unlimited wisdom.——Anonymous

Man is the only animal that can take advantage of the knowledge which has accumulated through the centuries. This fact is of particular importance in research, which operates as a continuous function of ever-closer approximation to the truth. The investigator can be sure that his problem does not exist in a vacuum, and that considerable work has already been done on topics which are directly related to his proposed investigation. The success of his efforts will depend in no small measure on the extent to which he capitalizes on the advances—both empirical and theoretical—made by previous researchers.

THE REVIEW OF THE LITERATURE

An essential aspect of the research project is the review of the related literature. Such a review represents the third step of the scientific method and the serious student of research will find an exhaustive survey of what has already been done on his problem an indispensable step in its solution. Unfortunately, students frequently fail to appreciate the importance of the review of the literature; they are likely to feel that they know enough about their problem and that their task is to get on with its solution. This feeling is frequently reflected in a tendency to dismiss the task as completed after a few articles have been reviewed and, especially, in the fact that the relevant literature, even when thoroughly reviewed, is not made an integral part of the total report. The student often fails to put his problem in the perspective of what has already been done and said.

The review of the literature is an exacting task, calling for a deep insight and clear perspective of the overall field. It is a crucial step which invariably minimizes the risk of dead-ends, rejected topics, rejected studies, wasted effort, trial-and-error activity oriented toward approaches already discarded by previous investigators, and—even more important—erroneous findings based on faulty research designs. It promotes a greater understanding of the problem and its crucial aspects and ensures the avoidance of unnecessary duplication; it provides comparative data on the basis of which to evaluate and interpret the significance of one's findings, and, in addition, contributes to the scholarship of the investigator.

The published literature is a fruitful source of hypotheses. Not only does it present suggestions made by previous investigators and writers concerning problems in need of investigation, but it also stimulates the research worker to devise hypotheses of his own. As he reacts to the designs, findings, and conclusions of other investigators, he can get insights which he can incorporate into an improved research design. Capitalizing on the successes and errors of others is certainly a more intelligent approach to a problem—especially one as broad as a thesis or dissertation—than is imagining that one is born equipped with a radar system that will guide him unerringly on target, and, at the same time, guard him against all pitfalls. Rarely does the neophyte have such insight into his problem that he cannot profit from the work of others; no experienced researcher would think of undertaking a study without acquainting himself with the contributions of previous investigators.

THE LIBRARY

The Organization of the Library

The library is the storehouse of the knowledge and wisdom which has accumulated since the beginnings of civilization. In a general sense, practically all of whatever is worth knowing has been put in written form and can be found in one of the volumes in the library if one knows how to locate it. Until relatively recently, man's progress was seriously hampered by the lack of source material. Until the invention of printing, and even for decades after, books were available only to the rich, and arriving at knowledge beyond that of personal experience was a relatively difficult task. In contrast, the rapidity and extensiveness of today's knowledge explosion, particularly in certain fields, by rendering yesterday's knowledge obsolete, if not false, has made it relatively impossible for the modern scholar to keep abreast even of his own specialty. The problem is no longer a lack of knowledge but rather such a wealth of knowledge that developing facilities for effective data-retrieval stands as one of the major problems facing today's researcher.

The problems concerning human knowledge fall into two main categories: 1. storage and 2. retrieval. So far we have been more concerned with storage, a function going back to the monasteries of medieval times which acted as depositories for existing information. The emphasis has now shifted toward retrieval. Such fields as chemistry, for example, have moved toward automated storage-and-retrieval systems from which the researcher can get on demand up-to-date information on all aspects of his problem. Education is also moving in this direction. This is not to minimize the storage function served by journals, books, etc. but, without efficiency in selective retrieval, all the storage is a relative waste of time.

Because of the library's tremendous assortments of material—of endless quantity, variety, and complexity—it is imperative that the researcher know how to locate and to use what is available, for without such a skill, he is simply a hunter lost in the forest. Effective research presupposes a good grasp of the organization of the library and of its contents.

Library work is a complex science. The wide variety of materials found in a library calls for a highly organized and involved system of classification. It is not expected that the graduate student will attain the proficiency of a librarian, but facility in the use of the library and its materials is, in a sense, the key to graduate studies. Although he occasionally will have to consult a librarian in order to locate unusual material, it is essential that the graduate student be able to locate the more common sources quickly and efficiently, and that he be able to extract the information contained therein with dispatch and accuracy—relying on librarians for help only in special cases.

The library is big: the library on the campus of a large university may have well over a million bound volumes specially cataloged, and in addition may subscribe to some 5,000 serials.

Through loans, the library can gain access to over a million articles published in the professional journals in any one year. (The total holdings of the Library of Congress are of the order of 50 million separate items.) Except in the smallest libraries, holdings are departmentalized—the circulation department, the reference room, the periodicals room, the government publications, the stack area, the reading rooms, etc.—each designed to provide a special service with maximum efficiency. Many of the larger libraries have special graduate-seminar rooms to which library books may be delivered for short periods of time; nearly all have carrels in the stack area where graduate students and faculty members can work close to the books they are likely to need. All of this can be rather complicated—in fact, hopelessly complicated—for the person who does not understand the system of organization. This, the graduate student needs to learn, and though it is hoped he has had contact with the library as an undergraduate, it must be recognized that his needs as a graduate student are much more complex than they were then.

Proficiency in the use of library—and thus in the review of the literature—consists of the ability to locate sources directly, to browse through multiple sources quickly, to cull relevant material, and to interpret and organize what one has accumulated. The specific procedures by which this can be done can be presented in further detail.

1. The logical starting point is to get a clear picture of the problem to be solved. Without this perspective, the review of the literature is a matter of reading at random, hoping that a problem will emerge. It is generally advisable to get first an overall view by consulting a general source, such as a textbook, which is more likely to give a coherent picture of the field than is a more specialized source. A textbook is also more likely to deal with the theoretical aspects of the problem and, thus, provide the prospective investigator with an overall framework within which his problem and its many aspects can be seen in perspective.

2. Having grasped the general nature of his problem, the investigator should orient himself toward the empirical research in the broad area in which his problem lies. The best reference for this phase is the *Encyclopedia of Educational Research,* and the *Review of Educational Research* for more up-to-date findings. An educational society yearbook in the

area is another ideal source. The student's major concern at this point should be to get a clear picture of the field as a whole; specific details are important only after he has achieved the structure into which they can fit meaningfully. Sources should not be read for their own sake, but rather for what they can contribute to rounding out a pattern which appears logical from the investigator's present view of his problem. This is a crucial consideration from the standpoint of effective library research. The investigator must be so familiar with his problem that he can judge the relevance of his readings. He should operate from a topical outline and a tentative set of classifications, so that whatever he reads can be immediately filed rather than merely accumulated. He must have such a clear perspective of his problem that any lack in his search to date becomes immediately noticeable.

3. A major prerequisite to effective library work is the ability to read at a high rate of speed. The student must learn to skim material to see what it has to contribute to the study; only after its relevance has been established should it be read in detail. Whatever is not pertinent to the study, regardless of its personal appeal, should be simply noted for later referral and dropped. Exploring all kinds of side issues merely sidetracks the investigation. Surveying the literature for the purpose of conducting research is not just "a pleasant excursion in the wonderful world of books;" it is a precise and exacting task of locating specific information for a specific purpose. Any tendency to wander should be curtailed.

4. The search for library material must be systematic and thorough. The investigator generally should begin by collecting his references, for unless the bibliography is developed systematically useful sources may be overlooked. In locating references from the *Education Index*, for example, it is generally desirable to work backward from the current volume. Judging the utility or the futility of an article by its title is always precarious; generally it is best to record anything that may be useful and to rely on one's ability to skim in order to save time and yet not overlook significant studies.

When a large number of references are to be copied, they should be typed, if possible; handwriting tends to be slow and is often illegible from the standpoint of the precision required here. Better still, why not Xerox pages on which a number of pertinent entries appear? These copies can then be used directly in the search for material or in typing out a set of cards. It is generally best to collect the bulk of the references at one time, so that the cards can be sorted and duplicates eliminated.

5. Notes should be taken systematically in the light of such criteria as uniformity, accuracy, and ease of assembly. Each entry should be separate; references should be recorded, one to a card, with complete bibliographic data entered on one side of the card. The content can be recorded below, or possibly on the reverse side. Consistency is important—a note on the back of a card may be overlooked, if one does not generally put notes there. Each note must be carefully labeled: nothing is more frustrating when it comes to writing than to find a note which is not clear as to why it was collected, where it came from, or what it is supposed to mean.

6. The investigator should take as complete notes as he might need. On the other hand, taking unnecessary notes is wasteful and, though it is better to err on the side of too much rather than too little, there is no substitute for knowing precisely what is useful and what is useless. While this ideal is never attained, the adequate researcher strikes a close balance between keeping notes to a minimum while, at the same time, also keeping to a minimum the need to check a source a second time because of failure to take adequate notes on first contact. It is also better not to recopy or to fill in details later. Recopying invites errors, and memory is invariably bad at the end of a full day of library work, when so much material of a relatively similar nature from relatively similar sources has been gathered.

It is essential that a general evaluation of each source be made, rather than simply a summary of its contents. Such an evaluation is necessary both in presenting the study in the review of the literature, and in using the study as background for the interpretation of the findings of the present investigation.

7. The actual note-taking process is always a chore. Long hours spent taking notes by hand can be torture. Too frequently, tediousness leads to impatience, to carelessness and illegibility, and to a tendency to cut corners and rely on one's memory in a misguided attempt to expedite the process. As a result, the final product is frequently short of ideal; at worst, it may be conducive to serious error.

The usual procedure for recording references is to take notes directly on 3 x 5 or 4 x 6 cards, labeling each as to topic. The author has found the IBM card superior to either size index card; it is thinner and of a better grade of material; it can be obtained blank on both sides except for a different color stripping at the top to identify topics; it can also be punched on any number of classifications and sorted by machine. It is even cheaper.

Probably the biggest stumbling block to effective library research is the tediousness of handwriting. One alternative is typing. Most libraries have typing rooms for the use of graduate students and faculty members. If typing facilities are available, half-sheets or even whole sheets of paper—with a carbon as a record—which can then be cut, sorted, pasted, and otherwise manipulated to expedite the writing of the first draft of the report, should be used. Another very satisfactory procedure is to dicate notes directly from the references into a portable tape recorder for transcription at one's convenience; this method is both simple and efficient.

The student should take advantage of modern facilities wherever possible. He should never copy tables, for example, but should have them Xeroxed so that he can have an authentic copy of the original when he is writing his report. Passages that may be used in a quotation should be reproduced rather than copied to preclude the risk of error. Most libraries have duplicating facilities available for a very nominal fee.* It also should be pointed out that quotations—and even other material—should never be taken from a secondary source, except as a last resort. The more removed from the original source the data are, the greater the risk of error.

The Card Catalog

The holdings of the library fall under two major classifications: *books* and *periodicals*—and a third category of *miscellany* which includes government documents, manuscripts, pamphlets, reference materials, maps, etc. The vast bulk of the library's collection is cataloged under *books* which includes books, booklets,

* The Library of the Future, based on LIBRARY-21 shown at the Seattle World Fair in 1962 (ALA., 1963) envisages a network of national and regional centers of unlimited storage and retrieval capacity equipped with all sorts of devices ranging from high-speed scanners and character and auditory recognition machines to various forms of photocopy, microphotography, photocomposition and magnetic tape with high-speed output printers made operative through instantaneous transmission by means of optical masers into video displays available in homes anywhere in the nation.

yearbooks, pamphlets, and certain serials, most of which can be obtained on loan from the circulation department. Each volume in this category ordinarily covers a single topic which can be identified by its title, and a reader interested in a given volume generally would want to read all, or a good part, of its contents.

In contrast, periodicals usually cover a wide variety of topics, and the reader is interested not in a whole volume but in particular articles which must be traced through the use of an index. Generally, periodicals are filed alphabetically in open stacks and cannot be taken out of the library. In addition, references—dictionaries, encyclopedias, and guides of various sorts—are housed in open shelves in the Reference Room. These are cataloged as regular bound volumes held by the library, but their circulation generally is limited to "room use."

All students generally have ready access to the open shelves of the Periodical and Reference Rooms, but only graduate students have access to the stacks. This special privilege is partially in recognition of the greater dependability of the graduate student, and partially in recognition of the fact that, in order to do research, graduate students must have the opportunity to browse through numerous sources quickly.

No matter how the student gets his books, however, he must be able to identify what he wants. This is done through the card catalog which generally lists all library holdings, except the periodicals and government documents. Although the Reference Room and the special libraries on campus have duplicate catalogs for their holdings, the card catalog of the Circulation Department is the master list of all material cataloged in any branch of the library, and any source can be traced from this catalog.

The primary purpose of the card catalog is to record what is contained in the library. In a sense, it is an index to the library. As its name implies, it is a listing of the library's holdings in various areas, describing each item briefly, and giving the classification code so that it can be readily identified. Books are shelved according to classification, so that they can be located quickly and efficiently.

Each volume is cataloged under author, title, and subject on separate 3 x 5 cards, arranged in alphabetical sequence in row after row of drawers. All cards pertaining to a given volume list essentially the same information, but they are filed differently. Thus John Doe's *Nuclear Physics* would be filed under *Doe* for the author card, under *Nuclear* for the title card, and under *Physics* for the subject card.

Both the general format of a catalog card, and the distinction between author, subject, and title card can be seen from the accompanying illustration. Each card lists the following basic information:

1. the name of the author;
2. the title of the book;
3. the imprint (edition, place, publisher, and date of publication);
4. special information (number of pages, preface, bibliography, size, illustration, number of volumes);

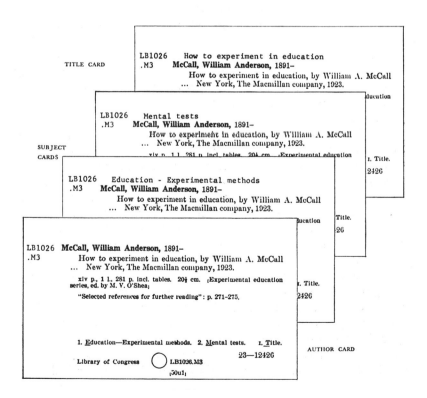

5. the subject classification(s) and other entries under which separate cards are to be found;
6. the Library of Congress and the Dewey Decimal call number; and
7. the L. C. (Library of Congress) card number.

In addition, each library types its own call number on the top left-hand corner of each card. If the library uses either the L. C. or the Dewey Decimal system, this may be the same number as that already printed on the card, or it may be whatever call number the volume carries in the particular library's classification system. Occasionally, a card will carry additional information —for example, a listing of the major parts of a volume.

The author card is the master card; on occasion, it may be the only card in the card catalog for a given volume, but a library would never fail to have an author card for each volume. Some of the peculiarities of the card catalog are: 1. Separate cards are made for co-authors of a book, but the book is listed under the name of the editor(s) when a number of authors have written separate chapters; 2. Pseudonyms are cross-referenced to the correct name—for example, *Twain, Mark, See Clemens, Samuel Langhorne;* 3. Societies are sometimes listed as authors for the works compiled under their sponsorship, though the author card may go to the editor or author.

Subject cards can be found for as many classifications as are listed on the L. C. card. Thus, a book in educational psychology would have a subject card under *Educational Psychology* (typed in red at the top of the card), and might have subject cards under *Psychology, Child Development,* and perhaps other headings. It should be noted that: 1. General topics are frequently broken down into subclassifications: *Psychology,* for example, could have subgroupings such as *Psychology, Abnormal; Psychology, Clinical; Psychology, Educational.* When the classification is extensive, special dividers are provided to facilitate ready location of a card. 2. Biographies are indexed by author, on the author card, and by biographee on the subject card. 3. Related subject areas are often identified by a *See also* card at the end of a subject classification, e.g., *Educational Psychology, See also Child Development.*

The title card carries the title of the volume, typed directly above the name of the author. It is filed alphabetically according to the first major word of the title. Some volumes do not have a sufficiently distinctive title—e.g., *A Short Introduction to the Study of History*—to warrant separate listing and therefore do not have a title card.

All cards are filed alphabetically with guide cards at intervals. Cards *about* an author come after cards *by* him—i.e., author cards take precedence over subject and title cards. A complete word is filed before compounds containing that word—e.g., *New York* is filed before *Newman*. Hyphenated words, like *pre-election*, are filed without regard to the hyphen. Names beginning with *Mc* are filed as if they were spelled *Mac*, and all abbreviations are filed as if they were spelled out in full—e.g., *Saint, Mister, United States,* etc. Titles beginning with a numeral are filed as though the number were spelled out—e.g., *The 100 Best Sellers* would be filed under *One Hundred Best Sellers*.

Classification Systems

The crucial features underlying library organization is the classification system. Most libraries in the United States operate either under the Library of Congress or the Dewey Decimal system, though some small libraries operate on a system of their own, and some of the older libraries may have a modified system. Undoubtedly, the L. C. system is the most flexible and comprehensive: it is designed for classifying unlimited quantities and varieties of material. On the other hand, it is a relatively new system and many libraries, already on a system of their own at the time the L. C. system was devised, did not elect to reclassify their holdings according to the new system. Many libraries operating on the Dewey Decimal system have found it adequate for their needs and are continuing with it; others have devised certain modifications in order to take advantage of some of the features of the L. C. system without, at the same time, incurring the expense of reclassifying all their holdings.

Both the L. C. and the Dewey Decimal systems are based on the allocation of a code for each field and the breaking down of these fields into finer and finer subclassifications. The major classifications of the two systems are shown on page 136.

	L. C. Classification		*Dewey Decimal Classification*
A.	General Works	000	General References
B.	Philosophy, Religion	100	Philosophy, Psychology
C.	History	200	Religion
D.	World History	300	Social Sciences
EF.	American History	310	Statistics
G.	Geography, Anthropology	320	Political Science
H.	Social Sciences	330	Economics
I.	Vacant	340	Law
J.	Political Science	350	Administration
K.	Law	360	Welfare Associations and
L.	Education (general)		Institutions
LA.	History of Education	370	Education (general)
LB.	Theory of Education	370.1	Theory and Philosophy
LC.	Special Forms and		of Education
	Applications	370.9	History of Education
LD.	U.S. Schools	371	Teachers—Methods,
LE.	American Education		Discipline
	(Outside U.S.)	372	Elementary Education
LF.	Education—Europe	373	Secondary Education
LG.	Education—Asia, Africa,	374	Adult Education
	Oceania	375	Curriculum
LH.	College and School Maga-	376	Education of Women
	zines, student periodicals	377	Religion, ethical
LJ.	Fraternities and their		education
	Publications	378	Higher Education
LT.	Textbooks	379	Public School, relation of
R.	Medicine		state to education
S.	Agriculture	380	Commerce, Communica-
T.	Technology		tion
U.	Military Science	390	Customs, Costumes,
V.	Naval Science		Folklore
W.	vacant	400	Philology
X.	vacant	500	Natural Science
Y.	vacant	600	Useful Arts
Z.	Library Science	700	Fine Arts
		800	Literature
		900	History

Inter-Library Loans

Materials not available in one library can often be borrowed from another library. The loan is always from the lender library to the library at which the student is enrolled and then to the student. Such loans are simply a courtesy, not an obligation, and the conditions and mechanics under which such loans can be effected are governed by American Library Association regulations. Thus, loans are limited to material not readily available through purchase, and they generally do not cover such items as irreplaceable manuscripts. Most loans are for two weeks, and the borrower usually pays transportation charges both ways.

The student should not overlook the possibility of purchasing some of the material he needs. Where extended use is indicated, the small cost may be more than repaid by a saving in time and convenience. If a journal article is needed, it can save time and even money to have a Xerox copy made. Most libraries can provide this kind of service. In fact, even a sizable volume can be microfilmed. Finally, when a certain amount of browsing needs to be done, the student should plan to visit a neighboring library where the needed volumes are available. Most libraries have the *National Union Catalog,* either in photoprint or card form, of the complete holdings of the Library of Congress. *The Union List of Serials in Libraries in the United States and Canada* and *New Serial Titles* will identify the major libraries having certain serials. If necessary, a student can write to a library asking if it has the publications he needs.

LOCATING LIBRARY SOURCES

The Periodical Literature

The other major component of the library collection is the periodicals. This section is of particular interest to the research worker, since it is here that he will find most of the material he needs for his review of the literature. The use of periodicals is predicated on an entirely different basis than that which governs the circulation material. Here we are interested not in a given volume, but in isolated articles which must be traced individually. Though certain journals tend to have articles related to certain topics, the effective use of journal material requires the use of a suitable index, the most important of which, as it applies to educational materials, is the *Education Index* (New York: Wilson, 1929–date). In fact, at times it may be necessary to use a number of indexes and guides—and this may involve complexities, many of which are beyond the scope of this text. The discussion will be simply suggestive, and the student is advised to consult other sources such as Burke and Burke, *Documentation in Education* (1967); Barton and Bell, *Reference Books: A Brief Guide for Students and Other Users of the Library* (6th ed., 1966); or Wynar, *Introduction to Bibliography and Reference Work: A Guide to Materials and Sources* (1966).

The *Education Index* (New York: Wilson, 1929–date) was until 1961 easily the most complete library tool of the worker in educational research. Issued nine times per year in paperbound editions which were cumulated quarterly, and annually, with three-year cumulations, 1929 through 1952, and two-year cumulations, 1953 through 1963, it listed practically all references to the educational literature, whether in the form of periodicals, books, or pamphlets. In 1961, its coverage was drastically curtailed to the point that it is now largely a subject index to the *periodical* literature in education, although it still indexes some of the publications of the U.S. Office of Education, the National Education Association, and other professional societies. This means that other sources have to be explored, for example, the *Cumulative Book Index* for books, the *Bulletin of Public Affairs Information Services* for government publications and the *NEA Publications Catalog* for the NEA publications.

Such a large number of other indexes, abstracts, and guides are available to the research worker that only a few can be mentioned here. References to periodicals include:

> 1. *Ulrich's International Periodical Directory* (formerly *Ulrich's Periodical Directory*, 1932–1965; Eileen C. Graves, ed., 12th ed., Bowker, 1967). Covers a selected list of current periodicals arranged by subject. Now in two volumes: Vol. 1, dealing with scientific, technical, and medical periodicals; Vol. 2, listing periodicals in arts, humanities, social sciences, and business.
> 2. *American Education Press Yearbook* (American Education Press, 1926–date). Gives rather complete information on American periodicals dealing with education.

3. *Union List of Serials in Libraries in the United States and Canada* (previously cited, 3rd ed., Wilson, 1966). It is supplemented by *New Serial Titles; A Union List of Serials Commencing Publication after December 31, 1949* (Library of Congress, 1953–date). Monthly with annual cumulations.

4. *Directory of Newspapers and Periodicals* (Philadelphia: Ayer & Son, 1880–date).

5. *Scholar's Guide to Journals of Education and Educational Psychology* (L. Joseph Lins and Robert Ries, eds., Madison: Dembar, 1965). Gives considerable detail on 135 educational and psychological journals, including editors, policies, etc. Indexed by title and subject.

The more common general indexes include:

1. *Readers' Guide to Periodical Literature* (New York: Wilson, 1900–date). Indexes all general sources covering education to 1929 when the Education Index took over that area. *Readers' Guide* is the successor to *Poole's Index to Periodical Literature* (Boston: Houghton Mifflin, 1802–1881) and *Nineteenth Century Guide to Periodical Literature* (New York: Wilson, 1890–1899). There is also an *Abridged Readers' Guide to Periodical Literature* (New York: Wilson, 1935–date).

2. *International Index to Periodicals* (New York: Wilson, 1920–1965). It indexes a somewhat more selected list of periodicals in the social sciences, including a number published abroad. It is now replaced by *Social Sciences and Humanities Index* (New York: Wilson, 1965–date). Quarterly with annual cumulations.

3. *Vertical File Index* (New York: Wilson, 1932–date). An excellent source of low cost materials.

4. *Facts on File* (New York: Facts on File, Inc., 1940–date). Weekly. Indexes current events, i.e., news items. It is cumulated into a single volume yearly (*Facts on File Yearbook*, 1941–date).

5. *Bulletin of Public Affairs Information Service* (New York: The Service, 1915–date). A selective index to periodical articles, government publications, and other publications relating to legislation and general public affairs.

6. *The New York Times Index* (New York: The New York Times, 1851–date). Indexes the content of *The New York Times* by subject, author, and date. Semimonthly with annual cumulations.

7. *The Christian Science Monitor: Subject Guide of the Christian Science Monitor* (Boston: The Christian Science Publishing Society, 1960–date). Monthly with annual cumulations.

The best known indexes and guides covering the periodical literature of a professional nature, in addition to the *Education Index,* include:

1. *Canadian Education Index* (Ottawa: Canad. Council on Res. in Educ., quarterly, 1965–date). Indexes, books, pamphlets, reports, and the periodical literature in education in Canada.

2. *The Catholic Periodical Index* (New York: Catholic Library Association, 1930–date) indexes the periodical literature dealing with Catholic education.

3. *Psychological Abstracts* (Washington: American Psychological Association, 1927–date). Abstracts the psychological literature. Bimonthly with yearly index.

4. *Child Development Abstracts and Bibliography* (Chicago: University of Chicago Press, for the Society for Research in Child Development, 1927–date). Three times annually.

5. *Sociological Abstracts* (Leo P. Chall, ed., 1952–date). Five times a year.

6. Special indexes and guides in specialized areas of education, e.g., business education, agriculture education, art education, music education, etc. *Occupational Index* (NYU: Personnel Service, 1936–date) indexes over 100 periodicals in the area of occupations by author, title, and subject. Journals which are not indexed systematically must be scanned individually through their table of contents.

Books and Textbook Materials

Probably because of their individual size and importance, regular books are most systematically and extensively covered by bibliographical services. In fact, a book published in any of the English-speaking countries generally can be located if one knows the author, the title, or even the approximate date of publication.

The most useful list of books published in the English language is the *Cumulative Book Index* (New York: Wilson,

1898–date). *The United States Catalog; Books in Print, Jan. 1, 1928* (4th ed., New York: Wilson, 1928) was the most complete list of American books published from 1898 to 1928. Books in English published since 1928 may be found in the various cumulations of the *Cumulative Book Index*. It lists all books in the English language indexed by author and subject. Semiannual and biennial cumulations. *The Cumulative Book Index* is supplemented by *Publishers' Weekly* (New York: Bowker, 1872–date). Weekly.

Other useful guides to books include:

1. *Publishers' Trade List Annual* (New York: Bowker, 1873 –date). Collection of publishers' catalogs.

2. *Books in Print; An Author-Title-Series Index* (New York: Bowker, 1948–date). Provides an author, title, and series index to the *Publishers' Trade List Annual.* See also *Textbooks in Print* (New York: Bowker, 1870–date).

3. *Subject Guide to Books in Print* (New York: Bowker, 1957–date).

4. *Forthcoming Books* (New York: Bowker, 1966). Bimonthly.

5. *National Union Catalog; A Cumulative Author List, 1958–1962.* Compiled by the Library of Congress. (New York: Row & Littlefield, 1963. 58 volumes).

6. *Book Review Digest* (New York: Wilson, 1905–date); and *Booklist and Subscription Books Bulletin: A Guide to Current Books* (Chicago: American Library Association, 1938–date). Both not only list books shortly after publication but also provide a review of their worth.

7. *Book Review Index* (Detroit: Gale Research Co., 1965– date). Monthly with quarterly cumulations, acts as a supplement to *Book Review Digest.*

8. Book reviews and listings are frequently found in the *Books Received* and *Book Reviews* section of certain journals. They can be located through the index of these journals. *Contemporary Psychology* (Washington APA, 1956–date) is devoted almost exclusively to reviews of books in psychology.

Most professional societies provide listings of their own publications. The National Education Association, for example, publishes an annual catalog of the publications of the parent organization and its member groups. The American Council of Education has available on request a complete listing of its publications since 1918 (some are out of print). The National

Society for the Study of Education has published a yearbook in two parts since 1901. The Association for Supervision and Curriculum Development also publishes a yearbook (1944–date). Most of these are listed in the card catalog, the *Education Index,* the *Cumulative Book Index,* and *Publishers' Weekly.*

General References

There are a number of good reference books with which the student aspiring to proficiency in the library should be familiar. The time spent in becoming acquainted with these sources is generally well repaid by smoother and speedier progress in library research. Practice in the use of these basic sources should be included early in the program of the graduate student. The following are particularly useful:

1. *Documentation in Education* (Arvid J. Burke and Mary A. Burke, New York: Teachers College Press, 1967; formerly, *How to Locate Educational Information and Data,* Carter Alexander and Arvid J. Burke, 4th ed., 1958).

2. *A Guide to Reference Books* (Constance M. Winchell, ed., Chicago: American Library Association, 8th ed. 1967; supplements usually at three-year intervals). This guide was edited by Mudge from 1936 to 1950.

3. *Introduction to Bibliography and Reference Work: A Guide to Materials and Sources* (B.S. Wynar, Denver: Libraries Unlimited, 1966).

4. *Reference Books: A Brief Guide for Students and Other Users of the Library* (Mary N. Barton and Marian V. Bell, Baltimore: Enoch Pratt Free Library, 6th ed., 1966).

5. *How and Where to Look it Up: A Guide to Standard Sources of Information* (Robert W. Murphey, New York: McGraw-Hill, 1958).

6. *The Modern Researcher* (Jacques Barzun and Henry F. Graff, New York: Harcourt, Brace, & World, 1957).

Among the more general references that can be found in any library, we might mention:

1. Encyclopedias: *Britannica; Americana; Collier's; World Book* (juvenile); *Columbia* (encyclopedia in one volume); and the *Lincoln Library of Essential Information* (1950).

2. Dictionaries: *Funk and Wagnall; Webster's New Third International;* and *Oxford English Dictionary.* Each comes in unabridged as well as in abridged form. We also have *Roget's Thesaurus of Words and Phrases* and *Rodale, the Word Finder.*

3. Almanacs (or general yearbooks): *World Almanac and Book of Facts* (New York: New York World, 1868–1931; New York: World Telegram, 1932–date); *Information Please Almanac* (John Kieran, ed., publisher varies, 1947–date); and *Statistical Abstracts of the United States* (Washington: Department of Commerce, 1897–date). *Reader's Digest Almanac* (Pleasantville, N.Y.: Reader's Digest Association, 1965–date) includes many charts, graphs, pictures, and maps; it is particularly readable and attractive.

A number of similar references exist that pertain more specifically to the field of education.

1. Encyclopedias: The best known and most useful is undoubtedly the *Encyclopedia of Educational Research* (Washington: American Educational Research Association, 3rd ed., 1960; 4th ed., 1969). Issued at ten-year intervals, it constitutes the primary tool in the hands of the educational researcher. *The Review of Educational Research* (Washington: American Educational Research Association, 1931–date) acts as a supplement to keep it current within a three-year span. *The Education Index* and the various periodicals can be used to fill in the gaps between issues of the *Review* and to deal with topics not covered therein.

Other important encyclopedias include: *Educator's Encyclopedia* (Englewood-Cliffs: Prentice-Hall, 1961); *International Encyclopedia of the Social Sciences* (David L. Sills, ed., New York: Macmillan, 1968); *The Encyclopedia of American Facts and Dates* (G. Carruth et al., 4th ed., New York: Crowell, 1966); and *Encyclopedia of American History* (Richard B. Morris, ed., New York: Harper & Row, 1965).

The *Annual Review of Psychology* (Paul Farnsworth, ed., Palo Alto: Stanford University, 1950–date; Calvin P. Stone, ed., vols. 1–6) constitutes the most up-to-date encyclopedia concerning the major aspects of psychology.

The 75-volume *Library of Education* (Washington: Center for Applied Research in Education, 1962–1965) and the various paperback series put out by some of the commercial book companies represent major contributions to the cause of education. A more recent publication is *Standard Education Almanac* (Los Angeles: Academic Media, 1968).

2. Dictionaries: The most adequate is Good's *Dictionary of Education* (New York: McGraw-Hill, 1959) which covers some 17,000 terms in education and related fields, e.g., psychology.

Other useful dictionaries include: *Comprehensive Dictionary of Psychological and Psychoanalytical Terms* (Horace B. English and Ava C. English, New York: Longmans, Green, 1958); *Dictionary of Sociology* (Henry P. Fairchild, ed., New York: Philosophical Library, 1944); and *A Dictionary of Statistical Terms* (Maurice G. Kendall and William R. Buckland, eds., London: Oliver & Boyd, 1957). Somewhat more specialized but of fundamental importance to counselors is the *Dictionary of Occupational Titles* (Washington: U.S. Employment Service, 1965) which lists nearly 36,000 job titles and 22,000 job descriptions. In the same area is *Occupational Literature* (Gertrude Forrester, ed., New York: Wilson, 1958) which lists over 4,000 books and pamphlets by occupation.

3. Yearbooks: (a) *The World Year Book of Education* (New York: Harcourt, Brace & World, 1932–date) now contains scholarly articles on various aspects of education; (b) *International Yearbook of Education* (Geneva: International Bureau of Education, UNESCO, 1933–date); (c) *Mental Measurement Yearbook* (Oscar Buros, ed., Highland Park: Gryphon Press, 6th ed., 1965); (d) the yearbooks of many educational societies ranging from such general societies as the National Society for the Study of Education to the more specialized such as the American Association of School Administrators.

4. Handbooks: A number of exceptionally comprehensive handbooks have been published, including the *Handbook of Research on Teaching* (N.L. Gage, ed., Washington: American Educational Research Association, Chicago: Rand McNally, 1963); *Handbook of Education* (A.W. Foshay, Chicago: Rand McNally, 1963); *Handbook of Research Methods in Child Development* (Paul H. Mussen, New York: Wiley, 1961).

5. Bulletins, manuals, and guides: (a) *Manual on Certification Requirements for School Personnel in the United States* (Washington: Department of Health, Education, and Welfare, 1951–date); (b) *A Guide to Graduate Study* (F.W. Ness, ed., Washington: American Council on Education, 3rd ed., 1965); (c) *The Random House Guide to Graduate Study* (E.R.

Wasserman, 1967); (d) *Accredited Institutions of Higher Learning* (Washington: American Council on Education, 1965–date) published every six months, it gives names and addresses and a few facts concerning higher education. It is the official directory of the Federation of Regional Accrediting Commissions of Higher Education; (e) *American Universities and Colleges* (Washington: American Council on Education, 1928–date) and *American Junior Colleges* (Washington: American Council on Education, 1940–date); (f) *Scholarships, Fellowships, and Loans* (S. Norman Feingold, Cambridge, Mass.: Bellman Publishing Company, 1949–date). It is kept current by *Scholarships, Fellowships, and Loans News Service*.

Government Documents

Government publications are so extensive and so specialized that they generally form a special division of the library organization. Much of the material is in pamphlet form published under the name of the issuing department and numbered according to series and subseries. As a result, the location of a specific item by the amateur is frequently a relatively difficult task. All publications of the Federal Government are listed according to the issuing agency in the monthly catalog of the *United States Government Publications* (1895–date). A subject index is provided monthly and cumulated yearly. Other references include:

1. *Education Index* which indexes many of the publications of the U.S. Office of Education. The Superintendent of Documents issues various price lists.*

2. *A Popular Guide to Government Publications* (William P. Leidy, New York: Columbia University Press, 2nd ed., 1963).

3. *Bulletin of Public Affairs Information Service,* previously cited (New York: The Service, 1915–date). Issued weekly except August and September; gives a selective index to articles dealing with government legislation and public affairs.

*Write the Superintendent of Documents, Washington, D.C., 20402, to be placed on the mailing list. Price list No. 31 pertains to education.

4. *American Education* (official organ of the U.S. Office of Education, HEW, formerly *School Life*). Each issue gives a a list of government publications of interest to educators.

5. *United Nations Document Index* (New York: United Nations, 1950–date) and *Education Abstracts* (Geneva: UNESCO, 1949–date).

Locating state and municipal documents is more difficult, not so much because of the quantity but because there is no systematic indexing or centralized agency responsible for the cataloging and circulation of the booklets and pamphlets issued by these various and separate units. Certain states have prepared indexes to their publications, e.g., *Index of Statistical Data Available in New York's State Departments,* New York State Division of Commerce. Probably the most adequate sources of state and municipal information are *The Book of the States* (Chicago: Council of State Governments, 1935–date) and *The Municipal Yearbook* (Chicago: International City Managers' Association, 1934–date). A number of state publications are listed in the *Library of Congress Monthly Checklist of State Publications* (Washington: Government Printing Office, 1910–date). Most studies conducted by the state are filed in the library of the state university and the librarians there are a fertile source of information on these studies. Some of the state and local studies pertaining to education may be found in *Education Index* but there is no systematic provision for this to occur.

Biographical Information

Biographical data on important persons are available in a wide variety of sources, most basic among which is any encyclopedia. Sources more specifically "biographical" include:

Who's Who (London: Black, 1849–date) and *Who Was Who* (London: Black, 1916–date); *Who's Who in America, Who Was Who in America, Who's Who in the East, Who's Who in the Midwest, Who's Who in the West, Who's Who in the South and the Southwest, Who's Who of American Women* (Chicago: Marquis Who's Who Inc., 1899–date); *Dictionary of American Biography* (New York: Scribner's Sons, 1928–1944) 20 vols., a most scholarly source, (abridged ed., 1964); *National Cyclopedia of American Biography* (New York:

White, 1892–date); *American Men of Science* (New York: Bowker, 2 vols., 1: Physical and Biological Sciences, 1906–date, 11th ed., 1965–67; and 2: Social and Behavioral Sciences, 1962–date); *The National Register of Scientific and Technical Personnel* (Washington: American Psychological Association and National Science Foundation, 1940–date). Data on persons currently in the news can be found in *Current Biography* (New York: Wilson, 1940–date); *Who's Who in American Current Biographical Reference Service* (Chicago: Marcus, 1940–date); and *The New York Times Index* (1913–date).

Biographical information concerning important educators can be found in any of the above sources. In addition, one can consult such volumes as *Who's Who in American Education* (Robert C. Cook, ed., Nashville: Who's Who in American Education, 1928–date); *Leaders in Education: A Biographical Directory* (Jacques Cattell and E.E. Ross, eds., Lancaster: Science Press, 1932, 1942, 1948); *Directory of American Scholars* (New York: Bowker, 1942–date; includes 4 vols. for different academic fields) and *American Men of Science,* previously cited, 1906–date.

Educators and Educational Agencies

The names and addresses of various persons and agencies connected with education can be found rather readily, although, at times, it may be difficult to be sure that such information is up-to-date, particularly with respect to the holders of specific offices. Probably the most up-to-date source of the mailing address of persons connected with education are the directories put out by the individual agencies, orientation to which can be obtained through *Guide to American Directories* (Detroit: Gale Research Co., 1956–date). The most comprehensive list of educators in the general sense is undoubtedly the U.S. Office of Education's *Education Directory* (Washington: U.S. Office of Education, 1912–date) which, among other things, lists officers of federal, state, county and city school systems, colleges, universities, and educational associations. Currently the Directory is issued in five parts: 1. State Government 2. Public School Systems; 3. Higher Education; 4. Educational Associations; and 5. Federal Government. Also pertinent here are *American Education* (formerly *Patterson's American Education;* Leona H. May, ed., Chicago: Educational Directories, 1904–date) which lists both public and private school officials; *American Universities and Colleges* (1920–date) and *American Junior Colleges* (1940–date), both previously mentioned; and the directories of various educational organizations. For example, the *NEA Handbook* (Washington: NEA, 1945–date) lists officers at the local, state, and national level in both the parent organization and its subsidiaries. *Official Guide to Catholic Educational Institutions* and *Religious Communities in the United States* (Rockville Center, New York: Catholic Institutional Directory Co., 1959–date) lists various officials of colleges, universities, schools, and religious orders of the Catholic faith.

For addresses and general information concerning educational agencies and institutions, particularly of higher learning, one can consult:

> *Encyclopedia of Associations* (Detroit: Gale Research Co., 1961, 3 vols.); *Directory of Research Agencies and Studies* (Raymond J. Young, Bloomington: Phi Delta Kappa, 1957–date); *National Register of Educational Researchers* (Bloomington: Phi Delta Kappa, 1966–date); *The Foundations Directory* (New York: Russell Sage Foundation, 1950–date); *Baird's Manual of American College Fraternities* (Menasha, Wisc.: George Banta Pub. Co., 1879–date); *American Library Directory* (Ann J. Richter, ed., New York: Bowker, 1923–date); *Handbook of Organizations* (Jane G. March, ed., Chicago: Rand McNally, 1965; and *American Education, American Universities and Colleges, American Junior Colleges,* and others previously cited. UNESCO provides a directory of educational organizations throughout the world in *Education Abstracts* (op cit.); *Research Centers Directory* (Detroit: Gale Research Co., 1960–date; formerly *Directory of University Research Bureaus and Institutes*) and *Research Units in Local School Systems* in *Education Research Circular,* No. 5, 1965 (Washington: NEA, 1965) describe various local school system research units and their research activities.

News Items

The primary source of news items is, of course, the newspaper; all newspapers retain back copies. Magazines also carry news some time after its occurrence. Probably the most adequate index of newspaper items are *The New York Times Index* (op. cit.), the *Subject Index of the Christian Science Monitor* (op. cit.) and *Facts on File* (New York: Facts on File Inc., 1940–date, weekly). The latter is best described as a current encyclopedia, indexed and cross-referenced semimonthly, monthly, quarterly, and annually. The annual compilations are known as *Facts on File Yearbook* (1941–date) and, more recently, *News Directory* (1965–date).

Bibliographies

Particularly helpful in the early stages of the review of the literature are the many excellent bibliographies prepared on a number of educational topics. Although many of these are not exhaustive and, of course, all are in various degrees of outdatedness, they can nevertheless save untold hours of searching. In a sense, the *Education Index,* the card catalog, and many other references previously cited constitute bibliographies. The extensive lists of references at the end of the articles of the *Encyclopedia of Educational Research* or the *Review of Educational Research* and other sources frequently constitute excellent bibliographies from which to start the research on the literature on a given topic.

The most comprehensive reference to bibliographies is *Bibliographic Index* (New York: Wilson, 1938–date), semiannually with annual and larger cumulations. In a sense, it is a bibliography of bibliographies. The U.S. Office of Education has also published bibliographies on selected topics; these can be located through *Education Index*. Special bibliographies are also found in such journals as *The Elementary School Journal, School Review,* and others. The U.S. Office of Education has also published bibliographies on *Administration, Higher Education: An Annotated Bibliography,* and *Research Related to Mentally Retarded Children,* both 1960.

Educational Research Studies

Obviously, the most significant of the recent developments in the retrieval and dissemination of research information is the Educational Research Information Center (ERIC), a nationwide service operated under USOE auspices designed to put the results of educational research into the hands of those who need it and to do so on an immediate and dependable basis (Burchinal, 1967a, 1967b). ERIC is an attempt to facilitate information exchange and to increase the value of research to the educational community by simply making its results readily available in a usable form.

ERIC consists of: 1. a network of 19 regional clearinghouses (as per September 1969), each responsible for collecting, abstracting, and indexing all relevant documents concerning a given area of education (e.g., the disadvantaged; Calkins and Grussow, 1967); and 2. ERIC CENTRAL, the headquarters office in Washington which coordinates the overall operation, stores the full text of the report on microfilm, and publishes *Research in Education* (1966–date*) announcing the various ERIC holdings, giving a résumé, and providing a system of index and cross-reference by subject, investigator, etc. The dissemination function is handled by Educational Reproduction Service (EDRS) operated by National Cash Register under contract with the Office of Education. It reproduces all documents listed in *Research in Education* for distribution to users in either hard copy or microfiche.†

A related service is School Research Information Service (SRIS), initiated by Phi Delta Kappa (Gephart, 1967) to provide an ERIC-type coverage of educational materials not fitting into the scope of the current ERIC clearinghouses and, therefore, not carried by ERIC, e.g., the reports of research or innovative educational practices sponsored by school personnel, curriculum study groups, etc.‡

Research studies are not listed separately in most sources. The *Education Index,* for example, is inclusive rather than selective and critical; it lists major research studies and expressions of unverified opinion side by side. Since both may have value depending on the student's needs and purposes, the *Index* brings both to the attention of the reader; it is up to him to check each

---

* A separate volume covers research reports previously submitted. The USOE has also initiated a program to get significant research into the hands of the practitioner and others who make educational decisions (Millman, 1967). The service includes the syntheses, integration, and repackaging of research results for a variety of nonresearch audiences.

† A microfilm reproduction capable of condensing up to 60 pages of text on a 4 by 6 slide, which can then be read with the use of a microfiche reader to bring the image back to normal page size.

‡ Somewhat less directly educational and yet of interest is the Armed Services Technical Information Agency (ASTIA) which serves as clearinghouse for technical reports of the various agencies within the Department of Defense. The agency prepares a *Title Announcement Bulletin* which is distributed to interested parties, who can then obtain an abstract of a given title or a reproduction of the complete document.

reference individually for whatever value it may have for him. The *Education Index* is still one of the more comprehensive sources of research studies, since most research studies are reported in the professional journals.

Another comprehensive source of educational research studies is the *Encyclopedia of Educational Research,* which synthesizes the significant research on major educational topics and provides an extensive bibliography of the research on the topics covered. Complementing the *Encyclopedia* is the *Review of Educational Research,* which reviews research on a series of 15 topics in three-year cycles and also provides extensive bibliographies of the research literature. The *Handbook of Research on Teaching* (op. cit.) and the earlier *Handbook of Research Methods in Child Development* (op. cit.) are excellent sources of a specialized nature. The series *What research says to the teacher* (Washington: NEA) is also a concentrated source of research findings presented from a consensus point of view. Of special interest to administrators is the *NEA Research Bulletin* (1923–date), which reports NEA-sponsored research in areas of school enrollment, teacher salaries, teacher supply and demand, and other matters concerning the profession.

Another comprehensive source of research studies in education is the list of theses and dissertations conducted in partial fulfillment of the doctoral degree. These are becoming progressively easier to locate through *Dissertation Abstracts* (Ann Arbor: University Microfilms, 1955–date; originally *Microfilm Abstracts,* 1938–1955), which abstracts a progressively greater percentage of the dissertations conducted in degree-granting institutions. The most comprehensive listing of theses, dissertations, research in progress, etc. is under "Dissertations, Academic" in each issue of the *Bibliographic Index.* Dissertations were indexed in *Education Index* up to 1961. The *Index to American Doctoral Dissertations* also gives a comprehensive list of the dissertations from a number of universities. These are, of course, summarized in *Dissertation Abstracts.* All dissertations abstracted are available on microfilm and, in most cases, on Xerox. University Microfilms also provides *Datrix,* a computerized data-retrieval service capable of scanning all dissertations on microfilm for any key word; it provides a computer-constructed bibliography of dissertations in which the topic is considered.

Other references to doctoral dissertations include the

Phi Delta Kappa series, *Research Studies in Education* (Mary L. Lyda et al., eds., Bloomington: Phi Delta Kappa, 1952–date) and *A Quarter Century of Educational Research in Canada: An Analysis of Dissertations in Education Accepted by Canadian Universities, 1930–1955* (Willard Brehaut, ed., Univ. of Toronto, 1958). Somewhat more specialized are such summaries as: Leo C. Fay et al., "Doctoral Studies in Reading, 1919–1960," *Indiana Univ. School of Education Bull.*, 40, No. 4; 1964 and, of course, the reviews of the literature on the teaching of individual subjects contained in the *Handbook of Research on Teaching* (1963, op. cit.).

Master's theses are not as completely covered by indexes and, therefore, not so readily or systematically identifiable. Nevertheless, a number of excellent references exist, e.g., *Master's Theses in Education* (Herbert M. Silvey, ed., Cedar Falls, Iowa: Research Publications, yearly, 1953–date) and *Guide to Lists of Master's Theses* (Dorothy M. Black, Chicago: American Library Association, 1966). Occasionally the author of a master's thesis will publish his results in a regular journal.

Non-degree-connected research is much more difficult to find. In fact, until the advent of the ERIC system, particularly as it relates to government-sponsored research, only haphazard success could be expected in locating such studies, whether they involved research conducted by university faculty, by military personnel, or by school systems. Some of this research is published in regular journals, but a good part probably still remains relatively unknown.

Educational Statistics

The most comprehensive source of statistics on all phases of American education, particularly at the national level, is *Digest of Educational Statistics* (Washington: Government Printing Office, 1962–date; formerly *Biennial Survey of Education,* 1917–1961). This is complemented by pamphlets, bulletins, etc. on special topics available on request from HEW, as well as other departments and agencies of the federal government.

Other useful sources of Educational Statistics include: *Statistical Abstracts of the United States,* annual (Dept. of Commerce, 1878–date); *Economic Almanac* (National Industrial Conference Board, 1940–date); *Handbook of Basic Economic Statistics* (Washington: Economic Statistics Bureau, 1947–date); various separate publications of HEW listed in *Price List* No. 31 available from the Supt. of Documents; and various issues of *American Education* (which replaced *School Life* as the official journal of the U.S. Office of Education and also *Higher Education*, which the U.S. Office published between 1945 and 1965). *Publication Trends* (Washington: HEW, 1959–date) has a section on school attendance, salaries, educational statistics, etc.

Economic Almanac gives up-to-date statistics on population, resources, cost of living, prices, income, etc. Also pertinent here are the various publications of the Bureau of the Census which, in addition to regular census figures, issues periodic reports on intercensus estimates of population, data on the labor force, educational level, income, etc. On each year ending in "2," for example, it gives special statistics on independent school systems. For population data, in addition to the census data, one might consult *Population Index,* a quarterly prepared by the Princeton University School of Public Affairs and Population Association of America (Washington). Not to be overlooked as potential sources of statistics affecting education and the administration of schools are such commercial series as the Dow Jones, Standard and Poor, Dodge (construction), and the various indexes of business activity, e.g., *Newsweek.*

Also of major interest is *Statistical History of the United States from Colonial Times to the Present* (New York: Horizon Press, 1965) which synthesizes two series: *Historical Statistics of the United States, Colonial Times to 1957,* and *Historical Statistics of the United States, Colonial Times to 1957; Continuation to 1962* (Washington: Government Printing Office, 1960, 1965).

The best single reference to local statistical data is the *Municipal Yearbook* (Chicago: International City Managers' Association, 1934–date, annual, op. cit.). Another useful source is *County and City Data Book* (Washington: Government Printing Office, 1952, 1957, 1962, 1967). Another important source of state statistical data is *The Book of the States* (Chicago: The Council of State Governments, 1935–date, biennial) which deals with legislation, taxation, finance, state services including education, etc.

At the municipal and individual school level, little can be done to locate research except to write directly to the local directors of research. The *Directory of Educational Research Agencies and Studies,* previously cited, would be useful in this connection, both in identifying some of the major studies that have been conducted and in providing the addresses of the research personnel to whom a request for information can be forwarded. *The Research*

Center's Directory (op. cit.) would be useful in identifying university and independent nonprofit research agencies. "Research in State Departments of Education," to be found in the U.S. Office of Education *Bull.* No. 26, 1965, describes research programs, publications, and research projects in various state education departments which might provide local data. Some of this research can also be located through ERIC and SRIS, previously mentioned.

Highlights of the Chapter

1. The concept of science as a series of successive approximations to the truth and the consequent need for the researcher to build on the efforts of previous investigators make it imperative for him to be thoroughly familiar with the writings in the field. A thorough review of the related literature is an integral part of the conduct of research, helping the researcher in the clarification of his problem and the avoidance of duplication, the formulation of insightful hypotheses, the planning of an adequate research design, and the rigorous and insightful interpretation of his findings.

2. The library is a relatively unlimited storehouse of knowledge. Because of the magnitude and complexity of the material housed therein, the student interested in its effective use must become familiar with its organization. Effectiveness in library work calls for speed, accuracy, and dependability in (a) locating the necessary source; (b) deciding what is to be extracted from each source; and (c) taking whatever notes are needed.

3. The review of the literature must be systematic and thorough, or it will produce inadequate results. It is particularly important for the researcher to have a clear conception of his problem so that he will keep the review of irrelevant material to a minimum while, at the same time, ensuring a complete coverage of what is relevant.

4. It is generally best for the researcher to orient himself to the general nature of his problem through such sources as a textbook and the *Encyclopedia* (and the *Review*) *of Educational Research* before investigating more isolated references to be traced through indexes.

5.   Library holdings fall under two major classifications: *books* and *periodicals*—with a third category of *miscellany*. The card catalog is the key to the *books* holdings of the library. Each volume has an author card, and generally a title card and one or more subject cards. Books are usually classified according to the Library of Congress or the Dewey Decimal system, although some libraries have a modified system of their own.

6.   Periodicals are generally housed in open shelves in the Periodicals Room. Their effective use is predicated on the use of an index to identify the articles on the subject under study.

7.   A wide variety of indexes and general references can be found to cover almost any area in which the modern researcher might be interested. He would do well to develop a certain familiarity with the more pertinent of these sources. General library sources such as Burke and Burke, *Documentation in Education* should be consulted for special problems.

8.   The current knowledge explosion makes selective data-retrieval the key to the research enterprise as well as to effective educational practice. The major developments in this respect as they relate to the educational literature are ERIC, SRIS, and Datrix.

Questions and Projects

1.   (a) If you have not already done so before, arrange for a guided tour of the library. Visit the stack areas in which books in education and in related disciplines are shelved.

(b) Develop a broad acquaintance with the journals pertinent to educational research, both through firsthand experience in the library and through a study of such sources as Lins and Ries, *Scholars' Guide to Journals of Education and Educational Psychology*.

2.   (a) Identify current leaders in the various areas of specialization—counseling, curriculum, reading, etc.

(b) Identify the pioneers in the field of educational research and their contributions. Justify your selection by listing their major contributions (for example: Thorndike: laws of learning, theory of identical components, development of tests and measurements).

3. Locate the report of a good research study from *Dissertation Abstracts*. Obtain the microfilm and analyze the study from the standpoint of the problem (statement, delimitation, and justification), hypothesis, research design, findings and conclusions, and implications and significance for educational practice.

Selected References

American Library Association. *The Library and Information Networks of the Future*. Chicago: The Assn., 1963.

Burchinal, Lee G. "ERIC—and the need to know," *NEA J.*, 65–72; 1967.

————. "ERIC and dissemination of research findings," *Theory into Practice*, 6: 77–84; 1967.

———— and Harold Haswell. "How to put two and a half tons of research into one handy little box," *Amer. Educ.*, 2: 23–24; Feb. 1966.

Burke, Arvid J. and Mary A. Burke. *Documentation in Education*. New York: T.C., Columbia Univ. Press, 1967.

Goldhammer, Keith and Stanley M. Elam (eds.) *Research Dissemination and Implementation*. 3rd Annual Symposium. Bloomington: Phi Delta Kappa, 1962.

Kent, Allen (ed.) *Library Planning for Automation*. Washington: Spartan Book, 1965.

Kochen, Manfred (ed.) *The Growth of Knowledge: Readings on Organization and Retrieval of Information*. New York: Wiley, 1967.

Walker, Fred L. "Automatic home library of 1980," *Sci. Dig.*, 29: 41–46; June 1951.

————."Blueprint for knowledge," *Sci. Monthly*, 72: 90–101; 1951.

6
STATISTICAL CONSIDERATIONS

Whatever contribution statistics can make to the whole problem lies not so much in the provision of cook-books by which problems are solved, but in providing a framework and a way of thinking about problems.——Oscar Kempthorne (1961)

This chapter presents an orientation to some of the more basic statistical concepts necessary for the conduct of research. It makes no attempt to deal with their derivation, and obviously makes no claim to a complete coverage.* This is an area in which the serious student of research needs to develop more than superficial skill, for proficiency in statistics is as fundamental to adequacy in research as proficiency in mathematics is to success in physics.

INTERPRETATION OF THE RESULTS OF RESEARCH

Research data become meaningful in the process of being analyzed and interpreted. If research is to be productive, therefore, the plans for analysis must be laid at the time the study is selected and designed, for unless the analysis of the data can be made sufficiently precise to permit interpretations and generalizations, there is no point in conducting the investigation. The analysis of research data follows rather closely the development

---

* The limited treatment here is in recognition of space limitations and the ready availability of a number of adequate sources; in no way does it imply its unimportance. On the contrary, in view of the modern emphasis on research, all graduate students should have at least one course beyond the introductory course. Elementary statistics should be made a requirement of all undergraduate training in Education.

of science, some of the principles of which will be repeated in brief for the sake of continuity in discussion. A prerequisite to interpretation is experience, which bears on the fundamental problem of obtaining accurate and adequate data, for no conclusion, regardless of the adequacy of analysis, can be more adequate than the data on which it is based. Implied here is the need for a thorough grounding in the area of tests and measurements and the principles governing the derivation of adequate data.

Generally, data are most easily processed when they are converted into numerical values. Quantification not only facilitates their manipulation, but also increases the precision with which they can be analyzed. On the other hand, this immediately raises the question as to what to include and on what basis—for instance, "price" must be defined as "wholesale price," "retail price," or other unambiguous notation. Even such elementary aspects as the number of rooms in a house, a person's age, and the number of students in a given university are subject to some degree of misrepresentation arising from a lack of clarity regarding the basis of classification. Before analysis can proceed, it is also necessary to decide whether cases for which complete data are not available should be eliminated or data "manufactured" to replace what is missing. Another problem that might arise is the extent to which one is justified in rejecting apparently incorrect scores or scores that are outside expectation. All of these are rather complicated problems calling for considerable research insight.

Although quantification is a fundamental step in the analysis and interpretation of data, it is not an end in itself, and conclusions must always be interpreted on the basis of the variables being investigated rather than on the basis of their numerical values. A statistic is an abstraction used to represent a large mass of data—it has no meaning of its own. Furthermore, the use of complex statistics where they are not warranted may impress the unsophisticated, but they are misleading and serve no useful purpose. Certainly, they do not improve the study.*

---

* There has been strong reaction against overemphasis on statistical methodology as a substitute for imaginative and significant research. The new orientation toward statistical sophistication is a healthy sign but it must not be allowed to give the student a false sense of the art of researching. We must avoid substituting statistical elegance for good ideas and overembellishing small studies with overelaborate analyses. The sharpening of statistical tools is to be commended; we must make sure that we use them where their use is warranted.

By synthesizing data, statistics can facilitate the derivation of conclusions. However, the interpretation of the findings and the process of arriving at decisions must always remain a matter of judgment and, for this reason, research must always be directed by a person familiar with the field rather than by a statistician alone. If an increase in the number of spelling errors were to attend a course in creative writing, for example, someone unfamiliar with the fact that creative writing encourages students to write more—and therefore, to make more spelling errors—might be misled into concluding that creative writing is conducive to poor spelling.

The processing of numerical data through statistics calls for competence in the use of statistical methods and for awareness of the assumptions that underlie their derivation. In order not to mislead or be misled, the researcher must know the strengths and the weaknesses of the statistics he uses. He must first remember that statistical manipulation does not endow data with a precision they did not have in the first place. He must recognize that, if one ignores assumptions or uses inappropriate measures, he can have his data "prove" anything he wants to prove. However, although some people use statistics as a drunk uses a lamppost—for support rather than enlightenment—this is not a failing of statistics, but rather of the misguided people who misuse a perfectly legitimate and useful tool.

STATISTICAL CONCEPTS

Statistics as a Tool of Research

Statistics is an indispensable tool for both the consumer and the producer of research; without it, one cannot even read the professional literature intelligently. It does not seem unreasonable, therefore, to expect the holders of an advanced degree to possess the statistical competence necessary to conduct simple research. Statistics is not particularly difficult when studied systematically, and anyone with an understanding of high school algebra need not be unduly restricted in understanding statistical concepts and even in using most statistical procedures in the analysis of research data. On the other hand, it would seem generally advisable to place the emphasis of courses in educational statistics on applications and proper use—with due caution with respect to underlying assumptions and limitations—rather than on their mathematical derivation.

Descriptive Statistics

The broad field of statistics can be divided into two major areas: *descriptive statistics* and *statistics of inference*. Descriptive statistics are used to synthesize data in order to describe the status of the phenomenon as it relates to the group under consideration. The superintendent, for example, may be interested in knowing that, on the average, each classroom uses 1.2 boxes of chalk per month. Or he may want to synthesize the IQ's obtained by individual students into an overall average for the whole student body. The measures of descriptive statistics most commonly used in education are the *mean,* the *standard deviation,* and the *coefficient of correlation,* each of which can be extended into other phases of statistical reasoning. The mean and the standard deviation, for instance, lead directly into the concept of statistical significance. The coefficient of correlation has direct bearing on predictive studies. Adequate treatment of the nature and purpose of these basic techniques can be found in any introductory text in statistics. The computational aspects will also be left to other sources. It should, however, be realized that, though computational proficiency is not a prerequisite to the use of statistical procedures as a research tool, a real understanding of these concepts is frequently best promoted through actual practice in computation.

Statistics of Inference

More pertinent from a research point of view are statistics of inference. Research is generally conducted by means of a sample on the basis of which generalizations concerning the population from which the sample was obtained are reached. More specifically, the investigator computes certain sample values as the basis for inferring what the corresponding population values might be; the principal, for example, might calculate the average IQ for a sample consisting of every 20th cumulative record card as the basis for estimating the average IQ of the whole school.

Underlying such an extension of a sample value to

the corresponding population value is the fundamental concept of *probability*. It is well known that individual sample values obtained in repeated random sampling from a given population will not be identical—except perhaps through coincidence—with the corresponding values of the population. One must, therefore, make allowances for the operation of chance in any inference relative to a population value based on an obtained sample value. This always involves an element of risk, and any generalization must be made on the basis of probability—never certainty. Furthermore, the investigator must fully realize the possibility—indeed, the general expectation—that he will be in error in a certain percentage of the decisions he bases on statistical inference. Chance fluctuations will invariably cause discrepancies to occur between sample data and expected values; it is the purpose of statistics of inference to help isolate differences that are real from those that are due to chance fluctuations. In other words, the investigator must first consider the possibility that the results obtained have simply occurred through the chance effects of uncontrolled variables, a hypothesis which he must subject to statistical test.

In the interest of clarity, it might be well to identify the following terms as they apply to a population and a sample, respectively, and the symbolism used to represent them.

	Value	Mean	Standard Deviation	Number of Cases
Population	Parameter	μ	σ	N
Sample	Statistic	$\overline{X}$	S	n

This terminology is fairly standard and needs to be clearly understood, thus, the mean of a sample, $\overline{X}$, is a statistic; the corresponding population mean is a parameter and is represented by the Greek letter μ.

The concept of statistical probability is perhaps best presented through what is known as the *binomial distribution*. If ten coins are tossed simultaneously a total of 1024 times, the number of heads in each of those 1024 throws will make a distribution that centers around 5 heads and 5 tails. However, in the 1024 tosses of the ten coins, there would be instances of 6 heads or 6 tails, of 7 heads or 7 tails, and even of 8 heads or 8 tails. In fact, theoretically, there could be as many as 10 heads in a single toss and

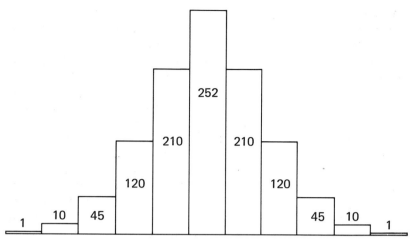

Fig. 6-1:   Hypothetical Distribution of Heads in 1024 Throws of 10 Coins

10 tails in another. The distribution that one might get on the basis of probability is shown in Figure 6-1.

Now, if a person were to toss ten coins only once, certainly, he would get one of the 1024 possibilities, and it could be any one from that showing 10 heads to that showing 10 tails. Suppose that he gets 9 heads: Is this so different from the expected value of 5 heads that he might have reason to suspect the operation of factors other than chance? Although it is recognized that the operation of chance will occasionally lead to unusual results, unusual results also occur for reasons other than chance, and there are times when it may be more logical to suspect that factors other than chance are responsible for an occurrence. The investigator has to make a judgment—and whether he attributes the occurrence to the operation of chance or to other factors, he can expect to be in error in a certain percentage of his decisions. It is a question of the level and the kind of risk he is willing to take, and if, for instance, he were to get 10 tails on the first toss of 10 coins, he might refuse to accept the operation of chance as the most logical explanation of this improbable event.

Sampling Distributions

If a statistic is to serve as the basis for making inferences concerning the population parameter, it is first necessary to ensure that the statistic is an unbiased estimate of this parameter—i.e., that the sample is a random sample of the population. For the sample statistic to provide the basis for inference regarding the population, it is also necessary that the general behavior of the statistic in repeated random sampling be known. For example, before we can decide whether a mean IQ of 105 for a given sample is indicative of a true superiority of the population surveyed over the general population, we need to know whether a discrepancy of 5 points from the expected 100 is relatively common in repeated sampling from the general population, or whether this constitutes a most unusual event. More specifically, we need to know the *mean* and the *standard deviation* of the distribution of the sample statistic in repeated random sampling. This would, of course, vary with the nature of the statistic in question, which, in turn, would depend on the nature of the problem.

A common research problem is to determine whether a sample statistic can be considered to be within the range of random sampling fluctuations of a given population parameter. For example, we might want to determine how the children of Community X compare with the national norm with respect to intelligence. Or we might want to test the relative difference in gains produced under two different methods of teaching. A number of basic formulas have been devised for dealing with problems of this kind; they are designed to yield answers which can be interpreted in the light of the problem under investigation.

There are really two problems here: one is computational; the other is logical. The more fundamental, of course, is the logical, and, since it appears that the computational aspects very frequently interfere with the understanding of what one is attempting to do and the rationale underlying such a procedure, it seems more profitable to deal first with the logical considerations.

To make the procedure more understandable, let us take the relatively familiar distribution of the Revised Stanford-Binet IQ's for the population of American-born whites. Let us simplify the discussion further by ignoring any question that might be raised regarding standardization procedures and by rounding out decimals to give the following parameters: $\mu = 100$ and $\sigma = 16$. The distribution is generally accepted to be normal, with the cases distributed more or less as shown in Figure 6–2.

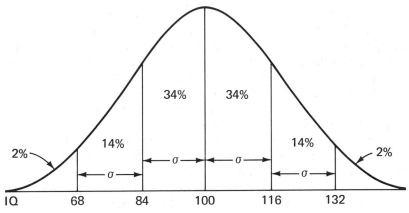

Fig. 6-2: The Normal Probability Distribution

Thus, approximately 34 percent of the general population of American-born whites have IQ's from 84 to 100, and a corresponding 34 percent between 100 and 116. Other percentages can be read directly from the figure, and finer breakdowns can be made by reference to the normal probability table, a copy of which can be found in any textbook on statistics.

If, from this population, repeated random samples of 64 cases are selected completely at random, the IQ of each of these cases obtained, and a mean IQ computed for each sample, it might be expected that the mean of each of the samples would be fairly close to 100—i.e., they would all center around the mean of the population $\mu = 100$, but would depart somewhat from this mean. These sample means would also form a distribution defined by a mean ($\overline{X}_{\overline{x}}$) and a standard deviation ($SE_{\overline{x}}$) of its own. Furthermore, this distribution would approximate the normal distribution, so that it is possible to bracket these sample means within intervals of their standard deviation in exactly the same way as in the distribution of raw scores (Figure 6-2). This point is fundamental to the interpretation of the results of research.

We have seen how the scores are distributed in a normal probability distribution. For example, 68 percent of the IQ's of the general population fall within one standard deviation (16 IQ points) of 100—i.e., 34 percent between 84 and 100 and 34 percent between 100 and 116. Nearly 96 percent of the scores fall within two standard deviations of the mean—i.e., between 68 and 132. A parallel interpretation can be made with respect to the distribution of sample means in repeated random sampling, except

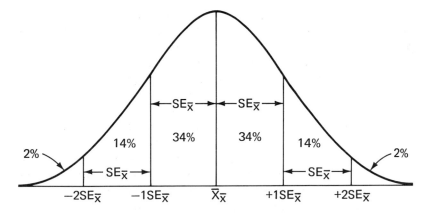

Fig. 6-3: Sampling Distribution of the Mean

that, instead of the concept of standard deviation used in connection with the distribution of a raw score like the IQ, we must substitute that of the *standard error of the mean** which is defined as
$SE_{\bar{x}} = \dfrac{\sigma}{\sqrt{n}}$ and which, therefore, in the present case has a value
of $\dfrac{16}{\sqrt{64}} = 2$.

Referring to Figure 6–3, we can establish that (a) the
sample means obtained in repeated random sampling ($n - 64$)
from a population of mean, $\mu = 100$, and $\sigma = 16$, distribute themselves normally† around a mean of their own (i.e., $\bar{X}_{\bar{x}}$) very nearly
equal to the population mean, μ; (b) this distribution has a standard
deviation of 2, so that we might expect 68 percent of our samples
to have a mean between $\mu \pm 1\ SE_{\bar{x}}$ (or between $\bar{X}_{\bar{x}} \pm 1\ SE_{\bar{x}}$)–i.e.,
between 98 and 102. We also might expect 96 percent of our sam-
ples to have a mean within the range from 96 to104. For a sample
to have a mean of less than 96, or more than 104, would be con-

---

* The distinction here is that the *standard deviation* pertains to a distribution of raw
scores whereas *standard error* is used to refer to the variability of a distribution of
sample statistics. The standard error of the mean then is simply the standard deviation of the distribution of sample means in repeated random sampling. The standard
error of any statistic is likewise the standard deviation of its sampling distribution.
† According to the *Central Limit Theorem*, even when the distribution of a given variable is not normal, the sampling distribution of its statistics, when based on large
samples selected at random from a given population, tends to approximate the normal
distribution.

sidered a rare event, since this would tend to occur on the basis of change alone in only two out of one hundred samples in repeated random sampling. A mean of 99.8, for example, would be well within the expected range. Conversely, a sample mean of 94 would be expected to occur only rarely through random sampling from the population. Were such a low mean to occur in a single trial, it would be rather difficult to conceive of its occurrence as resulting from chance alone. The exact probability involved could be read from a table of the normal probability distribution.

Similar reasoning and corresponding formulas can be used to deal with other statistics. The problem is a matter of logic and common sense. We have to explain research results in the simplest and most convincing manner. We know that the sample statistics obtained from random samples taken from a given population are not likely to coincide with the population parameter but rather will tend to deviate within the range of random sampling errors as computed from formulas such as those above. The most obvious way of explaining a discrepancy between a given sample statistic and the expected value, therefore, is to assume that this discrepancy is due to chance. This assumption can be tested, and if it appears reasonable, it can be accepted as the most logical explanation of the discrepancy noted. If, on the other hand, the discrepancy is so large—e.g., a sample mean of 94 in the example above—that it represents an event which is most improbable as the outcome of chance, the investigator must look for a more logical explanation of the difference obtained. Thus, he might consider this a real difference rather than one that arose through chance, and might conclude that the children of Community X, as a population, are significantly below average in IQ.

THE NULL HYPOTHESIS

Rationale Underlying the Null Hypothesis

As we previously noted, the investigator starts out with a *research* hypothesis stating what he considers likely to occur, e.g., the children with Head Start training will outperform comparable children without benefit of this experience. However, before he can accept this hypothesis, he must eliminate the factor of chance. This he does by postulating its opposite, namely, that the discrepancy in the performance of the two groups is adequately explained on the basis of chance. Stated in technical terminology, the investigator starts out with what is known as the *null hypothesis* —i.e., with the assumption that the difference between obtained and expected results is simply the result of chance. In keeping with the principle of parsimony which states that phenomena should be explained on the basis of the simplest explanation consistent with all of the facts of the case, he postulates that the difference noted is due to chance. Specifically, the null hypothesis denies the existence of any real difference between the expected value and that obtained in the sample until the factor of chance has been eliminated as the "causative" agent in the discrepancy noted. In an experiment comparing Method A and Method B, for example, it is unlikely that the experimental and control groups will make identical gains even if the two methods are exactly equal in effectiveness. By chance alone, one is likely to exceed the other by at least a small margin; only when the difference in the performance of the two groups is greater than might be accounted for on the basis of chance fluctuations can the investigator assume one method to be superior to the other. On this assumption then, the investigator proceeds to test the difference obtained by calculating the probability of obtaining similar results in repeated random sampling from identical populations, where the difference between sample means should then technically be zero. He can reject the null hypothesis if the probability of obtaining such a difference on the basis of chance alone is very small—or "accept"* the null hypothesis if the difference is within the range of differences adequately accounted for by chance.

The logic underlying such a test revolves around the probability or improbability of the occurrence through chance of a difference of the magnitude of that obtained. If the difference is so large that it makes such an event very improbable, the null hypothesis is rejected, with the implication that a more plausible explanation is to be sought. For example, if Group A decisively outperforms Group B, it can be concluded that Method A is more effective in promoting pupil growth than is Method B. The rejection of the null hypothesis in this case is tantamount to assuming

---

* A more precise expression might be "fail to reject" the null hypothesis. The fact that a difference between sample values is not large enough to cause us to reject the null hypothesis is not "proof" that the difference between corresponding population values is therefore zero. We "accept" the null hypothesis only in the sense that it *could be* true, not that it *is* true.

the superiority of one method over the other. If, on the other hand, the difference is so small that its occurrence on the basis of chance is relatively probable, the null hypothesis is accepted, with the understanding that chance *could* account for such a difference. All that is said is that chance is an acceptable explanation of the difference. The null hypothesis is never proved or disproved; it is simply accepted as plausible or rejected as implausible. Note also that what is being tested is not whether there is a difference between the two samples—this is obvious from the data—but rather that there is a real difference in the *populations* which the two samples represent—i.e., in this case, in the methods under comparison.

Confidence Levels

The level of improbability necessary to justify the rejection of the null hypothesis is obviously a matter of judgment, based on such considerations as the nature of the problem and the risk the investigator is willing to take. Two types of errors are involved here: Type 1 or *Alpha* errors refer to the rejection of the null hypothesis when it is actually true. This occurs when, even though two populations are actually equivalent—e.g., in a study of the standing height of boys and girls at age 11—yet, one of the samples by chance just turns out to be so different from the other that we reject the null hypothesis. Type 2 or *Beta* errors, on the other hand, refer to the acceptance of the null hypothesis when it is actually false. For instance, even though boys as a population may be taller than girls at age 15, this may not appear in a sample of, say 10 boys and 10 girls to a sufficient degree to cause the rejection of the null hypothesis.

Type 1 errors can be minimized by the simple expedient of rejecting the null hypothesis only when the differences are so fantastically great that the occurrence borders on the impossible, rather than the relatively improbable. However, this automatically increases correspondingly the likelihood of the occurrence of Type 2 errors, for many sizable sampling differences would then be accepted as being within the realm of chance while, in reality, they reflect real differences in the populations under test. Actually, the only two ways in which both types of errors can be reduced simultaneously—and not at the expense of one another—would be by taking larger samples and/or by reducing the sampling variability by selecting a more restricted population or by relying on a tighter sampling design.

It is, therefore, a matter of compromise. One type of error must be balanced against the other, and the level of acceptance and rejection of the null hypothesis must be set at what might be considered the optimal point, depending on the relative consequences of the two types of error. Custom and tradition in the fields of education and psychology favor balancing the two types of errors around the points at which there are either 5 chances out of 100 or 1 chance out of 100 of being in error. On a normal probability distribution, for example, critical cut-off points are established at 1.96 standard errors and 2.58 standard errors on either side of the mean representing the 5 percent and the 1 percent level of probability, respectively. Thus, if the difference being tested is such that as large a difference could be expected on the basis of chance 5 or more times out of 100 in repeated random sampling from equivalent populations, the null hypothesis is accepted on the grounds that the difference could be accounted for on the basis of chance. If, on the other hand, the difference is sufficiently large that such a difference would occur by chance less than once out of 100 trials, the null hypothesis is rejected on the premise that factors other than chance are probably involved in producing such a rare event. A difference of this magnitude is said to be statistically significant at the 1 percent level—or at the 99 percent

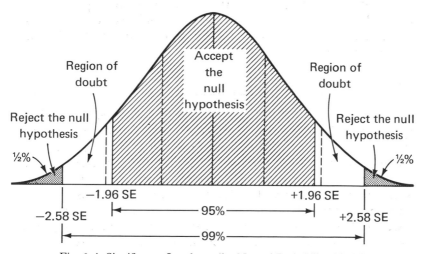

Fig. 6–4: Significance Levels on the Normal Probability Model

level of confidence—which is the equivalent to saying that the probability of a difference of this magnitude occurring through chance is only 1 out of 100, or less. Differences falling between the 5 percent and the 1 percent level may be said to be in the *region of doubt,* or perhaps considered *significant at the 5 percent level.*

On the normal probability distribution, the critical values that are generally considered are those at 1.96 and 2.58 standard errors on either side of the population parameter, which correspond to the 5 percent and the 1 percent levels of probability, respectively. However, it must be recognized that these are simply arbitrary values, and that other cut-off points could have been selected. In the early stages of exploration, for example, it might be advisable to set the level of rejection rather low so that variables are not eliminated before they have had a chance to prove themselves—i.e., so that they are not rejected prematurely. In the later stages of the investigation of a given problem, where precision is essential, the level of rejection should—other things being equal—be set higher so that relationships that are not really significant will be excluded.

It must be noted that the null hypothesis is rejected not because the probability that the populations are equivalent is low, but because there is a simpler and more adequate explanation. In other words, the basis for accepting or rejecting the null hypothesis is not so much probability as it is reasonableness—or parsimony. It should be noted further that probability applies not to the null hypothesis—which is either true or false—but to the risk the investigator is willing to take as to the truth or the falseness of the hypothesis.

Tests of Significance

Thus far, the discussion has centered around the rationale underlying the testing of the null hypothesis; we now turn to the computational aspects. The techniques for testing the tenability or the unacceptability of the null hypothesis vary with the type of problem and with the statistic which is appropriate in a given case. Probably the simplest formula concerns the comparison of a sample with a population where the parameters of the latter are known. For example, let us say that the mean IQ of the sample of 64 children from Community X (see page 163) was found to be 102.8 in contrast to the parameter, $\mu = 100$ and $\sigma = 16$, for the general population. The test of the null hypothesis in this case is the z test.*

$$z = \frac{\overline{X} - \mu}{\sigma/\sqrt{n}} = \frac{102.8 - 100}{16/\sqrt{64}}$$
$$= 1.4$$

The value of 1.4 is not significant, since it is less than the 1.96 required for significance at the 5 percent level. The null hypothesis is, therefore, accepted—i.e., we conclude that the difference, while favoring the children of Community X, is not large enough to exclude at a reasonable level the possibility that this may have been a chance superiority and that another sample of children from the same community might just as easily have shown them to be below national average in IQ.†

Not all tests of significance can be based on the theory of the normal probability distribution. Certain statistics do not yield a normal distribution in continued random sampling and cannot be interpreted according to the normal model. Statisticians have devised a number of models to deal with the common non-normal sampling distributions and have prepared tables listing the values corresponding to the commonly used probability levels—generally the 5 percent and the 1 percent—to permit the acceptance or rejection of the null hypothesis. These table values do not coincide numerically with those of the normal distribution, of course, but the rationale underlying their use is the same.

Among the more common tests of the null hypothesis, in addition to the normal theory test, are: 1. the *t* test, which very closely parallels the z test above, except that the standard devia-

* Sometimes known as the *critical ratio test,* a term less commonly used today. The symbol z is used, in a parallel sense with a z score, to refer to a test of significance the results of which are to be interpreted on the basis of the normal model.

† A common variant of the above *two-tailed* test of significance is the *one-tailed* test which involves a preconception as to the direction of the difference under test. Thus, in the two-tailed test, the point was simply whether or not a difference existed between the two means; the direction of this difference was not specified. If, on the other hand, we undertook to test whether, in view of the positive correlation among abilities, we might expect to find tall men superior to the general population in IQ, we are interested only in whether they are *superior* in IQ, not in whether they are *different*. The test involved here is identically the same as before, but the significance values corresponding to a given probability level have to be changed accordingly. Thus, the 1-percent level of significance corresponds to a z-value of 2.58 in a two-tailed test, (i.e., half of 1 percent of each tail), but 2.33 in a one-tailed test (i.e., 1 percent on whichever tail is specified in the hypothesis).

tion of the population is unknown, so that the standard deviation of the sample has to be used as the best estimate and the results interpreted on the probability table of the t distribution; 2. the F test, which is used in analysis of variance as a sort of multiple t test, permitting, for instance, the simultaneous comparison of the gains of three or more groups. It is also used in analysis of covariance, which permits the statistical adjustment of two or more groups on one or more independent variables on which equivalence was not established in the experimental design as the basis for a net comparison of their differences on the dependent variable; and 3. the *Chi-square* test which is used when the variables under discussion are in the form of frequencies relating to mutually exclusive categories in a two-way classification.

Highlights of the Chapter

1.   Statistical proficiency is fundamental to the proper analysis of research data, particularly in the more advanced stages of the investigation of a complex phenomenon.

2.   Descriptive statistics attempt to synthesize data in order to describe the status of phenomena. Statistics of inference are concerned with projecting sample data to provide a judgment concerning the phenomena as it actually exists.

3.   Research deals with a sample from which it derives certain statistics, which it then uses as the basis for inference concerning the corresponding population parameter. Basic to such inferences are the concepts of the sampling distribution of the statistics in repeated random sampling, of probability, and of limits within which the population parameter can be expected at a given level of confidence.

4.   In keeping with the principle of parsimony, the researcher refuses to attribute the occurrence of the phenomenon in question to the operation of the variable under study until the possibility of its having occurred through the operation of chance has been excluded at a given probability level. This is the essence of the null hypothesis.

5.   Like all hypotheses, the null hypothesis is never proved; it is simply accepted as plausible (perhaps as one of many plausible hy-

potheses that could be considered) or rejected as improbable. In this choice, two types of errors are possible: (a) rejecting the null hypothesis when it is true; and (b) accepting the null hypothesis when it is false. Since the risk of one and the other of the two errors varies inversely, it is a matter of balancing one risk against the other. In educational and psychological research, the critical probability levels for the acceptance and rejection of the null hypothesis are generally (arbitrarily) set at the 5 percent and the 1 percent level, respectively. The risk of both types of errors can be reduced simultaneously by increasing the sample size and/or the precision of the sampling design.

6.   A difference large enough to cause the rejection of the null hypothesis is said to be significant in the sense that, even though differences of this magnitude *can* occur by chance, there is a more parsimonious explanation in the present instance.

Questions and Projects

1.   Make a catalog survey of the statistics offerings and especially the statistics requirements for graduation in various disciplines. What implications might be read in the relative lack of emphasis on statistics in undergraduate—and even graduate—teacher education?

2.   What effect might the current lack of statistical sophistication on the part of education personnel both on the campus and in the field have on the success of the present emphasis on research?

3.   Alonzo Grace (AERA *Annual Report*, 1962) recommends that Education faculties be retrained in research and statistical methods. How might this be accomplished?

4.   Get acquainted with modern data-processing equipment. Obtain information on the potentialities of the computer for educational research purposes.

Selected References

Baier, Donald E. et al. "Can personnel researchers test and train themselves in statistics?" *Educ. psychol. Measmt.*, 12: 267–74; 1952.
Block, Jack. "On the number of significant findings to be expected by chance," *Psychometrika*, 25: 369–80; 1960.

Bolles, Robert C. "The difference between statistical hypotheses and scientific hypotheses," *Psychol. Rep.*, 11: 639–45; 1962.

Borko, Harold (ed.) *Computer Applications in the Behavioral Sciences.* Englewood Cliffs: Prentice-Hall, 1962.

Bross, E.J. *Design for Decision.* New York: Macmillan, 1953.

Caffrey, John and Charles Mosmann. *Computers on Campus.* Washington: Amer. Council Educ., 1967.

Dubois, Philip H. "Statistical controls in educational research," *Sci. Educ.*, 50: 156–59; 1966.

Edwards, Ward. "The theory of decision making" *Psychol. Bull.*, 51: 380–417; 1954.

Emmons, C.W. "The role of statistics in physiological research," *Biometrics*, 16: 161–75; 1960.

Fattu, Nicholas A. "Processing of data," in Chester W. Harris (ed.) *Encyclopedia of Educational Research.* New York: Macmillan, 1960. pp. 1047–56.

Fisher, Ronald A. *Statistical Methods and Scientific Inferences.* New York: Hafner, 1956.

Grant, D.A. "Statistical theory and research design," *Ann. Rev. Psychol.*, 1: 277–96; 1950. (And subsequent volumes.)

Harris, Chester W. "Statistical methods," in Chester W. Harris (ed.) *Encyclopedia of Educational Research.* New York: Macmillan, 1960. pp. 1397–1415.

Hjelm, Howard R. et al. "Symposium: The computer and educational research," *Harv. educ. Rev.*, 31: 235–80; 1961.

Johnson, Palmer O. "Modern statistical science and its function in educational and psychological research," *Sci. Monthly*, 72: 385–96; 1951.

Kish, Leslie. "Some statistical problems in research designs," *Amer. sociol. Rev.*, 24: 328–38; 1959.

Lindvall, C.M. "Tests of significance," *Phi Delta Kappan*, 38: 314–17; 1957.

Nunnally, Jum. "The place of statistics in psychology," *Educ. psychol. Measmt.*, 20: 641–50; 1960.

Ostle, Bernard. *Statistics in Research: Basic Concepts and Techniques for Research Workers.* Ames: Iowa State Coll. Press, 1963.

Rozeboom, W. "The fallacy of the null hypothesis significance test," *Psychol. Bull.*, 57: 416–28; 1960.

Savage, I. Richard. "Non-parametric statistics," *J. Amer. stat. Assn.*, 52: 331–44; 1957.

Tatsuoka, Maurice M. and David V. Tiedeman. "Statistics as an aspect of scientific method in research on teaching," in N.L. Gage (ed.) *Handbook of Research on Teaching.* Chicago: Rand McNally, 1963. pp. 142–70.

7
SAMPLING

All empirical knowledge is, in a fundamental sense, derived from incomplete or imperfect observation and is, therefore, a sampling of experience.——Frederick F. Stephan (1948)

Probably no concept is as fundamental to the conduct of research and the interpretation of its results as is sampling. Research is almost invariably conducted on the basis of a sample from which the investigator derives certain generalizations applicable to the population from which the sample was taken. Even when a complete census is taken, there is generally some thought of this particular population being a sample of future populations to which the results of the present investigation will apply. Indeed, all research can be considered a sample of the multitude of studies that could be done on a given subject. Rarely is research interested in a group for its own sake.

The Nature of Sampling

At its more advanced levels, sampling can involve a highly complex set of procedures which require an understanding not only of sampling techniques but also of the mathematics underlying their use. Precision in sampling is particularly important in normative-survey research, where the sample must be selected in complete compliance with the principles of sampling if it is to have meaning for the population. In experimental studies, on the other hand, such exact correspondence between sample and population is generally not as important, since the crucial point is the relative equivalence of the two groups being compared, rather than the complete agreement of the samples with the population.

Sampling is both necessary and advantageous. Taking a total census is costly and often difficult; in many cases it is completely impossible. What is not so clearly recognized by the layman, who feels that one takes a sample when he cannot poll the whole population is that sampling frequently results in more adequate data than a census. The modern statistician would argue that taking a census is frequently a sign of statistical incompetence. Not only is sampling more practical than a census but, by permitting greater control over every aspect of the selection and appraisal of the individual cases, it may actually produce more accurate results. In an interview study, for example, sampling allows for better training and coordination among the interviewers. It permits greater depth in interviewing; it also permits greater depth in analysis and greater accuracy in processing, and allows the interviews to be conducted in a relatively shorter period of time so that the distorting effects of the passage of time are minimized. As Hansen (1960) points out, "If we merely wanted to get national statistics, there would be no reason for taking a census every ten years. This could be done more accurately through sampling procedures, and at a fraction of the cost."

This is not to suggest that sampling is desirable in itself or that the smaller the sample, the better. Admittedly, research should be based on a substantial number of cases, but it must be recognized that the increase in precision obtained through increasing the sample size is frequently more than negated by the errors and other difficulties that accompany a vast operation. If a wine tester had to consume his entire consignment in order to determine its quality, he would certainly defeat any purpose that testing the wine is expected to serve. Furthermore, it is very likely that, as he proceeded with the task, errors of judgment would probably increase in proportion to the decrease in his sobriety. It might be better to settle for a sample—a small sample!

Obviously, a major reason for sampling is to reduce expense—in time, effort, and money—and the factor of cost must be balanced against the adequacy of the data that are obtained. Some of the problems involved include the question of the specific purpose the sample is to serve, the degree of precision the estimates should have, and the funds available to obtain the desired accuracy. Frequently, the money that can be saved by taking a small sample might be more profitably spent in carrying out a pilot study that would make the design of the study more meaningful.

Conversely, complicated sampling designs may so increase the cost of processing and analyzing the data that they negate any saving sampling affords. This is especially true if checks have to be introduced to forestall error.

If sample data are to be used as the basis for generalizing to a population, it is essential that the sample be representative of that population. While this is a principle with which everyone agrees, it is also a principle that is incapable of implementation. In the strict sense of the term, a representative sample would be a miniature or replica of the population, at least with respect to the characteristic under investigation. In order to check the representativeness of the sample, therefore, the corresponding population characteristics would have to be known—in which case there would be no need for a sample. The problem is resolved at the operational level by seeking a sample which is random as the best approximation to representativeness, i.e., a sample which falls within the range of random sampling errors of being representative with respect to the trait under study. The required population parameter can then be estimated at any desired level of probability to lie within an interval of a given magnitude centering around the sample value obtained.

A crucial point here is to define the population from which the sample is to be taken and to which the conclusions of the study are to apply. One must be very suspicious, for instance, of samples that select themselves—as in a questionnaire study with a low percentage of returns—or of samples selected simply on the basis of ready availability. In such instances, it is relatively impossible to establish the specific population to which the results apply, i.e., the population of which such a sample might reasonably be considered representative.

ERRORS IN SAMPLING

Classification of Sampling Errors

Sample data that are not representative can suffer from errors of a *random* and/or *systematic* nature. These errors can be classified further as errors of *sampling* and/or *measurement*, providing a four-way classification as shown in Figure 7-1. Cell A refers to the unavoidable errors that occur whenever sampling is done. If the investigator has decided on a sample of $n = 100$, and has already selected the first 99, the 100th case, selected at random, may be high, low, or average with respect to the trait in question and will, therefore, cause some shift in the sample statistic. These errors tend to cancel each other to the point that, if n is sizable, the sample statistic will tend to stabilize close to the population parameter. Furthermore, not only can these errors be minimized to any fractional value by increasing n, but their magnitude can also be estimated.

	Random	Constant
Sampling	A	B
Measurement	C	D

Fig. 7–1:   Classification of Errors

Cell B refers to errors of bias in sampling—i.e., sampling errors which do not cancel out, but rather lean systematically in one or the other direction of the population value. For example, if one were to attempt to determine the income of the residents of a given city by canvassing the four corner houses in each block, he would probably incorporate a bias in his data, since people living in corner houses probably draw above-average income in order to be able to afford these somewhat favored locations.

To the extent that systematic errors exist, the data are of limited use as the basis for generalizing to the population. For example, to determine the average IQ of a school by having each teacher select the first two students who complete an assignment, or two honor students, or two students who volunteer would most likely provide fictitious results as far as the overall school status is concerned.

Although Cells C and D refer to errors in measurement, rather than to errors in sampling per se, they are pertinent here since sampling results reflect not only the selection of sample cases but also the determination of the characteristics of those selected. The errors in Cell C are those which arise from the simple fact that measurements derived from any instrument of less than complete reliability are inevitably in some degree of error. These errors cannot be eliminated completely, but they can be minimized even for a given student by basing his score on an extended and comprehensive testing program that will permit such errors to cancel out. They can be minimized further with respect to the sample statistic by having a sizable sample, which permits the self-cancellation of whatever individual (random measurement) errors still remain.

Cell D concerns another bias—that due to systematic errors of measurement. If, in the testing of a sample of students for IQ, the examiner inadvertently allows an extra three minutes for the test, for instance, there will probably be a systematic tendency for the sample statistic to be higher than the corresponding population parameter. And this would be so regardless of the size of the sample for which the extra time was allowed.

Relative Magnitude of Sampling Errors

From the standpoint of research, the "bad" errors are the systematic errors—both in sampling and in measurement. Not only can the size of random errors be estimated, but they can be reduced to decimal values by the simple expedient of increasing the size of the sample and the reliability of the tests used. Furthermore, as explained in Chapter 4, while unreliability is serious when dealing with one individual—as in guidance, for example—these individual irregularities do not affect the overall sampling statistic appreciably since they tend to cancel out.

The magnitude of random sampling errors as they affect the sample statistic can best be appreciated by referring to the standard error of the mean, $SE_{\bar{x}} = \dfrac{\sigma}{\sqrt{n}}$, as presented on page 165. Thus, if the average IQ of repeated random samples of $n = 64$, taken from the general population, is calculated, chances are 96 out of 100 that a given sample mean will fall within 4 IQ points of the population mean. If greater accuracy is desired, it can be obtained by increasing either the size of the sample or the homogeneity of the variable under investigation, or by using a more adequate sampling design which will decrease the variability of the sampling distribution of the statistic under study for a given sample size.

Systematic errors, on the other hand, are frequently difficult to detect. One cannot tell by looking at a distribution whether or not the condition of randomness was fulfilled, nor is there any test of the randomness of sample data. Furthermore, the size of systematic errors cannot be estimated since they are outside the scope of statistical theory. To make matters worse, such errors can be large. The effects of selecting the corner house as a basis for sampling for income or of allowing an extra three minutes on a standardized test may well introduce sizable errors. Similarly, non-returns in a questionnaire study may incorporate a considerable bias, the extent and even the direction of which is sometimes difficult to estimate.

It might be well at this time to distinguish between what might be called the *parameter* and the *true* value for a population. The parameter is probably best conceived as an extension of the sample statistic. As the sample is increased in size to become a complete census—i.e., as n leads to N—the sample statistic becomes the population parameter. Generally, the larger the sample, the closer the sample statistic approaches the population parameter. Thus, using the IQ as the variable, the mean of a sample of two cases may be a long way from the population parameter. As the investigator increases his sample to three cases, then four cases, and finally n cases, the mean will swing back and forth, gradually stabilizing closer and closer to the parameter to the point that, as the sample comes progressively closer to including everyone in the population, the sample statistic comes progressively closer to the population parameter. If there are systematic errors, however, including in the sample more and more of the members of the population will not correct for such errors, and the sample statistic will stabilize near the parameter but not near the true value—if we define the *true* value as an errorless parameter.*

If the results obtained are systematically higher or lower than the corresponding true value, the sample is biased and the discrepancy is called an *error of bias*. This is a phenomenon with which even a census must cope. The United States Census, despite a relatively complete coverage, probably does not get a true value for the age of women, any more than the Bureau of Internal Revenue gets a true picture of the actual income of Americans or

---

* Mathematicians would probably prefer to think of the population parameter as the true value. It would then be necessary to recognize that the extension of the sample statistic does not necessarily give the parameter.

even Americans who file. In both instances, since we are no longer sampling, the discrepancies are due almost exclusively to systematic errors of measurement. Bias can also stem from systematic errors of sampling. Errors of bias are frequently as large as they are unnecessary, and it does not make sense to increase sample size and cost to reduce random errors to the third decimal place, and leave untouched king-size constant errors. The one thing that is unquestionably more misleading than a small biased sample is a large sample with an equal bias.

Random sampling errors can be reduced by increasing the sample size. They are, of course, eliminated completely when the sample size is increased to include everyone in the population. This can be seen from the formula for the standard error of the mean, for example, which when stated in full, becomes:

$$SE_{\bar{x}} = \frac{\sigma}{\sqrt{n}} \sqrt{\frac{N - n}{N - 1}}$$

It can be seen from the factor at the right that as n reaches N, the standard error becomes zero. Increasing the size of the sample can also eliminate systematic errors of sampling, since, obviously, there can be no errors of sampling—random or systematic—when one no longer samples. This would not, however, eliminate errors of measurement; it would not even affect systematic errors of measurement.

In practice, the investigator takes only a small fraction of the total population, and he can, therefore, continue with a bias even when the sample is numerically large. A Republican-party worker, for example, canvasses ten of his fellow party workers regarding the likely outcome of a coming election. Realizing that his sample is too small, he canvasses another ten of his fellow party workers. Even if he extends his sample to 100 by including the families and the close friends of his fellow workers, he is merely stabilizing his bias, not eliminating it. Only through increasing his sample to the point of exhausting the bias by running out of obviously Republcan groups will his sample become more representative.

This situation was illustrated by the *Literary Digest* fiasco of 1936. On the basis of a sample of nearly 2.5 million questionnaires returned from over 10 million mailed to potential voters, selected largely through its own subscription lists, automobile registrations, and telephone directories, the *Digest* predicted the overwhelming defeat of Roosevelt—only to end with a 20 percent error in their prediction. During the same election, *Fortune,* on the basis of a sample of 4500, was able to approximate the actual results within 1 percent, and also to predict the likely error of the *Digest* poll. Apparently, even with a sample of nearly 2.5 million, the *Digest* had not exhausted the bias to the point of including a sufficient representation of the unemployed and the lower socio-economic groups, who were highly partisan to Roosevelt's New Deal. There would have been a bias even if the poll had obtained complete returns ($n = 10,000,000 +$) since the bias was incorporated in the very criteria of selection.

SAMPLE SIZE

Other things being equal, the larger the sample, the greater the precision and accuracy of the data it provides. And, contrary to the common belief, the precision of the data is determined primarily by the size of the sample, rather than by the percentage of the population represented in the sample. This can be shown directly by the formula of the standard error of the mean

$$SE_{\bar{x}} = \frac{\sigma}{\sqrt{n}}\sqrt{\frac{N - n}{N - 1}}$$ for instance. Except in the case of a large

sample taken from a small finite population, the precision of the sample mean is determined by the term n in the denominator—and, of course, σ—rather than by the ratio $\sqrt{\frac{N - n}{N - 1}}$. In fact, when the population is large, the latter term does relatively little to improve precision and, for that reason, is generally omitted from the formula.

The size of the sample which he should take is invariably one of the first questions a graduate student asks his advisor. The exact procedure by which to determine the sample size required varies with the nature of the variable and its sampling distribution, but the basic procedure can be illustrated in connection with the mean of repeated random samples based on the normal probability distribution.

As we have seen (page 165), the chances are 95 to 5 that a sample mean in repeated random sampling will fall within the interval $\mu \pm 1.96\ SE_{\bar{x}}$. The next question is the degree of accuracy required. Would the purpose of the study be adequately served if the sampling errors were kept within 2 percent at the 95 percent confidence level—i.e., would it be satisfactory if the investigator could be confident at the 95 percent level that the sample mean does not differ from the population parameter by more than 2 points in the case of the IQ? If this is acceptable, the investigator can use the formula for the standard error of the mean to provide the required value of n.

$$1.96 \text{ SE}_{\bar{x}} = 2$$

$$1.96 \frac{\sigma}{\sqrt{n}} = 2$$

$$1.96 \frac{(16)}{2} = \sqrt{n}$$

$$15.68 = \sqrt{n}$$

$$246 = n$$

Thus, he would need a sample of 246 cases in order to meet the conditions of a 2 percent error at the 95 percent confidence level. If he insists on limiting the error to 1 IQ point and, simultaneously, on raising the confidence level to the 99 percent level, he will have to increase his sample size by a considerable margin, as indicated by the following relationship:

$$2.58 \text{ SE}_{\bar{x}} = 1$$

Similar computations will provide an estimate of the sample size necessary for obtaining any degree of precision at any confidence level in whatever statistic is being considered. Thus, the question of the size of the sample to be selected is answered on the basis of the precision (and the confidence level) desired. If one is content with a general approximation to the population parameter, the sample can be small; if, on the other hand, a greater degree of precision is required, the sample must be correspondingly larger.*

To summarize: the answer to the question of the size of the sample that is required is to be found in the margin of error that can be tolerated in the final estimate of the population parameter. Precision in the estimate of the population parameter

---

* Since in most formulas for the standard error, sample size features as the square root of n in the denominator, a doubling of the precision of a sample statistic generally calls for quadrupling the sample size. It may be more practical to increase the precision by restricting the population in order to increase its homogeneity, i.e., to reduce σ.

requires the application of methods of analysis which will extract maximum information from the data that are obtained. But, at the risk of monotony, it must be repeated that it is a fallacy to expect mere sample size to ensure accuracy, since sample size will not generally eliminate any bias inherent in the sampling or measurement techniques. The latter is the area that needs to be watched carefully, for the errors that may occur there can make any attempt at refinement and precision through increased sample size look relatively misguided.

THE MECHANICS OF SAMPLING

Definition of Population

Sampling procedures involve a number of considerations which must be clearly understood if adequate results are to be obtained. The first problem is to clarify the purposes of the study and, in the light of these purposes, to define the population to be sampled. This definition should be sufficiently clear that there is no question about the inclusion or exclusion of a specific case, or about the applicability of the conclusions to any given case or group. For example, in a study of juvenile delinquency, it must be clearly stated whether the population consists of those who have been delinquent or simply those who have been caught.

Although a population can be relatively unlimited— e.g., mankind—research must concern itself with *restricted* populations, such as school children, junior-high-school students in the state of . . . , school children in a given county, or perhaps freshmen attending the University of . . . . Generally, the more homogeneous the population from which one samples, the more precise the results that can be derived. However, since sample data can be generalized only to the population from which the sample is obtained, it is generally inadvisable to overrestrict the population under investigation. It is particularly important not to make a false definition of the population. The investigator cannot, for example, define the population of a given school as "the children present on the day of observation," if his problem is one of the health of these children, since the presence or absence of a given child may be related to the status of his health. Sample size must be related to such questions as the nature of the survey, the instrument to be used, and the means of access to the population, as well as to the particular sampling design. Thus, if the sample is to be contacted by questionnaire, the sample might be larger than if interviews are to be conducted. The unit of sampling is also important. If a group test is to be administered to an entire class at one time, a larger sample might be taken than if individual tests are required. In all cases, the size of the sample should be in line with the degree of precision required.

Basic Principles of Sampling

The crucial problem in sampling is obviously the actual selection of the sample. The theoretical considerations underlying this selection—representativeness, randomness, etc.—have been presented; it is now a matter of implementation. The task is probably best approached from the basic principle that every member of the population must have an equal chance of being included in the sample. This immediately poses a number of complications, the first of which is the relative impossibility of obtaining an adequate listing of any given population. The telephone directory is not an adequate listing of the residents of a given city, since some residents are listed more than once, while others are not listed at all; it is not even an adequate listing of telephone subscribers. It is almost impossible to get an adequate list of the students of a given college—unless defined arbitrarily—when one considers those who registered late, those who dropped out, those who are carrying a partial load, those who are registered for non-degree classes, etc. In fact, when considered critically, nearly every listing—the telephone directory, the city directory, the tax rolls, the voters' list, auto registration—is invariably incomplete, inaccurate, outdated, or otherwise inadequate from the standpoint of almost any sampling purpose one might have in mind. It is even more difficult to locate a usable listing of the substrata into which a given population might be divided. And, of course, proceeding without a list is not the solution: interviewing people on the street on any day of the week or hour of the day is very likely to give some segment of the local population a greater chance of being selected than others.

The basic principle of sampling can be restated as follows. There must be no logical connection between the method of sampling and the characteristic being sampled. Thus, using the corner house as a basis for sampling for income is a biased design because living in a corner house is not independent of income.

Of course, sampling on the basis of corner houses may be a perfectly random design if one is sampling for eye color, since there is no logical reason to believe that people living in corner houses are predominantly blue-eyed or brown-eyed. There is no reason to suspect that blue-eyed people, for example, would be denied an equal chance of being selected if we used corner houses as the basis for our sampling. This design may be biased, however, if the variable under investigation is standing height, since there are indications of a correlation between standing height and vocational success and, therefore, income.

Whether or not a sample is a random sample cannot be determined by inspection; a hand of 13 cards of the same suit, for example, can be dealt randomly. The criterion for randomness must be sought elsewhere, i.e., in the process itself. A random can be defined as a sample which has been obtained by a random method. Such a sample would give results that approximate the true population value more and more closely as the sample size increases. The problem can be resolved at the operational level by superimposing a new characteristic—e.g., the series of cardinal numbers—on the population, and sampling at random in accordance with this new characteristic. The problem of sampling then becomes a matter of enumerating the population (where this is possible) and of selecting certain numbers at random, say from a table of random numbers such as that in Table 7–1. These numbers, by definition, constitute a random sample of the numbers assigned to the population, and, therefore, provide a correspondingly random sample of the population of individuals. The numbers selected in this way can be assumed to be independent of any characteristic; their use as the basis for sampling probably provides as valid a guarantee of randomness as it is possible to devise.

Another approach which is sometimes used is to take a *systematic* sample consisting of every *i*th member of the population as necessary in order to obtain a sample of the size required. Systematic sampling is generally an acceptable sampling procedure since, if one starts at random, it gives every individual in the population an equal chance of being included in the sample. It is, however, a faulty design when there is a cyclical pattern in the variable being investigated. For example, taking a traffic count from five to six o'clock in the afternoon of every day would obviously provide a biased estimate of the number of cars that go by a particular intersection during a given week. It is necessary to break the rhythm of the pattern in order to eliminate the bias it

TABLE 7-1: Random Numbers (I)

03 47 43 73 86	36 96 47 36 61	46 98 63 71 62	33 26 16 80 45	60 11 14 10 95
97 74 24 67 62	42 81 14 57 20	42 53 32 37 32	27 07 36 07 51	24 51 79 89 73
16 76 62 27 66	56 50 26 71 07	32 90 79 78 53	13 55 38 58 59	88 97 54 14 10
12 56 85 99 26	96 96 68 27 31	05 03 72 93 15	57 12 10 14 21	88 26 49 81 76
55 59 56 35 64	38 54 82 46 22	31 62 43 09 90	06 18 44 32 53	23 83 01 30 30
16 22 77 94 39	49 54 43 54 82	17 37 93 23 78	87 35 20 96 43	84 26 34 91 64
84 42 17 53 31	57 24 55 06 88	77 04 74 47 67	21 76 33 50 25	83 92 12 06 76
63 01 63 78 59	16 95 55 67 19	98 10 50 71 75	12 86 73 58 07	44 39 52 38 79
33 21 12 34 29	78 64 56 07 82	52 42 07 44 38	15 51 00 13 42	99 66 02 79 54
57 60 86 32 44	09 47 27 96 54	49 17 46 09 62	90 52 84 77 27	08 02 73 43 28
18 18 07 92 46	44 17 16 58 09	79 83 86 19 62	06 76 50 03 10	55 23 64 05 05
26 62 38 97 75	84 16 07 44 99	83 11 46 32 24	20 14 85 88 45	10 93 72 88 71
23 42 40 64 74	82 97 77 77 81	07 45 32 14 08	32 98 94 07 72	93 85 79 10 75
62 36 28 19 95	50 92 26 11 97	00 56 76 31 38	80 22 02 53 53	86 60 42 04 53
37 85 94 35 12	83 39 50 08 30	42 34 07 96 88	54 42 06 87 98	35 85 29 48 39
70 29 17 12 13	40 33 20 38 26	13 89 51 03 74	17 76 37 13 04	07 74 21 19 30
56 62 18 37 35	96 83 50 87 75	97 12 25 93 47	70 33 24 03 54	97 77 46 44 80
99 49 57 22 77	88 42 95 45 72	16 64 36 16 00	04 43 18 66 79	94 77 24 21 90
16 08 15 04 72	33 27 14 34 09	45 59 34 68 49	12 72 07 34 45	99 27 72 95 14
31 16 93 32 43	50 27 89 87 19	20 15 37 00 49	52 85 66 60 44	38 68 88 11 80
68 34 30 13 70	55 74 30 77 40	44 22 78 84 26	04 33 46 09 52	68 07 97 06 57
74 57 25 65 76	59 29 97 68 60	71 91 38 67 54	13 58 18 24 76	15 54 55 95 52
27 42 37 86 53	48 55 90 65 72	96 57 69 36 10	96 46 92 42 45	97 60 49 04 91
00 39 68 29 61	66 37 32 20 30	77 84 57 03 29	10 45 65 04 26	11 04 96 67 24
29 94 98 94 24	68 49 69 10 82	53 75 91 93 30	34 25 20 57 27	40 48 73 51 92
16 90 82 66 59	83 62 64 11 12	67 19 00 71 74	60 47 21 29 68	02 02 37 03 31
11 27 94 75 06	06 09 19 74 66	02 94 37 34 02	76 70 90 30 86	38 45 94 30 38
35 24 10 16 20	33 32 51 26 38	79 78 45 04 91	16 92 53 56 16	02 75 50 95 98
38 23 16 86 38	42 38 97 01 50	87 75 66 81 41	40 01 74 91 62	48 51 84 08 32
31 96 25 91 47	96 44 33 49 13	34 86 82 53 91	00 52 43 48 85	27 55 26 89 62
66 67 40 67 14	64 05 71 95 86	11 05 65 09 68	76 83 20 37 90	57 16 00 11 66
14 90 84 45 11	75 73 88 05 90	52 27 41 14 86	22 98 12 22 08	07 52 74 95 80
68 05 51 18 00	33 96 02 75 19	07 60 62 93 55	59 33 82 43 90	49 37 38 44 59
20 46 78 73 90	97 51 40 14 02	04 02 33 31 08	39 54 16 49 36	47 95 93 13 30
64 19 58 97 79	15 06 15 93 20	01 90 10 75 06	40 78 78 89 62	02 67 74 17 33
05 26 93 70 60	22 35 85 15 13	92 03 51 59 77	59 56 78 06 83	52 91 05 70 74
07 97 10 88 23	09 98 42 99 64	61 71 62 99 15	06 51 29 16 93	58 05 77 09 51
68 71 86 85 85	54 87 66 47 54	73 32 08 11 12	44 95 92 63 16	29 56 24 29 48
26 99 61 65 53	58 37 78 80 70	42 10 50 67 42	32 17 55 85 74	94 44 67 16 94
14 65 52 68 75	87 59 36 22 41	26 78 63 06 55	13 08 27 01 50	15 29 39 39 43
17 53 77 58 71	71 41 61 50 72	12 41 94 96 26	44 95 27 36 99	02 96 74 30 83
90 26 59 21 19	23 52 23 33 12	96 93 02 18 39	07 02 18 36 07	25 99 32 70 23
41 23 52 55 99	31 04 49 69 96	10 47 48 45 88	13 41 43 89 20	97 17 14 49 17
60 20 50 81 69	31 99 73 68 68	35 81 33 03 76	24 30 12 48 60	18 99 10 72 34
91 25 38 05 90	94 58 28 41 36	45 37 59 03 09	90 35 57 29 12	82 62 54 65 60
34 50 57 74 37	98 80 33 00 91	09 77 93 19 82	74 94 80 04 04	45 07 31 66 49
85 22 04 39 43	73 81 53 94 79	33 62 46 86 28	08 31 54 46 31	53 94 13 38 47
09 79 13 77 48	73 82 97 22 21	05 03 27 24 83	72 89 44 05 60	35 80 39 94 88
88 75 80 18 14	22 95 75 42 49	39 32 82 22 49	02 48 07 70 37	16 04 61 67 87
90 96 23 70 00	39 00 03 06 90	55 85 78 38 36	94 37 30 69 32	90 89 00 76 33

From Ronald A. Fisher, and Frank Yates, *Statistical Tables for Biological, Agricultural, and Medical Research* (New York: Hafner, 1963).

TABLE 7-1: Random Numbers (II)

53 74 23 99 67	61 32 28 69 84	94 62 67 86 24	98 33 41 19 95	47 53 53 38 09
63 38 06 86 54	99 00 65 26 94	02 82 90 23 07	79 62 67 80 60	75 91 12 81 19
35 30 58 21 46	06 72 17 10 94	25 21 31 75 96	49 28 24 00 49	55 65 79 78 07
63 43 36 82 69	65 51 18 37 88	61 38 44 12 45	32 92 85 88 65	54 34 81 85 35
98 25 37 55 26	01 91 82 81 46	74 71 12 94 97	24 02 71 37 07	03 92 18 66 75
02 63 21 17 69	71 50 80 89 56	38 15 70 11 48	43 40 45 86 98	00 83 26 91 03
64 55 22 21 82	48 22 28 06 00	61 54 13 43 91	82 78 12 23 29	06 66 24 12 27
85 07 26 13 89	01 10 07 82 04	59 63 69 36 03	69 11 15 83 80	13 29 54 19 28
58 54 16 24 15	51 54 44 82 00	62 61 65 04 69	38 18 65 18 97	85 72 13 49 21
34 85 27 84 87	61 48 64 56 26	90 18 48 13 26	37 70 15 42 57	65 65 80 39 07
03 92 18 27 46	57 99 16 96 56	30 33 72 85 22	84 64 38 56 98	99 01 30 98 64
62 95 30 27 59	37 75 41 66 48	86 97 80 61 45	23 53 04 01 63	45 76 08 64 27
08 45 93 15 22	60 21 75 46 91	98 77 27 85 42	28 88 61 08 84	69 62 03 42 73
07 08 55 18 40	45 44 75 13 90	24 94 96 61 02	57 55 66 83 15	73 42 37 11 61
01 85 89 95 66	51 10 19 34 88	15 84 97 19 75	12 76 39 43 78	64 63 91 08 25
72 84 71 14 35	19 11 58 49 26	50 11 17 17 76	86 31 57 20 18	95 60 78 46 75
88 78 28 16 84	13 52 53 94 53	75 45 69 30 96	73 89 65 70 31	99 17 43 48 76
45 17 75 65 57	28 40 19 72 12	25 12 74 75 67	60 40 60 81 19	24 62 01 61 16
96 76 28 12 54	22 01 11 94 25	71 96 16 16 88	68 64 36 74 45	19 59 50 88 92
43 31 67 72 30	24 02 94 08 63	38 32 36 66 02	69 36 38 25 39	48 03 45 15 22
50 44 66 44 21	66 06 58 05 62	68 15 54 35 02	42 35 48 96 32	14 52 41 52 48
22 66 22 15 86	26 63 75 41 99	58 42 36 72 24	58 37 52 18 51	03 37 18 39 11
96 24 40 14 51	23 22 30 88 57	95 67 47 29 83	94 69 40 06 07	18 16 36 78 86
31 73 91 61 19	60 20 72 93 48	98 57 07 23 69	65 95 39 69 58	56 80 30 19 44
78 60 73 99 84	43 89 94 36 45	56 69 47 07 41	90 22 91 07 12	78 35 34 08 72
84 37 90 61 56	70 10 23 98 05	85 11 34 76 60	76 48 45 34 60	01 64 18 39 96
36 67 10 08 23	98 93 35 08 86	99 29 76 29 81	33 34 91 58 93	63 14 52 32 52
07 28 59 07 48	89 64 58 89 75	83 85 62 27 89	30 14 78 56 27	86 63 59 80 02
10 15 83 87 60	79 24 31 66 56	21 48 24 06 93	91 98 94 05 49	01 47 59 38 00
55 19 68 97 65	03 73 52 16 56	00 53 55 90 27	33 42 29 38 87	22 13 88 83 34
53 81 29 13 39	35 01 20 71 34	62 33 74 82 14	53 73 19 09 03	56 54 29 56 93
51 86 32 68 92	33 98 74 66 99	40 14 71 94 58	45 94 19 38 81	14 44 99 81 07
35 91 70 29 13	80 03 54 07 27	96 94 78 32 66	50 95 52 74 33	13 80 55 62 54
37 71 67 95 13	20 02 44 95 94	64 85 04 05 72	01 32 90 76 14	53 89 74 60 41
93 66 13 83 27	92 79 64 64 72	28 54 96 53 84	48 14 52 98 94	56 07 93 89 30
02 96 08 45 65	13 05 00 41 84	93 07 54 72 59	21 45 57 09 77	19 48 56 27 44
49 83 43 48 35	82 88 33 69 96	72 36 04 19 76	47 45 15 18 60	82 11 08 95 97
84 60 71 62 46	40 80 81 30 37	34 39 23 05 38	25 15 35 71 30	88 12 57 21 77
18 17 30 88 71	44 91 14 88 47	89 23 30 63 15	56 34 20 47 89	99 82 93 24 98
79 69 10 61 78	71 32 76 95 62	87 00 22 58 40	92 54 01 75 25	43 11 71 99 31
75 93 36 57 83	56 20 14 82 11	74 21 97 90 65	96 42 68 63 86	74 54 13 26 94
38 30 92 29 03	06 28 81 39 38	62 25 06 84 63	61 29 08 93 67	04 32 92 08 09
51 29 50 10 34	31 57 75 95 80	51 97 02 74 77	76 15 48 49 44	18 55 63 77 09
21 31 38 86 24	37 79 81 53 74	73 24 16 10 33	52 83 90 94 76	70 47 14 54 36
29 01 23 87 88	58 02 39 37 67	42 10 14 20 92	16 55 23 42 45	54 96 09 11 06

Directions: Having enumerated the population (in whatever order they happen to be listed) (say, N = 582), select at random any three columns (so as to allow for all cases); say, Columns 6, 7, and 8. Reading from page 1, individuals No. 373, 467, 227, 599 . . . would be part of the sample; 635 would be ignored since no one was assigned that number. The process would be continued—going on to the next page or any other 3-digit block—until the required sample size had been obtained.

would promote. A systematic sample is also unacceptable when the variable is increasing rapidly. If the sample consists of 1 case out of every 100, it would make a difference if the sample included Cases 1, 101, 201, 301, . . . or by contrast, Cases 99, 199, 299, 399, ...

One of the more questionable sampling practices is allowing the sample to select itself, as in the case of letters to the editor or incomplete questionnaire results. Also faulty is the practice of allowing the interviewer, or some expert, to select the sample on the basis of judgment. While this method is commonly used, especially in commercial polls, such an approach involves considerable risk, even when the investigator is trained and definite restrictions are imposed on his operations.

SAMPLING DESIGNS

Sampling designs range from very elementary to very elaborate sequential and multi-stage sampling designs. No perfect or universally adequate sampling design has, as yet, been devised. The method to be used in a given investigation depends on the nature of the problem, the subjects to be located, the resources available, as well as on such factors as cost and administrative convenience. Often a pilot study can save time and expense by uncovering potential sources of difficulty, and by providing the investigating staff with training both in statistics and in field work. Generally that method is best which gives the greatest degree of precision per unit of sampling cost, and the pilot study can help to obtain the values necessary for the derivation of the most effective design. It can be said that a sample is adequate when it is precise enough to allow the required confidence to be placed on the dependability of its results. More specifically, it is adequate when the standard error permits the bracketing of the population parameter within a band of precision sufficient to meet the requirements of the study.

Probability and Non-Probability Designs

Sampling designs can be classified into two broad categories: 1. *probability designs;* and 2. *non-probability designs.* In the former, randomness is the fundamental element of control. This was demonstrated in the binomial distribution based on the tossing of 10 coins a total of 1,024 times. Randomness causes such distributions to duplicate themselves time after time within random sampling errors as determined by formula. Such designs permit the specification of the precision that is obtained and the number of cases necessary to provide the required precision.

Non-probability designs, on the other hand, derive their control from the judgment of the investigator. For example, a pollster might be instructed to interview 100 persons passing a certain street corner, or to contact by phone so many storekeepers, so many housewives, so many clerks, etc. These cases are then selected on such bases as availability and interviewer judgment. Frequently, randomness is erroneously assumed to follow from the stratification of the population into relevant subpopulations. The advantage of non-probability designs lies largely in the area of convenience, which—along with the larger sample size sometimes possible for the same cost—is felt to compensate for the relative risk of possible bias. Commercial pools, for instance, frequently claim —with some degree of empirical justification—that the increase in the precision of probability sampling over non-probability sampling is too small to warrant the extra cost of a random sampling design, particularly since their procedures are adequate for present demands. The fact that the actual selection is done by experienced field workers is obviously involved in their relative success. Frequently, on the other hand, such samples are overweighted with the cooperative, the available, etc. They depend too exclusively on uncontrolled factors and, especially, on the investigator's insight, and there is no statistical procedure permitting the determination of the margin of sampling error.

Many people do not see the advantage of random sampling. It is their opinion that any person who has had vast experience in doing research can improve on chance in selecting a sample. This is, of course, erroneous. On the other hand, there are instances where the investigator does not want a representative sample, i.e. he does not want a sample that represents any particular population. In some studies—such as exploratory surveys in which the object is to obtain a wealth of ideas rather than simply a description of a given population—the investigator may choose as his sample only informed persons who can provide him with the maximum degree of insight into his problem. At times, it may be possible to combine probability and non-probability sampling. This complicates the statistical treatment of the resulting data, of course, and may add to the cost. It is possible that greater precision can be obtained for a given cost by simply taking a larger sample of a standard variety.

Simple, unrestricted random sampling is the least complex (probability) sampling design, calling for nothing more than selecting the required number of cases at random from the specified population. This can be done by using a table of random numbers, a roulette, or any haphazard scheme, or even a systematic design. It is also the most fundamental, inasmuch as it underlies most of the more advanced designs.

Stratified Sampling Designs

Stratified random sampling is a refinement of simple random sampling since, in addition to randomness, stratification introduces a secondary element of control as a means of increasing precision and representativeness. A stratified random sample is, in effect, a weighted combination of random subsamples combined to give an overall sample value. For instance, if we were to study the weight of the adult residents of a given island, perhaps with a view to a possible airlift, all one would have to do would be to take a completely random sample of the people regardless of sex, obtain the average per capita weight, and multiply by the total number to be evacuated. However, since men tend to weigh more than women, an error might be introduced if, by chance, we were to pick more (or less) than the proportionate number of men. The likelihood of a sizable error from this source is relatively small, since the basic elements of randomness would keep the sex ratio of the sample relatively coincident with that of the population. In general, where a sufficiently large sample is taken, a simple random sampling can be depended on to provide a usable answer. On the other hand, somewhat greater precision might be obtained if we were to make sure that the number of men and of women in our sample was proportional to the men-women ratio in the population (assuming this is known).

There may be times when it would be advantageous to take a disproportionate number of cases from the different strata. Sometimes the precision of a sample for a given cost can be increased by taking a smaller representation of the more homogeneous strata, and a larger sample of the more heterogeneous. Instead of taking a stratified sample in which the number in each of the strata are proportional to the number in the strata of the population, it is a rather common procedure, for example, to make the size of the sample per strata proportional to the product of the number and the standard deviation of the variable within each of the strata of the population. An even greater improvement over random sampling might be obtained by making the sampling in each of the strata proportional to the product of the number and the standard deviation of the strata in the population, and inversely proportional to the square root of the cost per sampling unit in that particular strata. One can also take a larger sample from the more doubtful strata, and then weight the mean of each of the strata according to their proportionality in the population. This would be desirable, for instance, in connection with the electoral college for the election of the President, where greater precision for a given sample size and cost would be obtained by sampling lightly the "obvious" states and more adequately the "doubtful" ones.

The usual stratification factors are sex, age, socio-economic status, educational background, residence (urban or rural), and occupation. Other factors which might be involved in special issues include political-party affiliation, religion, and race. Stratified sampling is generally difficult to conduct inasmuch as we rarely have a usable listing of each of the strata. On the other hand, it is generally not necessary to stratify on multiple bases inasmuch as these tend to be intercorrelated, and consequently, stratification on one or more of these factors will generally result in relatively adequate stratification on a number of other related factors.

Stratified random sampling provides more precise results than simple random sampling only if stratification results in greater homogeneity within the strata than would be found in the whole population taken as a unit. Stratification is profitable, in the sense of giving more precise results, whenever the population can be broken down into subpopulations with characteristic differences with respect to the trait under investigation. In the problem regarding the airlift, for example, one might profit from stratifying according to sex, since there is a characteristic sex difference with regard to weight. There would probably be no point in stratifying according to hair color since this appears to be independent of weight. Furthermore, even if we did find average differences in the weight of persons with different hair color, we would still have to determine the distribution of hair color in the population. This would, of course, increase the cost of our sample, and this would have to be balanced against the possibility of gaining more precise results by spending the same amount of money on getting a larger sample on the basis of simple random sampling.

Stratification is particularly appropriate in opinion polls where, on such issues as the appointment of Clare Boothe Luce as Ambassador to the Vatican, the expression of *strongly approve, approve, undecided, disapprove, strongly disapprove* might be related to such background factors as sex, political and religious affiliation, educational status, etc. There would be no point in stratifying with respect to a variable which is presumably unrelated to the issue under study—e.g., the month of birth. To be meaningful, the results of a study of this kind must be reported separately, according to strata, whenever characteristic differences exist among the subpopulations into which the population as a whole can be divided with respect to the issue under study.

It also must be pointed out that the stratification of the population according to such factors as sex is a matter of judgment based on evidence of a characteristic difference. However, once the strata are set, sampling within each of the strata must be at random in line with the principles presented in the previous sections, and it is a serious error to assume that stratification, as such, removes the need for random selection within the strata. On the contrary, it is stratification that is not essential to good sampling, for the basic element of control in sampling is randomness; stratification simply provides a secondary control.

Purposive Sampling

Purposive sampling can be considered a form of stratified sampling in that the selection of the cases is governed by some criterion acting as a secondary control. At one end of the continuum, we have the type of probability sampling illustrated by the standardization of the (1937) *Stanford-Binet*, in which the authors—on the premise that a correlation exists between socio-economic status and IQ, and that, therefore, any sample not representative of the population with respect to socio-economic status would also be suspect with respect to IQ—attempted to include a proportionate representation of each of the socio-economic strata of American society as revealed by the 1930 census.

Thus, the characteristic of socio-economic status acted as a secondary control in the selection of the sample.

Another form of purposive sampling is *quota sampling,* which is also a form of stratified sampling except that, as commonly used, the term refers to a nonprobability design in which the investigator, after having stratified his population, uses his judgment rather than randomness in selecting the cases. As such, it is, therefore, subject to the objection just presented. Generally, such sampling is best used where the object is not to get precise statistics, but rather to collect typical opinions on a given issue, or perhaps, in an exploratory study where the purpose is to develop insight so that later a more accurate study can be conducted with probability sampling. Quota sampling has advantages over probability sampling with respect to convenience. For instance, it permits the investigator to substitute one person for another in the case of a refusal. This does not solve the problem of the bias connected with non-response; it simply ignores it. According to the viewpoint expressed in this text, this represents over-confidence in the magic of having a given sample size, since ignoring bias is not the equivalent of resolving it.

Double Sampling

A rather frequent extension of the basic sampling design is multi-stage sampling, which is really a matter of sampling within samples. This might involve, for instance, sampling certain houses within certain blocks of a given city, or certain classrooms within certain schools. Another example might involve interviewing a few non-respondents to a questionnaire to determine the nature of the reactions of that particular segment of the overall sample, and then weighting their responses in order to give them fair representation in the final results of the total sample. It must, of course, be noted that double sampling complicates the statistical analysis of the data and increases the cost correspondingly.

In another form of the double sampling design, the investigator might select his sample on the basis of a characteristic which is readily available and highly correlated with the primary characteristic for which the collection of data is expensive and/or difficult. Since the two characteristics are correlated, an adequate sample with respect to the second characteristic should automatically be an adequate sample with respect to the first. Another variation of the double sampling design might involve obtaining the values of the primary characteristic by means of an equation relating it to a secondary characteristic for which an adequate sample can be readily obtained.

Cluster Sampling

A fundamental problem connected with sampling concerns the choice of the sampling unit. Although generally the sample is selected in units of one, this need not be so. In education it is frequently as easy to contact a whole classroom as it is to contact a single individual. A sampling design in which the unit of sampling consists of multiple cases—e.g., a family, a classroom, a school, or even a school system—is known as *cluster sampling.* Thus, in the standardization of the 1937 *Stanford-Binet,* Terman and Merrill selected a given community and tested every single child in that community who was within one month of his birthday.

Cluster sampling is particularly attractive from the standpoint of permitting the easy accumulation of large samples. This may be somewhat misleading, however, because, to the extent that the members of individual clusters are more homogeneous than an equal number of cases selected completely at random (i.e., to the extent that a positive intraclass correlation exists among the members), an overlapping effect takes place. Therefore, the effective number of cases from the standpoint of increasing the precision of the sample is somewhat less than the actual number of cases included.*

Nevertheless, even if a substantial intraclass correlation exists, a cluster sampling design generally is advantageous in that the loss of precision per individual case is more than compensated for by the possibility of taking larger samples for the same cost. It is agreed, however, that a sample obtained by taking a relatively large number of small clusters is preferable to a sample of equal size obtained from a small number of large clusters.

---

* The computation of the standard error in cluster sampling calls for a special formula which is somewhat more involved than that for the single sampling unit, especially when inequality in the size of the cluster is found. See Russell L. Ackoff, *The Design of Social Research* (Chicago: University of Chicago Press, 1953); Leon Festinger and Daniel Katz, *Research Methods in the Behavioral Sciences* (New York: Holt, Rinehart & Winston, 1965); or Eli S. Marks, "Sampling in the revision of the Stanford-Binet Scale," *Psychol. Bull.,* 44: 413–34; 1947.

Cluster sampling is independent of the other kinds and classifications of sampling designs, and one might sample in clusters according to a simple random sampling, a stratified random sampling, or any other sampling design. For example, in a study of high-school seniors, the sampling unit might be the English class; each English class in the state can be numbered; stratification can be made according to the size of the school; then, by means of random numbers certain English classes can be selected and tested as a unit.

Sequential Sampling

An interesting sampling design of somewhat recent origin is *sequential sampling* in which sampling is continued until a significant result on which to base a decision is obtained. For instance, a manufacturer who has devised a new light bulb would want to test it for life expectancy before placing it on the market. However, since testing the bulb implies its destruction, he would want to conduct the test as economically as possible. This he might do by testing, perhaps, fifty bulbs. If these proved to be significantly superior or inferior to the conventional bulbs, he would then have his answer. If, however, the test proved to be inconclusive, he could add, say, another fifty bulbs for an overall test of one hundred. This might provide a conclusive answer. If not, the test would be continued by the addition of one batch after another until the issue is settled one way or the other, at the lowest possible cost.

Sequential sampling introduces an interesting approach to research. Thus, instead of carrying out a study of five hundred cases, it might be advisable to carry, for example a five-stage sequential research program of one hundred cases each. If the first step provides a decisive answer, the study can be dropped immediately. If not, it can be continued until the answer is obtained, or until the five hundred cases are exhausted. In such an approach, if a basic flaw were to be found in the design of the study, the first stage could be considered a pilot study to the others, which would then be conducted on the basis of an improved design.

Synthesis

In summary, it might be repeated that there is no best sampling design. Validity of sample data, like validity of all data, is a specific concept to be evaluated from the standpoint of the specific case. It is, therefore, difficult to generalize. Nevertheless, it is generally true that the aspect of sampling to which investigators of educational problems might most profitably devote their attention is minimizing possible bias rather than devising complicated designs.

Highlights of the Chapter

1.   Research is invariably conducted on the basis of a sample from which inferences concerning the population can be derived. Sampling is both necessary and advantageous in the usual case. It is especially fundamental in survey research.

2.   If a sample is to serve as the basis for inferences concerning the population, it is essential that it be representative—i.e., that it be a replica—of the population in question. Since this principle is impossible to implement, statisticians have substituted the concept of randomness with the understanding that a random sample will provide statistics within random sampling errors of the corresponding population parameter. The magnitude of these errors can be estimated at any probability level, and the population parameter can, therefore, be estimated on the basis of probability to lie within specified intervals.

3.   A sample that is not representative can suffer from errors of a random and/or systematic nature and further from errors of sampling and/or measurement. Random errors of both sampling and measurement can be reduced to fractional values—even to the point of complete elimination—by increasing the sample size. Not only can their magnitude be estimated, but the size of the sample necessary to provide a desired degree of precision at a given probability level can be computed in advance if the sampling distribution of the statistic is known. Random errors can also be reduced through an improved sampling design. Constant errors, on the other hand, are simply stabilized (rather than eliminated) by taking even a substantial sample. Constant errors of measurement are not removed even by taking a complete census.

4.   The first problem in sampling is to define the population so that there is no doubt about who is to be included and to whom the results of the study are to apply.

5. A basic principle of sampling is that every member of the population must have an equal chance of being included in the sample. This immediately raises the complication that it is almost impossible to obtain an adequate listing of any population from which the sample might be selected. A somewhat more readily applicable principle of sampling is that there must be no logical connection between the method of sampling and the characteristic being sampled. Where the population can be enumerated, this principle is generally best implemented through the use of a table of random numbers.

6. Sampling can be based on a probability or a non-probability design. The latter derives its control from the judgment of the investigator; not only is it subject to serious error, but it does not provide the basis for calculating the magnitude of such error. Probability designs, on the contrary, derive their control from the concept of randomness and thus can provide an appraisal of random errors.

7. The basic sampling design is simple random sampling. Stratified sampling introduces a secondary control and provides greater precision in sampling whenever stratification results in greater homogeneity in the substrata with respect to the variable in question.

8. Cluster sampling is of interest to educational researchers who can frequently select their samples in units of a classroom as easily as in units of a single child.

9. A number of other sampling designs are possible, some of which are relatively complicated from the standpoint of both sampling and statistical treatment. In general, educational researchers might more profitably orient their efforts toward minimizing possible biases in sampling and measurement than toward experimenting with complex sampling designs.

Questions and Projects

1. Actually try tossing ten coins repeatedly to see how closely it would approximate the binomial distribution. Do the same with respect to two dice.

2. The U.S. Census reports are a source of fascinating data. Get acquainted with some of the data of relevance to education, e.g., the population in different age brackets, the educational attainment of Americans, etc.

3. Investigate the operation of the Gallup, the Harris, and other polls. Evaluate the influence they have had upon various aspects of American life.

Selected References

Abula-Ela, A.A. "Randomized response models for sample surveys of human populations," *Diss. Abstr.*, 27: 4012-B; 1967.

Cantril, Hadley. *Gauging Public Opinion*. Princeton: Princeton Univ. Press, 1947.

Cochran, William G. *Sampling Techniques*. New York: Wiley, 1963.

Cornell, Francis G. "Sampling methods," in Chester W. Harris (ed.) *Encyclopedia of Educational Research*. New York: Macmillan, 1960. pp. 1181-84.

Fiske, Donald W. and Lyle V. Jones. "Sequential analysis in psychological research," *Psychol. Bull.*, 51: 260-75; 1954.

Hansen, Morris H. "Modern methods in the sampling of human populations," *Amer. J. public Health*, 41. 662-68; 1951.

—— and William N. Hurwitz. "The problem of non-response of sample surveys," *J. Amer. stat. Assn.*, 41: 517-29; 1946.

—— et al. *Sample Survey Methods and Theory: 1. Methods and Applications; 2. Theory*. New York: Wiley, 1953.

Kendall, Maurice G. and B. Babington Smith. "Randomness and random sampling numbers," *J. Royal stat. Soc.*, 101: 147-56; 1938. (See also Suppl., 6: 51-61; 1939.)

Kish, Leslie. *Survey Sampling*. New York: Wiley, 1965.

McNemar, Quinn. "At random: Sense or nonsense," *Amer. Psychol.*, 15: 295-300; 1960.

Marks, Eli S. "Sampling in the revision of the Stanford-Binet Scale," *Psychol. Bull.*, 44: 413-34; 1947.

——. "Some sampling problems in educational research," *J. educ. Psychol.*, 42: 85-96; 1951.

Meier, Norman C. and Cletus J. Burke. "Laboratory tests of sampling techniques," *Public Opinion Quart.*, 11: 586-95, 1947; 12: 316-24, 1948.

Moonan, William J. "Some empirical aspects of the sequential analysis technique as applied to an achievement examination," *J. exper. Educ.*, 18: 195–207; 1950.

Rounding, Robert C. "A two-step sample size problem," *Diss. Abstr.*, 26: 1073; 1965.

Slonim, Morris J. "Sampling in a nutshell," *J. Amer. stat. Assn.*, 52: 143–61; 1957. (Also paperback; New York: Simon & Schuster, 1960.)

Stephan, Frederick F. "History of the uses of modern sampling procedures," *J. Amer. stat. Assn.*, 43: 12–39; 1948.

United States Department of Commerce, Bureau of the Census. *Population Estimates: Projections of the Population of the United States by Age, Sex, and Color to 1990, with Extensions of Population by Age and Sex to 2015.* Current Population Reports, Series P-25, No. 381. Washington: The Bureau, 1967.

———. *Population Estimates: Projection of Educational Attainment 1970 to 1985.* Current Population Reports, Series P-25, No. 390. Washington: The Bureau, 1968.

Van Dusseldorp, A. "A study of methods of gathering data for the Iowa State Department of Public Instruction through sampling," *Diss. Abstr.*, 26: 5796; 1966.

Each procedure that has been devised to produce scientific data does so by building certain constraints into what can take place and what can be observed. Consequently, the more precisely a technique can answer one kind of question, the more likely it will be that this same technique will give the wrong answer or actually obscure the answer to another type of question.——Ray Hyman (1964)

PART TWO

INTRODUCTION TO RESEARCH METHODS

Classification is inevitably an arbitrary process, resulting in a product of varying degrees of appropriateness and usefulness depending on the nature of the phenomena to be classified and the purposes to be served. The categorizing of educational research methods into logical and functional classes is doubly precarious because of the composite and overlapping nature of many of its procedures. Yet, despite this lack of clear-cut distinctions among the methods, it is desirable to attempt their classification for the insights into the overall organization and nature of educational research which such attempts provide.

That there is no natural system of classification of educational research methods which would cause each of the methods to fall neatly into place becomes evident when one considers the differences in the classification systems presented by the different authors of textbooks and articles in the field. As Barr (1960) points out, educational research methods can be categorized on the basis of end result (or goal), data-gathering technique, method of data-processing, degree of control exercised, approach, source of the data, and a number of other considerations. Educational research can also be classified as laboratory or field research, action or pure research, and, of course, according to such other dimensions as curriculum research, psychometric research, or sociometric research.

In practice, most authors agree on three basic categories:

1.   *Historical,* which is concerned with the past and which attempts to trace the past as a means of seeing the present in perspective.

2.   *Survey,* which is concerned with the present and attempts to determine the status of the phenomenon under investigation.

3.   *Experimental,* which is oriented toward the discovery of basic relationships among phenomena as a means of predicting and, eventually, controlling their occurrence.

This classification is based partially on time sequence though even more significant differences exist with respect to the purposes which the methods are to serve, the nature of the problems for which they are appropriate, and the procedures employed in the conduct of each.

This basic classification is used by Best (1959) in his text. Hillway (1956) adds a fourth category—the case study. Good and Scates (1954) also add a fourth category to cover the area of complex causal relationships. More specifically, they add research of a causal-comparative, correlational, case study, and genetic nature. Travers (1969), on the other hand, discusses essentially the same topics under a somewhat different organizational structure. Cornell and Monroe (1953) present a somewhat more complex system of classification: not only do they list five basic classes—descriptive, metric, clinical, correlational, and experimental—but they also mention as a possible sixth method: "theory construction or model building and the verification of theoretical systems."

The discussion of research methods in the present text will be organized according to the three basic categories outlined above. More specifically, the various educational research methods will be considered under the following headings:

Historical
    1.   historical
    2.   legal
    3.   documentary

Survey
    1.   descriptive
        (a)   survey testing
        (b)   questionnaire
        (c)   interview
    2.   analytical
        (a)   documentary-frequency
        (b)   observational
        (c)   rating
        (d)   critical incident
        (e)   factor analysis
    3.   school surveys
    4.   genetic

Experimental
    1.   simple experimental designs
    2.   multivariate analysis
    3.   case study
    4.   predictive (correlational)

The distinction between the various categories is, of course, imprecise, and the reader might be tempted to question the specific allocation of certain kinds of research to the particular category to which they have been assigned. From the standpoint of purpose —namely, determining the status of a given phenomenon—legal and documentary research are, for example, more closely related to survey than to historical research. On the other hand, the particular problems encountered, and the specific techniques to be applied in such research probably more closely resemble those of historical research, and, for the sake of organization, reader comprehension, and the avoidance of unnecessary repetition, they are discussed in that setting.

The particular allocation of the various methods to a category is a matter of judgment, and the classification of the different methods here is primarily a scheme for unified presentation rather than a rigid, mutually exclusive organization which is inherent in the different methods. In fact, though there are basic similarities in the methods grouped in each category, at times there are also considerable differences. No two problems can be solved in identically the same way; what constitutes the proper method for dealing with a specific problem can be decided only on the basis of its peculiarities. Furthermore, what is relatively the same analysis of essentially the same type of data might fall in one category or another depending on one's purpose. And, of course, a given method is frequently used in a subsidiary way in conducting research based on another classification —e.g., interviewing as a means of dealing with nonresponse in a questionnaire study.

No one system of classification can fit a field as complex as education. On the contrary, if they are to be effective in dealing with problems as complex as those in education, educational research methods must be varied, complex, and, inevitably, overlapping. This is especially true inasmuch as, at the present stage of its development as a science, education needs exploratory studies that have general significance in broad areas. Later, as the field becomes more clearly defined, it will become progressively more possible and necessary to emphasize controlled experimentation.

In a sense, it is relatively futile even to concentrate on the identification of research methods according to a rigid categorization. Our efforts might be more profitably directed toward seeing that the method used is in harmony with scientific principles and that it is adequate for the job. Conversely, any method, or any combination of methods, that leads to dependable generalization is automatically a good method. There is, however, a need to define and to evaluate the method used, and, as Hillway (1956) points out, if a researcher cannot describe his approach, chances are that his understanding of what he is doing is too vague and that his approach will prove ineffective. There is also the need for a thorough understanding of all research methods—with particular reference to their strengths, limitations, applicability, and appropriateness—for an inappropriate method can only lead to unsatisfactory results and disillusionment.

It is worthwhile to repeat that, while the methods listed entail obvious differences in purpose and approach, the significant aspect of the situation is their similarity as techniques of science. Despite their superficial differences, they qualify as research methods only as they adhere to the basic principles of science and scholarliness. This is demonstrated, in all research methods, by the precision with which the problem is formulated, the population defined, and the sample selected; the care with which the data are collected, validated, and interpreted; and the scholarship with which inferences are drawn and the report is written. It is only within the framework of this basic similarity that their differences exist.

8
HISTORICAL RESEARCH

Man is the only creature who is aware of and interested in his past.——James W. Thompson (1942)

Historical research is one of the most difficult types of investigation to conduct adequately. Although everyone is a "historian" in the sense of recalling and recounting what has occurred in the past, such "history" is typically at the level of the historical novel, the purpose of which is to entertain rather than to present historical truth. Rarely do such accounts meet the criteria of historical research which, if it is to be a science, must meet the same standards of excellence and scholarship as other forms of research.

THE NATURE OF HISTORICAL RESEARCH

In view of the ambiguity with which the term *history* is used, a brief overview or general orientation to its nature and development will be presented in order to place historical research in proper perspective. As used by the early Greeks, history meant an inquiry to establish what had actually happened, and, to some degree, history is still that branch of learning that studies and records past events. As it applies to research, history is primarily an inquiry, an attempt to discover what has happened. To historians of the later nineteenth century, this was its only function. They also believed that, by subscription to a scientific approach—reliance on dependable sources, the authentication of sources, and the validation of evidence through an elaborate system of internal criticism, together with as complete an objectivity as humanly possible—the past could be accurately reconstructed.

While some of these considerations are still valid today, few modern historians would be bold enough to claim that complete objectivity is possible—or perhaps even desirable. Nor do they ever hope to recreate the past as it actually happened. They no longer conceive of the function as that of recorders of past events who are concerned with the establishment of facts. More and more, the emphasis has been toward the interpretation of the data, toward giving meaning to the events described rather than simply producing an encyclopedic catalog of events. Many historians feel that overemphasis on facts is actually an obstacle to good history; facts must be selected for clarity and conciseness with respect to purpose as the criterion for their inclusion or omission. As Nash (1964) points out, "There is an increasing realization that interpretation is an essential aspect of historiography. 'Neutral' historians still exist, but they are becoming rarer." This places the historian on less sure ground; he must make certain that his conclusions are based on as verifiable data as he can gather. It is here that the historian stakes his claim to scholarliness.

The historian is inevitably influenced by some philosophy operating explicitly or implicitly in his interpretations. Historical philosophies generally fall into three major categories. The first interprets history as the expression of a plan or purpose set by divine or natural (scientific) law which simply leads man on to his destiny. The second conceptualizes civilization as a biological organism with the determinants of its development, achievements, and life span inborn. Finally, there is the humanistic view, which gives man an important role in determining his fate and that of the world in which he lives. The historian generally espouses a theoretical position and attempts to interpret his data with respect to the general positions listed above, or to some of the more specific theories, such as the scientific (technological), economic, geographic, "great man," or even the eclectic theory, in order to give meaning to the facts of history. Toynbee's interpretation of history, for example, stresses the indomitable quality of the spirit of man in overcoming difficulties and obstacles and postulates this trait as the basis for the flowering out of a civilization. He presents the history of the settlement of the North American continent in terms of this challenge-and-response theme.

Historical research can be classified according to 1. *approach*—e.g., the pragmatic approach used by Karl Marx to arrange all the facts of history to support his concept of socialism;

2. *subject*—e.g., the biography of a given person, the monography of a town, state, nation, or civilization, or, at a slightly higher level, the history of ideas, institutions, or trends; and 3. *technique*—i.e., based whether on documents or on relics.

Purposes of Historical Research

The purposes for which historical research is undertaken are probably as varied as the many individuals who engage in the activity. They can, however, be summarized into two major categories:

1. The foremost purpose of doing historical research is to gain a clear perspective of the present. Present problems—e.g., racial integration, or the recent opposition to federal aid to education—are understandable only on the basis of their historical background. Most current events have a past "history" and it is generally necessary for us to acquaint ourselves with this history if we are to appreciate their real significance. Historical research can provide us not only with hypotheses for the solution of current problems, but also with a greater insight into our culture and into the role which education is to play in the progress of society. Cremin (1961), for example, sees progressive education as the educational phase of the broader progressive movement which characterized American democracy a couple decades back. Likewise, Nash (1964) sees the conflict between a reverence for tradition and a desire for change as an important factor in some of the contemporary difficulties in Canadian education.

An understanding of the history of education should enable the educator to recognize fads and frills which are frequently advocated as the "just discovered" cures for educational ills when, in reality, they are simply rejuvenated versions of ideas tried years ago and found wanting. This does not mean that these ideas are not to be reconsidered, since changes in the interim may have put them in a new light, but it still should be noted that they are not new. Strict grading, for example, or the four-quarter school year are not inventions of the 1960's. An understanding of the historical background of education should provide American educators with a better perspective regarding the facts and values upon which important educational decisions can be based. Nash (1964), for example, cites Hawkins' book (1960) as an interesting example of the history of education, both in showing that many innovations are merely reintroductions of old ideas and in strengthening the hands of reformers by pointing to precedents for proposed reform. As Travers (1964) points out, such government leaders as Roosevelt and Churchill had a deep, scholarly interest in history, a knowledge which must have influenced their decisions. Travers suggests that the amateur reformers in the field of education would probably drop most of their plans for the remodeling of public education if they had a better understanding of the failure of such attempts in the past.

2. A common motive underlying historical research is the desire of the scientist to arrive at an accurate account of the past. This may involve nothing more than a scholarly interest in truth—i.e., the desire to know what happened and how, and why the men of the times allowed it to happen. There is even room for the scientist to be interested in giving an accurate account of the past without particular concern for its meaning for the present. On the other hand, the historian generally would not be satisfied with the mere discovery of truth, but would conceive his primary responsibility as a scientist to be the interpretation of the data in order to link the past to the present and to the future.

The Steps of Historical Research

Although slight adaptations from standard scientific methods need to be made because of its nature, historical research must meet the same criteria and generally follow the same procedures as the other forms of research.

1. The identification and delineation of the problem is frequently a difficult proposition, since it involves not only the location of a problem which has historical and current significance, but also the availability of adequate data. Many otherwise acceptable historical topics may have to be discarded because data simply are not available. Thus it might be a nice problem to determine conclusively the authorship of the Shakespearean plays, but probably little could be located that would add any light to the present uncertainty.

2. The collection of data may involve anything from digging up ancient ruins to stumbling on old documents, as in the case of the Dead Sea Scrolls. Although occasionally material may be found in old manuscripts located by chance,

most educational data probably have to be gathered in the routine fashion by going through minutes of meetings, diaries, etc.

3. The establishment of the validity of the data generally involves the dual process of first establishing the authenticity of the source, and then the validity of its contents.

4. The interpretation of the data must be made from the standpoint of whatever hypothesis or theory the data will most adequately support. Isolated facts have no meaning, and a mere listing of historical occurrences is not research. It is necessary that data be considered in relation to one another and synthesized into a generalization or conclusion which places their overall significance in focus.

HISTORICAL EVIDENCE

The Nature of Historical Evidence

The difficulty of deriving truth from historical evidence, and the methodical care used by historians in dealing with this fully recognized problem, must be realized if historical science is to be properly appreciated. The major problem is, of course, that the data on which such research is based are invariably relatively inadequate. Usually at the time a historical study is conducted, the sources are no longer available for complete investigation, and consequently much of the data has to be inferred—with all of the undependability this may entail. Lack of perspective, as well as lack of impartiality and disinterestedness, can, of course, make it equally difficult to deal with the more current events. Thus, in appraising the tons of data gathered during World War II, it would be difficult to maintain complete objectivity, especially with regard to events in which people are emotionally involved or which concern persons who are still living. Likewise, the exact circumstances attending the attack on Pearl Harbor or the assassination of President Kennedy, if known, may never be made public. Fear of a lawsuit may likewise deter historians from publishing evidence of wrongdoing by a public figure, for example.

The date of the occurrence of a given event is often difficult to determine, partly because of the confusion arising from the change to the present Gregorian calendar. The calendar was revised in the sixteenth century by Pope Gregory XIII, but the revision was not accepted in British countries until 1752, at which time the current calendar was eleven days behind the Gregorian calendar. As a result, we recognize Washington's birthday as February 22, even though, according to his family Bible, his birthdate was February 11. There was no year 0; the new calendar merely skipped from 1 B.C. to 1 A.D. Furthermore, there are reasons to believe that Jesus Christ was born in 7 B.C. rather than in the year 1.

It is frequently difficult to determine the date when a certain university was established, for it may have operated on a semiorganized basis, or at a lower level of education, for a number of years before it became fully chartered as an institution of higher learning. Or it may not have had any students or even its own physical plant for a number of years, even after the charter was granted. Brickman (1949) gives instances of a degree-granting college arbitrarily choosing as its official opening date, the date on which it first began as an elementary school.

The term *first* is also troublesome. For instance, the first psychological laboratory in America is variously credited to J. McKeen Cattell and William James, depending on whether keeping experimental animals in the basement constitutes a laboratory. Similarly, which school qualifies as the first *normal* school depends on whether we are thinking of the first school to perform the functions of a normal school, or whether we insist that it be chartered by the state under that title.

Sources of Historical Evidence

Historical sources may be classified in two major categories—*documents* and *relics* (or remains)—according to whether or not the source was intended to transmit the information, or whether it is simply an artifact. Documents are usually written, whereas relics, e.g., archaelogical remains such as tools and utensils, are not. But this is not the basic point of distinction. A letter written by Lincoln, for example, would be a document from the standpoint of the information it contains, but would be a relic from the standpoint of spelling errors, handwriting, or other features that provide information apart from the message Lincoln wished to convey.

Among the various documentary sources, we may list: 1. official records—minutes of meetings, committee reports, and legal documents; 2. institutional records—attendance rolls, university bulletins, etc.; 3. memoirs, biographies, diaries, personal letters, books on the philosophy of a given scholar; etc. There are, of course, a number of limitations inherent in each of these sources. In the wording of laws that are finally passed, for instance, there is a suggestion of unanimous agreement, whereas violent discussions may have preceded their acceptance and many modifications and amendments may have been suggested, until, eventually, a compromise was reached—perhaps to no one's liking. The policies listed in university bulletins frequently are nullified through numerous exceptions. In the memoirs of faculty members, occurrences of many years past frequently take on a new light as the author sees his career in retrospect. Manuscripts are frequently subjected to so many editorial changes that they no longer resemble their original form. Newspaper reports of educational events are particularly subject to distortion, either through careless reporting or through emphasis on the sensational, with a corresponding disregard of the educationally significant aspects of the situation.

Primary and Secondary Sources

The historian, evaluating the adequacy of his evidence, must distinguish between evidence from a primary source—i.e., data provided by actual witnesses to the incident in question—and evidence from secondary sources in which a middleman has come between the original witness and the present consumer. Secondary sources are subject to an inherent danger of inaccuracy; whenever evidence is transmitted from one person to another, it tends to become distorted. At times, such evidence represents nothing more than unverified hearsay or rumor. For this reason, reliable historians insist on primary sources wherever possible, using secondary sources only as hypotheses to bridge the gaps between the various pieces of primary evidence.

The historian, having to rely on secondary sources, must be fully aware of their limitations. When numerous gaps in the primary evidence cause overreliance on secondary sources, he should probably refrain from attempting the study at all. Unavailability of primary sources is a particular problem in education where, surprisingly enough, only fragmentary reports concerning the process of education are available. It seems that people in the past considered education so fundamental and so commonplace that they did not bother recording anything about its nature or its organization. Consequently, it is relatively difficult to locate suitable evidence to permit the conduct of a good historical study in education. Such personal documents as diaries and letters likewise leave too many gaps for the historian to get the required continuity without having to rely unduly on secondary sources and his own imagination.

On the other hand, though it is true that frequently what is called history is so far removed from the original source and so carelessly compiled that it is unacceptable, it is also true that secondary sources are sometimes particularly accurate. If the historian has an adequate insight into the situation so that he can balance one secondary source against another, he may come much closer to the truth than if he relied on a single original source. We frequently listen to news commentators for an orientation to a message from the President, for example. Because of their background, commentators are frequently able to synthesize significant factors in the situation and present a much clearer picture than could be obtained by most people from a first-hand report. For the same reason, it may be better to read a translation of a given passage than to read the original in a foreign language. It should also be understood that secondary sources often become more accurate with the passage of time, as historians gain impartiality as well as perspective and, of course, as more data become available. The historian, therefore, does not ignore or reject secondary sources; he investigates any lead he can uncover, but he does not accept anything until he has investigated its validity.

Criticism of Historical Data

Historians, fully aware of the limitations of the data with which they have to deal, have developed systematic means of evaluating such evidence. This evaluation involves the dual process of establishing the authenticity of the source and also the validity of its content. These are known as *external* and *internal* criticism, respectively, though the terms *lower* and *higher* criticism are also used.

The historian must first establish the authenticity of his sources. Stated negatively, he must save himself from being the victim of a fraud, such as those which have at times been perpetrated not only on the public but even on scientists. A classic example of such a fraud is the Cardiff Giant, presumably the fossilized skeleton of a prehistoric human monster, found near Syracuse in 1869. Cleverly made out of gypsum at the request of a farmer and buried in a spot where it would be found by well-diggers, it was acclaimed, even by some reputable scientists, as genuine. The fraud was finally exposed by a newspaper reporter who was able to establish that a shipment of gypsum had been made to a certain barn prior to the discovery of the skeleton and who secured a confession from one of the participants.

The motives that impel individuals to perpetrate frauds range from those involving monetary gain and personal glory to adventure and misguided humor. Frauds are common in the field of art, for example, where duplicate paintings of the masterpieces have been passed off as originals—at considerable profit. Likewise, it can be said that if all the pieces of the original Cross that have been sold to unsuspecting tourists along the Mediterranean were to be placed together they would form a very big cross, indeed. Also common are literary frauds, in which alleged letters or manuscripts of famous people are suddenly "discovered" and sold at a handsome profit, even to relatively sophisticated amateurs. Among these was a series of forged letters purporting to be the correspondence between Abraham Lincoln and Ann Rutledge, which was sold to the *American Monthly* in 1928. Fortunately, frauds in education have so far been relatively rare—probably because of the lack of financial incentive.

The detection of fraud is a highly developed science, involving everything from logic to the use of the most sensitive devices of modern science. For example, the philologist can detect frauds on the basis of the changes in the meaning of words over the years. Forgeries have been exposed through their use of words that were not yet coined or were obsolete at the time the document is alleged to have been written. A person, event or object that is chronologically misplaced, e.g., Lincoln's alleged reference to the state of Kansas at a time when the state did not exist, is a slip that can be detected through the science of anachronism. Fraudulent documents can sometimes be identified by dating the document through the chemical analysis of the paper, the water mark, the ink, or by investigating the spelling and the language in use at the alleged time of publication. Ultraviolet rays and fluorescent photography can be used to detect erasures and alterations in manuscripts. The fluorine and Carbon-14 tests can be used to establish the age of fossils and other remains. It is, however, likely that the best tool in the detection of frauds is the investigator's common sense, combined with a healthy sprinkling of skepticism.

Although, theoretically, the primary purpose of external criticism is the establishment of historical truth rather than the detection of fraud, its actual operation is largely restricted to the negative role. In fact, external criticism, in common with many other aspects of science, cannot "prove" the genuineness of a particular source except on the basis of plausibility and probability.* The matter is complicated further by the fact that imitators are fully aware of the means of detecting frauds so that, like counterfeiters of money, they make extremely clever forgeries. Furthermore, the range of their operation as it affects the historical researcher is much greater than in the case of counterfeit money and the frauds in question do not get the constant "expert" surveilance given to currency.

Among the more common problems encountered in establishing the authenticity of documents are plagiarism, alterations of documents, insertions, deletions, and even unintentional omissions. Biographies, for example, often attribute witty sayings to famous people who somehow always have the right word at the right time. Before being made part of the record, speeches are often reviewed for grammatical errors and, in some cases, for alteration of content. Such modifications can be found even in the *Congressional Record* (which, incidentally, also contains records of "speeches" that were never given on the floor, complete with applause). The relatively common practice of having reports ghost-written also causes difficulty; it is felt, for instance, that Washington's inaugural address was written by Jefferson. In fact, a government or a business executive may incorporate in a report material compiled by different subordinates—perhaps with different writing styles—which might lead later historians to suspect forgery or alteration of the original document.

Even more crucial from the standpoint of the basic purpose of science—the discovery of truth—is the establishment of the validity of the content of a document or source, regardless of its authorship or genuineness. This is frequently no simple

---

* The computer provides an interesting way of establishing authorship through the frequency of the appearance of prepositions, conjunctions, articles, and other discriminating stylistic details and features which characterize the writings of a given author.

achievement. For example, changes have occurred in older documents as a result of errors, omissions, additions, and transpositions in transcribing. Before the advent of printing, each document had to be copied by hand, and, though much of this was done with particular care by monks and other scholars, occasional errors crept in. These documents frequently were transcribed from copy to copy so that the document now available may be many times removed from the original—which may have been lost or simply destroyed. For example, we do not have an original copy of Chaucer's tales.* Furthermore, as the documents were copied over the centuries, interpretive notes placed in the margin by one scholar may have been included as part of the regular text when it was copied by the next scholar, so that the final copy, though genuine as a whole, may have any number of parts that were not in the original.†

In addition to copying errors, translation of some of the documents from one language to another, or from an earlier to current usage, may have resulted in distortion in meaning. Even contemporary writers in one's own language are frequently difficult to understand; many of them cannot be taken literally and can be understood only through knowledge of their style of writing. And, of course, the problem is not made any easier when socio-economic and cultural differences—with local idioms and slang expressions—are introduced. *Public schools* and *football* mean different things to British and American writers; American educators don't always mean the same thing when they talk about *team teaching* or the *ungraded school.*

The establishment of the general reputation, integrity, and competence of its author are of particular importance in determining the validity of the content of a historical document. At this point, internal and external criticisms are interdependent and complementary processes. For example, a document is less suspect if it can be established that it was written by Abraham Lincoln, George Washington, or some person in high office on a topic with which he was familiar. If, on the other hand, the witness is suspected of bias, or considered a poor observer because of errors

* Interesting in this connection is the recent discovery (1967) of two of Chopin's waltzes (Waltz in G Flat Major, Opus 70, No. 1, and Waltz in E Flat, Opus 18). These manuscripts bear Chopin's signature and are apparently authentic. They do differ noticeably from their counterparts that have been played these many years.

† Modern photocopying processes are a great help in this regard.

he is known to have made in similar circumstances, his testimony must be severely questioned—and, of course, more readily rejected. In a sense, this is similar to the situation in a court of law, and the student might profit from developing the parallel. Thus, the testimony of a reputable person in the area of his competence is generally accepted, while the witness found lying, even in part, is frequently discredited *in toto*. Of course, the historian cannot accept or reject an entire document because one part is correct or erroneous; he must appraise each fact by itself. Such questions as: Was the witness in a position to observe? Was he mentally competent? Did he stand to gain from his testimony or was he a disinterested observer? and so on, can help determine the acceptability of the testimony. On the other hand, the point can be carried too far; even the most adequate witness is sometimes in error, and conversely, the most disreputable witness tells the truth occasionally. Even a clock that is stopped is right twice a day!

Historians make extensive use of the concept of motives. The fact that behavior is purposive, rather than accidental, is an important tool historians use in interpreting historical events. It is understandable that the superintendent reporting on a controversy is likely to present his side in the best light, especially in his annual report where he can take advantage of hindsight to second-guess the event. Or, on the other hand, he may take the blame in order to protect others. In reporting to the public, he is likely to dwell on his successes rather than his failures. Critics of education, on the other hand, are likely to be basing their criticisms on their experiences in school years ago or on stories brought home by their children. The historian must recognize that behavior springs from a multiplicity of motives, and that using a single motive as his basic theme (e.g., Caesar's ambition or Hitler as a revengeful, power-hungry madman) will often provide a false perspective. A biography may present the picture of a politician as a ruthless pursuer of power, a humanitarian totally committed to the improvement of social conditions, or a scientist completely dedicated to the discovery of truth, as if the person's whole life centered around this one point.

The circumstances under which a document was written are also important. Frequently people are in a position in which they cannot be completely candid. People in public life often make very complimentary remarks, e.g., "I have the fondest feelings for the Honorable Senator . . . ," a statement which may have little bearing on the true feelings of the speaker. In the same way, political opponents may attack each other viciously in public and yet be very close friends in private. Biographies are particularly suspect from the standpoint of accuracy, especially if the subject is still alive. In fact, in evaluating biographical documents, the relationship of the writer to the subject must be fully explored. If he is to place proper interpretation on his findings, the historian must also analyze the motives of the writer. These may range all the way from monetary reward—though education is relatively free from this incentive—to friendship or enmity. It is generally accepted that the more disinterested the writer, the more likely he is to give a faithful reproduction of the facts.

Autobiographies are even more suspect. If the source is published after the death of the author, it is difficult to verify what a dead person has said, or even to know if what he recounts is something that he witnessed himself or information that he obtained secondhand. He may be taking full credit for events in which he was involved only as a very minor participant, or perhaps simply as a bystander. Thus, John Smith is generally considered such a braggart that historians question very seriously his story of Pocahontas. Here again, the general credibility of the author is frequently an important clue to the validity of the content.

The validity of a historical "fact" can sometimes be verified by comparing it with the statements of other authors, though agreement may mean nothing more than that they have obtained their information from the same, and perhaps erroneous, source. Thus, the common belief that the Declaration of Independence was signed on July 4, 1776 does not deny the fact that most of the signing was done on August 2, 1776. Likewise, there are tons of data in the Communist countries blaming Western imperialism for all the tensions of the world. When there is disagreement among authors, the historian must establish which, if any, is correct. This he attempts to do on the basis of overall plausibility, reputation, independent corroboration, and general compatability with other known facts. The story of the Dutch boy with his finger in the dyke, for example, stands up better as entertainment for naive children than it does as a historical fact.

The matter of numbers in historical writings is particularly bothersome. Not only are dates undependable, but it is generally accepted that numbers used in documents, even as late as the Middle Ages, are so unreliable that they are relatively meaningless. That Methuselah allegedly lived to the age of 969 means relatively little. The number 20 is used in Chaucer in the sense of many, and even today such expressions as 1001 cannot be taken literally. Similarly, statistics on enrollment, population, library holdings, etc. cannot always be accepted at face value. When there are conflicts between sources, one must depend on general credibility and give preference to the source with the greatest plausibility from the standpoint of internal consistency and agreement with other accepted facts. It is rather inconceivable, for example, that Xerxes' army numbered nearly two million men as reported; it would have taken almost forever to get that many men through the Pass of Thermopylae.

It is evident that historical research is an exacting task calling for a high level of scholarship. Invariably, the historian will have to rely partially on sources that he can no longer verify; on many occasions he will have to rely on inferences based upon logical deduction in order to bridge gaps. At times, the historian will be unable to verify or to discredit the evidence before him, and yet he has to accept it or reject it. In such cases, it is probably best for him to preface his remarks with the phrase "according to . . . ," and thus safeguard his reputation and avoid the misuse of his status as a scientist by misleading his readers.

If he is to be successful in grasping the true significance of his data, inadequate as they might be, the historical researcher must possess a rich fund of historical as well as general knowledge. He particularly needs an intelligent understanding of human nature, a keen mind, good common sense, and a strong grasp of both the present and the past. It is particularly important that he have good historical perspective. As Whitehead (1954) points out:

> The more history I read, the less I think of historians. Most of them strike me as men who presume to write authoritatively about events which they are not qualified to understand. Or else they accept the official documents of the epoch at their face value, omitting to reflect that its real significance lay in the emotional atmosphere which activated its people and the general ideas under whose sway they lived.

INTERPRETATION OF HISTORICAL DATA

Facts have no meaning in and of themselves. Having established the authenticity and validity of his facts, the historian must, therefore, address himself to the even more fundamental task of interpreting these facts in the light of his problem. In this, he must be especially aware of the limitations of his data. Because of the relative incompleteness and unverifiability of historical evidence, the interpretation of its significance requires the historian's greatest ingenuity and imagination, as well as caution, insight, and scholarliness. This constitutes a major test of his claim to scientific status. His first task is that of making sense out of the multitude of facts he has gathered, an operation which generally calls for a synthesis of data in relation to a hypothesis or theory rather than mere accumulation or summary. And yet he must avoid the undue projection of his personality onto the data and avoid fitting the data to his particular point of view to the disregard of a more logically parsimonious structure.

Causation is a troublesome concept in science; it is doubly so in historical research where "causes" are in the nature of antecedents, or precipitating factors, rather than "causes" in the restricted scientific sense. Historical causes are invariably complex, and a common error in interpretation is oversimplification. Since history is primarily a record of human behavior, causes in history are often best considered from the standpoint of the motives of the participants; the cause of World War II, for example, might be found in the motives underlying the behavior of Hitler and his Nazi followers. However, behavior is invariably based on a multiplicity of interacting motives of different vector strength, a fact which makes the task of the historian relatively difficult, and which suggests training in the dynamics of human behavior as necessary background.*

The historian must be cautious in his use of analogy as a source of hypothesis or as a frame of reference for interpretation. Because of the complexity of historical data, it is generally possible to draw parallels between one historical event and any number of others. Thus, the current administration, for example, can be compared to any one of the previous administrations from

---

* The task of the historian in placing historical events into perspective is complicated by the possibility of simple accident or happenstance.

one standpoint or another, and historical parallels can be oriented in a number of directions depending on the historian's viewpoint. In the late thirties, a parallel was often drawn between Spartan and Nazi education, for example. Any such comparison is invariably characterized as much by exceptions and differences in certain aspects, as it is by similarities in others, so that any attempt at extrapolation is risky. It is also imperative that the historian not interpret data of different cultures or different historical periods from the standpoint of his personal standards—which, of course, do not apply. For example, it is very difficult for modern man to put the brutality of the Middle Ages in proper focus.

The historian's goal, then, is not only to establish facts but also to determine trends which the data may suggest and generalizations which can be derived from the data. His task is one of synthesis and interpretation, rather than mere summation. This calls for some frame of reference, and, of course, it must be recognized that historians differ in their interpretations of the same facts. The present Vietnam conflict, for example, is the subject of major disagreement with respect to both the specific events and their interpretation—a disagreement resulting from the superimposition of different frames of reference on a somewhat confused set of data rather than from a deliberate attempt at distortion.

THE WRITING OF THE REPORT

The writing of the historical report is a task involving the highest level of scholarship. While conducting and reporting research is never simple, it is doubly difficult in the field of history where so much depends on the ingenuity and the scholarliness of the investigator. Because of the relative lack of conclusive evidence on which valid generalizations can be established, it is accepted that the writing of historical research has to be a little freer in allowing a somewhat greater reliance on subjective interpretation of data. This does not, however, condone the distortion of the truth. Though the approach to the collection of data needs to be flexible, it must be sufficiently systematic to prevent unnecessary gaps or omissions.

The discontinuous and incomplete nature of historical evidence places a particular burden on the investigator to provide the required continuity. At the same time, it allows him to demonstrate his scholarship through his insights into his subject, the plausibility and clarity of his interpretations, the ingenuity and creativity which he brings to the solution of his problem, and the adequacy of the writing of his report. But it also increases the danger of error, and if the gaps are such that an attempt at interpretation is unsafe, the historian must be careful not to part company with his scholarship. He may either indicate that the gaps exist and stop there, or he may suggest a number of alternate interpretations. He may even leave the task of presenting his data to the more reckless historical writer.

Although the historian is not permitted liberties with the truth, historical presentations need not be dull nor cumbersome. The historian, concerned over historical accuracy, may feel compelled to point out that Columbus is *alleged* to have landed on what is now Watling Island rather than make the simple statement, Columbus discovered America. Gottschalk (1950) feels that, though commendable, such precision is hardly warranted. Since one can say even dull things in an interesting way, there is no justification for writers to get bogged down in battles and discoveries—in "the same slough of uninspired verbiage." When the facts are such that they must be qualified so repeatedly that they would make cumbersome reading, the solution might again be to pass the task on to the historical writer, who is not subject to the same restrictions as the historical researcher.

HISTORICAL RESEARCH: IS IT SCIENTIFIC?

An issue which has been raised repeatedly—though perhaps not always profitably—concerns the scientific status of historical research. The question is essentially academic; it is considered here for whatever light it sheds on the nature of the historical method. The issue centers around the definition of terms and the criteria used. The status of historical research as a scientific endeavor can hardly be questioned, if the criteria are defined in terms of its reliance on critical methods of discovery and of scholarship. If, on the other hand, we insist that science be oriented toward the discovery of laws capable of conclusive verification, historical research probably does not qualify as a science. There are three main tasks in historical research: 1. the collection of data; 2. the treatment and interpretation of the data; and 3. the derivation of conclusions and generalizations. From a strict point of view, historical research can be criticized for failure to meet the criteria of science in all three.

1. The Collection of Data Historical data, as the basis for historical generalizations, are not comparable to the materials of the physical sciences. They have to be reconstructed, in many cases, from rather nebulous and essentially unverifiable sources. Historical facts are not "knowable" in the same sense as the facts of the physical sciences; they have to be inferred and accepted on the basis of plausibility. Also, though the scientific method attempts to arrive at a workable hypothesis on the basis of a comparison of a sufficiently large number of samples, historical research is generally based on unique events which occurred but once and which cannot occur again.

2. The Treatment and Interpretation of the Data The natural sciences are oriented toward experimentation. Historical problems, on the other hand, since they deal with unique events, are verifiable only on the basis of logical deduction. It is very difficult for the historian to make an adequate analysis of diaries, letters, etc.; often he must deal with a profusion and complexity of data produced under varying conditions of insight and incentive. Interpretation of the present is difficult, especially when satire, allusions, metaphors, and other figurative liberties are involved. It is even more difficult to deal with a different period of history and/or a different national or cultural group—which automatically introduces such complications as translation, differences in the use of words, and differences in customs and mental outlook.

3. The Products of Historical Research Historical research can also be criticized from the standpoint of the products it seeks to provide. Research is oriented to the derivation of laws and principles expressing certain regularities among phenomena. This borders on the concept of causation, which is especially confusing in the case of historical events. Thus, the assassination of Archduke Ferdinand can be considered the precipitating "cause" of World War I—just as perhaps marriage may be considered the only readily identifiable "cause" of divorce. Or, as Bertrand Russell

(1953) suggests, Eli Whitney can be considered the "cause" of the War between the States, since his invention of the cotton gin led to a renewed interest in slavery—but this is not the whole story.

In the physical sciences, the goal of the researcher is the derivation of verifiable conclusions that can eventually become laws. Generalizations of historical evidence, on the other hand, since they are based on unique events, are relatively meaningless. In fact, the concept of historical "laws" is perhaps self-contradictory. Of course, this point of view can be challenged on the grounds that the distinction between physical and historical laws is essentially a matter of degree rather than of kind. Certain laws of a historical nature—e.g., the law of supply and demand, the law of diminishing returns, and many others—possess the same basic properties as other scientific laws.

In summary, historical research can be considered lacking in a number of the characteristics of the scientific method, interpreted in its narrow sense. For that matter, many aspects of educational and sociological research today do not meet the strict requirements of science as defined by the physical sciences. On the other hand, a number of historical facts have been established beyond reasonable doubt: it is accepted that Christopher Columbus discovered America, that the Pilgrim Fathers landed at Plymouth Rock on December 21, 1620, that the Chinese invented gunpowder, that the Lincoln–Ann Rutledge letters are fabrications, and that Wild Bill Hickok died in Tombstone from a bullet in the back. In fact, as pointed out by Gottschalk (1950), the amazing thing is not that historians disagree but that they agree as much as they do. Indeed, the ingenious, systematic, and painstaking way in which they have proceeded in deciphering the Rosetta Stone or in establishing the historical existence of Moses, or the authorship of the Shakespearian plays reflects a fascinating degree of scholarship. It does not make sense to reject historical research as unscientific, and then, just because their results are amenable to the legerdemain of statistical treatment, to brand as scientific questionnaire studies, with their usual inadequacy in the areas of non-return, misinterpretation, and other inherent weaknesses—or, for that matter, experiments dealing with trivial problems.

Historians do find a common ground with other scientists in the scholarly nature of their efforts to seek truth within the framework of the data with which they have to deal. Historical research must adhere to the same principles and practices and the same scholarship and accuracy which characterize all scientific research. More specifically, the historian as a scientist must show a complete mastery of his material. He must display originality, ingenuity, creativity, and critical insight into the meaning of facts, and he must maintain the usual scientific objectivity, for, though many gaps in the data will have to be filled according to his best judgment, he is still bound by the rules of science.

At all times, the historian must operate inductively— i.e., rather than starting with a hypothesis and then marshalling the facts to support it, he must rely on deduction only to check the plausibility of his hypothesis or tentative generalization. In connection with the hypothesis that certain plays were written by a young playwright from Stratford named William Shakespeare, for example, one might reason deductively that, in order to have been the author, Shakespeare would have had to be rather well-educated. Such deductive reasoning can, of course, lead to the rejection of certain hypotheses, and thus orient the investigation toward more fruitful leads. Finally, the historical report must meet the usual standards of scientific and scholarly writing.

Because of the relative unavailability of adequate data and its excessive reliance on subjectivity, historical research has fallen into some degree of disrepute, and the choice of a historical problem for a doctoral dissertation has, in general, been discouraged. This is unfortunate for, along with philosophical research, historical studies can make a significant contribution by providing a perspective on many educational problems in relation to which we must constantly make important decisions. Whether the neophyte has the necessary background and insight to make such a contribution is, perhaps, another matter.

CRITERIA OF HISTORICAL RESEARCH

A number of criteria on the basis of which historical research may be evaluated can be obtained readily from the preceding discussion. A few of the major points are included in the following checklist.

1. PROBLEM. Has the problem been defined clearly? It is difficult enough to conduct historical research adequately without adding to the confusion by starting out with a nebulous problem. Is the problem capable of solution? Is it within the competence of the investigator?

2. DATA. Are data of a primary nature available in sufficient completeness to provide a solution, or has there been an overdependence on secondary or unverifiable sources?
3. ANALYSIS. Has the dependability of the data been adequately established? Has the relevance of the data been adequately explored?
4. INTERPRETATION. Does the author display adequate mastery of his data and insight into their relative significance? Does he display adequate historical perspective? Does he maintain his objectivity? Are his hypotheses plausible? Have they been adequately tested? Does he see the relationship between his data and other "historical facts?"
5. PRESENTATION. Does the style of writing attract as well as inform? Does the report make a contribution on the basis of newly discovered data or new interpretations, or is it simply "uninspired hackwork?" Does it reflect scholarliness?

CLASSICAL STUDIES IN HISTORICAL RESEARCH

The most significant discovery of historical data in recent years is, undoubtedly, that of the Dead Sea Scrolls which have been confirmed as genuine documents left by Jewish tribes at the approximate time of Christ. The first scrolls were discovered in 1947, but did not become usable until 1956 when scientists devised a process of spraying them with glue and baking them so that they could be sawed open and photographed without disintegrating. They constitute a significant contribution to the understanding of the Jews of that particular period of history as a background for the introduction of Christianity.

The deciphering of Egyptian hieroglyphics through the Rosetta Stone by Champollion (1822) opened for scientific study the whole of early Egyptian civilization. Important in our own country's history is the Kensington Stone found in Minnesota in 1898. Considered a fraud for some years—and, at one time, used as a doorstop—it is now accepted as valid evidence of the presence of Norwegian nationals in the Midwest in an early period of American history.

Although no such spectacular historical "discoveries" are to be found in the field of education, special mention must be made of Cubberley's *Public Education in the United States* (1947), which gives a comprehensive coverage of the various movements in American education and their sociological and philosophical significance. Graves' *A History of Education* (1909, 1910, and 1913) gives a correspondingly adequate coverage of world education from early times to the present. A more recent publication (1961) is Cremin's *Transformation of the School: 1876–1957.*

DOCUMENTARY RESEARCH

Very closely related to historical research is documentary research—i.e., research based on documents and records. Generally speaking, documentary research differs from historical research in that it usually excludes remains as a source of evidence, and, conversely, may include the study of contemporary documents, such as might be involved in deciphering enemy codes. On the other hand, this distinction is not always clear-cut or binding.

The location of documents is often a chance affair. Many stories are told of famous letters and other documents retrieved from attics or junk dealers and, not infrequently, from the edge of the furnace. More typically, it involves a great expenditure of time, energy, and effort, as well as ingenuity, in tracing one lead after another until documents are located and, frequently, a great deal of persuasion before they are obtained for study.

The crucial aspects of documentary research, like those of historical research, are validating the data and interpreting their significance. Legal documents tend to be dependable, but ordinary records frequently are in considerable error. Statistical data are not always comparable; in devising an index of business conditions, for instance, one frequently finds sizable discrepancies over the years in such things as whether office workers in industrial firms are included among *industrial workers*, whether sales data are adjusted for seasonal variations, etc. College enrollment figures or library holdings are rarely comparable from school to school. The problem is even greater when the data are obtained from different documentary sources. The federal government has established considerable uniformity in the data it reports, but there is no such uniformity in local data or in data collected by various industrial or commercial agencies. The problem becomes even more complicated when foreign nations are involved. Infant mortality rates in certain undeveloped nations appear to be abnormally low, for example, simply because the birth and death of many infants are never officially recorded.

Bibliographical Research

Bibliographical research is oriented toward the integration and synthesis of a given problem. In a sense, therefore, such research resembles a term paper, except that it is more critical and on a higher level of significance, comprehensiveness, and complexity. Generally, it is frowned on as a doctoral dissertation. On the other hand, such a study conducted by a person with considerable insight into the overall problem can frequently make a significant contribution to education by structuring the field and identifying the areas in need of further investigation. A great deal can be gained, for example, by having someone clarify various educational issues. Bibliographic research deserves a better status than it has had. However, it is difficult to conduct, particularly by a graduate student who is not likely to have the degree of insight necessary to do such a study justice. For that reason, the general reluctance of graduate faculties to accept bibliographic studies in fulfillment of the research requirements for the degree is probably justified.

Legal Research

In view of the legal responsibilities connected with the various aspects of managing the school, legal research is of particular interest not only to school administrators, but also, in various degrees of directness, to every member of the profession. Is the chemistry teacher responsible for accidents occurring in his laboratory? Is the football coach responsible for an injury to a player? Can a teacher detain a student so long that he will miss his bus? These are some of the questions which require answers, and, though answers are available, they are generally complex and involve a number of provisos, special considerations, and technicalities.

Legal research is subject to the same general requirements as are other forms of research. In nature, it most closely resembles bibliographical research. The task is to summarize pertinent statutes, to trace further legal developments through related court decisions, and finally to analyze the decisions in the light of the problem being investigated. The last step is the writing of the report to convey legal information to educators and laymen who are not themselves legally trained. Obviously, legal research calls for special training in the field of law, and anyone without this training is not competent to do this type of research. In fact, in view of their complexity, such studies are generally best undertaken by such organizations as the National Education Association, rather than by a graduate student working toward a degree.

Highlights of the Chapter

1. Because of the difficulty in obtaining dependable data, historical research is among the most difficult to conduct adequately. The student should exercise caution in selecting a historical problem for the fulfillment of the research requirement for his degree. On the other hand, a survey of the past can frequently provide valuable insights into present practices, and education might profit from a reevaluation of its present reluctance to sponsor historical research for thesis or dissertation purposes.

2. The historian generally conceives his task to be the interpretation of the past in the light of a certain point of reference, rather than simply the development of a chronicle of events. The three major points of view from which historical perspective is superimposed on historical data are the scientific, the biological, and the humanistic. Among the more specific orientations are the technological, the geographic, the "great man," and the eclectic theories.

3. Historical evidence is almost invariably inadequate: not only are historical events unique and incapable of verification through duplication, but records are invariably lacking from the standpoint of accuracy, completeness, impartiality, etc. This is particularly evident in some types of data, e.g., dates and numbers.

4. The historian must rely on primary sources for the bulk of his information and, where such gaps exist in available primary sources that he has to place undue reliance on secondary sources and/or his imagination to bridge the gaps, he should probably refrain from undertaking the study. It must, of course, be realized that,

while secondary sources are frequently undependable, they are sometimes, on the contrary, most trustworthy. The historian uses all the evidence at his disposal, but he must take special care to ensure its validity by subjecting it to rigorous test.

5.   Historical evidence must be carefully evaluated from the standpoint of both its authenticity and its validity, and very elaborate techniques have been devised to preclude the perpetration of frauds. While such methods of detection can lead to the rejection of historical evidence as false or fraudulent, they can lead to its acceptance only on the basis of plausibility.

6.   The accumulation and validation of historical data, while crucial, is only a step to the even more important task of interpreting their significance. Here the historian is on extremely subjective grounds, and he must be careful not to part company with his scholarship. The establishment of causation is particularly precarious. On the other hand, it is precisely through the display of his grasp of the field, the clarity and plausibility of his interpretations, his ability to bridge gaps, the continuity and the perspective which he superimposes on these data to make them meaningful that the historian establishes his claim to scientific status.

7.   While the writing of the historical report must unavoidably—and desirably—allow for a somewhat greater degree of freedom in the use of subjectivity than does the usual research report, this is not a license for the historian to let his imagination and his personal biases distort the facts.

8.   Whether historical research qualifies as a scientific endeavor depends on the criteria used. While historical research cannot meet some of the tests of the scientific method interpreted in the narrow sense of its use in the physical sciences, it does qualify from the standpoint of its subscription to the same principles and the same general scholarship and accuracy which characterize all scientific research.

9.   Documentary, bibliographic, and legal research, though not strictly "historical" in nature, share somewhat the same problems as historical research, particularly from the standpoint of the in-

completeness, discontinuity, and unverifiability of the data and the crucial role which the investigator's insight plays in the interpretation of their significance.

Questions and Projects

1.   Make a historical study of the development of historical research. Appraise its present status and current trends.

2.   Make a documentary study of the present status of educational research as revealed by the professional literature.

3.   Identify common points of agreement among the educational leaders whose influence is incorporated in present educational practice—e.g., Rousseau, Herbart, Dewey—with respect to such issues as the relative role of the teacher in the learning of the child.

4.   Trace the evolution of certain basic concepts underlying educational practice, e.g., the concept of pupil activity as a factor in the effectiveness of his learning. Other current educational practices worthy of historical study include independent study, modular scheduling, team teaching, merit pay, and the middle school.

Selected References

Ausubel, Herman. *Historians and Their Crafts: A Study of the Presidential Addresses of the American Historical Association, 1884–1945.* New York: Columbia Univ. Press, 1950.

Benjamin, Harold H. "An approach to the study of causation in educational history," *Hist. Educ. J.,* 6. 137–52; 1954.

Brickman, William W. *A Guide to Research in Educational History.* New York: New York Univ. Bookstore, 1949.

Carr, Edward H. *What is History?* New York: Knopf, 1962.

Committee on Historiography. *Theory and Practice in Historical Study.* New York: Soc. Sci. Res. Council, 1946.

Cremin, Laurence A. *Transformation of the School: 1878–1957.* New York: Knopf, 1961.

Gottschalk, Louis R. *Understanding History: A Primer of the Historical Method.* New York: Knopf, 1950.

Graves, Frank P. *A History of Education: 1. Before the Middle Ages, 1909;
2. During the Middle Ages, 1910; and 3. In Modern Times,
1913.* New York: Macmillan.

Hockett, Homer C. *The Critical Method in Historical Research and Writing.*
New York: Macmillan, 1955.

Hughes, H. Stuart. "The historian and the social scientist," *Amer. hist. Rev.,*
66: 20–46; 1960.

Johnson, Leighton H. "Education needs historical studies," *Phi Delta
Kappan,* 36: 157–59; 1955.

Kazamias, Andreas M. and Byron G. Massialas. *Tradition and Change in
Education: A Comparative Study.* Englewood Cliffs: Prentice-
Hall, 1965.

Kuhn, Thomas S. "Historical structure of scientific discovery," *Sci.,* 136:
760–64; 1962.

Mosteller, Frederick and David L. Wallace. "Inference of an authorship
problem," *J. Amer. stat. Assn.,* 58: 275–309; 1963.

Perdew, Philip W. "Criteria of research in educational history," *J. educ.
Res.,* 44: 217–23; 1950.

———. "Analysis of research in educational history," *Phi Delta Kappan,*
32: 134–36; 1950.

Renier, Gustaf J. *History: Its Purpose and Method.* New York: Beacon, 1950.

Smith, Wilson. "The new historian of American education," *Harv. educ.
Rev.,* 31: 136–43; 1961.

Starr, Richard. "The history of education: Some impressions," *Harv. educ.
Rev.,* 31: 124–35; 1961.

Strauss, William L. "The great Piltdown hoax," *Sci.,* 119: 265–69; 1954.

Wilson, Edmund. *The Scrolls from the Dead Sea.* New York. Oxford Univ
Press, 1955.

Woody, Thomas A. "Of history and its methods," *J. exper. Educ.,* 15: 175–
201; 1947.

9
THE SURVEY: DESCRIPTIVE STUDIES

If we want to know how people feel, what they experience and what they remember, what their emotions and motives are like, and the reasons for acting as they do— why not ask them?——Gordon W. Allport (1942)

No category of educational research is more widely used than the type known variously as the *survey*, the *normative-survey*, or *descriptive* research. This is a broad classification comprising a variety of specific techniques and procedures, all similar from the standpoint of purpose—namely, to establish the status of the phenomenon under investigation.

THE NATURE OF SURVEY RESEARCH

Although it is not possible to make clear-cut distinctions between descriptive studies and the other research classifications, general differences can be pointed out. A fairly clear line can be drawn between survey studies and historical studies on the basis of time: the latter deals with the past, the former with the present.* Surveys differ from experimental studies in purpose. Surveys are oriented toward the determination of the status of a given phenomenon rather than toward the isolation of "causative"

---

* Less clear is the distinction between surveys and documentary and legal research whose primary purpose is to "survey" existing documents. As previously noted, both documentary and legal research could have been included in the present rather than in the previous chapter.

factors accounting for its existence. Survey studies differ from case studies in that surveys are generally based on large cross-sectional samples, while case studies are oriented to the more intensive and longitudinal study of a smaller sample and, like experimentation, attempt to isolate antecedents of the phenomenon under investigation.

The distinction between survey studies and other forms of educational research is complicated by a number of subsidiary outcomes which often accrue as by-products. For instance, the comparison of the status of two or more groups subjected to differential treatment approximates the experimental method. Similarly, successive surveys can establish trends and permit the prediction of the likely status of phenomena. Changes in census figures over the years, for example, are a valuable gauge of national growth. Furthermore, when a distinct break in a given trend can be associated with a procedural change or with the introduction of a certain factor at that point, the break can be considered a rough experiment on the relative effect of the change. While these subsidiary results are frequently of major importance, the primary goal of the survey is the investigation of the present status of phenomena.

While, on the whole, less scientifically sophisticated than most other research techniques, surveys vary in complexity and sophistication. At one extreme, they constitute nothing more than a fact-finding approach to the study of local problems conducted on a one-shot basis, without any significant research purpose—e.g., a survey of the academic qualifications of school superintendents. At the other extreme are surveys that bear directly on significant interrelationships among phenomena. Surveys of the inmates of concentration camps, for example, have provided important insights into the dynamics of the human personality under conditions of psychological stress. Terman's studies of the gifted have likewise been of considerable practical and theoretical significance.

Historically, surveys date to the first census ordered by Caesar Augustus. They vary in subject from the duties and responsibilities of the school superintendent and the activities of the classroom teacher to the attitudes of school personnel or the public on a wide variety of educational and sociological issues. In scope, survey studies range from such vast undertakings as the decennial census of the U.S. Bureau of the Census to the spur-of-the-moment poll of the smoking preferences of college students.

Purpose of Surveys

Educational surveys are particularly versatile and practical, especially for the administrator, in that they identify present conditions and point to present needs. They cannot make the decisions for the administrator, but they can provide him with information on which to base sound decisions. Surveys are so obviously useful, in fact, that administrators tend to rely on them too exclusively, and to base crucial decisions on a survey of opinions —often poorly sampled. Surveys are of the present and, if used simply for the purpose of seeing what has been attained to date, are of limited value. On the other hand, by providing the basis for plans for improvement, they can be decidedly forward-looking and practical. As Trow (1963) points out, a survey of the characteristics of teachers planning to remain in teaching as against those planning to leave the profession has obvious implications in terms of the recruitment of teachers. Likewise, in view of the shortage of counselors, we might want to know just how much counseling a counselor actually does and what type of counseling seems to be most profitable from the standpoint of the child. Trow wonders how decisions of this kind can be made without some form of investigation. Furno (1966) suggests that "If the school administrator unquestioningly accepts statistics from census or sample surveys, he will be duped more often than not. If he distrusts statistics completely, he will be more ignorant than he need be."

Surveys must do more than merely uncover data; they must interpret, synthesize, and integrate these data and point to their implications and interrelationships. While the fact-finding aspects of the survey are occasionally semiclerical in nature, there is ample opportunity for the investigator to display ingenuity and scholarliness in his interpretation of the data and in his understanding of their strengths and weaknesses, interrelationships, apparent antecedents, and especially their implications.

To the extent that this is possible in the early stages of investigation, the survey, like all other research, must begin with a definite problem and be oriented toward the eventual derivation of valid generalizations. The survey makes its maximum contribution when it originates from a problem existing within the framework of theory, and is oriented toward the identification of factors and relationships worthy of investigation under more rigorously controlled conditions. Since it is rarely possible to achieve adequate control of extraneous factors within the setting of the natural situation, the survey is not generally capable of testing specific hypotheses. As a method of research, it represents a step of intermediate scientific sophistication by which semi-crude relationships among phenomena are explored. It is a scientific technique only insofar as it strives for all the precision of which it is capable.

The survey constitutes a primitive type of research in that the investigation of any problem must begin with a "survey" of its nature before it can move into the more structured and rigorous phases. At its most elementary stage, the survey is concerned with determining the immediate status of a given phenomenon. More important from the standpoint of its role as a technique in the development of educational science, however, is the extension of this clarification of the problem into the development of further insights and, eventually, into the derivation of hypotheses to be incorporated into more adequate investigations at the experimental level. Thus, its purpose is both immediate and long-range.

The survey is more realistic than the experiment in that it investigates phenomena in their natural setting. This is, of course, a great strength in the early stages of the investigation of a problem in that it affords flexibility and versatility. In the latter stages of investigation, however, this strength becomes a weakness since the lack of control precludes a definitive test of crucial hypotheses. Unfortunately, though the survey should be a steppingstone to more precise investigations, in practice this second step is frequently overlooked. Too often surveys are made of problems that lead nowhere, that have no significant purpose or that are oriented toward meaningless topics. On the other hand, it does not follow that the survey is an inferior type of research; the concept of inferiority does not belong here, for the answer that is needed depends on the type of question that is asked and, certainly, with respect to certain types of problems—e.g., the attitudes of children toward cheating—the answer must be derived from a survey rather than from some more sophisticated approach.*

* This does not negate the statement by Van Dalen (1966) that there have been too many descriptive studies. The time has come to move into more fundamental investigations of phenomena. Descriptive studies can only serve as useful exploratory tools; they can never establish cause-effect relationships.

Classification of Surveys

Survey studies can be divided into any number of subcategories, depending on the basis and purpose of classification. Probably the most basic breakdown is to separate them into *descriptive* studies, which are oriented toward the description of the present status of a given phenomenon, and *analytical* studies, in which phenomena are analyzed in terms of their basic components. Along a different continuum, survey studies can also be classified according to the instruments and techniques used—e.g., questionnaire, interview, observation, etc. Although neither of these breakdowns is clear-cut, this dual system of classification seems to have merit from an operational, as well as from an organizational, point of view, and will be used as the basis of the present discussion. This chapter is devoted to descriptive studies.

Special Problems

Two problems which are of importance in all research are particularly crucial in surveys.

1. The problem of sampling is of primary concern in all survey studies, for unless the sample on the basis of which the data are collected is representative of the population selected for investigation, the conclusions drawn cannot apply to that population.

2. The validity of the instruments or techniques used in gathering the data is crucial to the validity of the conclusions that are derived from surveys. To the extent that the instruments used are not valid—and one must remember that validity applies to a particular situation under specific conditions—the results obtained cannot be interpreted nor can generalizations be reached.*

SURVEY TESTING

Undoubtedly, the most systematic survey research conducted in our public schools is the standardized academic achievement testing program. Every year, school districts spend thousands of dollars to appraise the outcome of their teaching

---

* The researcher would have to be very careful of conducting a survey on the basis of pre-existing data. Reasons given to counselors by students for dropping out of school, for example, not having been collected with a research purpose in mind, probably cannot serve such a purpose.

efforts. In addition, there is the somewhat less comprehensive, but nonetheless highly organized, program of pupil appraisal in terms of intelligence, special aptitude, personality adjustment, and vocational interest.

A distinction needs to be made between the guidance function and the research function of testing since although the two are not independent, we are concerned here only with the latter. Research is interested in groups—i.e., it attempts to derive generalizations which are applicable beyond the individual case. Survey testing, as a research activity, usually is interested in evaluating the achievement of a class, a school, or a system in relation to the group on which the test was standardized.* In contrast, the guidance approach is focused on the child as an individual.

Problems in Survey Testing

Of the two major problems connected with survey research, sampling generally is of minor importance in survey testing, since in most school situations the total population in the grades concerned is tested. Any attempt to use volunteers or individuals selected on a judgmental basis to represent the school would, of course, be taboo. The problem of the validity of the instruments used, on the other hand, is both crucial and difficult to handle adequately. The major difficulty is the applicability of the test norms to the particular group under study. It must first be realized that many instruments have been inadequately standardized. But even more detrimental to meaningful results is the question of the applicability of the norms of a given test to a particular group. If we accept the principle that any test score is valid only to the extent that the background of the testee is comparable to that of the group on which the test was standardized, how does one interpret the performance of children in a rural community on a test standardized on city children? Or the performance of children on a test in arithmetic which covers decimals when, because of the arrangement of the local curriculum, the unit on decimals is postponed one grade? Just how much below national norms is it permissible for a school in the slums to be? All of these questions point to the inescapable fact that the measurement of performance is

---

* Interclass or interschool comparisons are sometimes made. From a research point of view, such comparisons are to be condemned, since the control necessary to make such comparisons meaningful is generally lacking.

simply a step to the more important task of interpreting that performance with respect to the objectives the school feels it can legitimately attain.

Test-wiseness on the part of the student is another important factor to consider in the interpretation of the results of testing. This factor would be particularly invalidating when teachers prepare their students for the administration of the survey instrument by reviewing with an equivalent form of the same test. Also worth mentioning is the all-too-frequent practice of invalidating the test norms by "teaching toward the test." Inasmuch as the norm group did not have the benefit of this orientation, any comparison of the performance of the practiced class and the norms is completely meaningless.

Uses of Survey Testing Results

The benefits to be derived from periodic appraisals of the work of the school are undoubtedly great. Such studies not only point to gaps and weaknesses in the school's program, but also serve to keep the whole system alert.* At the college level, entrance examinations enable the school to appraise its functions in relation to the students it undertakes to serve. Coupled with analyses of student grades, studies of admission-test performance help keep the school, and the units within it, on an even keel and can be useful in such policy decisions as calibrating grading policy to the level of the students admitted.

If testing studies are to be of benefit to the school system and to the children, however, they have to be carried out correctly—or not at all. Since policy decisions are generally no better than the data on which they are based, and since unwise decisions can cause considerable harm, there is no room for incompetence here. In any school system, the appointment of a director of testing who has considerable background both in the principles of measurements and in research methods, working through a relatively adequate test chairman in each of the schools, seems to be essential if we are to justify such a program.

---

* On the other hand, appraised from a philosophical and pedagogical point of view, overemphasis on such evaluation can have detrimental effects on the attainment of some of the school's most important objectives: creativity, character development, mental health, etc.; from a research point of view, it can invalidate any comparison with the test norms.

THE QUESTIONNAIRE

The Questionnaire as a Research Tool

Probably no instrument of research has been more subject to censure than the questionnaire. Yet it continues to be the most used and most abused instrument in educational research, as both graduate students and professional agencies continue to rely on it. The questionnaire apparently dates back to Horace Mann, who is credited with having used it as a research tool in 1847. Its abuse—both in quantity and in lack of quality—reached such proportions in the post-World War I period that the National Education Association in 1930 devoted an extensive article to the consideration of the problem. It was noted, for instance, that some school superintendents received as many as one hundred questionnaires per year, most of them of a very inadequate nature. Despite its recognition of flagrant abuses, the NEA study concluded that its findings pointed to an immediate need for the drastic improvement of the questionnaire as an instrument of science rather than to a blanket condemnation. The NEA made specific recommendations for dealing with the problem and advised its members to reply to a questionnaire only when its quality from the standpoint of sponsorship, significance of the topic, construction, etc. merited such a reply.

As a result of such resistance, there has been a decline in the use of the questionnaire as a research instrument, together with a clarification of its proper use and an improvement in its quality. Today, its weaknesses and limitations—as well as its strengths—are more clearly recognized, and a serious attempt is made to limit its use to appropriate situations. The problem is one of deciding when to use it, and then of ensuring that it meets acceptable levels of adequacy. In other words, the questionnaire has definite advantages which must be weighed against its disadvantages, and its validity must be considered in the specific case.

The first problem to be faced in planning a questionnaire survey is, obviously, to decide whether an adequate answer can be obtained by a survey, or whether recourse should be made to more precise techniques. This calls for an understanding of the relative advantages both of surveys and of other forms of research. A teacher might attempt to solve the problem of whether or not training in phonics promotes greater proficiency in reading by surveying the opinions of other teachers, who are equally ignorant of the answer. The decision must be based on a clear conception of specifically what the investigator wants to determine, and the kind of data necessary to answer the questions which the problem entails.

Assuming that a survey is indicated, the investigator needs to determine whether the questionnaire is the most adequate source of survey information in this particular case. This choice is made on the basis of the relative advantages and disadvantages of each of the relevant survey techniques in relation to the problem and the situation involved—or in technical terms, it is necessary to choose the best instrument from the standpoint of validity, reliability, and usability.

Advantages and Disadvantages of the Questionnaire

The discussion of the relative advantages of the questionnaire must be restricted to what constitutes a relevant comparison. There is nothing particularly enlightening about weighing the merits of the questionnaire against those of the experiment, for example, since they are designed for essentially different purposes. The choice of the questionnaire in preference to other survey techniques is generally a matter of weighing its strengths and weaknesses against those of the interview, with which it is most nearly interchangeable. In fact, some authors insist on the term *mailed questionnaire* to distinguish it from the questionnaire used as a guide in interviewing. The discussion will be oriented, therefore, toward a comparison of these two techniques on the basis of the usual criteria of validity, reliability and usability.

Among the major advantages of the questionnaire is that it permits wide coverage at a minimum expense both in money and effort. It not only affords wider geographic coverage but it also reaches persons who are difficult to contact. This greater coverage makes for greater validity in the results through promoting the selection of a larger and more representative sample.

Particularly when it does not call for a signature or other means of identification, the questionnaire may, because of its greater impersonality, elicit more candid and objective replies. Thus, depending on the topic—e.g., the reactions of students toward school—it may elicit more valid responses, although, to be sure, a skillfully conducted interview can also obtain good results. On the other hand, the questionnaire does not permit the investigator to note the apparent reluctance or evasiveness of his respondents, a matter which is better handled through the interview, nor does it permit the investigator to follow through on misunderstood questions or inadequate answers. The questionnaire also permits more considered answers. Its use would be indicated in situations in which the respondent needs to check his information or in which group consultation would result in more valid information. The questionnaire allows greater uniformity in the manner in which the questions are posed, and this ensures greater comparability in the answers. On the other hand, this does not necessarily ensure truth.

The advantages of the questionnaire are more apparent than its disadvantages. As a consequence, it frequently appeals to the amateur who uses it for all purposes regardless of its suitability and without sufficient awareness of its limitations. The major weakness of the questionnaire is undoubtedly the problem of non-returns. Not only do non-returns decrease the size of the sample on which the results are based—which is relatively unimportant wherever the sample is large—but it introduces a bias inasmuch as non-respondents are likely to differ from respondents in fundamental ways. Empirical studies have shown important differences to exist between respondents and non-respondents— and even between regular respondents and those who respond to follow-ups—in such factors as interest in the topic, attitude, conscientiousness, promptness, educational and socio-economic status, etc. It is logical to assume that, in many cases, the non-respondents' refusal to participate is not independent of such factors as a negative attitude toward the subject or toward the sponsor of the investigation, for example. While the motives that underlie non-response vary from situation to situation, it can be assumed that the non-respondent is different, at least in some way, from the respondent and that this difference may have a definite bearing on the validity of the results obtained.

The validity of questionnaire data also depends in a crucial way on the ability and willingness of the respondent to provide the information requested. Research has shown that respondents are, as a group, of superior intellectual and educational status. Members of the lower intellectual and educational groups tend not to answer and, if they do, to introduce an element of invalidity by their inability to interpret the questions or to express their responses clearly. It also is possible that a respondent, though capable of providing the information, is not willing to do so. This is true especially when the information concerns sensitive subjects or reflects on the respondent, or when he feels threatened by the questions asked. It also is possible for the respondent to be so uninterested in the topic under investigation that he will answer the questions more or less at random. The questionnaire frequently does not provide the investigator with sufficient opportunity for developing interest on the part of the respondent, nor does it allow him to develop the rapport necessary to permit him to ask questions of a personal nature. Unfortunately, the investigator has no way of knowing in how many instances both of response and non-response the above conditions of inability and/or unwillingness to provide the information prevailed, and consequently he cannot judge the extent of the invalidity of his data. His only salvation lies in selecting his population so as to avoid this sort of predicament.

A major disadvantage of the questionnaire is the possibility of the misinterpretation of the questions. This danger is increased when the questions are ambiguous because of improper formulation or variations in word meaning associated with differences in socio-economic and cultural status—weaknesses which are as much the result of misuse as they are limitations inherent in the method itself. Misinterpretations are more likely to occur when the respondent is not equal to the task expected of him, but they too frequently arise even under ideal conditions. To make matters worse, such misinterpretations are frequently impossible to detect, and they cannot be corrected as in the interview. Invalid responses can also occur as a result of leading questions. But this is not a weakness inherent in the method; in fact, it is less of a factor than in the interview, since the questionnaire is more objective. Furthermore, since the questionnaire is a matter of public record to be scrutinized whenever unusual results occur, the presence of such a bias is more readily discernible.

Construction of the Questionnaire

Next to the choice of a suitable topic and population, probably no other aspect of a questionnaire study is more crucial to its success than is the adequacy of construction of the questionnaire itself. The average student has no concept of the complexity of devising an adequate questionnaire. His general attitude, after he has thrown a few questions together, is "Everybody knows what I mean," and it is frequently necessary to prove to him that things are not that simple. The point can sometimes be driven home by having him administer his questionnaire to a group of his colleagues and then analyze their responses. When, as a result of such an experience, he realizes that his questions are in need of clarification, if not complete reformulation, he is generally more receptive to suggestions for the improvement of his instrument. The difficulty is that the student confuses the questionnaire with ordinary conversation in which it is possible to correct misinterpretations through repetition of the question or further explanation. He fails to realize that once the questionnaire is in the mail, nothing can be done to improve it. He needs to appreciate that a major determinant of the quality of a questionnaire study is the adequacy of the instrument through which the data are obtained. Devising a test of intelligence, for example, may take months and even years. There is no reason to believe that a questionnaire is something that one can put together in a single afternoon.

The first step in the construction of an adequate questionnaire is to attain a thorough grasp of the field, of the objectives of the study, and of the nature of the data needed. While a thorough review of the literature can point out the general area of significance that needs to be considered, it is usually necessary to structure the field even further, especially in an exploratory study. This is probably best done by conducting unstructured interviews with persons who are familiar with the field. Thus, in a questionnaire study of the reading interests and habits of gifted adolescents of low socio-economic status, the investigator would probably have to rely both on the literature and on interviews with such youngsters for an orientation as to what to include and how to formulate his items.

The investigator must realize that there is a limit to the demands he can make of the respondent, and that, consequently, he must delimit his study to the point that he is not expecting too much and yet is able to get a reasonable answer to his problem. Thus, he must eliminate all questions which pertain to data which can be found readily—and often more accurately—elsewhere. If the questionnaire is still too long, he must consider what can be sacrificed with the least loss to the final answer. Every item must serve a definite purpose or face elimination.

The more clearly the problem is stated, the more adequately each of the items can be related to the purpose of the study. This is essential not only to ensure that every item is functional, but also to encourage response, since respondents will tend to shy away from a questionnaire that is simply a fishing expedition aimed in the general direction of the target. Most frequently such an approach leaves unasked the very questions that would have made the study meaningful and purposeful. The following letter received by the Commissioner of Education for Alaska (Editor, 1939) is, let us hope, a classic in confusion never to be equalled; however, many questionnaires display some of the same symptoms.

> I am preparing a thesis upon the subject: "The Teaching of English as Revealed in the Courses of Study of the Countries of the English-Speaking Nations of the World." I am writing you for such information and suggestions as you may be able and will kindly give me. I shall certainly appreciate whatever help you may give me along this line. Life is full of duties and we all have our own work to do; but I find that sometimes there are those who from education, training, experience and contacts in life, know off-hand what it would take a long time for others to learn from research and a long period of reading.
>
> Do you know some interesting books on Alaska: her history, her economic problems, commerce, imports, exports, human relations, etc., etc.—everything of interest without our taking so much time to "think clearly" at this time.
>
> Of course, my subject is on Education and English; but these subjects require background which Alaska has.
>
> I have to present my subject in an original way, giving a new slant or fresh ideas or a definite contribution to knowledge.
>
> What is it then that Alaska has or does in a different way from other English-Speaking Countries or "outlying" parts of the United States? (May I state that we in "the States" consider you "an integral part" of the United States just as we do Hawaii. Of course you know these things. Are Alaska, American Samoa, Canal Zone, Guam, Hawaii, Philippine Islands, Puerto Rico, and Virgin Island—all in the same class

educationally as to organization? Alaska has one University
and from a perusal of it, you seem to have everything.

(*Marginal Note*): Could you give me the names of a few of
the best books on the teaching of English used in Alaska?
(All phases or just one branch of the work.)

I wonder if climate would be the determining factor in
some cases. Hawaii has her "tropical influences" in her curriculum as does the Philippines, Puerto Rico. (I always think
of Cuba and want to include her in the American School
System, just as I want to include Canal Zone which is a pro-
tectorate. I am always at a loss to know what to do with
Canal Zone. She only has about three cities, I believe.)

American Samoa, Guam and the Virgin Island—(How
about Wake Island?) As we think of these, what could we
say of them educationally? Could we tell something interesting about them, giving their climate, area, capitals or
principal cities and occupations and lead up to the need of
a certain kind of education which they have or do not have
and give the school census, the educational statistics including the number of teachers and the grades, classification and
organization of the schools and the language existing in the
islands or outlying parts and the efforts that are being made
to instruct the children and the citizens or parents. What
dialects have they in these "parts"?

(*Note at top of page 2*): Did your school children get a
chance to see the King and Queen or hear them on the Radio?

Of course we are interested in Alaska for your sake—and
because of the "Gold Rush"—her nearness to Asia—Anthropology,—her fisheries—and I am interested in the Indians and
the Esquimeaux and their carvings and also the Art of the
Indians as manifested in their carvings on the totem poles,
etc., etc.

I am especially interested in the railroad centers of Alaska
—the cities visited by Harding and those cities made famous
by the passing of Will Rogers. Keeping in mind my thesis,
will you tell me something of interest about education in these
cities? What Indian or Esquimeaux or other dialects have you
in Alaska? I think the Americans speak the same as the
Pacific Northwest or Van Couver if they are Canadians. May
I hear from you?

Thanks.

Very truly yours,

P.S. We are interested in Samoa because of Stevenson. I
wonder if very much attention is paid to education in Samoa

or Virgin Islands? I wonder what type of education is given there?

Questions on the same subtopic should probably be grouped to give the questionnaire a semblance of order, and to enable the respondent to orient himself to the trend of thought. The more general questions of a set should come first, and then the more detailed and specific—e.g., "Do you work after school?" "How many hours a week do you work?" "Does your work interfere with your studies?" The questions should be arranged so that they can be cross-interpreted rather than remain completely independent, for although the questionnaire is made up of separate questions, it should be organized so that it has unity from the standpoint of purpose.

1. Importance of Scholarly Construction   Constructing a questionnaire calls for numerous revisions in which variations of the same question should be submitted to experimental trial. The same question posed in different ways very frequently brings out different responses. The help of outsiders is essential; they are generally more objective and can see flaws that the investigator is invariably too close to see. This points to the need for a pilot study, in which competent persons are asked to fill out the questionnaire and to indicate their reactions to every phase of its organization. The pilot-study questionnaire can be given first to friends, then to persons who are familiar with questionnaire construction and the field in general, and finally to people of the same nature as those who are eventually to receive the final draft.

Professional people are aware of their responsibility to provide information which they feel is for a good cause. However, questionnaire studies have to compete with many other demands on the respondent's time and goodwill. Frequently resistance and annoyance toward questionnaires has been developed in potential respondents as a result of abuse by such groups as sales organizations. This only points to the challenge to be faced. If he is to expect the respondent to give of his time and energy, it behooves the investigator to prepare a scholarly questionnaire, for the obligation to respond to a questionnaire no longer binds when there is a legitimate question as to whether the proposed study will make a contribution. The primary responsibility lies with the investigator, and the respondent's obligation to reply vanishes when the problem is trivial, when the questions display signs of carelessness, when unnecessary questions are included, when the questions do not provide the means for giving valid answers, or when the investigator has not had the courtesy to keep his demands on the respondent's time and energy within reasonable limits.

2.   Open and Closed Questions   The form the questions and the responses are to take is an important consideration in the construction of the questionnaire. It is first necessary to determine whether the items of the questionnaire are to be *open questions,* requiring the respondent to reply in his own words—e.g., "What is your occupation?"—or *closed questions,* providing the respondent with ready-made alternatives—e.g., in answer to the above, banker, _____, lawyer, _____, etc. The choice is determined largely by the nature of the problem. It is generally desirable, for example, to use the open questionnaire in the early stages of investigation in order to define the field, and to use a closed questionnaire when the specific aspects of the problem are more precisely delineated.

Closed questions help keep the questionnaire to a reasonable length and, thus, encourage response—and increase validity from the standpoint of the representativeness of the returns—while open questions enable the respondent to give a more adequate presentation of his particular case. The open questionnaire possesses greater flexibility, which may or may not be desirable. It allows the respondent more leeway in stating his position, which may be equivalent to saying it allows for greater validity. On the other hand, it increases the risk of misinterpretation. For example, the answer "mechanic" in response to the question about the individual's occupation introduces considerably greater confusion in interpretation (with corresponding loss of validity) than would listing clearly defined occupational levels for the respondent to check.

The closed questionnaire with its list of alternatives structures the concept under study and minimizes the risk of misinterpretation. It permits easier tabulation and interpretation by the investigator. On the negative side, it may well provide the respondent who does not have an answer with an alternative that he can check whether it applies significantly in his case or not. For example, the drop-out who leaves school for such undefined reasons as "general discontent" may consider "need to work" a logically adequate, socially acceptable, and noncontroversial alternative, regardless of how prominently his need to work may have featured in his decision to leave school. This is akin to the well-recognized problem of interviewer bias, which is considered the major weakness of interview studies.

In a closed questionnaire it is essential to allow for all possible answers—i.e., the categories provided must be both exhaustive and mutually exclusive. This frequently requires adding an extra category asking for "Other—Please specify" for the respondent who does not find any of the alternatives suitable. On the other hand, experience suggests that the respondent rarely exercises this option; almost invariably he simply accepts one of the alternatives provided rather than devise his own. It should be noted that the more scientifically oriented the respondent is, the more precise he tends to be, and the more annoyed he is likely to become with preplanned alternatives, each of which he would have to qualify before it would cover his particular situation.

The question of whether to use the open or the closed questionnaire can be resolved only on the basis of the usual criteria of validity, reliability, and usability, and, inasmuch as most of the problems to be covered in education are varied and complex, a combination of the two is generally better than the exclusive use of one. Each has its merits and limitations, and it is a matter of using the proper one for the proper purpose. The closed questionnaire generally makes for greater coverage and more systematic tabulation. On the other hand, there may be the need for the respondent to clarify his position with regard to some of the items, and it is generally advisable to include an open question or two for any general reaction or comment at the end of each major section of the closed questionnaire. Neither the open nor the closed questionnaire is particularly effective for probing into a problem. When such a purpose is contemplated, the possibility of relying on the interview, particularly of the depth variety, should be considered.

The exact manner in which the respondent is to indicate his answers to a closed questionnaire depends largely on the individual questions. Certain questions can be answered by *yes* and *no*, but most answers dealing with complex aspects of a problem are not that clear-cut. The use of a five-point scale, such as *Strongly agree, Agree, Undecided, Disagree, Strongly disagree,* frequently elicits more valid responses and is probably less frustrating to the conscientious respondent who wants to be truthful. Whenever the respondent is asked to rate certain items, he should be given specific directions as to the number of items he should check—e.g., his three favorite TV programs. Otherwise there is no way of equating the response of the person who checks only one program with those of the person who has checked a large number in which he has varying degrees of interest. In some cases, greater uniformity and validity might be obtained by instructing the respondent to rate his favorite programs in a 1–2–3 order.

A number of rules and suggestions have been given for the construction of questionnaires (Cantril, 1947; Parten, 1950). These rules should be considered from the standpoint of the principles underlying scientific data-gathering rather than as factors peculiar to the questionnaire. The basic task is to provide a vehicle which will permit and encourage the respondent to provide meaningful answers. More specifically, the problem is one of devising an instrument of maximum validity and reliability, capable of obtaining the information relevant to a given topic. The concept of usability is also of utmost importance, since, unlike the tests administered in the captive setting of the school, the questionnaire finds that its weaknesses—e.g., excessive length—are immediately reflected in non-response and consequent loss of validity.

3. Content   A primary consideration in questionnaire construction is the content of the question. Obviously, questions should be restricted to those the investigator has reason to believe will elicit valid and reliable answers. For example, the questions, "Have you noticed any improvement in the health of your child since we instituted the milk program in our school?" cannot provide usable data since the average parent cannot conceivably know. Similarly, the use of the questionnaire for the measurement of attitudes and feelings raises the very pertinent questions, "Does the person understand himself sufficiently?" and "Is he willing to reveal his interpretation of himself?" Also to be avoided, for example, are questions with a "patriotic" overtone, for they are almost invariably answered in a "patriotic" direction, regardless of their content.

Each question must be justified on the basis of its contribution to the overall purpose of the study. This basic principle automatically precludes vague and ambiguous questions. Conversely, it implies clear, direct, and simple language, and subscription to the basic rules of effective communication.

The following are samples of the type of questions to be avoided: "What is your salary?" (9 or 12 months?); "What is the value of your house?" (Purchase or resale?); "Do you frequently encounter disciplinary problems?" (What is frequently?); "How late do you let your children watch TV?" (Weekdays or weekends?); "Do you believe in freedom of speech?" (Emotionally toned); "Do you think a veteran should have to join a union in order to get work?" (Emotionally toned); "Do you favor federal aid to education as a means of providing for the proper education of your child?" (Emotionally toned); "Are you in favor of labor unions?" (Too broad); "Do you believe that the whole testimony of a witness found to be inaccurate in part should *ipso facto* be stricken from the record?" (Unnecessary difficulty in vocabulary); "How would you rate your superintendent?" (Lack of frame of reference); "Do you think boys and girls should be in separate classes or should they be taught together, yes or no?" (Yes or no what?); "Do you favor old-age pension and socialized medicine?" (Two ideas in one); "Marital status? _____" (Unclear; can be answered by "satisfactory"); "Boy or girl? _____" (Unclear; can be answered "yes"); "Do you make announcements at the beginning or the end of the class period? _____" (Unclear); and many other similar questions which reflect not only a lack of scholarship, but also some lack of understanding of what constitutes intelligible communication.

The plight of the poor respondent is well illustrated by Bob Burns' story of Grandpa Snazzy as a witness in court:

> The attorney says: "Now Mr. Snazzy, did you or did you not, on the date in question or at any time previously or subsequently, say or even intimate to the defendant or anyone else, whether friend or mere acquaintance or in fact a total stranger, that the statement imputed to you, whether just or unjust and denied by the plaintiff, was a matter of no moment or otherwise? Answer—did you or did you not?"
>
> Grandpa thinks a while and then says, "Did I or did I not what?"

Questions must be worded so that they are meaningful to the person to whom they are addressed. Different expressions mean different things to different people, particularly when differences in cultural background are involved. The questionnaire calls for a substantial educational background, if it is to be answered adequately. It is generally agreed that some 40 percent of the general population are illiterate for questionnaire purposes. Abrams (1951) estimates that 90 percent of the people misinterpret at least 10 percent of the questions and that at least 10 percent of the people misinterpret 90 percent of the questions.

When there is reason to suspect that a question is susceptible to misinterpretation, it must be phrased carefully in order to counteract possible bias. Frequently this means orienting the respondent's mind-set to the purpose of the investigation. Respondents almost invariably have already formed certain mind-sets toward a number of problems and tend to answer questions according to this frame of reference. Thus, though "housework is never done," housewives usually answer "no" when asked if they work. They will frequently say "no" even when they hold a part-time job, such as keeping books or minding the store for their husband. Similarly, students will seldom list themselves as workers, though they may put in a forty-hour week in industry or business in addition to going to school. All these things must be foreseen and guarded against through specific questions and directions.

The Validation of Questionnaires

Although the criterion of validity to which the questionnaire, as an instrument of science, must subscribe has already been defined, there remains the task of identifying the specific ways in which this validity is established. It must be recognized that, though the whole instrument is oriented toward the whole problem, the questionnaire is comprised of specific and relatively independent questions, each dealing with a specific aspect of the overall situation. In a sense, then, it is the validity of the items rather than of the total instrument that is under consideration. For example, the question, "How many children do you have?" may elicit a valid answer, while, in the same questionnaire, the question "How much money do you make?" can easily foster varying degrees of error, if not of deceit. It must be recognized that there are circumstances under which it is relatively impossible to obtain valid answers. Certain questions by their very nature—e.g., "Do you cheat on examinations?"—are likely to promote falsification. On the other hand, that the validity of the individual items must be considered does not negate the fact that the questionnaire must have a unity and validity of its own with respect to the topic under investigation. This the investigator needs to bring out through the synthesis of the responses to the specific items and the interpretation of their relevance in bringing out the total picture.

The actual validation of a questionnaire utilizes the same principles and procedures as the validation of any instrument of testing and measurement. At the most elementary level, it is necessary for the questionnaire to have content validity—i.e., each question must be related to the topic under investigation; there must be an adequate coverage of the overall topic; the questions must be clear and unambiguous; etc. A more adequate approach to validation consists of checking the agreement between the responses elicited by the questionnaire with an external criterion. Factual questions about age and educational background, for example, can be readily checked against the records. However, it is somewhat more difficult to locate an adequate criterion for many of the more significant items. With regard to questions of opinion and attitudes, the investigator might have to rely on an interview to see whether the responses to the questionnaire actually represent the respondent's views on the subject discussed. Similarly, the validity of a child's statement that he views TV for a total of twelve hours a week might be checked by having him indicate the programs that he views regularly, by asking his parents, by having his siblings list the number of hours they view, etc., all of which are relatively inadequate criteria.

In some instances, it is possible to validate questionnaire responses against actual behavior. For example, LaPiere (1934) sent a questionnaire asking hotel and motel proprietors and restaurant keepers who had actually housed and fed a Chinese couple whether they accepted Chinese guests. The responses indicated considerable discrepancy between stated policy and actual practice. This, of course, raises the question of the suitability of overt behavior as a criterion of the validity of the response to a questionnaire item. A respondent may be willing to divulge his feelings in response to a questionnaire item and yet suppress such feelings in his behavior in a face-to-face contact. Establishing validity is even more complicated in open questionnaires where the greater flexibility may promote greater validity in the responses, but also increase the possibility of invalidity in their tabulation and interpretation.

Research has been conducted into the effects on the

validity of questionnaire data of requiring a signature as opposed to allowing the respondent to remain anonymous. Gerberich (1947), for instance, found that requiring signatures tended to inhibit honesty and frankness in filling out the *Mooney Problem Checklist*. Gerberich and Mason (1948), on the other hand, found that requiring signatures made no difference in answering such questions as "Have you had a course in high-school biology?" The contradiction is not surprising when the differences in the ego-involvement generated by the questions are considered in the light of the specificity of validity as a concept.

The validity of a questionnaire must be established prior to its use, for validation is an aspect of its development, not of its use in the solution of the problem. It should also be noted that invalidity is not restricted to the instrument itself. It can also result from systematic errors in coding or interpretation, or from a bias in orientation provided by the cover letter or the directions.

Reliability of Questionnaire Data

The question of the reliability of the questionnaire is often ignored, partly because it is difficult to establish with any degree of precision. The usual procedures for calculating the reliability of tests are difficult to apply here. Split-half reliability is, of course, out of the question because of the relative independence and non-additivity of the component items. The possibility of phrasing the questions in two different ways and interspersing these in the questionnaire as a means of testing the reliability of certain items is of dubious validity since the average respondent would probably see through such a trick and simply ignore the second question or answer it the same way he did the first. Besides adding to the length of the questionnaire, such a procedure is likely to annoy the respondent, who might not want to be a party to this type of carelessness. It might discourage him from participating in the study—especially in that it reflects on his integrity and/or intelligence.

The *test—retest* method is the only feasible approach to the establishment of the reliability of the questionnaire. An individual who has answered the questionnaire as part of its standardization can be asked to take it again, and his answers can be compared for consistency. This procedure is not foolproof, since on the retest the respondent will probably attempt to remember and duplicate his earlier responses rather than answer the questions as he sees them. For this reason such evidence of consistency can hardly testify to the validity of the instrument and is a questionable measure of its reliability. At the empirical level, such studies as that of Cuber and Gerberich (1946) and of Gerberich (1947) have shown considerable inconsistency in questionnaire responses, particularly in factual items, but the authors view the inconsistency to be typical of all personal communication rather than peculiar to the questionnaire. Gerberich suggests the need for the investigation of three separate but related problems: 1. the consistency of the questionnaire responses; 2. the accuracy of the questionnaire responses; 3. the comparison of the accuracy of the questionnaire responses with that of responses to the interview. He also urges caution in the acceptance of questionnaire data.

The Question of Non-Returns

Questionnaire studies are generally plagued by a relatively high percentage of non-return. Many studies in the literature report returns as low as 20 to 40 percent. Shannon (1948) reports an average of 65 percent return for "reputable" questionnaire studies reported in a sample of theses, dissertations, and professional articles. He mentions, however, that a discouragingly large number of studies did not report the percentage of returns, perhaps because of inadequacies therein. On the other hand, some studies have achieved a 100 percent return. Such high returns have tended to evolve from a number of follow-ups, coupled with a happy combination of a select population and a select topic; they would be difficult to obtain in the general case.

Among the many factors that promote a high percentage of returns, none is of greater importance than the selection of a worthwhile topic and the addressing of the questionnaire to a group for whom the topic has interest and psychological meaning. It is the responsibility of the investigator to prove the significance of his problem to the satisfaction of the prospective respondent. Conversely, while the percentage of returns is bound to vary from topic to topic, a low percentage of returns frequently implies a poor choice of topic or of population, or perhaps inadequacy in the construction of the questionnaire—all of which can be minimized through a pilot study.

Probably the next most important factor in promoting a high percentage of return is the follow-up. In any sample there will be a few individuals who will fail to return the questionnaire on first contact, and it is invariably necessary to institute the means for follow-up on the missing returns. In some instances, failure to return stems from a direct rejection of the questionnaire, but more frequently it implies nothing more than forgetfulness. It is necessary, therefore, to send out follow-up letters whenever the flow of returns starts to drop off. A series of follow-ups and, finally, perhaps a double postcard calling for a brief answer to a shortened version of the questionnaire, or an interview, may be necessary to bring the returns to an acceptable level. In sending out follow-up letters, it generally is wise to include a second copy of the questionnaire in case the respondent has thrown away the first.

Of course, numerous follow-ups can be an annoyance to the respondent, leading him to refuse to cooperate in future questionnaire studies. It may also lead to his sending back results that are completely invalid. Therefore, it is generally advisable in a follow-up for the investigator to attempt a new approach at convincing the potential respondent that his response is needed. The matter of follow-up is simpler when signatures on the questionnaires returned permit the identification of the delinquents to whom reminders can be sent. When signatures would be objectionable, it may be advisable to include a postcard to be mailed separately, indicating that the questionnaire has been returned under separate cover. This can be combined with the investigator's offer to mail the results of the study to those who are interested.*

1. The Length of the Questionnaire Another significant factor in the percentage of returns is the length of the questionnaire. Generally, the shorter the questionnaire and the less demand it makes on the respondent's time, the higher the percentage of

---

*Questionnaires are sometimes coded so that the respondent, though he believes that he is given complete anonymity, can actually be identified. This might be done where, say, student reaction to a course might need to be correlated with his background to be derived from his cumulative record. This procedure is fraught with danger; under no circumstances must the individual be identified per se, except to make possible the putting together of the two segments of information concerning him. While some people can see nothing ethically wrong with such a procedure, the student contemplating such a move should do so only after serious consideration of the matter with his advisor.

returns. The investigator must appreciate the fact that he cannot expect his respondents to cover every aspect of a broad problem, and that he might have to delimit his problem—consistent, of course, with its retaining its meaningfulness. It must, on the other hand, be noted that the significance of the problem and the proper choice of a population, as well as the scholarship in the construction of the questionnaire, are much more important determinants of returns than is the length per se. Sletto (1940) for example, was able to obtain a 69 percent return to a questionnaire of fifty-two pages of printed material. It would seem that brevity is not important in itself, but as a means of removing superfluous items and thus improving the overall quality of the instrument. Although one may adopt as a rule of thumb that a questionnaire should not take more than half an hour of the respondent's time, the time factor must be considered in the light of the nature of the topic, the loyalty of the group contacted, and other factors—many of which are of greater importance than time itself.

2.   The Choice of Population   The choice of the population is a prime consideration in determining the extent of response. If the topic is of interest to the respondent, he will take the time to fill out the questionnaire. Business people, for instance, would respond to a questionnaire from Dun and Bradstreet. Conversely, it is likely that the low percentage of return in many questionnaire studies in education results from the fact that the questionnaire has been sent to people who do not have the answers expected of them and/or who have no interest in the subject. The population needs to be defined in such a way that participation is restricted to those who are able to make a significant contribution to the success of the study. Some investigators have been able to obtain fairly high returns by asking people in advance if they are willing to cooperate in the study, and mailing the questionnaire only to those who have indicated a willingness to participate. This is a very questionable procedure; it tends to invalidate the results before starting, inasmuch as a bias in sampling is inherent in the original acceptance or rejection of the request for cooperation. One is likely to get a bias soon enough without deliberately incorporating it into the design.

3.   The Instrument   A factor not to be overlooked is the scholarship involved in the construction of the questionnaire. No one wants to be a party to slipshod work. If the questionnaire reflects quality, many people expect similar adequacy in the overall study and are willing to contribute to its success. Such scholarship is generally obtained at the expense of a number of revisions and, of course, a pilot study, which make possible the elimination of items that are defective, irrelevant, or otherwise objectionable. The attractiveness of the format is also conducive to higher returns; it generally pays dividends from the standpoint of returns, for instance, to have the questionnaire printed rather than mimeographed.

4. The Cover Letter   The cover letter is also of critical importance to the success of the study, since the investigator cannot rely on his personality to elicit cooperation but must depend on the printed word to "sell" his study. Sales organizations, in particular, have come to realize the crucial role of "sales talk." A good letter can make a real contribution to the success of a questionnaire study; a poor letter can serve only to alienate even cooperative individuals. The cover letter must be brief, courteous, and forceful; it must appeal to the recipient so that he will agree to cooperate. The investigator might ask himself: "Specifically, what am I offering the person in return for his cooperation in the study?" Among the motives which the investigator can tap are professional obligation, personal and professional pride, spirit of helpfulness, etc. Rarely is it adequate to base a request for cooperation on the proposition: "I have to write a thesis." Since it probably varies from study to study and from population to population, the kind of appeal that will work is probably best determined on the basis of a pilot study. It is possible, for instance, that the appeal "You will be helping to improve the situation of your fellow-students" would be effective where there is high group loyalty. In other instances, the appeal might be to the individual's personal and professional responsibility, or perhaps to the altruistic desire to help others.

The cover letter should be separate from the questionnaire itself, and should be addressed to the individual by name and title. It also should bear the investigator's name and title and his relation to the study. It should make particularly clear the purpose and importance of the study, the procedure on the basis of which the respondent happened to be included in the sample, the sponsorship of the study, if any, etc. When a student is writing to an authority in the field, the faculty advisor, as a courtesy, should also write a letter of sponsorship. Generally, sponsorship promotes the study but it may bias the responses; endorsement by the school board or by some teacher organization may encourage teachers to reply but perhaps to do so along party lines. It is generally agreed that the investigator should enclose a self-addressed envelope; he should also include two copies of his questionnaire so that the respondent will have one for his files.

5. Other Factors A number of other factors of a more minor nature frequently have a bearing on response. For instance, it has been found that the use of an ordinary stamp promotes somewhat greater returns than a prepaid stamp. Apparently people are reluctant to throw away a regular stamp, but feel that a business letter stamp is not going to cost anything if it is not used. The timing appears to have an effect on returns; it is probably best not to have the questionnaire arrive on a Monday or at the beginning of the year, when the teacher or administrator is busy. On the other hand, research in this area has not been entirely consistent; perhaps it is only in instances in which the status of the study is precarious in the first place that these factors assume significance.

6. Dealing with Non-Response The matter of non-response involves two major problems. One, of course, is the maximizing of the returns in the first place. The other consideration is the adjustment of the results to compensate for nonresponse. For example, if the lower socio-economic subgroups responded in a much lower percentage than did the middle and upper classes, the investigator might restrict the study to the upper and middle classes and restate his problem accordingly. Some investigators simply weight the responses of the lower class to bring the class up to quota. This, of course, is of doubtful validity. The fact that some members of the lower classes replied while others did not suggests that non-respondents are really different from respondents, despite the fact that they belong to the same socio-economic class. They cannot, therefore, be adequately represented by simple extrapolation of the respondents of their socio-economic class. Equally faulty is the scheme which takes a larger sample than is basically necessary and ignores those who do not respond. This assumes that the constant errors of sampling incorporated in such a procedure are of lesser magnitude than are random errors—an assumption which is very questionable, as we saw in Chapter 7. A more adequate scheme is advanced by Hansen and Hurwitz (1946) who suggest interviewing a random sample of the non-respondents to establish their pattern of response, which can then be weighted to give an overall picture. Note that it is necessary to get the actual response of non-respondents before including them in the study through weighting. This is, of course, a much more defensible approach to the problem, but it is also more complicated and, perhaps, still not entirely free from bias.

Evaluation of Questionnaire Research

In summary, it seems that the weaknesses of the questionnaire—while very real—are not insurmountable. It seems further that, today as in 1930, the criticisms of the questionnaire are aimed at its abuse rather than at its use. Recent opinions on the subject have run the gamut of the favorability-unfavorability continuum. On the negative side are such views as those of Charters (1955), who suggests that educational researchers must seek new ways to answer persistent questions. Even stronger positions against the questionnaire are taken by Ruckmick (1930), who knows of no other procedure which compels so much forethought, coupled with the avoidance of irretrievable errors as does the questionnaire; and by Duker (1948), who writes:

> The reliability and validity is low, the frequent use of the questionnaire is a vice and a weakness mitigating against the recognition of educational research as a science. It seeks secondary information, hearsay evidence concerning facts when primary evidence is at hand. It is the voice of expediency, not of science, justified on the basis of saving time and money.

Frequently, questionnaire research constitutes nothing more than a pooling of ignorance; the opinion of one single expert may be far superior to the compilation of the opinions of many persons who do not have the information and/or who are incapable or unwilling to convey the information they have.

More positive in their views are such people as Monroe and Engelhart who, in 1936, suggested that until experimental science relieves us of the need for human judgment, or removes from our minds interest in unique events, this wayward child of science, the questionnaire, feeble as it is, will remain an indispensable helper. Another comment favorable to the questionnaire is that of Phillips (1951) who points out that the weaknesses laid at the door of the questionnaire are primarily within the control of the investigator.

A number of studies have been reported on the relative adequacy of the questionnaire as a research instrument. Unfortunately, most of the studies have failed to point out that *adequacy* as used in this context must be spelled out in terms of the usual criteria of validity, reliability, and usability, and further, that validity is a specific concept. A questionnaire may be adequate for obtaining information on family size and yet not adequate for determining student reactions toward their teachers. Franzen and Lazarsfeld (1945), in their study of former college students, concluded that the mailed questionnaire obtained more information and more ready admission of unusual activities and interests than did interviews.

The present consensus is that, when properly used, the questionnaire has potentialities as an instrument of science. Conrad (1960) points out that the U.S. Office of Education makes considerable use of the questionnaire after attempting to validate it by checking for evidence of internal consistency and agreement with information already on hand. Ruckmick (1930) expresses the opinion that the questionnaire has been very useful in education and that we should not disparage it. Topp and McGrath (1950) make a particularly strong plea for answering questionnaires. They point out that the questionnaire is an economical way of accumulating information of significance to educators; that it saves both the sender and respondent time, effort, and cost; and that if it were eliminated, progress in many areas of education would be greatly handicapped and much useful information lost. They feel that answering a questionnaire is a professional obligation, particularly since education is a profession in which there is no ready means of communication among members, and that to say that it is not worthy of response is "to play God" and to imply that the person who sent it is lacking in common sense. They point out that the rationalization that one does not answer questionnaires because the rate of response is generally so low that valid generalizations cannot be derived is a circular argument.

None of these statements denies the need for improvement of the questionnaire. It is fully agreed, for instance, that unless the returns can be brought up to an acceptable level, there is no point in bothering anyone. Furthermore, whenever there is doubt as to the adequacy of the responses that can be obtained, the questionnaire should not be used. But there is, on the other hand, no justification for a complete across-the-broad condemnation of questionnaire studies. The general consensus is that the questionnaire can serve a very definite purpose in the advancement of education at its present stage of development— and perhaps for some time to come. It is clear, however, that there is urgent need for the improvement of its quality and for the restriction of its use to appropriate situations.

The following criteria may be used as a checklist for evaluating a questionnaire:

1. It deals with a significant topic; it makes an important contribution, and is worthy of professional participation.

2. The importance of the problem is clearly explained in the statement of the problem and in the cover letter.

3. It seeks only information not available elsewhere.

4. It is as brief as the study of the problem will allow.

5. The directions are clear, complete, and acceptable.

6. The questions are relatively free from ambiguity and other invalidating features; questions that may place the respondent on the defensive are avoided.

7. The questions are in good psychological order.

8. The questions are so arranged that they can be readily tabulated and interpreted.

INTERVIEW STUDIES

A research method very similar in nature and purpose to the questionnaire is the interview. In fact, except for certain relative advantages which need to be clearly recognized, the two techniques are, for some purposes at least, essentially interchangeable. As a research technique,* the interview is a conversation carried out with the definite purpose of obtaining certain information. It has the same purpose and, if it is to yield dependable gen-

---

*Although our interest is in the interview as a research technique, the interview is most frequently used in connection with nonresearch activities, e.g., counseling or hiring procedures.

eralizations, must subscribe to the same criteria as other scientific techniques. It is designed to gather valid and reliable information through the responses of the interviewee to a planned sequence of questions.

The interview can be either *structured* or *unstructured,* depending on the extent to which the content and procedures involved are standardized in advance. Thus, in the administration of the *Revised Stanford-Binet,* no deviation from standardization procedures is allowed. On the other hand, in a survey of the reactions of freshmen to their orientation program, a more conversational approach would allow the respondent greater freedom in discussing any aspect of the program of significance to him.

To some extent, the distinction between structured and unstructured interviews parallels that between the open and the closed questionnaire, although the unstructured interview, being even more flexible than the open questionnaire, is better suited to getting diverse responses and, of course, more capable of following through on tangential ideas. Both types of interviews have their purpose and their relative advantages. The unstructured interview is most appropriate for getting insight into a particular situation in the early stages of investigation; the structured interview, on the other hand, is used to derive more precise generalizations in the later stages. In the structured interview, the interviewer operates on the basis of an interview schedule, which is essentially an abbreviated questionnaire, often planned to the last detail.

The structured interview calls for less versatility and on-the-spot adaptability on the part of the interviewer. On the other hand, it requires a thorough knowledge of the problem—achieved in part from the try-out of the schedule—so that the questions can be phrased to function in the field with a minimum of modification. It can be used effectively, therefore, only when a careful exploratory survey has enabled the investigator to structure the field and to devise adequate questions from which deviations can be kept to an absolute minimum.

Comparison with the Questionnaire

In a sense, the interview can be considered an oral questionnaire, though, to be sure, it has definite characteristics of its own which must be considered in judging its suitability for the investigation of a given phenomenon. The similarity of the interview and the questionnaire is relatively obvious in the structured interview, where the major point of distinction is that the investigation is conducted through face-to-face contact rather than through the mails. In fact, the more structured an interview is, the more closely it resembles the questionnaire. Conversely, the less structured the interview is, the more evident its relative advantages and disadvantages in contrast to the questionnaire become.

The primary advantage of the interview over the questionnaire is its greater flexibility which permits the investigator to pursue leads that appear fruitful, to encourage elaboration of points which the respondent has not made clear or has partially avoided, and to clarify questions which the respondent has apparently misunderstood. While the questionnaire is out of the hands of the investigator the minute it is mailed, the interview allows the investigator to remain in command of the situation throughout the investigation. The flexibility of the interview is, of course, of greatest value in exploratory studies where the structure of the field emerges as the investigation proceeds. It is of correspondingly less importance where the field is more clearly defined. For example, in the early stages of an investigation of the characteristics considered by principals and superintendents in hiring new teachers, an interview may provide a number of ideas that otherwise would be overlooked. Later, as more studies are made, suggestions for drawing up a structured interview (or questionnaire) might be derived from the literature as well as from personal experience, so that the more precise structured approach becomes more appropriate.

Despite the rigid limits it places on the interviewer, the structured interview has a number of advantages over the questionnaire under certain circumstances. It permits the establishment of greater rapport and, thus, stimulates the respondent to give more complete and valid answers; it permits the canvassing of persons who are essentially illiterate for questionnaire purposes or who are reluctant to put things in writing; and it generally promotes a higher percentage of return. Another important strength of the interview is that it permits the interviewer to help the respondent clarify his thinking on a given point so that he will give a response where he would normally plead ignorance and, even more important, so that he will give a correct answer instead of a false one. Thus, if a respondent indicates that he cannot remember, the skillful interviewer may structure the field for him by pointing out some concurrent events in order to refresh his memory.

The interview also allows the observation of the respondent for signs of evasiveness, noncooperation, and other irregularities. Not only can the interviewer appraise the sincerity and cooperation of his respondent, but he can often combat negative attitudes by establishing a higher level of rapport, or, at least, take the factor into consideration in interpreting the results. And, of course, by allowing for the operation of the interviewer's personality in overcoming reluctance and resistance, the interview frequently results in successful contact with people who would refuse to participate under less compelling circumstances.

The flexibility of the unstructured interview is undoubtedly its greatest strength. Not only does it enable the investigator to pursue a given lead in order to gain insight into the problem and to obtain more adequate answers but, more important, it frequently leads to significant insights in unexpected directions. As he pursues various leads, the investigator may find his problem shift and become entirely different. Such flexibility can also lead to by-products which were not anticipated in the original plan of the study but which often have greater significance than the outcomes of the initial design. The unstructured interview is useful in probing into attitudes and motives of which even the respondent may not be aware. Depth interviewing permits getting below the surface of clichés in the case of the person who is reluctant to take a stand, who is not too clear on his own position, or who is reluctant to admit certain problems. The psychology of projective techniques might be useful here as background for understanding more adequately the possibility of the use of the interview in this context.

Interviewer Bias

The major weakness of the interview is interviewer bias which, ironically, stems in large part from its flexibility—which is, then, both its major advantage and disadvantage. To the extent that the interviewer is allowed to vary his approach to fit the occasion, he is likely not only to complicate the interpretation of his results, but, even more serious, to project his own personality into the situation and, thus, influence the responses he receives. Research has shown that interviewers tend to obtain data that agree with their own personal convictions. Part of this occurs as a result of ad-libbing by the interviewer in rephrasing or clarifying questions. The problem is more basic and fundamental than this, however. Research (e.g., Cahalan, 1947; Hanson and Marks, 1958; Lenski and Leggett, 1960; Williams, 1965; Fowler, 1967) has shown that the very presence of the interviewer—with all that he represents in the eyes of the interviewee—affects the responses he gets. This is unavoidable. Usually the respondent will orient his answers toward the sociable and courteous rather than simply toward the truth—especially if the investigator is a pleasant person. If, on the other hand, the interviewer is curt, the respondent is likely to evade questions or even to disagree just to register his annoyance. In either case, the responses will be colored somewhat from the truth.

No matter what he is or does, the interviewer is bound to have some effect upon his data. Research (Madge, 1953; Hyman, 1950) has shown that Negro respondents express fewer negative reactions when interviewed by whites than when interviewed by Negroes, and that interviewers who look Jewish or have Jewish names obtain fewer anti-semitic reactions than do other interviewers. While the degree of distortion present has to be appraised from the standpoint of the specific situation, this is a complication which is inherent in the method itself and of which the interviewer must be fully aware. The validity of the responses he derives depends on his ability to overcome such biases. A considerable amount of research pertinent to the interview has been conducted in the field of clinical counseling, and the research worker contemplating doing an interview study can profit from a thorough appraisal of the literature in that field.

Another disadvantage of the interview as a research technique is its cost. Not only can it be expensive, especially when the survey covers a wide geographic area, but it is also costly in time and effort since it almost invariably necessitates call-backs, long waits, and travel. Besides, a busy person may prefer to fill out a questionnaire at his leisure rather than submit to a long interview. Sometimes the advantages of the interview and questionnaire can be combined by leaving a questionnaire to be completed and calling back at an appointed time to pick it up and to check on aspects that need clarification.

Selection of Interviewers

Contrary to the opinion commonly held by the neo-phyte, interviewing is not a technique that can be mastered on the spur of the moment. Simply talking things over with people on an off-the-cuff basis is not interviewing, and it is certainly not the scientific interviewing required for research purposes. On the contrary, its very looseness makes extra competence all the more necessary. Even in the case of structured interviews, the interviewer must be able to make intelligent deviations from his schedule without violating the standardization of the procedure. Consequently, interviewing calls for the most rigorous selection of interviewers and, further, for their most thorough, meticulous, and painstaking preparation. First, the interviewer must be a person who reflects integrity, objectivity, and personal charm, and who has the tact and ability to meet and to communicate effectively with people, even of a different cultural background. He must have a good grasp of the dynamics of human behavior and must be able to make people feel at ease and willing to communicate. He must be sensitive to clues, which frequently make the difference between a successful and an unsuccessful interview, and between truth and falsehood. He must be particularly adept at making an effective primary contact, for the success of the interview frequently depends on the rapport established in the first minute or two; it may even determine whether there is an interview at all. In initiating the interview, he may have to depend on his friendliness and charm, while relying on other motives, such as the interviewee's natural willingness to talk to others about subjects in which he is interested, for its continuance.

While the interviewer must be able to understand the personality dynamics of his interviewees, he must not allow them to understand him to the point of orienting their responses to what they think he would like to have them say. Furthermore, he must be aware of his own dynamics so that he recognizes that his biases sensitize him to certain phenomena and lead him to certain interpretations. Unless he is careful, he will be looking for and seeing what he wants to see.

It is also necessary to realize that certain people just do not make good interviewers. Some cannot refrain from projecting their own personality into the problem they are investigating, especially with respect to certain topics and certain interviewees;

others do not inspire the necessary confidence in prospective interviewees and, as a result, get an excessive percentage of refusals or are not able to keep their interviews from becoming nonproductive. In practice, the unsuitability of an interviewer, either in general or with respect to a specific problem or type of interviewee, generally can be detected in a pilot study or in the training period conducted prior to the investigation.

Besides selecting suitable interviewers, it is necessary to fit the interviewer to the prospective interviewee. It is mandatory, for instance, that the person who interviews a housewife about some aspect of her status be sufficiently familiar with her responsibilities to permit two-way communication. Whether the interviewer should be a member of the same group, or acquaintance, or even a personal friend of the interviewee is a matter to be determined at the local level. Most experts would consider it more important for the interviewer to maintain his status as a scientific person and, except for areas of a very impersonal nature, to refrain from interviewing acquaintances where the relationship might be considered more personal than professional and where the interviewee might be placed on the defensive. In any case, however, a pilot study is a more adequate basis for decision than *a priori* reasoning.

The interviewer must first address himself to the general task of meeting people and understanding them so that he can establish rapport quickly and effectively, overcome resistance where it develops, lead the respondent over embarrassing topics, and generally guide the conversation toward the derivation of adequate answers. In short, he must be both a psychologist and a skillful manipulator of men of varying background and status. This is even more important, of course, in the case of the unstructured interview where, unless the interviewer is particularly skillful, the conversation can go in all directions without revealing anything worthwhile, or come to a standstill. He must also know his problem and have a keen and alert mind which can detect ideas worth exploring. He must be able to help people who are inarticulate and unsure of themselves and, yet, he must avoid projecting his personality into the situation to the point where they are simply acting as dummies on the knee of a ventriloquist.

The structured interview calls for an understanding of the problem sufficient to permit the devising of adequate questions. These must be phrased in such a way as to avoid their appearing stilted when used in conversation. Furthermore, the interviewer must be capable of deviating from the schedule to answer questions and to correct misinterpretations without violating the standardization of the procedure. This is particularly well-known to people who have administered individual tests of intelligence, for instance.*

Training of Interviewers

Before an interview study is undertaken, the prospective interviewer should undergo rigorous training. This is generally best done through a pilot study that would not only train the interviewer, but will also help structure the field and identify its problems and pitfalls. Training is particularly crucial in a study which involves a team of interviewers for, unless they synchronize their procedures, their findings will be essentially uninterpretable. Generally, the training program must incorporate the fourfold approach of: 1. convincing the prospective interviewers that they are in need of training; 2. impressing on them the importance of the problem to be investigated; 3. orienting them to the nature of the problem so that they can see the relevance of the responses they get; and 4. providing them with special skills on the basis of which they can accomplish their purposes. In structured interviews, for instance, the major task is to convince the interviewers of the necessity of abiding by standardization procedures. Supervised practice in interviewing is essential to the success of the study.

Interviewing is an art that calls for the highest level of competence—a fact fully recognized in such fields as counseling where the general requirements call for both a theoretical background in the dynamics of human behavior and for supervised practice in the art of interviewing. Generally, competence in interviewing comes after long years of experience coupled with a good background in the theory and the art of interviewing. In view of the complex problems inherent in the use of the method, and the ease and speed with which research data can be invalidated, the

---

* What is needed is equivalence of response and not necessarily equivalence of stimulus. The important thing is to get maximum validity of response, both in quantity and in accuracy, by whatever means possible and not necessarily by providing an identical stimulus to all respondents. In dealing with a deaf person, the interviewer would just have to talk a little louder; in dealing with a foreigner he would have to do some translating. Although this would entail some question as to the standardization, it would probably bring about more valid results than attempting to maintain uniformity.

use of the interview technique by the amateur—including the graduate student who has not had specific training under supervision in the field—is generally to be discouraged.

Note-Taking in Interviewing

It is desirable to take notes during an interview in order to preclude misrepresentation resulting from a failure in memory. In some instances, this poses no problem; if the topic under investigation is such that the respondent has no objection to being quoted, his remarks can be taken verbatim or recorded and edited later for answers significant to the study. This would be the ideal method, inasmuch as the purpose of the study may change as the analysis proceeds and certain data may assume an unanticipated significance. However, many interviewees become apprehensive when they see that their remarks are being recorded and become defensive, noncommittal, and noncommunicative. When there is danger of this occurring, it is probably best not to make note-taking too conspicuous an aspect of the interview.

Whatever notes are taken should not interfere with the interview. Taking longhand notes, for instance, generally is inadvisable since it slows down the interview and is likely to encourage the respondent to become progressively more laconic. A common solution to this problem is to devise a brief interview schedule on which to check the main points of the interview, according to a prearranged system of notation. This can be done as the interview progresses or, if any form of note-taking might be disturbing to the respondent, immediately after the interview. On the other hand, some interviewees would undoubtedly feel more comfortable if they saw the interviewer taking notes rather than relying on his memory.

Important Interview Studies

Undoubtedly the best known of the many interview studies conducted on a regular basis is the decennial census of the U.S. Bureau of the Census. The regular reports in which the findings of the nation-wide census are presented, and the many interim reports of the Bureau covering certain localities and aspects of the economy, are of interest to the businessman, the school administrator, and even to the average citizen. The Census is, obviously, the nation's most comprehensive interview investigation and, though it is not strictly educational, it has definite educational implications, particularly in such areas as population growth and enrollment, educational status, and income level.

Also of interest to the American public are the many polls conducted by Gallup, Roper, Crosley, Harris, and others, on a multitude of social and political issues. Polls are also conducted by a number of business firms. American Telephone and Telegraph and General Motors, for example, spend millions of dollars in questionnaires sent to their customers. General Mills and Metropolitan Life Insurance also conduct extensive polls, and radio and TV audiences are frequently canvassed by the Hooper Poll in its attempt to derive ratings of the relative popularity of the various programs.

The Kinsey studies (1948, 1953), of the sexual habits of the human male and the human female are of interest here because they exemplify some of the difficulties involved in conducting sociological research into areas which are of a confidential and personal nature. The major criticism of the Kinsey studies—in addition to loose reporting—centers around the problems of sampling and interviewing, both of which, because of the nature of the problem, necessarily introduce special difficulties. These studies have been reviewed by numerous critics, and the student is referred to more comprehensive sources for more adequate treatment of their net worth (Wallis, 1949; Cochran et al., 1953).

Validity of Interview Studies

Establishing the validity of the interview presents much the same problems as it does in the case of the questionnaire. Again, validity pertains to the separate items as well as to the overall operation. The fact that the interview permits a follow-through on misunderstood items and inadequate responses generally promotes validity, but suitable criteria, especially for the more sensitive and intangible issues, are essentially unavailable. The rather common practice of using inter-interviewer agreement as a criterion of validity is questionable in view of the inherent danger that, if interviewers have the same frame of reference because of similarity in background and training, they may simply duplicate each other's mistakes.

A crucial point in the validity of the interview is the

possibility, if not the likelihood, that the interviewer's very presence will affect the responses he gets. Unless special care to avoid
such a bias is exercised, the results can be misleading. The validity
of the interview appears to be directly proportional to the competence of the interviewer. This makes its use by the amateur in
any but the most psychologically simple situations precarious, and
the method, though most valuable when properly used, should be
approached cautiously.

The reliability of the interview also must be considered from the standpoint of the individual items, and, while it may
be possible to obtain reasonable consistency in certain items, a
similar consistency can hardly be expected in other matters. This
is probably not peculiar to the interview, however, but would be
true of any approach used to obtain the same data.

Highlights of the Chapter

1.   Survey studies are designed to determine the present status of
a given phenomenon and though, much too frequently, they are
simply fact-finding expeditions conducted under relatively ill-
defined circumstances, they are often of considerable immediate
value. They can also provide, as by-products, an indication of
trends, and even hypotheses as to the antecedents of the status
noted. Their flexibility makes them particularly suited to the early
exploration of phenomena. They are, however, of relatively limited
scientific sophistication. There is need for a greater utilization of
survey results as sources of hypotheses and for greater emphasis
on the interpretation and integration of the findings into theoretical
structure.

2.   Although the distinction is not clear-cut, surveys can be divided into descriptive and analytical. The questions of sampling
and of the validity of the various data-gathering instruments are of
crucial importance to the validity of all survey results.

3.   Survey testing probably represents the most systematic research program conducted in our schools. The proper interpretation of the results of survey testing requires considerable background in the field of tests and measurements, especially from the
standpoint of the validity of the instruments used in the particular
situation.

4.   The questionnaire is probably the most used and most abused survey instrument. Too frequently, it is used to provide a pooling of ignorance in situations where only a more adequate approach—experimentation, for example—can provide a meaningful answer. The question of non-returns is particularly troublesome since non-response generally introduces a bias in the data. The possibility of misinterpreting the items is another source of difficulty relatively inherent in the questionnaire method. On the other hand, it has obvious advantages, particularly from the standpoint of practicality.

5.   Among the more important considerations in the successful use of the questionnaire in educational research are the appropriateness of the questionnaire to the investigation of the particular problem, the significance of the study, the proper choice of the population, the scholarliness of the instrument, and the appeal of the cover letter.

6.   The questionnaire can be open or closed, or it can combine the two approaches, depending on the nature of the problem and the purpose of the study. The open questionnaire, for example, is more flexible and is generally better suited for the early exploration of a problem.

7.   Evaluations of the questionnaire range from outright condemnation to general endorsement. It is generally agreed that there is a need for its overall improvement and the restriction of its use to appropriate situations.

8.   Although for certain purposes, the interview is interchangeable with the questionnaire, it has definite characteristics—and advantages and disadvantages—of its own. The unstructured interview, for example, is particularly flexible and, therefore, suitable for the early stages of a problem. Its weakness lies in the bias which the very presence of the interviewer is likely to introduce in the data he collects. The rigorous selection and training of the interviewers is essential to the success of the interview.

9. Note-taking during the interview is sometimes a problem; the danger of distortion and omissions resulting from memory losses must be balanced against the distortion which may result when the interviewee realizes that his responses are being recorded.

Questions and Projects

1.   What are some of the limitations of the survey approach to the investigation of educational problems? What are some of the strengths?

2.   (a) Specifically, what benefits might be derived from the school's annual standardized achievement testing program?

(b) How might the school proceed in the selection of the instruments to be used?

3.   (a) Locate a questionnaire in the literature and appraise its overall quality in the light of the principles of test construction.

(b) As a class project, prepare and pretest a questionnaire. Include the cover and follow-up letters.

Selected References

Ackoff, Russell L. and Leon Pritzker. "The methodology of survey research," *Internat. J. opinion attitude Res.*, 5: 313–34; 1951.

Flanagan, John C. et al. *The Talents of American Youth: 1. Design for a Study of American Youth*. New York: Houghton-Mifflin, 1962.

————. *The Identification, Development, and Utilization of Human Talents: The American High-School Student*. C.R.P., No. 635. Pittsburgh: Project Talent Office, Univ. Pittsburgh, 1964.

Hyman, Herbert H. *Survey Design and Analysis: Principles, Cases, and Procedures*. New York: Free Press, 1955.

Sieber, Sam D. "The case of the misconstrued technique," *Phi Delta Kappan*, 49: 273–76; 1968.

Young, Pauline V. *Scientific Social Surveys and Research*. Englewood Cliffs: Prentice-Hall, 1966.

The Questionnaire

Bennett, C.M. and R.E. Hill. "Comparison of selected personality characteristics of respondents and nonrespondents to a mailed questionnaire study," *J. educ. Res.*, 58: 178–80; 1964.

Clausan, John A. "Controlling bias in mail questionnaires," *J. Amer. stat. Assn.*, 42: 497–511; 1947.

Couch, A. and K. Keniston. "Yeasayers and naysayers: Agreeing response set as a personality variable," *J. abnorm. soc. Psychol.*, 60: 151–74; 1960.

Di Vesta, Francis J. "Problems in the use of questionnaires for studying the effectiveness of educational programs," *Educ. psychol. Measmt*, 14: 138–50; 1954.

Marshall, Max S. "The questionnaire complex," *Educ. Forum*, 24: 173–79; 1960.

Nixon, John E. "The mechanics of questionnaire construction," *J. educ. Res.*, 47: 481–87; 1954.

Payne, Stanley L. "Thoughts about meaningless questions," *Public Opinion Quart.*, 14: 687–96; 1951.

Romine, Stephen A. "Criteria for a better questionnaire," *J. educ. Res.*, 42: 69–71; 1948.

Slocum, W.L. et al. "Increasing response to questionnaires and structured interviews," *Amer. sociol. Rev.*, 21: 221–25; 1956.

Suchman, Edward A. and Boyd R. McCandless. "Who answers questionnaires?" *J. appl. Psychol.*, 24: 758–69; 1940.

Voss, Robert B. "A procedure for reducing the effects of slanting questionnaire responses toward social acceptability," *Educ. psychol. Measmt*, 18: 337–45; 1958.

Wallace, David. "A case for and against mail questionnaires," *Public Opinion Quart.*, 18: 40–52; 1954.

The Interview

Cochran, William G. et al. "Statistical problems of the Kinsey Report," *J. Amer. stat. Assn.*, 48: 673–716; 1953.

Fowler, Floyd J. "Education, interaction, and interview performance," *Diss. Abstr.*, 27: 2195-A, 1967.

Hanson, R.H. and Eli S. Marks. "Influence of the interviewer on the accuracy of survey results," *J. Amer. stat. Assn.*, 53: 635–55; 1958.

Kann, Robert L. and Charles F. Cannell. *The Dynamics of Interviewing: Theory, Techniques, and Cases.* New York: Wiley, 1957.

Lenski, Gerhard E. and John C. Leggett. "Caste, class, and deference in the research interview," *Amer. J. Sociol.*, 65: 463–67; 1960.

Mosteller, Frederick. "Interviewing and questionnaire design," in *The Pre-Election Polls of 1948.* New York: Soc. Sci. Res. Council, 1949.

Parker, Clyde A. et al. "Questions concerning the interview as a research technique," *J. educ. Res.*, 51: 215–21; 1957.

Smith, Harry L. and Herbert H. Human. "The biasing effect of interviewer expectations on survey results," *Public Opinion Quart.*, 14: 491–506; 1950.

Williams, James A. "Interviewer-respondent interaction: A study of bias in the information interview," *Diss. Abstr.*, 25: 4857; 1965.

10
THE SURVEY:
ANALYTICAL STUDIES

*. . . the history of science is a history of relentless
analysis. We aim to break down gross phenomena into
subphenomena; we aim to break complex stimulus conditions into their unitary parts.*——Benton J. Underwood (1957)

Analysis as an Aspect of Science

One of the most basic of all research techniques is
analysis. Analysis as a method underlies the whole process of research, from the selection of a problem and its reduction to manageable size to the point where the data are processed and the
conclusions are reached. Since most educational problems are too
broad to be attacked as a unit, they must be analyzed into their
constituent parts as the preliminary step in deriving significant
relationships among them, in isolating relevant from irrelevant aspects, and in structuring them in their scientific context.

As we have seen in Chapter 2, an aspect of the early
development of a science is *classification*—a process of ordering
phenomena into subcategories on the basis of whatever properties
and characteristics prove relevant from the standpoint of the purpose at hand. By playing a critical role in identifying the crucial
aspects of phenomena, analysis not only promotes a better understanding of both the whole and its parts but also, thereby, permits
the allocation of phenomena into evermore precise and functional
categories for which increasingly precise relationships can be
discovered. It also permits combining into meaningful classes
phenomena having in common one or more aspects crucial with
respect to a given purpose despite, perhaps, vast differences in

irrelevant aspects. To a zoologist, for example, a whale is a mammal, not a fish.

Such a breakdown is essential to the development of a discipline into a precise science. Generally, the properties of a given phenomenon are predicated on the properties of its constituents, and the identification and understanding of these constituents, at one level or another of analysis, can usually lead to an understanding—or at least to hypotheses—of the nature of the phenomenon itself. Thus, the identification of a child as an underachiever provides considerable insight into many of his characteristics and his likely behavior under certain circumstances.

The point in the analysis at which the breakdown provides the greatest enlightenment depends on the purpose. Thus, the analysis of materials into the basic elements of the periodic table constitutes one of the greatest "discoveries" in the advancement of science; the more recent and further analysis of matter into its atomic structure constitutes an even more fundamental step in its progress. On the other hand, neither breakdown is too useful in understanding the nature and properties of table salt (NaCl), which does not have much in common with the properties of its constituent elements or of its constituent atoms.

Analysis can be carried too far for the purpose under consideration, and the investigator must decide on the degree of fineness with which he wants to analyze his data. The point to consider here is that, for certain purposes at least, a given phenomenon loses its meaningfulness if it is dissected past the point at which it really exists as an entity, and that the researcher must stop short of complete analysis or face the risk of destroying the very thing he is investigating. This is essentially the objection that Gestalt psychologists raise against analysis in their basic postulate that the whole is more than the sum of its parts. The analysis of a phenomenon into its constituents provides a greater understanding of its nature only to a point. Beyond that point, the basic laws which apply to its constituents may no longer apply to the phenomenon itself.

Analysis is worthwhile only to the extent that the breakdown is relevant from the standpoint of the study. Thus, while the analysis of a document with respect to such components as "appeal to emotion," "appeal to logic," etc. might provide increased insight into its psychology, analysis on the basis of vocabulary might be more appropriate for the purpose of appraising its readability and predicting likely success or failure in its comprehension. The analysis of the document into the letters that form the words would be of little value except possibly to a typesetter.

Analysis as a Research Method

In addition to being a fundamental method of science, analysis is also a legitimate research method in its own right. It is closely related to descriptive research with which it plays an essentially complementary role. Not only is analysis a form of description, but, without analysis to provide a deeper insight into their basic nature, the adequate description of phenomena is relatively impossible. The description of the nature of a textbook, for example, can be only superficial without some attempt to analyze its various characteristics. As a research method, analysis refers to a broad general category of analytical techniques ranging from simple frequency counts to observational studies of various degrees of precision, complexity, and sophistication, all attempting to identify the basic dimensions into which phenomena can be appraised in relation to a given problem.* The emphasis is on analysis of basic components rather than a simple overall description as discussed in the previous chapter.

CONTENT ANALYSIS

Content analysis encompasses a group of techniques concerned with the analysis of records already in existence, e.g., newspaper articles, textbooks, TV programs, or even cartoons. At its simplest level, as characterized by the old "documentary-frequency" studies, it includes frequency counts of any number of things—e.g., spelling errors, the spoken vocabulary of children, fractions in common use, etc.—often in isolation of the framework that would make them meaningful. This is not to malign such classic studies as that of Thorndike (1921, 1932, 1944) who identified the ten, twenty, and later, thirty thousand most used English words or that of M.E. Smith (1926) who investigated the size of the vocabulary of young children. The findings of these studies are unquestionably of importance in themselves.

---

* Analysis could also include case studies in which the purpose is to identify conditions in the individual's past or present circumstances involved in a "causative" or contributing way in the development of his present predicament or status. Case studies will be considered in Chapter 11, since their major orientation is to the discovery of the antecedents of phenomena rather than an analysis of their present status.

As presently used, the term *content analysis* represents a more sophisticated level of investigation, concerned with the identification of the more subtle and more significant dimensions into which a given phenomenon can be analyzed from the standpoint of a clear-cut research problem. Specifically, it differs from its predecessor in orientation from the earlier "frequency counts," often of a highly tedious clerical nature, to an emphasis on collecting data only after it has been fitted into a scientifically meaningful context, e.g., prejudice, propaganda, or emotional appeal in editorials, the character-building overtones of certain instruction, or other psychologically meaningful features of speeches, textbooks, novels, movies, etc. A particularly significant example of this new orientation are the two volumes of *The Taxonomy of Educational Objectives* (Bloom, 1956, *Cognitive Domain;* Krathwohl et al., 1964, *Affective Domain*).

Of considerable interest are the studies of readability aimed at determining the level of reading difficulty of written material. Such studies are usually accomplished by means of a formula, a number of which have been devised, each based on somewhat similar bases and yielding essentially similar but not identical results. Such studies have shown, for example, that textbooks frequently have a measured reading level beyond the grade placement for which they are prescribed.

Textbooks can also be analyzed from the standpoint of such aspects as emphasis on group discussion, advocacy of particular ideologies, treatment of minority problems, use of graphic material, format, etc. A more comprehensive approach to textbook analysis might involve investigation on a multiple basis. In selecting social studies textbooks for adoption by the school, for example, the investigator might base his analysis on such factors as historical accuracy, exposition of acceptable social ideals, emphasis on character formation, readability, attractiveness of format, motivational appeal, clarity of expression, etc. The analysis could be extended to a rating of each factor, weighted in proportion to its importance from the standpoint of the objectives of the school curriculum. This would then yield an overall score or index.

Also relevant in this context is job analysis, the purpose of which is to reveal the nature of a given job in order to permit more adequate coordination of the worker to the job. Job analysis in the field of education might include time-motion studies concerned with determining the duties and responsibilities of school personnel from the superintendent to the janitor. Such studies are useful to the administrator in selecting adequate personnel and in providing in-service training to meet job requirements. Knowing specifically what is required on the job would help teacher-training institutions in providing students with the skills conducive to effective teaching.

Studies of this kind can be particularly useful to the school administrator. While concerned primarily with present status, they are definitely oriented toward the improvement of future practice. On the other hand, too often, factors of availability and ease of measurement have oriented such surveys toward the investigation of the trivial to the neglect of the more fundamental aspects of phenomena. It must also be realized that such studies do not identify the reasons why certain phenomena exist; they simply point to their existence. Furthermore, frequency of occurrence is not synonymous with importance. The fact that adults make little use of fractions such as $7/19$ implies that they should be eliminated from the curriculum only if we can assume that, because something is not used, it is unnecessary. Similarly, a study revealing that a certain amount of duplication exists in the curriculum does not answer the question of how much duplication is permissible, or even desirable. This, of course, is not peculiar to analytical studies; research is never expected to provide decisions, but simply data on which intelligent decisions can be based.

OBSERVATIONAL STUDIES

Nature of Observation

Observation is at once the most primitive and the most refined of modern research techniques. It is, undoubtedly, the first procedure of science, inasmuch as all scientific data must originate in some experience or perception. As a scientific tool, it may range from the most casual and uncontrolled to the most scientific and precise, involving modern mechanical and electronic means of supplementing human powers of observation. Much of the observation of the layman is of a capricious nature and generally does not yield results of any great scientific value. It differs from scientific observation only in degree, however, and there is no specific point at which observation becomes or ceases to be scientific.

Observation underlies all research; it plays a particularly prominent part in the survey procedures now being considered, and even experimentation is simply observation under controlled conditions. As a research technique of its own, however, observation has made a relatively limited contribution to the development of education as a science. Thus far, most of the uses of observation as a research technique—with the obvious exception of child development studies—have been routine and scientifically imprecise. On the other hand, it must be recognized that many significant variables can be investigated in no other way.

Criteria of Scientific Observation

Contrary to the opinion of the amateur who may be inclined to think that observation is nothing more than what he has been doing all his life, observation is actually so loose and yet so complex that it is one of the most difficult techniques to harness in the service of science. It is, therefore, necessary to make a distinction between observation as a scientific tool—which must *ipso facto* comply with the usual requirements of all instruments of science—and the casual observation of the man in the street. Both the scientist and the layman observe, but the scientist starts with a hypothesis and arranges the conditions of his observations to avoid distortion. More specifically, scientific observation must comply with the following criteria:

1. Scientific observation is systematic rather than haphazard or opportunistic. In the early stages, where the problem is to survey the phenomenon as a whole, it is necessary to maintain maximum flexibility in order to gain insight into its nature and to permit structuring the field for more controlled investigation later. On the other hand, in the more refined states at which research operates, casual observation rarely provides anything of value. Scientific observation is directed at those aspects of the total situation which are considered to be significant from the standpoint of the purposes of the study. It is based on the assumption that orienting observation toward segments into which the phenomenon can be broken to permit closer examination leads to more dependable data. This, in turn, assumes that the phenomenon has been properly dissected and significant aspects correctly identified. Conversely, it involves the inherent

risk of overlooking significant dimensions of the situation outside the frame of the observer's mind-set.

The scientific observer has a good grasp of the theoretical foundation underlying his problem; he is an expert who knows precisely what he is looking for within the total situation. Not only does he structure the phenomenon he is to observe but he also plans his observations, perhaps by preparing in advance a checklist as a means of orienting his observations toward the aspects of the situation significant from the standpoint of his hypothesis. He is aware of the pitfalls to be avoided and has the necessary background of experience, both in research methods and in the problem area, for him to capitalize on the opportunities that present themselves.

2. Scientific observation must be objective and free from bias. This must be reconciled with the fact that scientific observation—as all research—should generally be guided by a clearly defined hypothesis, with the consequent danger of directing the search toward preconceived goals. It is obviously true that prejudgment on the part of the observer may color his perceptions and blind him to certain aspects of the situation; the teacher who is convinced that underachievers are "lazy" is likely to find many confirming instances. Prejudgment is a liability, particularly in the early stages of observation when the observer must maintain maximum openmindedness as to what is relevant from the standpoint of his purposes.

On the other hand, one cannot see anything in a complex situation if he simply looks at everything on a catch-as-catch-can basis. The observer might as well realize that his perceptions will be influenced by previous experience and to acknowledge openly his basic premises as working hypotheses and to rely on the scientific method and its imposition of restrictions on the operation of his judgment as a means of minimizing the biasing influence of such predispositions. This frequently means that he will have to fight his whole background, including his prejudices, in order to have them under control. It may even be that, under certain circumstances, he may have to disqualify himself on the grounds that he is too emotionally involved. A person with a high level of repressed hostility, for example, might not be able to conduct an impartial study of the disciplinary measures used in the classroom.

3. The observer must be in a good position to observe and he must have adequate sense organs. He must have a clear conception of the overall, as well as the specific, aspects of

the situation and be able to distinguish the significant from the insignificant. He must be alert and able to make adjustments on the spur of the moment. And while he must be systematic and objective in his observations, he must also display originality, flexibility, and imagination.

4. Wherever possible, scientific observation should be quantitative. Although many important phenomena cannot be quantified, it becomes almost imperative in the more refined stages of investigation to derive some means of quantifying observations in order to increase their precision and to facilitate their analysis.

5. Like all scientific data-gathering techniques, observation must comply with the usual criteria of reliability, usability, and, especially, validity. While these characteristics have to be appraised from the standpoint of the individual case, they suggest, among other things, the need for a number of observations covering a relatively large segment of the phenomenon under study. It is recognized in anecdotal records, for example, that the teacher must be careful not to report the atypical behavior of the child and, thus, present a misleading picture of his true nature. Furthermore, since scientific observation must be verifiable, it should be carefully recorded so as to permit validation.

Observation as a Scientific Procedure

Unlike the questionnaire and the interview which rely on the respondent to provide the data required, observation consists of allowing the phenomena to reveal themselves through their operation or characteristics. In a sense, observation is a more basic method of collecting data, since it attempts to get at the data directly rather than through the reports of the individuals involved. On the other hand, in cases such as the investigation of attitudes, one has to infer the data indirectly through behavior. Observation would be useful in situations where, for example, individuals are observed under conditions of stress to see the deterioration of behavior. Observation is particularly useful in situations involving infants or in the study of animals, where the human observer must of necessity emerge as the measuring instrument.

A major advantage of observation is that it permits the recording of behavior as it occurs and bypasses having to rely on the reports of untrained observers. Observation has the further advantage that it may not require the same degree of cooperation by the subject as the questionnaire or the interview. The observer's obvious limitation in this respect is the relative unlikelihood of his being on the spot when significant phenomena occur so that, for the sake of economy, he is more or less forced to rely on questioning people who happen to have been there. In some cases, he can stage the occurrence of certain phenomena, but then he must be careful not to introduce an element of artificiality to the situation and thus invalidate his observations.

The Training of Observers

Observation is no better than the people doing the observing. It is, therefore, mandatory for anyone who conducts an observational study to undergo extensive training. Sportscasters and announcers, for example, are much more adequate observers of a sports event than is the average fan; not only are their observations more accurate and dependable, but they also see many things that escape the layman. They can anticipate plays and, knowing what is likely to occur, they can orient their total observation to the significant components while the fan simply scatters his attention on irrelevant aspects. Training in observation is particularly important in the social sciences where the observer is frequently faced with determining which factors are significant out of the multiple phenomena occurring simultaneously. To complicate matters, the more significant aspects of a given situation are also the more subtle; a slight frown or a tightening of the lips may be much more meaningful than the more obvious "smile" and words of welcome.

Not only is there need for thorough training of observers before they are sent out in the field but there is further the need for continuous on-the-job training as the study proceeds. It is important that the observers-in-training be fully aware of the purposes of the observation in the light of the problem being investigated, so that they can adapt their observations to a given situation and make sound decisions in situations not specifically covered by the directions. It must also be remembered that some people are just not good observers, either in general or with respect to certain phenomena in which they may be emotionally involved, for example. Their unsuitability should be detected in the training period and they should be dropped as observers in the interest of the quality of the study.

Planning for Observation

Securing valid observations demands careful planning, for unless the observer is crystal clear as to the purpose of his investigation and the crucial aspects of the overall situation, his observations will necessarily be of limited validity. Accuracy of observation requires, first of all, that the observer be in a favorable position for observing. It is also necessary to decide the extent of the individual observations. It may be, for instance, that the observation of a tangible object requires only a quick glance. The adequate observation of complex intangibles calling for inferences about their nature—e.g., evidence of repressed hostility among teachers in the classroom—may, on the other hand, require extended observation and even the pooled judgments of many observers. Such problems are generally best resolved on the basis of a pilot study that permits the observer to appraise the situation beforehand to determine how he can best observe without distortion or oversight of significant aspects.

An important consideration in planning for observation is the adequacy of the sample of observations on which the conclusions are to be based. This calls for the dual process of deriving a representative sample of observations from a representative sample of the subjects under investigation—with "representativeness" in both cases defined from the standpoint of the purpose of the study. For example, in the determination of children's behavior patterns, a representative sample of children are placed in an observational situation in which they are likely to display their typical behavior. If, on the other hand, the problem is to determine the reactions of delinquent children to conditions of stress, one would have to choose, not a random sample of children, but a random sample of delinquent children, and to expose them not to ordinary conditions but rather to preplanned conditions of stress. Having identified a random sample of subjects, the investigator must then obtain a random sample of their behavior. This he can do by, say, taking spot checks of each of the children in a systematic order, say, at fifteen-second intervals.

The observer needs to know beforehand the type of observation he is to make: Is he merely to note the occurrence of a given event on a yes-no basis, or must he make a judgment as to its intensity, duration, and apparent effect. He needs to know whether he is simply to observe or whether he is to interpret what he observes: Is he to note that John shoved his neighbor or is he expected to relate the shoving to such psychological dimensions as hostility, social immaturity, restlessness, etc.? If he is to make interpretations, it is essential that he know the criteria on which he is to base his judgments. Furthermore, plans must be made for recording the information quickly, in order to keep distraction of the observer to a minimum, and inconspicuously, in order to prevent distortion of the situation.

Science has developed a number of instruments and devices of various degrees of scientific sophistication designed to promote more precise observation. While none of the instruments used in the social sciences has achieved the precision and accuracy of the gauges, meters, and other yardsticks of the physical sciences, we do have motion and still pictures, sound-recording equipment, one-way screens, projectors, and various psychological scales, as well as simple checklists. The video recorder is now being used to provide an exact picture of classroom operations just as the TV camera has been used over the past decade in athletics. Because they can be stopped at any moment and played any number of times, even in slow motion, without distortion, movies and video recorders are particularly useful in observing a complex situation such as the operation of democratic discussion in a large group. Instrumentation can also be valuable when used in connection with observation in a laboratory situation where, because of the restrictions placed on what is being observed and the control of irrelevant factors, such observation can be made relatively precise. Scientific progress has been made in the area of reading, for instance, where instruments have made possible the derivation of relatively dependable generalizations concerning eye movements and the other mechanical aspects of the act of reading.

Structured and Unstructured Observation

In the early stages of the investigation of a given phenomenon, it is necessary to allow maximum flexibility in observation in order to promote maximum perspective into its meaningful dimensions. Premature attempts to restrict the observations to areas considered significant on an *a priori* basis entail the risk of overlooking some of the more crucial aspects, particularly from the standpoint of interaction. Later, as the investigation proceeds and the phenomenon is seen with greater clarity, the investigator can restrict his observations to the more precise investigation of selected aspects of the situation in an attempt to derive more rigorous generalizations—i.e., he can orient his observations toward the systematic study of those aspects which previous search has shown to be significant. Eventually, these aspects can be subjected to even more precise investigation under experimental conditions.

Participant and Non-Participant Observation

When the subject of observation is the behavior of a human being—or even an animal—the relationship that exists between the observed and the observer is of primary concern, since the very presence of the latter is likely to cause some shift in the behavior he is trying to observe. Although the exact extent to which the observed party is affected varies with such factors as the nature of the activity, the characteristics of the observer and of the observed, etc., the subject's reaction to the observer and to the observation is obviously a factor to be considered in judging the validity of observation as a scientific technique. In fact, some research workers feel that, with the possible exception of observation through one-way screens and hidden microphones, it is not possible to observe without some distortion of the phenomenon being observed, and that all that can be done is to minimize such distortion and to take it into consideration in the interpretation of the results.*

Observation can be either *participant* or *non-participant*. In participant observation, the observer works his way into the group he is to observe so that, as a regular member, he is no longer regarded as an outsider against whom the group needs to guard. Sociological studies have been conducted in which the investigator joined groups of hoboes, hoodlums, and prisoners in jails in order to observe and understand them better. In non-participant observation, on the other hand, the observer remains aloof from the group. The fact that he is observing may be known to the group, but the matter of his observation is made as inconspicuous as possible. In other studies, the observer may simply

---

* Such distortion is not restricted to the social sciences: a similar phenomenon may be observed in physics, where, for instance, the apparatus used to detect the behavior of particles in atomic radiation actually distorts the movement of these particles (the Heisenberg effect).

pretend to be a bystander, or he may even hide behind one-way screens so that his presence is unsuspected.

The advantages and disadvantages of participant and non-participant observation depend largely on the situation. It is probably true that nothing can give a better insight into the life of hoboes, for instance, than living with them through inclement weather and other hardships. On the other hand, participation does not eliminate the distorting influence of the observer, for any member of a group must automatically play a role within that group. Furthermore, as the participant-observer adapts more and more to his role as a participating member of the group, he becomes increasingly blinded to the peculiarities he is supposed to observe. As a result, he is less likely to note what would be significant to a more objective observer. As he develops friendships with the members of the group, he is also likely to lose his objectivity and, along with it, his accuracy in rating things as they are.

Some research workers feel that the observer must restrict himself to no more than partial participation and maintain his status of scientific observer apart from the group. They claim that the distortion caused by his presence is not serious. It has been found that people, particularly children, get used to the observer to the point where they are no longer affected by being observed; after a short period of adjustment, they simply resume their usual behavior. At the empirical level, studies have shown little difference between the observations made by observers out in the open and observers sitting behind one-way screens (Bales, 1950), but this would vary with the nature of the phenomenon being observed and with other factors mentioned previously. It must also be remembered that certain observers are more capable than others of blending into a situation—either as participants or as external observers.

Recording Observation

An important aspect of observation concerns the recording of what is observed. Specifically, the need for immediate recording in order to minimize distortion due to forgetting needs to be balanced against the inherent danger that the process of recording will cause the observer to miss significant observations and will maximize distortion by making the fact of his observation conspicuous. The specific way in which the recording of observation can compromise with these two conflicting considerations varies from situation to situation. In certain circumstances, recording can be done directly, perhaps even with the help of cameras, sound tapes, and other mechanical means. This type of recording is ideal, since it gives an animated picture to be studied at leisure and capitalizes on the dynamic aspects of the situation. It also permits other observers to study the records and pass judgment on the adequacy of the interpretation.

In most instances, such ideal recording is out of the question. Taking longhand notes is generally inadvisable since it is too time-consuming and likely to cause impairment of the observational process. Probably the most commonly used, and generally the most practical, means of recording observational data is through the use of a checklist consisting of key words, which the observer can check as he goes along and from which he can later reconstruct the observation. The checklist is prepared in advance for the purpose of focusing the attention of the observer on relevant aspects of the situation and of systematizing his observation so that none of the significant aspects is overlooked. The checklist should be comprehensive and yet short enough to permit easy location of the items. The categories should be simple: a "yes," "no," or a key word to identify the alternatives is generally sufficient for an observer who is familiar with the situation.

There are times when any form of record-taking during an interview is inadvisable, and the observer must rely on his memory for the reconstruction of his observations. In such instances, he should record his observations as soon as possible after he leaves the setting so as to minimize the danger of distortion as a result of forgetting. There are, on the other hand, occasions when any premature attempt at judgment will produce only incomplete and inaccurate appraisals which will bias later observations. In such instances, postponed recording can promote greater validity in observation by permitting the total picture to be seen in perspective. Of course, even in such cases, some kind of observational guide can be used to prevent the observer from overlooking any significant aspect of the situation.

Interpretation of Observations

The more subtle aspect of observational studies, and from a scientific point of view perhaps the most crucial, is the interpretation of the data from the standpoint of the problem under investigation. The observer is more than a machine merely registering what is going on; he is a scientist investigating a problem. And, while the interpretation of certain observational data is relatively obvious, in other instances, drawing meaningful inferences from the data may require a high level of scientific sophistication and imagination combined with a thorough grasp of the subject area.

Interpretation has to be done by someone at some point in the course of investigation. It can be done directly by the investigator at the time of his observation. Favoring such an approach is the fact that the observer may be in a better position to interpret what he observes than someone who has to reconstruct the situation secondhand. It is obviously difficult for someone to evaluate an event he did not witness, particularly with respect to the more subtle aspects of human interaction or events whose meaning depends crucially on the intangible aspects of the setting in which they occur. It would be virtually impossible to decide *in absentia* whether the child reported to have sought information from his teacher was perhaps fundamentally seeking attention or support. On the other hand, the observer may have his hands full keeping up with all that is happening and to have to interpret as he goes along may actually detract from the completeness and validity of his observations. Furthermore, where several observers are involved, on-the-spot interpretation introduces the problem of uniformity in interpretation. In such instances, it may be best for the observer merely to record his observations and to leave the matter of interpretation to an expert who is more likely to provide a unified frame of reference. It must also be recognized that the interpreter's frame of reference is fundamental to any interpretation, and it might be advisable to insist on agreement between interpreters of somewhat different backgrounds and orientation as a means of counteracting possible bias in the results of a single observer.

Classroom Observation

Although pupil growth promoted by classroom procedures has been a matter of continuous concern, it is only recently that the classroom itself has been the subject of scientific investigation. This is precisely what might have been expected considering that observation, the obvious approach for this purpose, involves major difficulties with respect to time, cost, the disruption of classroom operation, the reluctance of teachers to be observed, and, perhaps above all, the relative unproductivity of early attempts in this direction. Actually, research into the activities of the classroom goes back to the work of Rice who, in 1897, (see Chapter 14), reported that the spelling ability of students bore little relationship to the amount of time devoted to its study. Continued interest in classroom operation was reflected in the concerted effort of the post–World War I period to identify the various aspects of teacher effectiveness. The Wisconsin studies (Barr, 1929, 1948), for example, represent a sustained effort at identifying teacher traits and behaviors that might distinguish between teachers judged by their supervisors to be at the opposite ends of the efficiency continuum. Unfortunately, these early efforts were not particularly rewarding: contrary to what one might logically expect—for, in the final analysis, teacher effectiveness must necessarily be defined in terms of its beneficial effects on people—research to date has failed to identify any significant relationship between teacher characteristics and/or performance and pupil growth. It seems that, whereas direct observation is a perfectly legitimate tool for learning something about the teaching process, it has not been possible to establish through classroom observation the relative effectiveness of various teaching procedures in promoting pupil gains. Morsh (1956) found that items of observed teacher behavior had little relationship to student gains in achievement; student behavior, on the other hand, was quite indicative of the extent to which learning was taking place. On second thought this is entirely logical: students who are daydreaming or "goofing off" cannot be expected to learn with any degree of effectiveness. In other words, student gains in achievement are related to pupil behavior, not teacher behavior, although Heil and Washburne (1962) did find that teachers who behaved in a well-organized manner had the greatest overall success in producing academic achievement.

As a result, research has changed its emphasis and concerned itself with identifying patterns of teacher behavior presumed desirable, on the premise that "correct" teacher behavior *should* result in adequate pupil gain. We hope that eventually we will be able to identify certain teacher behavior patterns that can be related to pupil growth. We also realize that, in the final analysis, teacher effectiveness will have to be determined with respect to how much is learned by the pupils. Meanwhile, the intermediate objective of teacher education is to get teachers to behave in certain ways while they teach—with the ultimate objective, pupil growth, to be expected as a secondary outcome. Presumably what is needed is to find out how teachers can encourage student behavior that will lead to learning; it would help, for example, if the teacher did something to keep students attentive and alert in class. There may be more than one single teacher behavior pattern that will achieve this objective.

A major aspect of the classroom that lends itself to observational research is its emotional climate. Anderson and his co-workers (Anderson et al. 1945; 1946; 1946), for example, found that teacher domination tended to incite pupil resistance. Another of the earlier studies of socio-emotional climate in relation to teacher behavior is that of Withall (1949) who, on the premise that a teacher's behavior is the most important single factor in creating classroom climate and, further, that the teacher's verbal behavior is a representative sample of his total behavior, classified classroom verbal behavior in seven categories from learner-supportive to reproving. Among other things, this study is a good example of the new trend toward the precise investigation of the specific aspects of behavior dictated by a clearly defined hypothesis.

More recently, there has been an increased recognition of the teaching process as a matter of pupil-teacher and pupil-pupil interaction—with a resulting shift in research on teacher effectiveness toward what is known currently as interaction analysis. In other words, the emphasis has shifted from the observation of the teacher in isolation to the consideration of reciprocal teacher and pupil behaviors. The assumption is that, rather than occurring independently of one another, classroom events occur as a consequence of one another or, at least, in sequence. This again reflects a trend in research dealing with classroom observation—namely, the development of theoretical perspective as the basis for the formulation of meaningful observational categories.

A major task in the implementation of classroom observation is the development of an adequate schedule for recording these observations. The task is that of identifying the range of teacher and/or pupil behaviors relevant to the purpose of the study, constructing items to be used in this context, and developing a schedule for quick tabulation. Because of the practical difficulty of recording, the classroom operation in all its complexity must be telescoped into a relatively small number of items. The development of such an observation schedule obviously requires considerable technical skill; in fact, that the whole enterprise is relatively complicated is best reflected in the concluding statement of the Medley-Mitzel article in the *Handbook of Research on Teaching* (1963): "Research in classroom behavior is not a pastime for amateurs; it is a full-time occupation for technically competent professionals."

One of the better known observation schedules is that developed by Ryans (1960) in his study of *The Characteristics of Teachers,* in which the observer makes assessments on a seven-point scale on each of 25 different dimensions of the behavior of teachers and pupils. His instrument structures classroom operation along three continua of teacher behavior patterns: X_0: friendly versus aloof; Y_0: responsible versus slipshod; and Z_0: stimulating versus dull. Eighteen of the bipolar statements pertain to teacher behavior and four to pupil behavior. Probably the best-known and, in a sense, the most comprehensive classroom observation schedule is the *Observation Schedule and Record* (OScAR) developed by Medley and Mitzel (1963) out of the earlier schedules by Withall (1949) and by Cornell et al. (1952). Originally devised to measure the behavior of beginning teachers, it has been used in a number of subsequent studies in an attempt to relate various measures of teacher effectiveness to certain teacher behavior variables. OScAR gives dependable information about three rather distinct dimensions of classroom behavior: the social-emotional climate, the relative emphasis on verbal learning, and the degree to which social structure centers about the teacher. Although still in need of refinement, particularly from the standpoint of relating classroom behavior to pupil achievement, OScAR seems to offer considerable promise as an instrument of research. One of its major strengths is that it provides data amenable to processing through some of the more adequate statistical procedures. Probably the most sophisticated approach to classroom interaction to date is that of Flanders (1960), who classifies the communication behavior of the classroom obtained at three-second intervals into one of ten categories and who, further, tabulates the events in pairs in a two-way chart so as to provide a picture of the continuity of the communication pattern. The student is referred to appropriate sources for a more complete discussion of the construction and use of observation schedules.

Evaluating Observation Studies

Observational research presents a number of practical difficulties. It is, first of all, not always possible to be on hand when some of the more significant events occur. Then, there is always the danger that the very presence of an observer will cause a distortion of the typical classroom operation. Often the more crucial the events, the greater the resistance to outside observers. Furthermore, certain events occur so infrequently that any systematic observation would be extremely time-consuming. Motion pictures, as a substitute, may conceivably be costly. Another major difficulty with observation is that the data resulting therefrom are not particularly amenable to precise statistical treatment, so that a good part of the hard-earned data collected is actually wasted. In addition, observational studies are subject to certain errors peculiar to this type of investigation.

Although established on essentially the same bases as for data derived from other survey techniques, establishing the validity and reliability of observational data presents certain unique problems:

> 1. Many of the variables that lend themselves to an observational approach cannot be defined with sufficient precision to permit the isolation of their various aspects into different levels of relevance and significance. To attempt to define or to isolate these aspects may involve false definitions and, consequently, invalidity. While the derivation of carefully defined categories bearing directly on what is observed in the light of the purposes of the study is generally a prerequisite to valid and reliable observation, there is a question of subjectivity involved in the reconstruction of the phenomenon through the addition of its component parts. Care must be taken not to concentrate on aspects of limited significance simply because they can be recorded objectively. The trend in recent years has been away from exhaustive surveys of all occurring behaviors in a given situation toward the more precise observation of particular aspects in order to answer specific questions as incorporated in a specific observational system designed to fit the investigator's purpose and the framework he is using.
>
> 2. Inherent in observation is the possible distortion of the phenomenon through the very act of observing. Such distortion is difficult to eliminate. It can be minimized through

hidden cameras, one-way mirrors, the proper choice and location of observers, inconspicuous recording, and other attempts at establishing observer neutrality. Video recorders present certain advantages over direct observation, not only in minimizing distortion, but also in providing a permanent record and thus the means for determining reliability and validity. They can, for example, permit an on-the-spot interpretation of the dynamics underlying the phenomena observed as well as their more subtle dimensions—e.g., the intensity of behavior as conveyed by the tone of voice, gestures, etc.—crucial factors which are often hard to detect in an ongoing situation.

3. A third difficulty peculiar to observation is that of obtaining an adequate sample of data on which to base conclusions. Since the observer has little control over the physical situation, it is frequently difficult to get information sufficiently free from complicating co-occurrences to give a clear picture of what is involved. This is particularly true in an unstructured situation where so many things can occur at once that it is difficult to attend to them all. The particular aspect of the situation in which the investigator is interested may occur so infrequently, and under such a variety of confounding circumstances, that it is difficult to establish its validity with any degree of precision.

4. The validity and reliability of observation depends primarily on the competence of the observer. Not only must he be fully trained in observational procedures and have a clear perspective of the nature of the phenomenon under study, but he must also have a valid frame of reference and a relative freedom from personal biases. Psychology has provided relatively conclusive evidence concerning the selectivity of perception and its distortion in the direction of one's motivation (Combs and Snygg, 1959; Ashley, 1951). The problem is complicated further, in the case of human beings in that the more significant aspects of behavior are often revealed through subtle cues which the observer must be able to detect. Generally, greater validity and reliability is obtained by having two or more observers make parallel observations. On the other hand, multiple observers are not a guarantee of validity, since they all may be subject to the same bias. If they have the same background and orientation, they are likely to look for the same things and to see and interpret them in the same way.

Because of the specific nature of the variables in question and the conditions under which the observation takes place, the empirical literature on the validity and reliability of observation is not very helpful. What works in one situation may not work in another; each situation has to be analyzed on its own merits. It seems reasonable to think, however, that when properly used by competent observers under good research conditions, observation can yield results of scientific value and usefulness at all stages of the investigation of a given phenomenon—from its early exploration to its final refinement. Furthermore, as previously noted, one must remember that observation is virtually the only means available for the investigation of certain phenomena, at least in their present stage of scientific development.

RATING STUDIES

Nature of Ratings

Research in the behavioral sciences is often concerned with phenomena's degree of existence which can only be estimated on the basis of subjective judgment. Some can only be assigned to different categories, e.g., *autocratic–democratic*. More commonly, these categories constitute steps of a continuous category system having a quantifiable relationship to each other, and the investigator's task is to assign ratings to the phenomenon in question in terms of these steps identified on either a numerical or a graphic scale ranging from, say, *excellent* to *poor*, or *favorable* to *unfavorable*. At a more sophisticated level, the separate ratings of the individual components are combined into an overall index of the individual's status on the phenomenon in question.

The concept of *rating* is probably best known in the area of tests and measurements where—in its basic sense as a form of classification of items into levels along a given continuum—it parallels measurement. It differs from measurement which often calls for nothing more than the skill to read a given instrument in that it implies the ability to estimate the status of the phenomenon or trait. It also differs from evaluation and appraisal in that it is not necessarily interested in relating such status, whether measured or estimated, to its adequacy from the standpoint of values, objectives, and other standards of reference. On the other hand, a value-judgment may be implicit at times in the scale values used, e.g., *excellent—poor*. As currently used in research, *rating* studies are generally considered essentially synonymous with *appraisal* studies, with the implication that considerable attention is to be devoted to the evaluation of what is discovered with reference to stated criteria of expectancy and desirability.

In their present stage of development, rating studies incorporate a high level of subjectivity and, while subjective judgment is involved in all research, there is need for restrictions to be placed on the extent and manner in which judgment is allowed to influence the study. Despite notable advances made in this area in the face of major complexities, rating as a research technique is still relatively undeveloped, particularly with respect to the more significant aspects of education, e.g., attitudes, character, adjustment, leadership, etc., the crucial aspects of which are still relatively undefined and the tools for the appraisal of which are generally of limited adequacy.

Mechanics of Rating

A simple and relatively crude way of dealing with data of the type considered here is *ranking*. The first attempt at rating personality characteristics, for example, devised during World War I, called for a panel of experts either to rate every individual in comparison to a "standard person" or to compare each individual in a group with every other individual. Such a technique is extremely laborious when it involves a number of people and, of course, requires that the raters be thoroughly acquainted with all the individuals to be rated. Such an approach could possibly be used in the rating of the faculty of a given department.

The more common and more practical method of rating is based on a *rating scale,* a procedure which consists of assigning for each trait whatever scale value seems a valid estimate of the trait in question and then combining the separate ratings into an overall score. The rating scale then is best conceived as an instrument which permits the quantification of observation through the assignment of numerical values to the ratings of the various components of a given phenomenon and the summation of these ratings into an index of overall status. The problems underlying scale construction, then, are twofold: 1. a series of items must be developed which elicit responses that are psychologically related to the attitude-object being appraised; and 2. the scale must differentiate among people at different points along the dimension being measured.

The scale on the basis of which the ratings are to be made has received considerable attention in the psychological literature and a number of specific rules can be given for its construction. It is necessary, for instance, that the wording of the items be clear and free from suggestion as to what the answer should be. The number of scale divisions to be used depends on the problem and purpose of the study. For example, for some items, a five-point scale of *excellent, very good, good, fair, poor* may be better than a three-point scale, which gives the rater less freedom of operation. On the other hand, a scale should probably never extend beyond seven scale points, since the categories provided should have psychological existence and be within the possibilities of accuracy in estimation. The more the scale construction structures the situation, the greater the uniformity of ratings it is likely to promote. However, such a structuring increases the danger of overlooking certain possibilities that were not anticipated, and thus places greater responsibility on the scale constructor and emphasizes the need for a pilot study to act as a basis for making the final judgments on the scale.

The problems encountered in the construction of a rating instrument range from the relative simplicity of preparing a checklist to the extreme complexity of devising a more advanced rating scale required for the study of complex variables. In its most primitive stage, the checklist might call for the rating of but one or two factors, or it might consist of an aggregate of separate ratings of semi-independent aspects of a given situation or phenomenon. In the rating scale an attempt is made to give the instrument overall unity in line with its stated purpose. Thus, though the term is sometimes used loosely, a rating scale is generally a relatively elaborate and comprehensive instrument with the items arranged on a single continuum which provides an overall score or index. Since this index is obtained through the combination of the items of the scale, it is essential to ensure that every significant aspect of the overall phenomenon is considered in its proper weighting, and that, conversely, nothing but components of the phenomenon is included.

Rating scales fall into one of three major types. In the summated (Likert-type) scale, the subject reacts, perhaps on a five-point scale, to a series of items in terms of whether he agrees or disagrees. The sum of the scores on the individual items is then interpreted on a continuum of favorableness–unfavorableness toward the object in question. The equal-appearing interval (Thurstone-type) scale likewise begins with a series of statements expressing various gradations of attitudes toward the attitude-object. These are placed on cards, and experts are asked to sort the cards into, say, eleven piles ranging from most strongly positive to most strongly negative, with the restriction that the piles be of approximately equal size. After discarding items which reflect great variation in placement, the remaining items are given a scale value representing the average of their placement by the expert panel. The cumulated (Guttman) scale is based on the concept of internal consistency or *scalability*. Items which are nonscalable are eliminated, since they are apparently related to aspects other than that toward which the overall scale is oriented and would, therefore, lower its validity. For instance, on a scale of *honesty–dishonesty*, the item: "Would you steal from a friend?" might be nonscalable in that it introduces a second dimension—loyalty—and thus makes it possible for a relatively dishonest person to rate himself at the "honest" end of the scale (see Mouly, 1968). An important development with respect to ratings is the *Q-technique* developed by Stephenson (1953) for the analysis of such data. The development of a scale and the techniques for analyzing the data which it provides entail a number of technicalities and complexities beyond the scope of the present text. The reader is referred to sources more specifically devoted to the principles and techniques of scale construction and analysis.*

The Importance of the Rater

The rater obviously plays a crucial role in the validity and reliability of the ratings. It is essential, for example, to ensure that the rater is sufficiently familiar with the phenomenon being studied for him to see its components in perspective. He must have a clear idea of the point of reference which is to act as a benchmark in his ratings; asking grade-school children to rate their

---

* See such sources as Allen L. Edwards, *Techniques of Attitude Scale Construction* (New York: Appleton-Century-Crofts, 1957); Harold Gulliksen and Samuel Messick (eds.), *Psychological Scaling: Theory and Application* (New York: Wiley, 1960); Fred N. Kerlinger, *Foundations of Behavioral Research* (New York: Holt, Rinehart and Winston, 1964); Orval H. Mowrer, "Q-technique—description, history and critique," in Orval H. Mowrer (ed.), *Psychotherapy: Theory and Research* (New York: Ronald Press, 1953), pp. 316–75; H.H. Remmers, *Introduction to Opinion and Attitude Measurement* (New York: Harper, 1954); Warren S. Torgerson, *Theory and Method of Scaling* (New York: Wiley, 1958); and Warren S. Torgerson, "Scaling and test theory," *Ann. Rev. of Psych.*, 12: 55–70; 1961.

teachers on a scale from *superior* to *average* to *inferior*, for example, presupposes that they have a clear concept of what an "average" teacher is or does. The layman would likewise have an inadequate point of reference with which to rate teachers and very frequently would have insufficient evidence on the basis of which to derive a valid and reliable rating.

It must also be remembered that sizable individual differences in ability to rate exist. Each rater brings to the situation his personal biases which may distort his perceptions and inter- pretations in varying degrees. Not only are certain individuals poor raters, but to complicate matters further, some individuals tend to be much poorer raters with respect to certain phenomena or cer- tain individuals than with respect to others. In the rating of indi- viduals, for instance, a new dimension is introduced by the fact that the rater must be familiar with the person he is rating, but yet must not be so close to him emotionally that he loses his perspec- tive. This need for emotional detachment would, of course, hold as well for other phenomena toward which the rater has definite attitudes.

In order to obtain relatively valid and reliable ratings, it is essential to clarify the nature of the phenomenon to be rated in the light of the objectives of the study. Ambiguity with respect to the specific aspects of the phenomenon that are to be included in the rating, for example, is likely to result in some degree of in- validity in the ratings that are made. Such a danger can be mini- mized by analyzing the phenomenon into its basic components and defining each in operational terms. For instance, if "teacher effec- tiveness" is broken down into fundamentals, such as "Is he or is he not tolerant of pupil mistakes?" which are probably considered only vaguely and nebulously when the rater's judgment is made on an overall basis, a more adequate rating is likely to result. Practice sessions, in which a group of raters attempt to reconcile the differ- ences in their ratings of a given phenomenon, are particularly effec- tive in clarifying the nature of the variables involved, in pointing out personal biases, and in calibrating the ratings to a common point of reference. Unless and until a relatively high degree of con- cordance in the ratings is obtained as a result of such practice sessions, there is no point in proceeding with the study.

As it relates to the rating of personality and other personal attributes, the ratings can be made either by the indi- vidual himself or by an external observer. Both approaches are in common use and, of course, each has advantages and disadvantages. The question of self-observation and self-report has received the attention of psychologists since the beginning of psychology as a science. Originally considered under the term *introspection,* self-rating was the basic tool of discovery in the early days of psychology. With the shift of psychology toward behaviorism, however, any data that was not sufficiently overt to be verifiable by outside observers became suspect. At present, a more lenient position has been taken toward self-observation and self-report on the obvious grounds that it is frequently the only means available for investigating certain crucial aspects of the individual's psychological makeup.

Psychologists are fully aware of the limitations and potential dangers of self-reports. They realize that self-reports are generally better measures of the person's self-concept than they are of the self as it exists. Self-reports are predicated on the assumption that the individual understands himself—an assumption which psychologists would question, since people typically have a very limited insight into their own dynamics. A prejudiced person, for example, does not see himself as prejudiced just as the humble person does not—and cannot—see himself as humble. The problem is further complicated by the reluctance of most people to reveal even the little they know about themselves. Thus, not only is the individual a poor judge of himself, but he is also a biased reporter. His report tells us not what he is but what he feels (perhaps unconsciously) he is, or would like to be, or would like us to believe he is.

These weaknesses, however, are not sufficient grounds for the absolute rejection of the self-report as a research technique. There is undoubtedly some degree of validity in the method, and it has been used with some success even in such delicate areas as the appraisal of attitudes. Its limitations, however, must be clearly recognized, and investigators should be cautious in its use. The self-report is probably best used in the early stages of investigation as a means of providing hypotheses which can then be tested by more rigorous means. Its use would have to be evaluated on the basis of the usual criteria of validity and reliability as they apply in the specific case.

External ratings are also subject to a number of limitations, one of which is the basic question of whether the object being rated is sufficiently well known to the rater for him to make a valid rating. Another is the extent to which the rater has the proper perspective as to what constitutes *average, above average,* and *below average* status in the trait in question. A more valid rating is generally obtained, for instance, by pooling the ratings of a number of judges who have been carefully selected on the basis of their expertness with respect to the trait in question. It is also best to allow for *no information* in order to prevent uninformed ratings from vitiating the overall index.

A common error in rating is the *halo effect,* which may be described as a general tendency for the rater to evaluate each of the individual's specific traits on the basis of a general overall impression or mental outlook, rather than on the basis of the traits as they appear independently. This is sometimes combined with the errror of *central tendency* in which the rater, whenever he is not sure of the rating he should give an individual, rates him close to the average. Some raters are particularly reluctant to rate anyone at the extremes; this sometimes stems from the *logical error* which involves a lack of clarity about the trait being rated, and a consequent tendency to play it safe. Another common error is the *generosity* or *leniency error,* in which a rater tends to rate almost everyone above (or below) average. This error is of particular concern when multiple raters are used, since a lack of a common point of reference makes for noncomparability of the ratings of the various judges. This lack of a common point of reference is further complicated by shifts in the point of reference of an individual rater, who may rate leniently at one time and severely at another. To minimize this difficulty it sometimes helps to identify certain scale values as points of reference—e.g., a "C" grade is performance typical of the average freshman—or to develop actual models— e.g., an "A" theme, a "B" theme, etc. This approach is used systematically in judging the adequacy of the responses to the *Stanford-Binet Scale of Intelligence,* for example.

THE CRITICAL INCIDENT TECHNIQUE

An important development in rating methodology is the critical incident technique (Flanagan, 1952). Its basic premise is that the validity with which a given trait can be appraised can be increased by identifying typical incidents that characterize the possesson or the lack of possession of the trait in question. It assumes, for example, that a better rating of a worker's efficiency can be obtained if "worker efficiency" is defined in operational terms, i.e., if it is related to specific and critical incidents of behavior that discriminate between a good and a poor worker: "A good worker is prompt; a poor worker is often tardy." "A good worker takes advice and suggestions; a poor worker resents criticisms and suggestions."

The critical incident technique has been used in the study of certain educational phenomena. Ryans (1960), for instance, clarifies the *apathetic–alert* continuum of pupil behavior by listing the following critical examples:

Apathetic	1 2 3 4 5 6 7 N	*Alert*
Pupils were inattentive; showed evidence of wandering attention; indifferent to teacher.		Pupils responded eagerly, appeared anxious to recite and participate.
Pupils were listless; spiritless.		Pupils watched teacher attentively when explanation was being made.
Pupils were restless.		Pupils worked concentratedly, appeared immersed in their work.
Pupils participated halfheartedly, assumed a "don't care attitude."		Pupils were prompt and ready to take part in activities.

These examples do not eliminate judgment but they help identify the continuum in question by relating it to actual instances which apparently distinguish between alert and apathetic pupil behavior. On the other hand, Travers (1964) points out that the method of selecting the critical incidents, i.e., by asking people to think of a very good and a very poor teacher and then to recall what each did respectively—actually favors the recall of unusual examples and incidents which, by their very rarity, are essentially useless as a guide in making valid judgments.

FACTOR ANALYSIS

Another analytic technique which is widely used, particularly in psychology, is factor analysis. Its primary purpose is to determine the factorial composition of a mass of data; more specifically, it attempts to reduce the matrix of intercorrelations among data to the smallest number of psychological dimensions or factors capable of accounting for the diversity of individual data. By looking at the various measures having a high loading on a given factor, the investigator postulates some underlying "hypothetical entity" or hypothetical construct, e.g., verbal facility, which apparently accounts for the relative performance of the different individuals on the test in question.

Factor analysis can provide valuable insights into the nature of phenomena, which can, in turn, be translated into a saving of time and effort. For example, to the extent that two tests are measures of the same psychological factor, each is a duplicate of the other and one is presumably unnecessary. Factor analysis can lead to the factorial purification of psychological tests and the consequent reduction in the degree of overlapping among them.*

Factor analysis is undoubtedly a powerful tool for the analysis of complex psychological and educational data. Now that the computer has reduced the computational labor, its use will undoubtedly increase. As a technique of science, on the other hand, it has certain limitations. It rests on the concept of correlation with all the inherent inaccuracies and weaknesses therein. Furthermore, only factors that have been included in the intercorrelational matrix can arise from factor analysis. Any factor that cannot be measured precisely with our present instruments is not likely to emerge as a factor, nor is a common denominator in the matrix, e.g., ability to read, likely to emerge as a factor.

There is no way of determining *the* factorial structure underlying human behavior; the only factors that can be discovered are those which have been included in the matrix. Consequently, the factorial pattern which is discovered in a particular study should not be interpreted as conclusive evidence of the existence or of the significance of the factors discovered. Wesman (1968), for example, points out in connection with the current search for *the* structure of the human intellect that the important distinction between the reality of such descriptive categories as primary mental abilities or cells in a three-dimensional model and the illusion of actual underlying functional entities is frequently overlooked. There are also certain assumptions underlying the procedures used that determine which factors will be extracted,

---

* Scale analysis has revealed that probably all tests are factorially impure, many of them to an objectionable degree. Many items on the average test are not directly on the continuum indicated by the purpose of the test, but constitute vector forces whose net contribution to what is being measured is somewhat reduced by the fact that such contribution is made only vectorially. Not only does this lead to unnecessary test length for a given degree of precision, but it also makes for a certain degree of invalidity in the results.

i.e., solutions are not unique but rather are dependent on the postulates that are accepted in the process of the derivation of the method. That the same factors tend to emerge from different studies simply reflects the fact that when investigations proceed from the same starting point and make the same assumptions they generally arrive at the same destination.

SCHOOL SURVEYS

Nature of School Surveys

A school survey generally is a comprehensive study of existing educational conditions undertaken to determine the overall effectiveness of the school's program with a view toward improvement where indicated. In a sense, it is a form of accounting or inventory. It gathers information about the various aspects of the school's program and evaluates them in the light of the objectives of the school. It can be restricted to one specific element or one specific department, but in general it is most useful when it is designed to encompass the school program in its entirety.

Although the school survey is primarily directed toward the practical aspects of education rather than toward the development of education as a science, under proper leadership such a survey can lead to a scientific investigation of the causes of the weaknesses it has uncovered. The school survey can help clarify educational goals at the local level and reduce the gap that exists between educational theory and practice. By forcing teachers to keep abreast of current developments, it helps to raise the standards of educational practice. School surveys vary in scope and complexity as well as in scientific sophistication, depending on the needs of the local situation and the capabilities of the personnel involved. The literature on the subject is voluminous and should be consulted for specific references. The various editions of the *Encyclopedia of Educational Research* have particularly good discussions of the nature and purpose of school surveys and their contribution to the cause of education.

Historical Development

The school survey is not new; well over a hundred years ago, Horace Mann and Henry Barnard were inspecting schools and making recommendations for their improvement. The general pattern of these early surveys was to invite a neighboring superintendent, a professor from a nearby university, or perhaps an official of the United States Office of Education to survey certain aspects of the school's program. These surveys were largely of an inspectional nature and frequently generated apprehension as well as opposition on the part of the local teachers. Furthermore, they generally lacked continuity from the standpoint of implementation of the recommendations and, consequently, were of limited overall value.

The current trend is to take a systems approach, i.e., to evaluate the school as a functional unit. The usual survey begins with a clarification of the objectives of the particular school and of education in general, and includes an appraisal of the administrative aspects, the instructional program, the physical plant, pupil transportation, personnel, pupil guidance, etc.—i.e., every aspect of the school is considered in the light of these objectives. It is felt that, because of the interdependence of the various aspects, a survey of the overall program generally gives a more meaningful picture than a survey restricted to a single department in isolation. The trend is toward the "development-type" of survey oriented toward making proposals for the improvement of the school, rather than simply the determination of existing conditions with emphasis on the discovery of weaknesses. It is common, furthermore, to attempt to maintain continuity from one survey to the next by orienting the attention of the investigating team to the strengths and weaknesses discovered in previous surveys and to the suggestions that were made. This generally acts as an incentive to implementing the recommendations of the previous evaluators and, thus, promotes a continuous program of self-improvement on the part of the school.

The school survey can be considered a case study of a school—utilizing the results of survey testing, questionnaires and interviews, observations, ratings, etc. and often enlisting the efforts of consultants and interested community leaders as well as local and neighboring school personnel. The specific steps of the survey vary with the purpose and the scope, as well as with the caliber of the personnel involved. Generally, however, the major steps include: 1. the determination of the aims and the goals of the school; 2. a critical appraisal of the present program and its outcomes; and 3. an evaluation of the present operation from the standpoint of the objectives. It usually ends with recommendations for improvements.

Organization of School Surveys

The school survey can be conducted in one of three ways: 1. by an outside consultant; 2. by the personnel of the local school; or 3. by a community-wide group consisting of local teachers, interested members of the community, and resource persons, headed by a specialist acting as consultant and survey leader. Each approach has its advantages and its disadvantages.

1.   The Consultant Survey   As we have noted, the early surveys were conducted by imported specialists; undoubtedly, a capable consultant can make such a survey meaningful and profitable. This method is, however, subject to certain limitations. Since a survey is generally of wide scope, a large number of weaknesses will probably be found so that the consultant is likely to find himself having to recite a long list of trouble spots. Anticipating this, teachers are likely to be reluctant to cooperate in the discovery of their weaknesses. Furthermore, since the teachers have almost no part in the survey, they are likely to be only mildly interested in implementing its recommendations; too often, the report is discarded the day it is filed, while teachers feel satisfied that they have done their bit when they have agreed, or denied, that the problems exist or that nothing can be done about them.

This is not to say that specialists should never be used for making a local survey. Cornell (1949) lists the following situations as pointing to the need for an outside expert: 1. when the local personnel have been unable to cope with a problem; 2. when the problems are so comprehensive that they create a burden on the teachers; and 3. when there has been such inbreeding that there is a need for an external perspective.

The consultant frequently has an advantage in that he can see the school in the light of his previous experience in similar schools. Not only is he likely to be more alert to the problems that may have become blind spots to people in the system, but he also can be more objective. The consultant often has highly specialized training in research, and he often has a research design that can be implemented with minor modifications. Generally, he has more prestige by virtue of being an outsider and frequently can command greater cooperation. On the other hand, it must be recognized that the problems of education are so complex that perhaps no one can be an expert in all areas. It must also be recognized that if the expert is to be effective, everyone must give him full cooperation, which may be too much to expect when one realizes that people do not cooperate even with their own physicians. It is imperative, for instance, that faculty rating not be combined with the survey, if maximum improvement of the school is to be achieved.

2. The Self-Survey The self-survey, involving teachers of the local school system working alone (except perhaps for a supervisor from the administration office) rarely accomplishes what a school survey should. Because they are close to their own problems, the teachers are likely to be blind to difficulties which have become so commonplace that they are no longer considered problems, or so ingrained that they are considered beyond solution. Furthermore, teachers frequently lack the insight into the true nature of their problems—and their potential solutions—which only the combined talents of the expert and of the teachers working as a team can provide. It is also true that teachers cannot shift gears easily; the reason their problems exist in the first place is that they have not had the competence to deal with them. Organizing a committee or a survey to give public testimony to the existence of the problem is not much help. Furthermore, to the extent that the survey represents added responsibility imposed on their regular duties, teachers are more likely to resent the extra work than they are to look for solutions. Self-surveys can be helpful when conducted in preparation for a more formal evaluation by a team of experts. In such instances, the teachers are more likely to be motivated to make improvements in preparation for the final survey, especially if they are encouraged to participate in and make contributions to the latter.

3. The Comprehensive Survey It is generally felt that the best approach to school evaluation is the comprehensive survey in which the school supplements its own personnel by enlisting the cooperation of teachers from nearby schools, interested community leaders, and consultants from neighboring universities and other school systems—all working together as a team under the direction of a steering committee headed by a survey leader. This broad approach is psychologically and administratively sound. Including the teachers in the survey—and in the improvement of their schools —is generally considered the best way of ensuring the success of the diagnostic aspects of the survey, as well as of promoting the implementation of the recommendations.

Participation of selected and interested community leaders is conducive to acquainting the community with its school, its philosophy, its operation, and the limitations under which it functions, and to promoting community goodwill. Laymen become less suspicious when they realize that the school has nothing to hide, that its problems are not insurmountable, and that its personnel is sincere in its desire to improve. The school needs to involve its patrons in identifying the problems which it faces. Community leaders can frequently bring a fresh approach to the problems of education that teachers have been too close to see. These are men of experience and often of wide and successful background who have much to contribute to the improvement of the school. Not to avail ourselves of their services is short-sighted.

4. Surveys by Accrediting Agencies Surveys of schools are also conducted by accrediting agencies. While, at one time, such surveys were oriented toward the policing of higher education and the maintenance of standards, the present emphasis is on helping the school develop a worthwhile program in line with its objectives and to plan for continuous improvement. It is invariably advisable for the school to conduct its own self-survey in preparation for the visit of the accrediting team. This not only expedites the work of the accreditors but it also permits the school to get a feel of its strengths, its weaknesses, and its potentialities.

Each survey must be conducted in the light of the objectives of the school—and the community which it is to serve—rather than on the basis of an absolute standard, and though the evaluation involves the use of criteria or guides, their use is largely to orient the thinking of the evaluators and to prevent the over-looking of significant aspects rather than to set definite goals that need to be met. It is realized that two schools with identical programs are not necessarily equivalent and that interschool comparisons are essentially meaningless, except in broad general terms. For this reason, it is no longer the practice of evaluators to give numerical ratings to the various items with a view to summating them in an index of overall quality. Again, the report must be precise in its recommendations concerning the specific ways in which weaknesses can be corrected, but it must especially emphasize the strengths on which the school can capitalize in developing a program capable of growth.

Evaluation of Social Surveys

Although no generalization can be made about the improvement which results from a school survey, there is no doubt that, when conducted under proper auspices, it can be effective. However, if maximum benefit is to be derived from such a survey, it is essential that the evaluators avoid promoting undue uniformity and conformity, thus stifling the initiative, originality, and individuality the school needs to possess if it is to provide a program adapted to the needs of the community it serves. The survey should, for example, avoid placing undue emphasis on test data to be used in interschool comparisons, to the corresponding neglect of more significant aspects which make a program functional, even though different. Of even greater importance from the standpoint of the benefits to be derived from a school survey is the need for the school to provide for continuous appraisal of the extent to which the recommendations are implemented. This is probably best effected through the efforts of a research bureau in the central office working closely with the community and the local school.

GENETIC RESEARCH

Because of the importance of child growth and development to the whole process of education, *genetic* or *developmental* research, though not strictly educational research, is of primary interest particularly to teachers in the elementary school. Largely because of the obvious difficulties encountered in research of this kind—the time element, the extensiveness of the facilities required, the cost, etc.—this interest has been primarily from a consumer point of view. Except for studies of academic and perhaps intellectual growth—the growth in the child's ability to grasp concepts such as time sequence, for example—genetic studies are rarely selected for thesis or even dissertation purposes. To date, the bulk of such research has been done in child-development clinics, among the most notable of which are those at Antioch, Berkeley, Chicago, Columbia, Harvard, Iowa, Michigan, Minnesota, Stanford, and Yale. Among the many studies conducted in this area, those of Gesell and of Terman are among the best known to professional personnel and lay people alike.*

Genetic research resembles a number of other research techniques described in this text. Like historical research, it is concerned with the occurrence of past events. It also approaches the experimental method, particularly in the comparison of identical twins under slightly different environmental conditions.† It is closely related to survey methods in that it is concerned with the status of a phenomenon at successive stages of growth. It differs from all of these in purpose, however. It is not primarily interested in the present status of development, nor in its historical background, nor even in the ways in which phenomena can be modified through the manipulation of environmental conditions—but simply in the pattern of development.

The techniques of genetic research have to be adapted to the age and nature of the subjects. In studying infants and preschool children, for instance, it may be necessary to use direct measurements, observations through one-way screens, etc. For older children, pencil-and-paper tests might be used instead. It can also vary in duration. Genetic studies of a short duration could be conducted with respect to such factors as academic growth, which is relatively rapid and for the measurement of which we have relatively adequate instruments. On the other hand, short-term genetic studies would not be effective for studying some of the more slowly developing aspects of growth, such as personality.

Genetic studies can be either *longitudinal* or *cross-sectional*. Longitudinal studies follow the same group of subjects over a relatively long period of time. For example, in 1958, Terman conducted his fourth follow-up of the one thousand gifted children whose study he began in 1925 (see Chapter 14). A cross-sectional approach, on the other hand, consists of taking random samples of children of successive ages as the basis for developing growth norms. The longitudinal approach is generally preferred over the cross-sectional; it has the advantage of continuity and permits the recording of individual fluctuations, which are frequently of greater interest than the overall growth pattern itself. The time

* See Kagan, Jerome and Howard A. Moss. *Birth to Maturity: A Study in Psychological Development.* New York: Wiley, 1962.

† See Arnold S. Gesell and Helen Thompson, "Learning and growth in identical infant twins," *Genet. Psychol. Monogr.,* 6: 5–120, 1929; Myrtle B. McGraw, *A Study of Johnny and Jimmy.* New York: Appleton-Century-Crofts, 1935.

factor poses a special problem, however, especially to doctoral or master's candidates. The maintenance of cooperation on the part of the subjects and the loss of subjects over long periods of time also present difficulties. The cross-sectional approach, on the other hand, is particularly vulnerable to sampling errors, so that a fairly large sample has to be used at each of the successive age levels in order to ensure valid data. It is sometimes possible to combine the two approaches by having, say, four overlapping groups at two-year intervals. In this way, one might conduct in two years a study that would normally take eight and, at the same time, validate each sample one to the other at the point of overlap. The time problem can also be overcome by conducting genetic studies through records, if adequate records have been kept. This condition is rarely fulfilled, however, unless careful plans have been made in advance. It is likely that even such simple items as the IQ, for example, are not recorded on a comparable basis over the years and are, therefore, lacking in the required continuity.

The major weakness of genetic studies is that they give growth patterns that represent the average of the group and, therefore, apply only indirectly to the individual case. In physical-growth curves, for instance, there is no place where the preadolescent growth spurt is shown, simply because it is neutralized from one person to the other—with the result that the overall pattern is, in a sense, erroneous and misleading. Another weakness is that, although psychology has recently made a beginning at formulating a theory of development (see Mussen, 1960; Baldwin, 1967), genetic research so far has been largely empirical in nature. The information it provides is, of course, useful, since it helps us to understand both the typical and the atypical child. Furthermore, such an empirical approach is necessary in the beginning stages of research. There is, however, a need to move on toward a science of growth and development. Science is concerned with the relationship among phenomena rather than simply with their existence; to note the status over the years and to develop a set of norms may be valuable, but it is only a preliminary step in the development of science which would be more concerned with the prediction and the control of the growth pattern.

Highlights of the Chapter

1.   Analysis is a fundamental technique of science underlying all scientific procedures. The analysis of a phenomenon into its com-

ponents permits the identification of its crucial aspects and provides a deeper insight into its nature and a more adequate basis for its allocation into meaningful classifications. The point in the analysis which provides the greatest insight varies with the nature of the phenomenon and, especially, with the purpose of the investigation.

2. Analysis is also a research method, comprising a variety of techniques designed to dissect phenomena into their constituents as a means of providing greater insight into their basic nature. One of the most elementary of these techniques is content-analysis.

3. Besides underlying all research, observation is also a research method in its own right and many phenomena can be investigated in no other way. Observation, especially unstructured observation, is probably the most flexible research technique and is consequently particularly suited to the early exploration of a given problem. However, because of its extreme flexibility and of the nature of the problems for which it is suited, it is frequently difficult to have observation meet the criteria of objectivity, reliability, and validity required of a scientific data-gathering instrument. Scientific observation must be distinguished from the capricious and haphazard observation of the layman.

4. Just as in the case of the interview, it is particularly difficult to prevent the very presence of the observer from vitiating the observation, and again, the selection and training of the observers is a crucial aspect of its success.

5. Although school procedures have always been of fundamental concern to educators, it is only recently that the classroom itself has been the subject of scientific observation. The relative failure of earlier investigations to relate teacher characteristics and behavior to pupil growth has led to a reconceptualization of the effective teacher in terms of pupil-teacher and pupil-pupil interaction. A number of observation schedules have been devised, the best known of which is probably OScAR.

6. Observation is frequently quantified through rating, a procedure consisting of assigning numerical values to represent the various degrees of the phenomenon in question. Ratings—and

especially ratings of some of the more important phenomena of concern to educators and psychologists—unavoidably incorporate a high level of subjectivity and imprecision. Among the more common errors are the halo effect, the error of central tendency, the logical error, and the generosity error. The critical incident technique attempts to promote greater validity in rating by orienting the rater's attention to specific instances of the phenomenon in question.

7.   Factor analysis attempts to telescope a vast array of different observations into a small number of underlying dimensions. Although factor analysis as a scientific technique has a number of limitations that must be clearly recognized, it serves a useful purpose in the clarification of phenomena.

8.   School surveys constitute a form of inventory of the operation of the school, considered in the light of its objectives. Although good results can sometimes be obtained through a survey conducted by an outside expert or by the personnel of the school, generally the most fruitful approach to school evaluation is the comprehensive survey which involves teachers from nearby schools, interested community leaders, and outside consultants working with and through the local school personnel. No matter what the approach, the emphasis should be on building up strengths rather than on identifying weaknesses, and plans must be instituted for the implementation of a program of continuous self-evaluation and self-improvement.

9.   Genetic research is interested in the pattern of growth over a period of time rather than simply in the measurement of its status at a given moment. Unfortunately, it is oriented toward the derivation of group norms and therefore tends to bury individual variations in growth, which are frequently the most significant aspect of the situation. To date, genetic research has been essentially empirical; there is need for a greater emphasis on the development of a theoretical orientation.

Questions and Projects

1.   Make a content analysis of a recent textbook in educational research. Develop evaluative criteria and rate its various components

to obtain an overall index of adequacy. Learn how to use a readability formula.

2.   Plan for the classroom observation of both teacher and pupil behavior and note interobserver agreement. Reconcile disagreements through discussion as a means of promoting validity, of gaining insight into the variables observed, and of getting a feel of observation as a research technique. Identify some of the characteristics of good and poor observers.

3.   Prepare a score card for evaluating the various research methods discussed in this text.

4.   Evaluate the report of a school survey in the light of its primary purpose of promoting improvement in the operation of the school. (Actual participation in an evaluation would be a most profitable experience.)

Selected References

Adkins, Dorothy C. "Principles underlying observational techniques of evaluation," *Educ. psychol. Measmt.,* 11: 29–51; 1951.

Berelson, Bernard. *Content Analysis in Communication Research.* New York: Free Press, 1952.

Burns, Hobert W. "The critical incident technique as an instrument of educational research: A philosophical analysis," *Diss. Abstr.,* 18: 520; 1958.

Chall, Jeanne S. *Readability: An Appraisal of Research and Application.* Columbus: Ohio State Univ., 1958.

Combs, Arthur W. et al. "The measurement of self-concept and self-report," *Educ. psychol. Measmt.,* 23: 493–500; 1963.

Coombs, Clyde H. "Theory and methods of social measurement," in Leon Festinger and Daniel Katz (eds.) *Research Methods in the Behavioral Sciences.* New York: Holt, Rinehart & Winston, 1965. pp. 471–75.

Corbally, John E. "Critical incident technique and educational research," *Educ. Res. Bull.,* 34: 57–62; 1956.

Cronbach, Lee J. and Goldine C. Gleser. "A review of Stephenson's *The Study of Behavior: Q-Technique and Its Methodology,*" *Psychometrika,* 19: 327–30; 1954.

Edwards, Allen L. and Katherine C. Kenney. "A comparison of the Thurstone and Likert techniques of attitude scale construction," *J. appl. Psychol.,* 30: 72–83; 1946.

Flanagan, John C. "The critical requirements approach to educational objectives," *Sch. & Soc.*, 71: 321–24; 1950.

———. *The Critical Incident Technique in the Study of Individuals.* Washington: Amer. Council Educ., 1952.

Flanders, Ned A. *Interaction Analysis in the Classroom.* Minneapolis: College of Education, Univ. Minnesota, 1960.

Gulliksen, Harold and Samuel Messick (eds.) *Psychological Scaling: Theory and Applications.* New York: Wiley, 1960.

Guttman, Louis A. "The Cornell technique for scale and intensity analysis," *Educ. psychol. Measmt.*, 7: 247–79; 1947.

Kerlinger, Fred N. "The attitude structure of the individual: A Q-sort of the educational attitudes of professors and laymen," *Genet. Psychol. Monogr.*, 53: 283–329; 1956.

Klare, George R. *The Measurement of Readability.* Ames: Iowa State Univ. Press, 1963.

Lee, Wayne D. "What does research in readability tell the classroom teacher?" *J. Read.*, 8: 141–44; 1964.

Lord, Frederick M. "Some relations between Guttman's principal components of scale analysis and other psychometric theories," *Psychometrika*, 23: 291–96; 1958.

McNemar, Quinn. "Opinion-attitude methodology," *Psychol. Bull.*, 43: 289–374; 1946.

Medley, Donald M. and Harold E. Mitzel. "Measuring classroom behavior by systematic observation," in N.L. Gage (ed.) *Handbook of Research on Teaching.* Chicago: Rand McNally, 1963. pp. 247–328.

Overall, John E. "Note on the scientific status of factors," *Psychol. Bull.*, 61: 270–76; 1964.

Pool, I. deS. (ed.) *Trends in Content Analysis.* Urbana: Univ. Illinois Press, 1960.

Remmers, H.H. "Rating methods in research on teaching," in N.L. Gage (ed.) *Handbook of Research on Teaching.* Chicago: Rand McNally, 1963. pp. 329–78.

Schaefer, Earl S. and Richard Q. Bell. "Development of a parent attitude research instrument," *Child Developm.*, 29: 339–61; 1958.

Shaw, Marvin E. and Jack M. Wright. *Scales for the Measurement of Attitudes.* New York: McGraw-Hill, 1967.

Stone, Philip J. et al. *The General Inquirer: A Computer Approach to Content Analysis.* Cambridge: Mass. Inst. Technology Press, 1956.

Torgerson, Warren S. *Theory and Methods of Scaling.* New York: Wiley, 1958.

Turner, Richard L. and Nicholas R. Fattu. "Skill in teaching: A reappraisal of the concepts and strategies in teacher effectiveness research," *Bull. Sch. Educ. (Indiana Univ.)* 36: No. 3, 1960.

Withall, John G. and W.W. Lewis. "Social interaction in the classroom," in N.L. Gage (ed.) *Handbook of Research on Teaching.* Chicago: Rand McNally, 1963. pp. 683–714.

Genetic Research

Carmichael, Leonard et al. "Symposium: Child development research—The next twenty-five years," *Child Developm.,* 31: 191–208; 1960.

Dearborn, Walter F. and John W.M. Rothney. *Predicting the Child's Development.* Cambridge: Sci-Art, 1941.

Gesell, Arnold S. *Studies in Child Development.* New York: Harper & Row, 1948.

Kagan, Jerome and Howard A. Moss. *Birth to Maturity: A Study in Psychological Development.* New York: Wiley, 1962.

Mussen, Paul H. (ed.) *Handbook of Research Methods in Child Development.* New York: Wiley, 1960.

New York Times Magazine: "Giant in the nursery—Jean Piaget," *New York Times Magazine,* May 26, 1968. pp. 25–27; 50–54; 62; 77–80.

Oakes, M.E. *Children's Explanation of Natural Phenomena.* New York: Bur. Publ., T.C., Columbia Univ., 1947.

Piaget, Jean. *The Moral Judgment of the Child.* New York: Harcourt, Brace & World, 1932.

———. *Judgment and Reasoning in the Child.* New York: Harcourt, Brace & World, 1948.

Terman, Lewis M. et al. *Genetic Studies of Genius.* Vols. 1–5. Stanford: Stanford Univ. Press, 1925, 1926, 1930, 1947, 1959.

11
THE EXPERIMENTAL METHOD

If we are to advance beyond the dark ages of educational pre-science, we must emulate the experimental proficiency and zeal of colleagues in other behavioral sciences.—Julian C. Stanley (1957)

Experimentation is undoubtedly the most sophisticated and, in a sense, the most powerful method for deriving dependable knowledge. Its worth has been shown repeatedly in the impressive advances made in the physical and biological sciences, ranging from Galileo's first "experiment" in 1589, the work of Pasteur in the discovery of bacteria, to the more recent control of the atom and of disease, not to mention the more dramatic current possibilities of the very creation of life in a test tube. The use of experimentation in the behavioral sciences, on the other hand, poses special problems from the standpoint of control, the basic concept underlying its operation. At the present stage of development of education as a science, the amenability of educational problems to the classical experimental design of the past is typically in direct proportion to their artificiality and/or unimportance. It is only since the recent development of multivariate analysis that experimentation has become applicable to the more realistic problems which a complex discipline like education presents. It must be recognized, however, that even though it has a major contribution to make to the cause of science, experimentation is not to be equated with science; at least one science, astronomy, has done quite well without it.

The purpose of experimentation is to identify functional relationships among phenomena through staging the occurrence of certain outcomes under conditions designed to control the effects of co-occurrences resulting from the simultaneous operation of extraneous factors. At the operational level, experimentation is a matter of varying the *independent* variable in order to study the effect of such a variation on the *dependent* variable. The investigator might vary the size of the type, for example, and appraise the effect of such manipulation on reading speed. Actually, what we know about our environment comes from observation, and all research is concerned with the observation of phenomena and the generalization of these observations into certain functional relationships whose validity can be tested. Experimentation simply enables us to improve the conditions under which we observe and, thus, to arrive at more precise results. It enables us to relate a given consequent to a specific antecedent rather than to a vague conglomeration of antecedents. This is the essence of the scientific method.

The Concept of Causation

The concept of *causation* is always troublesome, even in experimentation where it is most fundamental. In the earlier use of the term, as illustrated by Mill's canons, causation implied an invariant one-to-one relationship between a certain antecedent and a certain consequent. In keeping with the resulting emphasis on the *law of the single variable*, the investigator attempted to control all relevant variables except the experimental factor so that whatever results were obtained could be attributed unequivocally to the operation of the variable under investigation. Unfortunately, such ideal conditions are rarely, if ever, fulfilled—even in the physical sciences.*

Quite apart from the practical limitations of experimentation based on the law of the single variable is the even more damaging objection that such control is theoretically unsound, since it tends to make the situation artificial and the results meaningless. This is particularly true in the social sciences where to attempt to reduce an inherently complex situation to the operation of a single variable simply defeats the purpose of the experiment by seeking a partial answer out of the context of reality. In fact, the unwarranted transfer of the law of the single variable from the physical sciences—where it might conceivably be used—to educa-

---

* The student might profit from reviewing the section on *causation* in Chapter 2.

tion where it is essentially inappropriate is largely responsible for the relative unproductivity of educational experimentation to date.

This earlier interpretation of causation is unnecessarily narrow and mechanistic. Scientists are not interested in the effect of a single variable examined in isolation, but rather in the joint effect and interaction of relevant factors operating simultaneously. Furthermore, rather than an invariant one-to-one relationship between antecedent and consequent, the more realistic concept of causation is *predictability*—i.e., the statistical probability of the occurrence of a given phenomenon in response to a given set of antecedents. Basic to this modern view are the concepts of *multiple causation* and *concomitance,* both of which are fundamental, especially to experimentation in the social sciences. The present interpretation is that experimentation must operate in the context of the complex *multivariate* interaction which characterizes phenomena as they actually exist.

Nature of Experimentation

Experimentation is a precise technique designed to deal with a specific problem. In the sequence of the investigation of a problem, one might begin with casual observation, unstructured interviews, and open questionnaires. As the nature of the problem comes into clearer focus, he might turn to more rigorous survey techniques such as the structured interview, the closed questionnaire, and the various methods of analysis in order to identify a complex of significant factors and to formulate definite hypotheses regarding the possible relationships involved. The final step would be an experimental test of the precise hypotheses so derived. In contrast to the other methods of research which tend to be more appropriate for the exploratory stages of investigation, experimentation attempts to provide a precise answer to a precise question. Conversely, experimentation cannot be used effectively until the area of the investigation has been sufficiently defined—through some of the less rigorous and therefore more flexible techniques—to permit the identification of the factors that need to be controlled and the specific hypotheses that need to be tested.

Because it seeks a precise answer to a precise question, the experiment must be carefully planned; designing such a study can consume more time than conducting it. A pilot study covering every single aspect of the investigation should generally be conducted as a means of identifying difficulties before the experiment starts, for once the experiment is put into motion, it must be run off exactly as planned. If errors show up at this point the only alternative is to abandon it; it cannot be patched up as it goes along. Consequently, an experimental study must start with a rigorous analysis of the problem and a clear identification of the issues involved, for obviously an experimental study based on false assumptions cannot yield valid results. Students tend to underestimate the need for precision in the formulation of rigorous hypotheses; they often see experimentation as a matter of trying something to see what might happen. As a consequence, not only are their attempts at experimentation wasteful but quite frequently they capitalize on chance and/or error to announce false results. Every aspect of the investigation must be carefully preplanned. There is need to define the population; college sophomores as experimental subjects, for example, constitute a sample of a population that is, with respect to certain problems at least, extremely ill-defined. Careful consideration must be given to the selection of the measures with respect to which the results of the investigation are to be judged, for the fate of the experiment depends in no small measure on the validity of the criterion. If this criterion happens to be a test, it is essential that we define the objectives of the experiment in such a way that its validity can be related to these objectives.*

A major part of the planning of an experiment consists in identifying what variables are to be controlled and how this is to be accomplished. More specifically, the experimenter must control all "extraneous" variables whose influence might otherwise be *confounded* with that of the variable under investigation. It permits, thereby, a more rigorous allocation of the occurrence of a given phenomenon to the operation of a specific factor, i.e., it permits the more rigorous identification of the relationship between antecedent and consequent. He might, for example, neutralize the influence of IQ on learning by restricting his study to subjects of a single IQ level. He might even go further and actually determine the extent of the contribution of a given factor on the dependent variable to the point of being able to compensate for

---

* In no area of educational research is the need for competence in tests, measurements, and statistics so clearly indicated as in experimentation.

its influence; it is possible, for example, to adjust barometric pressure to sea level. Failure to provide this control means that the experimenter will not be able to determine whether the effect noted in the dependent variable is indeed the result of the operation of the independent variable or, on the contrary, of other factors allowed to operate in the situation.

The experiment is both precise and economical. Whereas in its natural setting, a phenomenon tends to occur but rarely and then generally under such a wide diversity of confounding conditions that the actual "cause" is difficult to isolate, the experiment sets up the conditions that bring about its occurrence under the most favorable conditions for observation. Making phenomena occur under specified conditions at a time when the investigator is ready to observe permits him not only to obtain more accurate answers at will and at once but also provides the basis for verification by other investigators. Thus, while all sciences depend on observation, experimentation permits precision in observation through controlling the conditions under which it takes place.

The fact that experimentation takes place in a prearranged setting does not imply that the experimental situation has to be created *in toto*. On the contrary, the experimenter frequently takes advantage of situations that already exist. For example, in investigating the effects of organic brain damage on test response, he does not start with identically normal individuals and subject some of them to varying degrees of brain damage in order to note the degree of impairment in mental functions. Rather, he utilizes groups of subjects as they already exist. Similarly, in the investigation of the effect of intelligence on academic performance, the comparison is made on the basis of pre-existing groups of children of different IQ's.* The problem has been simplified a hundredfold by the advent of modern statistical techniques, which have made it possible to use data from pre-existing groups, even though somewhat unequivalent, as the basis for precise experimental conclusions. Analysis of covariance, for example, provides a correction for initial differences in the IQ of the groups which would otherwise interfere with the meaningful interpretation of the relative effectiveness of two teaching methods being compared.

---

* Care must always be exercised in using pre-existing groups for research purposes, inasmuch as the investigator generally has no control over the complicating circumstances that may have been responsible for the groups being what they are. See the discussion on the *ex post facto* experiment.

CHARACTERISTICS OF AN EXPERIMENT

The purpose of experimentation is to identify functional relationships among phenomena through staging the occurrence of certain outcomes under controlled conditions designed to prevent the confounding effects of the operation of extraneous factors. Experimentation can be considered a technique of deliberately staging a situation designed to force nature to provide an unequivocal "yes" or "no" to a specific hypothesis concerning the phenomenon under discussion. For this to occur, it is essential that the experiment contain within itself the means for answering its own questions—i.e., the experiment be self-contained. This, in turn, calls for the satisfaction of three basic and interrelated conditions: *control, randomization,* and *replication.* Unless these conditions are fulfilled, the experiment cannot be interpreted, for it cannot eliminate the possibility that the results obtained were caused by factors other than the factor under investigation. More specifically, the experiment must provide the basis for calculating the probability that the phenomenon which did occur was the result of the experimental factor rather than of the operation of extraneous factors.

Control

The basic element of experimentation is *control.* The experiment must be designed so that the influence of extraneous factors not included in the hypothesis are prevented from operating and confounding the outcome that is to be appraised. To illustrate: Assume that eight out of ten rabbits inoculated with Serum X die within twenty-four hours. These results cannot be interpreted, because the "experiment" does not exclude the possible influence of extraneous factors. The rabbits may have died as a consequence of the fright attending their capture and inoculation, for example, or perhaps as a reaction to the disinfectant in which the needles had been lying. As Wilson (1955) points out, if one doubts the necessity of controls, all he has to do is to reflect on the statement: "It has been conclusively demonstrated by hundreds of experiments that the beating of tom-toms will restore the sun after an eclipse." For this experiment to be self-contained, it would have been necessary to have a *control group* of rabbits that paralleled the *experimental* group in all respects, except for the fact that one group was inoculated with the serum and the other group was not.

The control of relevant factors is often difficult to establish, especially in the social sciences. The number of variables to be controlled—intelligence, previous background, motivation, etc.—is large. Furthermore, there is a limit to the extent to which one can manipulate human beings for experimental purposes, and it is frequently necessary to compromise between what is scientifically rigorous and what is administratively feasible.

Although control is fundamental to experimentation, care must be taken not to overcontrol the situation so that it becomes artificial and the results, as a consequence, are inapplicable and meaningless from the standpoint of the actual situation. Page (1958), for example, discusses the choice between strict experimental control, so that while rigorous generalizations are reached they do not apply to any real situation, and investigation of the situation as it actually exists, which precludes generalization to other situations. The pure scientist would insist on generalizability on the premise that unless control is exercised the results are meaningless, since there would be no way of knowing what "caused" them. The practitioner, on the other hand, would insist on applicability to the real situation, regardless of whether the results can be generalized to any general class of events. He would contend that rigorous results that apply nowhere are automatically useless. This is the basic issue of *action research,* in which scientific rigor is frequently sacrificed in order to obtain an answer to a practical problem existing here and now. This dilemma is also illustrated by animal experimentation where, because of the strict degree of control possible, the results are highly generalizable but hardly applicable to the human situation. Unfortunately, it seems that in the social sciences—where phenomena are invariably complex—what is discovered most precisely is very frequently what is least useful because it is most artificial.

In classroom experiments, it is particularly difficult to control the enthusiasm and the zeal of the teacher and the motivation which he generates in his students. Almost any procedure—no matter how unsound—that stirs the imagination of the children and their teachers is likely to be found more effective than another method in which motivation is not at such a high pitch. To the extent that enthusiasm is frequently based on such transient factors as the novelty of the method, the findings concerning the true worth of the methods being compared are invalid. There would be nothing wrong, of course, with incorporating enthusiasm in the experiment when differences in enthusiasm are inherent in the methods. To the extent that the pupil-directed approach to learning is more closely synchronized with the child's needs, goals, and purposes, for example, it might be expected to promote greater pupil motivation than the teacher-directed method. It would be incorrect to attempt to equalize pupil motivation in such a study, for it would destroy the variables under investigation.

Another factor that needs to be considered very closely is the nature of the experimental design itself. Occasionally, the experiment is designed in such a way that it can lead to only one conclusion. Such a situation is described by Russell (1927) in relation to the classic studies in the psychology of learning:

> One may say broadly that all animals that have been carefully observed have behaved so as to confirm the philosophy in which the observer believed before his observations began. Nay, more, they have all displayed the national characteristics of the observer. Animals studied by Americans rush about frantically, with an incredible display of hustle and pep, and at last achieve the desired result by chance. Animals observed by Germans sit still and think, and at last evolve the solution out of their inner consciousness. To the plain man, such as the present writer, this situation is discouraging. I observe, however, that the type of problem which a man naturally sets to an animal depends upon his own philosophy, and that this probably accounts for the differences in the results.

Frequently, the criterion against which the outcomes of a given experiment are measured is directly related to the outcomes the experimental method was designed to produce, so that the experiment is a success from that standpoint, but nothing is said about the price that was paid because of the neglect of other equally desirable objectives. It seems logical that any program designed to emphasize one phase of the overall academic program is likely to be successful in that phase of it. To the extent that the criterion emphasizes one aspect or one objective and minimizes others, the results are likely to favor one or the other of the methods, depending on their emphasis relative to the criterion. Thus, in the comparison of the discussion with the lecture method of teaching, choosing as the criterion performance on standardized tests, with their typical emphasis on facts and memory work, is likely to favor the lecture method. On the other hand, it is frequently difficult to establish the fairness—i.e., the validity—of the test on the basis of which the results of the experiment are to be appraised. It is essential to define the objectives of the experiment so that the validity of the criterion relative to these objectives can be established.

Randomization

Our first goal, then, is to control all relevant factors operating in the situation. However, since complete control is impossible, the investigator must attempt to neutralize the effect of whatever factors have not been adequately controlled by assigning at random both the subjects to the different groups and the groups to the different treatments under study. As we have emphasized in Chapter 7, the basic element of control is randomness; alone, it will preclude directional differences caused by uncontrolled factors and will provide group equivalence within the limits of random sampling errors, the magnitude of which can be both estimated on the basis of probability and reduced to any desired level. The random assignment of subjects and treatments to groups, whenever feasible, constitutes our best approach to effective experimental control.

The effects of failure to randomize the influence of unequated factors are readily seen in the story of the captain who tested the effectiveness of seasickness tablets by conveniently giving the tablets to his own crew and using the passengers as control (Wilson, 1955). Obviously, the tablets were "effective"; a number of the passengers were seasick—but none of the crew. Similar biases due to a failure to randomize the assignment of subjects to the experimental treatments can be found, for instance, in studies of the effectiveness of a remedial-reading program when an attempt is made to select for the program those pupils who are most likely to profit from it, while the remainder act as a control group. This is apparently what occurred in the Lanarkshire investigation of the value of milk to the health of schoolchildren (Leighton and McKinley, 1930); the teachers, having been allowed some discretion in choosing the experimental group, actually chose children who were in the greatest need of milk. Similar violations of the principles of control and randomization are to be noted in studies in which the experimental group consists of volunteers or, for that matter, in studies comparing the performance of an experimental group with that of the group on which the norms of a test were derived. In both instances, since the subjects cannot be assumed to have been randomized in their assignment to the groups being compared, a bias in the results is almost sure to exist.

Replication

No matter how careful one is in equating a single pair of subjects and in assigning the subjects at random one to each group, there invariably remain slight differences between the two subjects that are bound to influence the results of the experiment. These differences must be neutralized by replicating the number of comparisons incorporated within a given experiment—i.e., by conducting what, in essence, amounts to a number of subexperiments within the framework of an overall experimental design. Rather than comparing a single control case with a single experimental case, the investigator makes a multiple comparison of a number of cases of the control group and a number of cases of the experimental group, all within the same experiment. Thus, in an experiment involving 50 cases in each of the experimental and control groups, he is really conducting 50 parallel "experiments" in one. In a more elaborate experiment, a number of control and experimental groups, each consisting of essentially equivalent individuals assigned at random to one or another of the two groups and the groups assigned at random to the different treatments, are combined within the framework of a single experiment. This is necessary in order to replicate all aspects of the situation which are not replicated when only two groups are compared— e.g., the teacher variable in a comparison of two teaching methods.

The precision of an experiment involves a balance between *control, randomization,* and *replication.* Randomness is, of course, essential. Without it, directional differences are likely to occur, the magnitude and direction of which are beyond interpretation. Assuming randomness, precision becomes a function of the degree of control and the extent of replication. Specifically, the precision of an experiment can be increased either by increasing the number of cases in the comparison groups, or by increasing the homogeneity of the samples through a greater degree of control, thus minimizing the influence of the many variables to which the differences in the outcome might be attributed. This implies that the greater the degree of control, the smaller the sample needed for a given level of precision. In practice, it is therefore a matter of balancing the degree of control that should be exercised against the possibility of relying on a larger number of cases of a somewhat less homogeneous nature. For example, Gossett (1931) suggested that greater precision in the overall results would have been obtained in the Lanarkshire experiment if the experimenters had used fifty pairs of identical twins instead of twenty thousand cases selected at random.

EXPERIMENTAL CONTROL

The Control of Extraneous Variables

The experimenter is concerned with the influence of the experimental factor on the dependent variable. However, the unequivocal appraisal of this effect presupposes the suppression of extraneous factors the effects of which might otherwise be confounded with that of the factor under study. In other words, before he can make a meaningful appraisal of the effect of the experimental factor on the dependent variable, he must establish experimental control. This can be effected in one of three major ways: 1. physical manipulation; 2. selective manipulation; and 3. statistical manipulation. The choice among these three methods is a function of the practical situation and, to some degree, the preferences of the investigator.

1. Physical Manipulation   In order to control nonexperimental variables that might affect the dependent variable, the experimenter might soundproof the laboratory, use a one-way screen or perhaps electrical devices that standardize the stimulus. The physical scientist, for whom physical controls are standard procedure, might control the temperature, the purity of the chemicals, or perhaps use a vacuum chamber where even air resistance is eliminated. In learning experiments it might be possible to control the amount of outside practice and the general interest (motivational) level of the participants. In learning experiments involving rats, one can generally control the various aspects of the experimental environment or even the genetic factors affecting learning.

2.   Selective Manipulation   In the behavioral sciences, particularly with human beings, it is frequently difficult to control the situation through physical means. The social scientist cannot set the intellectual or the motivational level of his subjects as the physical scientist can adjust the temperature by turning a dial or the specific gravity of a given solution by adding more acid. His alternative tends to be to counterbalance variables so as to neutralize their effects on the dependent variable. A common approach is to assign the subjects at random to the experimental and the control group. He must, likewise, randomize teachers so as to neutralize the teacher variable. He may even pair his subjects in terms of relevant variables and assign one member of each pair at random to each of the two groups so that whatever variables are involved will be controlled by contributing equally to the two groups. Control by selection would also be necessary with respect to the experimental factor. In studying the effect of intelligence, organic brain damage, or anxiety on learning speed, the investigator would have to rely on pre-existing groups. Certain variables such as motivation, neurotic tendencies, etc. tend to be inherent in certain subjects, and different levels of the experimental factors cannot just be assigned to different subjects in the way electrical current can be varied by simply turning a knob.*

3.   Statistical Manipulation   More and more, behavioral scientists are relying on statistical control for isolating the influence of extraneous factors on the dependent variable. Thus, in a study of the effects of two methods of teaching on pupil learning, analysis of covariance can be used to adjust the relative performance of the two groups for their initial unequivalence with respect to, say IQ. The more sophisticated multivariate designs actually apportion

---

* We need to make a distinction between *assigned* and *active* variables. Sex, grade level, maladjustment, etc. can only be assigned. Practice, deprivation, and various treatments can be active in the sense that they can be superimposed on one or the other of the groups at random.

the total variance in the dependent variable to the operation of two or more factors.*

It must be recognized that randomness is the primary element of control. The random assignment of subjects and of treatments to groups will generally assure experimental control. It is only when such randomness is not possible, a condition that occurs rather frequently in education where access is to preformed groups rather than to the whole population, that statistical manipulation becomes necessary. It should also be noted that even when physical or selective manipulation is used, it must be accompanied by the random assignment of the subjects to the groups in order to neutralize the variables on which the groups are not specifically equated.

Experimental Validity

Underlying the need for control is the more fundamental concept of validity of the experimental results. Two types of validity are involved: 1. internal (i.e., Are the results dependable?); and 2. external (i.e., To whom do they apply?). Internal validity is the basic minimum without which an experiment is useless. Yet both are necessary if experimental results are to be useful as well as dependable. It should also be noted that internal and external validity may, at times, be incompatible: the more controlled the experiment, the higher the internal validity but also the narrower the application, i.e., the greater the artificiality from the standpoint of practical usefulness.

1. Internal Validity Obviously crucial in any experiment is the question of whether the independent variable did indeed produce the effect noted in the dependent variable. Implied is the necessity of eliminating the possibility that some uncontrolled extraneous factor, either alone or in combination with other variables, did not, on the contrary, contribute in some indeterminate degree to producing the effect in question. In their classic treatment of the subject, Campbell and Stanley† (1963) identify eight

---

* A high level of statistical competence is essential to experimental sophistication. The student is referred to more adequate sources for a discussion of multivariate techniques.

† The following discussion of experimental validity and experimental designs is based on the contents of the Campbell-Stanley article (*Handbook of Research on Teaching,* 1963).

sets of extraneous factors which need to be controlled if misinterpretation of experimental results is to be avoided:

(a) Contemporary history: Specific events occurring during the course of the experiment—in addition to the experimental factor X—may affect the performance of the subjects on the dependent variable as measured by the posttest T_2. An experiment featuring an anti-virus drug designed to reduce instances of the common cold can easily be vitiated by an epidemic sweeping the community. The effect of the epidemic on the dependent variable would be *confounded* with the influence of the experimental factor to the point that the effect of the latter would be completely indeterminate.

(b) Maturation: Performance of the experimental subjects on the dependent variable—as measured by posttest T_2—is likely to be affected by any number of changes occurring within the subject with the passage of time. He may perform better or worse, not only because of the effect of the experimental factor but perhaps also because he is older, more intellectually mature, more tired, or perhaps even bored.

(c) Pretest: Experience with the pretest often reflects itself in performance on the posttest, whether through actual practice effects or through the sensitization of the experimental subject to the experimental factor.

(d) Instrumentation: Changes in the calibration of the measuring "instrument," whether a test, a gauge, or an observer, from pretest to posttest or perhaps from experimental to control group may also be confounded with the changes actually resulting from the experimental factor X. In grading an essay, the investigator may actually shift his point of reference toward greater leniency or greater severity. If he knows which essays were pretests and which were posttests—or if he knows which papers are associated with the method he prefers, he may well be looking for evidence of gain. This occurs even in physical instruments: a scale gets "tired" as the springs lose their resilience.

(e) Statistical regression toward the mean: The well-known tendency for extreme scores in a distribution obtained through instruments of less than complete reliability to regress toward the mean upon retesting biases the results against individuals and groups who scored high on the pretest and in favor of those who scored low.

(f) Differential selection of subjects: Initial differences between the two groups, as reflected in performance on the pretest T_1, are likely to continue to operate on the posttest

T_2; unless the groups are equated in the first place on all relevant variables, there is no way of appraising the effects of the experimental factor.

(g) Experimental mortality: Differential loss of subjects from the experimental and control groups will tend to bias the results of the experiment; if the less motivated members of one group drop out of the study, the relative performance of the two groups on the posttest will reflect to an indeterminate degree both the operation of the experimental variable and the relative unequivalence of the two groups on motivation as an extraneous variable.

(h) Interaction of selection and maturation, selection and history, etc.: Even when the experimental and control groups have equivalent prescores, other differences, e.g., in motivation, personality, etc. may still predispose one group to react better to the experimental factor. Volunteers, for example, are invariably suspect as experimental subjects.

2. External Validity

2. External Validity   The internal validity of the experimental results is obviously the first consideration but, given this validity, consideration must also be given to their generalizability. Specifically, what meaning do these findings concerning the effects of X have beyond the confines of this particular experiment? Do the results have validity for all men? for all children? or only for average children enrolled in a particular subject taught according to a given curriculum? Operationally, this means that the experimenter must define clearly, before he conducts his experiment, the population from which his samples were selected and to which the results are to apply. The effects of a given experimental factor obtained from an experiment conducted in a first-class school in a high-income community may not be the same as would be obtained in a ghetto school, for example. The following are the major factors that need to be controlled if the results are to have external validity:

(a) Interaction effects of selection biases and the experimental factor X: The particular characteristics of an experimental group—its intellectual level, its academic orientation, and other features of its particular background—may make it more or less responsive than average to the experimental factor. Experimental results can be generalized only to a population of which the particular sample in its particular setting is truly representative.

(b) Reactive or interaction effects of pretesting: Pretesting may sensitize the experimental subject to the experimental factor so that the results obtained can be generalized only to other pretested groups.

(c) Reactive effects of experimental procedures: The effects of the experimental procedures employed are often such as to restrict the generalizability of the findings to populations similarly treated. The very fact that a person is selected to participate in an experiment often motivates him to greater efforts so that the results are not applicable to other people exposed to the same experimental factor in a nonexperimental setting.* What this amounts to is that knowledge of the experiment may need to be kept secret from the experimental group or, if that is not possible, the control group might be made to feel equally singled out for special treatment.

(d) Multiple treatment interference: The effect of a treatment on a subject previously exposed to other treatments cannot be generalized to other subjects who have not undergone the same sequence of treatments. The effect of the repeated treatment of the same subject with, say, different antibiotics, would probably be cumulative.

EXPERIMENTAL DESIGNS

Although ideally, an experiment should incorporate full control, i.e., maximum validity, internal and external, undoubtedly a more realistic interpretation of the experimenter's task is for him to plan his research strategies so as to obtain dependable answers to the questions identified in his research hypotheses. More specifically, the research design must be appropriate to the task at hand and, in practice, experimental designs vary widely in complexity and adequacy, depending not only on the research sophistication of the investigator but more fundamentally on such factors as the complexity of the problem under investigation and the conditions under which it is investigated. Campbell and Stanley (1963) emphasize that situational realities are often such as to preclude a rigorous experimental design. The experimenter must then resort to what they call "quasi-experimental" designs that incorporate the most control that can be achieved under the conditions. He must be especially aware in such a case of specifi-

*This is the well-known "Hawthorne effect."

cally what factors of internal and external validity his design does not control so that he can keep these facts in mind when interpreting his experimental findings. The present discussion will present typical experimental designs ranging in adequacy of control from the loosest to the most rigorous; each needs to be considered with respect to the factors of validity previously mentioned.

Crude Designs—Inadequate Control

Design 1: One-Group, Pretest-Posttest. At a most elementary level, we might consider the case of the teacher attempting to increase the vocabulary of his students through teaching Latin roots. He gives a pretest, teaches for the period of a semester, and gives a posttest and measures the extent of gain from pretest to posttest. In paradigm form, we have:

$$T_1 \qquad X \qquad T_2$$

Such a design is so totally lacking in control that it is really not an experiment at all. Since the same students are used in the pre- and the posttest, selection variables are controlled but, if some of the subjects drop out, selective mortality may be involved. There is no way for the experimenter to decide whether the increase in vocabulary from T_1 to T_2 was produced by the experimental factor X or by factors of history, maturation, pretesting, regression, etc. In other words, alternative hypotheses have not been ruled out; any number of factors besides X might have caused a change in the students' vocabulary. Nor have the factors of external validity been adequately isolated.

True Designs—Adequate Control

The addition of a control group to the design above would help greatly; it would control history, maturation, pretesting, instrumentation, etc., since both the experimental and the control groups would undergo essentially the same experiences. However, if the subjects are not assigned at random to the experimental and control groups, initial differences between the two groups may introduce effects which are confounded with those of the experimental factor. One group may be brighter, better motivated, or more test-wise. In other words, the groups are not necessarily equivalent on all factors that might affect the experimental results beyond the exposure to the experimental factor.

Design 2: Parallel Group, Random Assignment. Assigning the subjects at random to the experimental and control groups, on the other hand, would provide the necessary control. In paradigm form, we would have:

$$E_R \qquad T_1 \qquad X \qquad T_2$$
$$C_R \qquad T_1 \qquad - \qquad T_2$$

This is the old workhorse of traditional experimentation. Generally speaking, this design controls history, maturation, and the other factors of internal validity. Except for special factors such as teacher personality, chaotic conditions on the final examination, or other biasing events occurring in one group only—all of which can be controlled through replication of groups—such a design is relatively adequate. The element of randomness as the basic factor of control should be noted. It provides a reasonable guarantee of the almost complete equivalence of the two groups—with the statistical tests of significance acting as a further safeguard against crediting to the experimental factors differences occurring through the element of chance.

One possible weakness of such a design concerns the reactive effects of testing on the external validity of the results. The pretest might sensitize the subjects of the experimental group to the experimental factor and restrict the generalizability of the results to a population similarly pretested. This may not be such a vitiating factor in education, where pretests can be readily hidden in the routine of the school's testing program and where all children are pretested anyway. External validity can also be impaired by the reactive effects of the experimental procedures: if the subjects know they are participating in an experiment, they may exert themselves harder to the point that the effect of this extra motivation will be confounded with that of the experimental factor.

Design 3: Parallel Groups, Random Assignment, Pretest-No Pretest. If pretesting is a vitiating factor, it can be dispensed with, since randomness as the primary element of control should guarantee initial equivalence. A rather complex design in this connection is the Solomon Four-Group design (Solomon, 1949) as presented in the following paradigm:

Group	Pretest	Treatment	Posttest	Difference*
E_{RT_1}	T_1	X	T_2	$D_1 = T_1, X, M, H$
C_{RT_1}	T_1	—	T_2	$D_2 = T_1 - M, H$
E_R	—	X	T_2	$D_3 = -, X, M, H$
C_R	—	—	T_2	$D_4 = - - M, H$

It should be noted that, since the posttest of the first two groups and those of the last two groups are not comparable, they cannot be combined into a single statistical test. On the other hand, the Solomon Four-Group design constitutes one of the most rigorous bivariate designs possible; it does present certain problems from the standpoint of practicality.

Design 4: Randomized, Control-Group, Posttest only. Contrary to the views of the traditional researcher who fails to appreciate the effectiveness of randomness as the true element of control, pretesting is not essential to rigorous experimentation. It would be detrimental when it introduces a reactive bias. It would even be impractical and inadvisable in experiments requiring a guarantee of anonymity to the participants. Substituting randomness for the pretest might facilitate the experiment, especially in cases where the experimental treatment and the posttest can be given in a single setting, e.g., change of attitude as a result of a motion picture. If we omit the pretest from Design 2, we have the following paradigm:

$$E_R \quad - \quad X \quad T_2$$
$$C_R \quad - \quad - \quad T_2$$

When combined with randomness and replication of the relevant aspects of the situation, this design is relatively adequate; it controls, even though it does not measure history, maturation, etc. It avoids the reactive effects of pretesting and, in certain cases, is preferred to Design 2. The latter, on the other hand, would be more rigorous in the usual case, since pretest-

---

* D_1 (the difference between T_1 and T_2 in Group E_{RT_1}) incorporates the effects of various combinations of the Pretest T_1, the experimental factor X, History H, and Maturation M. The effects of a given factor can be isolated by comparing appropriate differences between T_1 and T_2. Thus, the effects of the experimental factor X alone = $D_3 - D_4$; the effects of the Pretest T_1 alone = $D_2 - D_4$; the effects of the interaction of T_1 and X = $D_1 - (D_2 + D_3)$.

ing would provide evidence of initial equivalence and permit minor adjustment through analysis of covariance, where necessary.

Quasi-Experimental Designs

Design 5: Nonrandomized, Control-Group, Pretest-Posttest. In education, where experiments frequently have to be based on preformed groups, randomizing subjects among the treatment groups is out of the question. Under those circumstances Design 2 might be repeated on a nonrandomization basis to give the following paradigm:

$$
\begin{array}{cccc}
E & T_1 & X & T_2 \\
C & T_1 & - & T_2
\end{array}
$$

Because of its failure to randomize, this design cannot guarantee the equivalence of the experimental and control groups in initial status on all factors that may affect the dependent variable. It is not at all unlikely to have preformed groups differ in intelligence, motivation, etc. It would be possible to adjust for certain differences through analysis of covariance but one would never know what other factors may be operating in the situation which have not been included in the pretesting. A common procedure, for example, is to adjust through covariance for intelligence and initial knowledge of the subject. This leaves unquestioned differences in motivation, study habits, etc. A bias of impossible magnitude would be introduced if, for example, the willingness to accept an experimental class were to reflect a greater degree of teacher imagination, initiative, dedication, and/or flexibility. Such a bias can be avoided only through the random assignment of teachers to a number of experimental and controlled groups. This is not possible, of course, where the characteristics and competencies in question are inherent in certain teachers.

Design 6: Counter-Balanced Design. Another approach to generating experimental control when dealing with preformed groups of unknown initial status that have to be taken intact is to rotate the treatments among the groups so that all of the groups are subjected to all the treatments in a random order. The paradigm would look like this:

Time Sequence

Group	1st	2nd	3rd	4th
A	X_1	X_2	X_3	X_4
B	X_3	X_4	X_2	X_1
C	X_2	X_1	X_4	X_3
D	X_4	X_3	X_1	X_2

To the extent that individual differences are rotated in semi-random fashion among treatments, a group-treatment equivalence is established. If all the groups have had all the experimental factors, the results can not be attributed to pre-experimental differences among groups. A major weakness of this design that may interfere with its validity is that the effect of exposure to one experimental factor can carry over—and be confounded with—the effects of a subsequent experimental factor. The inoculative effects of one serum would affect the immunizing power of the next serum, unless enough time is allowed to elapse between treatments for the effect to dissipate. There is no guarantee that it will, nor any way of knowing that it did.

Design 7: One-Group, Time Series Design. Another quasi-experimental design is that shown below in which repeated measures are taken both before and after the introduction of the experimental factor as a means of establishing a bench mark from which the effects of the experimental factor can be gauged.

$$T_1 \quad T_2 \quad T_3 \quad T_4 \quad X \quad T_5 \quad T_6 \quad T_7 \quad T_8$$

If, for example, the introduction of the experimental factor causes a distinct break in the trend established from Test 1 through Test 4 and resumed from Test 5 through Test 8 (although the latter trend may be different from the first, depending on the permanence and cumulative nature of the experimental treatment), this break in the basic trend might be attributed to the experimental factor. An accident, or surgery, for example, might produce such a permanent shift. This design controls relatively well factors of maturation but is vulnerable to errors due to history: a major event occurring concurrently with the introduction of the experimental factor may produce effects which are likely to be confounded with those of the experimental factor. It might at times incorporate certain weaknesses from a generalizability point of view with regard to interaction with pretesting, for example. The number of consecutive tests that have to be taken favors children with perfect attendance; the results might not apply to less adequately domesticated subjects.

Design 8: Control-Group, Time Series. This is essentially Design 7 to which a control group has been added, giving us the following paradigm:

$$E \quad T_1 \quad T_2 \quad T_3 \quad T_4 \quad X \quad T_5 \quad T_6 \quad T_7 \quad T_8$$
$$C \quad T_1 \quad T_2 \quad T_3 \quad T_4 \quad - \quad T_5 \quad T_6 \quad T_7 \quad T_8$$

Such a design provides adequate control for most factors of internal validity. From the standpoint of generalizability, it is rather vulnerable to the reactive effects of treatment with multiple pretesting which is perhaps more objectionable in a nonschool situation than it is in education where frequent pretests are given anyway.

A relatively questionable quasi-experimental design is the *ex post facto* experiment, in which a particular characteristic of a given group is investigated with a view to identifying its antecedents. This is experimentation in reverse: instead of taking groups that are equivalent and exposing them to different treatment with a view to promoting differences to be measured, the *ex post facto* experiment begins with a given effect and seeks the experimental factor that brought it about. The obvious weakness of such an "experiment" is that we have no control over the situations that have already occurred and we can never be sure of how many other circumstances might have been involved. For example, if we note that many of our present civic and business leaders were boy scouts in their youth proportionately more frequently than nonleaders, we need to realize that leadership status is related to a number of factors in addition to membership or nonmembership in scouting. Similarly, statistics on the differential earning power of high school graduates and dropouts cannot be attributed to high school education alone, since a multitude of other factors, including intelligence, motivation, socio-economic background, etc. may have also played an important part in both their present earning capacity and their graduate *versus* dropout status.

By their very nature, *ex post facto* experiments can provide support for any number of different, and perhaps contradictory, hypotheses; they are so completely flexible that it is largely a matter of postulating hypotheses according to one's personal preferences. The point is that the evidence simply illustrates a hypothesis; it does not test the hypothesis since hypotheses cannot be tested on the same data from which they were derived. The relationship noted may actually exist but it is not necessarily the only relationship, or perhaps even the crucial relationship. Before we can accept high school graduation as the "cause" of the greater earning power of graduates, other alternative hypotheses have to be eliminated. This does not mean that the *ex post facto* experiment is completely worthless; many of our important studies in education and psychology are *ex post facto* studies. On the other hand, their failure to introduce the common elements of control, randomization, etc. makes them extremely vulnerable from a scientific point of view and the danger of their being misleading should be clearly recognized. Meanwhile, *ex post facto* "experiments" are probably better conceived as surveys, useful in the derivation of hypotheses to be tested through more conventional experimental approaches.

Factorial Designs

The experimental designs considered thus far are univariate—or perhaps, more correctly, bivariate—in the sense that they deal with the relationship between a single antecedent and its consequent, with the operation of other variables controlled. As a result, the situation is also made relatively artificial. Much more appropriate in dealing with problems of the complexity of those generally found in education are the multivariate (factorial) designs which permit the simultaneous investigation of a number of variables. In contrast to analysis of covariance which attempts to neutralize the possible influence of extraneous factors on the dependent variable, multivariate analysis actually provides separate tests of the effects of these factors on the dependent variable, both singly and in interaction, with a minimum of distortion of the natural situation in which they actually exist. Comparisons of the effects of autocratic and democratic teachers on pupil achievement, for example, generally reveal no great difference; nor do secure and insecure children differ significantly in achievement. However, when studied in interaction, it might be found that autocratic teachers are "better" for insecure children while democratic teachers are "better" for secure children. The existence of this type of interaction may explain some of the contradictions found in the professional literature.

Although multivariate designs are not a panacea for unlocking the secrets of the many problems with which education must cope, they constitute in most cases a more effective approach than the traditional methods in common use. Such designs are also economical in that they permit the simultaneous testing of a number of hypotheses, i.e., they provide answers to a number of questions within the framework of a single experiment. They have the added advantage of providing a measure of the interaction among the independent variables in their effect on the variable under study. On the other hand, multivariate analysis calls for a background in statistics beyond that of the majority of teachers. Besides, such an experiment can get unwieldy when the design gets past the three-dimensional model. The topic is obviously beyond the scope of the present text; the student is referred to the many excellent books in statistical designs for a discussion of the various models, their relative strengths and weaknesses, and the computational procedures involved.

Causal-Comparative Studies

Dealing with some of the more significant problems of education—e.g., teacher effectiveness, underachievement, or delinquency—with their multiplicity of "causal" factors, contributing factors, precipitating factors, as well as an unlimited number of other elements of various degrees of relevance, all operating in different degrees of interaction, presents obvious difficulties. Any attempt to investigate the effects of any one of these factors through a series of simple experiments in isolation of the other agents in the situation is not likely to yield anything but a series of half-answers, which is essentially the same as no answers at all. On the other hand, where a number of variables are involved, multivariate analysis soon becomes unwieldy.

The predicament stems in part from the relative lack of clarity with which many of these so-called complex problem situations have been defined. In our present development of educational science, we do not have a sufficient understanding of many of the more complex educational problems as they actually exist. Until their various aspects have been structured more definitively and the number of relevant factors brought down to manageable size, their investigation through factorial designs is relatively impractical. A common approach to structuring the field in order to gain greater insight into a complex situation is to select two groups at opposite ends of the continuum in order to identify the factors on the basis of which one group can be distinguished from the other. Research into the contrasting characteristics of juvenile delinquents and nondelinquents, for example, has shown the former to be more independent, extrovertive, vivacious, impulsive, aggressive, adventuresome, and, of course, more lacking in self-control (Glueck, 1953).

This approach, sometimes known as *causal-comparative,* presents certain difficulties. It places a particularly great burden on the imagination and insight of the investigator to identify the crucial aspects of the situation. Obviously he cannot consider everything, nor would he want to, since it is essential to keep the number of variables to be analyzed to a relative minimum if confusion is to be avoided. Yet, to the extent that he leaves out factors that are relevant, his solution will be lacking. This is complicated further by the fact that crucial factors are frequently subtle; good teachers, for example, differ from poor teachers principally in contributing rather than in critical factors. The computer provides new possibilities in processing the mass of data such an approach normally presents. A somewhat more scientifically oriented approach would be to rely on factor analysis to reduce the number of variables to be considered by identifying the fundamental psychological dimensions that underlie the operation of more superficial traits.

LABORATORY EXPERIMENTATION

Because of the relative difficulty of maintaining adequate control in a field experiment, scientists, particularly physical scientists, often resort to laboratory experimentation. Even though modern multivariate designs permit the relatively rigorous investigation of the multiple aspects of a complex variable in its natural setting, there are still many instances where laboratory experimentation seems indicated. The intensive investigation of a small segment of an overall problem can provide insights that can be converted into hypotheses to be tested under more normal conditions. Frequently, such studies are conducted on animals where an even greater degree of control can be exerted; this is the primary source of data on the psychology of learning, dating back to the work of Thorndike.

Because they permit almost complete control over the operation of extraneous factors, laboratory studies are generally more precise than the corresponding field investigations. On the other hand, the laboratory situation is automatically more artificial and the results are of correspondingly limited external validity. In extreme cases, the results are relatively useless, except as possible sources of hypotheses. The laboratory method is most appropriate to the physical sciences, where the conditions underlying the law of the single variable are more likely to be fulfilled without undue distortion of the natural situation. At any rate, laboratory experimentation is a precise technique whose use is generally restricted to problems of a specific and limited nature and designed to provide a picture of the operation of a given variable as it functions by itself. Once its operation in isolation is known, it may be easier to understand more adequately its operation in interaction with the other aspects of the overall situation.

The laboratory situation is made deliberately artificial with respect to the precision with which the nonexperimental factors can be controlled in order to derive more precisely the relationship of the phenomena under investigation. However, because of this artificiality, any conclusion based on laboratory experimentation—either in the testing of drugs or in the learning patterns of animals—has to be verified in the field before it is implemented or extended to the general case. As far as the general population is concerned, any conclusion derived in the laboratory is simply a hypothesis in need of testing. This is not to deny the crucial role played by laboratory experimentation both in the exploratory stages of locating workable ideas and in the final stages of deriving precise laws. Most of our knowledge of the highly complex phenomena in the physical—and, to some extent, the medical—world has been derived in the laboratory. Many of our more precise findings in psychology have also come from the laboratory, e.g., the work of Harlow, Hebb, Skinner, Underwood, not to mention Thorndike, or even Fechner and Wundt.

EVALUATION OF EXPERIMENTATION

Experimentation has been largely responsible for the tremendous development of the physical and biological sciences;

experimentation in the field of education, on the other hand, has not fulfilled its earlier promise. Not only has it failed to provide more than superficial answers to many educational problems, but it has also produced conflicting and contradictory outcomes. As a result, some educators have felt that experimentation is not suitable for the investigation of the more significant problems in education and that whatever answers they are to get must come from judgment, experience, common sense, and consensus, rather than experimentation.

That progress has not been as rapid as one might have wished can be understood in the light of the many obstacles which education, by its very nature, presents to rigorous experimentation. Many of its variables are both complex and scientifically unclear, e.g., motivation, attitudes, adjustment, etc. We are still lacking many of the basic tools necessary for the appraisal of significant educational variables. Furthermore, outcomes in the field of education frequently emerge only slowly, meanwhile being affected by so many variables that it is difficult to assign a certain outcome to a specific antecedent. To make matters worse, the gains obtained with respect to one criterion frequently are offset by losses with respect to another. The fact that we are dealing with human subjects poses problems of control and even of availability of a much more complex nature than those confronting the physical scientist. Human subjects even react to the experiment itself, e.g., with increased motivation, and thus vitiate the results.

Where appropriate, experimentation is the most rigorous means for obtaining dependable information. It is especially suited to deriving precise answers to precise questions through the control of the operation of extraneous variables. However, the very element of control, when applied to a field where variables are as inherently complex as they are in education presents a real danger of artificiality. In general, the more precise an experiment, the more artificial and the more meaningless its results. Much of the lack of progress in educational experimentation in the past can be attributed to our failure to see the inappropriateness of the univariate approach for dealing with the complex problems facing education. We are now giving long overdue attention to multivariate designs, which have much to contribute from this standpoint. On the other hand, it must be recognized that experimentation is not a cure-all; it is a matter of using it where it fits. There are many problems that are not amenable to an experimental investigation. In other words, there is not one single research method; different research methods are useful for different purposes. It must also be noted that experimental studies, like many other studies in education, tend to be discontinuous and contribute rather little to the advancement of education as a science.

As a profession, educators have done far too little experimentation of any kind, and especially of the long-range complex variety needed to provide adequate answers to educational problems. Rarely do the teachers who face the actual problems in the field have the time or the training necessary to solve their problems. Even teachers and administrators with advanced degrees are rarely sufficiently versed in research and statistical techniques to conduct adequate experiments. Although the situation is improving, university faculties in education, in contrast to those in psychology and the physical and biological sciences, are still relatively unoriented toward research and incompetent in the use of the more sophisticated research designs. Until a few years ago, a survey of university catalogs would have shown that advanced training in experimental and statistical methodology was rarely required of doctoral candidates in education; often these courses were not even offered in the School of Education. In other words, it would seem that, despite the need for exceptional competence in keeping with the complexity of our problems, we have until recently been lacking even the simplest basic skills. The new emphasis on statistical sophistication, on the other hand, can introduce a danger, namely, that statistical manipulation will be substituted for the selection of significant problems arising from sound theoretical premises; in fact, that significant problems will be avoided because they do not provide data amenable to elegant statistical methodologies in current favor.

Much of the experimentation conducted to date has been inadequate, if not incorrect. Norton and Lindquist (1951), in their review of the literature, point to numerous and damaging recurrent errors in experimental design and in the analysis of experimental results. Many of the reported studies reflect a glaring failure to comply with the basic conditions of control. Frequently, such relevant factors as teacher effectiveness are overlooked and become confounded with the effect of the variable under study. Other common errors include the invalidation of the criterion through the experimental design, failure to take into account the assumptions underlying the procedures used, the use of inappropriate and inadequate statistics, and carelessness in the definition of the population to which the results are to be generalized. The more experimentally adequate studies, on the other hand, are often of limited usefulness because of their relative artificiality. As pointed out by Stanley (1957), the professional literature is virtually devoid of well-controlled experimental studies conducted in the classroom. Fortunately, the situation is undergoing improvement as a result of the renewed interest in research, the availability of the computer, and the new sophistication of research and statistical methodology generated by such writers as Fisher, Lindquist, and more recently, Campbell and Stanley. Perhaps the situation is best synthesized in the words of McLean (1966), who summarizes his review of experimental designs by saying:

> That anyone should draw comfort from such modest gains as have been cited in the previous paragraphs is an indictment of the state of educational research; but in view of the nature of the problems faced by those who do research with human beings *in situ,* we can be thankful that at last attention is being given to the right questions.

CASE STUDIES

Closely related to experimentation from the standpoint of purpose is the *case study,* which is also designed to identify the antecedents responsible in a direct or indirect "causative" way for the occurrence of such problems as reading disabilities, maladjustment, emotional immaturity, or delinquency. Actually, the case study is not so much a unique method of investigation as it is the application of all relevant techniques to the study of a person, a group, an institution, or even a community. Consequently, it resembles almost all other types of research in some way or another. It borders on historical research, for example, in the sense that the present case can be understood only in relation to its past. It resembles the survey in that it is concerned with the present status of phenomena. More fundamentally, of course, it differs from the survey in that the determination of status is a secondary consideration; the more fundamental question is the discovery of how it got that way.

Case studies, as the term is generally used, are generally oriented toward the solution of a particular problem at the individual level rather than toward the derivation of generalizations having scientific validity. Although case studies used for purposes of individual guidance can lead to the identification of relationships having a definite bearing on research, in the strict sense of the term, research is concerned with the derivation of generalizations that apply beyond the individual case; consequently, case studies become research only to the extent that they lead to such generalizations. The study of five or six cases can provide insight into the dynamics of human behavior and its antecedents but, since it is not likely to permit the isolation of crucial factors, the extent to which it can lead to valid generalizations is extremely limited. Perhaps the case study is more fundamentally a clinical procedure and only secondarily a research technique. It probably makes its greatest contribution to the advancement of science as a source of hypotheses to be verified by more rigorous investigation.

Case Study Data

The major problem of a case study is essentially that of the historical method, namely, obtaining dependable data from which valid interpretations can be derived. Not only are wide gaps bound to exist, but the data that are available generally have not been collected to focus on the present problem and invariably are incomplete, inaccurate, and otherwise inadequate. The investigator's first task is to gather data that will supply a relatively complete picture of the case. Generally, this involves the use of observation, interviews, tests, and other data-gathering devices and techniques designed to provide information on the individual's life history including his health history, his scholastic record, his home and community background, and any other aspect of the situation that might clarify the present problem. Unfortunately, much of this information will be relatively unverifiable except on the basis of general plausibility.

Along with the gathering and verifying of the data, the investigator must devote himself to the even more demanding task of interpreting these data in the light of the present problem, with a view toward a diagnosis of the case and a prognosis of its likely disposition. This calls for insight into the past and present situation sufficient to permit the synthesis of the data relative to the present problem. This is invariably difficult to achieve since situations extending through a substantial portion of the individual's life are generally too comprehensive to permit a complete investigation of every aspect. To make matters worse, they cover a multitude of different facets of the individual's background and any attempt at their synthesis must rely heavily on the investigator's judgment, if not intuition, as to their relevance and significance.

In order to make sense out of the mountain of data which he may accumulate, the investigator must superimpose on them a general theoretical orientation. This calls for insight into human nature as it exists in its sociological context and always involves obvious risks of error. The investigator's mind-set may blind him to certain significant aspects of the situation. To the extent that his general orientation determines not only the data he collects, but also the relevance he attributes to them and the interpretation he gives them, he must be careful not to build out of his own personal experience and perspective a case which has little relation to the actual situation.

Rationale of Case Studies

Case studies generally involve the cooperation of a number of investigators pooling their resources toward the diagnosis, the prognosis, and perhaps the treatment of a problem. In the guidance of a child who is displaying antisocial behavior, for example, a team, consisting of the school psychologist, teachers, guidance workers, social workers, and other interested persons, may pool information and insights in order to gain an understanding of the case. Eventually a diagnosis is reached and remedial steps are prescribed. The latter validates the diagnosis; if the treatment alleviates the symptoms, it can be assumed that the source of difficulty has been properly identified, and that the problem is being resolved. Conversely, if the symptoms persist, it might be suspected either that the cause of the difficulty has not been properly identified or that an improper inference has been made about the treatment implied by the diagnosis.

The case study is, of course, a fundamental technique in medicine, where diagnosis and treatment as outlined above are standard procedures. However, we need to distinguish between diagnosis in medicine and diagnosis in education and psychology, where it is typically more complicated. In medicine, the diagnosis is relatively clear from the symptoms; a slight fever, a swelling of the lower jaw, etc. spells mumps with relative certainty. Once the identification is made, the treatment is generally prescribed, and the cure follows in rather short order so that the diagnosis can be validated. In education and psychology, on the other hand, the problem is not so simple. First, the symptoms rarely identify the cause except in a very tentative way. The child who is antisocial may be so for any number of reasons, ranging from feelings of parental rejection to perhaps hunger. Consequently, it is frequently necessary to collect a great deal of information about the individual and to pool the insight of a number of experts to arrive at a sound diagnosis.

In the social sciences, the problems of devising remedial procedures and of implementing the solution are also more difficult. Failure of the home to cooperate, for instance, may preclude a cure. Consequently, when treatment does not work, it is difficult to know who is to blame for the failure—or even to know if indeed a failure has occurred. Improvement frequently is slow, and even the most adequate technique can aggravate the symptoms while reorganization is taking place, which may cause the person in charge to give up the treatment just as improvement is about to be shown. It is also difficult to attribute success to any one cause; in reading, for instance, it is common to attribute the child's improvement in reading to the remedial exercises when it may stem, in part at least, from the greater attention the child is receiving. Thus, even when a cure is effected, the investigator may not have learned very much from a scientific point of view.

The Steps of the Case Study

If it is to be accepted as a scientific technique, the case study must follow essentially the same steps and meet essentially the same criteria as do the other research methods. On the other hand, it presents a number of problems which are relatively unique, either in kind or degree. These are probably best considered in connection with the steps through which such a study must proceed.

1. The first step of the case study is obviously the selection of the cases which exemplify the problem area under consideration. There is especially a need for typical cases—i.e., a random sample of cases considered representative of the

problem under investigation. The sample should be large enough to permit the derivation of valid generalizations. This often presents a problem. Since case studies cover many facets of the total picture and extend over a long period of time, it is common practice to restrict the study to the thorough investigation of a few cases. This, of course, raises the question of the representativeness of such small samples and of the degree of confidence with which the results can be generalized to the alleged population.

2. The collection of data on the individual cases must be guided by some tentative hypothesis. Some of the data will be readily available from records and will pose no problem of collection. There will, however, be the question of verification and interpretation. Generally when these data were collected, present needs were not anticipated, and, as a result, the data were probably not collected and recorded systematically enough to be dependable and understandable in the context of the present problem. The cumulative record, for example, may include test scores recorded without date or identification. Some data will be incorrect or invalid, or perhaps atypical or out of context, and therefore misleading. Some of the data will have to be collected from the community where the emphasis is often on hearsay, on the atypical and, of course, on memory. Some will have to come from parents who may not have insight into whether the child was insecure as a baby or whether he had unusual troubles at school, for example.

3. An important step in the case study is the derivation of hypotheses or tentative diagnoses of the likely antecedents of the difficulty. Generally, this is followed by some mental elaboration of the diagnosis in the light of the data already available and, where necessary, by the collection of further data.

4. Along with the diagnosis comes the suggested treatment and the prognosis of the likely response of the subject to such treatment, judged in the light of the severity of the case and the environmental circumstances under which the cure is to be effected. The situation calls for considerable insight into the dynamics of human behavior as they operate in a sociological setting which, in turn, calls for considerable training in the general area of psychology and sociology. A common practice when case studies are used in guidance is to implement multiple remedial procedures simultaneously on the assumption that one or the other will work. From a research point of view, such an approach does not provide

the generalizations which science requires in order to deal with subsequent cases.*

5. The final step is the follow-up of the case from the standpoint of its response to treatment. This constitutes a test of the validity of the diagnosis.

Highlights of the Chapter

1.   Experimentation is a scientifically sophisticated technique capable of providing precise answers to precise problems. Its use is, therefore, restricted to the later stages of the investigation of a problem, after it has become sufficiently structured to permit the derivation of specific hypotheses which can then be submitted to experimental test. The experiment is conducive to both economy and precision since it stages the occurrence of a phenomenon under conditions as free as possible from confounding co-occurrences, and thus permits its precise and rigorous allocation to the operation of the experimental factor.

2.   In the earlier conception, experimentation was based on the law of the single variable and was oriented toward the discovery of direct one-to-one cause-and-effect relationships. This interpretation was not only unnecessarily narrow and incapable of fulfillment, but it also introduced artificiality in the situation and thus tended to vitiate the very purpose of the investigation.

3.   If an experiment is to provide dependable answers, it must be self-contained—that is, it must provide the basis for the interpretation of its results. The basic condition underlying experimentation is control, without which there is no way of knowing whether the results noted are due to the operation of the variable under investigation or to some extraneous factor.

4.   Since control of all extraneous factors operating in the situation is impossible, it is necessary to assign the subjects at random to the experimental and the control groups to neutralize the effects of whatever variables have not been adequately controlled. This is often difficult to do in education where variables are often pre-assigned and groups preformed. However, no matter how carefully

---

* In practice, it is frequently inadvisable to postpone treatment indefinitely while a one-at-a-time approach is being tried. Furthermore, certain remedial procedures may not work in isolation.

extraneous factors are controlled, or how carefully subjects and treatments are randomized, slight discrepancies between the two groups are still likely to exist because of the operation of chance. It is therefore necessary to replicate the comparison with regard to each of the relevant variables.

5.   Operationally, the adequacy of an experimental design is best appraised from the standpoint of the factors of internal and external validity presented by Campbell and Stanley in the *Handbook of Research on Teaching*. Since, by their very nature and the situation in which they occur, educational phenomena typically preclude the complete control of all extraneous factors, the experimenter must almost invariably rely on quasi-experimental designs and take the various uncontrolled factors into consideration in the interpretation of his data. Despite the obvious limitations of its monistic premises, the parallel-group design has probably been the most commonly used experimental strategy to date.

6.   Laboratory experimentation is designed to provide a precise answer to a restricted aspect of a specific problem under rigorously controlled—and relatively artificial—conditions not possible in a field experiment. The resulting insights can then be transferred to the more adequate investigation of the overall phenomenon in the more realistic field setting. The method is more common to the physical sciences and medicine.

7.   Unfortunately, educational science has not attained the stage of development at which many of its significant problems are amenable to experimental procedures of the monistic approach which has dominated educational experimentation to date.

8.   The multiplicity of factors invariably involved in the occurrence of a complex phenomenon automatically makes its investigation through multivariate analysis laborious and complicated. Before multivariate analysis can be used effectively in the solution of the complex problems characteristic of education, there is need for clarification of their nature and the structuring of their components into a somewhat more fundamental organization. The causal-comparative approach, which is designed to identify the contrasting

characteristics of the two extremes of a given phenomenon, can sometimes provide insight into which factors need to be considered and which can perhaps be ignored.

9. The case study is concerned with the antecedents of such complex phenomena as delinquency or reading disability. The major difficulty generally centers around the accumulation of accurate background data and their interpretation in the light of the present predicament of the individual. The technique is most frequently used in a clinical rather than a research setting; it becomes research only to the extent that it permits the derivation of generalizations of relatively broad applicability. In general, case studies serve their greatest research functions through the suggestion of hypotheses that can then be investigated more adequately by more rigorous techniques.

Questions and Projects

1. (a) Evaluate two or three experiments reported in the literature from the standpoint of the factors of internal and external validity presented in this chapter. What changes, if any, might you make in the reported conclusions as a consequence of your analysis?

(b) What is the present status of the classical studies conducted in education? What might modern research, statistical, and technological sophistication contribute to a more adequate study of some of these earlier problems? Redesign one of these studies to conform more adequately to modern principles of experimental validity.

Selected References

Becker, Gary S. *Human Capital: A Theoretical and Empirical Analysis with Special Reference to Education.* New York: Columbia Univ. Press, 1964.

Boring, Edwin G. "The nature and history of experimental control," *Amer. J. Psychol.*, 67: 573–89; 1954.

Brooks, W.D. "Effects of a persuasive message upon attitudes: A methodological comparison of an offset before-after design with a pretest-posttest design," *J. Comm.*, 16: 180–88; 1966.

Campbell, Donald T. and Julian C. Stanley. "Experimental and quasi-experimental designs for research on teaching," in N.L.

Gage (ed.) *Handbook of Research on Teaching.* Chicago: Rand McNally, 1963. pp. 171–246.

Cattell, Raymond B. (ed.) *Handbook of Multivariate Experimental Psychology.* Chicago: Rand McNally, 1966.

Chen, M.K. "Critical look at the matching technique in experimentation," *J. exper. Educ.,* 35: 95–98; 1967.

Chernoff, Herman. "Sequential design of experiments," *Ann. math. Stat.,* 30: 755–60; 1959.

Cochran, William G. "Design of experiments," in *International Encyclopedia of the Social Sciences.* New York: Macmillan, 1968. Vol. 5, pp. 245–54.

Fen, Sing-nan. "The theoretical implications of multivariate analysis in the behavioral sciences," *Behav. Sci.,* 13: 138–42; 1968.

Ferguson, Eva D. "Ego-involvement: A critical examination of some methodological issues," *J. abnorm. soc. Psychol.,* 64: 407–17; 1962.

Fisher, Ronald A. *The Design of Experiments.* 6th ed. New York: Hafner, 1951.

Guba, Egon G. "Experiments, studies, and investigations," in Jack A. Culbertson and Stephen M. Hencley (eds.) *Educational Research: New Perspectives.* Danville: Interstate, 1963. pp. 237–48.

Johnson, Palmer O. and Leo C. Fay. "The Johnson-Neyman technique, its theory and application," *Psychometrika,* 15: 349–67; 1950.

——— and Fei Tsao. "Factorial design and covariance in the study of individual educational development," *Psychometrika,* 10: 133–62; 1945.

Kempthorne, Oscar. "The design and analysis of experiments with reference to educational research," in Raymond O. Collier and Stanley M. Elam (eds.) *Research Designs and Analysis.* 2nd Annual Symposium. Bloomington: Phi Delta Kappa, 1961. pp. 97–133.

Rosenthal, Robert. *Experimenter Effects in Behavioral Research.* New York: Appleton-Century-Crofts, 1966.

Ryan, Thomas A. "Multiple comparisons in psychological research," *Psychol. Bull.,* 56: 26–47; 1959.

Saupe, Joe L. "Factorial-design multiple discriminant analysis: A description and an illustration," *Amer. educ. Res. J.,* 2: 175–84; 1965.

Schutz, Richard E. "The control of error in educational experimentation," *Sch. Rev.,* 74: 150–58; 1966.

Stanley, Julian C. "Controlled experimentation in the classroom," *J. exper. Educ.,* 25: 195–201; 1957.

———. "Studying status vs. manipulating variables," in Raymond O. Collier and Stanley M. Elam (eds.) *Research Design and Analysis.* 2nd Annual Symposium. Bloomington: Phi Delta Kappa, 1961. pp. 173–208.

———. "Quasi-experimental designs," *Sch. Rev.*, 73: 197–205; 1965.

———. "A common class of pseudo-experiments," *Amer. educ. Res. J.*, 3: 79–87; 1966.

———. "The influence of Fisher's *The Design of Experiments* on educational research 30 years later," *Amer. educ. Res. J.*, 3: 223–29; 1966.

———(ed.) *Improving Experimental Design and Statistical Analysis.* 7th Annual Symposium. Bloomington: Phi Delta Kappa, 1967.

Tiedeman, David V. "Experimental method," in Chester W. Harris (ed.) *Encyclopedia of Educational Research.* New York: Macmillan, 1960. pp. 486–90.

12
PREDICTIVE METHODS

Outside of womankind, few topics have intrigued and tormented mankind more than the problem of predicting the future.——Nicholas A. Fattu (1958)

Man is forever predicting the likely outcome of his efforts. In fact, both at the personal and the professional level, man's behavior almost invariably implies some degree of expectancy. We invest our money because we expect to make a profit; we enroll in school because we expect to get a degree; we work hard because we expect a promotion or a raise. We also strive to improve the accuracy of our predictions. We classify people into subclasses because doing so allows us to set more accurate and precise expectations of them. We categorize students on the basis of intelligence and motivation, for example, so that we can more accurately predict their chances of academic success. Classifying people according to age and general conditions of health permits a closer estimation of their life expectancy. In fact, aptitude, readiness, guidance and personnel work are all predicated on the concept of prediction. Such expectations are based on probability of occurrence for, as Fattu (1958) emphasizes, the only 100 percent accurate method of prediction is hindsight, an activity which is almost as popular as it is precise.

BASES OF PREDICTION

The bases on which predictions are made range all the way from intuition and charlatanism to relatively precise empirically and theoretically derived relationships. Fortune-telling, for example, is simply guesswork made true by selective forgetting. Astronomers, on the other hand, are able to predict the position of a star at any given time in the future with almost complete accuracy.

Prediction Based on Trends

Prediction is often based on trends. It appears safe to predict, for example, that the enrollment of our schools will increase in the next decade; it has been rising for some time now and probably will continue to do so in the future. Trend prediction is a standard procedure in economics, where business conditions indexes, for instance, are based on the trend lines of relevant economic indicators. These are sometimes simply graphic extensions of the lines of growth of contributing factors. A more precise technique consists of deriving the mathematical equation of the line of growth and extrapolating it into the future. Some equations of this kind have relatively wide applicability: for example, the Gompertz curve, which displays an initial gradually increasing rate of acceleration followed by a gradual tapering off to a limit. It can be used to represent both population growth and the learning curve in the acquisition of a motor skill. The more basic equation of the straight line is applicable to a number of situations, including changes in a phenomenon over a short period of time in which growth can be assumed to be linear.

Prediction Based on Association

Prediction can also be based on the association between variables. For example, to the extent that IQ and academic achievement are positively correlated, it is possible to predict, with some degree of accuracy, that a person with a high IQ will probably do well academically. Such prediction is not free from exception since the association between IQ and academic achievement is not a one-to-one relationship. Prediction on the basis of association can be extended to more sophisticated and precise predictions, involving formulas of various degrees of complexity, the relative accuracy of which can be estimated through proper statistical techniques.

The most common basis for informal prediction used in education is performance on educational and psychological tests. By virtue of the correlation of the scores they yield with measures of certain other traits, all tests are in a sense prognostic. Intelligence tests, for example, are prognostic of academic and vocational success. Performance on an achievement test is predictive of later performance in the same area and, to a lesser degree, of performance in related areas. Every test allows for prediction, and tests are rarely given for purposes other than prediction. This is implied in the concept of test validity.

At an elementary level, prediction can be based on a simple charting of two variables, such as IQ and grades, on a scattergram. A line of best fit can then be drawn through the data to display the general trend. This idea can be extended to provide an expectancy table or chart showing expected performance for different IQ levels. Table 12–1, for example, lists the probability of getting a minimum grade-point average of C, B, or A for freshmen of different levels of ability as determined on the basis of a composite

TABLE 12–1: EXPECTANCY TABLE FOR ESTIMATING ACADEMIC PERFORMANCE FOR THE FRESHMAN YEAR OF ENTERING STUDENTS AT THE UNIVERSITY*

	All Students, Male and Female; N = 1,268			
	Student Will Get Average of:			*Proportion Admitted as Fall*
Index 2 V +	*C or*	*B or*		*Entering*
M + 4 H	*Better*	*Better*	*A*	*Freshmen*
400		93	49	↑
380		85	33	
360	98	73	20	
340	96	58	10	
320	90	42	5	100
300	81	27	2	↓
280	68	15	1	98
260	52	7		95
240	35	3		87
220	21			30
200	11			1
180	5			↑
160	2			0
140	1			↓
Per Cent of 1960 Freshmen Achieving:	58	21	1	

* From Hills (1964).

index. This expectancy concept can be extended, in turn, into a two-way (double-entry) classification to provide more precise prediction; Wesman (1966), for example, lists the probability associated with college grade-point averages of A & B, C, and D & E for different combinations of high, middle, and low high-school rank and high, middle, and low college qualification test scores.

Correlation

The concept of correlation is fundamental to prediction based on association among variables. Since this concept is adequately treated in introductory texts in statistics, the present discussion will be restricted to a brief overview of its use in predictive studies. It must first be realized that correlation is not synonymous with causation; correlation simply implies concomitance. It may suggest causation, but the latter would have to be shown since, frequently, the correlation between factors is nothing more than the reflection of the operation of a third factor. There is a positive correlation between the number of churches and the number of traffic accidents in a given community, for instance, a relationship which can be explained readily on the basis of the growth in population to which both factors are related.

To be valuable in prediction, the degree of association between two variables must be relatively substantial, and, of course, the greater the association, the more accurate the prediction it permits. What this means in practice, however, is not clear, except that anything short of perfect correlation between two variables will permit errors in predicting one from a knowledge of the other. The correlation must, of course, represent a real relationship rather than simply the operation of chance. Beyond this, what constitutes an adequate correlation between two variables can be appraised only on the basis of what can logically be expected, and, of course, what accuracy of prediction is required to serve the purpose of the study. A coefficient of correlation of 0.35 between motivation and grades, for example, is perhaps all that can be expected in view of the crudeness of our present measures of motivation and of grades.

Correlation is a group concept, a generalized measure which is useful primarily in predicting group performance. We can predict, for example, that gifted children as a group will succeed in school, but we cannot be sure that a particular gifted child will do well. Except where the correlation between two variables is ±1.00, prediction always involves an element of risk, the magnitude of which can be appreciated from a consideration of the index of forecasting efficiency (e) which is defined as follows:

$$e = 1 - \sqrt{1 - r^2}$$

where r is the coefficient of correlation between the two variables. This measure represents the predictability over and above pure chance, associated with a given coefficient of correlation. Thus, using as an example, a coefficient of 0.60 between X and Y, we find

$$
\begin{aligned}
e &= 1 - \sqrt{1 - .3600} \\
&= 1 - \sqrt{.6400} \\
&= 1 - .80 \\
&= 0.20 \text{ or } 20\%
\end{aligned}
$$

On the basis of correlation of 0.60 between X and Y, we can predict Y from a knowledge of X, 20 percent better than chance—i.e., we can reduce by 20 percent the range of error that would be involved if we had based our prediction on pure guesswork.

Similar calculations of the predictive efficiency of other values of the coefficient of correlation would give the following:

r	e
±1.00	100%
±0.80	40%
±0.60	20%
±0.40	8%
±0.20	2%
±0.00	0%

Since most of the correlations among the variables of interest in education are of the order of 0.50, relatively little confidence can be placed in such predictions in the individual case. It is, therefore, necessary to attempt to raise the correlation on the basis of which predictions are made, in order to increase their precision. This can be done by refining either or both the instruments used and the criterion being predicted, and, as we shall see, by combining a number of variables into a composite predictor of the criterion.

STATISTICAL PREDICTION*

Simple Regression

The usual procedure for predicting one variable from knowledge of another consists of converting the correlation between the two variables into a predictive or *regression* equation which expresses the relationship between them. Such an equation is simply the algebraic expression of the line of best fit through the data arranged in a scattergram on the X and Y coordinates. It gives the most probable value of the *dependent* variable (or *criterion*) for each of the values of the independent variable (or *predictor*).

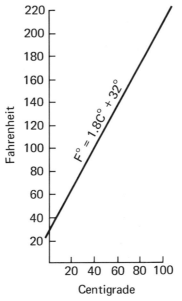

Fig. 12–1: Graphic Representation of a Regression Equation.

* This section will introduce the reader to simple mathematical reasoning. The concepts are not difficult; anyone who has had a course in elementary statistics should make it a point to follow the discussion. However, failure to understand the specific steps should not be a deterrent to grasping the general orientation of the presentation. Textbooks in statistics or in educational tests and measurements should be consulted for a more complete treatment.

† A common example of such a straight line is the formula, $F° = 1.8C° + 32°$, from which Centrigrade temperatures can be converted into Fahrenheit temperatures. The meaning of b and a are shown graphically in the chart in Figure 12–1.

The technique calls for the solution of the constants b and a in the equation of the straight line,

$$Y = bX + a$$

where the constants b and a simply indicate the slope and the "starting point" of the line of best fit.† This can be done directly either through the solution of the equations,

(1) $\Sigma Y = b\Sigma X + na$
(2) $\Sigma XY = b\Sigma X^2 + n\Sigma X$

or from their algebraic equivalent,

$$\tilde{Y} = r\frac{S_y}{S_x}X + (\overline{Y} - r\frac{S_y}{S_x}\overline{X})$$

where Y is the estimate of the variable to be predicted; $\overline{X}$ and $\overline{Y}$ are the means, and S_y and S_x are the standard deviations of the variables X and Y respectively, and r is the coefficient of correlation between X and Y.

Thus, given:

$\tilde{Y}$ = Robert's estimated grade-point average

X = Robert's IQ = 103

$\overline{Y}$ = School's average GPA = 2.3

$\overline{X}$ = School's average IQ = 122

S_y = Standard deviation of the school's distribution of GPA = 0.7

S_x = Standard deviation of the school's distribution of IQ = 11

r = the correlation between IQ and GPA at this school = .50

Substituting

$$\tilde{Y} = r\frac{S_y}{S_x}X + (\overline{Y} - r\frac{S_y}{S_x}\overline{X})$$

$$= .50\left(\frac{.7}{11}\right) + [2.3 - (.50)\left(\frac{.7}{11}\right)(122)]$$

$$= .032X + (2.3 - 3.9)$$

$$= .032X - 1.6$$

$$= 3.3 - 1.6 = 1.7$$

The equation gives Robert a predicted grade-point average of 1.7. What does this mean? Actually, 1.7 is the grade-point average to be expected by the multitude of "Roberts" with an IQ of 103 entering this particular college. It is simply an average to be expected from this hypothetical group—some will get more; some will get less. The next consideration is the variability to be expected in the grade-point average of this multitude of students of IQ of 103. This introduces the concept of the *standard error of estimate,* or *prediction,* which can be calculated as follows:

$$\text{S.E.}_{\text{est.}} = S_y \sqrt{1 - r^2}$$
$$= 0.7 \sqrt{1 - .2500}$$
$$= 0.7 \sqrt{.7500}$$
$$= 0.7(.87) = 0.609 \text{ (or 0.6 approximately)}$$

This can be interpreted on the basis of the normal probability distribution shown in Figure 12–2. Whereas the average grade-point to be expected by students of this caliber attending this college is 1.7, 34 percent and 34 percent can be expected to obtain grade-point averages from 1.7–0.6 and from 1.7+0.6—i.e., between 1.1 and 1.7 and between 1.7 and 2.3, respectively. Similarly, 14 percent of these students can be expected to obtain grade-point

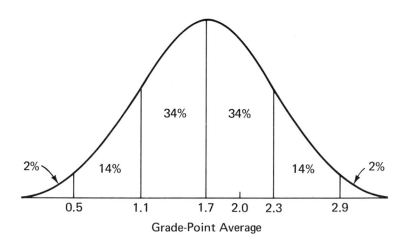

Fig. 12–2: Probable Distribution of Grades (Y = 1.7; SE$_{\text{est.}}$ = 0.6)

averages from 0.5 to 1.1 and from 2.3 and 2.9. And, some 2 percent can be expected to get a grade-point average of less than 0.5, and another 2 percent a grade-point average in excess of 2.9.

One can go further and note that, since graduation generally requires a grade-point average of 2.0, only some 30 percent of these students might be expected to attain this level of scholarship, a point that might be brought out in counseling a student of this caliber. It must be remembered, of course, that the odds refer to the group and have only indirect meaning for any one student.

Multiple Regression

A somewhat more complex—and more realistic and useful—approach to the prediction of a given variable is multiple regression, in which the estimate of the criterion measure is based on the linear combination of several independent variables. For example, grades in college might be predicted from a linear combination of such variables as high-school rank (X_1); *Scholastic Aptitude Test* score (X_2); and *Cooperative English Test* score (X_3) through an equation of the form,

$$\tilde{Y} = \beta_1 X_1 + \beta_2 X_2 + \beta_3 X_3 + a$$

where the Beta multipliers of the independent variables are computed to maximize the prediction of the dependent variable. The procedure consists of making the weight of each of the predictor variables proportional to its net contribution to the dependent variable. Thus, if Variable X_1 makes a greater contribution to the dependent variable Y than does a lesser predictor, it is weighted more heavily, so that a person high on an important predictor and low on a minor predictor would obtain a higher criterion score than the person with the reverse combination of high and low predictor scores.

The Beta-weights in the equation are derived from the solution of n equations in n unknowns. The procedure is essentially routine, and, for equations involving no more than three or four independent variables, the work is not particularly time-consuming. In fact, with the computer, the work is now largely clerical. The computation is beyond the scope of this text but it is not beyond the capabilities of any teacher willing to solve simultaneous equations.

Once the weights have been determined, an estimate of an applicant's likely success can be obtained by the simple process of substituting his scores on each of the independent variables in the equation. Again, this does not represent exactly what the student will get, but an average predicted by the equation for the multitude of applicants whose weighted summation of X_1, X_2, and X_3 gives such a predicted score. The procedure also permits the computation of the probability of a given student achieving any given grade-point average above or below that predicted.

1. Choice of Predictors A regression equation is only as good as the variables on which it is based. The specific combination of variables to be included in the equation—and the relative weights they are to be given—depends first of all on the nature of the problem; different variables would be needed, for instance, for predicting success in engineering than in education. They would also vary from subject to subject, from school to school (even in the same subject), and from year to year. Furthermore, in the present stage of development of the social sciences, one can never be sure of what to include, for some excluded variable, had it been included, might have tapped an important aspect of performance ignored by the other components of the predictive equation. It would be desirable, for instance, in developing an equation to predict performance in a relatively unknown area, to err on the side of including too many variables rather than too few, especially since those variables that do not contribute significantly to the prediction will be eliminated in the process of deriving the equation.

The variables selected as predictors should be correlated as highly as possible with the dependent variable, but, on the other hand, they should be as independent of each other as possible, since, obviously, if two variables are duplicates of one another, one or the other will carry the prediction all by itself and the other will add nothing.

A common misuse of regression equations is to include an unnecessarily large number of variables on a trial-and-error basis, thus increasing their complexity and unwieldiness. Although this may be permissible, and even advisable, in exploratory studies, the investigator should generally attempt to select predictors that fit into the theoretical structure of the variable to be predicted. Maximum effectiveness in prediction would tend to be obtained when factorially pure predictors are selected to cover each of the components of the criterion with a maximum of validity and a minimum of overlapping.

The variables included also have to be capable of reliable measurement and be available before the prediction is needed. The variables used in predicting college success, for example, have to be available at the time the student applies for admission. Yet, one must be careful not to select variables simply because they are available or easy to measure. Most predictive equations, for example, do not place sufficient emphasis on such variables as motivation and personality characteristics, principally because they are difficult to measure with sufficient precision for them to add significantly to the equation.

An interesting question in the use of multiple regression equations in personnel selection concerns the role that the judgment of the personnel interviewer is to play in the selection. Although sizable individual differences are bound to exist in the ability of interviewers to distinguish between potentially satisfactory and potentially unsatisfactory workers, there is sufficient evidence to suggest the relative inadequacy of personal judgment to warrant caution in its use. The problem can perhaps be resolved by having the interviewer's rating of the applicant included as one of the predictors in the equation. If the rating has validity with respect to the criterion scores over and above what is already contributed by the other variables in the equation, its Beta-weight will testify to its usefulness, and the rating should be kept either as part of the equation or as a separate step in the hiring process. If, on the other hand, nothing is added by the inclusion of the interview rating, employment procedures could be streamlined by the omission of the interview without loss in predictive efficiency.

2. Choice of Criterion The choice of the criterion of a regression equation is a vital factor in its effectiveness. It is an even more crucial factor in its validity since, obviously, what constitutes an adequate criterion depends on the purpose of the study. More specifically, the criterion should reflect the objectives of what is to be promoted. In practice, the dependent variable selected is too frequently an inadequate criterion of the true goals of the activity in question. Generally, the criterion predicted in schools of education, for example, is the grade-point average which, besides incorporating a considerable element of unreliability and invalidity as a measure of learning, is in itself only vaguely related to the crucial question "Will the student make a good teacher?" Similarly, it is conceivable that a predictive equation used in medical-school admissions will select scholars, and not necessarily promising physicians.

Even when grades are a legitimate criterion of college success, a number of questions still need to be answered: "What grades are to be counted—grades for the first semester, the first year, or the four years? Should we include all subjects, including electives or only grades in courses in the immediate area of the student's academic goal, etc.? To the extent that a criterion is unclear, it is relatively difficult to devise an equation for its adequate prediction. For example, before grades can be used as a criterion, it is necessary for the teachers to synchronize their grading procedures from the standpoint of validity and reliability and—when a number of teachers are involved—from the standpoint of calibration to a common point of reference. Predicting freshman grades in college, for example, is complicated by the fact that the different schools within a university enroll students in different courses, each with its own emphasis and its own grading standards. For this reason, it is generally necessary to prepare separate equations for the different schools.

A special problem with respect to the use of grades as a criterion is generally encountered in the graduate school, where "everybody gets a B." Because of the restriction in the range over which graduate grades are assigned, the correlation of the various predictors with grades as criterion is automatically negligible. In addition, the predictors—undergraduate record, aptitude, *Graduate Record Examination* scores, etc.—are generally highly intercorrelated. Before adequate prediction can be obtained, therefore, it is necessary to increase the range over which graduate success is measured and to seek predictors of greater mutual independence.

3. Shrinkage   A phenomenon peculiar to regression equations derived for the purpose of predicting a given criterion is that, when the formula is applied to any group other than the one on which its Beta-weights were obtained, there is a shrinkage in its degree of accuracy. This might be anticipated from the premises on which the equation is derived. Since the Beta-weights are obtained to maximize the prediction of the dependent variable in the particular group under study, even to the point of capitalizing on chance factors, it follows that for any other group the predictors will not fit as well, and that the overall prediction will shrink somewhat from this ideal level.

It has been suggested that, in predicting a given criterion from certain independent variables, two equations be derived from different samples, and that the weights obtained in these samples be averaged as the best estimate of the prediction in the overall population, freed from the idiosyncrasies of either of the particular samples. This is probably sound, since such an averaging would stabilize the Beta-weights and would provide for a more adequate prediction in the general case. Two implications are involved here: 1. a slight change in the Beta-weights of the predictors does not affect the prediction appreciably and is not particularly objectionable from a theoretical point of view, and 2. any regression equation should always be cross-validated on a second sample. There is also the need for periodic revision of the equation.

Other Forms of Prediction

1.   Canonical Correlation   Sometimes, the task at hand is to predict from some combination of predictor variables, not a single criterion (e.g., GPA) but rather some combination of several criteria. Canonical correlation, devised for this purpose, generates two sets of weights, one for the predictors and one for the criteria, to produce an equation of the form:

$$\beta_1 X_1 + \beta_2 X_2 + \beta_3 X_3 = \alpha_1 Y_1 + \alpha_2 Y_2$$

that will maximize the correlation between these two sets of weighted measures. Devised by Hotelling (1935, 1936), canonical correlation up to now has been ignored, largely because of the excessive labor involved in its calculation. With the advent of the computer and an increased awareness of its advantages over multiple correlation in situations involving multiple criteria, canonical correlation is now receiving increased attention in educational and psychological research.

2.   Pattern Analysis   An even more advanced prediction technique is *pattern* analysis (or *profile* or *configurational* analysis), which is generally considered more accurate than the traditional multiple regression approach when dealing with certain kinds of variables. This technique is beyond the scope of the present text.

3. Discriminant Functions It frequently occurs that the phenomenon to be predicted is qualitative rather than quantitative. It may be desirable, for example, to allocate freshmen to advanced, average, and introductory classes on the basis of such independent variables as IQ, high-school rank, and previous background in the subject. The problem is to weight the predictor variables so that the distinction between the categories into which the subjects are to be assigned is maximized. This can be done through discriminant analysis, a technique devised by Fisher (1936), which attempts to set up the linear combination of weighted measurements that will maximize the discrimination between groups with a minimum of overlapping and false classification. More specifically, the technique attempts to derive a weighted linear function of a set of variables that will maximize both the in-group homogeneity and the between-group distinction.

Evaluation of Multiple Regression

Multiple regression equations are obviously practical. Despite the shrinkage that accompanies their application to a different group, the increase in correlation between predictors and criterion, which multiple regression provides, frequently results in a considerable increase in accuracy of prediction. On the other hand, predictive studies are essentially, if not entirely, empirical, and their contribution to the development of education as a science is relatively limited. Regression equations, no matter how weighted, add little to the development of science and, though hypotheses and theory may be involved in the selection of the variables to be included in the equation, thus far the procedure has made little attempt at the discovery of the fundamental relationships among phenomena. Thus, the review of over 1000 studies attempting to relate one or more tests to the prediction of some aspect of academic achievement led Travers (1949) to conclude that the actual contribution to knowledge made by these studies was relatively small.*

* Actually, correlation can play an important role in generating hypotheses to be subjected to experimental test. Although correlation does not necessarily imply "causation," a causal law capable of producing a mean difference also tends to produce a significant correlation. Correlation can lead to a strengthening or a weakening of a causal hypothesis: a correlation of zero would disconfirm the likelihood of a causal relationship; a high correlation, on the other hand, would increase its credibility (see Campbell and Stanley, 1963).

Frequently any number of variables are thrown together in the equation, and reliance is placed on the statistical procedure to eliminate variables which make only a minor contribution to the prediction of the criterion. With the increased availability of the computer, this trial-and-error process has become more prevalent. This may add to the accuracy of the prediction and, especially, to the inclusion of variables that would otherwise be overlooked, but it provides relatively little insight into the basic reasons underlying their contribution. Including a whole slough of variables that might conceivably be useful increases the work of deriving the equation and of using it after it has been derived. In the meantime, it obviates the need for theory to guide the investigation and makes the process clerical rather than scholarly.

An interesting phenomenon of prediction is its tendency to be either self-fulfilling or self-destructive in that it stimulates a reaction which interferes with its fulfillment. If an applicant for college admission is told that he is a borderline case, for example, he is likely to exert himself a little more than he would normally and thus invalidate the prediction. Or, if, because his chances for success are slim, he is advised to carry a light load, his grades may be considerably above the level predicted.

SPECIAL CASES

Individual Prediction

Probability as it underlies prediction is a group concept whose applicability to the individual needs to be considered. Prediction in the individual case can be based either directly on the individual's past performance or on the assumption that the probability which pertains to the group of which he is a member somehow has a bearing on him. If, for example, we can determine by extended observation that the individual plays golf a couple of times a month, we might establish the probability of his playing in any one week to be 0.50. Such a prediction would, of course, be subject to the usual risk of error.

Individual prediction based on group probability is somewhat more theoretically complex. To say that an entering freshman has one chance in four of passing a certain test is a group concept which technically does not apply to the individual. What is said is that some 25 percent of the group will succeed. As it applies to the individual, however, the probability statement is in the form of a dichotomy; he will not be 25 percent successful, but will either pass or fail. Both the gifted and the dull student will either succeed or fail on a given test, each with the identical probability level of one or zero; it still seems relevant, however, to note that the underlying group probabilities of success may be 0.98 and 0.03 respectively.

Clinical versus Actuarial Prediction

The discussion so far has emphasized predictions based on the formal weighting of the variables in some form of a predictive equation. Predictions can also be made on a judgmental or clinical basis.

A fundamental aspect of clinical prediction involves the categorizing of phenomena into homogeneous subclassifications, each with a definite probability expectancy with respect to a certain outcome. Clinical predictions of longevity, for instance, might involve categorizing people into increasingly narrow subclassifications—i.e., not human beings but Americans; not Americans, but American men. Further subclassifications can be made by age, marital status, occupational status, etc. To the extent that the individual is pigeonholed correctly into a highly homogeneous subclassification for which group probabilities relative to outcome have been determined, a relatively accurate prediction can be made.

In practice, it is impossible to devise such classification on the basis of all factors related to a given phenomenon. Furthermore, even if it were possible to devise the categories and to determine the probability to be attached to each, it would be impossible to assign the individual to the particular subcategory representing each of his particular traits with any degree of certainty. The categorizing of the individual must be made, therefore, on the major bases of classification only, and, for that reason, such predictions—like all predictions—are only probable.

The question of the relative effectiveness of actuarial (statistical) and clinical prediction has received considerable attention since Meehl's publication (1954) of a booklet on the subject. The evidence reviewed by Meehl and others points to a rather consistent superiority of the statistical method of combining data into a prediction: ". . . in all but one . . . the predictions made actuarially were either approximately equal or superior to those made by a clinician." This generalization was again confirmed by Sawyer (1966) in a re-analysis of the evidence to cover the *measurement* as well as the *synthesis* component of the controversy—both of which can be either "mechanical" or clinical. The mechanical mode of combining data was again found consistently superior to the clinical, regardless of whether the data were collected mechanically or clinically. Conversely, the clinical mode of collecting data was found inferior whether used in conjunction with mechanical or clinical methods of synthesis. As it relates to prediction as a research function, it would seem that the clinician can best contribute by providing for inclusion by statistical means data concerning characteristics that would otherwise be ignored, and further that his contribution is probably best increased through training in making his judgments more suitable for inclusion in the statistical formula. Whether the increase in accuracy of prediction obtained through the inclusion of clinical judgment warrants the extra cost might be an important consideration, of course.

Prediction of Rare Events

A unique aspect of prediction concerns the case in which the phenomenon to be predicted has a very low probability of occurrence—for example, death as a result of an abscessed tooth. Meehl and Rosen (1955) suggest that in such cases a greater overall accuracy of prediction would be obtained by predicting for each person that he will not meet death in this way than by attempting to predict which person will and which will not die from such infection.

Prediction and Determinism

Another interesting point concerning prediction is discussed by Feigl and Brodbeck (1953), who raise the question of whether our ability to predict delinquency would absolve the individual of any blame when he becomes a delinquent according to prediction; or rob him of any credit when he refrains from becoming delinquent after research has predicted that he will not. This issue borders on the concepts of fatalism and determinism and is an interesting point in the philosophy of science. The reader is referred to the original source for further discussion.

Highlights of the Chapter

1. Man is perpetually predicting the likely outcome of his efforts. Basic to all such predictions is the element of risk at various levels of probability.

2. Prediction can be based on trends derived from past performance. As long as the same forces continue to act on a given object or factor, it seems logical to expect that it will continue in the same general direction at the same rate of speed or acceleration.

3. Prediction can also be based on association between variables as represented by the concept of correlation. At its most elementary level, prediction can be a matter of general expectancy of superior, average, or inferior status on one factor by virtue of its status on a related variable. A more precise prediction can be obtained by converting the measure of association into a regression equation involving one or more independent variables. Such an approach also provides an estimate of the margin of error in the prediction.

4. The choice of the variables (both predictor and criterion) is of primary importance in the adequacy of the equation derived. In a multiple regression equation, for example, the predictor variables should be as highly correlated with the criterion and as independent of one another as possible. Generally, the choice of predictors should make logical and theoretical—rather than simply empirical —sense. It is sometimes possible to cluster variables in order to prevent undue unwieldiness in the equation.

5. While statistical prediction generally entails the prediction of a single criterion through the weighted linear combination of relevant predictor variables, prediction can also be oriented toward the prediction of a composite criterion or based on the analysis of the profile of the data. Discriminant analysis is designed to provide the optimal allocation of individuals to different criterion groups rather than the derivation of a predicted criterion score.

6. Statistical prediction, thus far, has been empirically—if not, clerically—oriented and has contributed little to the advancement of education as a science. Greater emphasis needs to be placed on the theoretical considerations underlying the relationships on which the prediction is based.

7.   Prediction is a group concept that has only indirect meaning and application to the individual.

8.   Of considerable current interest is the relative effectiveness of clinical and actuarial prediction. Clinical prediction is based on the concept of the classification of the individual into relatively homogeneous subclasses for which a relatively high level of group probability has already been established. While it is difficult to generalize, it is likely that each approach is the more valid in situations for which it seems most appropriate. However, the two approaches are complementary rather than antagonistic.

Questions and Projects

1.   What procedures are currently used in your college for the admission of students? How satisfactory have present screening procedures been? With the use of the computer, devise an equation to predict the relative achievement of applicants. Choose the variables to be incorporated into the equation carefully on the basis of both practical and theoretical considerations. Check on the validity of your equation by relating predicted scores to actual performance at the end of the semester or year.

2.   Make a brief survey of employee-selection procedures of local industrial firms. What evidence do they collect systematically of the effectiveness of their procedures?

Selected References

Anderson, Harry E. and Benjamin Fruchter. "Some multiple correlation and predictor selection methods," *Psychometrika*, 25: 59–76; 1960.

Bloom, Benjamin and Frank R. Peters. *The Use of Academic Prediction Scales for Counseling and Selecting College Entrants.* New York: Free Press, 1961.

Borg, Walter S. "GRE aptitude scores as predictors of GPA for graduate students in education," *Educ. psychol. Measmt.*, 23: 379–82; 1963.

Bryan, Joseph G. "The generalized discriminant function: Mathematical foundation and computational routine," *Harv. educ. Rev.*, 21: 90–95; 1951.

Capps, Marian P. and Frank A. DeCosta. "Contributions of the Graduate Record Examinations and the National Teachers Examinations to the prediction of graduate school success," *J. educ. Res.*, 50: 383–89; 1957.

Cardinet, Jean. "The use of profiles for differential classification," *Educ. psychol. Measmt.*, 19: 191–205; 1959.

Fattu, Nicholas A. "Prediction: From oracle to automation," *Phi Delta Kappan*, 39: 409–12; 1958.

Fishman, Joshua A. "Unsolved criterion problems in the selection of college students," *Harv. educ. Rev.*, 28: 340–49; 1958.

Holzberg, Jules D. "The clinical and scientific methods: Synthesis or antithesis?" *J. proj. Techn.*, 21: 227–42; 1957.

Horst, Paul and C. MacEwan. "Optimal test length for multiple prediction: The general case," *Psychometrika*, 22: 311–24; 1957.

Johnson, Palmer O. "The quantification of qualitative data in discriminant analysis," *J. Amer. stat. Assn.*, 45: 65–76; 1950.

McHugh, Richard B. and Peter C. Apostolakos. "Methodology for the comparison of clinical and actuarial predictions," *Psychol Bull.*, 56: 301–08; 1959.

Meehl, Paul E. *Clinical versus Statistical Prediction: A Theoretical Analysis and a Review of the Evidence.* Minneapolis: Univ. Minnesota Press, 1954.

—— et al. "Symposium on clinical and statistical prediction," *J. couns. Psychol.*, 3: 163–73; 1956.

Mosier, Charles I. et al. "Symposium: The need and means of cross-validation," *Educ. psychol. Measmt.*, 11: 5–28; 1951.

Owens, Thomas R. and Arliss L. Roaden. "Predicting academic success in masters' degree programs in education," *J. educ. Res.*, 60: 124–26; 1966.

Pickrel, Evan W. "Classification theory and techniques," *Educ. psychol. Measmt.*, 18: 37–46; 1958.

Rulon, Phillip J. "Distinctions between discriminant and regression analysis and a geometric interpretation of the discriminant function," *Harv. educ. Rev.*, 21: 80–90; 1951.

Schine, Lester D. "Relative efficiency of test selection methods in cross-validation on generated data," *Educ. psychol. Measmt.*, 26: 833–46; 1966.

Shea, Joseph A. *The Predictive Value of Various Combinations of Standardized Tests and Subtests for Prognosis of Teaching Efficiency.* Educ. Res. Monogr., 19, No. 5. Washington: Catholic Univ. Amer. Press, 1955.

Tiedeman, David V. et al. "The multiple discriminant function—A symposium," *Harv. educ. Rev.*, 21: 71–95; 1951.

U.S. Department of Commerce, Bureau of the Census. *Projections of School and College Enrollment in the United States to 1985.* Current Population Report, Series P-25, No. 338. Washington: The Bureau, 1966.

PART THREE

OVERVIEW AND APPRAISAL

Experience in the management of any enterprise has shown the need for periodic evaluation of its operation. Evaluation is particularly important in education, where a wide array of variables operate in complex interaction, so that the coordination of the various components is typically the primary determinant of success or failure. It is doubly important today as the school attempts to realign itself so as to meet more effectively the challenges of our rapidly changing social order. Professional responsibility dictates that we approach this period of transition with a clear understanding of our present status projected against a background of what is desirable and what is feasible.

We cannot expect to transform the educational process overnight. The very nature and function of education in our society makes the process of change slow and deliberate. Inertia centered in the teacher-education program at both the undergraduate and the graduate level, and in the profession at large precludes an immediate about-face in our operation. Furthermore, programs inaugurated today, no matter how exciting and effective, are not likely to result in dramatic improvement in pupil growth by tomorrow, or even within a semester or a year. Progress here calls for imaginative and convincing innovations within a framework of stability and continuity. This, in turn, calls for a clear understanding of both our assets and our liabilities in the light of our current objectives as background for the development of effective strategies in the deployment of our resources for achieving these goals. We need to understand both where we are and where we want to go so that we can chart our progress in this period of opportunity. The matter is not one of idle speculation: the insights, imagination, and effort we bring to the task today will, in no small measure, determine not only our success as a profession but also the kind of schools, the kind of society—perhaps the kind of world—that will be ours to enjoy in the years to come.

13

EDUCATIONAL RESEARCH: A REVIEW AND EVALUATION

The promise of excellence in education rests on the willingness of the nation to support a comprehensive program of educational research and development to improve schools.——Lindley J. Stiles (1962))

THE PRESENT STATUS OF EDUCATION

Keynote on Progress

The advances we are witnessing in the various fields of scientific endeavor arc truly spectacular. Not only have we been able to accomplish feats that only a few years ago belonged to the realm of science fiction, but our achievements are becoming progressively more impressive. Underlying this progress is the all-out commitment of modern industry to research as the foundation for growth and, indeed, for survival. Progress in education has been far less impressive and the question is whether we can equip the students we are now teaching to live in this rapidly moving world. We have made gains—in fact, very definite gains—often under relatively adverse circumstances. Over the last few decades, we have attained a much better understanding of the child as a developing organism, of the learning process, and of the role of education in promoting his maximum growth. In the area of child development, for example, we have shifted from the theoretical premise of the immutability of the maturational process to a new emphasis on the role of the environment in the development of the child. This has had a bearing not only on preschool education but on all aspects of the operation of the schools. We have made definite progress in viewing the curriculum from the standpoint of the pupil and in adapting classroom organization, teaching methods, and curricular content to capitalize on pupil needs, goals, and purposes as a means of ensuring his maximum self-realization.

We have made worthwhile advances in research methods. We have come a long way from the crude work of Binet in testing and of Rice in experimentation. We have made significant gains in certain areas—e.g., in reading where yearly reviews present an impressive list of accomplishments. We are no longer in a sea of ignorance; we can now locate areas of knowledge and we have a fair idea of those areas that still need exploration. Most important, we are more aware of the importance of research in educational progress and have gained some understanding of the type of research on which educational gains can be based.

Each year, hundreds of studies are added to the large number already reported in the professional literature. The *Encyclopedia of Educational Research* stands as an impressive monument to the research activities of the profession. Not all of these studies have been earthshaking; in many areas, the evidence is still meager and fragmentary; most areas are still relatively unexplored. But it must be remembered that education as a scientific undertaking dates back only to the early 1900's. We must remember that it took centuries to turn quackery into medicine, astrology into astronomy, and alchemy into chemistry.

Early progress was particularly delayed by a lack of statistical techniques, of instruments of testing, and of adequate research methodology. Still very much with us as a retarding influence on the progress of education as a science is the immense complexity of human nature, the nebulous and intangible nature of educational phenomena, and the time it takes for change in these phenomena to take place. Educational progress has been hampered by the highly decentralized nature of our educational system which has minimized the interstimulation of the members of the profession, and which has led to considerable duplication of research effort.

Not only have we had to start from scratch in a field that does not lend itself easily to certain types of research but we have had to counteract such conditions as overcrowded classrooms, overworked and undertrained teachers, public indifference toward research, and traditionalism on the part of the teaching profession itself. Yet, despite these limitations, we have forged ahead. Davis (1963), for example, refers to the rather significant, though beginning, effort to organize knowledge in relation to the curriculum. We can point to a reasonable list of principles of teaching and learning based on research and accepted theoretical premises (e.g., Burton, 1958; Hilgard, 1956). Bloom (1966) refers to a number of areas in which research has altered or is likely to alter our way of thinking about educational phenomena; he suggests that, of the 70,000 studies listed in the *Review of Educational Research* over the past 25 years, about 70 are crucial for all that follows. Our progress should be relatively easier and faster as some of our earlier problems are gradually resolved.

Lag in Education as a Science

While we owe no apologies for professional unproductivity, education is characterized more by gaps than by solutions. After fifty years of research, we still know very little about the nature of the learning process, the development of personality, the conditions of personal adjustment, etc. Despite the many gains we have made, we cannot ignore the concern expressed by Kandel (1950) who, on looking at the *Encyclopedia of Educational Research,* wondered to what extent the mountain of material reviewed there would lead to improvement in educational practice. More recently, Buswell (1963), reviewing the *Handbook of Research on Teaching,* was likewise disappointed to find how small is the body of positive knowledge a half-century of research on teaching had produced. In a similar vein, Monroe (1950) suggests that research has played a rather minor role in the development of teacher education—or, at least, its influence has not been commensurate with the volume of studies pertaining to the education function. Most of the studies have focussed on existing inadequacies and have, consequently, brought about little change in teaching. Research in teacher effectiveness has likewise been relatively unproductive; much of it is basically faulty, failing, for example, to control such obvious nonexperimental factors as the Hawthorne effect.* Much research is oriented toward inadequate criteria (e.g., standardized test performance). Many studies overlook the interaction among the variables; many fail to consider the

* See Chapter 14.

total picture: for example, the teacher-aide program may actually promote effective learning, but, then, the cost is higher.

A particularly pessimistic view is presented by Lamke, who, in 1955, expressed the opinion that, had the research of the previous three years in medicine, agriculture, physics, or chemistry been wiped out, our life would have been changed materially, but, if research in teacher personnel in the same three years were to have vanished, educators and education would have continued much as usual. Similarly, Tate (1950) feels that, outside of the narrow field of psychometrics, the contribution of educational research has been wholly disappointing, that little scientific value can be derived from the tons of research that have been conducted, and that the majority of the studies are unreliable, trivial, and unworthy of serious consideration or application. A similar view is expressed by Eurich (1962), who suggests that much educational research can be characterized as "the accumulation of irrelevant statistics in order to proceed from an unwarranted hypothesis to a foregone conclusion." Kerlinger (1960) likewise feels that educational research is frequently characterized by triviality, superficiality, and scientific naiveté. As Buswell (1963) puts it, there may be nothing wrong with having things turn out to be trivial, but it is disturbing to see how many times and for how long we looked before turning to more important problems and more promising methods. He laments studies of "worn-out problems made with outmoded techniques." Outside observers are equally critical: sociologists (Trow, 1963; Sieber, 1968), for example, are amazed at the incompetence of educational researchers in the use of modern survey methods. Nor is the situation any better in Canada where, in Robinson's opinion (1965), education suffers a lack of inventiveness, of efficiency, and of independence from American goals. Furthermore, according to Nash (1962), the situation is becoming steadily worse: he refers to the insipid banality and monumental triviality of the topics, which, he feels, are matched only by the timid uniformity of the methodology. He insists that, if research is ever to make a significant alteration in Canadian education, it will have to rise above the level of the current trivia. Fattu (1960) argues that there are too many inadequate studies whose only justification is that it was the best that could be done under the circumstances. Apparently, only a small number of educators, either in the field or on the campus, are competent in the statistical and research strategies which have been available for years. Undoubtedly, much of the cluttering of educational journals with trivia stems from the inability of the writers to conduct the more sophisticated research called for by a more significant problem.

While it is true that education as a science is relatively young and that educational research is often conducted under conditions short of ideal, it is equally true that educational progress to date has been impeded by a number of weaknesses that must be remedied if education is to forge ahead. Our failure to keep pace with the progress in other fields of scientific endeavor can be traced directly to our insufficient appreciation of the importance of research as the vehicle on which scientific progress must depend. While research is an integral part of business and industry, this relationship is still far from clear in education, where the emphasis is on teaching rather than on a balance between teaching and research into *what* and *how* one should teach. As Stanley (1961) observes, "No modern competitive business could survive long if it put as little money, time, and effort into careful research and development as our public schools."

Research in education to date has been haphazard and discontinuous; the results have been incomplete, if not erroneous, answers. In contrast to the physical sciences, where professional researchers devote their lives to the study of a given problem, education has allowed the amateur and the hobbyist to carry the ball. A study by Brownell (1951) of articles in professional journals revealed that 44 percent of research studies reported in the field of arithmetic were done by individuals who apparently terminated their research efforts with this single study. Of the 778 authors of arithmetic articles, only 10.5 percent had published three or more articles. Similar figures were obtained with regard to reading and English. In other words, three published papers qualified researchers for membership in the highest 10 percent from the standpoint of productivity. More recently, Buswell et al. (1966) report that only one in four of the 1129 graduates with a doctorate in education in 1954 had published in 10 years; half of these had published only one study.

If one of the major functions of the school is to provide social leadership, it must first accelerate its efforts toward solving its own problems. Most of the major disciplines, and especially the physical sciences, have placed a strong emphasis on research—with excellent results. There is no comparable tradition for research in education. As Henry (1960) points out, 97 percent of all research in terms of dollars done in colleges and universities is conducted at 173 of the larger universities. It is high time for educators to realize the need for keeping pace with the world their efforts have helped to produce. While it is obvious that there are significant aspects of education that do not lend themselves to easy scientific determination, there is nevertheless the need for a reappraisal and reorientation of our research efforts in the light of the modern advances that surround us.

Overemphasis on Empiricism

It has been the thesis of the present text that probably no obstacle stands so clearly in the path of the progress of the science of education at this stage of development as does our failure to integrate into meaningful structure the reams of empirical findings that research has produced. Much of our research efforts thus far has been oriented to what Buswell (1941) calls "tinkering"; though this may be better than empty theorizing, we need to develop both the empirical and theoretical aspects of research to the point where they give each other mutual support. Our lack of theoretical development has not only prevented us from gaining adequate perspective into various educational problems but it has also allowed our research efforts to be expended in diverse and confusing directions. As a result, our research has been isolated, repetitious, and haphazard rather than continuous and systematic.

In contrast to psychology, which has maintained a nice balance between theory and empiricism, education has been far too oriented toward practicality: "If it works, it works; why bother finding out why? Why seek other methods when, after a lot of work, we might find nothing better? Anyway, education is too complex; it is affected by too many factors to permit generalizations." We tend to glorify empiricism as synonymous with science. There is a tendency to consider facts as the ultimate form of knowledge—a fact is a fact! A theory, on the other hand, is considered impractical and equivalent to speculation and guesswork. School personnel frequently use the cliché, "This is all right in theory but it won't work in practice," forgetting that a good theory must work in practice or it isn't worthy of being called a theory. Yet, these same people operate on the basis of their own unproven theories, untested and untestable assumptions, dogmatic assertions and unwarranted generalizations based on subjective impressions. They are convinced that good teaching is an art derived from experience and requiring no scientific verification, that a scientific foundation is not necessary or even useful for effective teaching, and that educational problems can be resolved by proclamation.

Inadequate Research Methodology

Although a case has been presented for the need for theoretical development, it is equally true that a theory can be no better than the empirical findings on which it is based. Unfortunately, we are still using research methods that are inadequate for the solution of many of the problems we face. We frequently act as if we considered a survey of group opinion an adequate approach to educational truth; even when we experiment, we often subscribe to the monistic concept of science, though it is essentially inadequate for dealing with the complex variables with which education must cope. We are still hampered by our unfamiliarity with research and statistical methods of the complexity required for the adequate attack on the more significant problems of education.

Many studies contain flaws that automatically make them null and void from the standpoint of scientific truth and potentially dangerous from the standpoint of application. These errors cover all aspects of research: improper formulation of the problem, inadequacy of control, nonrepresentativeness of the sample, invalidity of the data, invalidity of the criterion, inadequacy of the analysis, errors in interpretation, and so on.* Scriven (1960), for example, points out that research continues to use criteria ". . . that would not survive five minutes of critical and explicit discussion." Many studies are inconclusive. Even more disappointing, as Buswell (1963) suggests, is the frequency of contradictory results. Some studies have been conducted loosely and, it seems, for the purpose of confirming the investigator's biases. Conger (1960), for instance, notes that, in the field of driver edu-

* During 1967, the *American Educational Research Journal* received 168 manuscripts for publication (Millman, 1968); of these, 111 were rejected (perhaps because of unsuitability from the standpoint of the purposes of the journal rather than necessarily from the standpoint of adequacy). Of the remainder, 23 were accepted, 12 were returned for revision, and 22 were still out for review (as of March 1968).

cation, poor research and worse reporting have combined to produce some strange results. As he sees it, perhaps the only valid conclusion that can be reached in driver-education research is that factors other than driver education itself are the significant contributors to the reported differences in accident and violation rates between driver-education and non-driver-education groups.*

What is particularly discouraging is that, even when methodologically correct, research in education is relatively prosaic, repetitive and lacking in impact. Marquis in 1948 listed six recurrent types of research that make relatively little contribution to the advancement of science: 1. *wisdom* research which makes a thorough review of the literature but does not get to the point of testing anything; 2. *unfocussed* research which goes in all directions at once with no problem to guide it; 3. *practical* research which solves problems at the local level but does not contribute anything to theory or the solution of further problems; 4. *descriptive* research which simply describes a certain phenomenon; 5. *theoretical* research which, though essential to the development of science, does not suggest ways in which a theory might be tested; and 6. *critical ratio* research in which statistical manipulations are made but which lack a theoretical framework. Stoddard, in 1952, was likewise arguing that much of the current research was fragmentary, discontinuous, that it avoided basic issues and, further, that it was frequently divorced from the superstructure of human values. More recently, Skinner (1960) bemoaned the fact that:

> Reacting against the excesses of psychological quackery, psychologists have developed an enormous concern for scientific respectability. They constantly warn their students against questionable facts and unsupported theories. As a result, the usual Ph.D. thesis is a model of compulsive cautiousness, advancing only the most timid conclusions thoroughly hedged about with qualifications.

A particularly significant reaction is setting in against the mechanistic orientation of current psychological research. Maslow (1966), for example, claims that psychologists have allowed research methodology to dictate the kind of research they undertake. Because the research techniques of the mechanistic

---

* Serious questions as to the effectiveness of the driver-education program are also raised in a recent (1968) HEW report on traffic safety.

tradition serve so well in the study of animal behavior or even some aspects of human behavior, its practitioners have come to argue that research be restricted to these methods. Unfortunately, as long as we define research in terms of the "scientific method" as the exclusive avenue to scientific knowledge, all problems that do not lend themselves to this type of investigation automatically become nonscience. As a consequence, psychologists have avoided the investigation of values and other personal attributes while they focussed on the more trivial aspects of human behavior that lend themselves to the traditional research methods. When the only tool you have in hand is a hammer, it is awfully tempting to treat everything as if it were a nail. This emphasis on a mechanistic model tends to sponsor "safe" investigations limited to inquiries that can be managed easily by existing methodologies. Unfortunately, according to Nash (1962): "The scientific method cannot be used to study any but the most trivial of educational problems. The reason for this is that the mechanistic presuppositions of science cannot be applied to those higher prefaces of human life wherein lie all significant issues in the field of education." Hyman (1964) and Robinson (1965) also lament the fact that educational research has developed a sort of ritual that tends to camouflage what our discipline is really about. Halpin (1963), in a similar vein, argues that scientists choose their research topics not because of their importance but rather because the techniques of measurement in that particular domain happen to be available. This is again the story of the drunk looking for his wallet under the street light— it was too dark to look for it "out there" where he had lost it! Halpin raises the question: "Does the investigator have the guts to study what is worth studying or does he prefer to play with his little toys in the safety of his playpen?"

THE LAG IN EDUCATIONAL PRACTICE

The story is told of the agricultural agent who, visiting a farmer in the hinterland and noticing the dilapidated conditions of the farm, told the farmer he would send him pamphlets suggesting improvement he might make. Returning some months later, the agent found the farm in the same state of disrepair and asked the farmer: "Didn't you get my pamphlets?" Whereupon the farmer replied: "Oh, yeah, I did; but I ain't read them. Why, shucks, I ain't farming half as good as I already know how!" Probably nowhere is the moral of this story more pertinent than in connection with the dual lag which exists between educational research as we know it should be conducted, as it is conducted, and as the results are applied in the classroom.

The limitations of current educational research have been noted. We know what constitutes adequate research, yet much of the current research into educational problems is based on inadequate procedures and, as a consequence, yields only partial and inconclusive answers. An even greater gap exists between research results and their application in the classroom. Despite the hundreds of studies conducted in education and related fields each year, educational practice is generally based as much on tradition, common sense, and consensus as it is on research. The reasons for this gap are obviously multiple rather than single, but certainly among the more fundamental is the lack of appreciation of the crucial role of research in the advancement of educational practice. The lack of orientation toward research which characterizes educators as a group is probably even more characteristic of the practitioner who, because of his limited training in research and statistics, is frequently cut off from research both as an ally in the solution of his problems and as the foundation of good teaching.

The difficulty stems in large measure from the lack of orientation toward research of the whole teacher-education program, a program in which answers—even at the graduate level—are more frequently given than found and in which the answers that are given have unwarranted finality and universality of application. As suggested at a recent symposium (Silberman et al., 1966), we are training teachers to accept prevailing educational practices rather than to experiment and evaluate. As Coombs (1960) points out, we do not change simply because we are not trained to change.

Undoubtedly, the lag in educational practice is also related to the inconclusiveness of current research findings. Not only are there many educational problems for which we do not have a solution, but even where solutions are available, they are frequently only partial answers whose validity in a given situation is open to question. According to Johnson (1959): "The major service rendered by educational researchers . . . seems to be to provide other research workers with resource references to use in writing further research reports." A common criticism (Silberman et al.) is that educational researchers are more interested in producing articles for journal publication than viable, well-engineered, instructional products. Much of our current educational knowledge is really a matter of propaganda parading as science; much of it neither provides answers nor raises significant problems and issues. No wonder that the educational researcher frequently encounters opposition from the practitioner.

It is understandable that the busy administrator cannot keep up with the research on all aspects of educational practice to the point where he can balance one study against another to gain perspective into the validity and applicability of the literature he reads. His attempts at consulting the research literature frequently result in error, frustration, or both. Pertinent sources are often difficult, if not impossible, to find. Yet, he cannot defer action forever while he waits for conclusive research to be conducted, nor can he chase from one journal to another to find the most adequate study. As a result, he frequently latches on to the first study he finds even though it may not be scientifically sound, typical of the research on the subject, or even applicable to his present situation.

When he goes beyond the first article, he is likely to find contradictions and equivocations. No one has bothered to synthesize the evidence so that it can be grasped by a person who is primarily an administrator, not a professional researcher. Not only are many of the studies in various degrees of inadequacy and/or error, but even when conducted under ideal conditions of control, the results still have to be adapted to the local situation. All of this demands a greater competence in the evaluation and interpretation of research than the average practitioner is likely to possess. When he attempts to conduct his own research, his efforts generally meet with less than complete success, as limitations in time, in facilities, and in research competence, both on his part and on that of participating teachers, frequently take their toll.

Whether as a consequence of such discouragement or as compensation for insecurity with respect to research, many teachers and administrators subscribe to "practicality." They cite community opposition to research and insist "I don't have to do research to know that" as they continue to use procedures which they have found "effective" in the past. It has also been suggested that educators do not have to meet competition the way industry does and that, as a result, they can afford to go on with "half-good" procedures. Removed one step further is the classroom teacher, who usually has had very little orientation to educational research in his undergraduate preparation and who loses contact with research in his everyday practice. As a result, he teaches in much the same way as he was taught, unable and unwilling to relate his procedures to newer advances or even to findings of long standing.

The obvious question here is: If educators are opposed to research, specifically how do they propose to solve their problems? The answer seems to be in their reliance on personal experience and, of course, on crude control-less research. This is then coupled with "expert" opinion and, as Ausubel (1953) points out, it is generally believed that anyone who has been in the profession for 25 years is entitled to some opinion; indeed, the right to make dogmatic pronouncements on pedagogical procedures which are valid by fiat alone follows directly, it seems, from the wisdom which extended experience or administrative status presumably confers. Many educational practices are simply duplicates of what some successful teacher has found effective in his particular case—which is then assumed to be universally applicable, even though the teacher has frequently only limited understanding of why his methods work.

Educators need to realize that personal experience is not a dependable foundation for educational practice. Nor, as Lundberg (1946) points out, are good intentions an adequate substitute for effective and scientifically sound techniques in achieving desirable goals. It is time for us to take our cue from industry where the cost of research is both large and unquestioned. Perhaps rather than asking, "What is the cost of research?", we should be asking, "What is the cost of *not* doing research?" This cost is too often measured in units of retardation, of ineffective education, of dropouts, and of juvenile delinquency. If we are to continue to invest in education as we have in the past, perhaps it would be wise to ensure the maximum effectiveness of the operation. There is undoubtedly merit in Anderson's suggestion (1961b) that merely urging teachers to put more effort into their teaching may not be the solution. Rather than beat dead horses, teachers might do better to reallocate some of their efforts toward the discovery of more adequate methods.

THE GRADUATE SCHOOL

The graduate school is undoubtedly the key to the future of education for it really determines the kind of leadership education will get at both the local and national levels. If it is to discharge its crucial function, the graduate school must define clearly its purposes and its mode of operation. First, although graduate training is superimposed on undergraduate training, it must not be simply a continuation of undergraduate work. Rather, it must involve a considerable departure both in the degree and the kind of training it emphasizes. To the extent that graduate work is designed to provide insight and practice in professional leadership, graduate studies must not be a matter of regimentation of students to a curriculum of standard courses tailored to undergraduate specifications. Rather than concentrate on courses geared to the absorption of knowledge, the graduate program must place its emphasis on the development of a person capable of discovering his own answers as the basis for making his own decisions.

Unfortunately, although it might be expected to provide leadership for the radical changes taking place all around it, the graduate school is not known for its flexibility and innovation. In fact, as suggested by Heiss (1968):

> A comprehensive review of the literature on graduate and professional education leads to the conclusion that there have been practically no new ideas in the basic format of graduate study during the past three of four decades.
>
> If the degree and direction of their change is a reliable measure of institutional vigor, many graduate institutions are in deep trouble as far as their vitality or intellectual health are concerned. In too many cases, the basic pattern for graduate study appears to have been set in concrete.

As Berelson (1960), for example, points out, too frequently well-motivated, bright candidates are discouraged by the red tape and the busy work, the inaccessibility of professors, the unavailability of necessary facilities, etc. There is a tendency to favor the plodder over the challenging nonconformist. Carmichael (1961) presents a particularly thorough critique of every aspect of graduate education and makes a number of suggestions for improvement.

Revolution in Education

Education is undergoing a major revolution. In the past decade, educators, as participants in the current socio-political revolution, have pressured for major improvement and innovation in educational practice. Unfortunately, research can take neither credit nor blame here, for these innovations were, by and large, effected without benefit of research evidence as to their worth. The new curricula in mathematics and the sciences, for example, are based largely on *a priori* premises. Team teaching, modular scheduling, and other innovations are largely the product of common sense and experience rather than scientific discovery. The Conference on Innovation (IDEA) held in Hawaii in the summer of 1967 was likewise more concerned with the dissemination and implementation of imaginative educational procedures than with the testing of their effectiveness. It would seem clear that educational research will have to feature more prominently in the educational enterprise of the future if the latter is to achieve its true status as a science.

A number of substantial reports (Buswell et al., 1966; Clark and Worthen, 1967; Halpin, 1966; Jensen, 1962; Kerlinger, 1965; Lazarsfeld and Sieber, 1964) have focussed with alarm on a number of serious obstacles to be removed if this educational revolution is to move in fruitful and significant directions rather than expend itself in commotion. The underlying theme of a large number of the writings in the field is the deplorable lack of scholarship that characterizes the school of education on the average campus—and, thence, presumably, its graduates out in the field. Indeed, permeating the school of education is an anti-intellectualism, reflected in a strong tendency to substitute opinion, personal feeling, and experience for more substantial and convincing evidence. According to Kerlinger, there is a tendency to shy away from theory, away from the abstract and the intellectual, even though as Fattu (1961) points out, technical schools have discarded their "trade school" orientation in favor of an abstract and theoretical emphasis in the training of engineers on the premise that technology has to become abstract and theoretical if it is to cope with the problems of this extremely complex postwar world. According to Kerlinger:

> The basic purpose of any doctoral program is to train intellectual leaders who are highly skilled in objective, critical inquiry and dedicated to its importance. Without this dedication to critical inquiry as a way of life, the doctorate means nothing.

The basic problem—and in part, both the cause and the result of this anti-intellectualism—is the low standards of scholarship that too frequently prevail in educational classes, in both the caliber of the student body and the academic requirements of the content. *Graduate Record Examination* evidence, for example, shows education students below the standards of other graduate students; according to Jensen (1962) the best education students are equal to any, but there is a great proportion of lower ability students. The same pattern apparently prevails at the undergraduate level (Kidd, 1959). To the extent that no amount of course work, teaching experience, or even good intentions can compensate for lack of aptitude, the problem becomes self-contaminating: inadequacies in the caliber of the students automatically force inadequacies in the level of instruction and the standards that can be enforced. The result is too frequently inadequate undergraduate training as the basis for further inadequacies in graduate training.

Emerging as one of the major criticisms of education is a dreary picture of scholastic inadequacy deeply engrained in the fabric of every aspect of the operation of the school of education, centering around a mediocre faculty attracting mediocre students to whom it teaches inadequate courses, thus producing another generation of poorly trained educational "leaders." Whereas the criticism can undoubtedly be overdone, Halpin (1966) refers to education courses as "Mickey Mouse" courses which discourage high caliber students, who find a greater challenge in other academic areas. He suggests that the main problem is the kind of people who enter teaching in the first place: these are people who are dominated by the need for affiliation rather than the need for achievement which generally characterizes the scientist. More fundamentally, Halpin suggests that we have here a conflict between two cultural systems: 1. the culture of science, and 2. the culture of education, each operating by its own set of rules. Education operates on the idea that what the customer needs or wants is what we should provide. According to Halpin, we have, therefore, watered down education to the level of the comic strip. Furthermore, this has become contagious: administrators themselves, for example, do not want to read research in the original; they want it digested and simplified. They don't want to know too many details; they want simple prescriptions.

Actually, graduate training in education faces a number of unique problems. Because of the pressure placed on them to improve their qualifications, many teachers apply for graduate work despite limited suitability and, in many cases, with greater commitment to the degree for what it implies and what it pays than to the knowledge it is supposed to represent. The result is that graduate faculties in education are placed in a predicament: since these teachers are going to continue to teach anyway, why deprive them of the opportunity to improve their competence through further schooling, even if a graduate degree has to be thrown in to provide the necessary inducement? As a consequence, graduate education operates as a service function, and, as Berelson (1960) points out, master's work today is not graduate in character; it is simply on the order of a fifth year of undergraduate training. Under these circumstances, standards are often hard to maintain; any professor or any school attempting to emphasize scholarship is likely to be bypassed in favor of someone more "understanding."

Particularly lamentable from the standpoint of scholarship in graduate education is the part-time on-the-job approach to the master's—if not the doctor's—degree. What this means in effect is that frequently marginal students undertake graduate work on a sideline nothing-to-lose basis, while carrying the burden of a full-time teaching assignment. Since teachers are generally dedicated to their job, they tend to place their primary allegiance to their children rather than to the graduate program for which they may have only monetary and promotional interest and, consequently, find it difficult to disengage themselves from the demands of the classroom. The result is often poor scholarship which leaves the faculty with the embarrassing alternatives of: 1. denying them admission or failing them and thus denying them the opportunity of improving their teaching, or 2. awarding them a degree, sometimes in considerable violation of standards.

The Research Requirement

The graduate school's responsibility for providing graduate students with the research skills necessary for the advancement of education as a science is of particular interest from the standpoint of the present text. Almost invariably, graduate programs in education require an introductory course in educational research at the master's level and frequently an advanced course at the doctoral level. Such courses generally enroll students who range from those with a good mathematical and scientific background, interested in becoming professional researchers, to those of less adequate background, who simply want to continue classroom work with increased insight and efficiency. In organizing such courses a distinction is generally made between the *consumer* and the *producer* points of view, with an emphasis generally on the former. Among the topics usually included in such courses are the nature and the role of science and research; the different research methods and research designs; library usage; the collection, analysis, and interpretation of data; sampling; statistical inference; the preparation of the research report and an orientation toward the professional literature.

Obviously, a research course at the introductory level cannot provide an adequate coverage of the total field. All it can do is to provide an orientation to research methodology and an appreciation of its importance. It then becomes the responsibility of the courses in the student's specialization to pursue the topic further from the standpoint of the applications of research to his special field and to education in general. In other words, it is not the function of the introductory course in educational research to turn out qualified researchers, but simply to provide a basis on which graduate students can deal with educational problems with a greater degree of professional insight.

The relative lack of research competence on the part of educators, despite the almost universal requirement of a course in educational research at the graduate level, suggests a need for a reconsideration of the purpose, orientation, and content of such a course. It is important to realize, for example, that if education is to prosper, training in research must go beyond the development of technicians whose knowledge is restricted to the application of formal techniques and procedures. Statistical competence and research methodology are simply tools—means to an end—contributing to knowledge, but not ends in themselves. On the contrary, research training must place its emphasis on the conceptualization of science as the framework within which educational research must operate.

The trend toward abandoning the thesis as a requirement for the master's degree in education and a number of the social sciences is lamented by many who look on the thesis as the crowning glory of graduate studies. The reasons for dropping the thesis requirement are, of course, many and varied. It is argued, for example, that the large number of master's students in education make it relatively impossible to provide adequate supervision. It is also claimed that students at the master's level are not sufficiently advanced for them to select a suitable topic within the narrow range of their research and statistical competence and that, consequently, insisting on a thesis produces nothing more than a second-rate term paper or a simple clerical report of frequencies relative to a trivial problem. To the extent that these allegations are true, additional course work and a comprehensive examination might be a better alternative.

Considered from a logical point of view, however, abandoning the thesis requirement—and accepting a project for the Ed.D. as a substitute for the Ph.D. dissertation—implies that research experience is not important in the training of a graduate student in education, that education should be oriented toward the practical rather than toward the scientific, and that even the leaders of the teaching profession are practitioners who need less emphasis on the development of research skills than is required for the traditional research degrees. In practice, it frequently means that the distinction between the undergraduate and the graduate degree is simply one of the number of courses and examinations that the student has completed satisfactorily.

Another of the traditional requirements for an advanced degree which is getting progressively less emphasis is proficiency in a foreign language. Although there are differences of opinion, the trend toward minimizing the need for a foreign language is probably more defensible than that concerning the thesis. Inasmuch as nearly all of the worthwhile material concerning education and related fields published in a foreign language is readily available in translated form (in fact, in many libraries, it is available only in translated form), it would seem wise to allow the student to substitute other research tools, e.g. advanced experimental designs, computer programming, etc. This argument does not apply to certain other disciplines, nor does it apply to the education student working for a degree in comparative education, for example, where a foreign language would be an indispensible tool.

ACTION RESEARCH

Teachers are constantly faced with problems which may be best attacked through fundamental research designed to develop the general principles from which the solution to the specific problems can be deduced. Although the derivation of the required principles may call for extended and complicated research, once the basic principles are derived, they are applicable to a wide range of subproblems which no longer need to be investigated individually. However, many specific problems facing the educator require attention here and now, and it is frequently more expeditious to attack these problems directly. Such on-the-spot research aimed at the solution of an immediate problem is known in education as *action research*.* It represents the implementation of Dewey's suggestion of harnessing classroom teachers in the solution of their classroom problems.

In contrast to pure research which is concerned with the derivation of generalizations and only secondarily with any practical value they might have, action research is undertaken as a guide to action in relation to specific problems. The action researcher is a practical man who is willing to forego scientific rigor in order to obtain a usable answer to a problem existing at the local level; he is concerned with the situation as it is today on the assumption that this is the kind of situation he will continue to face and that his answers will be useful to the extent that he bases them on actual cases.

Advantages of Action Research

The person most responsible for the development of action research is Stephen M. Corey, whose *Action Research to Improve School Practice,* published in 1953, hit a responsive chord among teachers plagued with problems and unfamiliar with the means for their solution. It presents a number of significant benefits:

1.   The appeal of action research is based, in part, on the relative inadequacy of pure research in relation to the needs of the practitioner. The fundamental researcher, it would seem, cannot be bothered with the mundane problems of the man in the field; he is a scientist, a student of educational phenomena rather than a participant in education. He is concerned with the development of

* The term *quasi-experimental designs* is now being used with a somewhat similar connotation (Stanley, 1965).

educational science rather than with its use for the improvement of educational practice. He accepts the proposition that his studies will eventually lead to an improvement of school practice—but this is the work of someone else. As Corey suggests, he tends to pride himself on being a scientist and considers not having to deal with the practical situation a matter of virtue.

Unfortunately, applications are not implicit in the statement of a scientific principle; rather applications call for the extension of the principle to be worked out in the individual case. This is particularly troublesome in education where a multiplicity of relatively complex variables are forever interacting. This then leaves the practitioner, with his limited research background, with the difficult task of translating into an actual classroom program the outcomes of pure research derived under conditions of strict control. Action research, in contrast, provides him with solutions he can more readily understand and adopt. It is predicated on the conviction that teachers are more apt to learn from their own research and evaluation.

> I have lost much of the faith I once had in the consequences of asking only the professional educational investigator to study the schools and to recommend what they should do. Incorporating these recommendations into the patterns of practitioners involves some problems that so far have been insoluble . . . (Corey, 1953).

2.   The most obvious advantage of action research stems from the fact that any change in teacher behavior and teaching practice must be preceded by a corresponding change in the thinking and attitudes of the teacher. Such a change is more likely to take place as a result of research which the teacher has helped plan, conduct, and evaluate than as a result of research reported in some journal. Besides, it is often easier to inaugurate innovations on a school-wide basis than it is to convert each teacher individually.

> I have a strong personal conviction that improvement in educational practice and curriculum will continue to be exceedingly slow and involve discouraging regression until the time comes when a large number of individuals and groups are engaged in numerous action research of the type discussed above. This seems to be the alternative to improv-

ing the curriculum by telling people what to do. (Corey, 1949).

Under proper leadership, cooperative research of this kind utilizes all the advantages of group dynamics in drawing out the best participation of teachers involved, in overcoming inertia and resistance, and in making teachers feel secure while investigating sources of difficulty. The feeling of accomplishment at having tackled their problems constructively—at their own level—is often a morale booster and a revitalizer of teachers frustrated at having to face problems and not being able to do anything about them. Teachers benefit from seeing that others have problems too and that this is not a sign of incompetence. Combining their talents for the solution of mutual problems frequently results in a feeling of partnership in scholarship, an improved group feeling and enthusiasm, and a higher level of research consciousness.

3.   The planning of action research generally provides teachers with insight into the nature of educational problems and stimulates them to read the related literature. The general familiarity with their immediate problem which they gain is likely to promote a greater understanding of the many other problems of the classroom and a greater competence in deriving solutions, both from the published literature and from more adequate investigations of their own.

Limitations of Action Research

However, action research is subject to a number of pitfalls which must be clearly recognized. Since it is almost completely empirical and local in nature, its contributions to the development of education as a science are likely to be secondary. Under optimum conditions, it can contribute facts to be integrated into theory and can provide for the testing of hypotheses. Unfortunately, the maximum benefits from action research are seldom realized because of failure to generalize the results and to integrate them into the existing theoretical structure. A number of other limitations are more directly connected with the method itself.

1.   A major limitation of action research is its relatively poor quality. Teachers are not researchers, and are likely to experience

a number of difficulties in obtaining meaningful results, especially since action research involves maximum flexibility in the interaction of the multiplicity of variables operating in the situation. These difficulties may arise from failure to define the problem clearly, resulting in the gathering of tons of data without the guidance of a hypothesis, inability to develop effective research strategies, inability to control extraneous factors, inadequacies in the treatment of the data, misinterpretation of the results, etc. It is sometimes difficult to achieve academic usefulness while maintaining scientific adequacy. Teachers frequently undertake overambitious projects and expect results too soon; as a consequence, they become disappointed and discouraged. Because of the failure to maintain adequate control, it is often difficult to identify "causes," even when "results" are obtained.

Action research can become a case of the blind leading the blind: it must be recognized, for example, that the typical teacher-education program is not designed to provide teachers with research sophistication, nor is it particularly conducive to the development of respect for research as the basis for the solution of educational problems (Shumsky, 1958). According to Barnes (1960), the highly routine nature of some of the work they do tends to dull the intellectual edge of many of the teachers who man the nation's classrooms. They tend to be practical-minded and not too interested in the abstract thinking that characterizes the scientist. They are far too accustomed to *telling* and not sufficiently accustomed to *asking*. They tend to look for a gimmick, a prescription, a rule of thumb. They are likely to tackle big problems and look for big answers, e.g., how to teach reading. As a consequence, they often gather data in all directions only to find that they answer nothing. On the other hand, it is difficult to identify problems narrow enough and yet satisfying to all teachers.

These many sources of difficulty point to the need for a consultant working closely with the teachers, both directly and through a steering committee, in order to promote greater compliance with recognized principles of scientific inquiry. This consultant needs to be highly trained in public relations and group dynamics, as well as research methods; he must provide close supervision if he is to keep untrained and ego-involved teachers on the track.

On the other hand, it must be remembered that never before have teachers been as qualified and as professionally oriented as they are today. It does not make sense to think that teachers are incapable of doing research and yet allow them to make crucial decisions affecting children while, at the same time, denying them the training in research that might improve the quality of these decisions. Teacher participation in the solution of the problems of the school is crucial to effective education. In a sense, we have here a parallel between educational research and medicine: certainly, the layman cannot be expected to discover a cure for the health problems facing mankind; yet, his active and intelligent participation in maintaining his own health is essential to effective medicine.

2.   A major consideration in action research concerns the generalizability of its results. Fundamental research starts by defining a population from which it takes a representative sample to serve as the basis for inferences concerning this population. In contrast, action research starts with a sample, the exact nature of which is often unknown; it is simply taken as is. It is not clear, therefore, to what population the conclusions and insights reached in the study are to apply. There is an apparent assumption that the teacher's present class is sufficiently "representative" that the results can be legitimately applied to the groups he is likely to have in the future. As pointed out in Chapter 7, this sort of *populationing* is always risky, especially since, in action research, the problem is often ill defined, the procedures unclear, and the subjects inadequately identified. In fact, action research frequently violates the basic rules of scientific inquiry: not only is it generally conducted in an atmosphere of common sense rather than of scientific control, but it is frequently seriously lacking in the extent to which the various criteria of rigorous research are met.

Despite its limitations, action research is certainly to be encouraged; any movement which promotes problem-solving in educational practice is a step in the right direction. Unquestionably, action research serves a purpose when it adds to the teacher's functional knowledge of the phenomena with which he must cope. Action research has led to the solution of many classroom problems; it has also contributed to the advancement of education as a science by providing hypotheses and tentative generalizations of immediate practicality. Action research also raises the professional caliber of the participants. It enables teachers to see education as a science as well as an art. It enables them to see research as an integral part of teaching and a prerequisite to the solution of the problems they face in the classroom. As Barnes (1960) suggests, it would seem logical to postulate that good teaching is predicated on active teacher-involvement in the study of classroom problems. It seems that it is difficult to be an intelligent *consumer* of research without having been, at least in a small measure, a *producer* of research. On the other hand, this dictates that teacher-education reorient itself toward research. Until we make education a joint enterprise in which teachers participate in educational research just as researchers participate in educational practice, teaching will remain a matter of dogmatism or a series of fads. As Glaser (1962) points out:

> One should not expect the conclusions and principles derived from basic research to find their way into educational and training practice unless researchers make the translation themselves or develop a systematic technology through which such translation may be effected.

Education, to date, has not demonstrated the true partnership that must exist between teaching and research. This is unfortunate, for, as Corey (1953) points out, our schools cannot keep up with the life they are supposed to sustain and improve unless teachers, pupils, supervisors, administrators, and school patrons continue to examine what they are doing. Singly and in groups they must use their imagination creatively and constructively to identify the practices that give promise and methodologically and systematically gather evidence to test their worth.

Even though action research at times is not research at all but rather simply an activity in which professional people normally engage in as part of their regular responsibilities, yet one must be careful not to make a dichotomy of action and fundamental research. The distinction—whether considered from the standpoint of the method or the quality of the research or the breadth and immediacy of applicability of the results—simply has reference to the two ends of a continuum. There should be no conflict between the two; the difference is essentially one of emphasis. On the other hand, even when conducted under the close supervision of a competent consultant, the contribution of action research to the promotion of education as a science is likely to be relatively incidental. There is need, therefore, while encouraging action research, to recognize the importance of parallel fundamental research. It also behooves the scientist to broaden his thinking outside the laboratory to examine conditions in the actual framework of the school.

RESEARCH BUREAUS

It is generally recognized that the majority of the so-called research bureaus operating in public school systems and even in universities are not doing *research* in any meaningful sense of the word. School systems with financial disbursements in the millions—apparently unaware or unconvinced of the contribution of research to educational practice—are often content with staffing their "research departments" with one or two clerks whose major responsibilities are tabulating attendance or preparing charts of the sources and outlays of school funds. When they exist at all, the majority of research bureaus operated at the local school level fail to meet minimal standards as to the research competencies of the director and his staff, the financial support necessary for adequate staffing and facilities, and, consequently, the adequacy of the research services they provide.*

Many research and development centers are more appropriately labeled "curriculum development centers," with a major focus on curricular innovations. Even the formal validation of these innovations is often a matter of very secondary interest. These bureaus perform a useful service; the misfortune, according to Glaser (1962), is that they give the illusion that they are conducting scientific research. State departments of education and state educational associations from which real leadership might legitimately be expected—and again let us not minimize the usefulness of the data which they collect—likewise are not doing the type of solid research that needs to be done if the schools are to fulfill their obligation to society.

Role of the Research Bureau

It is obvious that, if educators do not do research, no one is going to do it for them. It is also obvious that teachers do not

---

* The situation is improving, largely as a result of the current emphasis on research and of the requirement for evaluation tied to government grants. Unfortunately, many school systems are finding it difficult to hire personnel with the necessary training.

have the time and the know-how to conduct the type of high-powered research that needs to be done if educational practice is to be placed on a truly scientific basis. A major solution, it would seem, lies in establishing within each school unit a research bureau capable of providing aggressive leadership in the solution of educational problems. Since many of the problems faced by any one teacher are also faced by other teachers in the system, only a system-wide attack on such problems will lead to their adequate solution. It seems reasonable, therefore, to expect the central office to initiate and coordinate such research and to become the logical center of operations. The integration of bilingual children, for example, or the dropout problem in relation to the suitability of the curriculum, are best handled on a total system basis.

A central research bureau can assume leadership for research projects of varying nature and scope to be conducted in any number of schools, or it might coordinate a system-wide attack on the various facets of a problem of common interest. It might be expected to discourage the choice of overambitious projects, to help in the formulation of the research design, to facilitate the selection of experimental and control groups, to enlist the cooperation of the necessary personnel—including outside consultants—and to assign specific responsibilities, to provide moral support and leadership, and finally to arrange for the dissemination of the results. This would enable the university faculty of education to keep in contact with the public schools; it would also provide graduate students with field experiences. Such a team—research bureau personnel, classroom teachers, university consultants, and graduate assistants—should be an adequate combination for a successful attack on the school's immediate as well as long-range problems.

Research Bureaus at the University, State and National Level

So far our setting has been the public schools; the need for research bureaus applies equally to the college situation and, even more specifically, to the school of education where problems are too frequently met at the discussion level, where what little research is conducted is done in a piecemeal fashion, where trivial problems are tackled with inadequate techniques by faculty members—on stolen time and minus facilities—as they run between classes and committee meetings. Although the situation is improving, educational research currently conducted on the average campus is of the same haphazard nature as that done in the public schools (Clarke, 1957; McArthur, 1958). Here, too, there is need for an agency with specifically delegated research responsibilities. Unfortunately, however, even when they exist, such research bureaus typically do little more than collect student data—e.g., enrollment, teaching loads, etc.—for institutional and administrative purposes.

Another common arrangement is the bureau of field services, generally associated with the Department of School Administration and primarily interested in surveys of a consultative nature. Sometimes field services are part of the Bureau of Educational Research, an arrangement which rarely works out for, as Lazarsfeld and Sieber (1964) point out, when both the service and the more basic research functions are combined in a single bureau, the former tends to crowd the latter into insignificance. This can be expected, inasmuch as most practitioners are eager to utilize the *services* provided by the school of education in solving their day-to-day problems, but they are far less interested in research designed simply to give them a better understanding of the overall educational process. A partial solution is to isolate the two functions into separate units, each with its own budget and its own staff, although perhaps coordinated through a steering committee and utilizing somewhat the same facilities. It would seem logical, for example, that, to the extent that fundamental research is a contribution to the profession and to the nation rather than specifically to the institution, it should probably be financed through outside funding agencies, wherever possible.

When staffed by adequate personnel, such a bureau can provide true leadership in the advancement of education. It can draw on university personnel and can make its facilities available to the community's schools and other agencies. It can serve as a training ground for graduate students and thus develop future educators capable of assuming their place among fellow-scientists. Probably no finer tool for upgrading the profession can exist than such a bureau dedicated to the solution of educational problems and the development of the future leaders of the profession. It can also provide consulting services to the various departments of the university, act in a liaison capacity with the computer center, facilitate communication among research workers, and generally help coordinate the research activities of the educational community.

A similar need for research leadership exists at the state and national levels. Administering education is big business, involving an annual expenditure of millions of dollars. Industry spending that kind of money would want to make sure it is spent in the most efficient way possible and would allocate a considerable percentage of this outlay to research. At the state level, there is need for a bureau of educational research to provide leadership for the research activities of the state department of education and the school systems under its jurisdiction, to coordinate research efforts within the state and from one state department of education to another, and to promote general improvement in educational practice through the dissemination and implementation of research findings—a function which has been taken over to some degree by the federally sponsored regional educational laboratories. To the extent that educational problems are often nationwide in nature, they are sometimes best approached through a nationwide attack. In a sense, the U.S. Office of Education has acted in the capacity of a superbureau of educational research, leading and coordinating the research efforts of the nation, and it might be expected to continue and to accelerate its efforts in these directions. Professional organizations operating at the national level—e.g., the American Educational Research Association and Phi Delta Kappa—might also be expected to assume continued leadership at all levels of the research enterprise.

REORGANIZATION OF OUR RESEARCH EFFORTS

Need for Reorganization

Education has made only limited progress in the resolution of its numerous and complicated problems—or, at least, its accomplishments have not kept pace with social demands. This is precisely what might have been expected for, as Sieber (1967) points out, the educational system is constantly under pressure to alleviate the maladjustments that social changes create. However, since social changes are bound to be more rapid in an industrial society than the modifications that can be wrought in a formal organizational structure as vast and complex as our educational system, education is inevitably and constantly "falling behind the times." Consequently, it tends to operate under conditions of per-

sistent crisis—a situation which may well prevent educational research from making its maximum contribution to the improvement
of education by continuously diverting its efforts and energies
away from a systematic and orderly attack on significant problems.

The general consensus among authorities (e.g., Kerlinger, 1968) is that, before any significant improvement can occur
as a consequence of the new emphasis on educational innovation
and research, a major and drastic change in the whole structure of
education will have to be effected. Analysis of the current status of
education, and of research as the means by which it is to be fur-
thered as a science, suggests a definite need for reorganization of
our efforts. The profession needs to devote itself more energetically
to a systematic attack on its problems, for, as Fattu (1961) has
emphasized, "only through inspired, sustained, and systematic
research in education similar to that which has graced the other
sciences can education become truly effective." More specifically,
if education is to participate in the scientific advances that characterize the world in which we live, we can no longer continue to
place major reliance for educational research on the haphazard
and incidental efforts of the amateur, the hobbyist, and the graduate student. Such an approach is not—and cannot be—adequate
for the demanding task of ensuring our scientific growth.

In contrast to other disciplines which have placed
their destiny in the hands of the professional researcher, we are
sporting our freshman team in a field so vital to our progress.
Furthermore, we are providing graduate students—on whom we
still depend for a large portion of the research done in education—
with only limited direction from relatively inexperienced coaches
who divide their time between teaching, advising students, writing
books and articles, and attending meetings and conventions. To
make matters worse, we systematically promote the coaches to
administrative positions so that, as soon as they develop proficiency
in research, their research activities are curtailed. Consequently,
as Fattu (1961) reports, agencies outside of education account for
two-thirds of the research conducted in education. Jensen (1962)
likewise points out that the bulk of the substance of educational
psychology has come from psychology, sociology, anthropology,
and other noneducation disciplines.

There is need for us to reconsider our overreliance on
the doctoral student and the amateur as the standard bearer of
education in its attempt at scientific growth. More specifically,

there is need to encourage the faculty of the school of education to become involved in worthwhile research projects as part of their regular professorial responsibilities. While the faculties of the physical sciences and other departments on campus engage in research as an integral component of their regular duties, the faculties of the schools of education still give inadequate recognition to the need for educational research and lack appreciation of its relevance to the improvement of education (Ausubel, 1953). There is no tradition for research in education as there is in other fields. As Keppel (1964a) points out, educational research is undervalued, underfinanced, and under a cloud. In a study by Fattu (1960) only 10 of the 94 colleges and universities granting the doctorate in education could be said to be making a serious effort to encourage educational research by maintaining a favorable intellectual climate, by giving adequate support, by making time and facilities available for research, and by giving significant consideration to research competence and orientation when appointing new members. Furthermore, as Clark (1963) and Herrick (1967) point out, education frequently loses the most productive research years of its faculty by requiring that the young professor attain a certain status before he is given the opportunity to do research through partial release from his regular teaching and service assignments.

Attempting to inculcate students with a strong understanding of and dedication to the cause of research in an atmosphere where the faculty itself is completely lacking in such orientation is as obviously futile as it is false. As Williams (1959) suggests, no professor can stimulate his students if he himself does not engage vigorously, seriously, and enthusiastically in the process of learning. To be an effective leader of graduate students, he must be an eager researcher whom students can respect for his scholarly achievements. Fattu (1961), Marsak (1966), and Lazarsfeld and Sieber (1964) likewise point to the importance of a favorable climate for research for the development of research interest and competence on the part of students; as Lazarsfeld and Sieber put it:

> In the absence of faculty members who are doing extensive research and, hence, in the absence of student apprenticeships, the only alternative is training in research through *formal courses*. It is difficult, however, to develop research orientation among graduate students through course work

only; for this leads to the use of "secondary" rather than "primary" research sources, and reviews of research rather than original reports.

Unfortunately, the bulk of the current educational leadership, both on the campus and in the field, is a product of the nonresearch orientation of the past two or three decades.

Actually, improvement is in the offing; education is emerging as a social process of broad sociological and scientific concern. We are caught in a major social upheaval in which education, along with the other behavioral sciences, will play a leading role. This is highlighted, for example, by the sudden surge in concern for the educational enterprise on the part of every segment of the educational community, the lay public, and perhaps even more dramatically, the various governmental agencies.*

This trend is being facilitated by the fortuitous advent of the computer and other technological advances, e.g., data-retrieval. We have achieved a more sophisticated level of statistical and research competence. Stanley (1966), for example, notes that educational research seems to be improving in its use of more appropriate techniques in the solution of important problems. We have yet to accumulate answers and solutions to our many problems but we have at least attained a certain degree of clarity as to the nature of the questions. Our progress will be especially facilitated by the current climate of urgency concerning the need for the improvement of education; former Commissioner Keppel (1964a, (1964b), for example, points to the general recognition of education as a matter of national necessity requiring the best effort of all and argues that

> the time for effective action is desperately short. We are caught in a revolution of change which demands an educational technology which is adequate to the role which only education can serve. Our opportunity to meet this demand will never be better than it is today.

Federal Participation in Education

The most significant single event underlying this new focus on educational research was the massive entry of the federal

* See the special issue of the *American Psychologist* (Vol. 22, Nov. 1967).

government into the field, beginning with the enactment of Public Law 531 (Cooperative Research Program) of 1954, authorizing the Commissioner of Education to enter into contract with universities, colleges, and state educational agencies, and jointly finance cooperative research into the field of education. The first appropriation of one million dollars in 1956 grew to twenty-five million before the program was absorbed in the reorganization of the Office of Education (Clark and Carriker, 1961; Stiles, 1962; Smith, 1964).

On the other hand, federal participation in educational research is probably better seen as part of a broad orientation of American society toward social progress as a parallel movement to advances in the physical realm. Federal support of education is, in a sense, an outgrowth of similiar support of research in the physical sciences by the Department of Defense, the Atomic Energy Commission, the National Aeronautic and Space Agency, the National Science Foundation, the National Institute of Mental Health, etc., going back over the past two or three decades. Various aspects of this new emphasis were anticipated by a number of educational leaders (e.g., Symonds, 1957; Walker, 1957; Clark and Carriker, 1961; Eurich, 1962; and Ryans, 1963, among others) before it become a federally sponsored actuality.

This new emphasis is also a reflection of the recent activities of various groups of college professors and scientists in devising new curricula in mathematics and the sciences, in the criticisms of education by scholars from other disciplines, and perhaps more directly the result of the efforts of the American Educational Research Association whose leadership was influential in obtaining governmental support of the Cooperative Research Program, of Phi Delta Kappa which in 1960 inaugurated its series of annual symposia in educational research and in 1965 appointed a full-time director of research, and of other professional groups. The current emphasis on research, in a sense spearheaded by the federal government, rests on a broad base of professional and public interest in the outcomes of American education as the medium for promoting social welfare in the America of tomorrow. More pointedly, it is serving notice that ". . . education cannot and will not remain . . . the exclusive province of the professional educator" (Levin, 1967). This current concern for education will infuse intellectual vigor into education. Undoubtedly, it represents a climate in which educational research can prosper; it is also a climate in which a direct mandate is placed on education for social, as well as self, improvement.

The full scope of the federal government's participation in education (Alford, 1965; Ianni, 1965; Boerrigter, 1966; HEW, 1967) is too broad to be considered here; the following is simply a brief and incomplete list of the major areas of federal involvement in American education.

A. The Elementary and Secondary Education Act (1965)

Title I   : Aid to schools in low-income areas

Title II   : Grants for the purchase of school library resources, textbooks, and other instructional materials

Title III : Supplementary services for elementary and secondary schools to provide services not currently available

Title IV : Support of educational research—provides support for the training of educational researchers, sponsors the establishment of research and development centers and of regional educational laboratories, operates the Educational Research Information Center (ERIC), etc.

Title V   : Support of certain operations of the State Departments of Education

An important provision of Title IV of interest in the context of the present discussion is that providing for the establishment of a national network of research and development centers and of regional educational laboratories. The latter are designed to bridge the gap between research and its implementation; the major emphasis is on development, demonstration, and dissemination. The R & D centers, on the other hand, deal with broad problems in education and are generally located on the campus of select institutions of higher learning and assume leadership for research in a broad educational area, e.g., early childhood education, teacher education, etc.

B. The National Defense Education Act (1958)—Select titles

Title III : Improvement of education—matching funds to states, loans to private schools to permit schools to buy special instructional equipment and materials in science, mathematics, etc.

Title IV : Graduate fellowships—provides support for graduate students in certain approved areas

Title V-B: Counseling and Guidance Institutes

Title VI : Support of training in foreign languages

Title VIII: Research into the educational use of communication media

Title X   : Improvement of State statistical services

C. Higher Education Act (1965)—Select titles

Title II   : Support to upgrade college and university libraries*

Title III : Strengthening of the educational program of smaller colleges

Title IV : (The Educational Opportunities Grants Program)—provides financial assistance to academically qualified students from low-income families to permit them to attend college

Title V-B : The National Teacher Corps—sponsors the training of teachers to work in slum schools

Title VI : Provides matching support of college programs for the improvement of undergraduate college instruction through the acquisition of instructional materials and equipment

D. The Higher Education Facilities Act (1963)—provides support for the construction of college classrooms, laboratories, and other facilities to accommodate the rapidly expanding college enrollment

E. The Civil Rights Act (1964)—has two titles which constitute the Equal Education Opportunities Program (EEOP):

Title IV : Provides assistance in handling problems resulting from racial integration

Title VI : Is concerned with the availability of equal opportunity to all qualified students regardless of race, color, or creed

F. The Economic Opportunity Act (1964)—sponsors the College Work-Study Program, under which students from low-income families can defray their educational expenses through part-time employment. The Office of Economic Opportunity also administers the Head Start Program as part of its war on poverty.

Reorientation Toward Research

A major stumbling block in the implementation of this vast federally sponsored program (and other programs stimulated thereby) is the dire shortage of adequately trained personnel. It would take thousands of persons trained to various degrees of proficiency just to staff existing programs, let alone expand to meet even minimal needs. This is especially critical inasmuch as we have no reserve pools from which to draw. This manpower shortage

---

* The Library Services Act of 1956 provides for library construction and makes library materials available to rural libraries. As amended in 1966, it allocates federal monies for library construction on a participating basis with the states.

will have a direct bearing on the kind of activities we undertake and will be a definite limiting factor in the success we are likely to have. It is obvious that multiplying research appropriations will not do the job, simply because, as Cronbach (1966) points out, incisive research calls for training and aptitudes that are now in very short supply. Even by vigorous recruiting from other faculties, we might be able to staff perhaps a dozen centers with adequate programs by 1970. He feels that, under the circumstances, research must not dilute its resources by tackling all aspects of the educational enterprise. Rather it must concentrate its talents where it can make an impact. Meanwhile, since the manpower shortage, and not the shortage of funds, will set present limits, the training of research personnel commands first priority.

What is called for is a drastic change affecting all aspects of our thinking—i.e., a new discipline of education, with complete orientation toward research as part of the nation's total commitment to the improvement of the educational enterprise. Walton (1966), for example, emphasizes the need to establish graduate faculties of education primarily concerned not with the immediate solution of the problems of education or with the training of practitioners but rather with the creation of a new discipline. He visualizes scholars of exceptional ability setting out to make theoretical sense out of education. Griffiths (1967) likewise insists that the central activity of the new school of education be the production of knowledge, i.e., research.

> The *centrality* of research is essential for it appears that this *is* an "either-or" situation . . . . Either instruction is research-based or it is a recitation of testimonials. Either research is the life-blood of the schools of education or practice is the norm.

This complete reorientation of the school of education toward research presents certain problems, of course. As Lazarsfeld and Sieber (1964) point out: "Schools of education have strong traditional obligations to the teaching profession and the educational efforts of the community at large." This will make it necessary for them to order their responsibilities as to priority and, as Sieber (1967) suggests, to resist the temptation to serve everyone.

Effectiveness of the overall program demands the clarification of the role assigned to the new school of education. The general consensus (e.g., Stiles, 1962; Cronbach, 1966;

Wittrock, 1967; Bright, 1968) seems to be that it should place its emphasis on basic research. Since we have so very few solid generalizations about the teaching-learning process and the educational enterprise in general, and since educational programs can be no better than the data from which they are created, it can be argued that all hands should turn to the development of a stockpile of basic knowledge before any attempt is made at evaluation, dissemination, or implementation. Ebel (1967), on the contrary, argues that basic research can promise very little improvement to the process of education—now or in the foreseeable future. He feels that professional educators should direct their efforts toward applied research designed to yield information immediately useful in the solution of contemporary educational problems. Without denying the value of basic research where it is appropriate, he feels that problems of the complexity of those found in education require the application of other sources of information and other processes of decision-making than those which pure science provides.

Before any significant improvement in the educational picture can be hoped for, there is need to effect a major upgrading of the school of education. Implied, first of all, is the recruitment and the nurture of a more adequate student body. At the graduate level, this means a more adequate undergraduate population from which to select, a more ruthless weeding of the unfit in the hope of attracting better prospects away from other disciplines, and a more rigorous and demanding sequence of courses. Perhaps even more important, this also implies upgrading of the faculty. A number of writers (Griffiths, 1967; Jensen, 1962; Lazarsfeld and Sieber, 1964; Sieber, 1967) have emphasized the need for recruiting faculty members from other disciplines where more adequate standards prevail. This would increase the research orientation of the school of education, bring into education people who are already oriented toward and experienced in research,* and provide an interdisciplinary perspective to educational prob-

---

* It must be recognized that the availability of research funds has lured into the laboratory some of the relatively scarce top-level educational researchers, this at a time when the increased enrollment and increased emphasis on research make their services all the more necessary in the classroom. Besvinick (1966) also suggests that it is often difficult for a university to maintain integrity in the face of the availability of research funds for certain defined purposes. There is always a danger of seeking what is funded rather than what is fundamental or even appropriate from the standpoint of urgency, educational benefit, or the competence of the researcher.

lems and their solution. Basic here is the point made by a number of writers that education is a field of study, not a discipline; Schutz (1967), for example, argues that education possesses no definable methodology, that there is nothing in the methodological sense that one can reasonably call "educational research"; education simply draws from the social sciences and the humanities and is unified by a common subject-matter, namely, learning and the setting in which this learning takes place. To the extent that this is true, scholars from other social disciplines can make a valuable contribution to the cause of education.

Training of Educational Researchers

A number of significant reports (Buswell et al., 1966; Clark and Worthen, 1967; Jensen, 1962; Lazarsfeld and Sieber, 1964; Stanley, 1967) have focussed attention on the training of researchers in the light of the current manpower shortage. One obvious possibility for meeting the research needs of the nation is to expand Title IV of the Elementary and Secondary Education Act, funding the training of research workers. But this is hardly the answer: in fact, according to Jensen, there may be too much money going down the drain now. Unless adequate research training facilities are available and an adequate student body can be recruited, the results are likely to be disappointing. As Schutz (1967) suggests, getting more students and staff to perpetuate the same kinds of programs and activities that have been conducted in the past does not seem to be the optimal course of action. As Sieber (1967) points out, unless there are changes in the basic structure and ideology of the new schools of education in the contemporary university, additional funds will simply enlarge and reinforce traditional types of training, with the result that an increased number of part-time researchers will engage as haphazardly and infrequently in more of the same fragmentary research as they have in the past.

Recruitment of potential educational researchers must be especially selective. Research is a complex and demanding task in which the ability of the researcher to explore insightfully numerous areas to tease out meaningful problems, convert them into research designs, collect and analyze the data into usable conclusions is often what makes the difference between a significant contribution and wasted motion. As Campbell (1963) points out, unless candidates of adequate caliber are selected, programs de-signed to prepare researchers are exercises in futility. With the current support of research training and the attractive employment opportunities, it should be possible to compete in the open market for the rather limited supply of high caliber students. Sieber (1967), for example, suggests that graduate departments which hope to produce researchers not look to the undergraduate educa-tion pool, but rather scan the other graduate horizons for bright youngsters who are attracted to education. In support of this posi-tion is the higher caliber of students in certain other disciplines and the more rigorous undergraduate training they have received. Halpin (1966) expresses a strong conviction that a person can be educated and scholarly only if he has a broad liberal arts back-ground. In an early article, Ryans (1955) also recommends a back-ground in liberal arts with a major in psychology or sociology, together with a minor in the physical or biological sciences.

There is considerable opposition to the requirement of teaching experience for admission to a research training pro-gram. Lazarsfeld and Sieber (1964), for example, recommend that undergraduate students with interest in research be encouraged to forego teaching and to enter immediately into graduate training: "Not only would this insure these students would not be side-tracked by experiences in the field, but it would inform more undergraduates that research is a valued activity, that is, a viable alternative to full-time teaching or administration." Travers (1964) feels that practical experience in the classroom is incompatible with the creative and inquisitive mind required in a research capacity; he argues that practical experience generates practi-tioners rather than investigators. At the empirical level, a canvass of current educators and educational researchers (Ellis, 1967) re-veals that, while the majority saw public school teaching experi-ence as "generally helpful" or "extremely helpful" for the overall effectiveness of performance of educational researchers, signifi-cantly less value was ascribed to teaching experience by those who: 1. were younger; 2. had published research in the past six years; 3. had not themselves completed a teacher-education program; and 4. had not themselves taught in the public school, than by their respective counterparts.

There is also a strong feeling (e.g., Stiles, 1962; Campbell, 1963; Stanley, 1967) that recruitment should focus on candidates who are young (as well as bright); not only would this enable them to have a longer period of service but it is also felt that early entry into research capitalizes on scholarship at an age when people are less tradition-bound. Half of the recipients of the doctor's degree in education are 38 or older at the time they receive their degree; one-quarter are 44 and older (King, 1961). Lazarsfeld and Sieber (1964) report that the typical recipient of the doctorate in education had spent seven years in teaching before getting his degree. To the extent that any candidate who has already established a career is likely to be reluctant to cast aside what has taken years to achieve, he is likely to view the doctorate as a means of advancing in the same direction he has already staked out. As Buswell et al. (1966) argue, for the Ph.D. group in particular, it is hard indeed to justify this large amount of previous teaching experience.

Research Training Programs

The exact nature of the research training program likely to be most effective is a matter of some disagreement. The joint PDK–AERA report (Clark and Worthen, 1967), for example, presents three different points of view: 1. Levin favors a close master-apprentice relationship; 2. Sieber prefers to scan the horizons for adequate students from other disciplines and then to insulate them from the regular professional education program. Jensen (1962) and Robinson (1965) also advocate separate departments, operating independently of each other, say by recognizing the Ph.D. as the symbol of research and the Ed.D. as the symbol of professional training, and devising separate programs for each degree; 3. Griffiths, on the other hand, favors the development of a new concept of a school of education in which a sizable number of well-prepared educational researchers are typically produced as part of the normal output: "The traditional concept of the school of education is untenable; if it is not abandoned, schools of education will shortly cease to exist." He argues that, if we are ever to train enough educational researchers with the necessary skills and acumen and, at the same time, develop a general receptivity for their services in the field, we must both upgrade and totally revamp schools of education around research as the primary focus. Such an approach would have the advantage of facilitating communication between researchers and practitioners; it would, moreover, be in line with the concept that, if it is to prosper, education must make use of the coordinated efforts of a diversity of talents in keeping with the diversity of tasks required in the educational endeavor. It would, however, require a vast effort if across-the-board mediocrity is to be avoided.

Another aspect of the situation is the nature of the actual training. Kerlinger (1959), Nash (1962), and Levin (1967), among others, deplore the current overemphasis on methodology per se. We have developed technicians with little orientation toward the major ideas on which to exercise their quantitative skills: "Such narrow research training will not work in the future." Buswell (1963) argues that:

> The most disturbing impression from examining the *Handbook (of Research on Teaching)* is that many researchers are far more competent in the technical process of research than they are in understanding the educational phenomena being studied. One gets the impression of being dressed in the latest styles of logical and statistical techniques and then having no important place to go.

This is again the reaction presented by Maslow (1966) and others against overreliance on the "scientific method" and the corresponding avoidance of significant problems.

At the operational level, writers in the field recommend a stiff curriculum, highlighting critical inquiry, the philosophy of science, mathematics, statistics, psychology, etc. Halpin (1963) and Travers (1964) emphasize the need for rigorous training designed to eliminate fuzzy thinking and the use of empty slogans; the latter, for example, suggests that a good starting point in the training of educational researchers is to have them consider some of the devices, theories, constructs, and models which the scientist uses to organize his thinking.

STRUCTURING OUR RESEARCH ACTIVITIES

Dissemination

Another critical consideration in the progress of education is that of the dissemination of knowledge, for no matter what effort the profession puts into research, it will be of no avail unless the results are known. What is required is an effective link between the generation of knowledge and its field testing and implementation—together with an adequate feedback for further research on a continuous spiral of increasing scientific sophistication and improved educational practice. More specifically, the problem is one of effective all-round communication among scientists as the basis for the identification of meaningful problems and imaginative approaches to their solution, parallel two-way communication between scientist and practitioner so as to permit the latter to make productive use of the knowledge so generated and the former to continuously reorient himself toward problems of higher priority and significance, and further, equally adequate communication among practitioners so as to ensure maximal use of educational science in the improvement of educational practice. Unfortunately, current dissemination patterns, which have just evolved much like Topsy, are running into a crisis which is threatening to jeopardize the whole scientific enterprise (see Board of Scientific Affairs, 1959). This is reflected dramatically in the relative clogging of the communication channels—including professional conventions—with such a superabundance of materials, much of it substandard, fragmentary, and unproductive, that the whole system is about to collapse under its own weight. In the meantime, it is impeding the ready exchange of key ideas necessary for progress in both science and practice.*

Dissemination begins with effective reporting. Certainly, the researcher has a moral responsibility to make his findings known to the profession and thereby contribute to the advancement of education. However, in view of the current overwhelming quantity of materials—as represented by the publication lag despite the vast increase in the number of journals and other publication media—he also has the responsibility to make his report brief, concise, clear, and maximally usable in the furtherance of educational science and educational practice. Interesting in this regard is the recommendation by Swanson (1966) of a new scientific information monitoring center, one of whose duties would be to stimulate summaries and reviews with a view to separating the

---

* The current concern of the academic community over the problem of dissemination is reflected in the fact that the *American Psychologist* devoted a whole issue (Vol. 21, Nov. 1966) to the topic. The current policy of the *American Education Research Journal* of publishing a brief synopsis of each article as part of the table of contents can be a valuable time-saver. Its synopses of articles accepted for eventual publication can be even more helpful, considering the publication lag. Tying such synopses to an ERIC-type system with immediate availability of the total text to those interested is a possibility worth considering as a means of expediting access to the literature and avoiding the cluttering of journals with articles in which a given subscriber is likely to have only passing interest.

substantial literature from the trivial. It would, for example, make known the judgment of the scientific community as to the quality of a given item and might, thereby, discourage the publication of inadequate articles. It could also serve the scientific community by repackaging scientific findings to serve the needs of a select audience. A similar idea is presented by Carter (1966), who suggests a national bureau acting as an overall management agency dealing with the information activities of the various departments of the federal government and related groups. This bureau would formulate policies and establish standards concerning various matters of publication, classification, storage, and retrieval.

The problem of storage is one of immediate urgency. With the current knowledge explosion, knowledge is being generated at such a steeply exponential rate that the very quantity of published material is totally overwhelming. Shera (1967) extending Rider's original projections (1944) postulates that, at the present rate of growth, the typical university library in the year 2040 might have some 200 million volumes; this would represent some 6,000 miles of shelf space. The card catalog files—if it had a card catalog— would consist of nearly three-quarters of a million catalog drawers, occupying no less than eight acres of floor space. The present system of storage is clearly doomed.*

Even more fundamental to the progress of education is the question of retrieval. With such an overwhelming abundance of material, it is essential for the scientist and the practitioner to be able to identify and to retrieve relevant data on call. Any storage system must, without question, incorporate within itself as a primary consideration the question of selective retrieval through the use of an index, or more realistically, a computer, along the lines of ERIC, SRIS, and Datrix (see Chapter 5).

A particularly crucial step to be taken in the reorganization of our research efforts is the clarification of the status of the major aspects of education, so that we can get a better perspective of our present position. The amount of material—of varying degrees of quality—that has accumulated helter-skelter in certain areas is so extensive that it is no longer possible to read it all, let alone digest its import. As pointed out by Underwood (1957), unless the data are synthesized periodically, the field is likely to

---

* Rider had suggested as a solution the use of microcards. National Cash Register can now produce a readable text at a reduction ratio of 48,000 to one.

become progressively more forbidding. As a consequence, it will scare away further research, particularly fundamental research.

What is needed is not just a summary of the literature but rather an integration of the vast accumulation of isolated knowledge into a logical framework which will place these empirical data into meaningful structure, deepen our understanding of their significance, and permit their more effective use. Particular emphasis must be given to identifying areas and directions in which the profession's research efforts might be most profitably exerted. This is a service for which each professional society might assume responsibility by providing periodic syntheses of its current status and trends as a means of providing perspective as to the nature of its specific problems and issues (see Atkin, 1966).* Such structuring of basic areas of education is crucial to the coordination of the efforts of the profession in its search for more adequate answers to more significant problems. In view of the relative lack of orientation of educators as a group toward research and the correspondingly greater need for specific guidance, such reviews probably constitute one of the major contributions that can be made to the cause of education at this time.

Emphasis on Systematic and Continuous Research

Much of the current educational research has been of a stop-gap nature oriented toward the solution of immediate problems. Such measures are inadequate; they cannot be depended on to provide the basis for systematic, continuous, and vigorous educational progress. A particularly strong statement against deluding ourselves that educational progress can come from our present "shoestring" operation was presented by the research committee of the American Educational Research Association (Grace, 1962) in the following recommendation:

---

*Reading has had yearly summaries dating back to 1924 (Gray, 1925–1960; Robinson, 1961, 1962–date; Harris, 1962–date). In addition, periodic summaries have been published (Traxler et al., 1941, 1946, 1955, 1960; Fay et al., 1964; and, of course, the *Review* and the *Encyclopedia of Educational Research*). The *Handbook of Research on Teaching* (1963) has particularly thorough reviews of the literature on selected topics related to teaching, including reading. The *Annual Review of Psychology* provides a relatively comprehensive analysis of the topics it covers on a yearly basis. *Psychological Bulletin* also provides the occasional in-depth review of select topics in psychology.

Promote the notion that research is difficult and is best done by the professional. Educational research can probably be promoted best if it is advertised as being hard, demanding, consuming, and requiring a lengthy period of preliminary professional training. Such a perception of research is standard when one thinks of physics, medicine, chemistry, but not so when education is considered. The popular interpretation of action research has so deluded public school teachers, supervisors, and administrators that they believe, first, that the required abilities are bestowed automatically when one announces his intentions to do research, and, second, that correlating the distance bus students travel to school and their IQ's epitomizes educational research in its most complex and penetrating aspects.

The type of progress education needs at this time can be promoted only through the implementation of long-range, comprehensive, and coordinated research programs as exemplified by the investigations of Gesell, Terman, Thurstone, Cattell, Guilford, Barr, Aikin, Ryans, and, more recently, Suppes. We need large-scale programs that will do for teaching and learning what such testing enterprises as Educational Testing Service have done for evaluation. We need to place emphasis on the R & D centers operating on an interdisciplinary basis under federal auspices. We need an equally strong "bench" out in the field involving the Regional Educational Laboratories, various state agencies, and the public schools. We need particularly a whole new orientation in the school of education, reflected in more active and systematic participation in research on the part of the faculty and a stronger emphasis toward research in the teacher-education program. If research is ever to have an impact on education, an informed teaching profession is essential to participate in the conduct of research and the implementation of research findings. Rigorous research training must be incorporated in the program of all graduate students in education; with the emphasis on research which is bound to dominate education of the future, there is no alternative.

We especially need to discard the piecemeal educational thinking of the past and substitute a program of continuous analysis of current status and alertness for improvement. What is especially important is that we address ourselves to the critical issues on which effectiveness in relation to the essentials of American education really revolves. We need to develop new high-level research strategies such as those responsible for the rapid progress of medicine, biology, and some of the other sciences. Platt (1964), for example, speaks of *strong inference,* a broad plan including a clear map of the current state of the problem, a search for crucial ways of asking questions, and research designs capable of yielding definitive answers. Such an approach would, among other things, reduce the redundancy which now characterizes educational research and educational practice. An enterprise as complex as American education needs an imaginative system-wide master plan— a strategy for innovation (Hilgard and Bower, 1966)—involving the cooperative efforts of educational philosophers, subject-matter experts, learning specialists and teaching methodologists, and researchers in identifying the major needs of education and developing the field-testing methods and materials necessary to meet these needs.

There is no excuse for continuing to deal, as Clark (1963) puts it, ". . . with all the children of all the people 'by guess and by gosh'."

> There is no reason to continue to conduct the affairs of education in this country in the knowledge vacuum which now exists. The way out of the present situation does not lie in half-way measures which are doomed to relative failure . . . . We can, if we have the will, change the character of American education in the next decade through research.

If the next war is to be won in the classroom rather than on the battlefield, it behooves American society to provide the means for the improvement of education, just as it behooves the profession to equip and to organize itself for effectiveness and productivity. A favorable climate now exists for the conduct of worthwhile research. In fact, the American public is looking to education for more answers to crucial problems than education is likely to be able to provide. Along with the scholars from related fields who have come to lend a hand, we will need to devise more effective educational methods if we are to meet the challenge of a rapidly changing society. But, it will do us little good to redouble our efforts and our output if we do not know which way we are supposed to go. It is time we look to research to provide the necessary enlightenment.

Highlights of the Chapter

1.   While education has made substantial progress in recent years, it has not kept pace with the rapid scientific advances which have characterized the past few decades. Our deficiencies stem primarily from 1. a lack of appreciation of research as the vehicle for scientific growth (and a corresponding glorification of practicality) and 2. a parallel lack of a theoretical framework on which to structure empirical findings and to orient the efforts of the profession. Equally serious is the current ritualization of the research process and the consequent avoidance of meaningful issues simply because they cannot be framed in the narrow and artificial conceptualization of "science."

2.   The graduate school holds the key to the future of the nation. Unfortunately, in addition to a number of general shortcomings, e.g., inflexibility in the face of the current socio-political revolution, graduate education suffers from a serious lack of scholarship in all aspects of its operation from the student body it attracts to the courses it teaches, the standards it maintains, and the "educational leaders" it graduates. At a more fundamental level, and pervading its whole operation, is a sort of anti-intellectualism, an important aspect of which is a general disinterest in research as the basis for knowledge, with the underlying implication that education should be practical rather than scientific. There is need for a serious reconsideration of the function of the graduate—as well as the undergraduate—program in education and its relation to research.

3.   In contrast to basic research, action research is oriented primarily toward the solution of immediate problems and only secondarily toward the derivation of generalizations of broad applicability. Action research presents a number of obvious advantages, but it has inherent weaknesses that need to be recognized. If they are to be effective in action research, teachers will need considerable guidance from a capable consultant.

4.   The relative lack of orientation of educators toward research is reflected in the correspondingly inadequate status of the research bureaus they operate. More adequate recognition of the importance of their potential contributions at all levels of the educational

enterprise could make such bureaus a major force in the improvement of educational practice. The Regional Education Laboratories and the R & D Centers initiated under federal auspices might likewise be expected to have a major impact on education.

5.   The massive entry of the federal government into education represents a clear recognition by American society of the crucial role of education in the welfare of the nation and a long-needed commitment to the improvement of educational practice through the development of educational science.

6.   Unfortunately, the nation's effort in educational research will be hampered for years to come by the dire shortage of qualified researchers and, further, by the relatively limited supply of talent from which to recruit. Attracting students and faculty from other disciplines is a necessary, albeit incomplete, solution.

7.   Before any significant improvement can be expected in the educational enterprise, there is need for a new discipline of education totally committed to research as the basis for educational and social progress.

8.   A fundamental aspect of this restructuring of education is a major upgrading of every facet of the school of education from its student body to its curriculum, standards, and faculty. The recruitment of educational research trainees must be highly selective and their training particularly rigorous. A greater research sophistication on the part of all teachers is essential to effective communication between the various components of the educational enterprise.

9.   A major problem to be resolved if educational progress is to be achieved is that of the effective dissemination of research findings. ERIC constitutes the best approach to date in the area of selective retrieval of research data. There is a parallel need for an insightful synthesis of empirical findings and the development of theoretical structure.

10.   If education is to prosper and to keep pace with the world its efforts have helped to create, it needs to devote itself to the sys-

tematic attack on its many problems, both at home and in society at large. With the current social upheaval, America is desperately looking to education for answers to many acute social problems; we, in turn, need to look to research for new insights with which to meet the challenge.

Questions and Projects

1.   How do you, as a teacher, learn of new research findings that might be incorporated in your teaching? To what extent might a greater orientation toward research in your undergraduate program have helped you become a better teacher?

2.   Describe any action research study conducted in your school within the past two years. What benefits are still visible? What was the feeling of the faculty as to the benefits derived in relation to cost in time and effort? What, if anything, could have been done to improve this benefit-cost balance?

3.   Make a critical analysis of the organization and functions of the research bureau of a nearby school system. Evaluate its contribution to the operation of the local school and to the advancement of education.

4.   Evaluate the effect of the massive entry of the federal government into the field of education. What is the rationale underlying these efforts? What are some of the more obvious benefits? What are some of the dangers? What do you see as the future of this venture? of education? To what extent is money the answer?

5.   Make a survey of school bulletins to determine the research requirements for the graduate degree of education at some of the country's leading institutions. What changes have taken place over recent years? Make an analysis of federally sponsored research training programs. What contribution might the latter make to the future of American education?

6.   What do you see as the benefits of the reconstruction of the School of Education toward research? Are there dangers? Can its functions be integrated within a research framework?

Selected References

American Association of Colleges of Teacher Education. *The Doctorate in Education*. Washington: The Assn., 1961.

American Psychological Association. "Basic research and national goals," *Amer. Psychol.*, 20: 662–86; 1965.

Atkin, J.M. "Basing curriculum change on research and demonstration," *Educ. Forum*, 31: 27–33; 1966.

Bagley, Clarence H. (ed.) *Design and Methodology in Institutional Research*. Proc. Fifth Annual Inst. Res. Forum. Pullman: Washington State Univ., 1965.

Bantock, G.H. "Educational research: A criticism," *Harv. educ. Rev.*, 31: 264–80; 1961.

Belth, Marc. "Prospects for a discipline of education," *Educ. Theory*, 12: 193–204; 1962.

Bereday, George Z.F. and Joseph A. Lauwerys (eds.) *Concept of Excellence in Education*. 1961 Year Book of Education. New York: Harcourt, Brace & World, 1961.

Berelson, Bernard. *Graduate Education in the United States*. New York: McGraw-Hill, 1960.

Blessing, James H. *Graduate Education: An Annotated Bibliography*. Office of Education Bull., No. 26, 1961. Washington: Govt. Printing Office, 1961.

Bloom, Benjamin S. "Twenty-five years of educational research," *Amer. educ. Res. J.*, 3: 211–21; 1966.

Brehaut, Willard. "An analysis of dissertations in education accepted by Canadian universities, 1930–55," *Ontario J. educ. Res.*, 2: 109–22; 1960.

Buswell, Guy T. et al. *Training of Educational Researchers*. Berkeley: Center for the Study of Higher Education, Univ. Calif., 1966.

Carmichael, Oliver C. *Graduate Education*. New York: Harper & Row, 1961.

Carter, Launor F. "National document-handling systems in science and technology," *Sci.*, 154: 1299–1304; 1966.

Clark, David L. and Blaine R. Worthen. *Preparing Research Personnel for Education*. Bloomington: Phi Delta Kappa, 1967.

Corey, Stephen M. *Action Research to Improve School Practices*. New York: T.C., Columbia Univ. Press, 1953.

Cronbach, Lee J. "The role of the university in improving education," *Phi Delta Kappan*, 47: 539–45; 1966.

Culbertson, Jack A. and Stephen P. Hencley (eds.) *Educational Research: New Perspectives*. Danville: Interstate, 1963.

Dyer, Henry S. "Can institutional research lead to a science of institutions?" *Educ. Rec.*, 47: 452–66; 1966.

Ebel, Robert L. "The limitations of basic research in education," *Phi Delta Kappa*, 49: 81–84; 1967.

Educational Researcher, Official Newsletter of the American Educational Research Association (formerly, *AERA Newsletter*). See various issues for latest developments in the field.

Edwards, R. "The training of educational researchers: A North American viewpoint," *Bull. Brit. Psychol. Soc.*, 21: 61–66; 1968.

Elam, Stanley M. (ed.) *Improving Teacher Education in the United States.* Bloomington: Phi Delta Kappa, 1967.

Elliott, David L. and Arthur W. Foshay. "Chart or charter: Recent developments in educational discourse," *Rev. educ. Res.*, 33: 233–44; 1963.

Engel, Mary. "Thesis—antithesis: Reflections on the education of researchers in psychology," *Amer. Psychol.*, 21: 781–87; 1966.

Eurich, Alvin C. "New dimensions in educational research," *AERA Newsletter*, 13: 4-10; April 1962.

Fattu, Nicholas A. "The teacher and educational research," *High Sch. J.*, 44: 194–203; 1961.

Flanagan, John C. "Implementing recent research findings in secondary education," *High Sch. J.*, 48: 377–82; 1965.

Foshay, Arthur W. et al. "The bureau of educational research and the problem of leadership," *Educ. Res. Bull.*, 31: 197–224; 1952.

Fox, James H. "Criteria of good research," *Phi Delta Kappan*, 39: 284–91; 1958.

Gideonse, H.D. "The national program of educational laboratories," *Phi Delta Kappan*, 47: 130–33; 1965.

Glaser, Robert. "Implications of training research in education," in E.R. Hilgard (ed.) *Theories of Learning and Instruction.* 63rd Yrbk., N.S.S.E., Pt. I. Chicago: Univ. Chicago Press, 1964. pp. 153–81.

Goldhammer, Keith and Stanley M. Elam (eds.) *Research Dissemination and Implementation.* 3rd Annual Symposium. Bloomington: Phi Delta Kappa, 1962.

Guba, Egon G. and Stanley M. Elam (eds.) *The Training and Nurture of Educational Researchers.* Bloomington: Phi Delta Kappa, 1965.

Harap, Henry. "A review of recent developments in teacher education," *J. teach. Educ.*, 18: 5–19; 1967.

Harrington, Fred H. "The Federal Government and the future of higher education," *Educ. Rec.*, 44: 155–60; 1963.

Hills, R.J. "Theory, research, and practice: Three legs of administrative science," *Sch. Rev.*, 71: 478–92; 1963.

Hodgkinson, Harold L. "Action research—A critique," *J. educ. Sociol.*, 31: 137–53; 1957.

Ianni, Francis A.J. "Federal concern for research in education," in John W. Duggan et al. *Research in Higher Education.* New York: College Entrance Examination Board, 1965. pp. 63–66.

Jackson, Robert W.B. *Educational Research in Canada Today and Tomorrow.* Toronto: W.J. Gage, 1961.

Jensen, Arthur R. "The improvement of educational research," *T. C. Rec.,* 64: 20–27; 1962.

Johnson, Loaz W. "What administrators want and will use from research workers," in *Growing Points in Educational Research.* 1959 Official Report. Washington: Amer. Educ. Res. Assn., 1959. pp. 7–12.

Johnson, Mauritz. "Research and secondary education," *Educ. Forum,* 31: 293–301; 1967.

Johnson, M.E.B. "Teachers' attitudes toward educational research," *Educ. Res.,* 9: 74–79, 1966.

Josephs, L.S. "Research and the training of teachers," *Sch. Life,* 46: 12–13; June 1964.

Keppel, Francis. "Research: Education's neglected hope," *J. Read.,* 8: 3–9; 1964.

——— . "On improving the diffusion of knowledge," *N.A.S.S.P. Bull.,* 48: 3–9; April 1964.

——— . "The national commitment to education," *Phi Delta Kappan,* 47: 167–68; 1965.

Kerlinger, Fred N. "Practicality and education," *Sch. Rev.,* 67: 281–91; 1959.

——— . "The mythology of educational research: The methods approach," *Sch. & Soc.,* 88: 149–51, 363–64; 1960.

——— . "The Ed.D. and the Ph.D.," *T. C. Rec.,* 66: 434–39; 1965.

——— . "The doctoral training of research specialists," *The Rec.* (formerly, *T. C. Rec.*), 69: 477–83; 1968.

Lazarsfeld, Paul F. and Sam D. Sieber. *Organizing Educational Research: An Exploration.* Englewood Cliffs: Prentice-Hall, 1964.

Levin, Harry. "Rationale and recommendations for a university-wide graduate training program in educational research," in David L. Clark and Blaine R. Worthen (eds.) *Preparing Research Personnel for Education.* Bloomington: Phi Delta Kappa, 1967. pp. 34–39.

Lewis, Lionel S. "Publish or perish," *J. Higher Educ.,* 38: 85–89; 1967.

Little, J. Kenneth. "Graduate education," in Chester W. Harris (ed.) *Encyclopedia of Educational Research.* New York: Macmillan, 1960. pp. 593–602.

——— . "Higher education and the national purpose," *Educ. Rec.,* 42: 161–72; 1961.

Mayhew, Lewis B. "Educational research, its capabilities and limitations," in John W. Duggan et al. *Research in Higher Education*. New York: College Entrance Examination Board, 1965. pp. 1–8.

Miller, Richard I. "Regional educational laboratories," *Phi Delta Kappan*, 48: 144–49; 1966.

Mitchell, Mildred B. "Trends toward multiple authorship in scientific publication," *J. Psychol.*, 52: 569–99; 1958.

Morse, Arthur D. *Schools of Tomorrow—Today*. Garden City: Doubleday, 1960.

Nash, Paul. "The future of educational research in Canada: A critique," *Canad. educ. Res. Dig.*, 2: 161–72; 1962.

National Education Association, Dept. Classroom Teachers, and American Educational Research Association. *What Research Says to the Teacher*. (Continuing series) Washington: The Assn., 1953–date.

Robinson, F.G. *Educational Research in Canada: An Analysis of Potential, Current Status, and Needed Development*. Ottawa: Canad. Council for Res. Educ., 1965. (draft)

Rosenzweig, Saul et al. "Operation Babel: A survey of the effectiveness of the foreign language requirements for the Ph.D. degree in psychology," *Amer. Psychol.*, 17: 237–43, 1962.

Ryans, David G. "Looking to the future in education," *Educ. Rec.*, 44: 360–68; 1963.

Sawyer, Jack and Howard Schechter. "Computers, privacy, and the National Data Center: The responsibility of social scientists," *Amer. Psychol.*, 23: 810–18; 1968.

Silberman, Harry F. et al. "The effect of educational research on classroom instruction," *Harv. educ. Rev.*, 36: 295–317; 1966.

Stephens, John M. *The Process of Schooling*. New York: Holt, Rinehart & Winston, 1967.

Stewart, M.A. et al. "Role and function of educational research," *Educ. Res.*, 9: 3–15; 1966.

Stiles, Lindley J. "Educational research: The source of better schools," *Theory into Practice*, 1: 70–74; 1962.

——. "Publish-or-perish policies in perspective," *J. teach. Educ.*, 17: 464–67; 1966.

Suppes, Patrick. "Modern learning theory and the elementary school curriculum," *Amer. educ. Res. J.*, 1: 79–93; 1964.

Swanson, Don R. "Scientific journals and information services of the future," *Amer. Psychol.*, 21: 1005–1010; 1966.

Tucker, Alan and Lee Sloan. "Graduate school talents sold to the highest bidder," *J. higher Educ.*, 35:12–16; 1964.

Tyler, Ralph W. "Specific contributions of research to education," *Theory into Practice*, 1: 75–80; 1962.

——. "The knowledge explosion: Implications for secondary education," *Educ. Forum*, 29: 145–53; 1965.

————. "The field of educational research," in Egon G. Guba and Stanley M. Elam (eds.) *The Training and Nurture of Educational Researchers.* 6th Annual Symposium. Bloomington: Phi Delta Kappa, 1965. pp. 1–12.

Wallace, J.G. "Some aspects of educational research: Development and evaluation in the U.S.A.," *Educ. Res.,* 9: 105–12; 1967.

Walters, Everett (ed.) *Graduate Education Today.* Washington: Amer. Council Educ., 1965.

———— and Frederic W. Ness. "The Ph.D.: New demands, same old responses," *Sat. Rev.,* Jan. 15, 1968, pp. 62–65+.

Walton, J. "Why universities are failing the schools: A discipline of education is needed," *Educ. Dig.,* 31: 22–24; 1966.

Whaley, W.G. "American academic degrees," *Educ. Rec.,* 47: 525–37; 1966.

Wittrock, M.C. "Product-oriented research," *Educ. Forum,* 31: 145–50; 1967.

Wolf, W. et al. "Research: The expanding concept," *Theory into Practice,* 6: 53–98; 1967.

Wright, Charles R. "Success or failure in earning graduate degrees," *Social. Educ.,* 38: 73–97; 1964.

14
SIGNIFICANT RESEARCH STUDIES

*. . . the most brilliant achievements of today will but
pave the way for even greater accomplishments in areas
which present work will have brought within focus.
Where barriers appear, new resources will be found;
when the horizon looms close, new vistas will open,
beckoning beyond. With vision continually freshened by
new accomplishments and by new conceptualizations,
man goes forever forward in his penetration of the unknown.*——Carter V. Good and Douglas E. Scates
(1954)

The number of investigations conducted in the field
of education is obviously large. An even larger number, having a
direct bearing on education, have been conducted in related fields.
The present chapter attempts to bring to the attention of the student a handful of classic studies of significance to educators; they
should be of interest from the standpoint of both content and
research design.

Space limitations permit the choice of only a few of
the many studies of sufficient significance to warrant discussion
here. The student is urged to check for additional titles in such
sources as the *Encyclopedia of Educational Research,* the *Review of
Educational Research,* the *Education Index* and the various professional journals, and even textbooks in the various areas of educational specialization. It has also been necessary to limit discussion
of the studies listed to a bare orientation—which, in some cases,

may not do them justice. More adequate treatment is to be found in the references cited; the student is strongly urged to consult the original source for a more adequate grasp of the specific nature of the study.

The Wisconsin Studies of Teacher Effectiveness
Arvil S. Barr

On the premise that the quality of the school revolves in a crucial way around the quality of its teachers, Barr in the mid-1920's undertook a series of studies of teacher effectiveness that extended over a period of nearly 40 years to the time of his death in 1962. These are reported in numerous journal articles and monographs, not to mention some 75 doctoral dissertations conducted under his direction at the University of Wisconsin. Some of the earlier studies were based on questionnaires designed to identify the major components and concomitants of teacher effectiveness; a number concentrated on the development and validation of the necessary instruments. A few were experimental, some utilized multiple regression techniques, while others attempted to abstract underlying factors from the results of earlier studies through factor analysis. However, most of the studies were status surveys; the basic approach was a matter of comparing contrasting groups of "good" and "poor" teachers with respect to either personal and behavioral characteristics or the performance of their students. Although based on a variety of data-gathering devices, instruments, and techniques, the underlying theme of this important series of studies was to discover relationships between teacher characteristics and/or behavior and some criterion of teacher effectiveness. The problem is, of course, of prime significance to every aspect of teacher selection, recruitment, preparation, and assignment.

In most studies, certain relationships, generally in line with expectations, were obtained. Although good and poor teachers were found to have many (in fact, most) characteristics in common—e.g., a tendency to dominate classroom communication—there were indications that "good" teachers were superior to their "poor" counterparts in intelligence, knowledge of subject matter, professional orientation, etc. They tended to be more flexible, sociable, and had a better sense of humor. On the other hand, no clear-cut contrasting profile was found, nor was the evidence conclusive or even consistent. Findings in one study were often not substantiated in another. A ten-year follow-up of the groups previously studied, for example, found only negligible correlation between any of the measures used in earlier studies and principals' ratings. In the same way, in one study, raising the minimum grade-point average for graduation from 1.3 to 1.5 would have eliminated 13 of the 24 teachers judged to be of below-average teaching ability. But it would have also eliminated a substantial number of teachers judged average, above-average, and superior.

An analysis of the results suggests that, unfortunately, Barr's extended series of studies did not produce the expected identification of factors crucially and unequivocally predictive of classroom effectiveness as defined on the basis of acceptable criteria of such effectiveness. Nor has subsequent research provided such identification. On second thought, this is not surprising in the light of the complexity of the problem and the tenuous assumptions on which these studies were based.

The study of teacher effectiveness implies that such an entity does indeed exist: it is predicated on the premise that some teachers are good teachers—i.e. "good" with respect to the various aspects of the complex activity called *teaching:* instruction, guidance, cooperation with parents and fellow-teachers, administrative routine, etc. It assumes that some teachers can teach effectively the bright and the dull, the young and the old, boys as well as girls; that they can teach one subject or another with equal competence. It may even suggest that good teachers are born, that they have natural "aptitude" for teaching, say on a par with musical aptitude, which perhaps can be made operational only through training but which is nevertheless the basic ingredient in teaching effectiveness. It suggests, for example, that certain personality patterns, e.g., one characterized by a dominant interest in children, are necessary and, other things being equal, sufficient for good teaching. These assumptions are obviously open to question.

The fact that the teacher performs a variety of services and is different things to different students, makes the choice of the criterion especially troublesome. Two major alternatives present themselves: 1. the product of teaching, namely, pupil growth; and 2. the process of teaching as evaluated through observation, ratings, etc. Unfortunately, besides being relatively inadequate indices of the quality of teaching in all its complexity, these two factors háve proved essentially independent of each other; apparently, they reflect different aspects of teaching.

Earlier attempts at measuring pupil growth were restricted to academic growth as measured through standardized achievement tests. This was gradually expanded to include the more personal goals of education, which introduced the immediate problem that the fundamental outcomes of good education are largely intangible and consequently difficult to measure with existing instruments. Many of the more crucial aspects of pupil growth —e.g., personality—are invariably subject to many influences besides that of the teacher. Results are often delayed, perhaps for years, so that it is difficult to isolate the specific effect a given teacher might have on a given student. In addition, there is the question of the emphasis to be placed on the various objectives of education, especially that the use of different aspects of pupil growth as criteria tends to produce conflicting results. The teacher who is particularly well-organized, precise, articulate, and "effective" in presenting complex subject matter to a class of gifted high school seniors is not necessarily (or even likely) to be equally effective from the standpoint of attitude and character development in a class of average ability. Factor analysis, for example, suggests that "pupil change" is really a composite of "information" and "non-information" change.

What constitutes teaching as a process presents equally complicated problems. That different observers, approaching the teaching act from the perspective of their individual biases, invariably come up with substantially different ratings of the teacher's classroom behavior can be expected; what is more discouraging is the failure of research to identify meaningful overall relationships between what the teacher does and what occurs in students as a consequence. It would seem that a given teacher action is not good or bad in itself but only in the context of the purposes, persons, and situations in relation to which it occurs. The same can be said of teacher characteristics. In short, years of research on the subject has failed to provide conclusive evidence of any real effect of any aspect of teacher characteristics and/or behavior on pupil growth.

The studies as a group are subject to a number of serious questions. 1. There is an obvious danger of circularity: it would be difficult to prevent the extent to which a teacher's characteristics and/or behavior reflect "approved" patterns of what a teacher should be or do from functioning as the basis for both his selection and his confirmation as a good or a poor teacher. 2. The lack of relationship between teacher effectiveness, on the one hand, and teacher intelligence, knowledge of subject matter, etc., on the other, can be accounted for, at least in part, by the restriction of these characteristics which the selection and screening process inherent in any teacher-education program invariably produces. 3. The fact that the raters were relatively untrained supervisors operating from different perspectives and points of reference would probably also tend to minimize the contrast between truly good and truly poor teachers; that inability to maintain classroom discipline constituted an overriding index of teacher ineffectiveness, for example, introduces a new dimension into the comparison.

Other basic difficulties with respect to assumptions and criteria have been mentioned. It does not seem possible, at least at present, to identify traits or behaviors exclusively associated with good and poor teachers; there is much overlapping between good and poor teachers on almost all criteria. It would appear that whatever differences exist are in the realm of contributing, rather than critical, factors. It would also seem logical to expect a number of effective teaching patterns, depending on the particular combination of teacher, students, and situations. Perhaps the best that can be done for the present is to evaluate teachers with respect to specific criteria in well-defined situations.

Undeterred by the relative unproductivity of the early research on teacher effectiveness conducted at Wisconsin and elsewhere (Barr, 1948), educators are now focussing on the classroom itself, presumably on the assumption that the ultimate goal of accelerated pupil growth can be achieved only through the operation of productive patterns of classroom interaction. More specifically, there has been an increased recognition of the classroom as the locus of a complex and dynamic multidirectional system of teacher-pupil and pupil-pupil interaction and of the need, therefore, for the study through direct observation of the various dimensions of its actual day-to-day operation. The task is obviously complex and demanding, necessitating, for example, the development of observational techniques and recording schedules, not to mention the adaptation of statistical procedures for processing the resulting data (see Medley and Mitzel, 1963). It is too soon to appraise the extent to which this new orientation can be expected to provide more positive results than previous efforts, but in the meantime, Barr's systematic investigation of the important problem of teacher effectiveness—by defining what it is not perhaps more than what it is—represents a significant contribution to the advancement of education.

References

Barr, Arvil S. *Characteristic Differences in the Teaching Performance of Good and Poor Teachers of the Social Studies*. Bloomington: Public School Publ. Co., 1929.
———— . "The measurement and prediction of teaching efficiency: A summary of investigations," *J. exper. Educ.*, 16: 203–83; 1948.
———— et al. *Wisconsin Studies for the Measurement and Prediction of Teaching Effectiveness*. Madison: Dembar Publications, 1961.
Biddle, Bruce J. and William J. Ellena. *Contemporary Research on Teacher Effectiveness*. New York: Holt, Rinehart & Winston, 1964.
Flanders, Ned A. *Interaction Analysis in the Classroom*. Minneapolis: Univ. of Minn., 1960.
Medley, Donald M. and Harold E. Mitzel. "Measuring classroom behavior by systematic observation," in N.L. Gage (ed.) *Handbook of Research on Teaching*. Chicago: Rand McNally, 1963. pp. 247–328.
Ryans, David G. *Characteristics of Teachers*. Washington: Amer. Council Educ., 1960.

The Measurement of Intelligence
Alfred Binet

Of particular practical, as well as historical, significance is the well-known derivation of the first intelligence test by Alfred Binet who, in 1904, at the request of the French Ministry of Public Instruction, headed a commission to investigate the problem of retardation in the Paris schools. Realizing the relationship of intelligence to academic progress, he saw the need for a test to identify those so mentally inadequate as to necessitate special care. Devoting himself to the task, Binet, with the help of Simon, published in 1905 what might be considered the first test of general intelligence. This first attempt was revised in 1908 and again in 1911.

Departing from the current emphasis on the measurement of narrow aspects of personality (e.g., rote memory, accuracy of perception, attention span, sensory discrimination, etc.)—which by this time had been shown to be relatively sterile—Binet oriented himself toward measures of general intelligence with particular emphasis on the higher mental processes as displayed in reasoning, imagination, judgment, attention, adaptability, and common sense. Putting together a number of items in rough order of difficulty, he attempted to allocate them to different age levels on the basis of the actual performance of children of different ages. In his 1908 revision, he arranged his items into age levels and coined the term "mental age." In his 1911 revision, which covered age three to the adult level, he attempted to provide a variety of problem situations and to eliminate those items in which the factor of the specific experiences peculiar to any one child might feature too prominently.

Binet-type tests were first introduced in America by Goddard who, in 1908, translated Binet's scale and extended it for use in connection with his work at the Vineland Training School. The most notable of the many revisions of the Binet scale in America is the Stanford revision by Terman (1916) and the later revisions by Terman and Merrill (1937, 1960). Terman also introduced the concept of IQ in his 1916 revision and, of course, incorporated a number of other improvements and extensions. Nevertheless, the various editions of the *Stanford-Binet* are based on essentially the same theoretical conceptions and general arrangement as the original Binet test. The 1937 revision has for years been considered a standby in the area of intelligence testing; the 1960 revision, obtained by combining forms L and M of the 1937 scale, will probably enjoy the same popularity.

Another milestone in the area of the measurement of intelligence is the derivation of the *Army Alpha* and *Army Beta* tests for the classification of soldiers in World War I. The *Army General Classification Test* of World War II is, in a sense, a revision of the *Army Alpha*. In addition, a vast array of group intelligence tests have been devised.

Binet's work is of particular interest in that it broke away from the futile approach to the measurement of intelligence used up to that point and set the pattern which is still the basis of the bulk of current tests of intelligence. The extent of his contribution to the field of education is best appreciated through a survey of the contributions which the measurement of the intelligence of thousands of youngsters the world over permits in terms of better calibration of curricular material and instruction to their level of understanding, more adequate vocational orientation, and the other possibilities which cause modern educators to recognize intelligence tests as an indispensable tool.

References

Binet, Alfred and T.H. Simon. *The Development of Intelligence in Children.* (trans. by E.S. Kite) Baltimore: Williams & Wilkins, 1916.

Terman, Lewis M. and Maud A. Merrill. *Measuring Intelligence.* Boston: Houghton-Mifflin, 1937.

———. *Stanford-Binet Intelligence Scale; Manual for the 3rd revision, Form L-M.* New York: Houghton-Mifflin, 1960.

Yerkes, Robert M. (ed.) *Psychological Examining in the United States Army.* Memoirs National Academy of Science, No. 15, 1921.

Yoakum, Clarence S. and Robert M. Yerkes. *Army Mental Tests.* New York: Holt, Rinehart & Winston, 1920.

The Harvard Growth Studies
Walter F. Dearborn and John W. M. Rothney

The investigation was inaugurated in the fall of 1922 at the Psycho-Educational Clinic of the Harvard Graduate School of Education and continued for 12 years, during the course of which approximately 3500 children entering first-grade in the metropolitan area of Boston were examined annually from the first-grade through adolescence. The study is a comprehensive longitudinal composite of a number of substudies aimed at getting a greater understanding of the general nature of growth or, more specifically, of differences in growth associated with individual variations, age, maturity, sex, and ethnic differences; of the nature of abnormal growth; of the relationship of physical growth to abnormalities in behavior; and of the relationship between mental and physical growth.

The results of the study led to the following conclusions (among others):

1. Physical and mental growth are essentially individual affairs; no two cases are the same; variability rather than consistency in growth is the rule, and comparison with average status has little value in the study of the development of individuals.

2. The relationship between physical measurement and mental

measurement is so low that the knowledge of one does not enable us to predict the other.

3. Prediction of growth at various ages—except for group averages—is extremely hazardous but it is particularly so during the period of adolescence.

4. The rate of development during the pre-pubescent growth spurt bears no significant relationship to learning of school material during this period. The rapid growth at adolescence need no longer be offered as an excuse for the slump in school performance during that period.

5. Classification of individuals into body types cannot be done with any substantial degree of accuracy.

6. The pre-pubescent growth spurt has been discovered to be much more abrupt than cross-sectional studies had led the authors to believe.

7. Average differences between sex, age and ethnic groups are much less important than the individual variations found within each group.

The study has shed considerable light on many aspects of growth during childhood and adolescence. It has probably made its greatest contribution in pointing out the highly individualistic nature of growth and the consequent limitations in the applicability of group norms to the individual.

The authors conducted a companion study of the relationship of anthropological, physical, sociological, psychological, educational, and economic factors to employment among young people. The employment status of 1360 out of a representative sample of 1541 subjects selected from the files of the 12-year growth study just reviewed showed no relationship with chronological age, high school attendance, absence and tardiness from school, school marks, IQ, attitude toward education, skeletal development, anthropological measurements, and other aspects of growth. There was a relationship between employment and schooling beyond high school. The authors point out that, while some of the findings may seem strange on the surface, e.g., the apparent nonsignificance of academic grades and IQ and employment, it must be remembered that these aspects are frequently not appraised as part of the employee-selection procedures. It must also be remembered that the study was conducted in a period of economic depression.

References

Cornell, Ethel L. and Charles M. Armstrong. "Forms of mental growth patterns revealed by reanalysis of the Harvard Growth Data," *Child Developm.*, 26: 169–204; 1955.

Dearborn, Walter F. and John W.M. Rothney. *Scholastic, Economic, and Social Backgrounds of Unemployed Youths.* Cambridge: Harvard Univ. Press, 1938.

_____. *Predicting the Child's Development.* Cambridge: Sci-Art, 1941.

The Eight Year Study of the Progressive Education Association

The Eight Year Study was undertaken for the purpose of obtaining dependable evidence regarding the effect of different patterns of high school education on subsequent college success. It has long been the contention of some educators that, if the control which college entrance requirements have had on the curriculum of the high school were to be abandoned, secondary schools could improve their curricular offerings to the benefit of their students. The opposite viewpoint is that, if these requirements were to be abandoned, chaos would result. The Eight Year Study put these conflicting notions to the test. In 1930, a committee of 26, exploring the possibilities of better articulation between high school and college, became convinced that the high school curriculum was too traditional to meet current student needs. They pointed particularly to the high school's neglect of its responsibility to those students for whom high school constitutes terminal education. They questioned further whether the current curriculum was necessary or even helpful for college success.

The study lasted from 1933 to 1941 during the course of which 30 high schools—both private and public—in various sections of the country that had indicated a willingness to liberalize their graduation requirements were allowed to make whatever changes they felt desirable with the full assurance from some 30 participating colleges and universities that their graduates would be accepted on the recommendation of the principal without reference to the usual Carnegie entrance requirements. The schools were selected on the basis of their willingness to make exploratory curricular changes and the general competence of the staff to make such changes effective. These curricular changes were varied in keeping with local needs and facilities: there is no easy way to describe them except in terms of the desire of the sponsoring school to replace inert subject matter by content more meaningful from the standpoint of the problems of youth in modern civilization.

A commission headed by Herbert E. Hawkes (of Columbia University) investigated the progress in college of the graduates of the liberalized high schools. Since a large majority of the graduates of the high schools had enrolled in 25 colleges, the investigation concerned itself with the 1475 students enrolled therein. Each of these was carefully matched with a student graduating from a traditional curriculum in terms of scholarship, age, sex, race, and home background. The results showed the graduates of the 30 schools to be on par with those of the traditional schools in the fundamentals but to be distinctly superior in ability to reason critically, to apply what they knew, and to integrate their experiences. They also tended to be superior in cooperation, self-confidence, sociability, effectiveness of expression, interests, and creativity—i.e., superior from the standpoint of the functionality of their learnings. Furthermore, the graduates from the schools that had departed most from the traditional curriculum did better than the graduates of those schools which had made lesser changes.

Apparently the students were not handicapped with respect to college achievement by their unorthodox curriculum; on the contrary, departure from the traditional curriculum seemed to improve rather than to lessen their chances of success. The study also pointed to the wisdom of relying on the judgment of the secondary school as to what constitutes adequate preparation for college. The study is particularly noted for the ingenuity and the comprehensiveness of the instruments which were devised by the evaluative committee under the direction of Ralph Tyler for the purpose of evaluating student progress. A similar series of studies was conducted by Wrightstone who compared traditional and "experimental" school practices in New York City. Using a matched-pair design over a six-year period, he also found the comparisons to favor the experimental group in all cases, particularly from the standpoint of social adequacy and critical thinking. Yet, despite the findings of these two studies, most colleges still subscribe to the traditional Carnegie unit entrance requirements. It might be a profitable exercise to relate the findings of this study to that of the Learned and Wood study of Pennsylvania high schools and colleges to be discussed later in the chapter.

References

Aikin, Wilford M. *The Story of the Eight Year Study.* New York: Harper & Row, 1942.

American Education Fellowship (Progressive Education Association). *Thirty Schools Tell Their Story.* Adventures in American Education Series, Vol. 5. New York: Harper & Row, 1943.

Chamberlain, Charles D. et al. *Did They Succeed in College?* New York: Harper & Row, 1942.

Giles, Harry H. et al. *Exploring the Curriculum.* New York: Harper & Row, 1942.

Smith, Eugene R. and Ralph W. Tyler. *Appraising and Recording Student Progress.* New York: Harper & Row, 1942.

Wrightstone, J. Wayne. *Appraisal of Newer Practices in Selected Public Schools.* New York: T. C., Columbia Univ., 1935.

——— . *Appraisal of Experimental High School Practices.* New York: T. C., Columbia Univ., 1936.

——— . *Appraisal of Newer Elementary School Practices.* New York: T. C., Columbia Univ., 1938.

Project Talent
John C. Flanagan

Project Talent, a longitudinal study still in progress, is an attempt to make a national inventory of the aptitudes and abilities among the boys and girls in the nation's secondary schools and to relate these aptitudes and abilities to their later adjustment as adults. The project is conducted jointly by the University of Pittsburgh and the American Institute for Research supported by funds from the U.S. Office of Education with assistance from the National Institute of Mental Health, the Office of Naval Research, and the National Science Foundation.

In March, 1960, a stratified sample of 440,000 students in 1353 secondary schools in all parts of the country were given a two-day battery of tests covering such areas as common information, English, reading comprehension, memory for words and sentences, arithmetic computation, arithmetic reasoning, creativity, etc. Also obtained was information on the student's background and plans, including his experiences, his study habits, and his family. In addition, an attempt was made to determine his interest in various occupations and activities. Detailed information was also collected concerning the guidance and counseling programs, the type of curriculum, and the various educational practices of the schools of the nation, with a view to determining what may be expected from students currently attending high schools. Follow-up studies of the original sample are to be made one, five, ten, and twenty years after graduation from high school and this information related to the data collected in 1960. (The one-year follow-ups are now completed; the five-year follow-up studies are currently under way.)

The goal of the study is to provide information that will promote improved educational practices and policies and thus educational experiences which will lead students toward a realization of their full potential. It is realized that there are too many youngsters with special talents and a great deal of promise who never develop these talents. It is the purpose of the project to identify these latent potentialities so as to enable young people to make better use of their particular patterns of aptitude; it is hoped that the study will contribute to the improvement of the whole process of identifying, developing, and utilizing the talents of the nation's youth. The project probably represents the most comprehensive educational survey of all times; the feasibility of the study is, of course, a tribute to modern electronics, without which the conduct of a study of such magnitude would obviously have been out of the question. Of particular significance—as harbinger of the future—is the data bank feature of the project; the vast quantity of data collected in connection with the project not only provide for multiple analyses within the project but are also being made available to other investigators for projects of their own.

Of a somewhat complementary nature is the Career Planning Study conducted under the direction of Donald E. Super in an attempt to conceptualize the process of vocational development. This is a longitudinal study concerned with the various aspects of vocational development with particular reference to the vocational implications and manifestations of the self-concept. It places major emphasis on the clarification of the process through which the life stages, developmental tasks, attitudes, and vocationally exploratory behavior eventually lead to vocational maturity and adjustment.

References

Flanagan, John C. *Project Talent: 1. Design for the Study of American Youth.* New York: Houghton-Mifflin, 1962.

————— et al. *The Identification, Development, and Utilization of Human Talents: The American High-School Student.* C.R.P., No. 635. Pittsburgh: Project Talent Office, Univ. of Pittsburgh, 1964.

—————. *The Project Talent Data Bank.* Pittsburgh: Project Talent Office, Univ. of Pittsburgh, 1965.

Orr, David B. "Project Talent: A national inventory of aptitudes and abilities," *Phi Delta Kappan,* 42: 237–43; 1961.

Schoenfeldt, Lyle F. *A National Data Resource for Behavioral, Social, and Educational Research.* Palo Alto: Amer. Inst. Res., 1968.

Shayloft, Marion F. *The High School Years: Growth in Cognitive Skills.* Pittsburgh: Amer. Inst. Res., 1967.

Super, Donald E. and Phoebe L. Overstreet. *The Vocational Maturity of Ninth-Grade Boys.* Career Pattern Study, Monogr., No. 2. New York: T. C., Columbia Univ., 1960.

————— et al. *Career Development: Self-Concept Theory.* New York: Coll. Entrance Examination Boards, 1963.

Genetic Studies
Arnold Gesell

Gesell's work extends over a half-century from the time he entered the Yale Clinic of Child Development in 1911 to his death in 1961, during the course of which 25 publications have appeared under his authorship and that of his associates. His investigations, sponsored under grants from the Rockefeller and Carnegie Foundations, cover all aspects of the development of motor and physical status, emotional expression, philosophic outlook, adaptive behavior, language, interpersonal relationships, and personal-social behavior during the period from infancy to age sixteen.

These investigations are reported in three major publications: 1. *The First Five Years of Life* (1940); 2. *The Child from Five to Ten* (1946); and 3. *Youth: The Years from Ten to Sixteen* (1956), each a longitudinal study of essentially the same children. The children in the first study were observed at 4, 16, 28, 40, 52, and 80 weeks and at 2, 3, 4, and 5 years. The subjects of the second investigation were examined at 5, 5½, 6, 7, 8, 9, and 10; many of these children had attended the nursery of the clinic and had been experimental subjects for some previous studies. His findings are reported in detailed description of growth patterns and norms of physical, mental, and personal-social development.

Gesell's emphasis has been consistently on the maturational aspects to the corresponding underestimation of the role of environmental factors in development. More specifically, he has operated on the premise of the relative immutability of basic developmental patterns, so that at a given age a child does this, at the next age level he does that, all on an essentially fixed maturational schedule somewhat analogous to Piaget's "stages" of development. This position Gesell has maintained in the face of the trend of the 1920's toward environmentalism sponsored by Watson, whose claims Gesell countered by showing that helping one twin achieve certain skills in advance of normal development gave him only temporary advantage; the other twin caught up "naturally" when the necessary maturation was attained. Gesell's position gave birth to the strong belief of the past few decades in the futility of early training and has provided the foundation for a number of rather pessimistic and apparently erroneous educational policies and practices concerning admission to first grade, the introduction of beginning reading, and other similar curricular and pedagogic issues (see Ausubel). His position is, of course, in substantial opposition to that of modern psychologists who see the environment, particularly in early years, as crucial to development and is gradually giving way to a more positive view of "ability" and "readiness" as the product of prior experience.

Gesell's studies have also been criticized for failure to use unselected populations. His subjects were in the main from the upper socio-economic and cultural strata, representing the more stable families in New Haven, Connecticut, and its suburbs. (The average IQ of his sample for his report on youth, for example, was in the neighborhood of 117.) His findings, therefore, have to be considered in the light of the rather convincing evidence of a differential developmental pattern for people of different socio-economic levels.

Nevertheless, Gesell's work constitutes a major contribution to the understanding of the child and his development. From the standpoint of research, his studies represent the type of systematic, programed research—involving an extensive staff of trained observers using a multiple approach of standardized tests, sequential examinations, clinical interviews, and observations supplemented by movie cameras, one-way screens, and other modern means—necessary for productive research and for the progress of education as a science.

References

Ausubel, David P. "Viewpoints from related disciplines; Human growth and development," *T. C. Rec.,* 60: 245-54; 1959.

Flavell, John H. *The Developmental Psychology of Jean Piaget.* Princeton: Van Nostrand, 1963.

Gesell, Arnold. *Infancy and Human Growth.* New York: Macmillan, 1928.

———. *The First Five Years of Life.* New York: Harper & Row, 1940.

——— and Ellen Thompson. *Learning and Growth in Identical Twin Infants.* Genet. Psychol. Monogr. 6, No. 1, 1929.

———. *Infant Behavior.* New York: McGraw-Hill, 1934.

——— and Frances L. Ilg. *The Child from Five to Ten.* New York: Harper & Row, 1946.

——— et al. *Youth: The Years from Ten to Sixteen.* New York: Harper & Row, 1956.

Ilg, Frances and Louise B. Ames. *The Gesell Institute of Child Behavior.* New York: Bell, 1955.

New York Times Magazine. "Giant in the nursery—Jean Piaget," *New York Times Magazine,* May 26, 1968, pp. 25-27, 50-54, 59, 62, 77-80.

The Character Education Inquiry
Hugh Hartshorne and Mark A. May

The Character Education Inquiry was undertaken in 1924 under the auspices of the Religious Education Association in an attempt to evaluate the results of moral education. The investigation had two major purposes: the study of deception and the development of instruments to appraise moral knowledge and attitude. It is reported in three volumes: 1. *Studies in Deceit* (1928); 2. *Studies in Service and Self-Control* (1929); and 3. *Studies in the Organization of Character* (1930), the best-known of which is the first. Originally planned for a three-year period, it was extended to five years, a considerable portion of which was spent in the development of the necessary instruments and procedures.

In the study of deceit over 10,000 students from both public and private schools from grades one through twelve and from all varieties of socio-economic, cultural, ethnic, intellectual, occupational, community, and religious backgrounds were placed in semi-laboratory situations where they could cheat, lie, steal—or refrain from so doing. These situations were kept as natural as possible in order to appraise the self and its integration with group standards and expectations, i.e., in order to see the individual under conditions of normal social interaction. Twenty-nine test situations, many of considerable ingenuity, were devised to measure the extent of deceit. Twenty-two of these "deception tests" involved ordinary classroom situations: four took place in an athletic setting, two at parties, and one involved work done at home. There were also two "lying" and two "stealing" tests. It was hoped that these tests would provide a relatively complete picture of the individual's tendencies to deceive.

The results revealed that children engage in a considerable amount of deceit and, further, that deceit is associated with such personal traits as dullness, retardation, emotional instability, low academic achievement, socio-economic and cultural limitations, certain national, racial, and religious groupings, disciplinary problems in school, and attendance at movies. The investigation suggested, for example, that deception runs in families in much the same way as, say, intelligence. This simply implies concomitance; in no way is there an implication of causation or inheritance. Deception seems to be affected by social interaction; the behavior of close friends and associates was a more basic indicator of a child's tendency to cheat than were his associations with adults. Deception in school was at a minimum when the classroom atmosphere was one of high morale and of goodwill and cooperation between teacher and pupils. Attendance at Sunday School or membership in scouting and other clubs oriented toward the teaching of integrity and honesty did not seem to have much, if any, influence; these children actually appeared less honest than average.

It was found that children were not consistent in their behavior; a child might be honest under one set of circumstances but not necessarily under another. The findings seemed to point to honesty as a conglomeration of specific acts governed largely by the specific situation in which the child found himself. Generally, the most common extraneous motive leading to cheating was a desire to do well in class. On this basis, it would seem that the social control of deceit is best approached through manipulating the situation in such a way as to make deceit unnecessary. This generalization runs counter to the integrative and directive nature of the self-concept as presented by Combs and Snygg and appears illogical from a psychological point of view, in that it makes the individual's behavior essentially haphazard, chaotic, and otherwise situational rather than organismic. Such a conception of character is undoubtedly oversimplified and misleading (see Mouly, 1968).

The authors acknowledge that they had measured deceit (or conduct) rather than character, i.e., that the tests used were measures of deception, helpfulness, cooperation, inhibition, and persistence, all of which are aspects of behavior which comprise character only when they are integrated into a functional entity. The inquiry constitutes a pioneer study in an important area; the findings have obvious implications for character education as sponsored both by the public schools and by specialized agencies such as the churches, youth agencies, and parochial schools. To the extent that the school accepts character formation as a major goal, it must be concerned with the effectiveness of its efforts in this direction. The findings also have broad sociological implications. The study is of particular interest from the standpoint of the conclusions presented by Jacob (1957) that four years of college has practically no influence on the value-structure of college students, except to make them more self-centered, more self-serving, and more prone to conform to the prevailing profile.

References

Combs, Arthur W. and Donald Snygg. *Individual Behavior.* New York: Harper & Row, 1959.

Hartshorne, Hugh. "Sociological implications of the Character Education Inquiry," *Amer. J. Sociol.,* 36: 251–62; 1930.

———— and Mark A. May. 1. *Studies in Deceit* (1928); 2. *Studies in Service and Self-Control* (1929); and 3. *Studies in the Organization of Character* (1930). New York: Macmillan.

————. "Recent improvements in devices for rating character," *J. soc. Psychol.,* 1: 66–77; 1930.

Jacob, Philip E. *Changing Values in College.* New York: Harper & Row, 1957.

Mouly, George J. *Psychology for Effective Teaching.* New York: Holt, Rinehart & Winston, 1968. pp. 103–05.

The Hawthorne Studies
Harvard School of Business

This well-known classic consists of a series of studies conducted at the Hawthorne plant (Chicago) of Western Electric Company, the manufacturer of telephone equipment for American Telephone and Telegraph Company. Originally designed as a one-year study of the effects of fatigue and monotony on worker output, the investigation has now become part of the company's standard program of operations research. The major report, published in 1939, covers the first twelve years of the study.

The results of the various substudies reveal a pattern of increase in worker productivity attending almost any and all changes in working conditions. In their study of illumination, for example, in which the production of four groups of supervisors, coil winders, and relay assemblers was compared under four different lighting conditions, output increased with an increase in lighting, but it also increased when the illumination was brought back to its original level and even when it was reduced to a mere three foot-candles. In fact, two girls who volunteered to work under lighting equivalent to that of ordinary moonlight were as efficient, reported no eyestrain, and showed less fatigue than when working under more normal lighting. Output also increased when light bulbs were simply exchanged for other bulbs of the same wattage after the workers had been led to believe that a change in light intensity was being made.

In order to exert greater control over the situation, the investigators separated five girls assembling relays from the regular working force and placed them in a special test room where changes could be made without disturbing the operation of the rest of the plant. A major part of the investigation concerned the output of this group under a series of experimental conditions relating to lighting, rest pauses, length of workday and workweek, wages and pay incentives, and other aspects of their working conditions. Production increased in nearly all cases, the increase reaching a maximum of about 30 percent above pre-experimental standards. It rose, for example, when the workweek was shortened and when rest pauses were introduced, and it rose again when both factors were returned to their original level.

The results suggest that social factors connected with the experimental changes—rather than the changes themselves—were responsible for the increase in output. A major feature of the study was the special status which the girls enjoyed. Their advice and reactions concerning the changes to be made in their working conditions were sought by no less than the plant superintendent, they were made to feel that the management was interested in their welfare, and they were given both special attention and special privileges. It seems that the increased output resulted not so much from the improved lighting or the rest pauses as from the feeling of status and morale.

The most significant aspect of the various changes that took place in the test room was the social transformation of the girls. There was not only a considerable increase in the morale and cohesiveness of the group but both grievances and absenteeism decreased sharply. As a result of the findings of the study, the study shifted from a consideration of the influence of the physical aspects of the working situation to an investigation of the more subtle and intangible factors of the psychology of personal and social adjustment in an industrial setting. A mass interviewing program in which over 200,000 interviews were held with employees of the plant bore out the investigators' premise that the employee's social status in his work group is a major cause of employee concern and complaint. The size and location of his desk or work position, for example, constitutes a status symbol frequently of greater concern to him than his salary.

Another phase of the study revealed that it is the standards of production of the group, rather than personal goals, that determine employee performance. Even with incentive pay, individual and group output is, to a large extent, dictated by the worker's fear of being a "rate buster" if he turns out too much, a "chiseler" if he turns out too little, and, of course, a "squealer" if he reports his fellow-workers. These considerations set definite limits to the individual's production performance and even his personal relations with "management." Furthermore, his need for group acceptance and status forces him to give group standards precedence over the more tangible company-employee relationships.

The studies are liable to certain criticism: for example, the investigation revolved around a very small group of volunteers and/or specially selected individuals. In fact, two of the five girls in the original test room situation were replaced because their low production created friction with the other three. Nevertheless, the investigation has made a significant contribution to our understanding of the complexity of the human relations problem in industrial production. More specifically, it has pointed out that wages, hours of work, working conditions, and the other aspects of the working situation are primarily symbols of social values concerning the individual's position or status among his immediate fellow-workers and in the company as a whole. It has shown that the worker's attitudes are basic determinants of production, affecting both individual and group effort, and, although many of his attitudes are perhaps irrational, an understanding—and where necessary, a reorientation—of these attitudes is essential to effective employee management. The study represents an honest and concerted effort to understand workers as individuals; it makes industrial efficiency no longer a mechanistic problem in engineering but rather one of personal and group dynamics. The study has undoubtedly had considerable influence in the evolvement of the pattern of modern industrial management-employee relationships. It has helped to introduce a new concept of "industrial psychology" with emphasis on leadership, democratic supervision, and human relations. Although conducted in an industrial rather than an academic setting, the investigation has direct bearing on classroom performance at both the individual and the group level. The modern emphasis in education on motivation, attitudes, and group dynamics is consistent with the findings of this study. More pertinent from the standpoint of the present text is the vitiating influence which the Hawthorne effect often has on the validity of experimental findings (see Cook, 1962).

References

Cook, Desmond L. "The Hawthorne effect in educational research," *Phi Delta Kappan*, 44: 116–22; 1962.

Mayo, E. *The Human Problems of an Industrial Civilization*. New York: Macmillan, 1933.

Roethlisberger, F.J. *Management and Morale*. Cambridge: Harv. Univ. Press, 1941.

—— and William J. Dickson. *Management and the Worker*. Cambridge: Harv. Univ. Press, 1939.

The Student and His Knowledge
William S. Learned and Ben D. Wood

This study, conducted in Pennsylvania as part of a sequence of inquiries financed by the Carnegie Corporation, placed primary emphasis on knowledge, with an underlying hope of ending the rule of the college credit as the measure of academic adequacy and status. While realizing the importance of such supplementary traits as character, attitude, and social efficiency, the authors operated on the premise that the basic criterion of college acceptability and college progress is still knowledge, or more specifically, permanent and available knowledge which is sufficiently defined and digested that it is readily available when needed so that it can serve as the basis for producing more advanced knowledge.

Three successive examinations were given as part of a comprehensive testing program involving 50,000 high school and college students: 1. the testing of high school seniors in 1928; 2. the testing of the same group at the end of the sophomore year (1930); and 3. a third testing of the same group in their senior year in college (1932). The tests used were devised especially for the inquiry and involved such phases as English, mathematics, history and social studies, and natural sciences. The examination, a copy of which is available in the appendix of the text, required twelve hours of testing at the senior high school level and eight hours for the college groups.

The most significant aspect of the findings was the great variability in performance among the participants—first, a great variation among the institutions, and a "much more striking" variation among the students of any one institution. In one phase of the study, tests were given to 5747 college sophomores attending 49 different institutions, to 3720 seniors, and to 1503 high school seniors. From the many significant comparisons presented, the authors point out that school status, as defined by the time spent and the courses passed in high school or college, has little relationship to any definite body of ideas, understood and available as a result of "education." The results showed that 28 percent of the college seniors did less well on the test than the average sophomore and that nearly 10 percent did less well than the average high school senior; conversely, 22 percent of the high school seniors surpassed the average college sophomore and 10 percent of the high school seniors surpassed the average college senior. Stated differently, the scores among sophomores ranged all the way from what might be considered inferior high school achievement to excellence that is attained only by the best ten percent of college seniors—in fact, the authors point out, performance that is perhaps above the average of faculty groups "if our experience on the earlier examination (1928) may be trusted."

The authors further point out that, instead of graduating seniors simply on the grounds that they have been on campus four years and have accumulated the required number of credits, if graduation had been based on knowledge as revealed by test performance, the graduating class of 1932 would have consisted of the top 28 percent of the seniors, the top 21 percent of the juniors, the top 19 percent of the sophomores, and the top 15 percent of the freshmen. These hypothetical graduates would have been head and shoulders in knowledge over the class of seniors that did graduate and, of course, nearly three years younger. It is particularly significant to note that, of the freshmen who qualified for this hypothetical graduating class, only two-thirds were still in attendance at the sophomore level and that two-thirds of those actually tested lower than they had tested as freshmen. This, the authors interpret as evidence that, as presently organized, courses lead to the accumulation of college credits rather than the accumulation of knowledge. In the high school study (1928) covering over 26,000 high school seniors, 25 percent of the non-college-preparatory students scored above the average of the college-bound group and vice versa.

A phase of the investigation concerned the comparison of the test performance of college seniors planning to teach with that of high school seniors. As might be expected, there was a substantial overlap between the two distributions not only in knowledge of subject matter but even in basic vocabulary. An even more pointed comparison showed 50 percent of the high school students specializing in science to have a higher science score than nearly 40 percent of the college seniors planning to teach science; conversely, 17 percent of the teacher specialists had lower scores than 31 percent of the corresponding high school students. In other words, many high school students actually surpassed their prospective teachers with respect to knowledge in their own field of specialization.

The authors interpret the results as indicative of the unsuitability of the present college curricular organization, where the goal is the passing of examinations and the accumulation of credits tied to specific courses, rather than to the accumulation of knowledge from broad and varied sources. They present a number of recommendations which need to be read in the original in order to be appreciated.

The study is, of course, dated; yet a repetition would, undoubtedly, reveal essentially the same conditions prevailing today. Whether this represents a lamentable condition, as Learned and Wood imply, and whether college credits and degrees should be awarded on the basis of academic competence, however acquired, is a question of educational philosophy and beyond the scope of research per se.

Reference

Learned, William S. and Ben D. Wood. *The Student and His Knowledge.* New York: Carnegie Foundation, 1938.

Patterns of Aggressive Behavior in Experimentally Created Social Climates
Kurt Lewin

This is a report of a number of experiments in group dynamics conducted in the Child Welfare Research Station of the State University of Iowa. In one of the experiments, Lippitt organized two clubs of ten-year-old boys engaged in making masks; one of the clubs was governed in an autocratic, authoritarian manner while the other operated on a democratic basis. In a second experiment by White and Lippitt, four new clubs of ten-year-old boys engaged in mask-making, mural painting, soap-carving, model airplane construction, etc., were organized on a voluntary basis, each under a different type of adult leadership: one group was governed democratically, the second had an autocratic leader, the third operated on a laissez-faire basis. Every six weeks, the groups changed leadership so that each of the groups had three different leaders in a five-month period. The groups were equated with respect to teacher ratings on such items as socio-economic background, social behavior, leadership potential, interpersonal relations, intellectual status, physical status, and other personality characteristics. There were eleven meetings of each group: the democratic group met first and engaged in activities of its own choosing. In order to maintain equivalence of the tasks, the autocratic group at its meetings two days later was assigned the activities which the democratic group had selected. The laissez-faire group was simply left on its own.

In the autocratic group, the policy was determined by the leader and each step—what should be done, by whom, with whom—was assigned one at a time so that future steps were always uncertain to a large degree. In general, the leader was aloof and impersonal rather than unfriendly. In the democratic group, all policies were determined by group discussion, encouraged and assisted by the adult leader. The laissez-faire group was given complete freedom for group and individual decision; the materials were supplied but the leader made it clear that he would provide information only when asked. He did not participate actively in any of the activities. It should be noted, however, that even in the autocratic group, participation was voluntary and the atmosphere was basically congenial.

As the meetings progressed, the authoritarian club members developed a pattern of aggressive domination toward one another, while their relationship to the leader became one of greater submission or of persistent demands for attention. The authoritarian group was significantly more aggressive and hostile than the democratic group. Not only was there scapegoating but two of the members ceased coming to the meetings. Interviews with the boys also showed complete agreement on the relative dislike of the autocratic leader, regardless of who he was. The aggressive pattern was even stronger in the laissez-faire group; this is probably best explained on the basis that the freer atmosphere permitted aggressiveness to be shown. Aggressiveness was frequently controlled and suppressed in the autocratic group when the leader was present; it showed itself, however, when he was absent. It also seems that autocratic control promotes apathy, and the autocratic group was found to be rather dull, lifeless, submissive and repressed; there was little joking, smiling, freedom of movement, or initiation of projects. In the second experiment, four of the five autocratic groups became rather apathetic and nonaggressive but apparently still hostile as revealed by aggressiveness toward one another when the leader left the room, by the general absence of smiling and joking, and by the boys' expressed dislike for the autocratic leader.

The democratic atmosphere, on the other hand, produced more constructive suggestions, more frequent matter-of-fact member-to-member behavior, greater individuality, and greater cooperation. The democratic group was more spontaneous and friendly; it was characterized by a great deal of "we-feeling" as opposed to the "I-feeling" found in the autocratic group.

It is also interesting to note that each of the two children who were switched from one group to another took on the characteristics of the group to which he was transferred. Likewise, as the groups were changed from autocratic to democratic leadership, the members assumed the behavior pattern characteristics of the group to which they were assigned. It did, however, take somewhat longer for the autocratic group to adjust to democratic procedures than for the democratic group to adjust to autocratic control, suggesting that, whereas autocracy is imposed on the individual, democracy has to be learned. It appears illogical to assume that, if left alone, individuals will form themselves naturally into democratic groups; chaos or a primitive pattern of organization through autocratic domination by a few members is a more likely outcome.

Whereas the study was not conducted in a classroom setting, it has very definite educational implications. Lewin concluded that the social climate in which a child lives is as important as the air he breathes and that the group to which he belongs has an all-important meaning in terms of his security. He points out further that the success a teacher is likely to have in a classroom depends not only on his skills but to a great extent on the classroom atmosphere he creates. This may be even more so in the intangible aspects of education. However, it must be recognized that the democracy and autocracy which Lewin discusses are rather extreme forms of what one might actually find in the field. It might be well to explore the possibilities of conducting a similar experiment under more normal conditions of a "standard" academic setting.

References

Lewin, Kurt. "Experiments in social space," *Harv. educ. Rev.*, 9: 21–32; 1939.
———. "The dynamics of group action," *Educ. Lead.*, 1: 195–200; 1943.
——— et al. "Pattern of aggressive behavior in experimentally created social climates," *J. soc. Psychol.*, 10: 271–99; 1939.
Lippitt, Ronald. *An Experimental Study of the Effects of Democratic and Autocratic Group Atmospheres*. Studies in Topological and Vector Psychologies, No. 1. Iowa City: Univ. Iowa Press, 1940.

The Quality of Group Decisions as Influenced by the Discussion Leader
Norman R.F. Maier

Research has shown that a decision which is arrived at collectively is more acceptable to the group than one which is imposed on it by someone in authority. It is also possible that group thinking may be superior to that of the individual since the thinking of a number of individuals is combined in a group decision. On the other hand, it must be recognized that the supervisor or leader is very frequently more informed and that he can, therefore, make a valuable contribution to the group's thinking. The question arises as to whether it is better for him to refrain from participating in order to ensure that the group will implement whatever decision it has reached. More precisely, the question is whether the leader can make his contribution to the group without incurring group resistance to the implementation of his ideas.

The study consisted of presenting a group of college students with the problem situation of an industrial assembly line in which production was being delayed by one of the men who was not as competent as his fellow-workers. In one of the experiments, the leader, who was well-versed in democratic processes and personality dynamics, restricted his contributions to summarizing, encouraging, analyzing, interpreting, supplying information, and preventing hurt feelings. He did suggest alternatives in the way he asked the questions and in his wording of the suggestions of others, but he did not make the solution obvious. In a second experiment, each of the subjects of the study took the place of one of the workers on the assembly line. The third experiment involved the use of untrained leaders who were merely given preliminary training as to procedures to be followed, the nature of the problem, and what might constitute an adequate solution. A control group discussed the problem without a discussion leader.

The results indicated that a group leader can greatly improve the quality of the group's thinking; in fact, the competence of the leader in a general sense determines the quality of the decision that is reached. More importantly, a leader who is skilled and who has ideas can also attain a higher degree of acceptance than a less skilled person. In fact, the quality of the decision which can be reached under skilled leadership very frequently increases the acceptability of the solution. However, even an unskilled leader, relying on basic democratic conference procedures, can apparently promote both decisions of quality and a high level of group acceptance of the decisions—suggesting that a leader who has ability in solving technical problems need not sacrifice his ability in order to maintain group goodwill. It must, of course, be recognized that a great deal depends upon the rapport the leader is able to establish with the group. It must also be noted that in this study even the untrained leader had the "correct" solution to the problem; this ideal situation may not prevail in an actual setting.

The study should be of interest to educators who, in a major sense, operate as classroom leaders. This would be even more important with the present emphasis on the problem-solving approach. Further, inasmuch as the teacher is likely to be an informed leader, his contributions to the classroom discussion, provided he operates in an atmosphere of cooperation, can probably lead to superior solutions without incurring the danger of resistance to their implementation.

Reference

Maier, Norman R.F. "The quality of group decisions as influenced by the discussion leader," *Hum. Rel.*, 3: 155–74; 1950.

Cooperation and Competition: An Experimental Study in Motivation
J. Bernard Maller

A study of considerable interest to educators in view of the importance of motivation in classroom performance is Maller's comparison of the relative motivational force of cooperation and competition. The study attempted to compare the performance in simple addition of children under conditions of 1. cooperation (self-motivation, i.e., appeal to desire for personal gain) and 2. competition (group motivation, i.e., appeal to desire for group gain). A secondary purpose was to discover the concomitant factors associated with either tendency. The major part of the study consists of three basic experiments involving 814 children in Grades 5 through 8 in four schools of different socio-economic status. The overall study involved 1530 children from ten different schools.

The first experiment compared pupil performance in twelve sessions of work, in six of which each child worked under conditions of competition and the remaining six under conditions of cooperation. A control group worked under no particular incentive. The results favored competition over cooperation and both competition and cooperation over the control situation. These differences were statistically significant; furthermore, the superiority of performance under conditions of competition over that under cooperation increased with the practice sessions. The greater motivational force of competition over cooperation tended to be more pronounced among girls than boys. On the other hand, about one-third of the students performed better under conditions of cooperation. In the second experiment, each child was allowed to choose whether he would work for himself or for the group. The subjects chose to work for themselves in three-quarters of the trials, and their performance also favored competition. Once again, certain children reversed the trend in performance.

With respect to the second purpose of the investigation, namely, to identify the traits associated with competitiveness and cooperation, Maller compared the 200 most cooperative and the 200 most competitive members of his overall group. The results were essentially negative: competitiveness and cooperation appeared to be relatively independent of sex, age, scholastic standing, health, nationality, etc. Cooperation was found to be slightly correlated with intelligence, moral knowledge, and resistance to suggestion.

In the third experiment, competition as an incentive was compared with various forms of cooperation: teamwork (teams chosen by captains), partnership (cooperation in pairs), boys versus girls, arbitrary grouping (class divided arbitrarily into two groups by the experimenter), and overall grouping of the class as a whole. Once again, pupil performance favored competition on an overall basis, although performance under conditions of competition was found to be inferior to that motivated through boys-versus-girls cooperation.

It is to be noted that Maller's design in the second experiment places cooperation in a setting of competition, i.e., he defines cooperation in terms of members cooperating as a group in order to compete more advantageously against another group. The superiority of cooperation over competition under conditions of sex rivalry (boys versus girls) must be considered in that light. He did not compare competition against cooperation with the latter devoid of obvious competition. Nor did he consider the factor of group cohesiveness. Also to be noted is the fact that the task which he imposed is hardly a group activity in which individual success is dependent on group cooperation. Furthermore, the study pertains to American children whose upbringing is possibly more competitive than that of certain other national groups. His results may also be a function of the age level. Maller suggests that the lack of practice in working with a group for a common goal precludes the formation of habits of cooperation and group loyalty, a possibility which may have been somewhat more true in the 1920's than it is of the present organization of the school. Thus, it might be desirable to repeat the study. Nevertheless, despite its possible limitations, Maller's study has interesting implications for our society and for the school, whose current orientation is still essentially competitive.

References

Deutsch, Morton. "A theory of cooperation and competition," *Hum. Rel.*, 2: 129–52; 1949.

Maller, J. Bernard. *Cooperation and Competition: An Experimental Study in Motivation*. T. C. Contributions to Education, No. 384. New York: Columbia Univ., 1929.

May, Mark A. et al. *Memorandum on Research in Competition and Cooperation*. Bull. No. 25. New York: Soc. Sci. Res. Council, 1937.

When Should Children Begin To Read?
Mabel V. Morphett and Carleton Washburne

This well-known study of the relationship between the reading of first-graders and their level of mental development was based on the total 1928–29 first-grade enrollment of the Winnetka (Illinois) public schools ($n = 141$). Beginning first graders were tested for intelligence by means of the *Stanford-Binet* and the *Detroit First-Grade Intelligence Test* and for reading proficiency by sight-word lists and the *Gray Standardized Oral Reading Check*. All eight of the Winnetka first-grade teachers cooperated in the study without knowledge of the mental age of their pupils. The results showed that, when the Detroit test was used as the basis for determining intellectual status, the children who had an MA of six years and six months made far greater progress than did those who were less mentally mature and made almost as satisfactory progress as did children of a higher mental age. When measured with respect to the *Stanford-Binet*, the children with an MA of six years and six months again made better progress in reading than did those of lesser mental maturity; they, however, made somewhat less satisfactory progress than did those of greater mental ages. A repetition of the experiment in 1929–30 with different teachers and different children confirmed the earlier experiments in all their basic conclusions.

The study is frequently cited in support of the position that it takes a mental age of six years and six months in order to learn to read, as reading is taught in our schools today. It is felt that having such a mental age decreases the likelihood of failure and discouragement attending the child's attempt to read when he is not "ready" and that, correspondingly, it increases the effectiveness of the school.

The study should be related to that of Gates conducted some eight years later in which he attempted to determine the optimum mental age at which reading should be introduced. In contradiction to the findings of Morphett and Washburne, Gates pointed out that the crucial mental age for reading varies with the material and the type of teaching; the mental age that is required for learning to read under one program or with one method may be entirely different from that required under other circumstances. The fact that children with a mental age of five years could be taught to read with essentially the same proficiency as normally found in first-grade led Gates to conclude that, within limits, there is no mental age that can be set as minimum, or even optimum, for beginning reading.

Skinner's success in training pigeons—or even more pertinently, Moore's success in teaching two- and three-year-olds to read—suggests that often it is not the difficulty of the learning task that overtaxes the child's ability but rather the rigidity of the adult thought-mold in which it is presented. According to the modern psychological concept of "learning sets," it would seem that previous development in visual and auditory discrimination is a more crucial determinant of reading readiness than mental age per se, and further, that this development is primarily a function of previous experience (see Mouly, 1968: 148 ff). Tyler (1964) goes one step further and suggests that: "Mental age does not seem to be a particularly useful index of readiness for whatever activity, practice, or skill we are planning to teach." Unfortunately, despite arguments and evidence against these "fixed maturation" premises, the notion of the immutability of maturation too frequently continues as the basis for educational decisions and policies (see Gesell, previously reviewed).

References

Ausubel, David P. "Viewpoints from related disciplines: Human growth and development," *T. C. Rec.*, 60: 245–54; 1959.

Gates, Arthur I. "The necessary mental age for beginning reading," *Elem. Sch. J.*, 37: 497–508; 1937.

Moore, Omar K. *Autoelic Responsive Environments and Exceptional Children.* Hamden (Conn.): Responsive Environment Foundation, 1963.

Morphett, Mabel V. and Carleton Washburne. "When should children begin to read?" *Elem. Sch. J.*, 31: 496–503; 1931.

Mouly, George J. *Psychology for Effective Teaching.* New York: Holt, Rinehart and Winston, 1968.

Skinner, B.F. "An operant analysis of problem solving," in B. Kleinmuntz (ed.) *Problem Solving: Research Methods and Theory.* New York: Wiley, 1966. pp. 225–57.

Tyler, F.T. "Issues related to readiness to learn," in E.R. Hilgard (ed.) *Theories of Learning and Instruction.* 63rd Yrbk., N.S.S.E., Pt. I. Chicago: Univ. Chicago Press, 1964. pp. 210–39.

Washburne, Carleton. "Ripeness," *Progr. Educ.*, 13: 125–30; 1936.

Spelling Inquiry
Joseph M. Rice

Probably none of the pioneers in educational research deserves more credit than J. M. Rice, whose spelling inquiry marks education's first attempt at the objective study of educational problems. Whereas experimentation in the physical sciences had preceded his relatively crude investigation by over a century, Rice's field study of spelling, conducted in the early 1890's, nevertheless constitutes a landmark in educational research.

Born in 1857, Rice received his M.D. degree in 1881. After a brief practice of medicine, he went to Europe to study pedagogics and psychology at the major educational centers of Germany. On his return to America, he devoted his energies to the improvement of American schools which he felt were inferior to those of Europe, particularly those of Germany. As editor of the *Forum,* he undertook an extensive tour of the nation's schools, visiting some 1200 teachers in the eastern and midwestern states. He was particularly disappointed at the mechanical way in which learning took place, the emphasis on isolated facts, and the failure to relate education to pupil interest.

Unfortunately, the articles which he wrote in support of more effective teaching were largely ignored. But Rice was not so easily discouraged; he proceeded to collect evidence to prove his point. Among the problems current at that time was a movement to extend the curriculum to include such subjects as home economics and manual training. This extension was opposed by many educators who felt that any such addition would be at the expense of the basic curriculum. Rice disagreed on the premise that much of the school day was wasted. He argued that the benefits derived from instruction in any one subject was far from proportional to the time devoted to it. Choosing spelling as an area in which he felt much of the instruction was essentially unprofitable, he devised a test which he had teachers administer to their classes. This did not work out, inasmuch as the teachers vitiated the study through their enunciation of the words. He, therefore, devised a second test which he personally administered to some 100,000 children. His results showed little relationship between spelling ability and the class time spent on the subject: schools devoting 10 to 15 minutes a week to the subject achieved gains equal to those spending three or four times as much.

Rice did not limit himself to the investigation of spelling; as editor of the *Forum,* he published some twenty articles oriented toward the improvement of educational practice. His contributions are most adequately reported in his book, *Scientific Management in Education* (1914).

That Rice's findings were not particularly well received is an understatement. They were ignored wherever possible or disputed and discounted; they had relatively little effect on educational practice for at least a couple of decades. It is only in retrospect that his study attains significance, for it marks the beginning of education's reliance on research evidence in the solution of educational problems. Accordingly, it represents a major step toward the modern view that educational problems must be settled by investigation rather than by argumentation. The rejection of his findings point to a common problem faced by research workers. Generally, the efforts of an outsider uncovering weaknesses in the educational program are resented and accomplish little. If they are to bring about improvement, outsiders must first gain the confidence and cooperation of the responsible school personnel. It is an error to assume, as Rice apparently did, that the simple presentation of evidence will lead to an improvement in school practice.

References

Rice, Joseph M. "The futility of the spelling grind," *Forum*, 23: 163-72, 409-19; 1897.

————. *Scientific Management in Education.* New York: Hinds, Noble, and Eldredge, 1914.

Scates, Douglas E. "Fifty years of objective measurement and research in education," *J. educ. Res.*, 41: 241-64; 1947.

Levels of Aspiration in Academically Successful and Unsuccessful Children
Pauline S. Sears

The meaning which a task has for the individual must be considered from the standpoint of its relationship to the self-concept he has developed over the years. Generally, the individual's tendency to strive to make a good showing is guaranteed by his need to maintain status and to derive from the situation in which he finds himself some degree of social approval from persons whose appraisal he values. Sears' study was concerned with the effect which past success or failure might have on the level of aspiration of ego-involved subjects who have characteristically experienced continued success or continued failure with regard to a particular task, and who, therefore, have certain expectations relative to their ability to perform adequately. It was her hypothesis that one's level of aspiration in the performance of a given task is a function of the success-failure status of the past experiences which he associates with the task.

The subjects were children of the fourth through sixth grades, and the tasks dealt with reading and arithmetic with which the children had already had some contact. The success group was composed of children who during their entire school life had shown evidence of success in academic subjects, including reading and arithmetic. The failure group, on the other hand, had the opposite experience. A third group was made up of children who had had success experiences with reading but failure experiences with arithmetic. All the children selected were ego-involved in the sense of being interested in the quality of their performance. The three groups were equated on such variables as CA, MA, and sex; they were different, on the other hand, from the standpoint of previous academic success.

After a preliminary trial or neutral session, the success group was advised that it had done exceedingly well and each member was told: "You did the first test in so many seconds: what are you going to try to do it in this time?" The failure group, on the other hand, was rebuked for its lack of performance and urged to try to improve. Each child was also asked how long he thought it would take him to do the test this time. In all cases, the variable involved was the discrepancy between the performance time required for a given trial and the level of aspiration the child set for the next trial. The study concerned itself with both the average discrepancy and the variability of these discrepancies for each of the groups over a set of twenty trials.

The results showed the success group capable of keeping its aim rather close to target; they maintained throughout the experiment a relatively small positive discrepancy. The failure group, on the other hand, showed a significantly larger discrepancy between their level of aspiration and their previous performance and a greater variability in this discrepancy. By contrast to the success group, the failure group scattered its estimates widely in both directions from the performance they might logically expect to achieve in the light of their previous performance.

Their reaction to the frustration situation apparently follows several different patterns: in some cases, it seems as if apathetic behavior developed, perhaps due to the subjects having reached the frustration level with the result that they then simply continued to tolerate a slight positive discrepancy. Others continued to strive for the improbable, while still others appeared to lose perspective, vacillating from a realistic estimate to estimates that were either unrealistically high or unrealistically low.

There is obviously no simple formulation that will adequately explain the complicated state of affairs represented by the above reactions to failure; it may well differ from subject to subject and from situation to situation depending upon such things as the nature of the individual's self-concept, his ego-involvement in the task, etc. It is possible that some failure subjects assumed that their willingness to try would be rewarded, at least for effort, if not for success; they perhaps considered the statement of their goal as a goal in itself. Others may have verbally aimed below what they could achieve as a means of attaining "success" by doing better than expected. It is also possible that certain subjects, faced with an unpleasant situation, behaved in a trial-and-error fashion; they may even have generated a certain degree of anxiety causing them to lose perspective and to behave in a rather erratic fashion. Others perhaps continued to pursue impossible goals apparently in a desperate attempt to maintain their self-concept of personal , adequacy.

The study has very definite implications for education and should be considered in connection with the self-concept, motivation, and other aspects of the dynamics of student behavior and classroom achievement. It has obvious bearings, for instance, on grading and other forms of reward. If we are to accept the conclusions and implications of this experiment, it would seem that success tends to lead the individual to set appropriate goals in line with his abilities and, therefore, leads to further success; continued failure, on the other hand, leads him to set goals that are unrealistic and thereby deprive himself of the reward and satisfaction which only true achievement can provide. The results would also mean that, if he is to promote the development of a positive self-concept and a realistic level of aspiration on the part of his students—and thereby place achievement on a self-perpetuating basis—the teacher must provide them with individualized attainable goals.

Reference

Sears, Pauline S. "Levels of aspiration in academically successful and unsuccessful children," *J. abnorm. soc. Psychol.*, 35: 498–536; 1940.

Studies of Unreliability in Grading
Daniel Starch and Edward C. Elliott

Also of major importance to education, in view of the prominent position occupied by academic testing in the operation of the school, are the well-known studies of the unreliability of grading essay examinations conducted by Starch and Elliott just prior to World War I.

The first study concerned the unreliability of grading English examinations. Two examinations in first-year high school

English were duplicated in their original form and copies were sent to 200 high schools with a request that the principal teacher in first-year English grade the two papers according to the practices and standards of the school. Of the 152 papers returned, ten had to be rejected because of wide differences in the grading standards of the schools involved, leaving a total of 142 usable grades. It was further necessary to weight the grades of the schools using 70 as a passing grade to calibrate the grades given to the level of the schools using 75 as a passing grade. The results showed startling discrepancies—up to some 35–40 points in some cases. Not only were the papers that were passed by some graders failed by others, but the order of quality of the two papers was reversed in many instances.

The same two papers were graded by 86 university students enrolled in a course in the teaching of English (very few having teaching experience). Except for their grading somewhat more leniently, the students gave approximately the same distribution of grades as the teachers above. The papers were also graded by a class of superintendents, principals, and teachers taking a course in educational measurements; they likewise gave a distribution of grades essentially similar to that given by the first set of teachers.

The wide discrepancy in the grading of these papers led some people to question whether the unreliability was peculiar to grading in English. To test this hypothesis, Starch and Elliott investigated unreliability in grading in geometry, where greater objectivity and accuracy might have been expected. A geometry paper was reproduced and sent to 180 high schools, again with the request that the principal teacher in mathematics grade it according to the practices and standards of the school. A total of 128 usable returns were obtained. Even greater deviations in grading were obtained than in the case of English; even after adjustment for differences between the passing standards of the various schools involved, the grades given ranged from 28 to 92.

In a third investigation, ten papers in freshman English were graded independently by ten instructors of the various sections of college freshman English. All instructors had given the same final examination, and each had already graded the papers of his own sections. It was found, among other things, that two instructors graded much lower and two instructors graded much higher than the average. Even when the grades were weighted in order to overcome the lack of uniformity in leniency, sizable differences still existed, especially with respect to two papers which were graded from 44 to 81 for one and from 20 to 65 for the other. Another phase of the study checked the extent to which an instructor agreed with his own grade when he regraded the same paper. An average difference of over four points was noted. This difference also held in other subjects, such as foreign languages and science.

These studies were probably instrumental to a considerable degree in the relative wane of the essay examination and the rise of the objective test. Starch's interpretation of his results as supporting coarser grading was probably also influential in the shift from numerical to letter grades.

References

Marshall, Jon C. "Composition errors and essay examination grades re-examined," *Amer. educ. Res. J.*, 4: 375–66; 1967.

Starch, Daniel. "Reliability of grading work in mathematics," *Sch. Rev.*, 21: 254–59; 1913.

———. "Reliability and distribution of grades," *Sci.*, 38: 630–36; 1913.

——— and Edward C. Elliott. "Reliability of the grades of high school work in English," *Sch. Rev.*, 20: 442–67; 1912.

Genetic Studies of Genius
Lewis M. Terman

One of the most significant studies relating to education is the comprehensive investigation of gifted children conducted by Terman and his co-workers under grant from the Commonwealth Fund and Stanford University. It is published in five volumes, each describing one stage of the investigation: Volume 1, probably the most widely known, analyses the intellectual and personality traits of 1000 gifted children located in central California in the early 1920's. Volumes 3, 4, and 5 represent a follow-up of the same group after five, twenty-five, and thirty-five years respectively. Volume 2 deals with the childhood and youth of the "geniuses" of history and attempts to set a minimum estimate of their likely intellectual level.

The major sample for the first study consisted of 648 gifted children in grades 1 through 8. A second group of 356 children of the same age living outside the main areas of the study were also included but less data were collected about them. A third group consisted of 378 high school students. In addition, a small number of cases were also selected because of outstanding status in such areas as music and art. A fifth group of 800 nonselected students from the same schools were used as control. On each of the cases in the major sample, some 100 pages of data were gathered, 65 pages of which concerned test and measurement data—including two intelligence tests; one education achievement test; tests of general information in the areas of science, history, literature, and the arts; tests of interests and knowledge of sports and games; reading records, etc. The additional 35 pages included questionnaire data regarding home and school background, medical history, rating of the home and the neighborhood, etc.

The investigation suggested that gifted children as a group were superior in all desirable traits; this evidence refuted the notion prevailing at the time that intellectual precocity was invariably accompanied by inferiority in nonintellectual areas. Terman's data showed the gifted group to display physical superiority, acceleration in school, interest in school subjects particularly of an abstract nature, versatility, breadth of reading interest, early maturation, and decisive superiority in such character and personality traits as self-confidence, persistence, and strength of character. They also surpassed normal children in honesty and other moral traits. They showed no lack of interest or of ability in sports.

These gifted children enjoyed both hereditary and environmental advantages. The number of eminent relatives was impressive: one-quarter had relatives in the Hall of Fame. They also came from homes superior in socio-economic status; 81 percent of the parents were professional and semi-professional, 18 percent were skilled and semi-skilled. Most of the children had at least one parent who was a college graduate. Among the interesting sidelights of the study was the fact that the sample included an excess of boys and of first-born. It was also noted that the investigators could identify the gifted child in a given classroom by selecting the youngest member of the class somewhat more accurately than could the teacher on the basis of judgment.

The second volume of the series deals with the study of 301 outstanding men in history with a view to discovering the minimum level of mental endowment that they must have possessed in order to have accomplished what they did. A case study was compiled for each of the subjects; it was found, for example, that many of them had been able to read at the age of three or had studied Greek and Latin at a preschool age. The geniuses of history gave evidence of both superior hereditary and environmental advantages; they also displayed the usual characteristics of the gifted.

The third volume reports the five-year follow-up and covers 97 percent of the original group. It was found, for instance, that the average IQ of the group had dropped slightly, as might have been expected on the basis of regression toward the mean. The fourth volume deals with the findings of the twenty-five-year follow-up, in which data were again collected through information blanks, interest and personality inventories and other means. It was found, for instance, that the offspring of the gifted sample had an average IQ of approximately 127 which, again, is in line with the concept of regression toward the mean. There was evidence of greater marital adjustment among the gifted than for the general population, a lower death rate, a lower incidence of delinquency, a better record of employment, a higher level of professional accomplishment, and a continuation of such personality characteristics as a sense of humor, cheerfulness, optimism, willpower and perseverance, desire to excel, and self-confidence. They gave every indication that giftedness in youth is a fairly good indication of similar giftedness throughout life. On the other hand, a number did not achieve in keeping with their potentialities. These could not be distinguished from the more successful with respect to intellectual status; whatever differences were involved appeared to center around such personality characteristics as drive and perseverance. The fifth volume presents a thirty-five-year follow-up of the group and suggests a continuation of the same life of success and outstanding achievement.

Terman's study is an especially good example of a carefully planned and executed longitudinal investigation. His success in obtaining cooperation and maintaining contact with his subjects is in large part a reflection of the intellectual and cultural level of the subjects involved. The study is obviously a classic in the field; its contribution to the understanding of the gifted child is of major importance with respect to the present emphasis on the education of the gifted. Not only has it answered a number of questions concerning the gifted, but it has also set the pattern for further investigation in this area.

References

Burks, Barbara S. et al. *Genetic Studies of Genius; 3. The Promise of Youth*. Stanford: Stanford Univ. Press, 1930.

Cox, Catherine M. *Genetic Studies of Genius; 2. The Early Mental Traits of 300 Geniuses*. Stanford: Stanford Univ. Press, 1926.

Terman, Lewis M. and Melita H. Oden. *Genetic Studies of Genius; 4. The Gifted Child Grows Up*. Stanford: Stanford Univ. Press, 1947.

————. *Genetic Studies of Genius; 5. The Gifted Group at Mid-Life*. Stanford: Stanford Univ. Press, 1959.

———— et al. *Genetic Studies of Genius; 1. Mental and Physical Traits of 1000 Gifted Children*. Stanford: Stanford Univ. Press, 1925.

The Disciplinary Value of High School Studies
Edward L. Thorndike

Thorndike's early contributions in the area of educational psychology, and more particularly in the area of transfer of training, led him to question the transfer value of the classical subjects. He, therefore, undertook to determine whether certain subjects had greater disciplinary value than others with respect to the improvement of reasoning ability. The study was based on the comparison of the gains in reasoning made by students enrolled in the various high school curricula and involved the testing of over 8000 pupils in Grades 9 through 11 with Form A of the *I.E.R. Test of Selective Relational Thinking* and the *I.E.R. Test of Generalization and Organization* in the fall of 1922 and again in the spring of 1923 with Form B of the same tests. The study was again repeated under Thorndike's direction by Broyler and Woodyard on a sample of approximately 5000.

The results did not show any major superiority on the part of any one curriculum in its ability to promote gains in reasoning ability. Not only were the differences relatively small but the studies were not particularly consistent in the ranking of the various subjects from the standpoint of their transfer potential.

Combining the results of the two studies, the subject areas came out in the following order: 1. algebra, geometry, trigonometry; 2. civics, economics, psychology, sociology; 3. chemistry, physics, general sciences; 4. arithmetic, bookkeeping; 5. physical training; 6. Latin and French, business, drawing, English, history, music, shop, Spanish; 7. cooking, sewing, stenography; 8. biology, physiology, agriculture; and 9. dramatic art. It was Thorndike's conclusion that "the expectation of any large difference in general improvement of the mind from one study rather than another seemed doomed to disappointment." He pointed out further that the balance in favor of any study is certainly not large; disciplinary values may be real and deserve weight in planning the curriculum, but the weight should be reasonable.

A more adequate study of the same problem is that of Wesman who overcame one of the basic weaknesses of the previous studies, namely, the fact that no distinction had been made between being merely enrolled in a given curriculum and mastering its content. Wesman's study duplicated the other two with the added feature of measuring the degree of achievement in the subjects being compared. His results agree relatively closely with those of the two previous studies, and, in general, confirm the conclusion that the disciplinary value of the various academic curricula as it transfers to the improvement of reasoning ability is not appreciably different from subject to subject. He concluded that "in general, the study fails to reveal superior transfer to intelligence for any one of the achievement areas measured and indicates the desirability of direct training in mental processes rather than dependence on transfer from school subjects."

These studies constitute an important landmark from the standpoint of curriculum construction and mark the beginning of the de-emphasis of the classic subjects on the strength of their disciplinary potential. It is the general consensus today that there is no superior subject matter for transfer; rather there are only superior learning experiences and transfer is more a function of the way learning takes place than of the subject matter involved. It should also be noted that in all three studies considerable relationship was noted between the extent of transfer and the intellectual status of the individual. The studies are important from the standpoint of the newer concepts of "learning how to learn" and of ability as something one develops through experience.

References

Broyler, Cecil R. et al. "A second study of mental discipline in high school studies," *J. educ. Psychol.*, 18: 377–404; 1927.

Harlow, Harry F. "The formation of learning sets," *Psychol. Rev.*, 56: 51–65; 1949.

Thorndike, Edward L. "Mental discipline in high school studies," *J. educ. Psychol.*, 15: 1–22, 83–98; 1924.

Wesman, Alexander G. "A study of transfer of training from high school subjects to intelligence," *J. educ. Psychol.*, 39: 254–64; 1945.

The Laws of Learning
Edward L. Thorndike

Probably no other research studies have had more effect on American education than Thorndike's studies in learning. They mark the beginning of experimental attack on the problem of learning and of the modern development of learning theories. Although his experiments were conducted on animal subjects, they have had tremendous impact on educational practice in the first few decades of this century and even to the present day.

His investigation comprised a number of experiments with various animals, designed to determine the factors governing the process of learning. In some of his early studies, Thorndike taught fish to swim through a small hole in a dividing plate in order to escape from sunlight to shade. Motivated by their aversion to strong light, the fish had progressively greater success in finding the hole. In his experiments with chicks, Thorndike had them find their way through a maze in order to get food. In all cases, the animals showed a progressive, although erratic, decline in the time needed to achieve a solution.

Probably his best-known experiments are those in which a hungry cat was placed in a box from which it could free itself by pulling a string or pressing a lever. After trying to squeeze through the slats of the box or clawing at the door, the cat finally hit upon the escape device—generally by accident—and was able to get to the food outside. In later trials, the cat's activities became progressively more directly oriented toward the escape mechanism until, after a number of trials, its escape was relatively automatic. In all instances, however, learning proceeded largely through the gradual elimination of error through a trial-and-error approach. The display of insight, as Thorndike saw it, was minimal, if not completely lacking. Dogs displayed essentially the same learning pattern, except that their progress tended to be somewhat smoother, perhaps because of their greater intelligence. Racoons and monkeys did even better, possibly because of greater curiosity and manipulative ability; the latter, for example, learned to discriminate between stimuli, e.g., to react when the food was in the experimenter's left hand but not when it was in his right hand. However, certain discriminations proved too difficult. Thorndike concluded that the reasoning ability of animals was relatively limited—that trial-and-error, rather than insight, was the dominant factor in their learning.

Thorndike's conclusions have been subjected to considerable criticism for not giving sufficient credit to the operation of reasoning as a component of problem-solving. His interpretations have been partially contradicted by other investigations, at least from the standpoint of emphasis. The issue revolves around the definition of "reasoning;" apparently, apes and monkeys are able to solve problems which demand a fairly high degree of abstraction or ability to discover relationships, as well as memory, but whether that constitutes "reasoning" is a matter of definition. Thorndike was unduly pessimistic in this regard and conceived of learning as relatively mechanical. Köhler, on the other hand, was able to demonstrate a number of instances of reasoning or "insight" in chimpanzees, such as piling boxes on top of one another in order to reach a banana hanging from the ceiling, or putting two sticks together in order to reach a banana placed outside the cage. More recently, Harlow has presented rather convincing evidence in support of "insight" as an aspect of the more general framework of "learning how to learn." Ausubel presents the concept of "advance organizers" in a similar context.

Thorndike's principal contribution to the psychology of learning, namely, the *law of effect*, originally had two components: 1. S–R bonds followed by satisfying after-effects tend to be strengthened; and 2. S–R bonds followed by annoying after-effects tend to be weakened, but the latter component was eventually discarded. The law of effect—along with the more general concept of reinforcement—is, generally speaking, the most important law in the psychology of learning, relating as it does to the concept of motivation. It has, of course, not received complete endorsement; recent emphasis on the stimulation theories of motivation has centered on certain inadequacies in the drive-reduction theory. Nevertheless, regardless of its theoretical validity, the law of effect, in its broad sense, is still of very definite theoretical as well as operational usefulness. Thorndike's second law of learning, the *law of exercise* which postulated that the strength of a neural bond was associated with the frequency of its use, is more vulnerable. At one time it provided the justification for drill as the basis of instruction, a practice which has more or less been superseded by the present emphasis on meaningfulness. It is now realized that practice is a necessary, but not a sufficient, condition for learning to take place. Both of these laws have been subjected to considerable discussion in the psychological literature and a definitive evaluation of their status would call for a more thorough background in the psychology of learning than can be presented in the short space here. In general, the major objections to Thorndike's laws of learning center around the relatively mechanical interpretation of learning which they imply.

References

Ausubel, David P. "The use of advance organizers in the learning and retention of meaningful verbal material," *J. educ. Psychol.*, 51: 267–72; 1960. (See also *The Psychology of Meaningful Verbal Learning: An Introduction to School Learning.* New York: Grune & Stratton, 1963)

Hilgard, Ernest R. and Gordon H. Bower. *Theories of Learning.* New York: Appleton-Century-Crofts, 1966.

Köhler, Wolfgang. *The Mentality of Apes.* New York: Harcourt, Brace & World, 1928.

Marx, Melvin H. "Spread of effect: A critical review," *Genet. Psychol. Monogr.*, 53: 119–86; 1956.

Postman, Leo J. "The history and present status of the law of effect," *Psychol. Bull.*, 44: 489–563; 1947.

Thorndike, Edward L. *Animal Intelligence.* New York: Macmillan, 1911.

———. *Human Learning.* New York: Appleton-Century-Crofts, 1931.

Woodworth, Robert S. *Contemporary Schools of Psychology.* Rev. ed. New York: Ronald Press, 1948.

The Teacher's Word Book
Edward L. Thorndike

Of considerable interest to teachers in the elementary school are Thorndike's vocabulary studies in which he identified the 10,000, 20,000, and 30,000 most widely used words. Although some work in this direction had been done prior to his and although more adequate studies have been conducted since, Thorndike's studies still remain among the better known. The magnitude of the task alone is of frightening proportions. The first word list (10,000 words) published in 1921 was selected from a count of over 7,000,000 words taken from elementary school textbooks, children's literature, English classics, the Bible, personal correspondence, newspapers, etc. The words are listed in 1000, 2000, 3000, . . . levels in terms of their frequency of occurrence, with a further breakdown of the first 1000 words into the various 100 levels and the next 4000 in 500 levels in frequency of use. The words are also rated as to "range" with respect to the extent of use in the 41 sources consulted in the derivation of the list. His word lists of 20,000 (1932) and of 30,000 words (1944) are essentially a continuation of his first study. Again, the words are rated as to range and frequency of use.

Thorndike felt the word lists would be of benefit to the teacher in judging the importance and difficulty of a given word as the basis for deciding the emphasis to be placed on it at a given grade level. He acknowledged that the lists were not perfect measures of the relative importance of the word listed; a word may be of personal interest and value to a student and yet not be of common currency in the world's readings. He also acknowledged the possibility that some one thousand words might be more deserving of inclusion in the lists and that the order of the words was not necessarily exact and final. It would also follow that the list would become out of date with the inclusion of new words and the dropping out of older words. It would also be true that regional differences, e.g., rural-urban differences, exist that would make such a list somewhat short of being a perfect guide. Nevertheless, in addition to promoting further studies in this area, the lists have had definite influence on the concept of controlled vocabulary load, particularly in the primary grades and, to some extent, in the field of readability.

References

Lindsay, Edward Y. *An Etymological Study of Ten Thousand Words in Thorndike's Teacher Word Book.* Indiana University Studies, 12, No. 65. Bloomington: Indiana Univ., 1925.

Thorndike, Edward L. *The Teacher's Word Book.* New York: T. C., Columbia Univ., 1921, 1932, 1944.

Factorial Studies of the Mind
Louis L. Thurstone and Thelma G. Thurstone

Particularly well-known in the field of intelligence is the series of investigations conducted by the Thurstones into the basic components of the mind. These and later studies have isolated a number of mental factors or abilities, primary among which is the verbal factor (V). Other factors that are commonly accepted include the numerical factor (N), the word fluency factor (W), the spatial factor (S), the memory factor (M), the reasoning factor (R), and the perceptual factor (P).

The major study involved in the identification of the primary mental abilities is a study conducted in the 1930's involving 60 tests, many of which were devised specifically for the study. In addition, data on chronological age, mental age, and sex were added for a total of 63 variables to be processed through factor analysis. The subjects were 710 out of 1154 eighth-grade children for whom complete records were available. The factors were rotated by means of the centroid method to provide seven identifiable factors (N, W, S, V, M, R, and P) and three relatively indeterminate factors. The results were checked in a second factorial study involving 437 cases, and the data again yielded the same factors.

The Thurstones have made a large number of valuable contributions to the general area of psychometrics, particularly with respect to the measurement of attitudes, interests, and intelligence and the development of rating scales and factor analysis. From a theoretical point of view, their position regarding intelligence is in apparent conflict with that of Spearman, although the difference is one of orientation and emphasis rather than of outright disagreement. The Thurstone approach is particularly appropriate in vocational guidance which is based in large measure on the differential adequacy of the counselee's primary mental abilities. Guilford's recent extension of the Thurstone approach to a three-dimensional solid model representing processes, contents, and products constitutes the most complete conceptualization of the complex nature of the human intellect. Although it structures the various components of human intelligence into a logical system, it emphasizes the fact that intelligence is not a single composite factor and, obviously, complicates no end the task of measuring it.

References

Guilford, J.P. "Three faces of intellect," *Amer. Psychol.*, 14: 469–79; 1959.

———. *The Nature of Human Intelligence*. New York: McGraw-Hill, 1967.

Thurstone, Louis L. *Primary Mental Abilities*. Chicago: Univ. Chicago Press, 1938.

——— and Thelma G. Thurstone. *Factorial Studies of Intelligence*. Psychometric Monogr. No. 2. Chicago: Univ. Chicago Press, 1941.

Teachers' Attitudes Toward Children's Behavioral Problems
E.K. Wickman

This widely quoted study, conducted in 1928 under the auspices of the Commonwealth Fund, concerned the rating as to relative severity of 50 behavior problems by a total of 511 teachers and 30 clinicians. The results revealed a substantial reversal in the ratings of teachers and clinicians: of the 12 behavior problems rated most severe by teachers, 2 were rated among the least severe by the clinicians while, of the 12 behavior problems rated least severe by teachers, 3 were rated among the most severe by the clinicians. In general, it might be said that teachers considered shyness, sensitivity, unsociability, fearfulness, daydreaming, and other purely "personal" problems which did not interfere with the teacher's immediate purpose among the least serious, whereas the clinicians rated these factors among the most serious. Teachers, on the other hand, rated behavior problems relating to sex, dishonesty, and disobedience as much more serious than did the clinicians. More simply, teachers placed emphasis on antisocial tendencies (defiance of authority and violation of rules), whereas clinicians saw greatest danger in unsocial tendencies (shyness and sensitivity). The study revealed, for example, a tendency for teachers to counterattack the "attacking" type of problem behavior and to indulge habits of withdrawal and dependency—thereby aggravating both unhealthy conditions.

The study is often quoted as evidence of the fact that teachers do not understand what constitutes a severe mental health problem. This interpretation is somewhat gratuitous, revealing some lack of understanding of the nature of the study. Wickman points to differences in professional interest; the clinician is interested in the social and emotional adjustment of the child, whereas the teacher is interested in his educational accomplishment.

Wickman also points very clearly to differences in the directions given to the two groups: "the directions to teachers for rating were phrased in such a way as to secure responses to the *present* problem, and the question of the significance of the present behavior disorder upon the *future* development of the child, though possibly unavoidably implied, was not definitely raised. The task set was to rate the degree of maladjustment represented by the immediate problem." The emphasis was on the amount of difficulty produced by the particular type of troublesome behavior. The clinicians, on the other hand, instead of evaluating the present problem, rated its significance in terms of its future effects in limiting the child's happiness, success, and general welfare after leaving school. The differences in ratings between teachers and clinicians become more understandable in terms of the differences in the directions they received.

It should be noted that more recent studies incorporating equivalence in the directions given to the clinicians and teachers have revealed much closer agreement in their attitudes as to the severity of children's behavior problems. Schrupp and Gjerde, in a repetition of Wickman's study using the same set of directions for both groups, found a correlation of 0.56 in the ratings of the two groups in contrast to the correlation of -0.04 found by Wickman. Whether one needs to be disturbed over the discrepancy in outlook that still exists between teachers and clinicians is a matter of opinion. There may be a need for a further shift of teachers away from concern over breaches of classroom decorum to a more objective consideration of behavior from the standpoint of the long-term development of the whole child. On the other hand, it is questionable whether there should ever be complete agreement in view of their different purposes and the different settings in which they operate.

References

Schrupp, Manfred H. and Clayton M. Gjerde. "Teacher growth in attitudes towards behavior problems of children," *J. educ. Psychol.*, 44: 204–14; 1953.

Wickman, E.K. *Children's Behavior and Teacher's Attitudes.* New York: Commonwealth Fund, 1928.

APPENDIX

THE THESIS
AND DISSERTATION

The research paper with which most people studying this text are concerned is the master's thesis or the doctoral dissertation. It seems advisable, therefore, to devote a section to this important project, especially since, although such a project should be the achievement of a lifetime, the end product too frequently turns out to be a disappointment. Unfortunately, no magic formula can be given that will ensure an adequate product. And although this section will attempt to present a few ideas on the various aspects of conducting and reporting research, these ideas are simply suggestive. Generally speaking, the giving of specific rules is incompatible with the whole process of research which, to be fruitful, must remain flexible. A good research study cannot be equated with step-by-step directions; anyone who needs such help probably should not be doing research in the first place.

THE RESEARCH PROPOSAL

Research starts with the identification of a problem. This is the first step in the sequence; it is also among the most important, for probably no aspect of the study has a greater bearing on the success of the overall venture than the wise choice of a problem. As we have seen in Chapter 3, it is both the prerogative and the responsibility of the graduate student to identify a suitable topic; to devise a suitable plan of attack; to collect, process, and interpret the required data; and finally to write the report. It is here that the student establishes his claim to status as a leader in the profession.

The early stages of the selection of a topic are generally a matter of considerable trial and error as the student traces one lead after another, dropping an idea here, gradually developing another, until finally a problem emerges. An important part of this search is discussing ideas with others, whose reactions invariably lead to a refinement of the proposed study. Research seminars conducted for students working on their dissertations can be of great help in this connection. There is probably no better way of having the student clarify his thinking relative to every phase of his proposed investigation than requiring him to defend his proposal before a seminar prior to submission for approval by his committee. A key person in the process of choosing a topic is the student's advisor, who, because of his familiarity with the field, can generally save him much aimless wandering and exploration of blind alleys. Major professors in the field are also valuable sources of help in formulating a tentative proposal.

On the other hand, the student seeking faculty help should come with ideas to discuss, with tentative topics formulated as clearly as he knows how. These ideas generally should be presented in writing as evidence that the student has done some thinking about his problem. It is rather difficult to give constructive advice to the student who "wants to write a thesis . . . ", who isn't sure of the area, "Administration, I guess . . . . Maybe something in how to deal with personnel." Before he can be helped, short of being handed a topic ready-made, he needs to get his ideas more clearly delimited—and, as much as possible, he must do this himself. If the thesis or dissertation is to provide the student with training in scholarship and leadership, he must not be allowed to rely on his advisor to make the decisions for him. Graduate study loses its true meaning if it subjects the student to the same type of minute-by-minute direction and support given to high school students or college freshmen.

The proposal submitted for committee approval should be sufficiently detailed and clear to serve as an actual blueprint for the study to follow. It should present the general nature and the current status of the problem, the theoretical and empirical framework within which it exists, the hypotheses to be tested, its significance and likely contribution, its feasibility, the method of attack (including the proposed analysis of the data), etc. Although it is a proposal and not the final draft, it must give evidence of careful planning and insightful anticipation of problems. Deviations from original plans may have to be made, but meticulous formulation of the proposal will keep such modification to a reasonable minimum.

WRITING THE REPORT

The specific arrangement of the thesis or dissertation from the standpoint of such details as chapter organization varies from topic to topic. A short master's thesis might be organized in three chapters: 1. The Problem; 2. The Design and Results of the Study; 3. The Summary and Conclusions. A doctoral dissertation, on the other hand, might have as many chapters as a good-sized book, with separate chapters devoted to the review of the literature, to the findings, and to the interpretation of the data, for example. The length of the report also varies. Historical and survey studies tend to be longer than experimental studies. The criterion is not the number of pages, but rather the adequacy of the scope of the problem and its treatment.

The general format also varies somewhat with the topic, its nature, its scope, and its complexity, as well as with the individual preferences of the writer. Generally, however, the research report divides itself into three major parts: 1. The preliminary section which includes the title page, the acknowledgments, the table of contents, and the list of tables; 2. The report itself which is divided into the introduction, the statement and delineation of the problem, the development of the data, and the conclusions; and 3. The bibliography and other supplementary material.

The Problem

The first section of the report must present the problem—its nature, scope, and significance. Usually this section begins with a general orientation to the problem area and leads directly into a statement of the problem to be investigated. This section should be appealing and challenging; it is generally difficult to write it well.

The statement of the problem is crucial since it delineates specifically what is to be investigated and, thus, what is relevant, what is irrelevant, and what constitutes an effective approach to its solution. The problem should be stated directly and, wherever possible, should be translated into a specific hypothesis to be investigated. The statement must distinguish clearly between what the study will investigate and what it will exclude from consideration. It should also leave no doubt about the assumptions being made. The statement should come early; it is frustrating to read page after page of discussion before finding out what the problem is that will make such discussion relevant. Special terms or special meanings given to common words should be clearly defined.

A section which is frequently underemphasized is the significance of the problem—i.e., the justification of the proposed study and its implications for educational practice. Whereas to the student his study may be all-important, the reader may not be so enlightened as to its significance and the possible contributions it might make. This should be included in the proposal, and, of course, should form the basis for the implications of the study discussed in the final chapter.

The Review of the Literature

The review of the literature is essential to the development of the problem and to the derivation of an effective approach to its solution. Not only must this part be thorough and exhaustive, but it must also be organized with respect to subheadings which will structure the literature according to the specific aspects of the problem. The review of the various sources should be analytical rather than merely cumulative, i.e., the studies should be evaluated as to adequacy and relevance rather than simply listed. Furthermore, the various sources must be integrated and synthesized to give the reader a clear picture of the status of the problem as background for placing the present investigation in perspective. Any review of the literature that is left hanging—that does not eventuate in a clear-cut generalization—is simply incomplete. Often, the literature is so extensive that the student must be selective as to what he includes: whereas this involves certain risks, the writer should be in a position to make a judgment as to whether listing one study after another on a given point is likely to clarify or to becloud the issue.

Generally, students do a rather thorough job of reviewing the empirical literature. Frequently, however, they do not present an adequate conceptual framework within which their problem exists; nor do they relate their findings to their theoretical implications. For example, in investigating the personality characteristics of nonreaders, there is apparently an assumption of perhaps reciprocal interaction of nonreading and personality maladjustment. On the other hand, an investigation of good readers might be approached from the hypothesis that an exceptionally good reader may be either extremely well-adjusted or, on the contrary, a maladjusted individual who compensates through overachievement in reading. These hypotheses are simply illustrative; the point is that it is best not just to investigate the relationship between reading and personality without presenting the hypothetical conception from which the study might have originated.

The Design

A study cannot be evaluated unless its procedures are reported in sufficient detail to make such an evaluation possible. The section on the design should be particularly clear and precise in order to allow the reader to grasp exactly what was done and, in the event of a need for verification or refutation, to permit its exact replication. Furthermore, since a primary purpose of reporting research is to permit a more effective attack upon a given problem, the procedures used in a study should be reported, even to the point of reporting on the more important blind alleys that were abandoned.

The specific aspects of the design that need to be emphasized vary with the nature of the study. In a survey study, for example, it is generally important to describe the locale in which the study is conducted, for the findings of a survey cannot be interpreted apart from such a consideration. In a survey of the reactions of teachers to the twelve-month school year, it would be essential to know whether the school buildings are air-conditioned, whether the community is rural or urban, etc., just as a survey of the reactions of teachers toward merit pay would have meaning only in terms of the present morale of the teachers, the facilities for adequate teacher evaluation, as well as the specific plan of merit pay proposed. On the other hand, the locale would be less important in an experimental study of the effects of increased emphasis on phonics in reading in the primary grades. Here, the specific procedures incorporated into the "experimental" method in contrast to those of the "control" method would have to be described at length. Sample lessons and a detailed list of guidelines and principles for the guidance of the participating teachers might also be included. Similarly, the specific steps used in selecting a random sample would be more important in a normative survey study, while the establishment of the equivalence of the experimental and control groups would be the point to emphasize in an experimental design.

When instruments are used, they should be described from the standpoint of their validity in the present case. The report of a questionnaire study should indicate the specific steps taken to devise and to improve the questionnaire and should provide concrete evidence of the adequacy of the final product. Copies of all but well-known instruments should be included in the appendices. In a questionnaire study, copies of the cover letters and the follow-up attempts should also be included, since they have direct bearing on the results achieved. When descriptions of this kind are particularly lengthy, a few summary statements should be made in the text of the report and a more complete description included in the appendix.

Collection and Interpretation of Data

No study can be better than the data on which it is based and the interpretation they are given. The adequacy of the data relates not only to the adequacy of the research design but even more directly to that of the instruments used. Skill in the choice and use of research instruments is, therefore, crucial to the success of the study and the validity of its results and conclusions. What is particularly important, since the validity of an instrument and of the data which it yields is a concept specific to the circumstance in which it is used, is the proper interpretation of the results in the light of the problem. In an experimental study, for example, if the instrument is not equally "fair" to the two methods, only misinformation as to the relative effectiveness of the methods being compared can be obtained. In view of the critical role which instruments of measurement play in the conduct of research, anyone without background in the theory and practice of tests and measurement is bound to be very much restricted as a research worker.

Summary and Conclusions

The final section of the report proper consists of a review of the significant aspects of the whole study structured so as to lead directly to the conclusions. This summary is important in that it places the whole study in perspective. It must be carefully written, especially since frequently this is the only section of the report that the busy person reads.

No part of a study is more important than any other since a defect in one section will automatically affect the whole study. If, however, one part can be singled out as all-important, it is the section which states the conclusions, for this presents what the study has to contribute to the advancement of education as a science. It is frequently a difficult section to write, inasmuch as it must be particularly accurate and precise as well as insightful.

Drawing the conclusions is a matter of clarifying "just what did the study reveal?" The conclusions can be a simple answer to the question or hypothesis raised in the statement of the problem. In more complex designs, and especially in a survey where the findings are usually multiple rather than single, the student must orient himself to the significant aspects of his study. Ordinarily, the findings should be organized into a small number of meaningful groupings of ideas, each with a definite significance relative to the problem under study. Particularly useless—in fact, confusing—from the standpoint of the conclusions to follow, for example, is the long recitation of "findings" cited pell-mell without regard to their implications or relative significance.

Once the findings have been organized into a few clusters, the conclusions should follow directly. Conversely, if the student has difficulty with his conclusions, it is generally because he is not clear as to his findings. Perhaps he needs to go back and analyze his data further; he may need to establish more clearly the interrelationships among his findings and between these findings and those of other investigators. He may even have to get a clearer perspective of the whole field. Incidentally, a very common fault in research reports is that of confusing findings with conclusions and vice-versa; they are, of course, different and any student who takes the time should be able to tell them apart.

It must also be noted that, at this point, the investigator abandons his role as a scientist and becomes a philosopher. This, of course, puts him in a vulnerable position since interpretation always involves an element of subjectivity. On the other hand, this is a responsibility which the investigator has to assume, for certainly he should have a more adequate understanding of his area of investigation than anyone else and he is obligated to provide a "learned" interpretation of his findings. He is, for example, in the best position to see the limitations of his study, and to point out the need for certain cautions in the interpretations and applications. He should also be capable of pointing out the direction which further research might take, the pitfalls to be avoided and the best utilization of research talent in the pursuit of the solution. This is an area in which the investigator can make a real contribution to the field. Certainly, he must have learned something from his experience that he can share with future investigators.

The conclusions are the expression of the investigator's personal interpretation of the facts he has uncovered. The object is to establish as clear-cut an answer to the questions posed in the statement of the problem as the data of the present study analyzed in the light of the situation and of the work of previous investigators will permit. The investigator must be particularly careful not to go beyond his findings and project his personal biases onto the data. He must be alert to such errors of logic as confusing concomitance for causation or the cause for the effect (reverse causality). He must not disregard contrary evidence, and he must not fail to recognize the limitations of his study. He must maintain his objectivity and, if faced with negative evidence, admit readily that his hypotheses are in error, rather than make lame excuses about the inadequacy of the study.

A common shortcoming of research reports concerns their failure to relate the findings and conclusions of the present study to those of other investigators as presented in the review of the literature. It is essential that the conclusions of the study constitute the final word on the subject, incorporating all research on the subject to date (including the present study). The findings and conclusions of the present studies must be integrated—reconciled where necessary—with those of previous investigators. Any limitations which might have influenced his results or those of others should be clearly pointed out. No study is perfect: compromises from an ideal design generally have to be made to conform to situational realities. The important thing is that a clear exposition of the present empirical and theoretical status of the problem be presented with a definite statement of the degree of confidence that can be placed on what appears to be known about it. This is, of course, the essence of the Campbell-Stanley emphasis on quasi-experimentation.

MECHANICS OF THE REPORT

Graduate students sometimes fail to appreciate the importance of having the report radiate the same high level of scholarship that went into the investigation itself. Nothing can detract from a good study more than carelessness in its report. Conversely, in the absence of contrary evidence, the display of carelessness and incompetence in the report is of itself sufficient grounds for suspicion of equal carelessness and incompetence in the conduct of the study. What is more, such carelessness is inexcusable in a candidate for a graduate degree.

A major aspect of faulty reporting concerns grammatical usage—i.e., simple failure to adhere to accepted rules of grammatical structure, coherent organization, and attention to the many details necessary for producing a first-rate piece of work. Another aspect concerns precision and effectiveness in expression. Although there appears to be a close relation between effective writing and clear thinking, it is also probably true that clear, concise, and forceful expression does not come, even to the clearest thinker, without the expenditure of considerable time and effort. Regardless of his literary talent, the writer will invariably find that many revisions are necessary to bring the report into acceptable form. Attention to details is the price one must pay for scholarly work. This insistence on quality is one of the major features that distinguishes the graduate from the undergraduate student, the educational leader from the educational follower.

The writing of the thesis or dissertation is governed by a number of regulations. Some merely emphasize the obvious while others are relatively mechanical and arbitrary. In the main, these regulations make good sense, and failure to comply generally invites trouble. Practice and experience have led to the development of a format and an organization designed to promote maximum clarity in reporting and maximum effectiveness of use by the reader who can then devote his whole attention to the content. For example, the statement of the problem comes first because only when the reader knows what the problem is can he evaluate the relevance of the literature reviewed and the adequacy of the research design. Likewise, the fact that the last chapter contains the study in a nutshell is a boon to the busy reader. This is not a matter of stifling the writer; there is plenty of opportunity to show one's ingenuity within the framework of a standard format. Indeed, there is no limit to the extent to which the writer can display originality, creativity, and initiative in the design of the study, in the style of presentation, in the choice of vocabulary, etc.

Format

The format of the report is generally specified in some detail by each individual school. The sample pages and suggestions provided here are, therefore, simply "acceptable" models from which deviations will probably have to be made to comply with local regulations. Some graduate schools are more specific than others. Many use a standard style: some have their own manual of style; others allow the student to use any acceptable style, provided he is consistent in its use. The differences that do exist tend to concern details rather than major points. For example, there is agreement on the need to include volume number, page numbers, and date of an article in a bibliographical entry; disagreement is frequently found, however, with respect to the order in which they are to be listed.

In general, it may be argued that the style adopted for educational writings should conform to the usual style of writing in the field of education. There might be value, for instance, in adopting a style which is consistent with that of the major publishers of textbooks in education. It should, of course, meet such criteria as completeness, uniformity, convenience, clarity, and appearance. Thus, it would seem acceptable to omit the publisher in a footnote notation since this data is included in the bibliography, but the date should not be omitted since it may be important to know if the item was written in 1900 or in 1960.

The Title Page   The importance of the wise choice of a title is sometimes overlooked. Theses and dissertations sometimes carry a title of such comprehensiveness that the reader might wonder if the writer is attempting to write his whole report on the title page. The title must be sufficiently indicative of the study that it does not mislead the reader. Note, for example, how annoying it is to run down a source that from its title seems relevant, only to find that its content covers an entirely different subject. There is also the opposite danger of overlooking an article of importance to one's study simply because its title made it appear irrelevant. The general format of a title page is shown in the specimen page. Note, for example, that the title is spaced in inverted pyramid when its length calls for more than one line of writing.

THE RELATIONSHIP OF SOCIO-ECONOMIC STATUS

TO PERFORMANCE ON THE ITEMS OF

THE REVISED STANFORD-BINET

A Thesis Submitted to the Graduate Faculty of

the University of . . .

in Partial Fulfillment of the Requirements

for the Degree of

Master of Education

by

John C. Doe

City, State

Month, Year

TABLE OF CONTENTS

CHAPTER 1

THE PROBLEM AND ITS BACKGROUND

Few scientific problems have been the subject of so much speculation and controversy as have the estimation of the influence of
environment on intelligence and the determination of the degree to
which intelligence tests now in common use can be considered valid
instruments for the measurement of the mental ability of subjects
who deviate widely in one or more respects from the average of the
group on which the norms of such tests were derived. Inasmuch as
the Revised Stanford-Binet Scale of Intelligence is used extensively to test children from all socio-economic levels, there is a need
to investigate the reliance which can be placed on the results of
this scale when it is used to test children whose socio-economic
background is either extremely favorable or extremely unfavorable.

The Problem

Statement and delimitation of the problem. It was the purpose
of this investigation to compare the performance on the items of
the Revised Stanford-Binet Scale of Intelligence, Form L, of pupils
from homes of low socio-economic status with that of pupils of equal
mental age coming from homes of high socio-economic status with a
view to determining the items, and particularly the types of items,
if any, on which performance is greatly affected by differences in

1

The Acknowledgments   The acknowledgment page frequently appears to clash with the objective and scientific tone which a paper of this kind should reflect. Although it is natural for the student to feel some degree of obligation toward a number of persons who have contributed to his study, sentimental expressions of "deep gratitude" to his advisor, his spouse, his typist, and innumerable other contributors are hardly called for. Certainly, helping graduate students with their research has high priority among the responsibilities the faculty is willing to assume; professional people do not consider this "beyond the call of duty" and deserving of special thanks.

The Table of Contents   Since there is no index in a thesis or dissertation, the table of contents becomes the only means of locating material within the report. Even more important, it provides the framework around which the report is organized and is, therefore, the base of operations. It should be very carefully done. Certainly, a graduate student should be able to organize his report into the chapter headings, subheadings, and sub-subheadings called for by his material. It must be consistent in indentation, capitalization, etc. and must agree with the actual organization of the text of the report.

The Chapter-Title Pages   Usually pages headed by a chapter title carry the line CHAPTER . . . down about two inches from the top of the page, followed three spaces lower by the title of the chapter in full capital letters. The first line of text begins three spaces below the title. The page number should be centered one inch from the bottom of the page and two spaces below the last line.

Headings   Major headings are centered on the line, and capitalized on the major words. They are separated from the preceding and succeeding line of the text by three spaces. Subheadings are underscored and indented three, five, or seven spaces. Only the first words and proper nouns are capitalized. They are followed by a period, and the text begins on the same line. All headings should maintain parallel structure.

Margins   Margins of 1¾ inches on the left and 1¼ inches on the right-hand sides of the page are commonly used. The last line of writing should be one inch above the bottom edge of the page. Except on chapter-title pages, the page number should come at the top right-hand corner of the page, one inch from the top edge and 1¼ inches from the right edge. The first line of text should be two or three spaces below the page number.

Pagination   Pages should be numbered consecutively in Arabic numerals from the first page of text to the end of the manuscript (including the appendices). The pages in the introductory sections are numbered ii, iii, iv, . . . one inch from the bottom of the page. Exceptions to this rule include the title page, which is counted but not numbered, and the approval page, which is neither numbered nor counted. All page numbers should stand alone, without period, hyphens, or dashes.

Bibliography   The bibliography tells the reader the sources of the investigator's information; it is always required in a thesis or dissertation. Generally, it should include only sources that have a direct bearing on the study and should be labeled SELECTED BIBLIOGRAPHY rather than simply BIBLIOGRAPHY. It must include every reference cited in the report and perhaps others of significance to the study.* On the other hand, the bibliography must not appear padded. Generally, the bibliography is not annotated, since the review of the literature is actually a form of annotation from the standpoint of the study. It should be preceded by a fly-sheet bearing the word BIBLIOGRAPHY. The fly-sheet and the first page of the bibliography, like all title pages, are numbered at the bottom of the page. The bibliography must, of course, be accurate and complete, since errors and omissions automatically render it useless. It should also be in good form.

Appendix   Material which, though pertinent to the study, would impede the flow of the report rather than aid in its understanding should ordinarily be placed in the appendix rather than in the main body of the text. Thus, whereas summary tables and other materials necessary for interpretation of the study are placed in the text, tables of raw data should be put in the appendix. Similarly, the discussion of the general nature and orientation of the questionnaire used must be included in the chapter on the de-

---

* When this section is called *References* (instead of *Bibliography*), in accordance with APA style, it is restricted to sources specifically cited.

sign of the study, but the actual questionnaire, together with the cover and the follow-up letters, should be placed in the appendix. The appendices should be preceded by a numbered fly-sheet with the word APPENDIX or APPENDICES centered on the page.

Footnote and Bibliographic Form   Credit must always be given for material that is borrowed—verbatim or paraphrased— from other sources; failure to do so constitutes plagiarism. The exact form through which such credit is given is, to some extent, a matter of personal preference, consistent with such criteria as convenience and clarity of identification of the source in question and graduate school or journal policy, where pertinent. The APA style manual (1967), for example, uses the date of publication in parentheses directly following the name of the author as the basis for identifying a particular entry, e.g., "Smith (1955) found . . . ." or "Smith (1955a) found . . . .", if the bibliography lists more than one Smith, 1955 entry. This style is particularly appropriate in a fast-moving field, where the date of publication may be a crucial factor in evaluating a source; it is standard in all APA and AERA publications and is becoming more accepted, if not recommended, for theses and dissertations in Psychology and Education. A some- what similar system also used occasionally in dissertations assigns a number to each item of the bibliography as the basis for its iden- tification. The bibliography is first alphabetized and numbered consecutively; reference to a given entry is then made by placing its number in parentheses directly following the author's name, e.g., "Smith (79) reports . . . .", where "79" is the number of the Smith reference in the bibliography. If, for any reason, the page number is needed, it can be added in the parenthesis, e.g., "Smith (79:174) reports . . . ." This system becomes cumbersome when a large number of references are involved: if a last-minute addition or deletion is made to the bibliography, for example, every refer- ence higher on the alphabet would presumably have to be renum- bered accordingly both in the bibliography and the text.

The older system consisted of footnotes listed at the bottom of the page and referenced in the text by superscripts placed immediately following the name of the author, at the end of the sentence in which the reference is made, or at the end of the quotation. Although any of these forms is acceptable, the first is easier to handle in such instances as: "Both Smith[1] and Brown[2] express . . . ." This system is also cumbersome when many references are to be listed; it is totally impractical in such publications as the *Review of Educational Research,* where the large number of footnotes would simply pile higher and higher at the bottom of each page.

Stylistic details pertaining to footnotes and bibliographic entries vary to such an extent that it is relatively impossible to cover all situations. A number of "acceptable" forms for some of the more common types of reference are illustrated below:

Books:

1. Footnote : John C. Smith and Robert B. Case. *Principles of Research,* 1960. p. 111.
2. Bibliography : Smith, John C. and Robert B. Case. *Principles of Research.* New York: Doe Publications, 1960.

Later footnotes may be abbreviated to *Ibid; Ibid,* p. 112; Smith and Case, *op   ,* or Smith and Case, *op. cit.,* p. 112; depending on the circumstances.

Periodicals:

1. Footnote : John C. Smith. "A study of common errors in spelling," *Journal of English Usage,* 16: 116–29; 1957.
2. Bibliography : Smith, John C. "A study of common errors in spelling," *Journal of English Usage,* 16: 116–29; 1957.

Later footnotes may be abbreviated as above.

Articles in an encyclopedia or yearbook:

1. Footnote : John C. Smith. "Spelling," in James L. Brown (ed.) *Encyclopedia of Language,* 1950. pp. 345–56.
2. Bibliography : Smith, John C. "Spelling," in James L. Brown (ed.) *Encyclopedia of Language.* New York: Doe Publications, 1950. pp. 345–56.

Unpublished theses or manuscripts:

1. Footnote : John C. Smith. *An Investigation of Common Errors in Scientific Writings.* Unpublished Master's Thesis. New York: Midtown University, 1955.
2. Bibliography : Smith, John C. *An Investigation of Common Errors in Scientific Writings.* Unpublished Master's Thesis. New York: Midtown University, 1955.

Quotations   Wholesale use of quotations is to be discouraged, since most quotable material can be paraphrased (with citation) to better advantage in terms of the particular orientation of the report. Quotations are appropriate: 1. when a point is to be challenged or there is need for special clarity in the issue being engaged—e.g., when a point of law is involved; 2. when two conflicting positions are to be compared; and 3. when a point is so well-stated, perhaps by a recognized authority, that it would add prestige to the idea being expressed and respectability to the study. It must be remembered, however, that notes should be taken for their significance rather than for their wit or literary flavor. The inclusion of a quotation simply because it comes from an authority or is cleverly stated, is an indication that the investigator is not too clear as to what he is about.

Short quotations generally are included as part of the regular text with quotation marks; longer quotations are indented and single spaced, without quotation marks. All quotations are footnoted. Omissions from a quotation are indicated by three spaced dots, with an additional dot to represent the period when the omission occurs at the end of the sentence—for example, "The validity of a rating scale . . . is always difficult to determine . . . ."

Tables   The usual format of a table is shown below:

TABLE 2
REPRESENTATIVENESS OF THE SAMPLE

Stratum	Population		Sample	
	Number	Percent	Number	Percent
1	2803	11.9	67	12.1
2	2759	11.7	63	11.3
3	3550	15.1	87	15.6
4	2638	11.2	63	11.3
. . . .				
9	2119	9.1	51	9.2
TOTAL	23 481	100.0	556	100.0

The word TABLE and the table title are capitalized, and the table number is in Arabic numerals. Double lines appear at the top and a single line separates the heading section. The title should be concise; avoid for instance, "TABLE SHOWING . . ." Tables should be simple and clear; making two tables is generally preferable to attempting to cover too many points in one table. Vertical lines should not be used to separate the columns; to be understandable and attractive, a table should not be so crowded that vertical lines are necessary. Footnotes to tables should be referenced through such symbols as *, †, ‡, ||, and ¶ (in order) rather than through superscripts which might be confused with the numbers in the table. Also note that, unless absolutely necessary, tables should not be broken to fall on two pages; with modern Xerox equipment, a large table can be reduced to a standard 8½ by 11 at nominal cost. When a table must be placed crosswise on a page, it should be placed so that the title is next to the binding.

TYPING

Typing is always a chore. If the student can type he probably should type his rough drafts, inasmuch as he gains insight into his study by going through the actual motions of putting it together. His first drafts will have to be revised and he should use double spacing in order to permit easy correction and revision.

A carbon copy is an absolute necessity. Copies of basic data should also be made (by photocopy, if necessary) and one copy stored in a safe place. Besides being insurance against loss or misplacement, a carbon copy also permits the student to continue with his work when the manuscript is in the hands of his advisor or the typist.

Generally, the student should not type his final draft. Unless he is an expert typist, he should allow himself the luxury of having the final step toward his degree custom-made. The final draft calls for many carbons* and almost erasure-free copy, a task that is better placed in the hands of a professional typist. On the other hand, the student must assume all responsibility for providing the typist with a usable copy and for checking her work. Needless to say, the better the draft presented to the typist, the fewer the errors and the nicer the arrangement of the final product. A good typist can catch an occasional error, but a sloppy rough draft is an open invitation to unsatisfactory work.

* Xeroxed copies are obviously to be preferred over multiple onionskin carbons.

STYLE

Effective Writing

Invariably, the greatest weakness of the research report is in expression and organization. Faculty advisors, almost without fail, spend more time on the grammatical and organizational aspects of the report than they do on the research design. Frequently, the trouble is a matter of carelessness—certainly, a graduate student should be able to make verbs agree with their subject, to avoid split infinitives, and to express his ideas clearly and effectively.

Unfortunately, however, inability to write is not restricted to graduate students; educators in general have been charged repeatedly with similar incompetence. Shannon (1951), for example, points out that "the evidence [of incompetence or indifference in writing] against education is too consistent and too convincing to be shrugged off as inconsequential." He goes on to say that dull writing is no more excusable than a dull wit, that effective writing is an art that can be learned, and that it is hard to believe that a person intelligent enough to do a reputable piece of research cannot report what he did with an equal degree of competence.

Dullness and monotony probably head the list of the specific criticisms of educational writings, but ineffectiveness and incoherence in organization, lack of clarity and forcefulness in sentence and paragraph structure, lack of precision in vocabulary, and even common grammatical errors are also frequently mentioned. Other faults more directly related to the research report include lack of precision in the statement and delineation of the problem, the making of sweeping generalizations, the use of flowery and ineffective language, and the inadequate synthesis of the various parts of the report.

To make matters worse, this is an area in which it is difficult to give constructive advice. The advisor is occasionally faced with having to rewrite each sentence and reorganize one section after another, or to give such advice as "be more careful," "write better," or "rewrite this section"—all of which are rather futile. Another consideration concerns the wisdom of twisting every sentence to the advisor's writing style; each person has his own way of saying things which generally should be respected. Undoubtedly, many research reports need to be improved, but there is a need for some degree of tolerance and appreciation of the fact that there is frequently more than one style of good writing. On the other hand, poor writing and carelessness cannot be condoned—and there might be a time when the student should be told to start again.

Some graduate students have not learned how to organize a research paper. The advisor would do well to insist that, before he undertakes to write one single line of his report, the student read half-a-dozen of the better organized and written dissertations in his field. With the small cost of microfilms, providing such models should impose far less financial strain on the institution than the failure to do so imposes academic stress on the advisor. Thus, a student familiar with good thesis writing would know that: 1. the research report is written in the past tense (e.g., the study was conducted . . . . , Group A gained . . . . , etc.). On the other hand, the conclusions supposedly representing a fact applicable to more than the single instance are written in the present tense (e.g., Motivation is conducive to effective learning). Certain parts of the description of the locale of the study should also be in the present (e.g., Miami is located on the gold coast of Florida). 2. Personal pronouns of the first person (I, me, my, we, our, etc.) are to be avoided; a research report should be impersonal. In general, references to the writer or the investigator should be kept to a minimum. 3. The active voice is generally to be preferred to the passive. 4. Numbers up to ten and all numbers beginning a sentence should be written out in full. The local thesis manual should be consulted for more specific and detailed suggestions. Specialized sources such as the *Manual for Writers of Term Papers, Theses, and Dissertations* (Turabian, 1967) and the American Psychological Association *Publication Manual* (1967) should be consulted for special problems that may arise.

Vocabulary

The purpose of the report is to communicate with one's colleagues relative to what was done and what was found—not to impress them with one's vocabulary and with one's ability to understand something "so obviously complicated." The writing should, therefore, aim for simplicity, clarity, and conciseness; conversely, it should avoid flowery language and other forms of verbal gymnastics. This does not imply the exclusive use of simple vocabulary, but rather the "art of plain talk" within the framework of the complexity of the materials presented.

Sentence Organization

Every sentence must convey its meaning with a maximum degree of precision. It is a good exercise, for example, to go over the report with a view to removing phrases, sentences, and even paragraphs that contribute nothing to the report. It is not uncommon, for instance, to see a paragraph begin with: "Dr. John K. Smith of the University of . . . in 1950 wrote an article entitled: . . . ." or even "Smith conducted a study . . . . He found . . . ." Why all the verbiage? What does it all contribute to the study?

The report should be organized to promote the straightest path to reader comprehension. This is sometimes made difficult by the fact that the investigator is so familiar with his topic that he loses perspective and cannot see what needs to be said, what needs to be emphasized, and what can be left out. As a result, he may leave out a key idea and leave the poor reader perplexed on the very point that is crucial to his understanding. Before giving the report a final polish, it is generally advisable, therefore, to have some other person read the rough manuscript with a view to improving its general organization.

THE RESEARCH REPORT

No matter how significant a study may be, it is useless if it is not reported. If one spent the time and energy to conduct a research project, it becomes his professional responsibility to make the results available to others, for this is the only way in which the profession can prosper.

The reasons why an investigator does not report his study are varied. He may feel that the reporting is something of an anti-climax; he may have been with the project so long that it has become stale. Some investigators feel that they are interested only in the results and that the labor and precision required for writing a complete report loom rather large, especially when many find effective writing difficult. A partial solution that has much to recommend it is for the investigator to write his report as he goes along. The review of the literature and the design of the study should be written in semi-final form before the study is under-taken. For the investigator to put himself in a position to have to explain what he is doing and why is obviously one of the most effective ways for him to clarify his thinking relative to his problem and the procedures he should follow in its investigation. Not only will it bring his study into focus but it also will result in an im-provement both in the design of the study and the adequacy of the report. Obviously, the written report cannot be in final form until the whole study is completed. The investigator may have to go back and rewrite his problem in line with the conclusions he has been able to derive from his data, but he should take every oppor-tunity to project his study as far as he can. He should, for example, anticipate the type of data he is likely to obtain, the type of analysis he will be able to make and even the format of the tables he will need to devise. When this is done systematically, the writing of the report is not a chore but a companion step to the investigation itself.

Even when the study is conducted primarily to fulfill a degree requirement, some attempt should be made to publish an article that will bring the study to the attention of the profession. This is simply a fee the student should expect to pay the profession for the services he has received from his advisor and his committee. This is especially important in the case of the master's thesis, which often remains relatively unknown. It is also possible that a doctoral candidate can make a contribution by publishing an article on an aspect of his study which is not adequately covered in his summary in *Dissertation Abstracts*.

This raises the question of the contributions such articles might make to the advancement of education. Obviously, anything that would advance the cause of education should be made available and, as a general rule, anything that a member of the profession in good standing has taken time and energy to in-vestigate probably is not devoid of merit: it must contain at least one idea that will stimulate others. The converse viewpoint is that the professional literature is so cluttered with articles—many of poor quality—that journal space should be restricted to articles that make a significant contribution. This points to the need for concise writing. In view of the shortage of journal space, it be-comes a matter of professional courtesy for the writer to strive for brevity within the framework of the necessary clarity. It may be possible to say in one sentence what might normally be said in two and to tabulate material which would take pages to describe in detail. This, of course, has its drawbacks in that overemphasis on brevity may result in the omission of certain details that would make the study meaningful.

EVALUATION OF THE RESEARCH REPORT

The production of a good research report calls for meticulous attention to innumerable details involving all the points considered here and many more. This is a most crucial aspect of graduate training, and the quality of the final product is a direct reflection of the "quality" of the student. It must be recognized that quality in as complex a matter as a thesis or dissertation is frequently a matter of intangibles which are difficult to identify. It is generally easier to identify areas of weakness that make a report inadequate than it is to spell out the specific points, attention to which will guarantee its adequacy. It must be realized that producing a good thesis—just like winning a football game—is more than mere compliance with rules.

Judging the adequacy of a research report after it has been submitted—although even then a difficult task—is apparently easier than listing definite criteria which will fit every study that might be undertaken. The following items are, therefore, simply some of the points a student might consider in the evaluation—and especially in the improvement—of his report.

1. *General Format*	attractiveness; conformity to external mechanics of good form: margins, pagination, etc.; freedom from typographical errors and erasures.
2. *Title*	appropriateness to the problem actually investigated; clarity and conciseness.
3. *Problem*	significance and possible contribution; clarity and conciseness of the statement of the problem; parsimony and tenability of the basic hypotheses; feasibility and suitability of the study.
4. *Review of the Literature*	thoroughness and comprehensiveness; evaluation and synthesis of the sources.

5. *Design*	adequacy and appropriateness to the problem under investigation; adequacy of the description of the design; adequacy of the instruments and procedures.
6. *Analysis of the Data*	validity of the data; reliability; adequacy of the analysis; appropriateness of statistical procedures; objectivity and insight in interpretation; effectiveness of the tables and other means of presentation.
7. *Conclusions*	validity of the conclusions; foundation on basic evidence; recognition of assumptions and limitations; integration with the statement of the problem; synthesis of the status of the problem and suggestions for further investigation.
8. *General Scholarship*	logical and coherent organization; breakdown into an effective system of headings and subheadings; evidence of insight into the nature of the problem; imagination in the design of the study and the interpretation of the results; evidence of adequate grasp of research and statistical tools; display of a scientific attitude; effectiveness in presentation of the report.

Selected References

American Psychological Association. *Publication Manual.* Washington: The Assn., 1967.

Baumol, William J. and Peggy Heim. "On contracting with publishers: Or what every author should know," *A.A.U.P. Bull.*, 53: 30-46; 1967.

Dugdale, Kathleen. *A Manual for Theses and Term Papers.* Bloomington: Indiana Univ. Bookstore, 1962.

Flesch, Rudolph F. *The Art of Plain Talk.* New York: Harper & Row, 1946.

———. *The Art of Readable Writing.* New York: Harper & Row, 1949.

———. *How to Make Sense.* New York: Harper & Row, 1954.

——— and A.H. Lass. *The Way to Write.* New York: McGraw-Hill, 1955.

Frankel, Charles. "John Dewey: Where he stands," *Teach. educ. Quart.*, 17: 84-89; 1960.

Guba, Egon G. "Guides for the writing of proposals," in Jack A. Culbertson and Stephen P. Hencley (eds.) *Educational Research: New Perspectives.* Danville: Interstate, 1963. pp. 289-305.

Holt, Robert R. "Researchmanship—Or how to write a dissertation in psychology without really trying," *Amer. Psychol.*, 14: 151; 1959.

Hoppin, Richard. "On the use and abuse of footnotes," *Grad. Sch. Rec.*, 20: 3–4; 1966.

Jent, H.C. "Inverse plagiarism," *Sch. & Soc.*, 95: 314–16; 1967.

Johnson, Granville B. "A method of evaluating research articles in education," *J. educ. Res.*, 51: 149–51; 1957.

Kooker, Earl W. "How to prove a point," *Educ. Forum*, 29: 99–103; 1964.

Lindvall, C.M. "Improving research: The review of related research," *Phi Delta Kappan*, 40: 179–80; 1959.

Lipson, Shirley and Anne W. Abrams. *The College of Education Style Manual.* Columbus: Ohio State Univ., 1960.

McIntyre, Kenneth. "How to write a thesis without really trying," *Phi Delta Kappan*, 46: 123–25; 1964.

Reisman, S.J. *A Style Manual for Technical Writers and Editors.* New York: Macmillan, 1962.

Sanford, Fillmore. "How to write a textbook," *Amer. Psychol.*, 6: 127–28; 1961.

Seeber, Edward D. *A Style Manual for Authors.* Bloomington: Indiana Univ. Press, 1965.

Shannon, John R. "Style in reporting research," *Calif. J. educ. Res.*, 1: 215–18; 1950.

———. "Art in writing for educational periodicals," *J. educ. Res.*, 44: 599–610, 1951; 46: 333–45, 1953; 47: 489–504, 1954.

Sherman, Theodore A. *Modern Technical Writing.* Englewood Cliffs: Prentice-Hall, 1966.

Strang, Ruth M. "Principles of readability applied to reporting research," *T. C. Rec.*, 49: 449–51; 1948.

Suydam, Marilyn N. "An instrument for evaluating empirical educational research projects," *J. educ. Res.*, 61: 200–03; 1968.

Thoma, Henry F. "Good morning, Professor; Want to write a textbook?" *Coll. Engl.*, 19: 45–50; Nov. 1957.

Turabian, Kate L. *Manual for Writers of Term Papers, Theses, and Dissertations.* Chicago: Univ. of Chicago Press, 1967.

U.S. Government Style Manual. Washington: Govt. Printing Office, 1959.

Woodford, F. Peter. "Sound thinking through clear writing," *Sci.*, 156: 743–45; 1967.

BIBLIOGRAPHY

Abrams, Mark. *Social Surveys and Social Action*. London: Heinemann, 1951.

Ackoff, Russell L. *The Design of Social Research*. Chicago: Univ. of Chicago Press, 1953.

Aikin, Wilford M. *The Story of the Eight Year Study*. New York: Harper & Row, 1942.

Alford, Albert L. "The Elementary and Secondary Education Act of 1965— What to anticipate," *Phi Delta Kappan*, 46: 483–88; 1965.

Allport, Gordon W. *The Use of Personal Documents in Psychological Science*. Bull., No. 49. New York: Soc. Sci. Res. Council, 1942.

American Association for Advancement of Science. *Symposium in Basic Research*. Publ., No. 56. Washington: The Assn., 1959.

American Council on Education. *Educational Research: Its Nature, Essential Conditions, and Controlling Concepts*. Studies, Ser. I, Vol. 3, No. 10. Washington: The Council, 1939.

American Educational Research Association. *Improving Educational Research*. Washington: The Assn., 1948.

——. *Growing Points in Educational Research*. Washington: The Assn., 1949.

——. "Twenty-five years of educational research," *Rev. educ. Res.*, 26: 199–344; 1956.

American Library Association. *The Library and Information Networks of the Future*. Chicago: The Assn., 1963.

American Psychological Association. "Basic research and national goals," *Amer. Psychol.*, 20: 662–86; 1965.

——. "Testimony before House Special Sub-Committee on Invasion of Privacy of the Committee on Governmental Operations," *Amer. Psychol.*, 21: 404–22; 1966.

——. *Casebook of Ethical Standards of Psychologists*. Washington: The Assn., 1967.

——. *Publication Manual*. Washington: The Assn., 1967.

Anderson, H.H. et al. *Studies of Teachers' Classroom Personalities.* Appl. Psychol. Monogr., No. 6, 1945; No. 8, 1946; No. 11, 1946.

Anderson, Kenneth E. "Avenues for the improvement of research," *Sci. Educ.,* 45: 418–24; 1961a.

———. "Improving the competence of teachers in measurements and evaluation," *Sci. Educ.,* 45: 424–29; 1961b.

Andrews, F.E. *Philanthropic Foundations.* New York: Russell Sage Foundation, 1956.

Andrews, J.H.M. "Practical function of research," *Canad. educ. Res. Dig.,* 3: 169–80; 1963.

Ash, Lee (compiler). *Subject Collections.* New York: Bowker, 1958.

Ashley, W.R. et al. "The perceived size of coins in normal and hypnotically induced economic states," *Amer. J. Psychol.,* 64: 564–72; 1951.

Atkin, J.M. "Basing curriculum change on research and demonstration," *Educ. Forum,* 31: 27–33; 1966.

Ausubel, David P. "The nature of educational research," *Educ. Theory,* 3: 314–20; 1953.

Bacon, Francis. *Bacon's Novum Organum* (T. Fowler, ed.) Oxford: Clarendon Press, 1889.

Baldwin, Alfred L. *Theories of Child Development.* New York: Wiley, 1967.

Bales, R. F. *Interaction Process Analysis.* Cambridge: Addison-Wesley, 1950.

Barbour, John "Human brain can be controlled by button," *Miami Herald,* Nov. 20, 1966, p. 11-C. (Reference to the work of Dr. Robert Heath and Dr. José Delgado.)

Barnes, John B. *Educational Research for Classroom Teachers.* New York: Putnam, 1960.

Barr, Arvil S. *Characteristic Differences in the Teaching Performance of Good and Poor Teachers in the Social Studies.* Bloomington: Public School Publ. Co., 1929.

———. "The measurement and prediction of teaching efficiency: A summary of investigations," *J. exper. Educ.,* 16: 203–83; 1948.

———. "Research methods," in Chester W. Harris (ed.) *Encyclopedia of Educational Research.* New York: Macmillan, 1960. pp. 1160–66.

Barton, Mary N. and Marian V. Bell. *Reference Books: A Brief Guide for Students and Other Users of the Library.* Baltimore: Enoch Pratt Free Library, 1966.

Barzun, Jacques and Henry F. Graff. *The Modern Researcher.* New York: Harcourt, Brace & World, 1957.

Bayles, Ernest E. *Democratic Educational Theory.* New York: Harper & Row, 1950 (rev., 1960).

Bellack, Arno A. (ed.) *Theory and Research in Teaching.* New York: Bur. Publ., T. C., Columbia Univ., 1963.

Berelson, Bernard. *Graduate Education in the United States.* New York: McGraw-Hill, 1960.

Best, John W. *Research in Education.* Englewood Cliffs: Prentice-Hall, 1959.

Besvinick, Sidney L. "Universities and sponsored research policy," *Phi Delta Kappan,* 48: 72–74; 1966.

Binet, Alfred and T.H. Simon. *The Development of Intelligence in Children.* (trans. by E.S. Kite) Baltimore: Williams & Wilkins, 1916.

Bishop, Jerry E. "Surgeons ponder ways to obtain vital organs for future transplants," *Wall Str. J.,* 170, No. 118: 1, 20; Dec. 18, 1967.

Black, Dorothy M. *Guide to Lists of Master's Theses.* Chicago: Amer. Library Assn., 1966.

Blauch, Lloyd E. (ed.) *Education for the Professions.* Washington: H.E.W., 1955.

Bloom, Benjamin S. (ed.) *The Taxonomy of Educational Objectives, I: Cognitive Domain.* New York: McKay, 1956.

———. "Twenty-five years of educational research," *Amer. educ. Res. J.,* 3: 211–21; 1966.

Board of Scientific Affairs. "Technical communication in psychology: A statement of the problem," *Amer. Psychol.,* 14: 267–71; 1959.

Boerrigter, Glenn C. "The USOE's support of extramural research," *Phi Delta Kappan,* 47: 554–57; 1966.

Bogue, Jesse P. (ed.) *American Junior Colleges.* Washington: Amer. Council Educ., 1940–date.

Bonner, James. "The next ninety years," in Richard P. Schuster (ed.) *The Next Ninety Years.* Pasadena: Calif. Inst. Technology, 1967. p. 78.

——— et al. *The Next Hundred Years.* Pasadena: Calif. Inst. Technology, 1957.

Bowman, Claude C. "Must the social sciences foster moral skepticism?" *Amer. sociol. Rev.,* 10: 709, 715; 1945.

Boyd, Ann M. and Rae E. Rips. *United States Government Publications.* New York: Wilson, 1949.

Brehaut, Willard. *A Quarter Century of Educational Research in Canada: An Analysis of Dissertations in Education Accepted by Canadian Universities, 1930–55.* Toronto: College of Education, Univ. of Toronto, 1958.

———. "An analysis of dissertations in education accepted by Canadian universities, 1930–55," *Ont. J. educ. Res.,* 2: 109–22; 1960.

Brickell, Henry M. "The dynamics of educational change," *Theory into Practice,* 1: 81–88; 1962.

Brickman, William W. *A Guide to Research in Educational History.* New York: New York Univ., 1949.

Bridgman, Percy W. *The Logic of Modern Physics.* New York: Macmillan, 1927.

———. "The present state of operationalism," in Phillip G. Frank (ed.)

The Validation of Scientific Theories. New York: Collier, 1961. pp. 75–80.

Bright, R. Louis. "Bright seeks 'basic' ed. research," *Educ. Res.,* 19: 1–2, 8; 1968.

Bronowski, Jacob. "Science and human values," *Univ. Quart.,* 10: 247–59; 324–38, 1955; 11: 26–42, 1956.

Brown, Clarence W. and Edwin E. Ghiselli. *Scientific Method in Psychology.* New York: McGraw-Hill, 1955.

Brown, Edwin J. "Some of the less measurable outcomes of education," *Educ. psychol. Measmt,* 2: 353–58; 1942.

Brownell, Samuel M. "The case for educational research," *Phi Delta Kappan,* 37: 203–06; 1956.

Brownell, William A. "Critique of research on learning and on instruction in the school," in Ralph Tyler (ed.) *Graduate Study in Education.* 50th Yrbk., N.S.S.E., Pt. I. Chicago: Univ. of Chicago Press, 1951. pp. 52–66.

Bryan, Roy C. *Keys to Professional Information for Teachers.* Kalamazoo: Western Michigan Univ., 1957.

Buckingham, B.R. "The editor turns professor," *Res. Bull.,* 6: 252–53; 1927.

Bunge, Mario. *Scientific Research, I: The Search for System.* New York: Springer-Verlag, 1967.

Burchinal, Lee G. "ERIC—and the need to know," *NEA J.,* 56: 65–72; 1967a.

———. "ERIC and dissemination of research findings," *Theory into Practice,* 6: 77–84; 1967b.

——— and Harold Haswell. "How to put two and a half tons of research into one handy little box," *Amer. Educ.,* 2: 23–24; Feb. 1966.

Burke, Arvid J. and Mary A. Burke. *Documentation in Education.* New York: Teachers College Press, 1967.

Buros, Oscar K. (ed.) *Tests in Print.* Highland Park: Gryphon Press, 1961.

———. *The Sixth Mental Measurement Yearbook.* Highland Park: Gryphon Press, 1965. (See also earlier editions.)

Burt, Cyril and W.L. Gregory. "Scientific method in psychology, II," *Brit. J. stat. Psychol.,* 11: 105–32; 1958.

Burton, William H. "Basic principles in a good teaching-learning situation," *Phi Delta Kappan,* 39: 242–48; 1958.

——— et al. *Education for Effective Thinking.* New York: Appleton-Century-Crofts, 1960.

Buswell, Guy T. "Structure of educational research," *Phi Delta Kappan,* 24: 167–69; 1941.

———. "Review of N.L. Gage (ed.) *Handbook of Research on Teaching,*" *Phi Delta Kappan,* 44: 55–57; 1963.

——— and T.R. McConnell. *Training for Educational Research.* Berkeley: Center for the Study of Higher Education, Univ. of Calif., 1966.

Cahalan, Don et al. "Interviewer bias involved in certain types of opinion survey questions," *Int. J. opinion attitude Res.*, 1: 63–77; 1947.

Calkins, Patricia and Joan Grussow. "ERIC—Data on the disadvantaged," *Phi Delta Kappan*, 48: 372–84; 1967.

Campbell, Donald T. and Julian C. Stanley. "Experimental and quasi-experimental designs for research in teaching," in N.L. Gage (ed.) *Handbook of Research on Teaching*. Chicago: Rand McNally, 1963. pp. 171–246.

Campbell, Roald F. "Training of research professors in educational administration," in Jack A. Culbertson and Stephen P. Hencley (eds.) *Educational Research: New Perspectives.* Danville: Interstate, 1963. pp. 341–54.

Canadian Education Association. *Invitational Conferences on Educational Research*. Toronto: The Assn., 1959–date.

Cantril, Hadley. *Gauging Public Opinion*. Princeton: Princeton Univ. Press, 1947.

Carmichael, Oliver C. *Graduate Education: A Critique and a Program*. New York: Harper & Row, 1961.

Carter, Launor F. "National document-handling systems in science and technology," *Sci.*, 154: 1299–1304; 1966.

Cattell, Jacques (ed.) *Directory of American Scholars: A Biographical Directory*. Lancaster: Science Press, 1957.

—— and E.E. Ross (eds.) *Leaders in Education: A Biographical Directory*. Lancaster: Science Press, 1948.

Cattell, Raymond B. (ed.) *Handbook of Multivariate Experimental Psychology*. Chicago: Rand McNally, 1966.

Charters, W.W. "Beyond the survey in school board research," *Educ. Admin. Superv.*, 41: 449–52; 1955.

Clark, David L. "Educational research: A national perspective," in Jack A. Culbertson and Stephen P. Hencley (eds.) *Educational Research: New Perspectives*. Danville: Interstate, 1963. pp. 7–18.

—— and W.R. Carriker, "Educational research and the Cooperative Research Program," *Phi Delta Kappan*, 42: 226–30; 1961.

—— and Blaine R. Worthen. *Preparing Research Personnel for Education*. Bloomington: Phi Delta Kappa, 1967. (or Washington: Amer. Educ. Res. Assn.)

Clarke, Stanley C.T. "Trends and problems in educational research," *Alta. J. educ. Res.*, 3: 209–19; 1957.

Cochran, William G. et al. "Statistical problems of the Kinsey Report," *J. Amer. stat. Assn.*, 48: 673–716; 1953.

Combs, Arthur W. and Donald Snygg. *Individual Behavior: A Perceptual Approach to Behavior*. New York: Harper & Row, 1959.

Conant, James B. "The role of science in our unique society," *Sci.*, 107: 77–83; 1948.

Conger, John J. "Personality factors in driver education," *Phi Delta Kappan*, 41: 396–97; 1960.

Conrad, Herbert S. "Contributions of the Federal Government to educational research methodology," in Frank W. Banghart (ed.) *Educational Research*. 1st Annual Symposium. Bloomington: Phi Delta Kappa, 1960. pp. 23–41.

———. "Clearance of questionnaires with respect to invasion of privacy, etc.: Principles and viewpoints in the Bureau of Research, U.S.O.E.," *Sociol. Educ.*, 40: 170–75; 1967.

Cook, Desmond L. "The Hawthorne effect in educational research," *Phi Delta Kappan*, 44: 116–22; 1962.

Cook, Robert C. (ed.) *Who's Who in American Education*. Nashville: Who's Who in American Education, 1928–date.

———. *Presidents and Deans of American Colleges and Universities*. Nashville: Who's Who in American Education, 1935–date.

———. *Trustees and Presidents in American Colleges and Universities*. Nashville: Who's Who in American Education, 1955–date.

Coombs, P.H. "Education's greatest need: A vice-president in charge of heresy," *Phi Delta Kappan*, 41: 243–47; 1960.

Corey, Arthur (chrman.) *Education and the Spirit of Science*. Washington: Educ. Pol. Comm., N.E.A., 1966.

Corey, Stephen M. "Action research, fundamental research, and educational practices," *T. C. Rec.*, 50: 509–14; 1949. (Also in *Growing Points in Educational Research*. Washington: Amer. Educ. Res. Assn., 1949. pp. 261–65.)

———. *Action Research to Improve School Practice*. New York: T. C., Columbia Univ., 1953.

Cornell, Francis G. "Getting action by means of the school survey," in *Growing Points in Educational Research*. Washington: Amer. Educ. Res. Assn., 1949. pp. 62–67.

——— and Walter S. Monroe. "Productive methods in research," *Phi Delta Kappan*, 35: 29–34; 1953.

——— et al. *An Exploratory Measurement of Individualities of Schools and Classrooms*. Urbana: Bur. Educ. Res., Univ. of Illinois, 1952.

Cremin, Lawrence A. *The Transformation of the School: Progressivism in American Education, 1876–1957*. New York: Knopf, 1961.

Cronbach, Lee J. "The role of the university in improving education," *Phi Delta Kappan*, 47: 539–45; 1966.

Cubberley, Ellwood P. *Public Education in the United States*. Boston: Houghton-Mifflin, 1934.

Cuber, J.F. and J.B. Gerberich. "A note on consistency in questionnaire responses," *Amer. sociol. Rev.*, 11: 13–15; 1946.

Culbertson, Jack A. and Stephen P. Hencley (eds.) *Educational Research: New Perspectives*. Danville: Interstate, 1963.

Cureton, Thomas K. *Masters' Theses in Health, Physical Education, and Recreation.* Washington: N.E.A., 1930–date.

Davis, O.L. "Organized knowledge influencing curriculum decisions," *Rev., educ. Res.,* 33: 245–53; 1963.

Dearborn, Walter F. and John W.M. Rothney. *Predicting the Child's Development.* Cambridge: Sci-Art, 1941.

Dewey, John. *How We Think.* Boston: Heath, 1933.

Draper, S. cited by J. Spivak. "Manned Mars landing, moon base are seen as likely space feats," *Wall Str. J.,* 169, No. 4, Jan. 6, 1967, pp. 1, 14.

Duggan, John W. et al. "Research in higher education," in *Harvard University Invitational Conference in Educational Research.* New York: College Entrance Examination Board, 1965.

Duker, Sam. "The questionnaire is questionable," *Phi Delta Kappan,* 29: 386, 392; 1948.

Ebel, Robert L. "The role of educational research," *A.E.R.A. Newsletter,* 9: 1–2; Jan. 1958.

———. "The limitations of basic research in education." *Phi Delta Kappan,* 49: 81–84; 1967.

——— (ed.) *Encyclopedia of Educational Research.* New York: Macmillan, 1969.

Edel, Abraham. *Science and the Structure of Ethics.* Int. Encyclopedia of Unified Science, Vol. 2, No. 3. Chicago: Univ. of Chicago Press, 1961.

Editor. "How would you answer this one?" *Alaskan Sch. Bull.,* 22: 12–13; 1939.

Edwards, Allen L. *Techniques of Attitude Scale Construction.* New York: Appleton-Century-Crofts, 1957.

Einstein, Albert. "Physics and reality," *J. Franklin Inst.,* 222: 349–89; 1936.

Ellis, Joseph R. *Opinions Regarding the Value of Teaching Experience in the Elementary and Secondary Schools for Educational Researchers.* DeKalb: Northern Illinois Univ., 1967. (dittoed)

English, Horace B. and Ava C. English. *Comprehensive Dictionary of Psychological Terms.* New York: Longmans, Green, 1958.

Estes, Nolan. cited by Richard Martin. "Education will become a life-long process," *Wall Str. J.,* 169, No. 30, Feb. 3, 1967, p. 1, 10.

Eurich, Alvin C. "New dimensions in educational research," *A.E.R.A. Newsletter,* 13: 4–10; 1962.

Fairchild, Henry P. (ed.) *Dictionary of Sociology.* New York: Philosophical Library, 1944.

Farnsworth, Paul (ed.) *Annual Review of Psychology.* Palo Alto: Stanford Univ., 1950–date. (Calvin P. Stone, ed., Vols. 1–6)

Fattu, Nicholas. "Prediction: From oracle to automation," *Phi Delta Kappan,* 39: 409–12; 1958.

————. "A survey of educational research at selected universities," in Frank W. Banghart (ed.) *Educational Research.* 1st Annual Symposium. Bloomington: Phi Delta Kappa, 1960. pp. 1–21.

————. "The teacher and educational research," *High Sch. J.*, 44: 194–203; 1961.

Fay, Leo C. et al. "Doctoral studies in reading, 1919–1960," *Indiana Univ. Sch. Educ. Bull.*, 40, No. 4, 1964.

Feigl, Herbert and May Brodbeck (eds.) *Readings in the Philosophy of Science.* New York: Appleton-Century-Crofts, 1953.

Festinger, Leon and Daniel Katz. *Research Methods in the Behavioral Sciences.* New York: Holt, Rinehart & Winston, 1965.

Fisher, Ronald A. *Statistical Methods for Research Workers.* Edinburgh: Oliver & Boyd, 1932.

————. "The use of multiple measurements in taxonomic problems." *Ann. Eugenics,* 7: 179–88; 1936.

————. *The Design of Experiments.* 7th ed. New York: Hafner, 1956.

———— and Frank Yates. *Statistical Tables for Biological, Agricultural, and Medical Research.* New York: Hafner, 1963.

Flanagan, John C. *The Critical Incident Technique in the Study of Individuals.* Washington: Amer. Council Educ., 1952.

————. "The critical incident technique," *Psychol. Bull.*, 51: 327–58; 1954.

————. "Project Talent," in American Council on Education. *Measurement and Research in Today's Schools.* 1960 Educational Conference. Washington: The Council, 1961. pp. 99–108.

————et al. *The Talents of American Youth: 1. Design for a Study of American Youth.* New York: Houghton-Mifflin, 1962.

————. *The Identification, Development, and Utilization of Human Talents: The American High-School Student.* C.R.P., No. 635. Pittsburgh: Project Talent Office, Univ. of Pittsburgh, 1964.

Flanders, Ned A. *Teacher Influence, Pupil Attitudes, and Achievement.* C.R.P., No. 397. Minneapolis: Univ. of Minnesota, 1960a.

————. *Interaction Analysis in the Classroom.* Minneapolis: College of Education, Univ. of Minnesota, 1960b.

Floyd, Dick. "Tomorrow's wonders not far off," *Miami Herald,* 341: 1-K, 4-K; Nov. 6, 1966.

Forrester, Gertrude (ed.) *Occupational Literature.* New York: Wilson, 1958.

Foshay, Arthur W. *Handbook of Education.* Chicago: Rand McNally, 1963.

————. "Issues and dilemmas in nurturing the educational researcher in an organizational setting," in Egon G. Guba and Stanley M. Elam (eds.) *The Training and Nurture of Educational Researchers.* 6th Annual Symposium. Bloomington: Phi Delta Kappa, 1965. pp. 163–79.

Fowler, Floyd J. "Education, interaction, and interview performance," *Diss. Abstr.*, 27: 2195–A; 1967.

Franzen, Raymond and Paul F. Lazarsfeld. "Mail questionnaire as a research problem," *J. Psychol.*, 20: 293–320; 1945.

Freeman, Frank N. "The contributions of science to education," *Sch. & Soc.*, 30: 107–12; 1929.

Furno, Orlando F. "Sample survey design in education—Focus on administrative utilization," *Rev. educ. Res.*, 36: 552–65; 1966.

Gage, N.L. (ed.) *Handbook of Research on Teaching.* Chicago: Rand McNally, 1963.

———. "Can science contribute to the art of teaching?" *Phi Delta Kappan*, 49: 399–403; 1968

Gephart, William J. (ed.) "How to use new school research service," *News, Notes, & Quotes*, 11: 1, 3; 1967.

Gerberich, John B. "A study of the consistency of informal responses to questions in a questionnaire," *J. educ. Psychol.*, 38: 299–306; 1947.

——— and J.M. Mason. "Signed versus unsigned questionnaires," *J. educ. Res.*, 42: 122–26; 1948.

Gesell, Arnold. *Infant Development: The Embryology of Early Human Behavior.* New York: Harper & Row, 1952.

——— and Frances L. Ilg. *Child Development.* New York: Harper & Row, 1949.

——— and Helen Thompson. *Learning and Growth in Identical Infant Twins.* Genet. Psychol. Monogr., 6, No. 1. Worcester: Clark Univ. Press, 1929.

——— et al. *The First Five Years of Life.* New York: Harper & Row, 1940.

———. *The Child from Five to Ten.* New York: Harper & Row, 1946.

———. *Youth: The Years from Ten to Sixteen.* New York: Harper & Row, 1956.

Ghiselli, Edwin E. *Theory of Psychological Measurement.* New York: McGraw-Hill, 1964.

Gideonse, H.D. "The national program of educational laboratories," *Phi Delta Kappan*, 47: 130–33; 1965.

Glaser, Robert (ed.) *Training Research and Education.* Pittsburgh: Univ. of Pittsburgh Press, 1962.

Glueck, Sheldon. "The home, the school, and delinquency," *Harv. educ. Rev.*, 23: 17–32; 1953.

Good, Carter V. (ed.) *Dictionary of Education.* New York: McGraw-Hill, 1959.

——— and Douglas E. Scates. *Methods of Research.* New York: Appleton-Century-Crofts, 1954.

Goodlad, John I. et al. *Computers and Information Systems in Education.* New York: Harcourt, Brace & World, 1966.

Gores, Harold B., cited by Richard Martin. "Education will become a lifelong process, lean on electronic aids," *Wall Str. J.*, 169, No. 30, Feb. 13, 1967, p. 1, 10.

Gorlow, Leon and Walter Katkovsky. *Readings in the Psychology of Adjustment.* New York: McGraw-Hill, 1959.

Gossett, William S. "The Lanarkshire experiment," *Biometrika*, 23: 398–406; 1931.

Gottschalk, Louis R. *Understanding History: A Primer of Historical Method.* New York: Knopf, 1950.

Goulet, Richard R. (ed.) *Educational Change: The Reality and the Promise.* New York: Citation Press, 1968.

Grace, Alonzo G. (chrman.) "Recommendations of the Committee on Research Promotion," in *Annual Report.* Washington: Amer. Educ. Res. Assn., 1962. pp. 19–26.

Graves, Albert D. *A History of Education: 1. Before the Middle Ages, 1909; 2. During the Middle Ages, 1910; 3. In Modern Times, 1913.* New York: Macmillan.

Graves, Eileen C. (ed.) *Ulrich's International Periodical Directory.* New York: Bowker, 1932–date.

Gray, William S. "Summary of reading investigations," *J. educ. Res.* (Feb. issue), 1924–1960. (Continued, Helen M. Robinson, 1961; Theodore L. Harris, 1962–date; See also Helen M. Robinson, 1962–date.)

Griffiths, Daniel E. "Some assumptions underlying the use of models in research," in Jack A. Culbertson and Stephen P. Hencley (eds.) *Educational Research: New Perspectives.* Danville: Interstate, 1963. pp. 121–39.

————. "An interdisciplinary staffing plan for schools of education: A new approach to training researchers for education," in David L. Clark and Blaine R. Worthen (eds.) *Preparing Research Personnel for Education.* Bloomington: Phi Delta Kappa, 1967. pp. 22–26.

Guilford, J.P. *The Nature of Human Intelligence.* New York: McGraw-Hill, 1967.

Gulliksen, Harold and Samuel Messick (eds.) *Psychological Scaling: Theory and Applications.* New York: Wiley, 1960.

Guttman, Louis A. "The quantification of a class of attributes: A theory and method of scale construction," in Paul Horst et al. *The Prediction of Personal Adjustment.* New York: Soc. Sci. Res. Council, 1941. pp. 321–45.

————. "The Cornell Technique for scale and intensity analysis," *Educ. psychol. Measmt.*, 7: 247–79; 1947.

Halpin, Andrew W. "A rationale for training research workers," in Jack A. Culbertson and Stephen P. Hencley (eds.) *Educational Research: New Perspectives.* Danville: Interstate, 1963. pp. 311–24.

————. *Theory and Research in Administration.* New York: Macmillan, 1966.

Hansen, Morris. "More than noses will be counted," *Bus. Week*, 1591: 30–31, Feb. 27, 1960.

———— and W.N. Hurwitz. "The problem of non-response in sample surveys," *J. Amer. stat. Assn.*, 41: 517–29; 1946.

Hanson, R.H. and Eli S. Marks. "Influence of the interviewer on the accuracy of survey results," *J. Amer. stat. Assn.*, 53: 635–55; 1958.

Harlow, Harry F. "Mice, monkeys, and motives," *Psychol. Rev.*, 60: 23–32; 1953.

————. "The nature of love," *Amer. Psychol.*, 13: 673–85; 1958.

Harris, Chester W. (ed.) *Encyclopedia of Educational Research*. New York: Macmillan, 1960.

———— (ed.) *Problems in Measuring Change*. Madison: Univ. of Wisconson Press, 1963.

Harris, Theodore L. et al. "Summary and review of investigations relating to reading," *J. educ. Res.* (Feb. issue), 1962–date.

Hartley, William D. "Huge nuclear facilities will help U.S. meet surging power demands," *Wall Str. J.*, 168, No. 123, Dec. 27, 1966, p. 1, 10.

Hartmann, George W. "The field theory of learning and its educational consequences," in N.B. Henry (ed.) *Psychology of Learning*. 41st Yrbk., N.S.S.E., Pt. II. Chicago: Univ. of Chicago Press, 1942. pp. 165–214.

Hartshorne, Hugh and Mark A. May. *Studies in Deceit*. New York: Macmillan, 1928.

Hawkins, Hugh. *Pioneer: A History of the Johns Hopkins University, 1874–1889*. Ithaca: Cornell Univ. Press, 1960.

Hebb, Donald O. *The Organization of Behavior*. New York: Wiley, 1949.

Heil, L.M. and C. Washburne. "Brooklyn College research in teacher effectiveness," *J. educ. Res.*, 55: 347–51; 1962.

H.E.W. *Fact Book on Office of Education Programs*. Washington: U.S.O.E., H.E.W., 1967.

————. *Report of the Secretary's Advisory Committee on Traffic Safety*. Washington: H.E.W., 1968.

Heiss, Ann. "Graduate education today: An instrument for change?" *J. higher Educ.*, 39: 1–10; 1968.

Henry, David P. "New priorities in research," *Educ. Rec.*, 41: 148–53; 1960.

Herrick, Virgil E. "Guides for facilitating research in universities," in David L. Clark and Blaine R. Worthen (eds.) *Preparing Research Personnel for Education*. Bloomington: Phi Delta Kappa, 1967.

Hilgard, Ernest R. *Theories of Learning*. New York: Appleton-Century-Crofts, 1956.

———— and Gordon H. Bower. *Theories of Learning*. New York: Appleton-Century-Crofts, 3rd edition, 1966.

Hills, John R. "College expectancy tables for high school counselors," *Pers. Guid. J.*, 42: 479–83; 1964.

Hillway, Tyrus. *Introduction to Research*. Boston: Houghton-Mifflin, 1956, 1964.

Hirshberg, Herbert S. and Carl H. Melinat. *Subject Guide to United States Government Publications*. Chicago: Amer. Library Assn., 1947.

Holmes, Henry W. et al. *Educational Research: Its Nature, Essential Conditions, and Controlling Concepts*. Series 1, Vol. 3, No. 10. Washington: Amer. Council Educ., 1939.

Hotelling, Harold. "The most predictable criterion," *J. educ. Psychol.*, 26: 139–42; 1935.

————. "Relations between two sets of variates," *Biometrika*, 28: 321–77; 1936.

Hyman, Herbert H. "Problems in the collection of opinion-research data," *Amer. J. Sociol.*, 55: 362–70; 1950.

Hyman, Ray. *The Nature of Psychological Inquiry*. Englewood Cliffs: Prentice-Hall, 1964.

Ianni, Francis A.J. "Research and experimentation in education," *Phi Delta Kappan*, 46: 489–94; 1965.

Jackson, Robert W.B. *Educational Research in Canada Today and Tomorrow*. Toronto: W.J. Gage, 1961.

Jacob, Philip E. *Changing Values in College*. New York: Harper & Row, 1957.

Jacobson, A.L., cited by Herbert G. Lawson. "Intelligence pills," *Wall Str. J.*, 167, No. 100: 1, 16; May 23, 1966.

Jensen, Arthur R. "The improvement of educational research," *T. C. Rec.*, 64: 20–27; 1962.

Johnson, Loaz W. "What administrators want and will use from research workers," in *Growing Points in Educational Research*. 1959 Official Report. Washington: Amer. Educ. Res. Assn., 1959. pp. 7–12.

Johnson, Lyndon B. *Learning and Liberty—Three Statements on Education*. Washington: Govt. Printing Office, 1967. p. 3.

Johnson, Palmer O. "Introductory remarks at opening of the Symposium on Educational Research," in Frank W. Banghart (ed.) *Educational Research*. 1st Annual Symposium. Bloomington: Phi Delta Kappa, 1960. pp. xv–xvi.

Johnson, Wendell. *People in Quandaries*. New York: Harper & Row, 1946.

Kagan, Jerome and Howard A. Moss. *Birth to Maturity: A Study in Psychological Development*. New York: Wiley, 1962.

Kahn, Herman and Anthony J. Wiener. *The Year 2000: A Framework for Speculation on the Next Thirty-Three Years*. New York: Macmillan, 1967.

Kandel, Isaac L. "Educational research," *Sch. & Soc.*, 72: 232; 1950.

Kempthorne, Oscar. "The design and analysis of experiments with some reference to educational research," in Raymond O. Collier and Stanley M. Elam (eds.) *Research Design and Analysis.* 2nd Annual Symposium. Bloomington: Phi Delta Kappa, 1961. pp. 97–133.

Keppel, Francis. "Research: Education's neglected hope," *J. Read.*, 8: 3–9; 1964a.

———. "On improving the diffusion of knowledge," *N.A.S.S.P. Bull.*, 48: 3–9, April 1964b.

Kerlinger, Fred N. "Practicality and education," *Sch. Rev.*, 67: 281-91; 1959.

———. "The mythology of educational research: The methods approach," *Sch. & Soc.*, 88: 149-64; 1960.

———. *Foundations of Behavioral Research.* New York: Holt, Rinehart & Winston, 1964.

———. "The Ed.D. and the Ph.D.," *T. C. Rec.*, 66: 434-39; 1965.

———. "The doctoral training of research specialists," *Rec. (T. C. Rec.)*, 69: 477-83; 1968.

Kidd, Charles V. *American Universities and Federal Research.* Cambridge: Harv. Univ. Press, 1959.

King, John E. "The doctorate in education," *Phi Delta Kappan*, 42: 382-86; 1961.

Kinsey, A.C. et al. *Sexual Behavior in the Human Male.* Philadelphia: Saunders, 1948.

———. *Sexual Behavior in the Human Female.* Philadelphia: Saunders, 1953.

Krathwohl, David R. et al. *The Taxonomy of Educational Objectives, II: Affective Domain.* New York: McKay, 1964.

Krech, David. "The chemistry of learning," *Sat. Rev.*, Jan. 20, 1968. pp. 48-50+.

———. "Psychoneurobiomeducation," *Phi Delta Kappan*, 50: 370-75, 1969.

Kruglak, Haym. "The delusion of the scientific method," *Amer. J. Physics*, 17: 23-29; 1949.

Lamke, Tom A. "Preface," *Rev. educ. Res.*, 25: 192; 1955.

——— and Herbert M. Silvey (eds.) *Master's Theses in Education.* Cedar Falls: Research Publications, 1952–date. (now Silvey.)

LaPiere, Richard T. "Attitude vs. action," *Soc. Forces*, 13: 230-37; 1934.

Larrabee, Harold A. *Reliable Knowledge.* Boston: Houghton-Mifflin, 1945.

Lazarsfeld, Paul F. and Sam D. Sieber. *Organizing Educational Research: An Exploration.* Englewood Cliffs: Prentice-Hall, 1964.

Learned, William S. and Ben D. Wood. *The Student and His Knowledge.* Boston: Merrymount Press, 1938.

Leighton, Gerald and Peter L. McKinley. *Milk Consumption and the Growth of School Children.* Dept. of Health for Scotland. London: H.M. Stationery Office, 1930.

Lenski, G.E. and J.C. Leggett. "Caste, class, and deference in the research interview," *Amer. J. Sociol.,* 65: 463–67, 1960.

Levin, Harry. "Rationale and recommendations for a university-wide graduate training program in educational research." in David L. Clark and Blaine R. Worthen (eds.) *Preparing Research Personnel for Education.* Bloomington: Phi Delta Kappa, 1967. pp. 34–39.

Lewin, Kurt et al. "Pattern of aggressive behavior in experimentally created social climates," *J. soc. Psychol.,* 10: 271–99; 1939.

Likert, Rensis. "A technique for the measurement of attitudes," *Arch. Psychol.,* No. 140, 1932.

Lindquist, Everett F. *Design and Analysis of Experiments in Psychology and Education.* Boston: Houghton-Mifflin, 1953.

Lins, L. Joseph and Robert A. Rees. *Scholars' Guide to Journals of Education and Educational Psychology.* Madison: December, 1965.

Lundberg, George A. *Can Science Save Us?* New York: Longmans, Green, 1946, 1961.

Lyda, Mary Louise et al. (compilers) *Research Studies in Education: A Subject-Author Index and Research Methods Bibliography.* Bloomington: Phi Delta Kappa, 1952–date.

MacArthur, R. S. "Organization for educational research in universities of Midwestern United States," *Alta. J. educ. Res.,* 4: 131–41; 1958.

McCall, William A. *How to Experiment in Education.* New York: Macmillan, 1923.

McConnell, James V. "Worm learns," *Sat. Eve. Post,* 237: 66–67; March 28, 1964.

McConnell, Thomas R. et al. *The Conceptual Structure of Educational Research.* Suppl. Educ. Monogr., No. 55. Chicago: Univ. of Chicago Press, 1942.

McGraw, Myrtle B. *Growth: A Study of Jimmy and Johnny.* New York: Appleton-Century-Crofts, 1935.

MacKinnon, Donald W. "Fact and fancy in personality research," *Amer. Psychol.,* 8: 138–46; 1953.

McLean, Leslie D. "Design and analysis methodology: An overview," *Rev. educ. Res.,* 36: 491–502; 1966.

Madge, John. *The Tools of Social Science.* New York: Longmans, Green, 1953.

Maier, Norman R.F. "The quality of group decisions as influenced by the discussion leader," *Hum. Rel.,* 3: 155–74; 1950.

Maller, J. Bernard. "Cooperation and competition: An experimental study in motivation," *T.C. Contributions to Education,* No. 384. New York: T.C., Columbia Univ., 1929.

March, Jane G. (ed.) *Handbook of Organizations.* Chicago: Rand McNally, 1965.

Marks, Eli S. "Sampling in the revision of the Stanford-Binet Scale," *Psychol. Bull.,* 44: 413–34; 1947.

———. "Some sampling problems in educational research," *J. educ. Psychol.,* 42: 85–95; 1951.

Marquis, Donald G. "Research planning at the frontiers of science," *Amer. Psychol.,* 3: 430–38; 1948.

Marsak, R.E. "Basic research in the university and industrial setting," *Sci.,* 154: 1521–24; 1966.

Martin, Richard. "Education will become a life-long process, lean on electronic aids," *Wall Str. J.,* 169, No. 30: 1, 10; Feb. 13, 1967.

Maslow, Abraham H. *The Psychology of Science.* New York: Harper & Row, 1966.

May, Leona H. (ed.) *Patterson's American Education.* Chicago: Educational Directories, 1904–date.

Medley, Donald M. and Harold E. Mitzel. "Measuring classroom behavior by systematic observation," in N.L. Gage (ed.) *Handbook of Research on Teaching.* Chicago: Rand McNally, 1963. pp. 247–328.

Meehl, Paul E. *Clinical versus Statistical Prediction: A Theoretical Analysis and a Review of the Evidence.* Minneapolis: Univ. of Minnesota Press, 1954.

——— and Albert Rosen. "Antecedent probability and the efficiency of psychometric signs, patterns, or cutting scores," *Psychol. Bull.,* 52: 194–216; 1955.

Michels, Walter C. "Limits of a scientist's responsibility," *Amer. J. Physics,* 16: 289–94; 1948.

Mill, John S. *A System of Logic.* New York: Harper & Row, 1873.

Millet, John D. (ed.) *Atlas of Higher Education in the United States.* New York: Columbia Univ., 1952.

Millman, Jason (ed.) "Washington notes," *Educ. Res.,* 18, No. 8, Aug. 1967.

———. "Editorial," *Educ. Res.,* 18, No. 2, Feb. 1967.

———. "AERJ acceptance data," *Educ. Res.,* 19, No. 3, Mar. 1968.

Minsky, Marvin L. "Artificial intelligence," *Sci. Amer.,* 215: 246–52+; Sept. 1966.

Monroe, Walter S. (ed.) *Encyclopedia of Educational Research.* American Educational Research Association. New York: Macmillan, 1950.

——— and Max D. Engelhart. *The Scientific Study of Educational Problems.* New York: Macmillan, 1936.

Morsh, J.E. *Development Report—Systematic Observation of Instructor Be-*

havior. USAF Pers. Trng. Res. Cent. Developm. Rep. No. AFPTRC-TN-56-52, 1956.

Mouly, George J. *Psychology for Effective Teaching.* New York: Holt, Rinehart & Winston, 1968.

Mowrer, O.H. "Q-technique—Description, history, and critique," in O.H. Mowrer (ed.) *Psychotherapy, Theory, and Research.* New York: Ronald Press, 1953. pp. 316–75.

Mussen, Paul H. (ed.) *Handbook of Research Methods in Child Development.* New York: Wiley, 1960.

Nash, Paul. "The future of educational research in Canada: A critique," *Canad. educ. Res. Dig.,* 2: 161–72; 1962.

——. "History of education," *Rev. educ. Res.,* 34: 5–21; 1964.

Ness, Frederick W. (ed.) *A Guide to Graduate Study Programs Leading to the Ph.D. Degree.* Washington: Amer. Council Educ., 1960.

Norton, Dee W. and Everett F. Lindquist. "Applications of experimental designs and analysis," *Rev. educ. Res.,* 21: 350–67; 1951.

Nyhan, William L. "A new metabolic disease," *Inquiry,* 1: 13–15; 1968.

Oppenheimer, Robert J. "Analogy in science," *Amer. Psychol.,* 11: 127–35; 1956.

Page, Ellis B. "Educational research: Replicable or generalizable?" *Phi Delta Kappan,* 39: 302–04; 1958.

Parten, Mildred. *Surveys, Polls, and Samples: Practical Procedures.* New York: Harper & Row, 1950.

Phillips, William M. "Weakness of the mail questionnaire: A methodological study," *Sociol. soc. Res.,* 35: 260–67; 1951.

Platt, John R. "Strong inference," *Sci.,* 146: 347–53; 1964.

Powell, Arthur G. *Educational Careers and the Missing Elite.* Cambridge: Harv. Grad. Sch. Educ., 1964.

Remmers, H.H. *Introduction to Opinion and Attitude Measurement.* New York: Harper & Row, 1954.

Rice, Joseph M. "The futility of the spelling grind," *Educ. Forum,* 23: 163–72; 1897.

Richter, Ann J. (ed.) *American Library Directory.* New York: Bowker, 1951.

Rider, Fremont. *The Scholar and the Future of the Research Library.* New York: Hadham, 1944.

Robinson, Francis G. *Educational Research in Canada: An Analysis of Potential, Current Status, and Needed Development.* Ottawa: Canad. Council Res. Educ., 1965. (draft)

Robinson, Helen M. "Summary of investigations relating to reading," *J. educ. Res.* (Feb. 1961); *Read. Teach.* (Jan. issue), 1962–64; Robinson et al. *Read Res. Quart.* (Winter issue), 1965–date.

Roethlisberger, F.J. *Management and Morale.* Cambridge: Harv. Univ. Press, 1941.

Rogers, Carl R. and B.F. Skinner. "Some issues concerning the control of human behavior," *Sci.* 124: 1057–66; 1956.

Romig, Walter (ed.) *Guide to Catholic Literature.* Washington: Catholic Library Assn., 1888–date.

Ruckmick, C.A. "The uses and abuses of the questionnaire procedure," *J. appl. Psychol.,* 14: 32–41; 1930.

Russell, Bertrand. *Philosophy.* New York: Norton, 1927.

———. *Mysticism and Logic.* New York: Norton, 1929.

———. "On the importance of logical form," in Otto Neurath et al. *International Encyclopedia of Unified Science.* Vol. 1, No. 1. Chicago: Univ. of Chicago Press, 1938. pp. 39–41.

———. *The Impact of Science on Society.* New York: Simon & Schuster, 1953.

———. "On the notion of cause with applications to the free-will problem," in Herbert Feigl and May Brodbeck (eds.) *Readings in the Philosophy of Science.* New York: Appleton-Century-Crofts, 1953. pp. 387–407.

Ryans, David G. "Preparation of educational research workers," *J. educ. Res.,* 49: 195–202; 1955.

———. *Characteristics of Teachers.* Washington: Amer. Council Educ., 1960.

———. "Looking to the future in education," *Educ. Rec.,* 44: 360–68; 1963.

Sawyer, Jack. "Measurement and prediction, Clinical and statistical," *Psychol. Bull.,* 66: 178–200; 1966.

Schuster, Richard P. *The Next Ninety Years.* Pasadena: Calif. Inst. Technology, 1967.

Schutz, Richard E. "Strategy for the development of training programs for educational researchers," in David L. Clark and Blaine R. Worthen (eds.) *Preparing Research Personnel for Education.* Bloomington: Phi Delta Kappa, 1967. pp. 40–44.

Scriven, Michael. "The philosophy of science in educational research," *Rev. educ. Res.,* 30: 422–29; 1960.

Sears, Pauline S. "Levels of aspiration in academically successful and unsuccessful children," *J. abnorm. soc. Psychol.,* 35: 498–536; 1940.

Selltiz, Claire and Stuart W. Cook. "Can research in social science be both socially useful and scientifically meaningful?" *Amer. sociol. Rev.,* 13: 454–59; 1948.

Shannon, John R. "Traits of research workers," *J. educ. Res.,* 40: 513–21; 1947.

———. "Percentage of returns of questionnaires in reputable educational research," *J. educ. Res.,* 42: 138–41; 1948.

Shera, Jesse H. "Librarians against machine," *Sci.,* 156: 746–50; 1967.

Shoben, Edward J. "Toward a concept of normal personality," *Amer. Psychol.,* 12: 183–89; 1957.

Shumsky, Abraham. "Teachers explore their attitudes toward research," *Educ. Res. Bull.*, 37: 31–38, 56; 1958.

Sieber, Sam D. "Existing organizational patterns in educational research," in Egon G. Guba and Stanley M. Elam (eds.) *The Training and Nurture of Educational Researchers.* 6th Annual Symposium. Bloomington: Phi Delta Kappa, 1965. pp. 139–62.

——— . "Proposals for a radical revision of research training in schools of education," in David L. Clark and Blaine R. Worthen (eds.) *Preparing Research Personnel for Education.* Bloomington: Phi Delta Kappa, 1967. pp. 27–33.

——— . "The case of the misconstrued technique," *Phi Delta Kappan*, 49: 273–76; 1968.

Silberman, Harry F. et al. "The effect of educational research on classroom instruction," *Harv. educ. Rev.*, 36: 295–317; 1966.

Silvey, Herbert M. (ed.) *Master's Theses in Education.* Cedar Falls: Research Publications, 1959–date. (See Lamke)

Skinner, B.F. "Are theories of learning necessary?" *Psychol. Rev.*, 57: 193–216; 1950.

——— . "A case history in scientific method," *Amer. Psychol.*, 11: 221–33; 1956.

——— . "Reinforcement today," *Amer. Psychol.*, 13: 94–99; 1958.

——— . "Pigeons in a pelican," *Amer. Psychol.*, 15: 28–37; 1960.

Sletto, Raymond F. "Pretesting of questionnaires," *Amer. sociol. Rev.*, 5: 193–200; 1940.

Smith, Donald E. and Patricia M. Carrigan. *The Nature of Reading Disability.* New York: Harcourt, Brace & World, 1959.

Smith, Gerald C. "Progress through the Cooperative Research Program," *Phi Delta Kappan*, 45: 303–10; 1964.

Smith, M. Brewster. "Mental health reconsidered," *Amer. Psychol.*, 16: 299–306; 1961.

Smith, M.E. "An investigation of the development of the sentence and the extent of vocabulary in young children," *Univ. of Iowa Studies in Child Welfare*, 3, No. 5, 1926.

Solomon, R. "An extension of control group design," *Psychol. Bull.*, 46: 137–50; 1949.

Spilhaus, A. "Experimental cities," in Richard P. Schuster (ed.) *The Next Ninety Years.* Pasadena: Calif. Inst. Technology, 1967. pp. 149–69.

Stanley, Julian C. "Controlled experimentation in the classroom," *J. exper. Educ.*, 25: 195–201; 1957.

——— . "Studying status vs. manipulating variables," in Raymond O. Collier and Stanley M. Elam (eds.) *Research Design and Analysis.* 2nd Annual Symposium. Bloomington: Phi Delta Kappa, 1961. pp. 173–208.

——— . "Quasi-experimental designs," *Sch. Rev.*, 73: 197–205; 1965.

————. "The influence of Fisher's *The Design of Experiments* on educational research 30 years later," *Amer. educ. Res. J.*, 3: 223–29; 1966.

———— (ed.) *Improving Experimental Designs and Statistical Analysis.* 7th Annual Symposium. Bloomington: Phi Delta Kappa, 1967.

Starch, Daniel and Edward C. Elliott. "Reliability of the grading of high school work in English," *Sch. Rev.*, 20: 442–57; 1912.

————. "Reliability of grading work in mathematics," *Sch. Rev.*, 21: 254–59; 1913.

Stephan, Frederick F. "History of the uses of modern sampling procedures," *J. Amer. stat. Assn.*, 43: 12–39; 1948.

Stephenson, William. *The Study of Behavior: Q-Technique and its Methodology.* Chicago: Univ. of Chicago Press, 1953.

Stiles, Lindley J. "The Cooperative Research Program," *Phi Delta Kappan*, 43: 231–36; 1952.

————. "Educational research: The source of better schools," *Theory into Practice*, 1: 70–74; 1962.

Stoddard, George D. "Educational research lacks impact; it avoids controversy and human values," *Nation's Sch.*, 49: 44–46; May 1952.

Stouffer, Samuel A. "Notes on the case study and the unique case," *Sociometry*, 4: 349–57; 1941.

Swanson, Don R. "Scientific journals and information service of the future," *Amer. Psychol.*, 21: 1005–1010; 1966.

Symonds, Percival M. "The organization of educational research in the United States," *Harv. educ. Rev.*, 27: 159–67; 1957.

Tate, Merle W. "Operationalism, research, and a science of education," *Harv. educ. Rev.*, 20: 11–27; 1950.

Terman, Lewis M. et al. *Genetic Studies of Genius.* 1. *The Mental and Physical Traits of a Thousand Gifted Children*, 1925; 2. Catherine M. Cox. *The Early Mental Traits of Three Hundred Geniuses*, 1926; 3. Barbara S. Burks et al. *The Promise of Youth: Follow-up Studies of a Thousand Gifted Children*, 1930; 4. Lewis M. Terman and Melita H. Oden. *The Gifted Child Grows Up: Twenty-five Years of Genius*, 1947; 5. *The Gifted at Mid-Life*, 1959. Stanford: Stanford Univ. Press.

———— and Maud A. Merrill. *Measuring Intelligence.* Boston: Houghton-Mifflin, 1937, 1960.

Thompson, James W. *A History of Historical Writing.* New York: Macmillan, 1942.

Thorndike, Edward L. *Educational Psychology. II: The Psychology of Learning.* New York: Bur. Publ., T. C., Columbia Univ., 1913.

————. *The Teacher's Word Book: Ten Thousand Words*, 1921; *Twenty Thousand Words*, 1932; *Thirty Thousand Words*, 1944. New York: T. C., Columbia Univ.

————. *Human Learning*. New York: Appleton-Century-Crofts, 1931.

Thurstone, Louis L. *The Vectors of the Mind*. Chicago: Univ. of Chicago Press, 1935.

————. *Primary Mental Abilities*. Chicago: Univ. of Chicago Press, 1938.

Topp, Robert F. and G.D. McGrath. "About that questionnaire—Answer it," *Sch. Exec.*, 70: 59–60; 1950.

Torgerson, Warren S. *Theory and Methods of Scaling*. New York: Wiley, 1958.

————. "Scaling and test theory," *Ann. rev. Psychol.*, 12: 51–70; 1961.

Travers, Robert M.W. "The prediction of achievement," *Sch. & Soc.*, 70: 293–94; 1949.

————. *An Introduction to Educational Research*. New York: Macmillan, 1964, 1969.

Traxler, Arthur E. *Ten Years of Research in Reading: Summary and Bibliography*. Educational Record Bulletin. New York: Educ. Rec. Bur., 1941. (See also subsequent summaries, Traxler et al. Educ. Rec. Bur., 1946, 1955, 1960.)

————. "Some comments on educational research at mid-century," *J. educ. Res.*, 47: 359–66; 1954.

Trow, Martin. "Survey research in educational administration," in Jack A. Culbertson and Stephen P. Hencley (eds.) *Educational Research: New Perspectives*. Danville: Interstate, 1963. pp. 249–63.

Turabian, Kate L. *Manual for Writers of Term Papers, Theses, and Dissertations*. Chicago: Univ. of Chicago Press, 1967.

Underwood, Benton J. *Psychological Research*. New York: Appleton-Century-Crofts, 1957.

U.P.I. "Will body in deep freeze still get social security benefits?" Washington: U.P.I., June 2, 1968.

U.S. Employment Service, Dept. of Labor. *Dictionary of Occupational Titles*, Vols. I and II. Washington: The Service, 1965.

Van Dalen, Deobold B. "Role of hypotheses in educational research," *Educ. Admin. Superv.*, 42: 457–60; 1956.

————. "Relationship of fact and theory in research," *Educ. Admin. Superv.*, 45: 271–74; 1959.

————. *Understanding Educational Research*. New York: McGraw-Hill, 1966.

Van Vleck, David. "Wall-to-wall people feared by professor," *Miami Herald*, Sunday, Nov. 20, 1966, p. 16-F.

Von Braun, Wernher (cited by J. Spivak). "Manned Mars landing, moon base are seen as likely space feats," *Wall Str. J.*, 169, No. 4, Jan. 6, 1967. pp. 1, 14.

Walker, Helen M. "Preparation of research workers in education," *Elem. Sch. J.*, 58: 9–15; 1957.

Wallis, W. Allen. "Statistics of the Kinsey report," *J. Amer. stat. Assn.*, 44: 463–84; 1949.

Walton, J. "Why universities are failing the schools: A discipline of education is needed," *Educ. Dig.*, 31: 22–24; 1966.

Wasserman, Elga R. *The Random House Guide to Graduate Study.* New York: Random House, 1967.

Weir, John. "The next ninety years," in Richard P. Schuster (ed.) *The Next Ninety Years.* Calif. Inst. Technology, 1967. pp. 53–78.

Wesman, Alexander G. *Double-Entry Expectancy Tables.* Test Service Bull., No. 56. New York: Psychol. Corp., 1966. (See also No. 38.)

Whitehead, Alfred North. *Dialogues of Alfred North Whitehead* (Lucien Price, recorder). New York: New American Library of World Literature, 1954.

Wickman, E.K. *Children's Behavior and Teachers' Attitudes.* New York: Commonwealth Fund, 1928.

Williams, George. "Teaching and research in the university," *NEA J.*, 48: 13–14; May 1959.

Williams, James A. "Interviewer-respondent interaction: A study of bias in the information interview," *Diss. Abstr.*, 25: 4857, 1965.

Wilson, Edmund. *The Scrolls from the Dead Sea.* New York: Oxford Univ. Press, 1955.

Winchell, Constance M. (ed.) *Guide to Reference Books.* Chicago: Amer. Library Assn., 1960. Supplements. (formerly, Isaac G. Mudge, ed.)

Winn, Ralph B. (ed.) *John Dewey: Dictionary of Education.* New York: Philosophical Library, 1959.

Withall, J. "Development of a technique for the measurement of socio-emotional climate in classrooms," *J. exper. Educ.*, 17: 347–61; 1949.

Wittrock, M.C. "Focus on educational psychology," *Educ. Psychol.*, 4: 17, 20; Mar. 1967.

Woellner, Robert C. et al. *Requirements for Certification of Teachers, Counselors, Librarians, and Administrators in Elementary and Secondary Schools and Junior Colleges.* Chicago: Univ. of Chicago Press, 1894–date.

Wolfle, Dael. "Fetish of an experiment," *Sci.*, 125: 177; 1957.

Wynar, B.S. *Introduction to Bibliography and Reference Work: A Guide to Materials and Sources.* Denver: Libraries Unlimited, 1966.

Young, Raymond (compiler). *A Directory of Educational Research Agencies and Studies.* Bloomington: Phi Delta Kappa, 1965.

INDEX